A NORTON CRITICAL EDITION

Joseph Conrad

LORD JIM

AUTHORITATIVE TEXT

BACKGROUNDS

SOURCES

CRITICISM

SECOND EDITION

Edited by

THOMAS C. MOSER

STANFORD UNIVERSITY

W • W • NORTON & COMPANY • *New York* • *London*

Printed in the United States of America.

The text of this book is composed in Electra
with the display set in Bernhard Modern.
Composition by PennSet, Inc.
Manufacturing by Courier.

Library of Congress Cataloging-in-Publication Data
Conrad, Joseph, 1857–1924.
Lord Jim : an authoritative text, backgrounds, essays in criticism /
Joseph Conrad ; edited by Thomas C. Moser ; sources edited by
Norman Sherry. — 2nd ed.
p.   cm. — (A Norton critical edition)
Includes bibliographical references.
I. Moser, Thomas C.   II. Title.
PR6005.O4L6   1996
823′.912—dc20   95-1667
ISBN 0-393-96335-7

W. W. Norton & Company, Inc., 500 Fifth Avenue, New York, N.Y. 10110
W. W. Norton & Company Ltd., Castle House, 75/76 Wells Street,
London W1T 3QT

7 8 9 0

The Editor

THOMAS C. MOSER received his Ph.D. from Harvard University. He is Professor of English Emeritus at Stanford University. He is the author of *Joseph Conrad: Achievement and Decline* and *The Life in the Fiction of Ford Madox Ford*. He is the editor of *Wuthering Heights: Text, Sources, Criticism* and *The Good Soldier*. He has published numerous articles, including a psychobiographical study of William Faulkner and reflective essays on Albert Guerard and Ian Watt.

Contents

Criticism

Illustrations

Preface to the First Edition

Lord Jim has the rare distinction of being a masterpiece in two separate and apparently conflicting genres. It is at once an exotic adventure story of the Eastern seas in the popular tradition of Kipling and Stevenson and a complexly wrought "art novel" in the tradition of Flaubert and James.

Strong, taciturn men face the terrors of the sea; European idealists try to bring peace and civilization to the benighted heathen; a handsome young Englishman who funks it during a disaster at sea attempts to redeem himself on a remote tropical isle and briefly finds happiness in the arms of a beautiful Eurasian girl. Melodrama abounds: murder, suicide, treachery, intrigue, cowardice, bravery, romantic love, heroic sacrifice, and even a pitched battle with pirates.

At the same time *Lord Jim* explores moral and psychological questions with a subtlety and complexity unknown in novels of adventure. Moreover, it refuses finally to find clear-cut answers to difficult questions. Conrad accomplishes this with such an array of narrative techniques as had never before been employed in the English novel. Even Henry James had tended to avoid a personal narrator like Marlow and had used subordinate narrators ("reflectors") much less profusely. And no previous novelist had ever so dislocated chronological narration or so skillfully played upon the reader's responses. Partly at least this masterpiece of literary impressionism is about how hard, how ultimately impossible, it is ever to tell precisely the way events happened and, especially, what one's attitude toward those events ought properly to be.

This edition of *Lord Jim* tries to pay adequate attention to its twin aspects—romantic Eastern subject matter and sophisticated literary method.

The material in the footnotes, glossary and gazetteer, and Norman Sherry's section on sources represents the culmination of decades of work by many Conrad scholars. In a letter to the *Times Literary Supplement* in 1923 (the year before Conrad's death), Sir Frank Swettenham identified the *Patna* story with that of the *Jeddah*, abandoned in the Indian Ocean by her white officers in August 1880. Both John D. Gordan in *Joseph Conrad: The Making of a Novelist* (1940) and Jocelyn Baines in *Joseph Conrad: A Critical Biography* (1960) refer to and enlarge upon Swettenham's letter although they do not identify the particular officer who probably inspired the creation of Jim. Augustine Podmore Williams, first mate of the *Jeddah* and later employed by a ship chandler in Singapore, has come to be widely known as the precursor of Jim through two recent books: Miss Jerry Allen's *The Sea Years of Joseph Conrad* (1965) and Norman Sherry's *Conrad's Eastern World* (1966). These books also describe in considerable detail the people and geography of Berau, the town in Eastern Borneo that probably suggested Patusan in the novel. But Mr. Gordan actually visited the neighborhood of Berau in 1939, and he discusses the town itself in his book. Mr. Baines mentions Berau and provides a photograph. Again, although Miss Allen and Mr. Sherry explain in detail how Conrad's reading about Rajah James Brooke and about various travelers to the East Indies enriches *Lord Jim*, Mr. Gordan and Miss Florence Clemens[1] had long before opened up the subject.

Besides presenting a detailed account of the Eastern background, Mr. Sherry's special contribution, elaborated on in this Norton Critical Edition, is to suggest how intimate was Conrad's personal relationship to the story of the *Jeddah*. Conrad must first have read in London newspapers this unexampled tale of cowardly British maritime officers just after he passed his second mate's examination and just before he got his first berth as a ship's officer. Conrad would actually have seen the *Jeddah* in harbor on his first trip to Singapore in 1883, after experiencing as second mate the disastrous burning and sinking of the *Palestine*. The *Jeddah* was referred to in Singapore newspapers during Conrad's second stay in Singapore in 1885. Most striking of all, in late 1887 Conrad found himself precisely in the shoes of A. P. Williams: he served as first mate of the little steamer *Vidar* just as Williams had done in 1882. Sensing from the novels and from his life Conrad's strong tendency to sympathetic identification, we can readily imagine how he must have felt while acting in the same capacity as Williams, the first mate who had jumped from the *Jeddah*. It is unlikely that Williams's failure was far from Conrad's consciousness a few months later when, on the occasion of his first and only command, of the barque *Otago*, Conrad underwent the most desperate and exhausting test of his maritime career: being the captain of a ship becalmed for days with virtually her entire crew disabled by malaria, an experience memorably evoked in his late novel *The Shadow-Line* (1917).

If *Lord Jim* differs from ordinary adventure stories in the actuality of its materials and the author's personal involvement with those materials, the novel differs even more in the artistry of its composition. Yet *Lord Jim* was written under amazing circumstances: Conrad thought he was writing a short story of twenty to forty thousand words and instead wrote a novel of well over one hundred thousand words. More incredible still, he wrote much of that novel while it was coming out in *Blackwood's Magazine*, and therefore he could not rewrite the early portions to fit in with later developments. Not surprisingly, he heavily revised the periodical version for book publication, as Mr. Gordan long ago pointed out.

By enabling the reader to trace the process of composition, this edition tries to provide materials for a deeper understanding of Conrad's art: a transcription of the earliest manuscript fragment, "Tuan Jim: A Sketch"; a history of the novel's composition as revealed in Conrad's correspondence, especially with his publishers; and most important, textual notes giving every substantive change likely to have been made by Conrad after the periodical version.

Joseph Conrad would, I fear, have had, at best, mixed feelings about this

1. "Conrad's Favorite Bedside Book: Wallace's *Malay Archipelago*," *South Atlantic Quarterly* 38 (1939):305–15.

edition. No doubt he would not have liked the footnotes, gazetteer, and source material, which would seem to identify the people and places and, to his mind, to deny the fictional creation. In a late, famous letter (July 14, 1923), Conrad berated Richard Curle for such identification: he begged Curle to free him of "that infernal tail of ships."[2] Of course, Conrad is right; *Lord Jim* is *his* created world, not the "real" world. (Although the *Jeddah* crossed the Bay of Bengal, the *Patna* crossed only "the bay.") For us to read *Lord Jim* as thinly disguised actuality rather than an heroic achievement of the creative imagination is simply to miss the whole book.

Nevertheless, the factual material in this edition has, I hope, two useful functions. Partly it provides information likely to have been known to a reader in 1900 but lost to us because of the evolution of place names and because of our remoteness from nineteenth-century British maritime life. Partly, too, the factual information should remind us forcibly that this impressionist novelist—disciple of James, mentor of Ford Madox Ford, friend of Galsworthy, Wells, and Gide—had been first of all a seaman, really a seaman, and for twenty years. He thus brought to his fiction an authenticity almost unprecedented in the history of the novel.

Because this edition is genuinely a labor of love, because it tries to be the best that could possibly be done,[3] it no doubt contains many and gross errors unrecognized by its complacent editor. These are not, however, the fault of the very numerous students, colleagues, and Conradians who gave unstinting assistance. My greatest debt is to three Stanford students: Betty Moore slaved on the notes and glossary; Robin Roney Hayeck and Peter Verdurmen collated endlessly. I am grateful, too, to certain other students: Jane Curry, the Kenneth Lincolns, Robin Macdonald, and David Thorburn. Three colleagues read through the entire edition: Albert J. Guerard was particularly helpful on things Conradian and French; Claude M. Simpson, Jr., on sticky editorial matters; Ian P. Watt on things Conradian, maritime, and Eastern. When asked, these other Conradians gave good advice: John D. Gordan, Bruce Harkness, Kenneth B. Newall, Norman Sherry, and Donald C. Yelton. I wish also to thank Bruce Haywood of Kenyon College and Clive E. Driver of the Philip H. and A. S. W. Rosenbach Foundation. Finally, John Benedict, the Norton editor, provided patient support far more complete than I would ever have attributed to a mere "commercial" publisher.

THOMAS C. MOSER

2. *Conrad to a Friend*, edited by Richard Curle (Garden City, N.Y.: Doubleday, Doran, 1928) 147.
3. Unfortunately, I could not collate the Rosenbach manuscript of *Lord Jim* for the textual notes. Scholars may consult but may not copy it.

Preface to the Second Edition

The 1968 Norton Critical Edition of *Lord Jim* was, so far as I know, the first fully annotated, scholarly edition of Conrad's masterpiece. Since then, a great deal has happened in Conrad studies, necessitating a thorough revision of all aspects of the original Norton Critical Edition. First, whereas textual experts of the 1960s favored the Heinemann, third English edition as the proper copy text for Conrad's works, now the Blackwood, first English edition is strongly preferred for *Lord Jim*. Therefore, I have used the latter as the new copy text, albeit with some emendations. Second, Conrad scholars over the past quarter-century have illuminated many historical and literary allusions in *Lord Jim* that previously went unnoted. Here I am indebted to Dwight H. Purdy, *Joseph Conrad's Bible* (Norman: Oklahoma UP, n.d.) and Adam Gillon, *Conrad and Shakespeare* (New York: Astra, 1976). I have been significantly aided, as well, by the editions of *Lord Jim* edited by John Batchelor (Oxford: Oxford UP, 1983) and by Cedric Watts and Robert Hampson (Harmondsworth: Penguin, 1986). Third, *The Collected Letters of Joseph Conrad*, edited by Frederick R. Karl and Laurence Davies, 8 vols. (Cambridge: Cambridge UP, 1983—), has supplanted all previous printings of the letters and is thus the one I now use in the Backgrounds section. Fourth, while Norman Sherry's richly detailed account of the historical and geographical sources of *Lord Jim* remains authoritative, it has been augmented and qualified by subsequent scholars, especially by Hans van Marle and Pierre Lefranc. Their topographical and geographical essay and Lefranc's brand-new sea piece appear in this volume. Finally, literary criticism has changed much, particularly since the late 1970s. All the critical essays in this edition are from the recent past except the selection from Albert J. Guerard's *Conrad the Novelist* from the first Norton Critical Edition. Guerard's book seems to me still much the best analysis and celebration of Conrad's artistry. In choosing the new critical pieces, my aim has been not to represent dutifully a variety of "approaches" but rather to apply Henry James's admittedly subjective standard, "the quality of the mind of the producer." Joseph Conrad, James's greatest disciple, surely deserves no less. Excerpts are indicated with three spaced asterisks (* * *): run in when the opening, middle, or close of a paragraph has been omitted and centered between full lines when a full paragraph or more is omitted.

This second Norton Critical Edition of *Lord Jim* is indebted to an embarrassing number of people, more than I can hope to mention, all lovers of Joseph Conrad. They comprise undergraduate and graduate students, colleagues, and friends, including correspondents. Two of the last merit special thanks. Ernest W. Sullivan II initially gave expert advice on editing the text. Later, using his own collations of all the editions of *Lord Jim* in Conrad's lifetime, he twice went through my textual notes, made numerous corrections and additions, and then double-checked the discrepancies between our findings against the original texts. In the last stage of the edition, Pierre Lefranc, serious sailor as well as literary scholar, determined for me, on the basis of the available evidence, the most likely route of the historical pilgrim ship the *Jeddah*, and plotted the course, tentatively, on his own chart. But many other Conradians offered helpful suggestions. I call to mind Daphna Erdinast-Vulcan, Leon Higdon, Alex Kurczaba, Hans van Marle, Gene Moore, Donald Rude. Norman Sherry long ago gave me his wonderful photographs. Dr. Gomer Evans and Ruth Gelber put me onto the photograph of the *Jeddah*'s rigging plan. Two distinguished Stanford Ph.D.'s and old friends, Paul Armstrong and Marianne De Koven, gave much good advice about recent Conrad critics. The latter also offered invaluable practical help, which I deeply appreciate. Three Stanford undergraduates provided faithful and intelligent research assistance: Dave Kunstle, Jacqueline Mohalley, Dean Stier. Stanford doctoral candidate Diana Maltz was a lifesaver at the end of the project, especially in cross-referencing the textual notes. In the Stanford Library, Mark G. Dimunation, former rare book librarian, and William McPheron, curator of the English and American Literature Collections, were most helpful. So, too, was Ms. Leslie Morris, curator of the Rosenbach Library in Philadelphia. Stanford's two great Conradians have long been strongly supportive, Ian Watt for thirty years and Albert Guerard for over forty-five. Supportive, too, have been fellow Norton editors, sympathetic colleagues, and dear friends Albert J. Gelpi and Barbara Charlesworth Gelpi. Polly Tooker remains the model of an expert typist and copy editor. At Norton, Kate Lovelady and Marian Johnson were very helpful in securing permissions and overseeing proofs, respectively. Carol Bemis is the ideal editor for Norton Critical Editions: patient, empathetic, smart, energetic. Still, the greatest support has been my wife, Joyce Penn Moser, whose warm presence and wise counsel have sustained me from start to finish.

T. C. M.

The Text of
LORD JIM

LORD JIM

A Tale

BY

JOSEPH CONRAD

*" It is certain my Conviction gains infinitely,
the moment another soul will believe in it."*
—NOVALIS.

WILLIAM BLACKWOOD AND SONS
EDINBURGH AND LONDON
MDCCCC

TO

MR AND MRS G. F. W. HOPE,

WITH GRATEFUL AFFECTION

AFTER MANY YEARS

OF

FRIENDSHIP.

Author's Note[1]

When this novel first appeared in book form a notion got about that I had been bolted away with. Some reviewers maintained that the work starting as a short story had got beyond the writer's control. One or two discovered internal evidence of the fact, which seemed to amuse them. They pointed out the limitations of the narrative form. They argued that no man could have been expected to talk all that time, and other men to listen so long. It was not, they said, very credible.[2]

After thinking it over for something like sixteen years, I am not so sure about that. Men have been known, both in the tropics and in the temperate zone, to sit up half the night "swapping yarns." This, however, is but one yarn, yet with interruptions affording some measure of relief; and in regard to the listeners' endurance, the postulate must be accepted that the story *was* interesting. It is the necessary preliminary assumption. If I hadn't believed that it *was* interesting I could never have begun to write it. As to the mere physical possibility we all know that some speeches in Parliament have taken nearer six than three hours in delivery; whereas all that part of the book which is Marlow's narrative can be read through aloud, I should say, in less than three hours. Besides— though I have kept strictly all such insignificant details out of the tale —we may presume that there must have been refreshments on that night, a glass of mineral water of some sort to help the narrator on.

But, seriously, the truth of the matter is, that my first thought was of a short story, concerned only with the pilgrim ship episode; nothing more. And that was a legitimate conception. After writing a few pages, however, I became for some reason discontented and I laid them aside for a time. I didn't take them out of the drawer till the late Mr. William Blackwood suggested I should give something again to his magazine.

It was only then that I perceived that the pilgrim ship episode was a good starting-point for a free and wandering tale; that it was an event, too, which could conceivably colour the whole "sentiment of existence" in a simple and sensitive character. But all these preliminary moods and stirrings of spirit were rather obscure at the time, and they do not appear clearer to me now after the lapse of so many years.

1. The epigraph is by the German romantic author Friedrich von Hardenberg (1772–1801), whose pen name was Novalis. The passage comes from fragment 153 of *Das Allgemeine Brouillon*, but Conrad probably used Thomas Carlyle's version in his *On Heroes, Hero-Worship, and the Heroic in History* (1841). Conrad requotes the sentence in his 1912 memoir, *A Personal Record*. The dedicatees were Conrad's oldest English friends. G. F. W. Hope, a businessman, was an ex-officer in the British Merchant Service and an amateur yachtsman. He appears anonymously as a "director of companies" and "Conway boy" in "Youth" (1898) and *Heart of Darkness* (1899); in the latter his yawl, *Nellie*, serves as the primary setting. At the time of writing *Lord Jim*, Conrad felt particular sympathy for the Hopes. They had lost not only all their investments but also their seventeen-year-old son, who was murdered. The Author's Note was written for the second English edition (London: Dent, 1917).
2. See Hugh Clifford in "Criticism" below.

The few pages I had laid aside were not without their weight in the choice of subject. But the whole was re-written deliberately. When I sat down to it I knew it would be a long book, though I didn't foresee that it would spread itself over thirteen numbers of "Maga."

I have been asked at times whether this was not the book of mine I liked best. I am a great foe to favouritism in public life, in private life, and even in the delicate relationship of an author to his works. As a matter of principle I will have no favourites; but I don't go so far as to feel grieved and annoyed by the preference some people give to my *Lord Jim*. I won't even say that I "fail to understand. . . ." No! But once I had occasion to be puzzled and surprised.

A friend of mine returning from Italy had talked with a lady there who did not like the book. I regretted that, of course, but what surprised me was the ground of her dislike. "You know," she said, "it is all so morbid."

The pronouncement gave me food for an hour's anxious thought. Finally I arrived at the conclusion that, making due allowances for the subject itself being rather foreign to women's normal sensibilities, the lady could not have been an Italian. I wonder whether she was European at all? In any case, no Latin temperament would have perceived anything morbid in the acute consciousness of lost honour. Such a consciousness may be wrong, or it may be right, or it may be condemned as artificial; and, perhaps, my Jim is not a type of wide commonness. But I can safely assure my readers that he is not the product of coldly perverted thinking. He's not a figure of Northern Mists either. One sunny morning, in the commonplace surroundings of an Eastern roadstead, I saw his form pass by—appealing—significant—under a cloud—perfectly silent. Which is as it should be. It was for me, with all the sympathy of which I was capable, to seek fit words for his meaning. He was "one of us."[3]

J. C.

1917.

---

3. After Adam ate the forbidden fruit, God said to the angels: "Behold the man is become as one of us, to know good and evil" (Genesis 3.22).

Lord Jim

Chapter I

He was an inch, perhaps two, under six feet, powerfully built, and he advanced straight at you with a slight stoop of the shoulders, head forward, and a fixed from-under stare which made you think of a charging bull. His voice was deep, loud, and his manner displayed a kind of dogged self-assertion which had nothing aggressive in it. It seemed a necessity, and it was directed apparently as much at himself as at anybody else. He was spotlessly neat, apparelled in immaculate white from shoes to hat, and in the various Eastern ports where he got his living as ship-chandler's water-clerk he was very popular.

A water-clerk need not pass an examination in anything under the sun,[1] but he must have Ability in the abstract and demonstrate it practically. His work consists in racing under sail, steam, or oars against other water-clerks for any ship about to anchor, greeting her captain cheerily, forcing upon him a card—the business card of the ship-chandler—and on his first visit on shore piloting him firmly but without ostentation to a vast, cavern-like shop which is full of things that are eaten and drunk on board ship; where you can get everything to make her seaworthy and beautiful, from a set of chain-hooks for her cable to a book of gold-leaf for the carvings of her stern; and where her commander is received like a brother by a ship-chandler he has never seen before. There is a cool parlour, easy-chairs, bottles, cigars, writing implements, a copy of harbour regulations, and a warmth of welcome that melts the salt of a three months' passage out of a seaman's heart. The connection thus begun is kept up, as long as the ship remains in harbour, by the daily visits of the water-clerk. To the captain he is faithful like a friend and attentive like a son, with the patience of Job,[2] the unselfish devotion of a woman, and the jollity of a boon companion. Later on the bill is sent in. It is a beautiful and humane occupation. Therefore good water-clerks are scarce. When a water-clerk who possesses Ability in the abstract has also the advantage of having been brought up to the sea, he is worth to his employer a lot of money and some humouring. Jim had always good wages and as much humouring as would have

1. See Ecclesiastes 1.9: "And there is no new thing under the sun." Also, see below, p. 185.
2. The Old Testament patriarch who undergoes afflictions with fortitude and faith.

bought the fidelity of a fiend. Nevertheless, with black ingratitude he would throw up the job suddenly and depart. To his employers the reasons he gave were obviously inadequate. They said "Confounded fool!" as soon as his back was turned. This was their criticism on his exquisite sensibility.

To the white men in the waterside business and to the captains of ships he was just Jim[3]—nothing more. He had, of course, another name, but he was anxious that it should not be pronounced. His incognito, which had as many holes as a sieve, was not meant to hide a personality but a fact. When the fact broke through the incognito he would leave suddenly the seaport where he happened to be at the time and go to another—generally farther east. He kept to seaports because he was a seaman in exile from the sea, and had Ability in the abstract, which is good for no other work but that of a water-clerk. He retreated in good order towards the rising sun, and the fact followed him casually but inevitably. Thus in the course of years he was known successively in Bombay, in Calcutta, in Rangoon, in Penang, in Batavia—and in each of these halting-places was just Jim the water-clerk. Afterwards, when his keen perception of the Intolerable drove him away for good from seaports and white men, even into the virgin forest, the Malays of the jungle village, where he had elected to conceal his deplorable faculty, added a word to the monosyllable of his incognito. They called him Tuan Jim: as one might say—Lord Jim.

Originally he came from a parsonage. Many commanders of fine merchant-ships come from these abodes of piety and peace. Jim's father possessed such certain knowledge of the Unknowable as made for the righteousness of people in cottages without disturbing the ease of mind of those whom an unerring Providence enables to live in mansions. The little church on a hill had the mossy greyness of a rock seen through a ragged screen of leaves. It had stood there for centuries, but the trees around probably remembered the laying of the first stone. Below, the red front of the rectory gleamed with a warm tint in the midst of grass-plots, flower-beds, and fir-trees, with an orchard at the back, a paved stable-yard to the left, and the sloping glass of greenhouses tacked along a wall of bricks. The living had belonged to the family for generations; but Jim was one of five sons, and when after a course of light holiday literature his vocation for the sea had declared itself, he was sent at once to a "training-ship for officers of the mercantile marine."[4]

He learned there a little trigonometry and how to cross top-gallant yards. He was generally liked. He had the third place in navigation and pulled stroke in the first cutter. Having a steady head with an excellent

---

3. Probably comes from James Lingard; the early life resembles that of A. P. Williams. See Norman Sherry in "Sources," below.
4. Probably the *Conway*. A mercantile marine school ship for boys who intended to make the merchant service their profession, she was anchored in the estuary of the River Mersey at Liverpool, accepting her first cadets in 1859.

physique, he was very smart aloft. His station was in the fore-top, and often from there he looked down, with the contempt of a man destined to shine in the midst of dangers, at the peaceful multitude of roofs cut in two by the brown tide of the stream, while scattered on the outskirts of the surrounding plain the factory chimneys rose perpendicular against a grimy sky, each slender like a pencil, and belching out smoke like a volcano. He could see the big ships departing, the broad-beamed ferries constantly on the move, the little boats floating far below his feet, with the hazy splendour of the sea in the distance, and the hope of a stirring life in the world of adventure.

On the lower deck in the babel of two hundred voices he would forget himself, and beforehand live in his mind the sea-life of light literature. He saw himself saving people from sinking ships, cutting away masts in a hurricane, swimming through a surf with a line; or as a lonely castaway, barefooted and half naked, walking on uncovered reefs in search of shellfish to stave off starvation. He confronted savages on tropical shores, quelled mutinies on the high seas, and in a small boat upon the ocean kept up the hearts of despairing men—always an example of devotion to duty, and as unflinching as a hero in a book.

"Something's up. Come along."

He leaped to his feet. The boys were streaming up the ladders. Above could be heard a great scurrying about and shouting, and when he got through the hatchway he stood still—as if confounded.

It was the dusk of a winter's day. The gale had freshened since noon, stopping the traffic on the river, and now blew with the strength of a hurricane in fitful bursts that boomed like salvoes of great guns firing over the ocean. The rain slanted in sheets that flicked and subsided, and between whiles Jim had threatening glimpses of the tumbling tide, the small craft jumbled and tossing along the shore, the motionless buildings in the driving mist, the broad ferry-boats pitching ponderously at anchor, the vast landing-stages heaving up and down and smothered in sprays. The next gust seemed to blow all this away. The air was full of flying water. There was a fierce purpose in the gale, a furious earnestness in the screech of the wind, in the brutal tumult of earth and sky, that seemed directed at him, and made him hold his breath in awe. He stood still. It seemed to him he was whirled around.

He was jostled. "Man the cutter!" Boys rushed past him. A coaster running in for shelter had crashed through a schooner at anchor, and one of the ship's instructors had seen the accident. A mob of boys clambered on the rails, clustered round the davits. "Collision. Just ahead of us. Mr Symons saw it." A push made him stagger against the mizzenmast, and he caught hold of a rope. The old training-ship chained to her moorings quivered all over, bowing gently head to wind, and with her scanty rigging humming in a deep bass the breathless song of her youth at sea. "Lower away!" He saw the boat, manned, drop swiftly

below the rail, and rushed after her. He heard a splash. "Let go; clear
the falls!" He leaned over. The river alongside seethed in frothy streaks.
The cutter could be seen in the falling darkness under the spell of tide
and wind, that for a moment held her bound, and tossing abreast of the
ship. A yelling voice in her reached him faintly: "Keep stroke, you young
whelps, if you want to save anybody! Keep stroke!" And suddenly she
lifted high her bow, and, leaping with raised oars over a wave, broke
the spell cast upon her by the wind and tide.

Jim felt his shoulder gripped firmly. "Too late, youngster." The captain of the ship laid a restraining hand on that boy, who seemed on the
point of leaping overboard, and Jim looked up with the pain of conscious
defeat in his eyes. The captain smiled sympathetically. "Better luck next
time. This will teach you to be smart."

A shrill cheer greeted the cutter. She came dancing back half full of
water, and with two exhausted men washing about on her bottom boards.
The tumult and the menace of wind and sea now appeared very contemptible to Jim, increasing the regret of his awe at their inefficient
menace. Now he knew what to think of it. It seemed to him he cared
nothing for the gale. He could affront greater perils. He would do so
—better than anybody. Not a particle of fear was left. Nevertheless he
brooded apart that evening while the bowman of the cutter—a boy with
a face like a girl's and big grey eyes—was the hero of the lower deck.
Eager questioners crowded round him. He narrated: "I just saw his head
bobbing, and I dashed my boat-hook in the water. It caught in his
breeches and I nearly went overboard, as I thought I would, only old
Symons let go the tiller and grabbed my legs—the boat nearly swamped.
Old Symons is a fine old chap. I don't mind a bit him being grumpy
with us. He swore at me all the time he held my leg, but that was only
his way of telling me to stick to the boat-hook. Old Symons is awfully
excitable—isn't he? No—not the little fair chap—the other, the big one
with a beard. When we pulled him in he groaned, 'Oh, my leg! oh,
my leg!' and turned up his eyes. Fancy such a big chap fainting like a
girl. Would any of you fellows faint for a jab with a boat-hook?—I
wouldn't. It went into his leg so far." He showed the boat-hook, which
he had carried below for the purpose, and produced a sensation. "No,
silly! It was not his flesh that held him—his breeches did. Lots of blood,
of course."

Jim thought it a pitiful display of vanity. The gale had ministered to
a heroism as spurious as its own pretence of terror. He felt angry with
the brutal tumult of earth and sky for taking him unawares and checking
unfairly a generous readiness for narrow escapes. Otherwise he was rather
glad he had not gone into the cutter, since a lower achievement had
served the turn. He had enlarged his knowledge more than those who
had done the work. When all men flinched, then—he felt sure—he
alone would know how to deal with the spurious menace of wind and

seas. He knew what to think of it. Seen dispassionately, it seemed contemptible. He could detect no trace of emotion in himself, and the final
effect of a staggering event was that, unnoticed and apart from the noisy
crowd of boys, he exulted with fresh certitude in his avidity for adventure,
and in a sense of many-sided courage.

Chapter II

After two years of training he went to sea, and entering the regions so
well known to his imagination, found them strangely barren of adventure. He made many voyages. He knew the magic monotony of existence
between sky and water: he had to bear the criticism of men, the exactions
of the sea, and the prosaic severity of the daily task that gives bread—
but whose only reward is in the perfect love of the work. This reward
eluded him. Yet he could not go back, because there is nothing more
enticing, disenchanting, and enslaving than the life at sea. Besides, his
prospects were good. He was gentlemanly, steady, tractable, with a
thorough knowledge of his duties; and in time, when yet very young,
he became chief mate of a fine ship, without ever having been tested
by those events of the sea that show in the light of day the inner worth
of a man, the edge of his temper, and the fibre of his stuff; that reveal
the quality of his resistance and the secret truth of his pretences, not
only to others but also to himself.

Only once in all that time he had again the glimpse of the earnestness
in the anger of the sea. That truth is not so often made apparent as
people might think. There are many shades in the danger of adventures
and gales, and it is only now and then that there appears on the face of
facts a sinister violence of intention—that indefinable something which
forces it upon the mind and the heart of a man, that this complication
of accidents or these elemental furies are coming at him with a purpose
of malice, with a strength beyond control, with an unbridled cruelty
that means to tear out of him his hope and his fear, the pain of his
fatigue and his longing for rest: which means to smash, to destroy, to
annihilate all he has seen, known, loved, enjoyed, or hated; all that is
priceless and necessary—the sunshine, the memories, the future; which
means to sweep the whole precious world utterly away from his sight
by the simple and appalling act of taking his life.

Jim, disabled by a falling spar at the beginning of a week of which
his Scottish captain used to say afterwards, "Man! it's a pairfect meeracle
to me how she lived through it!" spent many days stretched on his back,
dazed, battered, hopeless, and tormented as if at the bottom of an abyss
of unrest. He did not care what the end would be, and in his lucid
moments overvalued his indifference. The danger, when not seen, has

the imperfect vagueness of human thought. The fear grows shadowy; and Imagination, the enemy of men, the father of all terrors, unstimulated, sinks to rest in the dulness of exhausted emotion. Jim saw nothing but the disorder of his tossed cabin. He lay there battened down in the midst of a small devastation, and felt secretly glad he had not to go on deck. But now and again an uncontrollable rush of anguish would grip him bodily, make him gasp and writhe under the blankets, and then the unintelligent brutality of an existence liable to the agony of such sensations filled him with a despairing desire to escape at any cost. Then fine weather returned, and he thought no more about it.

His lameness, however, persisted, and when the ship arrived at an Eastern port[1] he had to go to the hospital. His recovery was slow, and he was left behind.

There were only two other patients in the white men's ward: the purser of a gunboat, who had broken his leg falling down a hatchway; and a kind of railway contractor from a neighbouring province, afflicted by some mysterious tropical disease, who held the doctor for an ass, and indulged in secret debaucheries of patent medicine which his Tamil servant used to smuggle in with unwearied devotion. They told each other the story of their lives, played cards a little, or, yawning and in pyjamas, lounged through the day in easy-chairs without saying a word. The hospital stood on a hill, and a gentle breeze entering through the windows, always flung wide open, brought into the bare room the softness of the sky, the languor of the earth, the bewitching breath of the Eastern waters. There were perfumes in it, suggestions of infinite repose, the gift of endless dreams. Jim looked every day over the thickets of gardens, beyond the roofs of the town, over the fronds of palms growing on the shore, at that roadstead which is a thoroughfare to the East,— at the roadstead dotted by garlanded islets, lighted by festal sunshine, its ships like toys, its brilliant activity resembling a holiday pageant, with the eternal serenity of the Eastern sky overhead and the smiling peace of the Eastern seas possessing the space as far as the horizon.

Directly he could walk without a stick, he descended into the town to look for some opportunity to get home. Nothing offered just then, and, while waiting, he associated naturally with the men of his calling in the port. These were of two kinds. Some, very few and seen there but seldom, led mysterious lives, had preserved an undefaced energy with the temper of buccaneers and the eyes of dreamers. They appeared to live in a crazy maze of plans, hopes, dangers, enterprises, ahead of civilisation, in the dark places of the sea; and their death was the only event of their fantastic existence that seemed to have a reasonable certitude of achievement. The majority were men who, like himself, thrown there by some accident, had remained as officers of country ships. They

1. Singapore. Conrad suffered a similar injury and was hospitalized in Singapore in the summer of 1887. See below, p. 355.

had now a horror of the home service, with its harder conditions, severer view of duty, and the hazard of stormy oceans. They were attuned to the eternal peace of Eastern sky and sea. They loved short passages, good deck-chairs, large native crews, and the distinction of being white. They shuddered at the thought of hard work, and led precariously easy lives, always on the verge of dismissal, always on the verge of engagement, serving Chinamen, Arabs, half-castes—would have served the devil himself had he made it easy enough. They talked everlastingly of turns of luck: how So-and-so got charge of a boat on the coast of China—a soft thing; how this one had an easy billet in Japan somewhere, and that one was doing well in the Siamese navy; and in all they said —in their actions, in their looks, in their persons—could be detected the soft spot, the place of decay, the determination to lounge safely through existence.

To Jim that gossiping crowd, viewed as seamen, seemed at first more unsubstantial than so many shadows. But at length he found a fascination in the sight of those men, in their appearance of doing so well on such a small allowance of danger and toil. In time, beside the original disdain there grew up slowly another sentiment; and suddenly, giving up the idea of going home, he took a berth as chief mate of the *Patna*.[2]

The *Patna* was a local steamer as old as the hills, lean like a greyhound, and eaten up with rust worse than a condemned water-tank. She was owned by a Chinaman, chartered by an Arab, and commanded by a sort of renegade New South Wales German, very anxious to curse publicly his native country, but who, apparently on the strength of Bismarck's victorious policy, brutalised all those he was not afraid of, and wore a "blood-and-iron"[3] air, combined with a purple nose and a red moustache. After she had been painted outside and whitewashed inside, eight hundred pilgrims (more or less) were driven on board of her as she lay with steam up alongside a wooden jetty.

They streamed aboard over three gangways, they streamed in urged by faith and the hope of paradise, they streamed in with a continuous tramp and shuffle of bare feet, without a word, a murmur, or a look back; and when clear of confining rails spread on all sides over the deck, flowed forward and aft, overflowed down the yawning hatchways, filled the inner recesses of the ship—like water filling a cistern, like water flowing into crevices and crannies, like water rising silently even with the rim. Eight hundred men and women with faith and hopes, with affections and memories, they had collected there, coming from north

2. Name of a city, district, and division of eastern India, a common variety of rice, and a ship known to Conrad. (Typically, Conrad uses the names of real ships, e.g., the *Pelion*, the *Wolverine*, and the *Sephora*, and of real ship lines, e.g., The Blue Star and The Dale.) The actual pilgrim ship was called the *Jeddah* after Mecca's port on the Red Sea. See Norman Sherry in "Sources," below.

3. Epithet applied to Otto von Bismarck (1815–1898), first chancellor of the German Empire, who said in a speech to the Prussian Diet in 1862: "Not by speechifying and counting majorities are the great questions of the time to be solved . . . but by iron and blood."

and south and from the outskirts of the East, after treading the jungle paths, descending the rivers, coasting in praus along the shallows, crossing in small canoes from island to island, passing through suffering, meeting strange sights, beset by strange fears, upheld by one desire. They came from solitary huts in the wilderness, from populous campongs, from villages by the sea. At the call of an idea they had left their forests, their clearings, the protection of their rulers, their prosperity, their poverty, the surroundings of their youth and the graves of their fathers. They came covered with dust, with sweat, with grime, with rags—the strong men at the head of family parties, the lean old men pressing forward without hope of return; young boys with fearless eyes glancing curiously, shy little girls with tumbled long hair; the timid women muffled up and clasping to their breasts, wrapped in loose ends of soiled head-cloths, their sleeping babies, the unconscious pilgrims of an exacting belief.

"Look at dese cattle," said the German skipper to his new chief mate.

An Arab, the leader of that pious voyage, came last. He walked slowly aboard, handsome and grave in his white gown and large turban. A string of servants followed, loaded with his luggage; the *Patna* cast off and backed away from the wharf.

She was headed between two small islets, crossed obliquely the anchoring-ground of sailing-ships, swung through half a circle in the shadow of a hill, then ranged close to a ledge of foaming reefs. The Arab, standing up aft, recited aloud the prayer of travellers by sea. He invoked the favour of the Most High upon that journey, implored His blessing on men's toil and on the secret purposes of their hearts; the steamer pounded in the dusk the calm water of the Strait;[4] and far astern of the pilgrim ship a screw-pile lighthouse, planted by unbelievers on a treacherous shoal, seemed to wink at her its eye of flame, as if in derision of her errand of faith.

She cleared the Strait, crossed the bay,[5] continued on her way through the "One-degree" passage.[6] She held on straight for the Red Sea under a serene sky, under a sky scorching and unclouded, enveloped in a fulgor[7] of sunshine that killed all thought, oppressed the heart, withered all impulses of strength and energy. And under the sinister splendour of that sky the sea, blue and profound, remained still, without a stir, without a ripple, without a wrinkle—viscous, stagnant, dead. The *Patna*, with a slight hiss, passed over that plain, luminous and smooth, unrolled a black ribbon of smoke across the sky, left behind her on the water a white ribbon of foam that vanished at once, like the phan-

---

4. The Strait of Malacca, a channel five hundred miles long between the southern Malay peninsula and the island of Sumatra.
5. The Bay of Bengal.
6. The One and a Half Degree Channel: a seaway of the Indian Ocean, roughly along 1° 30' N, between Haddummati Atoll and Suvadiva Atoll of the Maldive Islands; about fifty-five miles wide. See below, pp. 379–80.
7. Dazzling brightness.

tom of a track drawn upon a lifeless sea by the phantom of a steamer.

Every morning the sun, as if keeping pace in his revolutions with the progress of the pilgrimage, emerged with a silent burst of light exactly at the same distance astern of the ship, caught up with her at noon, pouring the concentrated fire of his rays on the pious purposes of the men, glided past on his descent, and sank mysteriously into the sea evening after evening, preserving the same distance ahead of her advancing bows. The five whites on board lived amidships, isolated from the human cargo. The awnings covered the deck with a white roof from stem to stern, and a faint hum, a low murmur of sad voices, alone revealed the presence of a crowd of people upon the great blaze of the ocean. Such were the days, still, hot, heavy, disappearing one by one into the past, as if falling into an abyss for ever open in the wake of the ship; and the ship, lonely under a wisp of smoke, held on her steadfast way black and smouldering in a luminous immensity, as if scorched by a flame flicked at her from a heaven without pity.

The nights descended on her like a benediction.

Chapter III

A marvellous stillness pervaded the world, and the stars, together with the serenity of their rays, seemed to shed upon the earth the assurance of everlasting security. The young moon recurved, and shining low in the west, was like a slender shaving thrown up from a bar of gold, and the Arabian Sea, smooth and cool to the eye like a sheet of ice, extended its perfect level to the perfect circle of a dark horizon. The propeller turned without a check, as though its beat had been part of the scheme of a safe universe; and on each side of the *Patna* two deep folds of water, permanent and sombre on the unwrinkled shimmer, enclosed within their straight and diverging ridges a few white swirls of foam bursting in a low hiss, a few wavelets, a few ripples, a few undulations that, left behind, agitated the surface of the sea for an instant after the passage of the ship, subsided splashing gently, calmed down at last into the circular stillness of water and sky with the black speck of the moving hull remaining everlastingly in its centre.

Jim on the bridge was penetrated by the great certitude of unbounded safety and peace that could be read on the silent aspect of nature like the certitude of fostering love upon the placid tenderness of a mother's face. Below the roof of awnings, surrendered to the wisdom of white men and to their courage, trusting the power of their unbelief and the iron shell of their fire-ship, the pilgrims of an exacting faith slept on mats, on blankets, on bare planks, on every deck, in all the dark corners, wrapped in dyed cloths, muffled in soiled rags, with their heads resting on small bundles, with their faces pressed to bent forearms: the men, the women, the children; the old with the young, the decrepit with the lusty—all equal before sleep, death's brother.

A draught of air, fanned from forward by the speed of the ship, passed steadily through the long gloom between the high bulwarks, swept over the rows of prone bodies; a few dim flames in globe-lamps were hung short here and there under the ridge-poles, and in the blurred circles of light thrown down and trembling slightly to the unceasing vibration of the ship appeared a chin upturned, two closed eyelids, a dark hand with silver rings, a meagre limb draped in a torn covering, a head bent back, a naked foot, a throat bared and stretched as if offering itself to the knife. The well-to-do had made for their families shelters with heavy boxes and dusty mats; the poor reposed side by side with all they had on earth tied up in a rag under their heads; the lone old men slept, with drawn-up legs, upon their prayer-carpets, with their hands over their ears and one elbow on each side of the face: a father, his shoulders up and his knees under his forehead, dozed dejectedly by a boy who slept on his back with tousled hair and one arm commandingly extended; a woman covered from head to foot, like a corpse, with a piece of white sheeting, had a naked child in the hollow of each arm; the Arab's belongings, piled right aft, made a heavy mound of broken outlines, with a cargo-lamp swung above, and a great confusion of vague forms behind: gleams of paunchy brass pots, the foot-rest of a deck-chair, blades of spears, the straight scabbard of an old sword leaning against a heap of pillows, the spout of a tin coffee-pot. The patent log on the taffrail periodically rang a single tinkling stroke for every mile traversed on an errand of faith. Above the mass of sleepers a faint and patient sigh at times floated, the exhalation of a troubled dream; and short metallic clangs bursting out suddenly in the depths of the ship, the harsh scrape of a shovel, the violent slam of a furnace-door, exploded brutally, as if the men handling the mysterious things below had their breasts full of fierce anger: while the slim high hull of the steamer went on evenly ahead, without a sway of her bare masts, cleaving continuously the great calm of the waters under the inaccessible serenity of the sky.

Jim paced athwart, and his footsteps in the vast silence were loud to his own ears, as if echoed by the watchful stars: his eyes roaming about the line of the horizon, seemed to gaze hungrily into the unattainable, and did not see the shadow of the coming event. The only shadow on the sea was the shadow of the black smoke pouring heavily from the funnel its immense streamer, whose end was constantly dissolving in the air. Two Malays, silent and almost motionless, steered, one on each side of the wheel, whose brass rim shone fragmentarily in the oval of light thrown out by the binnacle. Now and then a hand, with black fingers alternately letting go and catching hold of revolving spokes, appeared in the illumined part; the links of wheel-chains ground heavily in the grooves of the barrel. Jim would glance at the compass, would glance around the unattainable horizon, would stretch himself till his joints cracked, with a leisurely twist of the body, in the very excess of wellbeing; and, as if made audacious by the invincible aspect of the peace, he felt he cared for nothing that could happen to him to the end of his days. From time to time he glanced idly at a chart pegged out with four drawing-pins on a low three-legged table abaft the steering-gear case. The sheet of paper portraying the depths of the sea presented a shiny surface under the light of a bull's-eye lamp lashed to a stanchion, a surface as level and smooth as the glimmering surface of the waters. Parallel rulers with a pair of dividers reposed on it; the ship's position at last noon was marked with a small black cross, and the straight pencil-line drawn firmly as far as Perim figured the course of the ship—the path of souls towards the holy place, the promise of salvation, the reward of eternal life—while the pencil with its sharp end touching the Somali coast lay round and still like a naked ship's spar floating in the pool of a sheltered dock. "How steady she goes," thought Jim with wonder, with something like gratitude for this high peace of sea and sky. At such times his thoughts would be full of valorous deeds: he loved these dreams and the success of his imaginary achievements. They were the best parts of life, its secret truth, its hidden reality. They had a gorgeous virility, the charm of vagueness, they passed before him with an heroic tread; they carried his soul away with them and made it drunk with the divine philtre of an unbounded confidence in itself. There was nothing he could not face. He was so pleased with the idea that he smiled, keeping perfunctorily his eyes ahead; and when he happened to glance back he saw the white streak of the wake drawn as straight by the ship's keel upon the sea as the black line drawn by the pencil upon the chart.

The ash-buckets racketed, clanking up and down the stoke-hold ventilators, and this tin-pot clatter warned him the end of his watch was near. He sighed with content, with regret as well at having to part from that serenity which fostered the adventurous freedom of his thoughts. He was a little sleepy too, and felt a pleasurable languor running through every limb as though all the blood in his body had turned to warm milk. His skipper had come up noiselessly, in pyjamas and with his sleeping-jacket flung wide open. Red of face, only half awake, the left eye partly closed, the right staring stupid and glassy, he hung his big head over the chart and scratched his ribs sleepily. There was something obscene in the sight of his naked flesh. His bared breast glistened soft and greasy as though he had sweated out his fat in his sleep. He pronounced a professional remark in a voice harsh and dead, resembling the rasping sound of a wood-file on the edge of a plank; the fold of his double chin hung like a bag triced up close under the hinge of his jaw. Jim started, and his answer was full of deference; but the odious and fleshy figure, as though seen for the first time in a revealing moment, fixed itself in his memory for ever as the incarnation of everything vile and base that lurks in the world we love: in our own hearts we trust for our salvation, in the men that surround us, in the sights that fill our eyes, in the sounds that fill our ears, and in the air that fills our lungs.

The thin gold shaving of the moon floating slowly downwards had lost itself on the darkened surface of the waters, and the eternity beyond the sky seemed to come down nearer to the earth, with the augmented glitter of the stars, with the more profound sombreness in the lustre of the half-transparent dome covering the flat disc of an opaque sea. The ship moved so smoothly that her onward motion was imperceptible to the senses of men, as though she had been a crowded planet speeding through the dark spaces of ether behind the swarm of suns, in the appalling and calm solitudes awaiting the breath of future creations. "Hot is no name for it down below," said a voice.

Jim smiled without looking round. The skipper presented an unmoved breadth of back: it was the renegade's trick to appear pointedly unaware of your existence unless it suited his purpose to turn at you with a devouring glare before he let loose a torrent of foamy, abusive jargon that came like a gush from a sewer. Now he emitted only a sulky grunt; the second engineer at the head of the bridge-ladder, kneading with damp palms a dirty sweat-rag, unabashed, continued the tale of his complaints. The sailors had a good time of it up here, and what was the use of them in the world he would be blowed if he could see. The poor devils of engineers had to get the ship along anyhow, and they could very well do the rest too; by gosh they—"Shut up!" growled the German stolidly. "Oh yes! Shut up—and when anything goes wrong you fly to us, don't you?" went on the other. He was more than half cooked, he expected; but anyway, now, he did not mind how much he sinned, because these last three days he had passed through a fine course of training for the place where the bad boys go when they die—b'gosh, he had—besides being made jolly well deaf by the blasted racket below. The durned, compound, surface-condensing, rotten scrap-heap rattled and banged down there like an old deck-winch, only more so; and what made him risk his life every night and day that God made amongst the refuse of a breaking-up yard flying round at fifty-seven revolutions, was more than *he* could tell. He must have been born reckless, b'gosh. He . . . "Where did you get drink?" inquired the German, very savage, but motionless in the light of the binnacle, like a clumsy effigy of a man cut out of a block of fat. Jim went on smiling at the retreating horizon; his heart was full of generous impulses, and his thought was contemplating his own superiority. "Drink!" repeated the engineer with amiable scorn: he was hanging on with both hands to the rail, a shadowy figure with flexible legs. "Not from you, captain. You're far too mean, b'gosh. You would let a good man die sooner than give him a drop of schnapps.[1]

---

1. Strong liquor resembling Hollands gin.

That's what you Germans call economy. Penny wise, pound foolish."
He became sentimental. The chief had given him a four-finger nip
about ten o'clock—"only one, s'elp me!"—good old chief; but as to
getting the old fraud out of his bunk—a five-ton crane couldn't do it.
Not it. Not to-night anyhow. He was sleeping sweetly like a little child,
with a bottle of prime brandy under his pillow. From the thick throat
of the commander of the *Patna* came a low rumble, on which the sound
of the word *schwein*[2] fluttered high and low like a capricious feather in
a faint stir of air. He and the chief engineer had been cronies for a good
few years—serving the same jovial, crafty, old Chinaman, with horn-
rimmed goggles and strings of red silk plaited into the venerable grey
hairs of his pigtail. The quay-side opinion in the *Patna*'s home-port was
that these two in the way of brazen peculation "had done together pretty
well everything you can think of." Outwardly they were badly matched:
one dull-eyed, malevolent, and of soft fleshy curves; the other lean, all
hollows, with a head long and bony like the head of an old horse, with
sunken cheeks, with sunken temples, with an indifferent glazed glance
of sunken eyes. He had been stranded out East somewhere—in Canton,
in Shanghai, or perhaps in Yokohama; he probably did not care to
remember himself the exact locality, nor yet the cause of his shipwreck.
He had been, in mercy to his youth, kicked quietly out of his ship twenty
years ago or more, and it might have been so much worse for him that
the memory of the episode had in it hardly a trace of misfortune. Then,
steam navigation expanding in these seas and men of his craft being
scarce at first, he had "got on" after a sort. He was eager to let strangers
know in a dismal mumble that he was "an old stager out here." When
he moved, a skeleton seemed to sway loose in his clothes; his walk was
mere wandering, and he was given to wander thus around the engine-
room skylight, smoking, without relish, doctored tobacco in a brass bowl
at the end of a cherrywood stem four feet long, with the imbecile gravity
of a thinker evolving a system of philosophy from the hazy glimpse of
a truth. He was usually anything but free with his private store of liquor;
but on that night he had departed from his principles, so that his second,
a weak-headed child of Wapping, what with the unexpectedness of the
treat and the strength of the stuff, had become very happy, cheeky, and
talkative. The fury of the New South Wales German was extreme; he
puffed like an exhaust-pipe, and Jim, faintly amused by the scene, was
impatient for the time when he could get below: the last ten minutes
of the watch were irritating like a gun that hangs fire; those men did
not belong to the world of heroic adventure; they weren't bad chaps
though. Even the skipper himself . . . His gorge rose at the mass of
panting flesh from which issued gurgling mutters, a cloudy trickle of
filthy expressions; but he was too pleasurably languid to dislike actively

2. Swine.

this or any other thing. The quality of these men did not matter; he rubbed shoulders with them, but they could not touch him; he shared the air they breathed, but he was different. . . . Would the skipper go for the engineer? . . . The life was easy and he was too sure of himself—too sure of himself to . . . The line dividing his meditation from a surreptitious doze on his feet was thinner than a thread in a spider's web.

The second engineer was coming by easy transitions to the consideration of his finances and of his courage.

"Who's drunk? I? No, no, captain! That won't do. You ought to know by this time the chief ain't free-hearted enough to make a sparrow drunk, b'gosh. I've never been the worse for liquor in my life; the stuff ain't made yet that would make *me* drunk. I could drink liquid fire against your whisky peg for peg,[3] b'gosh, and keep as cool as a cucumber. If I thought I was drunk I would jump overboard—do away with myself, b'gosh. I would! Straight! And I won't go off the bridge. Where do you expect me to take the air on a night like this, eh? On deck amongst that vermin down there? Likely—ain't it! And I am not afraid of anything you can do."

The German lifted two heavy fists to heaven and shook them a little without a word.

"I don't know what fear is," pursued the engineer, with the enthusiasm of sincere conviction. "I am not afraid of doing all the bloomin' work in this rotten hooker, b'gosh! And a jolly good thing for you that there are some of us about the world that aren't afraid of their lives, or where would you be—you and this old thing here with her plates like brown paper—brown paper, s'elp me? It's all very fine for you—you get a power of pieces out of her one way and another; but what about me— what do I get? A measly hundred and fifty dollars a-month and find yourself.[4] I wish to ask you respectfully—respectfully, mind—who wouldn't chuck a dratted job like this? 'Tain't safe, s'elp me, it ain't! Only I am one of them fearless fellows . . ."

He let go the rail and made ample gestures as if demonstrating in the air the shape and extent of his valour; his thin voice darted in prolonged squeaks upon the sea, he tiptoed back and forth for the better emphasis of utterance, and suddenly pitched down head-first as though he had been clubbed from behind. He said "Damn!" as he tumbled; an instant of silence followed upon his screeching: Jim and the skipper staggered forward by common accord, and catching themselves up, stood very stiff and still gazing, amazed, at the undisturbed level of the sea. Then they looked upwards at the stars.

What had happened? The wheezy thump of the engines went on. Had the earth been checked in her course? They could not understand;

3. Measure for measure.
4. Provide your own equipment.

and suddenly the calm sea, the sky without a cloud, appeared formidably insecure in their immobility, as if poised on the brow of yawning destruction. The engineer rebounded vertically full length and collapsed again into a vague heap. This heap said "What's that?" in the muffled accents of profound grief. A faint noise as of thunder, of thunder infinitely remote, less than a sound, hardly more than a vibration, passed slowly, and the ship quivered in response, as if the thunder had growled deep down in the water. The eyes of the two Malays at the wheel glittered towards the white men, but their dark hands remained closed on the spokes. The sharp hull driving on its way seemed to rise a few inches in succession through its whole length, as though it had become pliable, and settled down again rigidly to its work of cleaving the smooth surface of the sea. Its quivering stopped, and the faint noise of thunder ceased all at once, as though the ship had steamed across a narrow belt of vibrating water and of humming air.

Chapter IV

A month or so afterwards, when Jim, in answer to pointed questions, tried to tell honestly the truth of this experience, he said, speaking of the ship: "She went over whatever it was as easy as a snake crawling over a stick." The illustration was good: the questions were aiming at facts, and the official Inquiry was being held in the police court of an Eastern port.[1] He stood elevated in the witness-box, with burning cheeks in a cool lofty room: the big framework of punkahs moved gently to and fro high above his head, and from below many eyes were looking at him out of dark faces, out of white faces, out of red faces, out of faces attentive, spellbound, as if all these people sitting in orderly rows upon narrow benches had been enslaved by the fascination of his voice. It was very loud, it rang startling in his own ears, it was the only sound audible in the world, for the terribly distinct questions that extorted his answers seemed to shape themselves in anguish and pain within his breast,—came to him poignant and silent like the terrible questioning of one's conscience. Outside the court the sun blazed—within was the wind of great punkahs that made you shiver, the shame that made you burn, the attentive eyes whose glance stabbed. The face of the presiding magistrate, clean shaved and impassible, looked at him deadly pale between the red faces of the two nautical assessors.[2] The light of a broad window under the ceiling fell from above on the heads and shoulders of the three men, and they were fiercely distinct in the half-light of the

---

1. Geographically speaking, Conrad is thinking of Bombay; but some of the details come from Singapore. See below, pp. 355–56 and 374–78.
2. Persons appointed to assist a judge or magistrate; especially those with professional knowledge of the subject to be decided (as legal assessors, nautical assessors, etc.).

big court-room where the audience seemed composed of staring shadows. They wanted facts. Facts! They demanded facts from him, as if facts could explain anything!

"After you had concluded you had collided with something floating awash, say a water-logged wreck, you were ordered by your captain to go forward and ascertain if there was any damage done. Did you think it likely from the force of the blow?" asked the assessor sitting to the left. He had a thin horseshoe beard, salient cheek-bones, and with both elbows on the desk clasped his rugged hands before his face, looking at Jim with thoughtful blue eyes; the other, a heavy, scornful man, thrown back in his seat, his left arm extended full length, drummed delicately with his finger-tips on a blotting-pad: in the middle the magistrate upright in the roomy arm-chair, his head inclined slightly on the shoulder, had his arms crossed on his breast and a few flowers in a glass vase by the side of his inkstand.

"I did not," said Jim. "I was told to call no one and to make no noise for fear of creating a panic. I thought the precaution reasonable. I took one of the lamps that were hung under the awnings and went forward. After opening the forepeak hatch I heard splashing in there. I lowered then the lamp the whole drift of its lanyard, and saw that the forepeak was more than half full of water already. I knew then there must be a big hole below the water-line." He paused.

"Yes," said the big assessor, with a dreamy smile at the blotting-pad; his fingers played incessantly, touching the paper without noise.

"I did not think of danger just then. I might have been a little startled: all this happened in such a quiet way and so very suddenly. I knew there was no other bulkhead in the ship but the collision bulkhead separating the forepeak from the forehold. I went back to tell the captain. I came upon the second engineer getting up at the foot of the bridge-ladder: he seemed dazed, and told me he thought his left arm was broken; he had slipped on the top step when getting down while I was forward. He exclaimed, 'My God! That rotten bulkhead 'll give way in a minute, and the damned thing will go down under us like a lump of lead.' He pushed me away with his right arm and ran before me up the ladder, shouting as he climbed. His left arm hung by his side. I followed up in time to see the captain rush at him and knock him down flat on his back. He did not strike him again: he stood bending over him and speaking angrily but quite low. I fancy he was asking him why the devil he didn't go and stop the engines, instead of making a row about it on deck. I heard him say, 'Get up! Run, fly!' He swore also. The engineer slid down the starboard ladder and bolted round the skylight to the engine-room companion which was on the port-side. He moaned as he ran. . . ."

He spoke slowly; he remembered swiftly and with extreme vividness; he could have reproduced like an echo the moaning of the engineer for

the better information of these men who wanted facts. After his first
feeling of revolt he had come round to the view that only a meticulous
precision of statement would bring out the true horror behind the appalling face of things. The facts those men were so eager to know had
been visible, tangible, open to the senses, occupying their place in space
and time, requiring for their existence a fourteen-hundred-ton steamer
and twenty-seven minutes by the watch; they made a whole that had
features, shades of expression, a complicated aspect that could be remembered by the eye, and something else besides, something invisible,
a directing spirit of perdition that dwelt within, like a malevolent soul
in a detestable body. He was anxious to make this clear. This had not
been a common affair, everything in it had been of the utmost importance, and fortunately he remembered everything. He wanted to go on
talking for truth's sake, perhaps for his own sake also; and while his
utterance was deliberate, his mind positively flew round and round the
serried circle of facts that had surged up all about him to cut him off
from the rest of his kind: it was like a creature that, finding itself imprisoned within an enclosure of high stakes, dashes round and round,
distracted in the night, trying to find a weak spot, a crevice, a place to
scale, some opening through which it may squeeze itself and escape.
This awful activity of mind made him hesitate at times in his
speech. . . .

"The captain kept on moving here and there on the bridge; he seemed
calm enough, only he stumbled several times; and once as I stood
speaking to him he walked right into me as though he had been stone-
blind. He made no definite answer to what I had to tell. He mumbled
to himself; all I heard of it were a few words that sounded like 'confounded
steam!' and 'infernal steam!'—something about steam. I thought . . .' "

He was becoming irrelevant; a question to the point cut short his
speech, like a pang of pain, and he felt extremely discouraged and weary.
He was coming to that, he was coming to that—and now, checked
brutally, he had to answer by yes or no. He answered truthfully by a
curt "Yes, I did"; and fair of face, big of frame, with young, gloomy
eyes, he held his shoulders upright above the box while his soul writhed
within him. He was made to answer another question so much to the
point and so useless, then waited again. His mouth was tastelessly dry,
as though he had been eating dust, then salt and bitter as after a drink
of sea-water. He wiped his damp forehead, passed his tongue over
parched lips, felt a shiver run down his back. The big assessor had
dropped his eyelids, and drummed on without a sound, careless and
mournful; the eyes of the other above the sunburnt, clasped fingers
seemed to glow with kindliness; the magistrate had swayed forward; his
pale face hovered near the flowers, and then dropping sideways over the
arm of his chair, he rested his temple in the palm of his hand. The
wind of the punkahs eddied down on the heads, on the dark-faced natives

wound about in voluminous draperies, on the Europeans sitting together very hot and in drill[3] suits that seemed to fit them as close as their skins, and holding their round pith hats on their knees; while gliding along the walls the court peons, buttoned tight in long white coats, flitted rapidly to and fro, running on bare toes, red-sashed, red turban on head, as noiseless as ghosts, and on the alert like so many retrievers.

Jim's eyes, wandering in the intervals of his answers, rested upon a white man who sat apart from the others, with his face worn and clouded, but with quiet eyes that glanced straight, interested and clear. Jim answered another question and was tempted to cry out, "What's the good of this, what's the good!" He tapped with his foot slightly, bit his lip, and looked away over the heads. He met the eyes of the white man. The glance directed at him was not the fascinated stare of the others. It was an act of intelligent volition. Jim between two questions forgot himself so far as to find leisure for a thought. This fellow—ran the thought—looks at me as though he could see somebody or something past my shoulder. He had come across that man before—in the street perhaps. He was positive he had never spoken to him. For days, for many days, he had spoken to no one, but had held silent, incoherent, and endless converse with himself, like a prisoner alone in his cell or like a wayfarer lost in a wilderness. At present he was answering questions that did not matter though they had a purpose, but he doubted whether he would ever again speak out as long as he lived. The sound of his own truthful statements confirmed his deliberate opinion that speech was of no use to him any longer. That man there seemed to be aware of his hopeless difficulty. Jim looked at him, then turned away resolutely, as after a final parting.

And later on, many times, in distant parts of the world, Marlow[4] showed himself willing to remember Jim, to remember him at length, in detail and audibly.

Perhaps it would be after dinner, on a verandah draped in motionless foliage and crowned with flowers, in the deep dusk speckled by fiery cigar-ends. The elongated bulk of each cane-chair harboured a silent listener. Now and then a small red glow would move abruptly, and expanding light up the fingers of a languid hand, part of a face in profound repose, or flash a crimson gleam into a pair of pensive eyes overshadowed by a fragment of an unruffled forehead: and with the very first word uttered Marlow's body, extended at rest in the seat, would become very still, as though his spirit had winged its way back into the lapse of time and were speaking through his lips from the past.

---

3. A strong durable cotton fabric, having a diagonal weave.
4. The narrator also of Conrad's "Youth," *Heart of Darkness,* and *Chance* (1913).

Chapter V

"Oh yes. I attended the inquiry," he would say, "and to this day I haven't left off wondering why I went. I am willing to believe each of us has a guardian angel, if you fellows will concede to me that each of us has a familiar devil as well. I want you to own up, because I don't like to feel exceptional in any way, and I know I have him—the devil, I mean. I haven't seen him, of course, but I go upon circumstantial evidence. He is there right enough, and, being malicious, he lets me in for that kind of thing. What kind of thing, you ask? Why, the inquiry thing, the yellow-dog thing—you wouldn't think a mangy, native tyke would be allowed to trip up people in the verandah of a magistrate's court, would you?—the kind of thing that by devious, unexpected, truly diabolical ways causes me to run up against men with soft spots, with hard spots, with hidden plague spots, by Jove! and loosens their tongues at the sight of me for their infernal confidences; as though, forsooth, I had no confidences to make to myself, as though—God help me!—I didn't have enough confidential information about myself to harrow my own soul till the end of my appointed time. And what I have done to be thus favoured I want to know. I declare I am as full of my own concerns as the next man, and I have as much memory as the average pilgrim in this valley, so you see I am not particularly fit to be a receptacle of confessions. Then why? Can't tell—unless it be to make time pass away after dinner. Charley, my dear chap, your dinner was extremely good, and in consequence these men here look upon a quiet rubber as a tumultuous occupation. They wallow in your good chairs and think to themselves, 'Hang exertion. Let that Marlow talk.'

"Talk! So be it. And it's easy enough to talk of Master Jim, after a good spread, two hundred feet above the sea-level, with a box of decent cigars handy, on a blessed evening of freshness and starlight that would make the best of us forget we are only on sufferance here and got to pick our way in cross lights, watching every precious minute and every irremediable step, trusting we shall manage yet to go out decently in the end—but not so sure of it after all—and with dashed little help to expect from those we touch elbows with right and left. Of course there are men here and there to whom the whole of life is like an after-dinner hour with a cigar; easy, pleasant, empty, perhaps enlivened by some fable of strife to be forgotten before the end is told—before the end is told—even if there happens to be any end to it.

"My eyes met his for the first time at that inquiry. You must know that everybody connected in any way with the sea was there, because the affair had been notorious for days, ever since that mysterious cable message came from Aden to start us all cackling. I say mysterious, because it was so in a sense though it contained a naked fact, about as

naked and ugly as a fact can well be. The whole waterside talked of
nothing else. First thing in the morning as I was dressing in my state-
room, I would hear through the bulkhead my Parsee Dubash jabbering
about the *Patna* with the steward, while he drank a cup of tea, by favour,
in the pantry. No sooner on shore I would meet some acquaintance,
and the first remark would be, 'Did you ever hear of anything to beat
this?' and according to his kind the man would smile cynically, or look
sad, or let out a swear or two. Complete strangers would accost each
other familiarly, just for the sake of easing their minds on the subject:
every confounded loafer in the town came in for a harvest of drinks over
this affair: you heard of it in the harbour office, at every ship-broker's,
at your agent's, from whites, from natives, from half-castes, from the
very boatmen squatting half-naked on the stone steps as you went up—
by Jove! There was some indignation, not a few jokes, and no end of
discussions as to what had become of them, you know. This went on
for a couple of weeks or more, and the opinion that whatever was
mysterious in this affair would turn out to be tragic as well, began to
prevail, when one fine morning, as I was standing in the shade by the
steps of the harbour office, I perceived four men walking towards me
along the quay. I wondered for a while where that queer lot had sprung
from, and suddenly, I may say, I shouted to myself, 'Here they are!'

"There they were, sure enough, three of them as large as life, and
one much larger of girth than any living man has a right to be, just
landed with a good breakfast inside of them from an outward bound
Dale Line steamer that had come in about an hour after sunrise. There
could be no mistake; I spotted the jolly skipper of the *Patna* at the first
glance: the fattest man in the whole blessed tropical belt clear round
that good old earth of ours. Moreover, nine months or so before, I had
come across him in Samarang. His steamer was loading in the Roads,
and he was abusing the tyrannical institutions of the German empire,
and soaking himself in beer all day long and day after day in De Jongh's
back shop, till De Jongh, who charged a guilder for every bottle without
as much as the quiver of an eyelid, would beckon me aside, and, with
his little leathery face all puckered up, declare confidentially, 'Business
is business, but this man, captain, he make me very sick. Tfui!'

"I was looking at him from the shade. He was hurrying on a little in
advance, and the sunlight beating on him brought out his bulk in a
startling way. He made me think of a trained baby elephant walking on
hind-legs. He was extravagantly gorgeous too—got up in a soiled sleeping
suit, bright green and deep orange vertical stripes, with a pair of ragged
straw slippers on his bare feet, and somebody's cast-off pith hat, very
dirty and two sizes too small for him, tied up with a manilla rope-yarn
on the top of his big head. You understand a man like that hasn't the
ghost of a chance when it comes to borrowing clothes. Very well. On
he came in hot haste, without a look right or left, passed within three

feet of me, and in the innocence of his heart went on pelting up-stairs into the harbour-office to make his deposition, or report, or whatever you like to call it.

"It appears he addressed himself in the first instance to the principal shipping-master. Archie Ruthvel had just come in, and, as his story goes, was about to begin his arduous day by giving a dressing-down to his chief clerk. Some of you might have known him—an obliging little Portuguese half-caste with a miserably skinny neck, and always on the hop to get something from the shipmasters in the way of eatables—a piece of salt pork, a bag of biscuits, a few potatoes, or what not. One voyage, I recollect, I tipped him a live sheep out of the remnant of my sea-stock: not that I wanted him to do anything for me—he couldn't, you know—but because his child-like belief in the sacred right to per-quisites quite touched my heart. It was so strong as to be almost beautiful. The race—the two races rather—and the climate . . . However, never mind. I know where I have a friend for life.

"Well, Ruthvel says he was giving him a severe lecture—on official morality, I suppose—when he heard a kind of subdued commotion at his back, and turning his head he saw, in his own words, something round and enormous, resembling a sixteen-hundred-weight sugar-hogshead wrapped in striped flannelette, up-ended in the middle of the large floor space in the office. He declares he was so taken aback that for quite an appreciable time he did not realise the thing was alive, and sat still wondering for what purpose and by what means that object had been transported in front of his desk. The archway from the anteroom was crowded with punkah-pullers, sweepers, police peons, the coxswain and crew of the harbour steam-launch, all craning their necks and almost climbing on each other's backs. Quite a riot. By that time the fellow had managed to tug and jerk his hat clear of his head, and advanced with slight bows at Ruthvel, who told me the sight was so discomposing that for some time he listened, quite unable to make out what that apparition wanted. It spoke in a voice harsh and lugubrious but intrepid, and little by little it dawned upon Archie that this was a development of the *Patna* case. He says that as soon as he understood who it was before him he felt quite unwell,—Archie is so sympathetic and easily upset,—but pulled himself together and shouted 'Stop! I can't listen to you. You must go to the Master Attendant. I can't possibly listen to you. Captain Elliot[1] is the man you want to see. This way, this way.' He jumped up, ran round that long counter, pulled, shoved: the other let him, surprised but obedient at first, and only at the door of the private office some sort of animal instinct made him hang back and snort like a frightened bullock. 'Look here! what's up? Let go! Look here!' Archie flung open the door without knocking. 'The master of the *Patna*, sir,'

---

1. Based on Captain Henry Ellis, the Master Attendant at Singapore in the 1880s. See below, pp. 356–57.

he shouts. 'Go in, captain.' He saw the old man lift his head from some
writing so sharp that his nose-nippers[2] fell off, banged the door to, and
fled to his desk, where he had some papers waiting for his signature: but
he says the row that burst out in there was so awful that he couldn't
collect his senses sufficiently to remember the spelling of his own name.
Archie's the most sensitive shipping-master in the two hemispheres. He
declares he felt as though he had thrown a man to a hungry lion. No
doubt the noise was great. I heard it down below, and I have every
reason to believe it was heard clear across the Esplanade as far as the
band-stand. Old father Elliot had a great stock of words and could
shout—and didn't mind who he shouted at either. He would have
shouted at the Viceroy himself. As he used to tell me: 'I am as high as
I can get; my pension is safe. I've a few pounds laid by, and if they don't
like my notions of duty I would just as soon go home as not. I am an
old man, and I have always spoken my mind. All I care for now is to
see my girls married before I die.' He was a little crazy on that point.
His three daughters were awfully nice, though they resembled him
amazingly, and on the mornings he woke up with a gloomy view of
their matrimonial prospects the office would read it in his eye and
tremble, because, they said, he was sure to have somebody for breakfast.
However, that morning he did not eat the renegade, but, if I may be
allowed to carry on the metaphor, chewed him up very small, so to
speak, and—ah! ejected him again.

"Thus in a very few moments I saw his monstrous bulk descend in
haste and stand still on the outer steps. He had stopped close to me for
the purpose of profound meditation: his large purple cheeks quivered.
He was biting his thumb, and after a while noticed me with a sidelong
vexed look. The other three chaps that had landed with him made a
little group waiting at some distance. There was a sallow-faced, mean
little chap with his arm in a sling, and a long individual in a blue flannel
coat, as dry as a chip and no stouter than a broomstick, with drooping
grey moustaches, who looked about him with an air of jaunty imbecility.
The third was an upstanding, broad-shouldered youth, with his hands
in his pockets, turning his back on the other two who appeared to be
talking together earnestly. He stared across the empty Esplanade. A
ramshackle gharry, all dust and venetian blinds, pulled up short opposite
the group, and the driver, throwing up his right foot over his knee, gave
himself up to the critical examination of his toes. The young chap,
making no movement, not even stirring his head, just stared into the
sunshine. This was my first view of Jim. He looked as unconcerned and
unapproachable as only the young can look. There he stood, clean-
limbed, clean-faced, firm on his feet, as promising a boy as the sun ever
shone on; and, looking at him, knowing all he knew and a little more

2. Eyeglasses clipped to the nose by a spring.

too, I was as angry as though I had detected him trying to get something out of me by false pretences. He had no business to look so sound. I thought to myself—well, if this sort can go wrong like that . . . and I felt as though I could fling down my hat and dance on it from sheer mortification, as I once saw the skipper of an Italian barque do because his duffer of a mate got into a mess with his anchors when making a flying moor in a roadstead full of ships. I asked myself, seeing him there apparently so much at ease—is he silly? is he callous? He seemed ready to start whistling a tune. And note, I did not care a rap about the behaviour of the other two. Their persons somehow fitted the tale that was public property, and was going to be the subject of an official inquiry. 'That old mad rogue up-stairs called me a hound,' said the captain of the *Patna*. I can't tell whether he recognised me—I rather think he did; but at any rate our glances met. He glared—I smiled; hound was the very mildest epithet that had reached me through the open window. 'Did he?' I said from some strange inability to hold my tongue. He nodded, bit his thumb again, swore under his breath: then lifting his head and looking at me with sullen and passionate impudence—'Bah! the Pacific is big, my friendt. You damned Englishmen can do your worst; I know where there's plenty room for a man like me: I am well aguaindt in Apia, in Honolulu, in . . .' He paused reflectively, while without effort I could depict to myself the sort of people he was 'aguaindt' with in those places. I won't make a secret of it that I had been 'aguaindt' with not a few of that sort myself. There are times when a man must act as though life were equally sweet in any company. I've known such a time, and, what's more, I shan't now pretend to pull a long face over my necessity, because a good many of that bad company from want of moral—moral—what shall I say?—posture, or from some other equally profound cause, were twice as instructive and twenty times more amusing than the usual respectable thief of commerce you fellows ask to sit at your table without any real necessity—from habit, from cowardice, from good-nature, from a hundred sneaking and inadequate reasons.

" 'You Englishmen are all rogues,' went on my patriotic Flensborg or Stettin Australian. I really don't recollect now what decent little port on the shores of the Baltic was defiled by being the nest of that precious bird. 'What are you to shout? Eh? You tell me? You no better than other people, and that old rogue he make Gottam fuss with me.' His thick carcass trembled on its legs that were like a pair of pillars; it trembled from head to foot. 'That's what you English always make—make a tam' fuss—for any little thing, because I was not born in your tam' country. Take away my certificate. Take it. I don't want the certificate. A man like me don't want your verfluchte[3] certificate. I shpit on it.' He spat. 'I vill an Amerigan citizen begome,' he cried, fretting and fuming and

3. Confounded, damned.

shuffling his feet as if to free his ankles from some invisible and mysterious grasp that would not let him get away from that spot. He made himself so warm that the top of his bullet head positively smoked. Nothing mysterious prevented me from going away: curiosity is the most obvious of sentiments, and it held me there to see the effect of a full information upon that young fellow who, hands in pockets, and turning his back upon the sidewalk, gazed across the grass plots of the Esplanade at the yellow portico of the Malabar Hotel with the air of a man about to go for a walk as soon as his friend is ready. That's how he looked, and it was odious. I waited to see him overwhelmed, confounded, pierced through and through, squirming like an impaled beetle—and I was half-afraid to see it too—if you understand what I mean. Nothing more awful than to watch a man who has been found out, not in a crime but in a more than criminal weakness. The commonest sort of fortitude prevents us from becoming criminals in a legal sense; it is from weakness unknown, but perhaps suspected, as in some parts of the world you suspect a deadly snake in every bush,—from weakness that may lie hidden, watched or unwatched, prayed against or manfully scorned, repressed or maybe ignored more than half a lifetime, not one of us is safe. We are snared into doing things for which we get called names, and things for which we get hanged, and yet the spirit may well survive,—survive the condemnation, survive the halter, by Jove! And there are things— they look small enough sometimes too—by which some of us are totally and completely undone. I watched the youngster there. I liked his appearance; I knew his appearance; he came from the right place; he was one of us. He stood there for all the parentage of his kind, for men and women by no means clever or amusing, but whose very existence is based upon honest faith, and upon the instinct of courage. I don't mean military courage, or civil courage, or any special kind of courage. I mean just that inborn ability to look temptations straight in the face,—a readiness unintellectual enough, goodness knows, but without a pose,—a power of resistance, don't you see, ungracious if you like, but priceless—an unthinking and blessed stiffness before the outward and inward terrors, before the might of nature and the seductive corruption of men—backed by a faith invulnerable to the strength of facts, to the contagion of example, to the solicitation of ideas. Hang ideas! They are tramps, vagabonds, knocking at the backdoor of your mind, each taking a little of your substance, each carrying away some crumb of that belief in a few simple notions you must cling to if you want to live decently and would like to die easy!

"This has nothing to do with Jim, directly; only he was outwardly so typical of that good stupid kind we like to feel marching right and left of us in life, of the kind that is not disturbed by the vagaries of intelligence and the perversions of—of nerves, let us say. He was the kind of fellow you would, on the strength of his looks, leave in charge of the deck—

figuratively and professionally speaking. I say I would, and I ought to know. Haven't I turned out youngsters enough in my time, for the service of the Red Rag, to the craft of the sea, to the craft whose whole secret could be expressed in one short sentence, and yet must be driven afresh every day into young heads till it becomes the component part of every waking thought—till it is present in every dream of their young sleep! The sea has been good to me, but when I remember all these boys that passed through my hands, some grown up now and some drowned by this time, but all good stuff for the sea, I don't think I have done badly by it either. Were I to go home to-morrow, I bet that before two days passed over my head some sunburnt young chief mate would overtake me at some dock gateway or other, and a fresh deep voice speaking above my hat would ask: 'Don't you remember me, sir? Why! little So-and-so. Such and such a ship. It was my first voyage.' And I would remember a bewildered little shaver, no higher than the back of this chair, with a mother and perhaps a big sister on the quay, very quiet but too upset to wave their handkerchiefs at the ship that glides out gently between the pier-heads; or perhaps some decent middle-aged father who had come early with his boy to see him off, and stays all the morning, because he is interested in the windlass apparently, and stays too long, and has got to scramble ashore at last with no time at all to say good-bye. The mud pilot on the poop sings out to me in a drawl, 'Hold her with the check line for a moment, Mister Mate. There's a gentleman wants to get ashore. . . . Up with you, sir. Nearly got carried off to Talcahuano, didn't you? Now's your time; easy does it. . . . All right. Slack away again forward there.' The tugs, smoking like the pit of perdition, get hold and churn the old river into fury; the gentleman ashore is dusting his knees—the benevolent steward has shied his umbrella after him. All very proper. He has offered his bit of sacrifice to the sea, and now he may go home pretending he thinks nothing of it; and the little willing victim shall be very sea-sick before next morning. By-and-by, when he has learned all the little mysteries and the one great secret of the craft, he shall be fit to live or die as the sea may decree; and the man who had taken a hand in this fool game, in which the sea wins every toss, will be pleased to have his back slapped by a heavy young hand, and to hear a cheery sea-puppy voice: 'Do you remember me, sir? The little So-and-so.'

"I tell you this is good; it tells you that once in your life at least you had gone the right way to work. I have been thus slapped, and I have winced, for the slap was heavy, and I have glowed all day long and gone to bed feeling less lonely in the world by virtue of that hearty thump. Don't I remember the little So-and-so's! I tell you I ought to know the right kind of looks. I would have trusted the deck to that youngster on the strength of a single glance, and gone to sleep with both eyes—and, by Jove! it wouldn't have been safe. There are depths of horror in that

thought. He looked as genuine as a new sovereign,[4] but there was some
infernal alloy in his metal. How much? The least thing—the least drop
of something rare and accursed; the least drop!—but he made you—
standing there with his don't-care-hang air—he made you wonder
whether perchance he were nothing more rare than brass.

"I couldn't believe it. I tell you I wanted to see him squirm for the
honour of the craft. The other two no-account chaps spotted their captain, and began to move slowly towards us. They chatted together as
they strolled, and I did not care any more than if they had not been
visible to the naked eye. They grinned at each other—might have been
exchanging jokes, for all I know. I saw that with one of them it was a
case of a broken arm; and as to the long individual with grey moustaches
he was the chief engineer, and in various ways a pretty notorious personality. They were nobodies. They approached. The skipper gazed in
an inanimate way between his feet: he seemed to be swollen to an
unnatural size by some awful disease, by the mysterious action of an
unknown poison. He lifted his head, saw the two before him waiting,
opened his mouth with an extraordinary, sneering contortion of his
puffed face—to speak to them, I suppose—and then a thought seemed
to strike him. His thick, purplish lips came together without a sound,
he went off in a resolute waddle to the gharry and began to jerk at the
door-handle with such a blind brutality of impatience that I expected
to see the whole concern overturned on its side, pony and all. The
driver, shaken out of his meditation over the sole of his foot, displayed
at once all the signs of intense terror, and held with both hands, looking
round from his box at this vast carcass forcing its way into his conveyance.
The little machine shook and rocked tumultuously, and the crimson
nape of that lowered neck, the size of those straining thighs, the immense
heaving of that dingy, striped green-and-orange back, the whole burrowing effort of that gaudy and sordid mass, troubled one's sense of
probability with a droll and fearsome effect, like one of those grotesque
and distinct visions that scare and fascinate one in a fever. He disappeared. I half expected the roof to split in two, the little box on wheels
to burst open in the manner of a ripe cotton-pod—but it only sank with
a click of flattened springs, and suddenly one venetian blind rattled
down. His shoulders reappeared, jammed in the small opening; his head
hung out, distended and tossing like a captive balloon, perspiring, furious, spluttering. He reached for the gharry-wallah with vicious flour-
ishes of a fist as dumpy and red as a lump of raw meat. He roared at
him to be off, to go on. Where? Into the Pacific, perhaps. The driver
lashed; the pony snorted, reared once, and darted off at a gallop. Where?
To Apia? To Honolulu? He had 6000 miles of tropical belt to disport
himself in, and I did not hear the precise address. A snorting pony

4. A British gold coin worth one pound (five dollars at that time).

snatched him into 'ewigkeit'[5] in the twinkling of an eye, and I never saw him again; and, what's more, I don't know of anybody that ever had a glimpse of him after he departed from my knowledge sitting inside a ramshackle little gharry that fled round the corner in a white smother of dust. He departed, disappeared, vanished, absconded; and absurdly enough it looked as though he had taken that gharry with him, for never again did I come across a sorrel pony with a slit ear and a lackadaisical Tamil driver afflicted by a sore foot. The Pacific is indeed big; but whether he found a place for a display of his talents in it or not, the fact remains he had flown into space like a witch on a broomstick. The little chap with his arm in a sling started to run after the carriage, bleating, 'Captain! I say, Captain! I sa-a-ay!'—but after a few steps stopped short, hung his head, and walked back slowly. At the sharp rattle of the wheels the young fellow spun round where he stood. He made no other movement, no gesture, no sign, and remained facing in the new direction after the gharry had swung out of sight.

"All this happened in much less time than it takes to tell, since I am trying to interpret for you into slow speech the instantaneous effect of visual impressions. Next moment the half-caste clerk, sent by Archie to look a little after the poor castaways of the *Patna*, came upon the scene. He ran out eager and bareheaded, looking right and left, and very full of his mission. It was doomed to be a failure as far as the principal person was concerned, but he approached the others with fussy importance, and, almost immediately, found himself involved in a violent altercation with the chap that carried his arm in a sling, and who turned out to be extremely anxious for a row. He wasn't going to be ordered about—'not he, b'gosh.' He wouldn't be terrified with a pack of lies by a cocky half-bred little quill-driver. He was not going to be bullied by 'no object of that sort,' if the story were true 'ever so'! He bawled his wish, his desire, his determination to go to bed. 'If you weren't a God-forsaken Portuguee,' I heard him yell, 'you would know that the hospital is the right place for me.' He pushed the fist of his sound arm under the other's nose; a crowd began to collect; the half-caste, flustered, but doing his best to appear dignified, tried to explain his intentions. I went away without waiting to see the end.

"But it so happened that I had a man in the hospital at the time, and going there to see about him the day before the opening of the Inquiry, I saw in the white men's ward that little chap tossing on his back, with his arm in splints, and quite light-headed. To my great surprise the other one, the long individual with drooping white moustaches, had also found his way there. I remembered I had seen him slinking away during the quarrel, in a half prance, half shuffle, and trying very hard not to look scared. He was no stranger to the port, it seems, and in his

5. Eternity.

distress was able to make tracks straight for Mariani's billiard-room and grog-shop near the bazaar. That unspeakable vagabond, Mariani, who had known the man and had ministered to his vices in one or two other places, kissed the ground, in a manner of speaking, before him, and shut him up with a supply of bottles in an up-stairs room of his infamous hovel. It appears he was under some hazy apprehension as to his personal safety, and wished to be concealed. However, Mariani told me a long time after (when he came on board one day to dun my steward for the price of some cigars) that he would have done more for him without asking any questions, from gratitude for some unholy favour received very many years ago—as far as I could make out. He thumped twice his brawny chest, rolled enormous black-and-white eyes glistening with tears: 'Antonio never forget—Antonio never forget!' What was the precise nature of the immoral obligation I never learned, but be it what it may, he had every facility given him to remain under lock and key, with a chair, a table, a mattress in a corner, and a litter of fallen plaster on the floor, in an irrational state of funk, and keeping up his pecker[6] with such tonics as Mariani dispensed. This lasted till the evening of the third day, when, after letting out a few horrible screams, he found himself compelled to seek safety in flight from a legion of centipedes. He burst the door open, made one leap for dear life down the crazy little stairway, landed bodily on Mariani's stomach, picked himself up, and bolted like a rabbit into the streets. The police plucked him off a garbage-heap in the early morning. At first he had a notion they were carrying him off to be hanged, and fought for liberty like a hero, but when I sat down by his bed he had been very quiet for two days. His lean bronzed head, with white moustaches, looked fine and calm on the pillow, like the head of a war-worn soldier with a child-like soul, had it not been for a hint of spectral alarm that lurked in the blank glitter of his glance, resembling a nondescript form of a terror crouching silently behind a pane of glass. He was so extremely calm, that I began to indulge in the eccentric hope of hearing something explanatory of the famous affair from his point of view. Why I longed to go grubbing into the deplorable details of an occurrence which, after all, concerned me no more than as a member of an obscure body of men held together by a community of inglorious toil and by fidelity to a certain standard of conduct, I can't explain. You may call it an unhealthy curiosity if you like; but I have a distinct notion I wished to find something. Perhaps, unconsciously, I hoped I would find that something, some profound and redeeming cause, some merciful explanation, some convincing shadow of an excuse. I see well enough now that I hoped for the impossible—for the laying of what is the most obstinate ghost of man's creation, of the uneasy doubt uprising like a mist, secret and gnawing like a worm, and more chilling

---

6. Beak, nose; here British slang phrase similar to "keep your chin up."

than the certitude of death—the doubt of the sovereign power enthroned in a fixed standard of conduct. It is the hardest thing to stumble against; it is the thing that breeds yelling panics and good little quiet villainies; it's the true shadow of calamity. Did I believe in a miracle? and why did I desire it so ardently? Was it for my own sake that I wished to find some shadow of an excuse for that young fellow whom I had never seen before, but whose appearance alone added a touch of personal concern to the thoughts suggested by the knowledge of his weakness—made it a thing of mystery and terror—like a hint of a destructive fate ready for us all whose youth—in its day—had resembled his youth? I fear that such was the secret motive of my prying. I was, and no mistake, looking for a miracle. The only thing that at this distance of time strikes me as miraculous is the extent of my imbecility. I positively hoped to obtain from that battered and shady invalid some exorcism against the ghost of doubt. I must have been pretty desperate too, for, without loss of time, after a few indifferent and friendly sentences which he answered with languid readiness, just as any decent sick man would do, I produced the word *Patna* wrapped up in a delicate question as in a wisp of floss silk. I was delicate selfishly; I did not want to startle him; I had no solicitude for him; I was not furious with him and sorry for him: his experience was of no importance, his redemption would have had no point for me. He had grown old in minor iniquities, and could no longer inspire aversion or pity. He repeated *Patna*? interrogatively, seemed to make a short effort of memory, and said: 'Quite right. I am an old stager out here. I saw her go down.' I made ready to vent my indignation at such a stupid lie, when he added smoothly, 'She was full of reptiles.'

"This made me pause. What did he mean? The unsteady phantom of terror behind his glassy eyes seemed to stand still and look into mine wistfully. 'They turned me out of my bunk in the middle watch to look at her sinking,' he pursued in a reflective tone. His voice sounded alarmingly strong all at once. I was sorry for my folly. There was no snowy-winged coiff of a nursing sister to be seen flitting in the perspective of the ward; but away in the middle of a long row of empty iron bedsteads an accident case from some ship in the Roads sat up brown and gaunt with a white bandage set rakishly on the forehead. Suddenly my interesting invalid shot out an arm thin like a tentacle and clawed my shoulder. 'Only my eyes were good enough to see. I am famous for my eyesight. That's why they called me, I expect. None of them was quick enough to see her go, but they saw that she was gone right enough, and sang out together—like this.' . . . A wolfish howl searched the very recesses of my soul. 'Oh! make 'im dry up,' whined the accident case irritably. 'You don't believe me, I suppose,' went on the other, with an air of ineffable conceit. 'I tell you there are no such eyes as mine this side of the Persian Gulf. Look under the bed.'

"Of course I stooped instantly. I defy anybody not to have done so.

'What can you see?' he asked. 'Nothing,' I said, feeling awfully ashamed
of myself. He scrutinised my face with wild and withering contempt.
'Just so,' he said, 'but if I were to look I could see—there's no eyes like
mine, I tell you.' Again he clawed, pulling at me downwards in his
eagerness to relieve himself by a confidential communication. 'Millions
of pink toads. There's no eyes like mine. Millions of pink toads. It's
worse than seeing a ship sink. I could look at sinking ships and smoke
my pipe all day long. Why don't they give me back my pipe? I would
get a smoke while I watched these toads. The ship was full of them.
They've got to be watched, you know.' He winked facetiously. The
perspiration dripped on him off my head, my drill coat clung to my wet
back: the afternoon breeze swept impetuously over the row of bedsteads,
the stiff folds of curtains stirred perpendicularly, rattling on brass rods,
the covers of empty beds blew about noiselessly near the bare floor all
along the line, and I shivered to the very marrow. The soft wind of the
tropics played in that naked ward as bleak as a winter's gale in an old
barn at home. 'Don't you let him start his hollering, mister,' hailed
from afar the accident case in a distressed angry shout that came ringing
between the walls like a quavering call down a tunnel. The clawing
hand hauled at my shoulder; he leered at me knowingly. 'The ship was
full of them, you know, and we had to clear out on the strict Q.T.,'[7]
he whispered with extreme rapidity. 'All pink. All pink—as big as mas-
tiffs, with an eye on the top of the head and claws all round their ugly
mouths. Ough! Ough!' Quick jerks as of galvanic shocks disclosed under
the flat coverlet the outlines of meagre and agitated legs; he let go my
shoulder and reached after something in the air; his body trembled
tensely like a released harp-string; and while I looked down, the spectral
horror in him broke through his glassy gaze. Instantly his face of an old
soldier, with its noble and calm outlines, became decomposed before
my eyes by the corruption of stealthy cunning, of an abominable caution
and of desperate fear. He restrained a cry—'Ssh; what are they doing
now down there?' he asked, pointing to the floor with fantastic precautions of voice and gesture, whose meaning, borne upon my mind in a
lurid flash, made me very sick of my cleverness. 'They are all asleep,'
I answered, watching him narrowly. That was it. That's what he wanted
to hear; these were the exact words that could calm him. He drew a
long breath. 'Ssh! Quiet, steady. I am an old stager out here. I know
them brutes. Bash in the head of the first that stirs. There's too many
of them, and she won't swim more than ten minutes.' He panted again.
'Hurry up,' he yelled suddenly, and went on in a steady scream: 'They
are all awake—millions of them. They are trampling on me! Wait! Oh,
wait! I'll smash them in heaps like flies. Wait for me! Help! H-e-elp!'
An interminable and sustained howl completed my discomfiture. I saw

7. Slang for quiet.

in the distance the accident case raise deplorably both his hands to his bandaged head; a dresser,[8] aproned to the chin, showed himself in the vista of the ward, as if seen in the small end of a telescope. I confessed myself fairly routed, and without more ado, stepping out through one of the long windows, escaped into the outside gallery. The howl pursued me like a vengeance. I turned into a deserted landing, and suddenly all became very still and quiet around me, and I descended the bare and shiny staircase in a silence that enabled me to compose my distracted thoughts. Down below I met one of the resident surgeons who was crossing the courtyard and stopped me. 'Been to see your man, Captain? I think we may let him go to-morrow. These fools have no notion of taking care of themselves, though. I say, we've got the chief engineer of that pilgrim ship here. A curious case. D.T.'s of the worst kind. He has been drinking hard in that Greek's or Italian's grog-shop for three days. What can you expect? Four bottles of that kind of brandy a-day, I am told. Wonderful, if true. Sheeted with boiler-iron inside, I should think. The head, ah! the head, of course, gone, but the curious part is there's some sort of method in his raving. I am trying to find out. Most unusual—that thread of logic in such a delirium. Traditionally he ought to see snakes, but he doesn't. Good old tradition's at a discount nowadays. Eh! His—er—visions are batrachian.[9] Ha! ha! No, seriously, I never remember being so interested in a case of jim-jams[1] before. He ought to be dead, don't you know, after such a festive experiment. Oh! he is a tough object. Four-and-twenty years of the tropics too. You ought really to take a peep at him. Noble-looking old boozer. Most extraordinary man I ever met—medically, of course. Won't you?'

"I had been all along exhibiting the usual polite signs of interest, but now assuming an air of regret I murmured of want of time, and shook hands in a hurry. 'I say,' he cried after me; 'he can't attend that inquiry. Is his evidence material, you think?'

" 'Not in the least,' I called back from the gateway."

Chapter VI

"The authorities were evidently of the same opinion. The inquiry was not adjourned. It was held on the appointed day to satisfy the law, and it was well attended because of its human interest no doubt. There was no incertitude as to facts—as to the one material fact, I mean. How the *Patna* came by her hurt it was impossible to find out; the court did not expect to find out; and in the whole audience there was not a man who

8. One that serves as a doctor's assistant, especially in the dressing of wounds.
9. An order of Amphibia comprising the frogs, toads, and tree toads.
1. Slang for *delirium tremens*, a violently disordered mental state of alcoholics, characterized by trembling, anxiety, hallucinations.

cared. Yet, as I've told you, all the sailors in the port attended, and the waterside business was fully represented. Whether they knew it or not, the interest that drew them there was purely psychological,—the expectation of some essential disclosure as to the strength, the power, the horror, of human emotions. Naturally nothing of the kind could be disclosed. The examination of the only man able and willing to face it was beating futilely round the well-known fact, and the play of questions upon it was as instructive as the tapping with a hammer on an iron box, were the object to find out what's inside. However, an official inquiry could not be any other thing. Its object was not the fundamental why, but the superficial how, of this affair.

"The young chap could have told them, and, though that very thing was the thing that interested the audience, the questions put to him necessarily led him away from what to me, for instance, would have been the only truth worth knowing. You can't expect the constituted authorities to inquire into the state of a man's soul—or is it only of his liver? Their business was to come down upon the consequences, and frankly, a casual police magistrate and two nautical assessors are not much good for anything else. I don't mean to imply these fellows were stupid. The magistrate was very patient. One of the assessors was a sailing-ship skipper with a reddish beard, and of a pious disposition. Brierly was the other. Big Brierly. Some of you must have heard of Big Brierly—the captain of the crack ship of the Blue Star line. That's the man.

"He seemed consumedly bored by the honour thrust upon him. He had never in his life made a mistake, never had an accident, never a mishap, never a check in his steady rise, and he seemed to be one of those lucky fellows who know nothing of indecision, much less of self-mistrust. At thirty-two he had one of the best commands going in the Eastern trade—and, what's more, he thought a lot of what he had. There was nothing like it in the world, and I suppose if you had asked him point-blank he would have confessed that in his opinion there was not such another commander. The choice had fallen upon the right man. The rest of mankind that did not command the sixteen-knot steel steamer *Ossa* were rather poor creatures. He had saved lives at sea, had rescued ships in distress, had a gold chronometer presented to him by the underwriters, and a pair of binoculars with a suitable inscription from some foreign Government, in commemoration of these services. He was acutely aware of his merits and of his rewards. I liked him well enough, though some I know—meek, friendly men at that—couldn't stand him at any price. I haven't the slightest doubt he considered himself vastly my superior—indeed, had you been Emperor of East and West, you could not have ignored your inferiority in his presence—but I couldn't get up any real sentiment of offence. He did not despise me for anything I could help, for anything I was—don't you know? I was a negligeable quantity simply because I was not *the* fortunate man of the earth, not Montague Brierly in command of the *Ossa*, not the owner of an inscribed gold chronometer and of silver-mounted binoculars testifying to the excellence of my seamanship and to my indomitable pluck; not possessed of an acute sense of my merits and of my rewards, besides the love and worship of a black retriever, the most wonderful of its kind—for never was such a man loved thus by such a dog. No doubt, to have all this forced upon you was exasperating enough; but when I reflected that I was associated in these fatal disadvantages with twelve hundred millions of other more or less human beings, I found I could bear my share of his good-natured and contemptuous pity for the sake of something indefinite and attractive in the man. I have never defined to myself this attraction, but there were moments when I envied him. The sting of life could do no more to his complacent soul than the scratch of a pin to the smooth face of a rock. This was enviable. As I looked at him, flanking on one side the unassuming pale-faced magistrate who presided at the inquiry, his self-satisfaction presented to me and to the world a surface as hard as granite. He committed suicide very soon after.[1]

"No wonder Jim's case bored him, and while I thought with something akin to fear of the immensity of his contempt for the young man under examination, he was probably holding silent inquiry into his own case. The verdict must have been of unmitigated guilt, and he took the secret of the evidence with him in that leap into the sea. If I understand anything of men, the matter was no doubt of the gravest import, one of those trifles that awaken ideas—start into life some thought with which a man unused to such a companionship finds it impossible to live. I am in a position to know that it wasn't money, and it wasn't drink, and it wasn't woman. He jumped overboard at sea barely a week after the end of the inquiry, and less than three days after leaving port on his outward passage; as though on that exact spot in the midst of waters he had suddenly perceived the gates of the other world flung open wide for his reception.

"Yet it was not a sudden impulse. His grey-headed mate, a first-rate sailor and a nice old chap with strangers, but in his relations with his commander the surliest chief officer I've ever seen, would tell the story with tears in his eyes. It appears that when he came on deck in the morning Brierly had been writing in the chart-room. 'It was ten minutes to four,' he said, 'and the middle watch was not relieved yet of course. He heard my voice on the bridge speaking to the second mate, and called me in. I was loth to go, and that's the truth, Captain Marlow, —I couldn't stand poor Captain Brierly, I tell you with shame; we never know what a man is made of. He had been promoted over too many heads, not counting my own, and he had a damnable trick of making

---

1. Brierly's suicide recalls the death of Captain Wallace of the *Cutty Sark*. See below, pp. 357–58.

you feel small, nothing but by the way he said "Good morning." I never addressed him, sir, but on matters of duty, and then it was as much as I could do to keep a civil tongue in my head.' (He flattered himself there. I often wondered how Brierly could put up with his manners for more than half a voyage.) 'I've a wife and children,' he went on, 'and I had been ten years in the Company, always expecting the next command—more fool I. Says he, just like this: "Come in here, Mr Jones," in that swagger voice of his—"Come in here, Mr Jones." In I went. "We'll lay down her position," says he, stooping over the chart, a pair of dividers in hand. By the standing orders, the officer going off duty would have done that at the end of his watch. However, I said nothing, and looked on while he marked off the ship's position with a tiny cross and wrote the date and the time. I can see him this moment writing his neat figures: seventeen, eight, four A.M. The year would be written in red ink at the top of the chart. He never used his charts more than a year, Captain Brierly didn't. I've the chart now. When he had done he stands looking down at the mark he had made and smiling to himself, then looks up at me. "Thirty-two miles more as she goes," says he, "and then we shall be clear, and you may alter the course twenty degrees to the southward."

" 'We were passing to the north of the Hector Bank that voyage. I said, "All right, sir," wondering what he was fussing about, since I had to call him before altering the course anyhow. Just then eight bells were struck: we came out on the bridge, and the second mate before going off mentions in the usual way—"Seventy-one on the log." Captain Brierly looks at the compass and then all round. It was dark and clear, and all the stars were out as plain as on a frosty night in high latitudes. Suddenly he says with a sort of a little sigh: "I am going aft, and shall set the log at zero for you myself, so that there can be no mistake. Thirty-two miles more on this course and then you are safe. Let's see—the correction on the log is six per cent additive; say, then, thirty by the dial to run, and you may come twenty degrees to starboard at once. No use losing any distance—is there?" I had never heard him talk so much at a stretch, and to no purpose as it seemed to me. I said nothing. He went down the ladder, and the dog, that was always at his heels whenever he moved, night or day, followed, sliding nose first, after him. I heard his boot-heels tap, tap on the after-deck, then he stopped and spoke to the dog—"Go back, Rover. On the bridge, boy! Go on—get." Then he calls out to me from the dark, "Shut that dog up in the chart-room, Mr Jones—will you?"

" 'This was the last time I heard his voice, Captain Marlow. These are the last words he spoke in the hearing of any living human being, sir.' At this point the old chap's voice got quite unsteady. 'He was afraid the poor brute would jump after him, don't you see?' he pursued with a quaver. 'Yes, Captain Marlow. He set the log for me; he—would you

believe it?—he put a drop of oil in it too. There was the oil-feeder where
he left it near by. The boatswain's mate got the hose along aft to wash
down at half-past five; by-and-by he knocks off and runs up on the
bridge,—"Will you please come aft, Mr Jones," he says. "There's a
funny thing. I don't like to touch it." It was Captain Brierly's gold
chronometer watch carefully hung under the rail by its chain.

    " 'As soon as my eyes fell on it something struck me, and I knew,
sir. My legs got soft under me. It was as if I had seen him go over; and
I could tell how far behind he was left too. The taffrail-log marked
eighteen miles and three-quarters, and four iron belaying-pins were
missing round the mainmast. Put them in his pockets to help him down,
I suppose; but, Lord! what's four iron pins to a powerful man like Captain
Brierly. Maybe his confidence in himself was just shook a bit at the last.
That's the only sign of fluster he gave in his whole life, I should think;
but I am ready to answer for him, that once over he did not try to swim
a stroke, the same as he would have had pluck enough to keep up all
day long on the bare chance had he fallen overboard accidentally. Yes,
sir. He was second to none—if he said so himself, as I heard him once.
He had written two letters in the middle watch, one to the Company
and the other to me. He gave me a lot of instructions as to the
passage—I had been in the trade before he was out of his time—and
no end of hints as to my conduct with our people in Shanghai, so that
I should keep the command of the *Ossa*. He wrote like a father would
to a favourite son, Captain Marlow, and I was five-and-twenty years his
senior and had tasted salt water before he was fairly breeched. In his
letter to the owners—it was left open for me to see—he said that he
had always done his duty by them—up to that moment—and even now
he was not betraying their confidence, since he was leaving the ship to
as competent a seaman as could be found—meaning me, sir, meaning
me! He told them that if the last act of his life didn't take away all his
credit with them, they would give weight to my faithful service and to
his warm recommendation, when about to fill the vacancy made by his
death. And much more like this, sir. I couldn't believe my eyes. It made
me feel queer all over,' went on the old chap, in great perturbation,
and squashing something in the corner of his eye with the end of a
thumb as broad as a spatula. 'You would think, sir, he had jumped
overboard only to give an unlucky man a last show to get on. What
with the shock of him going in this awful rash way, and thinking myself
a made man by that chance, I was nearly off my chump[2] for a week.
But no fear. The captain of the *Pelion* was shifted into the *Ossa*—came
aboard in Shanghai—a little popinjay, sir, in a grey check suit, with
his hair parted in the middle. "Aw—I am—aw—your new captain,
Mister—Mister—aw—Jones." He was drowned in scent—fairly stunk

2. Insane, crazy.

with it, Captain Marlow. I daresay it was the look I gave him that made him stammer. He mumbled something about my natural disappointment—I had better know at once that his chief officer got the promotion to the *Pelion*—he had nothing to do with it, of course—supposed the office knew best—sorry. . . . Says I, "Don't you mind old Jones, sir; dam' his soul, he's used to it." I could see directly I had shocked his delicate ear, and while we sat at our first tiffin[3] together he began to find fault in a nasty manner with this and that in the ship. I never heard such a voice out of a Punch and Judy show. I set my teeth hard, and glued my eyes to my plate, and held my peace as long as I could; but at last I had to say something. Up he jumps tiptoeing, ruffling all his pretty plumes, like a little fighting cock. "You'll find you have a different person to deal with than the late Captain Brierly." "I've found it," says I, very glum, but pretending to be mighty busy with my steak. "You are an old ruffian, Mister—aw—Jones; and what's more, you are known for an old ruffian in the employ," he squeaks at me. The damned bottle-washers stood about listening with their mouths stretched from ear to ear. "I may be a hard case," answers I, "but I ain't so far gone as to put up with the sight of you sitting in Captain Brierly's chair." With that I lay down my knife and fork. "You would like to sit in it yourself—that's where the shoe pinches," he sneers. I left the saloon, got my rags together, and was on the quay with all my dunnage about my feet before the stevedores had turned to again. Yes. Adrift—on shore—after ten years' service—and with a poor woman and four children six thousand miles off depending on my half-pay for every mouthful they ate. Yes, sir! I chucked it rather than hear Captain Brierly abused. He left me his night-glasses—here they are; and he wished me to take care of the dog—here he is. Hallo, Rover, poor boy. Where's the captain, Rover?' The dog looked up at us with mournful yellow eyes, gave one desolate bark, and crept under the table.

"All this was taking place, more than two years afterwards, on board that nautical ruin the *Fire-Queen* this Jones had got charge of—quite by a funny accident, too—from Matherson—mad Matherson they generally called him—the same who used to hang out in Häi-phong, you know, before the occupation days. The old chap snuffled on—

" 'Ay, sir, Captain Brierly will be remembered here, if there's no other place on earth. I wrote fully to his father and did not get a word in reply—neither Thank you, nor Go to the devil!—nothing! Perhaps they did not want to know.'

"The sight of that watery-eyed old Jones mopping his bald head with a red cotton handkerchief, the sorrowing yelp of the dog, the squalor of that fly-blown cuddy which was the only shrine of his memory, threw a veil of inexpressibly mean pathos over Brierly's remembered figure,

---

3. Usual Anglo-Indian word for a meal; normally, for a light midday meal.

the posthumous revenge of fate for that belief in his own splendour which had almost cheated his life of its legitimate terrors. Almost! Perhaps wholly. Who can tell what flattering view he had induced himself to take of his own suicide.

" 'Why did he commit the rash act, Captain Marlow—can you think?' asked Jones, pressing his palms together. 'Why? It beats me! Why?' He slapped his low and wrinkled forehead. 'If he had been poor and old and in debt—and never a show—or else mad. But he wasn't of the kind that goes mad, not he. You trust me. What a mate don't know about his skipper isn't worth knowing. Young, healthy, well off, no cares. . . . I sit here sometimes thinking, thinking, till my head fairly begins to buzz. There was some reason.'

" 'You may depend on it, Captain Jones,' said I, 'it wasn't anything that would have disturbed much either of us two,' I said; and then, as if a light had been flashed into the muddle of his brain, poor old Jones found a last word of amazing profundity. He blew his nose, nodding at me dolefully: 'Ay, ay! neither you nor I, sir, had ever thought so much of ourselves.'

"Of course the recollection of my last conversation with Brierly is tinged with the knowledge of his end that followed so close upon it. I spoke with him for the last time during the progress of the inquiry. It was after the first adjournment, and he came up with me in the street. He was in a state of irritation, which I noticed with surprise, his usual behaviour when he condescended to converse being perfectly cool, with a trace of amused tolerance, as if the existence of his interlocutor had been a rather good joke. 'They caught me for that inquiry, you see,' he began, and for a while enlarged complainingly upon the inconveniences of daily attendance in court. 'And goodness knows how long it will last. Three days, I suppose.' I heard him out in silence; in my then opinion it was a way as good as another of putting on side.[4] 'What's the use of it? It is the stupidest set-out[5] you can imagine,' he pursued hotly. I remarked that there was no option. He interrupted me with a sort of pent-up violence. 'I feel like a fool all the time.' I looked up at him. This was going very far—for Brierly—when talking of Brierly. He stopped short, and seizing the lapel of my coat, gave it a slight tug. 'Why are we tormenting that young chap?' he asked. This question chimed in so well to the tolling of a certain thought of mine that, with the image of the absconding renegade in my eye, I answered at once, 'Hanged if I know, unless it be that he lets you.' I was astonished to see him fall into line, so to speak, with that utterance, which ought to have been tolerably cryptic. He said angrily, 'Why, yes. Can't he see that wretched skipper of his has cleared out? What does he expect to happen? Nothing can save him. He's done for.' We walked on in silence a few steps. 'Why

4. Holding myself aloof.
5. An arrangement or display.

eat all that dirt?' he exclaimed, with an oriental energy of expression—
about the only sort of energy you can find a trace of east of the fiftieth
meridian. I wondered greatly at the direction of his thoughts, but now
I strongly suspect it was strictly in character: at bottom poor Brierly must
have been thinking of himself. I pointed out to him that the skipper of
the *Patna* was known to have feathered his nest pretty well, and could
procure almost anywhere the means of getting away. With Jim it was
otherwise: the Government was keeping him in the Sailors' Home for
the time being, and probably he hadn't a penny in his pocket to bless
himself with. It costs some money to run away. 'Does it? Not always,'
he said, with a bitter laugh, and to some further remark of mine—
'Well, then, let him creep twenty feet underground and stay there! By
heavens! I would.' I don't know why his tone provoked me, and I said,
'There is a kind of courage in facing it out as he does, knowing very
well that if he went away nobody would trouble to run after him.'
'Courage be hanged!' growled Brierly. 'That sort of courage is of no use
to keep a man straight, and I don't care a snap for such courage. If you
were to say it was a kind of cowardice now—of softness. I tell you what,
I will put up two hundred rupees if you put up another hundred and
undertake to make the beggar clear out early to-morrow morning. The
fellow's a gentleman if he ain't fit to be touched—he will understand.
He must! This infernal publicity is too shocking: there he sits while all
these confounded natives, serangs, lascars, quartermasters, are giving
evidence that's enough to burn a man to ashes with shame. This is
abominable. Why, Marlow, don't you think, don't you feel, that this
is abominable; don't you now—come—as a seaman? If he went away
all this would stop at once.' Brierly said these words with a most unusual
animation, and made as if to reach after his pocket-book. I restrained
him, and declared coldly that the cowardice of these four men did not
seem to me a matter of such great importance. 'And you call yourself
a seaman, I suppose,' he pronounced angrily. I said that's what I called
myself, and I hoped I was too. He heard me out, and made a gesture
with his big arm that seemed to deprive me of my individuality, to push
me away into the crowd. 'The worst of it,' he said, 'is that all you fellows
have no sense of dignity; you don't think enough of what you are supposed
to be.'

"We had been walking slowly meantime, and now stopped opposite
the harbour office, in sight of the very spot from which the immense
captain of the *Patna* had vanished as utterly as a tiny feather blown
away in a hurricane. I smiled. Brierly went on: 'This is a disgrace. We've
got all kinds amongst us—some anointed scoundrels in the lot; but,
hang it, we must preserve professional decency or we become no better
than so many tinkers going about loose. We are trusted. Do you
understand?—trusted! Frankly, I don't care a snap for all the pilgrims
that ever came out of Asia, but a decent man would not have behaved

like this to a full cargo of old rags in bales. We aren't an organised body of men, and the only thing that holds us together is just the name for that kind of decency. Such an affair destroys one's confidence. A man may go pretty near through his whole sea-life without any call to show a stiff upper lip. But when the call comes. . . . Aha! . . . If I . . .'

"He broke off, and in a changed tone, 'I'll give you two hundred rupees now, Marlow, and you just talk to that chap. Confound him! I wish he had never come out here. Fact is, I rather think some of my people know his. The old man's a parson, and I remember now I met him once when staying with my cousin in Essex last year. If I am not mistaken, the old chap seemed rather to fancy his sailor son. Horrible. I can't do it myself—but you. . . .'

"Thus, apropos of Jim, I had a glimpse of the real Brierly a few days before he committed his reality and his sham together to the keeping of the sea. Of course I declined to meddle. The tone of this last 'but you' (poor Brierly couldn't help it), that seemed to imply I was no more noticeable than an insect, caused me to look at the proposal with indignation, and on account of that provocation, or for some other reason, I became positive in my mind that the inquiry was a severe punishment to that Jim, and that his facing it—practically of his own freewill—was a redeeming feature in his abominable case. I hadn't been so sure of it before. Brierly went off in a huff. At the time his state of mind was more of a mystery to me than it is now.

"Next day, coming into court late, I sat by myself. Of course I could not forget the conversation I had with Brierly, and now I had them both under my eyes. The demeanour of one suggested gloomy impudence and of the other a contemptuous boredom; yet one attitude might not have been truer than the other, and I was aware that one was not true. Brierly was not bored—he was exasperated; and if so, then Jim might not have been impudent. According to my theory he was not. I imagined he was hopeless. Then it was that our glances met. They met, and the look he gave me was discouraging of any intention I might have had to speak to him. Upon either hypothesis—insolence or despair—I felt I could be of no use to him. This was the second day of the proceedings. Very soon after that exchange of glances the inquiry was adjourned again to the next day. The white men began to troop out at once. Jim had been told to stand down some time before, and was able to leave amongst the first. I saw his broad shoulders and his head outlined in the light of the door, and while I made my way slowly out talking with some one —some stranger who had addressed me casually—I could see him from within the court-room resting both elbows on the balustrade of the verandah and turning his back on the small stream of people trickling down the few steps. There was a murmur of voices and a shuffle of boots.

"The next case was that of assault and battery committed upon a money-lender, I believe; and the defendant—a venerable villager with a straight white beard—sat on a mat just outside the door with his sons, daughters, sons-in-law, their wives, and, I should think, half the population of his village besides, squatting or standing around him. A slim dark woman, with part of her back and one black shoulder bared, and with a thin gold ring in her nose, suddenly began to talk in a high-pitched, shrewish tone. The man with me instinctively looked up at her. We were then just through the door, passing behind Jim's burly back.

"Whether those villagers had brought the yellow dog with them, I don't know. Anyhow, a dog was there, weaving himself in and out amongst people's legs in that mute stealthy way native dogs have, and my companion stumbled over him. The dog leaped away without a sound; the man, raising his voice a little, said with a slow laugh, 'Look at that wretched cur,' and directly afterwards we became separated by a lot of people pushing in. I stood back for a moment against the wall while the stranger managed to get down the steps and disappeared. I saw Jim spin round. He made a step forward and barred my way. We were alone; he glared at me with an air of stubborn resolution. I became aware I was being held up, so to speak, as if in a wood. The verandah was empty by then, the noise and movement in court had ceased: a great silence fell upon the building, in which, somewhere far within, an oriental voice began to whine abjectly. The dog, in the very act of trying to sneak in at the door, sat down hurriedly to hunt for fleas.

" 'Did you speak to me?' asked Jim very low, and bending forward, not so much towards me but at me, if you know what I mean. I said 'No' at once. Something in the sound of that quiet tone of his warned me to be on my defence. I watched him. It was very much like a meeting in a wood, only more uncertain in its issue, since he could possibly want neither my money nor my life—nothing that I could simply give up or defend with a clear conscience. 'You say you didn't,' he said, very sombre. 'But I heard.' 'Some mistake,' I protested, utterly at a loss, and never taking my eyes off him. To watch his face was like watching a darkening sky before a clap of thunder, shade upon shade imperceptibly coming on, the gloom growing mysteriously intense in the calm of maturing violence.

" 'As far as I know, I haven't opened my lips in your hearing,' I affirmed with perfect truth. I was getting a little angry, too, at the absurdity of this encounter. It strikes me now I have never in my life been so near a beating—I mean it literally; a beating with fists. I suppose I had some hazy prescience of that eventuality being in the air. Not that he was actively threatening me. On the contrary, he was strangely passive—don't you know? but he was lowering, and, though not exceptionally big, he looked generally fit to demolish a wall. The most reassuring symptom I noticed was a kind of slow and ponderous hesitation, which I took as a tribute to the evident sincerity of my manner and of my tone. We faced each other. In the court the assault case was proceeding. I caught the words: 'Well—buffalo—stick—in the greatness of my fear. . . .'

" 'What did you mean by staring at me all the morning?' said Jim at last. He looked up and looked down again. 'Did you expect us all to sit with downcast eyes out of regard for your susceptibilities?' I retorted sharply. I was not going to submit meekly to any of his nonsense. He raised his eyes again, and this time continued to look me straight in the face. 'No. That's all right,' he pronounced with an air of deliberating with himself upon the truth of this statement—'that's all right. I am going through with that. Only'—and there he spoke a little faster—'I won't let any man call me names outside this court. There was a fellow with you. You spoke to him—oh yes—I know; 'tis all very fine. You spoke to him, but you meant me to hear. . . .'

"I assured him he was under some extraordinary delusion. I had no conception how it came about. 'You thought I would be afraid to resent this,' he said, with just a faint tinge of bitterness. I was interested enough to discern the slightest shades of expression, but I was not in the least enlightened; yet I don't know what in these words, or perhaps just the intonation of that phrase, induced me suddenly to make all possible allowances for him. I ceased to be annoyed at my unexpected predicament. It was some mistake on his part; he was blundering, and I had an intuition that the blunder was of an odious, of an unfortunate nature. I was anxious to end this scene on grounds of decency, just as one is anxious to cut short some unprovoked and abominable confidence. The funniest part was, that in the midst of all these considerations of the higher order I was conscious of a certain trepidation as to the possibility—nay, likelihood—of this encounter ending in some disreputable brawl which could not possibly be explained, and would make me ridiculous. I did not hanker after a three days' celebrity as the man who got a black eye or something of the sort from the mate of the *Patna*. He, in all probability, did not care what he did, or at any rate would be fully justified in his own eyes. It took no magician to see he was amazingly angry about something, for all his quiet and even torpid demeanour. I don't deny I was extremely desirous to pacify him at all costs, had I only known what to do. But I didn't know, as you may well imagine. It was a blackness without a single gleam. We confronted each other in silence. He hung fire for about fifteen seconds, then made a step nearer, and I made ready to ward off a blow, though I don't think I moved a muscle. 'If you were as big as two men and as strong as six,' he said very softly, 'I would tell you what I think of you. You . . .' 'Stop!' I exclaimed. This checked him for a second. 'Before you tell me what you think of me,' I went on quickly, 'will you kindly tell me what it is I've said or done?' During the pause that ensued he surveyed me with indignation, while I made supernatural efforts of memory, in which I was hindered by the oriental voice within the court-room expostulating with impassioned volubility against a charge of falsehood. Then we spoke almost together. 'I will soon show you I am not,' he said, in a tone suggestive of a crisis. 'I declare I don't know,' I protested earnestly at the same time. He tried to crush me by the scorn of his glance. 'Now that you see I am not afraid you try to crawl out of it,' he said. 'Who's a cur now—hey?' Then, at last, I understood.

"He had been scanning my features as though looking for a place where he would plant his fist. 'I will allow no man,' . . . he mumbled threateningly. It was, indeed, a hideous mistake; he had given himself away utterly. I can't give you an idea how shocked I was. I suppose he saw some reflection of my feelings in my face, because his expression changed just a little. 'Good God!' I stammered, 'you don't think I . . .' 'But I am sure I've heard,' he persisted, raising his voice for the first time since the beginning of this deplorable scene. Then with a shade of disdain he added, 'It wasn't you, then? Very well; I'll find the other.' 'Don't be a fool,' I cried in exasperation; 'it wasn't that at all.' 'I've heard,' he said again with an unshaken and sombre perseverance.

"There may be those who could have laughed at his pertinacity. I didn't. Oh, I didn't! There had never been a man so mercilessly shown up by his own natural impulse. A single word had stripped him of his discretion—of that discretion which is more necessary to the decencies of our inner being than clothing is to the decorum of our body. 'Don't be a fool,' I repeated. 'But the other man said it, you don't deny that?' he pronounced distinctly, and looking in my face without flinching. 'No, I don't deny,' said I, returning his gaze. At last his eyes followed downwards the direction of my pointing finger. He appeared at first uncomprehending, then confounded, and at last amazed and scared as though a dog had been a monster and he had never seen a dog before. 'Nobody dreamt of insulting you,' I said.

"He contemplated the wretched animal, that moved no more than an effigy: it sat with ears pricked and its sharp muzzle pointed into the doorway, and suddenly snapped at a fly like a piece of mechanism.

"I looked at him. The red of his fair sunburnt complexion deepened suddenly under the down of his cheeks, invaded his forehead, spread to the roots of his curly hair. His ears became intensely crimson, and even the clear blue of his eyes was darkened many shades by the rush of blood to his head. His lips pouted a little, trembling as though he had been on the point of bursting into tears. I perceived he was incapable of pronouncing a word from the excess of his humiliation. From disappointment too—who knows? Perhaps he looked forward to that hammering he was going to give me for rehabilitation, for appeasement? Who can tell what relief he expected from this chance of a row? He was naïve enough to expect anything; but he had given himself away for nothing in this case. He had been frank with himself—let alone with me—in the wild hope of arriving in that way at some effective refutation, and the stars had been ironically unpropitious. He made an inarticulate noise in his throat like a man imperfectly stunned by a blow on the head. It was pitiful.

"I didn't catch up again with him till well outside the gate. I had even to trot a bit at the last, but when, out of breath at his elbow, I taxed him with running away, he said, 'Never!' and at once turned at bay. I explained I never meant to say he was running away from *me*. 'From no man—from not a single man on earth,' he affirmed with a stubborn mien. I forbore to point out the one obvious exception which would hold good for the bravest of us; I thought he would find out by himself very soon. He looked at me patiently while I was thinking of something to say, but I could find nothing on the spur of the moment, and he began to walk on. I kept up, and anxious not to lose him, I said hurriedly that I couldn't think of leaving him under a false impression of my—of my—I stammered. The stupidity of the phrase appalled me while I was trying to finish it, but the power of sentences has nothing to do with their sense or the logic of their construction. My idiotic mumble seemed to please him. He cut it short by saying, with courteous placidity that argued an immense power of self-control or else a wonderful elasticity of spirits—'Altogether my mistake.' I marvelled greatly at this expression: he might have been alluding to some trifling occurrence. Hadn't he understood its deplorable meaning? 'You may well forgive me,' he continued, and went on a little moodily, 'All these staring people in court seemed such fools that—that it might have been as I supposed.'

"This opened suddenly a new view of him to my wonder. I looked at him curiously and met his unabashed and impenetrable eyes. 'I can't put up with this kind of thing,' he said, very simply, 'and I don't mean to. In court it's different; I've got to stand that—and I can do it too.'

"I don't pretend I understood him. The views he let me have of himself were like those glimpses through the shifting rents in a thick fog—bits of vivid and vanishing detail, giving no connected idea of the general aspect of a country. They fed one's curiosity without satisfying it; they were no good for purposes of orientation. Upon the whole he was misleading. That's how I summed him up to myself after he left me late in the evening. I had been staying at the Malabar House for a few days, and on my pressing invitation he dined with me there."

Chapter VII

"An outward-bound mail-boat had come in that afternoon, and the big dining-room of the hotel was more than half full of people with a-hundred-pounds-round-the-world tickets in their pockets. There were married couples looking domesticated and bored with each other in the midst of their travels; there were small parties and large parties, and lone individuals dining solemnly or feasting boisterously, but all thinking, conversing, joking, or scowling as was their wont at home; and just as intelligently receptive of new impressions as their trunks upstairs. Henceforth they would be labelled as having passed through this and that place, and so would be their luggage. They would cherish this distinction of their persons, and preserve the gummed tickets on their portmanteaus as documentary evidence, as the only permanent trace of their improving enterprise. The dark-faced servants tripped without noise over the vast and polished floor; now and then a girl's laugh would be heard, as innocent and empty as her mind, or, in a sudden hush of crockery, a few words in an affected drawl from some wit embroidering for the benefit of a grinning tableful the last funny story of shipboard scandal. Two nomadic old maids, dressed up to kill, worked acrimoniously through the bill of fare, whispering to each other with faded lips, wooden-faced and bizarre, like two sumptuous scarecrows. A little wine opened Jim's heart and loosened his tongue. His appetite was good, too, I noticed. He seemed to have buried somewhere the opening episode of our acquaintance. It was like a thing of which there would be no more question in this world. And all the time I had before me these blue, boyish eyes looking straight into mine, this young face, these capable shoulders, the open bronzed forehead with a white line under the roots of clustering fair hair, this appearance appealing at sight to all my sympathies: this frank aspect, the artless smile, the youthful seriousness. He was of the right sort; he was one of us. He talked soberly, with a sort of composed unreserve, and with a quiet bearing that might have been the outcome of manly self-control, of impudence, of callousness, of a colossal unconsciousness, of a gigantic deception. Who can tell! From our tone we might have been discussing a third person, a football match, last year's weather. My mind floated in a sea of conjectures till the turn of the conversation enabled me, without being offensive, to remark that, upon the whole, this inquiry must have been pretty trying to him. He darted his arm across the tablecloth, and clutching my hand by the side of my plate, glared fixedly. I *was* startled. 'It must be awfully hard,' I stammered, confused by this display of speechless feeling. 'It is—hell,' he burst out in a muffled voice.

"This movement and these words caused two well-groomed male globe-trotters at a neighbouring table to look up in alarm from their iced pudding. I rose, and we passed into the front gallery for coffee and cigars.

"On little octagon tables candles burned in glass globes; clumps of stiff-leaved plants separated sets of cosy wicker chairs; and between the pairs of columns, whose reddish shafts caught in a long row the sheen from the tall windows, the night, glittering and sombre, seemed to hang like a splendid drapery. The riding lights of ships winked afar like setting stars, and the hills across the roadstead resembled rounded black masses of arrested thunder-clouds.

" 'I couldn't clear out,' Jim began. 'The skipper did—that's all very well for him. I couldn't, and I wouldn't. They all got out of it in one way or another, but it wouldn't do for me.'

"I listened with concentrated attention, not daring to stir in my chair; I wanted to know—and to this day I don't know, I can only guess. He would be confident and depressed all in the same breath, as if some conviction of innate blamelessness had checked the truth writhing within him at every turn. He began by saying, in the tone in which a man would admit his inability to jump a twenty-foot wall, that he could never go home now; and this declaration recalled to my mind what Brierly had said, 'that the old parson in Essex seemed to fancy his sailor son not a little.'

"I can't tell you whether Jim knew he was especially 'fancied' but the tone of his references to 'my Dad' was calculated to give me a notion that the good old rural dean was about the finest man that ever had been worried by the cares of a large family since the beginning of the world. This, though never stated, was implied with an anxiety that there should be no mistake about it, which was really very true and charming, but added a poignant sense of lives far off to the other elements of the story. 'He has seen it all in the home papers by this time,' said Jim. 'I can never face the poor old chap.' I did not dare to lift my eyes at this till I heard him add, 'I could never explain. He wouldn't understand.' Then I looked up. He was smoking reflectively, and after a moment, rousing himself, began to talk again. He discovered at once a desire that I should not confound him with his partners in—in crime, let us call it. He was not one of them; he was altogether of another sort. I gave no sign of dissent. I had no intention, for the sake of barren truth, to rob him of the smallest particle of any saving grace that would come in his way. I didn't know how much of it he believed himself. I didn't know what he was playing up to—if he was playing up to anything at all—and I suspect he did not know either; for it is my belief no man ever understands quite his own artful dodges to escape from the grim shadow of self-knowledge. I made no sound all the time he was wondering what he had better do after 'that stupid inquiry was over.'

"Apparently he shared Brierly's contemptuous opinion of these proceedings ordained by law. He would not know where to turn, he confessed, clearly thinking aloud rather than talking to me. Certificate gone, career broken, no money to get away, no work that he could obtain as far as he could see. At home he could perhaps get something; but it meant going to his people for help, and that he would not do. He saw nothing for it but ship before the mast—could get perhaps a quartermaster's billet in some steamer. Would do for a quartermaster. . . . 'Do you think you would?' I asked pitilessly. He jumped up, and going to the stone balustrade looked out into the night. In a moment he was back, towering above my chair with his youthful face clouded yet by the pain of a conquered emotion. He had understood very well I did not doubt his ability to steer a ship. In a voice that quavered a bit he asked me why did I say that? I had been 'no end kind' to him. I had not even laughed at him when—here he began to mumble—'that mistake, you know—made a confounded ass of myself.' I broke in by saying rather warmly that for me such a mistake was not a matter to laugh at. He sat down and drank deliberately some coffee, emptying the small cup to the last drop. 'That does not mean I admit for a moment the cap fitted,' he declared distinctly. 'No?' I said. 'No,' he affirmed with quiet decision. 'Do you know what *you* would have done? Do you? And you don't think yourself . . . he gulped something . . . 'you don't think yourself a—a—cur?'

"And with this—upon my honour!—he looked up at me inquisitively. It was a question it appears—a *bona fide*[1] question! However, he didn't wait for an answer. Before I could recover he went on, with his eyes straight before him, as if reading off something written on the body of the night. 'It is all in being ready. I wasn't; not—not then. I don't want to excuse myself; but I would like to explain—I would like somebody to understand—somebody—one person at least! You! Why not you?'

"It was solemn, and a little ridiculous too, as they always are, those struggles of an individual trying to save from the fire his idea of what his moral identity should be, this precious notion of a convention, only one of the rules of the game, nothing more, but all the same so terribly effective by its assumption of unlimited power over natural instincts, by the awful penalties of its failure. He began his story quietly enough. On board that Dale Line steamer that had picked up these four floating in a boat upon the discreet sunset glow of the sea, they had been after the first day looked askance upon. The fat skipper told some story, the others had been silent, and at first it had been accepted. You don't cross-examine poor castaways you had the good luck to save, if not from cruel death, then at least from cruel suffering. Afterwards, with time to think it over, it might have struck the officers of the *Avondale* that there was 'something fishy' in the affair; but of course they would keep their doubts to themselves. They had picked up the captain, the mate, and two engineers of the steamer *Patna* sunk at sea, and that, very properly, was

1. Made in good faith (Latin).

enough for them. I did not ask Jim about the nature of his feelings during the ten days he spent on board. From the way he narrated that part I was at liberty to infer he was partly stunned by the discovery he had made—the discovery about himself—and no doubt was at work trying to explain it away to the only man who was capable of appreciating all its tremendous magnitude. You must understand he did not try to minimise its importance. Of that I am sure; and therein lies his distinction. As to what sensations he experienced when he got ashore and heard the unforeseen conclusion of the tale in which he had taken such a pitiful part, he told me nothing of them, and it is difficult to imagine. I wonder whether he felt the ground cut from under his feet? I wonder? But no doubt he managed to get a fresh foothold very soon. He was ashore a whole fortnight waiting in the Sailors' Home, and as there were six or seven men staying there at the time, I had heard of him a little. Their languid opinion seemed to be that, in addition to his other shortcomings, he was a sulky brute. He had passed these days on the verandah, buried in a long chair, and coming out of his place of sepulture only at meal-times or late at night, when he wandered on the quays all by himself, detached from his surroundings, irresolute and silent, like a ghost without a home to haunt. 'I don't think I've spoken three words to a living soul in all that time,' he said, making me very sorry for him; and directly he added, 'One of these fellows would have been sure to blurt out something I had made up my mind not to put up with, and I didn't want a row. No! Not then. I was too—too . . . I had no heart for it.' 'So that bulkhead held out after all,' I remarked cheerfully. 'Yes,' he murmured, 'it held. And yet I swear to you I felt it bulge under my hand.' 'It's extraordinary what strains old iron will stand sometimes,' I said. Thrown back in his seat, his legs stiffly out and arms hanging down, he nodded slightly several times. You could not conceive a sadder spectacle. Suddenly he lifted his head; he sat up; he slapped his thigh. 'Ah! what a chance missed! My God! what a chance missed!' he blazed out, but the ring of the last 'missed' resembled a cry wrung out by pain.

"He was silent again with a still, far-away look of fierce yearning after that missed distinction, with his nostrils for an instant dilated, sniffing the intoxicating breath of that wasted opportunity. If you think I was either surprised or shocked you do me an injustice in more ways than one! Ah, he was an imaginative beggar! He would give himself away; he would give himself up. I could see in his glance darted into the night all his inner being carried on, projected headlong into the fanciful realm of recklessly heroic aspirations. He had no leisure to regret what he had lost, he was so wholly and naturally concerned for what he had failed to obtain. He was very far away from me who watched him across three feet of space. With every instant he was penetrating deeper into the impossible world of romantic achievements. He got to the heart of it at last! A strange look of beatitude overspread his features, his eyes sparkled in the light of the candle burning between us; he positively smiled! He had penetrated to the very heart—to the very heart. It was an ecstatic smile that your faces—or mine either—will never wear, my dear boys. I whisked him back by saying, 'If you had stuck to the ship, you mean!'

"He turned upon me, his eyes suddenly amazed and full of pain, with a bewildered, startled, suffering face, as though he had tumbled down from a star. Neither you nor I will ever look like this on any man. He shuddered profoundly, as if a cold finger-tip had touched his heart. Last of all he sighed.

"I was not in a merciful mood. He provoked one by his contradictory indiscretions. 'It is unfortunate you didn't know beforehand!' I said with every unkind intention; but the perfidious shaft fell harmless—dropped at his feet like a spent arrow, as it were, and he did not think of picking it up. Perhaps he had not even seen it. Presently, lolling at ease, he said, 'Dash it all! I tell you it bulged. I was holding up my lamp along the angle-iron in the lower deck when a flake of rust as big as the palm of my hand fell off the plate, all of itself.' He passed his hand over his forehead. 'The thing stirred and jumped off like something alive while I was looking at it.' 'That made you feel pretty bad,' I observed casually. 'Do you suppose,' he said, 'that I was thinking of myself, with a hundred and sixty people at my back, all fast asleep in that fore-'tween-deck alone—and more of them aft; more on the deck—sleeping—knowing nothing about it—three times as many as there were boats for, even if there had been time? I expected to see the iron open out as I stood there and the rush of water going over them as they lay. . . . What could I do—what?'

"I can easily picture him to myself in the peopled gloom of the cavernous place, with the light of the globe-lamp falling on a small portion of the bulkhead that had the weight of the ocean on the other side, and the breathing of unconscious sleepers in his ears. I can see him glaring at the iron, startled by the falling rust, overburdened by the knowledge of an imminent death. This, I gathered, was the second time he had been sent forward by that skipper of his, who, I rather think, wanted to keep him away from the bridge. He told me that his first impulse was to shout and straightway make all those people leap out of sleep into terror; but such an overwhelming sense of his helplessness came over him that he was not able to produce a sound. This is, I suppose, what people mean by the tongue cleaving to the roof of the mouth. 'Too dry,' was the concise expression he used in reference to this state. Without a sound, then, he scrambled out on deck through the number one hatch. A wind-sail rigged down there swung against him accidentally, and he remembered that the light touch of the canvas on his face nearly knocked him off the hatchway ladder.

"He confessed that his knees wobbled a good deal as he stood on the foredeck looking at another sleeping crowd. The engines having been stopped by that time, the steam was blowing off. Its deep rumble made the whole night vibrate like a bass string. The ship trembled to it.

"He saw here and there a head lifted off a mat, a vague form uprise in sitting posture, listen sleepily for a moment, sink down again into the billowy confusion of boxes, steam-winches, ventilators. He was aware all these people did not know enough to take intelligent notice of that strange noise. The ship of iron, the men with white faces, all the sights, all the sounds, everything on board to that ignorant and pions multitude was strange alike, and as trustworthy as it would for ever remain incomprehensible. It occurred to him that the fact was fortunate. The idea of it was simply terrible.

"You must remember he believed, as any other man would have done in his place, that the ship would go down at any moment; the bulging, rust-eaten plates that kept back the ocean, fatally must give way, all at once like an undermined dam, and let in a sudden and overwhelming flood. He stood still looking at these recumbent bodies, a doomed man aware of his fate, surveying the silent company of the dead. They *were* dead! Nothing could save them! There were boats enough for half of them perhaps, but there was no time. No time! No time! It did not seem worth while to open his lips, to stir hand or foot. Before he could shout three words, or make three steps, he would be floundering in a sea whitened awfully by the desperate struggles of human beings, clamorous with the distress of cries for help. There was no help. He imagined what would happen perfectly; he went through it all motionless by the hatchway with the lamp in his hand,—he went through it to the very last harrowing detail. I think he went through it again while he was telling me these things he could not tell the court.

" 'I saw as clearly as I see you now that there was nothing I could do. It seemed to take all life out of my limbs. I thought I might just as well stand where I was and wait. I did not think I had many seconds . . .' Suddenly the steam ceased blowing off. The noise, he remarked, had been distracting, but the silence at once became intolerably oppressive.

" 'I thought I would choke before I got drowned,' he said.

"He protested he did not think of saving himself. The only distinct thought formed, vanishing, and re-forming in his brain, was: eight hundred people and seven boats; eight hundred people and seven boats.

" 'Somebody was speaking aloud inside my head,' he said a little wildly. 'Eight hundred people and seven boats—and no time! Just think of it.' He leaned towards me across the little table, and I tried to avoid his stare. 'Do you think I was afraid of death?' he asked in a voice very fierce and low. He brought down his open hand with a bang that made the coffee-cups dance. 'I am ready to swear I was not—I was not. . . . By God—no!' He hitched himself upright and crossed his arms; his chin fell on his breast.

"The soft clashes of crockery reached us faintly through the high windows. There was a burst of voices, and several men came out in high good-humour into the gallery. They were exchanging jocular reminiscences of the donkeys in Cairo. A pale anxious youth stepping softly on long legs was being chaffed by a strutting and rubicund globe-trotter about his purchases in the bazaar. 'No, really—do you think I've been done to that extent?' he inquired, very earnest and deliberate. The band moved away, dropping into chairs as they went; matches flared, illuminating for a second faces without the ghost of an expression and the flat glaze of white shirt-fronts; the hum of many conversations animated with the ardour of feasting sounded to me absurd and infinitely remote.

" 'Some of the crew were sleeping on the number one hatch within reach of my arm,' began Jim again.

"You must know they kept Kalashee watch in that ship, all hands sleeping through the night, and only the reliefs of quartermasters and look-out men being called. He was tempted to grip and shake the shoulder of the nearest lascar, but he didn't. Something held his arms down along his sides. He was not afraid—oh no! only he just couldn't—that's all. He was not afraid of death perhaps, but I'll tell you what, he was afraid of the emergency. His confounded imagination had evoked for him all the horrors of panic, the trampling rush, the pitiful screams, boats swamped—all the appalling incidents of a disaster at sea he had ever heard of. He might have been resigned to die, but I suspect he wanted to die without added terrors, quietly, in a sort of peaceful trance. A certain readiness to perish is not so very rare, but it is seldom that you meet men whose souls, steeled in the impenetrable armour of resolution, are ready to fight a losing battle to the last; the desire of peace waxes stronger as hope declines, till at last it conquers the very desire of life. Which of us here has not observed this, or maybe experienced something of that feeling in his own person—this extreme weariness of emotions, the vanity of effort, the yearning for rest? Those striving with unreasonable forces know it well—the shipwrecked castaways in boats, wanderers lost in a desert, men battling against the unthinking might of nature, or the stupid brutality of crowds."

Chapter VIII

"How long he stood stock-still by the hatch expecting every moment to feel the ship dip under his feet and the rush of water take him at the back and toss him like a chip, I cannot say. Not very long—two minutes perhaps. A couple of men he could not make out began to converse drowsily, and also, he could not tell where, he detected a curious noise of shuffling feet. Above these faint sounds there was that awful stillness preceding a catastrophe, that trying silence of the moment before the crash; then it came into his head that perhaps he would have time to rush along and cut all the lanyards of the gripes, so that the boats would float off as the ship went down.

"The *Patna* had a long bridge, and all the boats were up there, four on one side and three on the other—the smallest of them on the port side and nearly abreast of the steering-gear. He assured me, with evident anxiety to be believed, that he had been most careful to keep them ready for instant service. He knew his duty. I daresay he was a good enough mate as far as that went. 'I always believed in being prepared for the worst,' he commented, staring anxiously in my face. I nodded my approval of the sound principle, averting my eyes before the subtle unsoundness of the man.

"He started unsteadily to run. He had to step over legs, avoid stumbling against the heads. Suddenly some one caught hold of his coat from below, and a distressed voice spoke under his elbow. The light of the lamp he carried in his right hand fell upon an upturned dark face whose eyes entreated him together with the voice. He had picked up enough of the language to understand the word water, repeated several times in a tone of insistence, of prayer, almost of despair. He gave a jerk to get away, and felt an arm embrace his leg.

" 'The beggar clung to me like a drowning man,' he said impressively. 'Water, water! What water did he mean? What did he know? As calmly as I could I ordered him to let go. He was stopping me, time was pressing, other men began to stir; I wanted time—time to cut the boats adrift. He got hold of my hand now, and I felt that he would begin to shout. It flashed upon me it was enough to start a panic, and I hauled off with my free arm and slung the lamp in his face. The glass jingled, the light went out, but the blow made him let go, and I ran off—I wanted to get at the boats; I wanted to get at the boats. He leaped after me from behind. I turned on him. He would not keep quiet; he tried to shout; I had half throttled him before I made out what he wanted. He wanted some water—water to drink; they were on strict allowance, you know, and he had with him a young boy I had noticed several times. His child was sick—and thirsty. He had caught sight of me as I passed by, and was begging for a little water. That's all. We were under the bridge, in the dark. He kept on snatching at my wrists; there was no getting rid of him. I dashed into my berth, grabbed my water-bottle, and thrust it into his hands. He vanished. I didn't find out till then how much I was in want of a drink myself.' He leaned on one elbow with a hand over his eyes.

"I felt a creepy sensation all down my backbone; there was something peculiar in all this. The fingers of the hand that shaded his brow trembled slightly. He broke the short silence.

" 'These things happen only once to a man and . . . Ah! well! When

I got on the bridge at last the beggars were getting one of the boats off
the chocks. A boat! I was running up the ladder when a heavy blow fell
on my shoulder, just missing my head. It didn't stop me, and the chief
engineer—they had got him out of his bunk by then—raised the boat-
stretcher again. Somehow I had no mind to be surprised at anything.
All this seemed natural—and awful—and awful. I dodged that miserable
maniac, lifted him off the deck as though he had been a little child,
and he started whispering in my arms: "Don't! don't! I thought you were
one of them niggers." I flung him away, he skidded along the bridge
and knocked the legs from under the little chap—the second. The
skipper, busy about the boat, looked round and came at me head down,
growling like a wild beast. I flinched no more than a stone. I was as
solid standing there as this,' he tapped lightly with his knuckles the wall
beside his chair. 'It was as though I had heard it all, seen it all, gone
through it all twenty times already. I wasn't afraid of them. I drew back
my fist and he stopped short, muttering—

" ' "Ah! it's you. Lend a hand quick."

" 'That's what he said. Quick! As if anybody could be quick enough.
"Aren't you going to do something?" I asked. "Yes. Clear out," he snarled
over his shoulder.

" 'I don't think I understood then what he meant. The other two had
picked themselves up by that time, and they rushed together to the boat.
They tramped, they wheezed, they shoved, they cursed the boat, the
ship, each other—cursed me. All in mutters. I didn't move, I didn't
speak. I watched the slant of the ship. She was as still as if landed on
the blocks in a dry dock—only she was like this.' He held up his hand,
palm under, the tips of the fingers inclined downwards. 'Like this,' he
repeated. 'I could see the line of the horizon before me, as clear as a
bell, above her stem-head; I could see the water far off there black and
sparkling, and still—still as a pond, deadly still, more still than ever sea
was before—more still than I could bear to look at. Have you watched
a ship floating head down, checked in sinking by a sheet of old iron too
rotten to stand being shored up. Have you? Oh yes, shored up? I thought
of that—I thought of every mortal thing; but can you shore up a bulkhead
in five minutes—or in fifty for that matter? Where was I going to get
men that would go down below? And the timber—the timber! Would
you have had the courage to swing the maul for the first blow if you
had seen that bulkhead? Don't say you would: you had not seen it;
nobody would. Hang it—to do a thing like that you must believe there
is a chance, one in a thousand, at least, some ghost of a chance; and
you would not have believed. Nobody would have believed. You think
me a cur for standing there, but what would you have done? What! You
can't tell—nobody can tell. One must have time to turn round. What
would you have me do? Where was the kindness in making crazy with
fright all those people I could not save single-handed—that nothing

could save? Look here! As true as I sit on this chair before you . . .'

"He drew quick breaths at every few words and shot quick glances at my face, as though in his anguish he were watchful of the effect. He was not speaking to me, he was only speaking before me, in a dispute with an invisible personality, an antagonistic and inseparable partner of his existence—another possessor of his soul. These were issues beyond the competency of a court of inquiry: it was a subtle and momentous quarrel as to the true essence of life, and did not want a judge. He wanted an ally, a helper, an accomplice. I felt the risk I ran of being circumvented, blinded, decoyed, bullied, perhaps, into taking a definite part in a dispute impossible of decision if one had to be fair to all the phantoms in possession—to the reputable that had its claims and to the disreputable that had its exigencies. I can't explain to you who haven't seen him and who hear his words only at second hand the mixed nature of my feelings. It seemed to me I was being made to comprehend the Inconceivable—and I know of nothing to compare with the discomfort of such a sensation. I was made to look at the convention that lurks in all truth and on the essential sincerity of falsehood. He appealed to all sides at once,—to the side turned perpetually to the light of day, and to that side of us which, like the other hemisphere of the moon, exists stealthily in perpetual darkness, with only a fearful ashy light falling at times on the edge. He swayed me. I own to it, I own up. The occasion was obscure, insignificant—what you will: a lost youngster, one in a million—but then he was one of us; an incident as completely devoid of importance as the flooding of an ant-heap, and yet the mystery of his attitude got hold of me as though he had been an individual in the forefront of his kind, as if the obscure truth involved were momentous enough to affect mankind's conception of itself. . . ."

Marlow paused to put new life into his expiring cheroot, seemed to forget all about the story, and abruptly began again.

"My fault of course. One has no business really to get interested. It's a weakness of mine. His was of another kind. My weakness consists in not having a discriminating eye for the incidental—for the externals,— no eye for the hod[1] of the rag-picker or the fine linen of the next man. Next man—that's it. I have met so many men," he pursued, with momentary sadness—"met them too with a certain—certain—impact, let us say; like this fellow, for instance—and in each case all I could see was merely the human being. A confounded democratic quality of vision which may be better than total blindness, but has been of no advantage to me—I can assure you. Men expect one to take into account their fine linen. But I never could get up any enthusiasm about these things. Oh! It's a failing; it's a failing; and then comes a soft evening; a lot of men too indolent for whist—and a story. . . ."

1. Possibly from *hodden*, a coarse cloth of undyed wool.

He paused again to wait for an encouraging remark, perhaps, but nobody spoke; only the host, as if reluctantly performing a duty, murmured—

"You are so subtle, Marlow."

"Who? I?" said Marlow in a low voice. "Oh no! But *he* was; and try as I may for the success of this yarn I am missing innumerable shades —they were so fine, so difficult to render in colourless words. Because he complicated matters by being so simple, too—the simplest poor devil! . . . By Jove! he was amazing. There he sat telling me that just as I saw him before my eyes he wouldn't be afraid to face anything—and believing in it too. I tell you it was fabulously innocent and it was enormous, enormous! I watched him covertly, just as though I had suspected him of an intention to take a jolly good rise out of me.[2] He was confident that, on the square,[3] 'on the square, mind!' there was nothing he couldn't meet. Ever since he had been 'so high'—'quite a little chap,' he had been preparing himself for all the difficulties that can beset one on land and water. He confessed proudly to this kind of foresight. He had been elaborating dangers and defences, expecting the worst, rehearsing his best. He must have led a most exalted existence. Can you fancy it? A succession of adventures, so much glory, such a victorious progress! and the deep sense of his sagacity crowning every day of his inner life. He forgot himself; his eyes shone; and with every word my heart, searched by the light of his absurdity, was growing heavier in my breast. I had no mind to laugh, and lest I should smile I made for myself a stolid face. He gave signs of irritation.

" 'It is always the unexpected that happens,' I said in a propitiatory tone. My obtuseness provoked him into a contemptuous 'Pshaw!' I suppose he meant that the unexpected couldn't touch him; nothing less than the unconceivable itself could get over his perfect state of preparation. He had been taken unawares—and he whispered to himself a malediction upon the waters and the firmament, upon the ship, upon the men. Everything had betrayed him! He had been tricked into that sort of high-minded resignation which prevented him lifting as much as his little finger, while these others who had a very clear perception of the actual necessity were tumbling against each other and sweating desperately over that boat business. Something had gone wrong there at the last moment. It appears that in their flurry they had contrived in some mysterious way to get the sliding bolt of the foremost boat-chock jammed tight, and forthwith had gone out of the remnants of their minds over the deadly nature of that accident. It must have been a pretty sight, the fierce industry of these beggars toiling on a motionless ship that floated quietly in the silence of a world asleep, fighting against time for the freeing of that boat, grovelling on all-fours, standing up in despair,

2. To outwit or make a person the subject of a jest.
3. Fairly, honestly.

tugging, pushing, snarling at each other venomously, ready to kill, ready to weep, and only kept from flying at each other's throats by the fear of death that stood silent behind them like an inflexible and cold-eyed taskmaster. Oh yes! It must have been a pretty sight. He saw it all, he could talk about it with scorn and bitterness; he had a minute knowledge of it by means of some sixth sense, I conclude, because he swore to me he had remained apart without a glance at them and at the boat— without one single glance. And I believe him. I should think he was too busy watching the threatening slant of the ship, the suspended menace discovered in the midst of the most perfect security—fascinated by the sword hanging by a hair over his imaginative head.[4]

"Nothing in the world moved before his eyes, and he could depict to himself without hindrance the sudden swing upwards of the dark skyline, the sudden tilt up of the vast plain of the sea, the swift still rise, the brutal fling, the grasp of the abyss, the struggle without hope, the starlight closing over his head for ever like the vault of a tomb—the revolt of his young life—the black end. He could! By Jove! who couldn't? And you must remember he was a finished artist in that peculiar way, he was a gifted poor devil with the faculty of swift and forestalling vision. The sights it showed him had turned him into cold stone from the soles of his feet to the nape of his neck; but there was a hot dance of thoughts in his head, a dance of lame, blind, mute thoughts—a whirl of awful cripples. Didn't I tell you he confessed himself before me as though I had the power to bind and to loose.[5] He burrowed deep, deep, in the hope of my absolution, which would have been of no good to him. This was one of those cases which no solemn deception can palliate, where no man can help; where his very Maker seems to abandon a sinner to his own devices.

"He stood on the starboard side of the bridge, as far as he could get from the struggle for the boat, which went on with the agitation of madness and the stealthiness of a conspiracy. The two Malays had meantime remained holding to the wheel. Just picture to yourselves the actors in that, thank God! unique, episode of the sea, four beside themselves with fierce and secret exertions, and three looking on in complete immobility, above the awnings covering the profound ignorance of hundreds of human beings, with their weariness, with their dreams, with their hopes, arrested, held by an invisible hand on the brink of annihilation. For that they were so, makes no doubt to me: given the state of the ship, this was the deadliest possible description of accident

4. Reference to Damocles, a fourth-century B.C. courtier of Dionysius the Elder of Syracuse. When Damocles spoke in flattering terms of the happiness of his ruler, Dionysius invited him to a banquet and seated him under a sword suspended by a single hair, thus reminding him of the vulnerability of everyone's life.
5. Allusion to Jesus' words to his disciples: "Whatsoever ye shall bind on earth shall be bound in heaven; and whatsoever ye shall loose on earth shall be loosed in heaven" (Matthew 18.18). In Roman Catholic theology, this passage is the basis for the authority of the priest to give absolution to a penitent following private confession.

that could happen. These beggars by the boat had every reason to go distracted with funk. Frankly, had I been there, I would not have given as much as a counterfeit farthing[6] for the ship's chance to keep above water to the end of each successive second. And still she floated! These sleeping pilgrims were destined to accomplish their whole pilgrimage to the bitterness of some other end. It was as if the Omnipotence whose mercy they confessed had needed their humble testimony on earth for a while longer, and had looked down to make a sign, 'Thou shalt not!' to the ocean. Their escape would trouble me as a prodigiously inexplicable event, did I not know how tough old iron can be—as tough sometimes as the spirit of some men we meet now and then, worn to a shadow and breasting the weight of life. Not the least wonder of these twenty minutes, to my mind, is the behaviour of the two helmsmen. They were amongst the native batch of all sorts brought over from Aden to give evidence at the inquiry. One of them, labouring under intense bashfulness, was very young, and with his smooth, yellow, cheery countenance looked even younger than he was. I remember perfectly Brierly asking him, through the interpreter, what he thought of it at the time, and the interpreter, after a short colloquy, turning to the court with an important air—

" 'He says he thought nothing.'

"The other with patient blinking eyes, a blue cotton handkerchief, faded with much washing, bound with a smart twist over a lot of grey wisps, his face shrunk into grim hollows, his brown skin made darker by a mesh of wrinkles, explained that he had a knowledge of some evil thing befalling the ship, but there had been no order; he could not remember an order; why should he leave the helm? To some further questions he jerked back his spare shoulders, and declared it never came into his mind then that the white men were about to leave the ship through fear of death. He did not believe it now. There might have been secret reasons. He wagged his old chin knowingly. Aha! secret reasons. He was a man of great experience, and he wanted *that* white Tuan to know—he turned towards Brierly, who didn't raise his head—that he had acquired a knowledge of many things by serving white men on the sea for a great number of years—and, suddenly, with shaky excitement he poured upon our spellbound attention a lot of queer-sounding names, names of dead-and-gone skippers, names of forgotten country ships, names of familiar and distorted sound, as if the hand of dumb time had been at work on them for ages. They stopped him at last. A silence fell upon the court,—a silence that remained unbroken for at least a minute, and passed gently into a deep murmur. This episode was *the* sensation of the second day's proceedings—affecting all the audience, affecting everybody except Jim, who was sitting moodily at

6. Bronze coin at the time worth one-half of a U.S. cent.

the end of the first bench, and never looked up at this extraordinary and damning witness that seemed possessed of some mysterious theory of defence.

"So these two lascars stuck to the helm of that ship without steerageway, where death would have found them if such had been their destiny. The whites did not give them half a glance, had probably forgotten their existence. Assuredly Jim did not remember it. He remembered he could do nothing; he could do nothing, now he was alone. There was nothing to do but to sink with the ship. No use making a disturbance about it. Was there? He waited upstanding, without a sound, stiffened in the idea of some sort of heroic discretion. The first engineer ran cautiously across the bridge to tug at his sleeve.

" 'Come and help! For God's sake, come and help!'

"He ran back to the boat on the points of his toes, and returned directly to worry at his sleeve, begging and cursing at the same time.

" 'I believe he would have kissed my hands,' said Jim savagely, 'and, next moment, he starts foaming and whispering in my face, "If I had the time I would like to crack your skull for you." I pushed him away. Suddenly he caught hold of me round the neck. Damn him! I hit him. I hit out without looking. "Won't you save your own life—you infernal coward," he sobs. Coward! He called me an infernal coward! Ha! ha! ha! ha! He called me—ha! ha! ha! . . .'

"He had thrown himself back and was shaking with laughter. I had never in my life heard anything so bitter as that noise. It fell like a blight on all the merriment about donkeys, pyramids, bazaars, or what not. Along the whole dim length of the gallery the voices dropped, the pale blotches of faces turned our way with one accord, and the silence became so profound that the clear tinkle of a teaspoon falling on the tesselated floor of the verandah rang out like a tiny and silvery scream.

" 'You mustn't laugh like this, with all these people about,' I remonstrated. 'It isn't nice for them, you know.'

"He gave no sign of having heard at first, but after a while with a stare that, missing me altogether, seemed to probe the heart of some awful vision, he muttered carelessly—'Oh! they'll think I am drunk.'

"And after that you would have thought from his appearance he would never make a sound again. But—no fear! He could no more stop telling now than he could have stopped living by the mere exertion of his will."

Chapter IX

" 'I was saying to myself, "Sink—curse you! Sink!" ' These were the words with which he began again. He wanted it over. He was severely left alone, and he formulated in his head this address to the ship in a tone of imprecation, while at the same time he enjoyed the privilege of witnessing scenes—as far as I can judge—of low comedy. They were still at that bolt. The skipper was ordering. 'Get under and try to lift'; and the others naturally shirked. You understand that to be squeezed flat under the keel of a boat wasn't a desirable position to be caught in if the ship went down suddenly. 'Why don't you—you the strongest!' whined the little engineer. 'Gott-for-dam! I am too thick,' spluttered the skipper in despair. It was funny enough to make angels weep.[1] They stood idle for a moment, and suddenly the chief engineer rushed again at Jim.

" 'Come and help, man! Are you mad to throw your only chance away? Come and help, man! Man! Look there—look!'

"And at last Jim looked astern where the other pointed with maniacal insistence. He saw a silent black squall which had eaten up already one-third of the sky. You know how these squalls come up there about that time of the year. First you see a darkening of the horizon—no more; then a cloud rises opaque like a wall. A straight edge of vapour lined with sickly whitish gleams flies up from the south-west, swallowing the stars in whole constellations; its shadow flies over the waters, and confounds sea and sky into one abyss of obscurity. And all is still. No thunder, no wind, no sound; not a flicker of lightning. Then in the tenebrous immensity a livid arch appears; a swell or two like undulations of the very darkness run past, and, suddenly, wind and rain strike together with a peculiar impetuosity as if they had burst through something solid. Such a cloud had come up while they weren't looking. They had just noticed it, and were perfectly justified in surmising that if in absolute stillness there was some chance for the ship to keep afloat a few minutes longer, the least disturbance of the sea would make an end of her instantly. Her first nod to the swell that precedes the burst of such a squall would be also her last, would become a plunge, would, so to speak, be prolonged into a long dive, down, down to the bottom. Hence, these new capers of their fright, these new antics in which they displayed their extreme aversion to die.

" 'It was black, black,' pursued Jim with moody steadiness. 'It had sneaked upon us from behind. The infernal thing! I suppose there had been at the back of my head some hope yet. I don't know. But that was all over anyhow. It maddened me to see myself caught like this. I was angry, as though I had been trapped. I *was* trapped! The night was hot, too, I remember. Not a breath of air.'

"He remembered so well that, gasping in the chair, he seemed to sweat and choke before my eyes. No doubt it maddened him; it knocked him over afresh—in a manner of speaking—but it made him also re-

---

1. See Isabella's words in Shakespeare's *Measure for Measure* 2.2.117–22: "but man, proud man, . . . like an angry ape / Plays such fantastic tricks before high heaven / As makes the angels weep."

member that important purpose which had sent him rushing on that bridge only to slip clean out of his mind. He had intended to cut the life boats clear of the ship. He whipped out his knife and went to work slashing as though he had seen nothing, had heard nothing, had known of no one on board. They thought him hopelessly wrong-headed and crazy, but dared not protest noisily against this useless loss of time. When he had done he returned to the very same spot from which he had started. The chief was there, ready with a clutch at him to whisper close to his head, scathingly, as though he wanted to bite his ear—

" 'You silly fool! do you think you'll get the ghost of a show when all that lot of brutes is in the water? Why, they will batter your head for you from these boats.'

"He wrung his hands, ignored, at Jim's elbow. The skipper kept up a nervous shuffle in one place and mumbled, 'Hammer! hammer! Mein Gott! Get a hammer.'

"The little engineer whimpered like a child, but, broken arm and all, he turned out the least craven of the lot as it seems, and, actually, mustered enough pluck to run an errand to the engine-room. No trifle, it must be owned in fairness to him. Jim told me he darted desperate looks like a cornered man, gave one low wail, and dashed off. He was back instantly clambering, hammer in hand, and without a pause flung himself at the bolt. The others gave up Jim at once and ran off to assist. He heard the tap, tap of the hammer, the sound of the released chock falling over. The boat was clear. Only then he turned to look—only then. But he kept his distance—he kept his distance. He wanted me to know he had kept his distance; that there was nothing in common between him and these men—who had the hammer. Nothing whatever. It is more than probable he thought himself cut off from them by a space that could not be traversed, by an obstacle that could not be overcome, by a chasm without bottom. He was as far as he could get from them—the whole breadth of the ship.

"His feet were glued to that remote spot and his eyes to their indistinct group bowed together and swaying strangely in the common torment of fear. A hand-lamp lashed to a stanchion above a little table rigged up on the bridge—the *Patna* had no chart-room amidships—threw a light on their labouring shoulders, on their arched and bobbing backs. They pushed at the bow of the boat; they pushed out into the night; they pushed, and would no more look back at him. They had given him up as if indeed he had been too far, too hopelessly separated from themselves, to be worth an appealing word, a glance, or a sign. They had no leisure to look back upon his passive heroism, to feel the sting of his abstention. The boat was heavy; they pushed at the bow with no breath to spare for an encouraging word: but the turmoil of terror that had scattered their self-command like chaff before the wind, converted their desperate exertions into a bit of fooling, upon my word, fit for knockabout clowns in a farce. They pushed with their hands, with their heads, they pushed for dear life with all the weight of their bodies, they pushed with all the might of their souls—only no sooner had they succeeded in canting[2] the stem clear of the davit than they would leave off like one man and start a wild scramble into her. As a natural consequence the boat would swing in abruptly, driving them back, helpless and jostling against each other. They would stand nonplussed for a while, exchanging in fierce whispers all the infamous names they could call to mind, and go at it again. Three times this occurred. He described it to me with morose thoughtfulness. He hadn't lost a single movement of that comic business. 'I loathed them. I hated them. I had to look at all that,' he said without emphasis, turning upon me a sombrely watchful glance. 'Was ever there any one so shamefully tried?'

"He took his head in his hands for a moment, like a man driven to distraction by some unspeakable outrage. These were things he could not explain to the court—and not even to me; but I would have been little fitted for the reception of his confidences had I not been able at times to understand the pauses between the words. In this assault upon his fortitude there was the jeering intention of a spiteful and vile vengeance; there was an element of burlesque in his ordeal—a degradation of funny grimaces in the approach of death or dishonour.

"He related facts which I have not forgotten, but at this distance of time I couldn't recall his very words: I only remember that he managed wonderfully to convey the brooding rancour of his mind into the bare recital of events. Twice, he told me, he shut his eyes in the certitude that the end was upon him already, and twice he had to open them again. Each time he noted the darkening of the great stillness. The shadow of the silent cloud had fallen upon the ship from the zenith, and seemed to have extinguished every sound of her teeming life. He could no longer hear the voices under the awnings. He told me that each time he closed his eyes a flash of thought showed him that crowd of bodies, laid out for death, as plain as daylight. When he opened them, it was to see the dim struggle of four men fighting like mad with a stubborn boat. 'They would fall back before it time after time, stand swearing at each other, and suddenly make another rush in a bunch. . . . Enough to make you die laughing,' he commented with downcast eyes; then raising them for a moment to my face with a dismal smile, 'I ought to have a merry life of it, by God! for I shall see that funny sight a good many times yet before I die.' His eyes fell again. 'See and hear. . . . See and hear,' he repeated twice, at long intervals, filled by vacant staring.

"He roused himself.

" 'I made up my mind to keep my eyes shut,' he said, 'and I couldn't.

2. Pushing sideways.

I couldn't, and I don't care who knows it. Let them go through that kind of thing before they talk. Just let them—and do better—that's all. The second time my eyelids flew open and my mouth too. I had felt the ship move. She just dipped her bows—and lifted them gently—and slow! everlastingly slow; and ever so little. She hadn't done that much for days. The cloud had raced ahead, and this first swell seemed to travel upon a sea of lead. There was no life in that stir. It managed, though, to knock over something in my head. What would you have done? You are sure of yourself—aren't you? What would you do if you felt now—this minute—the house here move, just move a little under your chair. Leap! By heavens! you would take one spring from where you sit and land in that clump of bushes yonder.'

"He flung his arm out at the night beyond the stone balustrade. I held my peace. He looked at me very steadily, very severe. There could be no mistake: I was being bullied now, and it behoved me to make no sign lest by a gesture or a word I should be drawn into a fatal admission about myself which would have had some bearing on the case. I was not disposed to take any risk of that sort. Don't forget I had him before me, and really he was too much like one of us not to be dangerous. But if you want to know I don't mind telling you that I did, with a rapid glance, estimate the distance to the mass of denser blackness in the middle of the grass plot before the verandah. He exaggerated. I would have landed short by several feet—and that's the only thing of which I am fairly certain.

"The last moment had come, as he thought, and he did not move. His feet remained glued to the planks if his thoughts were knocking about loose in his head. It was at this moment too that he saw one of the men around the boat step backwards suddenly, clutch at the air with raised arms, totter and collapse. He didn't exactly fall, he only slid gently into a sitting posture, all hunched up, and with his shoulders propped against the side of the engine-room skylight. 'That was the donkey-man. A haggard, white-faced chap with a ragged moustache. Acted third engineer,' he explained.

" 'Dead,' I said. We had heard something of that in court.

" 'So they say,' he pronounced with sombre indifference. 'Of course I never knew. Weak heart. The man had been complaining of being out of sorts for some time before. Excitement. Over-exertion. Devil only knows. Ha! ha! ha! It was easy to see he did not want to die either. Droll, isn't it? May I be shot if he hadn't been fooled into killing himself! Fooled—neither more nor less. Fooled into it, by heavens! just as I . . . Ah! If he had only kept still; if he had only told them to go to the devil when they came to rush him out of his bunk because the ship was sinking! If he had only stood by with his hands in his pockets and called them names!'

"He got up, shook his fist, glared at me, and sat down.

" 'A chance missed, eh?' I murmured.

" 'Why don't you laugh?' he said. 'A joke hatched in hell. Weak heart! . . . I wish sometimes mine had been.'

"This irritated me. 'Do you?' I exclaimed with deep-rooted irony. 'Yes! Can't *you* understand,' he cried. 'I don't know what more you could wish for,' I said angrily. He gave me an utterly uncomprehending glance. This shaft had also gone wide of the mark, and he was not the man to bother about stray arrows. Upon my word, he was too unsuspecting; he was not fair game. I was glad that my missile had been thrown away,—that he had not even heard the twang of the bow.

"Of course he could not know at the time the man was dead. The next minute—his last on board—was crowded with a tumult of events and sensations which beat about him like the sea upon a rock. I use the simile advisedly, because from his relation I am forced to believe he had preserved through it all a strange illusion of passiveness, as though he had not acted but had suffered himself to be handled by the infernal powers who had selected him for the victim of their practical joke. The first thing that came to him was the grinding surge of the heavy davits swinging out at last—a jar which seemed to enter his body from the deck through the soles of his feet, and travel up his spine to the crown of his head. Then, the squall being very near now, another and a heavier swell lifted the passive hull in a threatening heave that checked his breath, while his brain and his heart together were pierced as with daggers by panic-stricken screams. 'Let go! For God's sake, let go! Let go! She's going.' Following upon that the boat-falls ripped through the blocks, and a lot of men began to talk in startled tones under the awnings. 'When these beggars did break out, their yelps were enough to wake the dead,' he said. Next, after the splashing shock of the boat literally dropped in the water, came the hollow noises of stamping and tumbling in her, mingled with confused shouts: 'Unhook! Unhook! Shove! Unhook! Shove for your life! Here's the squall down on us. . . .' He heard, high above his head, the faint muttering of the wind; he heard below his feet a cry of pain. A lost voice alongside started cursing a swivel hook. The ship began to buzz fore and aft like a disturbed hive, and, as quietly as he was telling me all this—because just then he was very quiet in attitude, in face, in voice—he went on to say without the slightest warning as it were, 'I stumbled over his legs.'

"This was the first I heard of his having moved at all. I could not restrain a grunt of surprise. Something had started him off at last, but of the exact moment, of the cause that tore him out of his immobility, he knew no more than the uprooted tree knows of the wind that laid it low. All this had come to him: the sounds, the sights, the legs of the dead man—by Jove! The infernal joke was being crammed devilishly down his throat, but—look you—he was not going to admit of any sort of swallowing motion in his gullet. It's extraordinary how he could cast upon you the spirit of his illusion. I listened as if to a tale of black magic at work upon a corpse.

" 'He went over sideways, very gently, and this is the last thing I remember seeing on board,' he continued. 'I did not care what he did. It looked as though he were picking himself up: I thought he was picking himself up, of course: I expected him to bolt past me over the rail and drop into the boat after the others. I could hear them knocking about down there, and a voice as if crying up a shaft called out "George!" Then three voices together raised a yell. They came to me separately: one bleated, another screamed, one howled. Ough!'

"He shivered a little, and I beheld him rise slowly as if a steady hand from above had been pulling him out of the chair by his hair. Up, slowly—to his full height, and when his knees had locked stiff the hand let him go, and he swayed a little on his feet. There was a suggestion of awful stillness in his face, in his movements, in his very voice when he said 'They shouted'—and involuntarily I pricked up my ears for the ghost of that shout that would be heard directly through the false effect of silence. 'There were eight hundred people in that ship,' he said, impaling me to the back of my seat with an awful blank stare. 'Eight hundred living people, and they were yelling after the one dead man to come down and be saved.[3] "Jump, George! Jump! Oh, jump!" I stood by with my hand on the davit. I was very quiet. It had come over pitch dark. You could see neither sky nor sea. I heard the boat alongside go bump, bump, and not another sound down there for a while, but the ship under me was full of talking noises. Suddenly the skipper howled "Mein Gott! The squall! The squall! Shove off!" With the first hiss of rain, and the first gust of wind, they screamed, "Jump, George! We'll catch you! Jump!" The ship began a slow plunge; the rain swept over her like a broken sea; my cap flew off my head; my breath was driven back into my throat. I heard as if I had been on the top of a tower another wild screech, "Geo-o-o-orge! Oh, jump!" She was going down, down, head first under me. . . .'

"He raised his hand deliberately to his face, and made picking motions with his fingers as though he had been bothered with cobwebs, and afterwards he looked into the open palm for quite half a second before he blurted out—

" 'I had jumped . . .' He checked himself, averted his gaze. . . . 'It seems,' he added.

"His clear blue eyes turned to me with a piteous stare, and looking at him standing before me, dumfounded and hurt, I was oppressed by a sad sense of resigned wisdom, mingled with the amused and profound pity of an old man helpless before a childish disaster.

" 'Looks like it,' I muttered.

3. See the derisive words of the crowd at Jesus' crucifixion: ". . . save thyself. If thou be the Son of God, come down from the cross" (Matthew 27.40).

" 'I knew nothing about it till I looked up,' he explained hastily. And that's possible too. You had to listen to him as you would to a small boy in trouble. He didn't know. It had happened somehow. It would never happen again. He had landed partly on somebody and fallen across a thwart. He felt as though all his ribs on his left side must be broken; then he rolled over, and saw vaguely the ship he had deserted uprising above him, with the red side-light glowing large in the rain like a fire on the brow of a hill seen through a mist. 'She seemed higher than a wall; she loomed like a cliff over the boat. . . . I wished I could die,' he cried. 'There was no going back. It was as if I had jumped into a well—into an everlasting deep hole. . . .' "

Chapter X

"He locked his fingers together and tore them apart. Nothing could be more true: he had indeed jumped into an everlasting deep hole. He had tumbled from a height he could never scale again. By that time the boat had gone driving forward past the bows. It was too dark just then for them to see each other, and, moreover, they were blinded and half drowned with rain. He told me it was like being swept by a flood through a cavern. They turned their backs to the squall; the skipper, it seems, got an oar over the stern to keep the boat before it, and for two or three minutes the end of the world had come through a deluge in a pitchy blackness. The sea hissed 'like twenty thousand kettles.' That's his simile, not mine. I fancy there was not much wind after the first gust; and he himself had admitted at the inquiry that the sea never got up that night to any extent. He crouched down in the bows and stole a furtive glance back. He saw just one yellow gleam of the mast-head light high up and blurred like a last star ready to dissolve. 'It terrified me to see it still there,' he said. That's what he said. What terrified him was the thought that the drowning was not over yet. No doubt he wanted to be done with that abomination as quickly as possible. Nobody in the boat made a sound. In the dark she seemed to fly, but of course she could not have had much way. Then the shower swept ahead, and the great, distracting, hissing noise followed the rain into distance and died out. There was nothing to be heard then but the slight wash about the boat's sides. Somebody's teeth were chattering violently. A hand touched his back. A faint voice said, 'You there?' Another cried out shakily, 'She's gone!' and they all stood up together to look astern. They saw no lights. All was black. A thin cold drizzle was driving into their faces. The boat lurched slightly. The teeth chattered faster, stopped, and began again twice before the man could master his shiver sufficiently to say, 'Ju-ju-st in ti-ti-me. . . . Brrrr.' He recognised the voice of the chief engineer saying surlily, 'I saw her go down. I happened to turn my head.' The wind had dropped almost completely.

"They watched in the dark with their heads half turned to windward as if expecting to hear cries. At first he was thankful the night had covered up the scene before his eyes, and then to know of it and yet to have seen and heard nothing appeared somehow the culminating-point of an awful misfortune. 'Strange isn't it?' he murmured, interrupting himself in his disjointed narrative.

"It did not seem so strange to me. He must have had an unconscious conviction that the reality could not be half as bad, not half as anguishing, appalling, and vengeful as the created terror of his imagination. I believe that, in this first moment, his heart was wrung with all the suffering, that his soul knew the accumulated savour of all the fear, all the horror, all the despair of eight hundred human beings pounced upon in the night by a sudden and violent death, else why should he have said, 'It seemed to me that I must jump out of that accursed boat and swim back to see—half a mile—more—any distance—to the very spot . . .'? Why this impulse? Do you see the significance? Why back to the very spot? Why not drown alongside—if he meant drowning—why back to the very spot, to see—as if his imagination had to be soothed by the assurance that all was over before death could bring relief? I defy any one of you to offer another explanation. It was one of those bizarre and exciting glimpses through the fog. It was an extraordinary disclosure. He let it out as the most natural thing one could say. He fought down that impulse and then he became conscious of the silence. He mentioned this to me. A silence of the sea, of the sky, merged into one indefinite immensity still as death around these saved, palpitating lives. 'You might have heard a pin drop in the boat,' he said with a queer contraction of his lips, like a man trying to master his sensibilities while relating some extremely moving fact. A silence! God alone, who had willed him as he was, knows what he made of it in his heart. 'I didn't think any spot on earth could be so still,' he said. 'You couldn't distinguish the sea from the sky; there was nothing to see and nothing to hear. Not a glimmer, not a shape, not a sound. You could have believed that every bit of dry land had gone to the bottom; that every man on earth but I and these beggars in the boat had got drowned.' He leaned over the table with his knuckles propped amongst coffee-cups, liqueur-glasses, cigar-ends. 'I seemed to believe it. Everything was gone and—all was over . . .' he fetched a deep sigh . . . 'with me.' "

Marlow sat up abruptly and flung away his cheroot with force. It made a darting red trail like a toy rocket fired through the drapery of creepers. Nobody stirred.

"Hey, what do you think of it?" he cried with sudden animation. "Wasn't he true to himself, wasn't he? His saved life was over for want of ground under his feet, for want of sights for his eyes, for want of voices in his ears. Annihilation—hey! And all the time it was only a clouded sky, a sea that did not break, the air that did not stir. Only a night; only a silence.

"It lasted for a while, and then they were suddenly and unanimously moved to make a noise over their escape. 'I knew from the first she would go.' 'Not a minute too soon.' 'A narrow squeak, b'gosh!' He said · nothing, but the breeze that had dropped came back, a gentle draught freshened steadily, and the sea joined its murmuring voice to this talkative reaction succeeding the dumb moments of awe. She was gone! She was gone! Not a doubt of it. Nobody could have helped. They repeated the same words over and over again as though they couldn't stop themselves. Never doubted she would go. The lights were gone. No mistake. The lights were gone. Couldn't expect anything else. She had to go. . . . He noticed that they talked as though they had left behind them nothing but an empty ship. They concluded she would not have been long when she once started. It seemed to cause them some sort of satisfaction. They assured each other that she couldn't have been long about it—'Just shot down like a flat-iron.' The chief engineer declared that the mast-head light at the moment of sinking seemed to drop 'like a lighted match you throw down.' At this the second laughed hysterically. 'I am g-g-glad, I am gla-a-a-d.' His teeth went on 'like an electric rattle,' said Jim, 'and all at once he began to cry. He wept and blubbered like a child, catching his breath and sobbing "Oh dear! oh dear! oh dear!" He would be quiet for a while and start suddenly, "Oh, my poor arm! oh, my poor a-a-a-arm!" I felt I could knock him down. Some of them sat in the stern-sheets. I could just make out their shapes. Voices came to me, mumble, mumble, grunt, grunt. All this seemed very hard to bear. I was cold too. And I could do nothing. I thought that if I moved I would have to go over the side and— . . .'

"His hand groped stealthily, came in contact with a liqueur-glass, and was withdrawn suddenly as if it had touched a red-hot coal. I pushed the bottle slightly. 'Won't you have some more?' I asked. He looked at me angrily. 'Don't you think I can tell you what there is to tell without screwing myself up?'[1] he asked. The squad of globe-trotters had gone to bed. We were alone but for a vague white form erect in the shadow, that, being looked at, cringed forward, hesitated, backed away silently. It was getting late, but I did not hurry my guest.

"In the midst of his forlorn state he heard his companions begin to abuse some one. 'What kept you from jumping, you lunatic?' said a scolding voice. The chief engineer left the stern-sheets, and could be heard clambering forward as if with hostile intentions against 'the greatest idiot that ever was.' The skipper shouted with rasping effort offensive epithets from where he sat at the oar. He lifted his head at that uproar,

---

1. Getting intoxicated; a synonym of *tight*, the metaphor being the same.

and heard the name 'George,' while a hand in the dark struck him on the breast. 'What have you got to say for yourself, you fool?' queried somebody, with a sort of virtuous fury. 'They were after me,' he said. 'They were abusing me—abusing me . . . by the name of George.'

"He paused to stare, tried to smile, turned his eyes away and went on. 'That little second puts his head right under my nose, "Why, it's that blasted mate!" "What!" howls the skipper from the other end of the boat. "No!" shrieks the chief. And he too stooped to look at my face.'

"The wind had left the boat suddenly. The rain began to fall again, and the soft, uninterrupted, a little mysterious sound with which the sea receives a shower arose on all sides in the night. 'They were too taken aback to say anything more at first,' he narrated steadily, 'and what could I have to say to them?' He faltered for a moment, and made an effort to go on. 'They called me horrible names.' His voice, sinking to a whisper, now and then would leap up suddenly, hardened by the passion of scorn, as though he had been talking of secret abominations. 'Never mind what they called me,' he said grimly. 'I could hear hate in their voices. A good thing too. They could not forgive me for being in that boat. They hated it. It made them mad. . . .' He laughed short. . . . 'But it kept me from—Look! I was sitting with my arms crossed, on the gunwale! . . .' He perched himself smartly on the edge of the table and crossed his arms. . . . 'Like this—see? One little tilt backwards and I would have been gone—after the others. One little tilt—the least bit—the least bit.' He frowned, and tapping his forehead with the tip of his middle finger, 'It was there all the time,' he said impressively. 'All the time—that notion. And the rain—cold, thick, cold as melted snow—colder—on my thin cotton clothes—I'll never be so cold again in my life, I know. And the sky was black too—all black. Not a star, not a light anywhere. Nothing outside that confounded boat and those two yapping before me like a couple of mean mongrels at a tree'd thief. Yap! yap! "What you doing here? You're a fine sort! Too much of a bloomin' gentleman to put your hand to it. Come out of your trance, did you? To sneak in? Did you?" Yap! yap! "You ain't fit to live!" Yap! yap! Two of them together trying to out-bark each other. The other would bay from the stern through the rain—couldn't see him—couldn't make it out—some of his filthy jargon. Yap! yap! Bow-ow-ow-ow-ow! Yap! yap! It was sweet to hear them; it kept me alive—I tell you. It saved my life. At it they went, as if trying to drive me overboard with the noise! . . . "I wonder you had pluck enough to jump. You ain't wanted here. If I had known who it was, I would have tipped you over—you skunk! What have you done with the other? Where did you get the pluck to jump—you coward? What's to prevent us three from firing you overboard?" . . . They were out of breath; the shower passed away upon the sea. Then nothing. There was nothing round the boat, not even a sound. Wanted to see me overboard, did they? Upon my

soul! I think they would have had their wish if they had only kept quiet.
Fire me overboard! Would they? "Try," I said. "I would for twopence."
"Too good for you," they screeched together. It was so dark that it was
only when one or the other of them moved that I was quite sure of
seeing him. By heavens! I only wish they had tried.'

"I couldn't help exclaiming, 'What an extraordinary affair!'

" 'Not bad—eh?' he said, as if in some sort astounded. 'They pretended to think I had done away with that donkey-man for some reason
or other. Why should I? And how the devil was I to know? Didn't I get
somehow into that boat? into that boat—I . . .' The muscles round his
lips contracted into an unconscious grimace that tore through the mask
of his usual expression—something violent, short-lived and illuminating
like a twist of lightning that admits the eye for an instant into the secret
convolutions of a cloud. 'I did. I was plainly there with them—wasn't
I? Isn't it awful a man should be driven to do a thing like that—and be
responsible? What did I know about their George they were howling
after? I remembered I had seen him curled up on the deck. "Murdering
coward!" the chief kept on calling me. He didn't seem able to remember
any other two words. I didn't care, only his noise began to worry me.
"Shut up," I said. At that he collected himself for a confounded screech.
"You killed him! You killed him!" "No," I shouted, "but I will kill you
directly." I jumped up, and he fell backwards over a thwart with an
awful loud thump. I don't know why. Too dark. Tried to step back, I
suppose. I stood still facing aft, and the wretched little second began to
whine, "You ain't going to hit a chap with a broken arm—and you call
yourself a gentleman, too." I heard a heavy tramp—one—two—and
wheezy grunting. The other beast was coming at me, clattering his oar
over the stern. I saw him moving, big, big—as you see a man in a mist,
in a dream. "Come on," I cried. I would have tumbled him over like
a bale of shakings. He stopped, muttered to himself, and went back.
Perhaps he had heard the wind. I didn't. It was the last heavy gust we
had. He went back to his oar. I was sorry. I would have tried to—
to . . .'

"He opened and closed his curved fingers, and his hands had an eager
and cruel flutter. 'Steady, steady,' I murmured.

" 'Eh? What? I am not excited,' he remonstrated, awfully hurt, and
with a convulsive jerk of his elbow knocked over the cognac bottle. I
started forward, scraping my chair. He bounced off the table as if a mine
had been exploded behind his back, and half turned before he alighted,
crouching on his feet to show me a startled pair of eyes and a face white
about the nostrils. A look of intense annoyance succeeded. 'Awfully
sorry. How clumsy of me!' he mumbled, very vexed, while the pungent
odour of split alcohol enveloped us suddenly with an atmosphere of a
low drinking-bout in the cool, pure darkness of the night. The lights
had been put out in the dining-hall; our candle glimmered solitary in

the long gallery, and the columns had turned black from pediment to capital. On the vivid stars the high corner of the Harbour Office stood out distinct across the Esplanade, as though the sombre pile had glided nearer to see and hear.

"He assumed an air of indifference.

" 'I dare say I am less calm now than I was then. I was ready for anything. These were trifles. . . .'

" 'You had a lively time of it in that boat,' I remarked.

" 'I was ready,' he repeated. 'After the ship's lights had gone, anything might have happened in that boat—anything in the world—and the world no wiser. I felt this, and I was pleased. It was just dark enough too. We were like men walled up quick in a roomy grave. No concern with anything on earth. Nobody to pass an opinion. Nothing mattered.' For the third time during this conversation he laughed harshly, but there was no one about to suspect him of being only drunk. 'No fear, no law, no sounds, no eyes—not even our own, till—till sunrise at least.'

"I was struck by the suggestive truth of his words. There is something peculiar in a small boat upon the wide sea. Over the lives borne from under the shadow of death there seems to fall the shadow of madness. When your ship fails you, your whole world seems to fail you; the world that made you, restrained you, took care of you. It is as if the souls of men floating on an abyss and in touch with immensity had been set free for any excess of heroism, absurdity, or abomination. Of course, as with belief, thought, love, hate, conviction, or even the visual aspect of material things, there are as many shipwrecks as there are men, and in this one there was something abject which made the isolation more complete,—there was a villainy of circumstances that cut these men off more completely from the rest of mankind, whose ideal of conduct had never undergone the trial of a fiendish and appalling joke. They were exasperated with him for being a half-hearted shirker: he focussed on them his hatred of the whole thing; he would have liked to take a signal revenge for the abhorrent opportunity they had put in his way. Trust a boat on the high seas to bring out the Irrational that lurks at the bottom of every thought, sentiment, sensation, emotion. It was part of the burlesque meanness pervading that particular disaster at sea that they did not come to blows. It was all threats, all a terribly effective feint, a sham from beginning to end, planned by the tremendous disdain of the Dark Powers whose real terrors, always on the verge of triumph, are perpetually foiled by the steadfastness of men. I asked, after waiting for a while, 'Well, what happened?' A futile question. I knew too much already to hope for the grace of a single uplifting touch, for the favour of hinted madness, of shadowed horror. 'Nothing,' he said. 'I meant business, but they meant noise only. Nothing happened.'

"And the rising sun found him just as he had jumped up first in the bows of the boat. What a persistence of readiness! He had been holding the tiller in his hand, too, all the night. They had dropped the rudder overboard while attempting to ship it, and I suppose the tiller got kicked forward somehow while they were rushing up and down that boat trying to do all sorts of things at once so as to get clear of the side. It was a long heavy piece of hard wood, and apparently he had been clutching it for six hours or so. If you don't call that being ready! Can you imagine him, silent and on his feet half the night, his face to the gusts of rain, staring at sombre forms, watchful of vague movements, straining his ears to catch rare low murmurs in the stern-sheets! Firmness of courage or effort of fear? What do you think? And the endurance is undeniable too. Six hours more or less on the defensive; six hours of alert immobility while the boat drove slowly or floated arrested, according to the caprice of the wind; while the sea, calmed, slept at last; while the clouds passed above his head; while the sky from an immensity lustreless and black, diminished to a sombre and lustrous vault, scintillated with a greater brilliance, faded to the east, paled at the zenith; while the dark shapes blotting the low stars astern got outlines, relief, became shoulders, heads, faces, features,—confronted him with dreary stares, had dishevelled hair, torn clothes, blinked red eyelids at the white dawn. 'They looked as though they had been knocking about drunk in gutters for a week,' he described graphically; and then he muttered something about the sunrise being of a kind that foretells a calm day. You know that sailor habit of referring to the weather in every connection. And on my side his few mumbled words were enough to make me see the lower limb of the sun clearing the line of the horizon, the tremble of a vast ripple running over all the visible expanse of the sea, as if the waters had shuddered, giving birth to the globe of light, while the last puff of the breeze would stir the air in a sigh of relief.

" 'They sat in the stern shoulder to shoulder, with the skipper in the middle, like three dirty owls, and stared at me,' I heard him say with an intention of hate that distilled a corrosive virtue[2] into the commonplace words like a drop of powerful poison falling into a glass of water; but my thoughts dwelt upon that sunrise. I could imagine under the pellucid emptiness of the sky these four men imprisoned in the solitude of the sea, the lonely sun, regardless of the speck of life, ascending the clear curve of the heaven as if to gaze ardently from a greater height at his own splendour reflected in the still ocean. 'They called out to me from aft,' said Jim, 'as though we had been chums together. I heard them. They were begging me to be sensible and drop that "blooming piece of wood." Why *would* I carry on so? They hadn't done me any harm—had they? There had been no harm. . . . No harm!'

"His face crimsoned as though he could not get rid of the air in his lungs.

---

2. An active quality or power whether of physical or of moral nature.

" 'No harm!' he burst out. 'I leave it to you. You can understand. Can't you? You see it—don't you? No harm! Good God! What more could they have done? Oh yes, I know very well—I jumped. Certainly. I jumped! I told you I jumped; but I tell you they were too much for any man. It was their doing as plainly as if they had reached up with a boat-hook and pulled me over. Can't you see it? You must see it. Come. Speak—straight out.'

"His uneasy eyes fastened upon mine, questioned, begged, challenged, entreated. For the life of me I couldn't help murmuring, 'You've been tried.' 'More than is fair,' he caught up swiftly. 'I wasn't given half a chance—with a gang like that. And now they were friendly—oh, so damnably friendly! Chums, shipmates. All in the same boat. Make the best of it. They hadn't meant anything. They didn't care a hang for George. George had gone back to his berth for something at the last moment and got caught. The man was a manifest fool. Very sad, of course. . . . Their eyes looked at me; their lips moved; they wagged their heads at the other end of the boat—three of them; they beckoned—to me. Why not? Hadn't I jumped? I said nothing. There are no words for the sort of things I wanted to say. If I had opened my lips just then I would have simply howled like an animal. I was asking myself when I would wake up. They urged me aloud to come aft and hear quietly what the skipper had to say. We were sure to be picked up before the evening—right in the track of all the Canal[3] traffic; there was smoke to the north-west now.

" 'It gave me an awful shock to see this faint, faint blur, this low trail of brown mist through which you could see the boundary of sea and sky. I called out to them that I could hear very well where I was. The skipper started swearing, as hoarse as a crow. He wasn't going to talk at the top of his voice for *my* accommodation. "Are you afraid they will hear you on shore?" I asked. He glared as if he would have liked to claw me to pieces. The chief engineer advised him to humour me. He said I wasn't right in my head yet. The other rose astern, like a thick pillar of flesh—and talked—talked. . . .'

"Jim remained thoughtful. 'Well?' I said. 'What did I care what story they agreed to make up?' he cried recklessly. 'They could tell what they jolly well liked. It was their business. I knew the story. Nothing they could make people believe could alter it for me. I let him talk, argue —talk, argue. He went on and on and on. Suddenly I felt my legs give way under me. I was sick, tired—tired to death. I let fall the tiller, turned my back on them, and sat down on the foremost thwart. I had enough. They called to me to know if I understood—wasn't it true, every word of it? It was true, by God! after their fashion. I did not turn my head. I heard them palavering together. "The silly ass won't say

3. Suez Canal, joining the Mediterranean with the Gulf of Suez and thus with the Red Sea and the Orient.

anything." "Oh, he understands well enough." "Let him be; he will be all right." "What can he do?" What could I do! Weren't we all in the same boat. I tried to be deaf. The smoke had disappeared to the northward. It was a dead calm. They had a drink from the water-breaker, and I drank too. Afterwards they made a great business of spreading the boat-sail over the gunwales. Would I keep a look-out? They crept under, out of my sight, thank God! I felt weary, weary, done up, as if I hadn't had one hour's sleep since the day I was born. I couldn't see the water for the glitter of the sunshine. From time to time one of them would creep out, stand up to take a look all round, and get under again. I could hear spells of snoring below the sail. Some of them could sleep. One of them at least. I couldn't! All was light, light, and the boat seemed to be falling through it. Now and then I would feel quite surprised to find myself sitting on a thwart. . . .'

"He began to walk with measured steps to and fro before my chair, one hand in his trousers-pocket, his head bent thoughtfully, and his right arm at long intervals raised for a gesture that seemed to put out of his way an invisible intruder.

" 'I suppose you think I was going mad,' he began in a changed tone. 'And well you may, if you remember I had lost my cap. The sun crept all the way from east to west over my bare head, but that day I could not come to any harm, I suppose. The sun could not make me mad. . . .' His right arm put aside the idea of madness. . . . 'Neither could it kill me. . . .' Again his arm repulsed a shadow. . . . '*That* rested with me.'

" 'Did it?' I said, inexpressibly amazed at this new turn, and I looked at him with the same sort of feeling I might be fairly conceived to experience had he, after spinning round on his heel, presented an altogether new face.

" 'I didn't get brain fever, I did not drop dead either,' he went on. 'I didn't bother myself at all about the sun over my head. I was thinking as coolly as any man that ever sat thinking in the shade. That greasy beast of a skipper poked his big cropped head from under the canvas and screwed his fishy eyes up at me. "Donnerwetter![4] you will die," he growled, and drew in like a turtle. I had seen him. I had heard him. He didn't interrupt me. I was thinking just then that I wouldn't.'

"He tried to sound my thought with an attentive glance dropped on me in passing. 'Do you mean to say you had been deliberating with yourself whether you would die?' I asked in as impenetrable a tone as I could command. He nodded without stopping. 'Yes, it had come to that as I sat there alone,' he said. He passed on a few steps to the imaginary end of his beat, and when he flung round to come back both his hands were thrust deep into his pockets. He stopped short in front

---

4. Exclamation; literally, "thunderweather."

of my chair and looked down. 'Don't you believe it?' he inquired with tense curiosity. I was moved to make a solemn declaration of my readiness to believe implicitly anything he thought fit to tell me.'"

Chapter XI

"He heard me out with his head on one side, and I had another glimpse through a rent in the mist in which he moved and had his being. The dim candle spluttered within the ball of glass, and that was all I had to see him by; at his back was the dark night with the clear stars, whose distant glitter disposed in retreating planes lured the eye into the depths of a greater darkness; and yet a mysterious light seemed to show me his boyish head, as if in that moment the youth within him had, for a second, glowed and expired. 'You are an awful good sort to listen like this,' he said. 'It does me good. You don't know what it is to me. You don't' . . . words seemed to fail him. It was a distinct glimpse. He was a youngster of the sort you like to see about you; of the sort you like to imagine yourself to have been; of the sort whose appearance claims the fellowship of these illusions you had thought gone out, extinct, cold, and which, as if rekindled at the approach of another flame, give a flutter deep, deep down somewhere, give a flutter of light . . . of heat! . . . Yes; I had a glimpse of him then, . . . and it was not the last of that kind. . . . 'You don't know what it is for a fellow in my position to be believed—make a clean breast of it to an elder man. It is so difficult—so awfully unfair—so hard to understand.'

"The mists were closing again. I don't know how old I appeared to him—and how much wise? Not half as old as I felt just then; not half as uselessly wise as I knew myself to be. Surely in no other craft as in that of the sea do the hearts of those already launched to sink or swim go out so much to the youth on the brink, looking with shining eyes upon that glitter of the vast surface which is only a reflection of his own glances full of fire. There is such magnificent vagueness in the expectations that had driven each of us to sea, such a glorious indefiniteness, such a beautiful greed of adventures that are their own and only reward. What we get—well, we won't talk of that; but can one of us restrain a smile? In no other kind of life is the illusion more wide of reality—in no other is the beginning *all* illusion—the disenchantment more swift—the subjugation more complete. Hadn't we all commenced with the same desire, ended with the same knowledge, carried the memory of the same cherished glamour through the sordid days of imprecation? What wonder that when some heavy prod gets home the bond is found to be close; that besides the fellowship of the craft there is felt the strength of a wider feeling—the feeling that binds a man to a child. He was

there before me, believing that age and wisdom can find a remedy against
the pain of truth, giving me a glimpse of himself as a young fellow in
a scrape that is the very devil of a scrape, the sort of scrape greybeards
wag at solemnly while they hide a smile. And he had been deliberating
upon death—confound him! He had found *that* to meditate about
because he thought he had saved his life, while all its glamour had gone
with the ship in the night. What more natural! It was tragic enough and
funny enough in all conscience to call aloud for compassion, and in
what was I better than the rest of us to refuse him my pity. And even
as I looked at him the mists rolled into the rent, and his voice spoke—

" 'I was so lost, you know. It was the sort of thing one does not expect
to happen to one. It was not like a fight, for instance.'

" 'It was not,' I admitted. He appeared changed, as if he had suddenly
matured.

" 'One couldn't be sure,' he muttered.

" 'Ah! You were not sure,' I said, and was placated by the sound of
a faint sigh that passed between us like the flight of a bird in the night.

" 'Well, I wasn't,' he said courageously. 'It was something like that
wretched story they made up. It was not a lie—but it wasn't truth all
the same. It was something. . . . One knows a downright lie. There
was not the thickness of a sheet of paper between the right and the wrong
of this affair.'

" 'How much more did you want?' I asked; but I think I spoke so low
that he did not catch what I said. He had advanced his argument as
though life had been a network of paths separated by chasms. His voice
sounded reasonable.

" 'Suppose I had not—I mean to say, suppose I had stuck to the ship?
Well. How much longer? Say a minute—half a minute. Come. In
thirty seconds, as it seemed certain then, I would have been overboard;
and do you think I would not have laid hold of the first thing that came
in my way—oar, life-buoy, grating—anything. Wouldn't you?'

" 'And be saved,' I interjected.

" 'I would have meant to be,' he retorted. 'And that's more than I
meant when I' . . . he shivered as if about to swallow some nauseous
drug . . . 'jumped,' he pronounced with a convulsive effort, whose
stress, as if propagated by the waves of the air, made my body stir a little
in the chair. He fixed me with lowering eyes. 'Don't you believe me?'
he cried. 'I swear! . . . Confound it! You got me here to talk, and . . .
You must! . . . You said you would believe.' 'Of course I do,' I protested,
in a matter-of-fact tone which produced a calming effect. 'Forgive me,'
he said. 'Of course I wouldn't have talked to you about all this if you
had not been a gentleman. I ought to have known . . . I am—I am—
a gentleman too . . .' 'Yes, yes,' I said hastily. He was looking me
squarely in the face, and withdrew his gaze slowly. 'Now you understand
why I didn't after all . . . didn't go out in that way. I wasn't going to

be frightened at what I had done. And, anyhow, if I had stuck to the ship I would have done my best to be saved. Men have been known to float for hours—in the open sea—and be picked up not much the worse for it. I might have lasted it out better than many others. There's nothing the matter with *my* heart.' He withdrew his right fist from his pocket, and the blow he struck on his chest resounded like a muffled detonation in the night.

" 'No,' I said. He meditated, with his legs slightly apart and his chin sunk. 'A hair's-breadth,' he muttered. 'Not the breadth of a hair between this and that. And at the time . . .'

" 'It is difficult to see a hair at midnight,' I put in, a little viciously I fear. Don't you see what I mean by the solidarity of the craft? I was aggrieved against him, as though he had cheated me—me!—of a splendid opportunity to keep up the illusion of my beginnings, as though he had robbed our common life of the last spark of its glamour. 'And so you cleared out—at once.'

" 'Jumped,' he corrected me incisively. 'Jumped—mind!' he repeated, and I wondered at the evident but obscure intention. 'Well, yes! Perhaps I could not see then. But I had plenty of time and any amount of light in that boat. And I could think too. Nobody would know, of course, but this did not make it any easier for me. You've got to believe that too. I did not want all this talk. . . . No . . . Yes . . . I won't lie . . . I wanted it: it is the very thing I wanted—there. Do you think you or anybody could have made me if I . . . I am—I am not afraid to tell. And I wasn't afraid to think either. I looked it in the face. I wasn't going to run away. At first—at night, if it hadn't been for those fellows I might have . . . No! by heavens! I was not going to give them that satisfaction. They had done enough. They made up a story, and believed it for all I know. But I knew the truth, and I would live it down—alone, with myself. I wasn't going to give in to such a beastly unfair thing. What did it prove after all? I was confoundedly cut up. Sick of life—to tell you the truth; but what would have been the good to shirk it—in—in —that way? That was not the way. I believe—I believe it would have —it would have ended—nothing.'

"He had been walking up and down, but with the last word he turned short at me.

" 'What do *you* believe?' he asked with violence. A pause ensued, and suddenly I felt myself overcome by a profound and hopeless fatigue, as though his voice had startled me out of a dream of wandering through empty spaces whose immensity had harassed my soul and exhausted my body.

" '. . . Would have ended nothing,' he muttered over me obstinately, after a little while. 'No! the proper thing was to face it out—alone— for myself—wait for another chance—find out . . .' "

Chapter XII

"All around everything was still as far as the ear could reach. The mist of his feelings shifted between us, as if disturbed by his struggles, and in the rifts of the immaterial veil he would appear to my staring eyes distinct of form and pregnant with vague appeal like a symbolic figure in a picture. The chill air of the night seemed to lie on my limbs as heavy as a slab of marble.

" 'I see,' I murmured, more to prove to myself that I could break my state of numbness than for any other reason.

" 'The *Avondale* picked us up just before sunset,' he remarked moodily. 'Steamed right straight for us. We had only to sit and wait.'

"After a long interval, he said, 'They told their story.' And again there was that oppressive silence. 'Then only I knew what it was I had made up my mind to,' he added.

" 'You said nothing,' I whispered.

" 'What could I say?' he asked, in the same low tone. . . . 'Shock slight. Stopped the ship. Ascertained the damage. Took measures to get the boats out without creating a panic. As the first boat was lowered ship went down in a squall. Sank like lead. . . . What could be more clear' . . . he hung his head . . . 'and more awful?' His lips quivered while he looked straight into my eyes. 'I had jumped—hadn't I?' he asked dismayed. 'That's what I had to live down. The story didn't matter.' . . . He clasped his hands for an instant, glanced right and left into the gloom: 'It was like cheating the dead,' he stammered.

" 'And there were no dead,' I said.

"He went away from me at this. That is the only way I can describe it. In a moment I saw his back close to the balustrade. He stood there for some time, as if admiring the purity and the peace of the night. Some flowering-shrub in the garden below spread its powerful scent through the damp air. He returned to me with hasty steps.

" 'And that did not matter,' he said, as stubbornly as you please.

" 'Perhaps not,' I admitted. I began to have a notion he was too much for me. After all, what did I know?

" 'Dead or not dead, I could not get clear,' he said. 'I had to live; hadn't I?'

" 'Well, yes—if you take it in that way,' I mumbled.

" 'I was glad of course,' he threw out carelessly, with his mind fixed on something else. 'The exposure,' he pronounced slowly, and lifted his head. 'Do you know what was my first thought when I heard? I was relieved. I was relieved to learn that those shouts—did I tell you I had heard shouts? No? Well, I did. Shouts for help, . . . blown along with the drizzle. Imagination, I suppose. And yet I can hardly . . . How stupid. . . . The others did not. I asked them afterwards. They all said

No. No? And I was hearing them even then! I might have known—
but I didn't think—I only listened. Very faint screams—day after day.
Then that little half-caste chap here came up and spoke to me. "The
Patna . . . French gunboat . . . towed successfully to Aden . . .
Investigation . . . Marine Office . . . Sailors' Home . . . arrangements
made for your board and lodging!" I walked along with him, and I
enjoyed the silence. So there had been no shouting. Imagination. I had
to believe him. I could hear nothing any more. I wonder how long I
could have stood it. It was getting worse, too . . . I mean—louder.'

"He fell into thought.

" 'And I had heard nothing! Well—so be it. But the lights! The lights
did go! We did not see them. They were not there. If they had been, I
would have swam back—I would have gone back and shouted
alongside—I would have begged them to take me on board. . . . I would
have had my chance. . . . You doubt me? . . . How do you know how
I felt? . . . What right have you to doubt? . . . I very nearly did it as it
was—do you understand?' His voice fell. 'There was not a glimmer—
not a glimmer,' he protested mournfully. 'Don't you understand that if
there had been, you would not have seen me here? You see me—and
you doubt.'

"I shook my head negatively. This question of the lights being lost
sight of when the boat could not have been more than a quarter of a
mile from the ship was a matter for much discussion. Jim stuck to it
that there was nothing to be seen after the first shower had cleared away;
and the others had affirmed the same thing to the officers of the *Avondale*.
Of course people shook their heads and smiled. One old skipper who
sat near me in court tickled my ear with his white beard to murmur,
'Of course they would lie.' As a matter of fact nobody lied; not even the
chief engineer with his story of the mast-head light dropping like a match
you throw down. Not consciously, at least. A man with his liver in such
a state might very well have seen a floating spark in the corner of his
eye when stealing a hurried glance over his shoulder. They had seen
no light of any sort though they were well within range, and they could
only explain this in one way: the ship had gone down. It was obvious
and comforting. The foreseen fact coming so swiftly had justified their
haste. No wonder they did not cast about for any other explanation. Yet
the true one was very simple, and as soon as Brierly suggested it the
court ceased to bother about the question. If you remember, the ship
had been stopped, and was lying with her head on the course steered
through the night, with her stern canted high and her bows brought low
down in the water through the filling of the fore-compartment. Being
thus out of trim, when the squall struck her a little on the quarter, she
swung head to wind as sharply as though she had been at anchor. By
this change in her position all her lights were in a very few moments
shut off from the boat to leeward. It may very well be that, had they

been seen, they would have had the effect of a mute appeal—that their
glimmer lost in the darkness of the cloud would have had the mysterious
power of the human glance that can awaken the feelings of remorse and
pity. It would have said, 'I am here—still here' . . . and what more can
the eye of the most forsaken of human beings say? But she turned her
back on them as if in disdain of their fate: she had swung round, burdened, to glare stubbornly at the new danger of the open sea which she
so strangely survived to end her days in a breaking-up yard, as if it had
been her recorded fate to die obscurely under the blows of many ham-
mers. What were the various ends their destiny provided for the pilgrims
I am unable to say; but the immediate future brought, at about nine
o'clock next morning, a French gunboat homeward bound from Réunion. The report of her commander was public property. He had swept
a little out of his course to ascertain what was the matter with that
steamer floating dangerously by the head upon a still and hazy sea.
There was an ensign, union down, flying at her main gaff (the serang
had the sense to make a signal of distress at daylight); but the cooks were
preparing the food in the cooking-boxes forward as usual. The decks
were packed as close as a sheep-pen: there were people perched all along
the rails, jammed on the bridge in a solid mass; hundreds of eyes stared,
and not a sound was heard when the gunboat ranged abreast, as if all
that multitude of lips had been sealed by a spell.

"The Frenchman hailed, could get no intelligible reply, and after
ascertaining through his binoculars that the crowd on deck did not look
plague-stricken, decided to send a boat. Two officers came on board,
listened to the serang, tried to talk with the Arab, couldn't make head
or tail of it: but of course the nature of the emergency was obvious
enough. They were also very much struck by discovering a white man,
dead and curled up peacefully on the bridge. '*Fort intrigués par ce
cadavre*,'[1] as I was informed a long time after by an elderly French
lieutenant whom I came across one afternoon in Sydney, by the merest
chance, in a sort of café, and who remembered the affair perfectly.
Indeed this affair, I may notice in passing, had an extraordinary power
of defying the shortness of memories and the length of time: it seemed
to live, with a sort of uncanny vitality, in the minds of men, on the tips
of their tongues. I've had the questionable pleasure of meeting it often,
years afterwards, thousands of miles away, emerging from the remotest
possible talk, coming to the surface of the most distant allusions. Has
it not turned up to-night between us? And I am the only seaman here.
I am the only one to whom it is a memory. And yet it has made its way
out! But if two men who, unknown to each other, knew of this affair
met accidentally on any spot of this earth, the thing would pop up
between them as sure as fate, before they parted. I had never seen that

1. Much intrigued by that corpse. (Marlow translates many of the subsequent French phrases as
   he narrates.)

Frenchman before, and at the end of an hour we had done with each other for life: he did not seem particularly talkative either; he was a quiet, massive chap in a creased uniform, sitting drowsily over a tumbler half full of some dark liquid. His shoulder-straps were a bit tarnished, his clean-shaved cheeks were large and sallow; he looked like a man who would be given to taking snuff—don't you know? I won't say he did; but the habit would have fitted that kind of man. It all began by his handing me a number of 'Home News,' which I didn't want, across the marble table. I said 'Merci.' We exchanged a few apparently innocent remarks, and suddenly, before I knew how it had come about, we were in the midst of it, and he was telling me how much they had been 'intrigued by that corpse.' It turned out he had been one of the boarding officers.

"In the establishment where we sat one could get a variety of foreign drinks which were kept for the visiting naval officers, and he took a sip of the dark medical-looking stuff, which probably was nothing more nasty than *cassis à l'eau*,[2] and glancing with one eye into the tumbler, shook his head slightly. '*Impossible de comprendre—vous concevez*,' he said, with a curious mixture of unconcern and thoughtfulness. I could very easily conceive how impossible it had been for them to understand. Nobody in the gunboat knew enough English to get hold of the story as told by the serang. There was a good deal of noise, too, round the two officers. 'They crowded upon us. There was a circle round that dead man (*autour de ce mort*),' he described. 'One had to attend to the most pressing. These people were beginning to agitate themselves—*Par-bleu!*[3] A mob like that—don't you see?' he interjected with philosophic indulgence. As to the bulkhead, he had advised his commander that the safest thing was to leave it alone, it was so villainous to look at. They got two hawsers on board promptly (*en toute hâte*) and took the *Patna* in tow—stern foremost at that—which, under the circumstances, was not so foolish, since the rudder was too much out of the water to be of any great use for steering, and this manœuvre eased the strain on the bulkhead, whose state, he expounded with stolid glibness, demanded the greatest care (*éxigeait les plus grands ménagements*). I could not help thinking that my new acquaintance must have had a voice in most of these arrangements: he looked a reliable officer, no longer very active, and he was seamanlike too, in a way, though as he sat there, with his thick fingers clasped lightly on his stomach, he reminded you of one of those snuffy, quiet village priests, into whose ears are poured the sins, the sufferings, the remorse of peasant generations, on whose faces the placid and simple expression is like a veil thrown over the mystery of pain and distress. He ought to have had a threadbare black *soutane*[4]

2. Black currant cordial and water.
3. Mild oath (euphemism for *par Dieu*: "By God!").
4. The style of cassock (a long, light outer garment) worn by Roman Catholic priests.

buttoned smoothly up to his ample chin, instead of a frockcoat with
shoulder-straps and brass buttons. His broad bosom heaved regularly
while he went on telling me that it had been the very devil of a job, as
doubtless (*sans doute*) I could figure to myself in my quality of a seaman
(*en votre qualité de marin*). At the end of the period he inclined his
body slightly towards me, and, pursing his shaved lips, allowed the air
to escape with a gentle hiss. 'Luckily,' he continued, 'the sea was level
like this table, and there was no more wind than there is here.' . . .
The place struck me as indeed intolerably stuffy, and very hot; my face
burned as though I had been young enough to be embarrassed and
blushing. They had directed their course, he pursued, to the nearest
English port '*naturellement*,' where their responsibility ceased, '*Dieu
merci.*'[5] . . . He blew out his flat cheeks a little. . . . 'Because, mind
you (*notez bien*), all the time of towing we had two quartermasters
stationed with axes by the hawsers, to cut us clear of our tow in case
she . . .' He fluttered downwards his heavy eyelids, making his meaning
as plain as possible. . . . 'What would you! One does what one can (*on
fait ce qu'on peut*),' and for a moment he managed to invest his ponderous
immobility with an air of resignation. 'Two quartermasters—thirty
hours—always there. Two!' he repeated, lifting up his right hand a little,
and exhibiting two fingers. This was absolutely the first gesture I saw
him make. It gave me the opportunity to 'note' a starred scar on the
back of his hand—effect of a gunshot clearly; and, as if my sight had
been made more acute by this discovery, I perceived also the seam of
an old wound, beginning a little below the temple and going out of
sight under the short grey hair at the side of his head—the graze of a
spear or the cut of a sabre. He clasped his hands on his stomach again.
'I remained on board that, that—my memory is going (*s'en va*). Ah!
Patt-nà. C'est bien ça.[6] Patt-nà. Merci. It is droll how one forgets. I
stayed on that ship thirty hours. . . .'

    " 'You did!' I exclaimed. Still gazing at his hands, he pursed his lips
a little, but this time made no hissing sound. 'It was judged proper,' he
said, lifting his eyebrows dispassionately, 'that one of the officers should
remain to keep an eye open (*pour ouvrir l'oeil*)' . . . he sighed idly . . .
'and for communicating by signals with the towing ship—do you
see—and so on. For the rest, it was my opinion too. We made our
boats ready to drop over—and I also on that ship took measures. . . .
Enfin![7] One has done one's possible. It was a delicate position. Thirty
hours! They prepared me some food. As for the wine—go and whistle
for it—not a drop.' In some extraordinary way, without any marked
change in his inert attitude and in the placid expression of his face, he

5. Thank God.
6. That's it exactly.
7. Untranslatable. Suggests shift in thinking. Literally, "enough."

managed to convey the idea of profound disgust. 'I—you know—when it comes to eating without my glass of wine—I am nowhere.'

"I was afraid he would enlarge upon the grievance, for though he didn't stir a limb or twitch a feature, he made one aware how much he was irritated by the recollection. But he seemed to forget all about it. They delivered their charge to the 'port authorities,' as he expressed it. He was struck by the calmness with which it had been received. 'One might have thought they had such a droll find (*drôle de trouvaille*) brought them every day. You are extraordinary—you others,' he commented, with his back propped against the wall, and looking himself as incapable of an emotional display as a sack of meal. There happened to be a man-of-war and an Indian Marine steamer in the harbour at the time, and he did not conceal his admiration of the efficient manner in which the boats of these two ships cleared the *Patna* of her passengers. Indeed his torpid demeanour concealed nothing: it had that mysterious, almost miraculous, power of producing striking effects by means impossible of detection which is the last word of the highest art. 'Twenty-five minutes—watch in hand—twenty-five, no more.' . . . He unclasped and clasped again his fingers without removing his hands from his stomach, and made it infinitely more effective than if he had thrown up his arms to heaven in amazement. . . . 'All that lot (*tout ce monde*) on shore—with their little affairs—nobody left but a guard of seamen (*marins de l'État*) and that interesting corpse (*cet intéréssant cadavre*). Twenty-five minutes.' . . . With downcast eyes and his head tilted slightly on one side he seemed to roll knowingly on his tongue the savour of a smart bit of work. He persuaded one without any further demonstration that his approval was eminently worth having, and resuming his hardly interrupted immobility, he went on to inform me that, being under orders to make the best of their way to Toulon, they left in two hours' time, 'so that (*de sorte que*) there are many things in this incident of my life (*dans cet épisode de ma vie*) which have remained obscure.' "

Chapter XIII

"After these words, and without a change of attitude, he, so to speak, submitted himself passively to a state of silence. I kept him company; and suddenly, but not abruptly, as if the appointed time had arrived for his moderate and husky voice to come out of his immobility, he pronounced, '*Mon Dieu!* how the time passes!' Nothing could have been more commonplace than this remark; but its utterance coincided for me with a moment of vision. It's extraordinary how we go through life with eyes half shut, with dull ears, with dormant thoughts. Perhaps it's just as well; and it may be that it is this very dulness that makes life to the incalculable majority so supportable and so welcome. Nevertheless, there can be but few of us who had never known one of these rare moments of awakening when we see, hear, understand ever so much —everything—in a flash—before we fall back again into our agreeable somnolence. I raised my eyes when he spoke, and I saw him as though I had never seen him before. I saw his chin sunk on his breast, the clumsy folds of his coat, his clasped hands, his motionless pose, so curiously suggestive of his having been simply left there. Time had passed indeed: it had overtaken him and gone ahead. It had left him hopelessly behind with a few poor gifts: the iron-grey hair, the heavy fatigue of the tanned face, two scars, a pair of tarnished shoulder-straps; one of those steady, reliable men who are the raw material of great reputations, one of those uncounted lives that are buried without drums and trumpets under the foundations of monumental successes. 'I am now third lieu- tenant of the *Victorieuse*' (she was the flagship of the French Pacific squadron at the time), he said, detaching his shoulders from the wall a couple of inches to introduce himself. I bowed slightly on my side of the table, and told him I commanded a merchant vessel at present anchored in Rushcutters' Bay. He had 'remarked' her,—a pretty little craft. He was very civil about it in his impassive way. I even fancy he went the length of tilting his head in compliment as he repeated, breath- ing visibly the while, 'Ah, yes. A little craft painted black—very pretty—very pretty (*très coquet*).' After a time he twisted his body slowly to face the glass door on our right. 'A dull town (*Triste ville*),' he observed, staring into the street. It was a brilliant day; a southerly buster was raging, and we could see the passers-by, men and women, buffeted by the wind on the side-walks, the sunlit fronts of the houses across the road blurred by the tall whirls of dust. 'I descended on shore,' he said, 'to stretch my legs a little, but . . .' He didn't finish, and sank into the depths of his repose. 'Pray—tell me,' he began, coming up ponderously, 'what was there at the bottom of this affair—precisely (*au juste*)? It is curious. That dead man, for instance—and so on.

" 'There were living men too,' I said; 'much more curious.'

" 'No doubt, no doubt,' he agreed half audibly, then, as if after mature consideration, murmured, 'Evidently.' I made no difficulty in com- municating to him what had interested me most in this affair. It seemed as though he had a right to know: hadn't he spent thirty hours on board the *Patna*—had he not taken the succession, so to speak, had he not done 'his possible'? He listened to me, looking more priest-like than ever, and with what—probably on account of his downcast eyes—had the appearance of devout concentration. Once or twice he elevated his eyebrows (but without raising his eyelids), as one would say 'The devil!' Once he calmly exclaimed, 'Ah, bah!' under his breath, and when I had finished he pursed his lips in a deliberate way and emitted a sort of sorrowful whistle.

"In any one else it might have been an evidence of boredom, a sign of indifference; but he, in his occult way, managed to make his immobility appear profoundly responsive, and as full of valuable thoughts as an egg is of meat. What he said at last was nothing more than a 'Very interesting,' pronounced politely, and not much above a whisper. Before I got over my disappointment he added, but as if speaking to himself, 'That's it. That *is* it.' His chin seemed to sink lower on his breast, his body to weigh heavier on his seat. I was about to ask him what he meant, when a sort of preparatory tremor passed over his whole person, as a faint ripple may be seen upon stagnant water even before the wind is felt. 'And so that poor young man ran away along with the others,' he said, with grave tranquillity.

"I don't know what made me smile: it is the only genuine smile of mine I can remember in connection with Jim's affair. But somehow this simple statement of the matter sounded funny in French. . . . 'S'*est enfui avec les autres*,' had said the lieutenant. And suddenly I began to admire the discrimination of the man. He had made out the point at once: he did get hold of the only thing I cared about. I felt as though I were taking professional opinion on the case. His imperturbable and mature calmness was that of an expert in possession of the facts, and to whom one's perplexities are mere child's-play. 'Ah! The young, the young,' he said indulgently. 'And after all, one does not die of it.' 'Die of what?' I asked swiftly. 'Of being afraid.' He elucidated his meaning and sipped his drink.

"I perceived that the three last fingers of his wounded hand were stiff and could not move independently of each other, so that he took up his tumbler with an ungainly clutch. 'One is always afraid. One may talk, but . . .' He put down the glass awkwardly. . . . 'The fear, the fear—look you—it is always there.' . . . He touched his breast near a brass button, on the very spot where Jim had given a thump to his own when protesting that there was nothing the matter with his heart. I suppose I made some sign of dissent, because he insisted, 'Yes! yes! One talks, one talks; this is all very fine; but at the end of the reckoning one is no cleverer than the next man—and no more brave. Brave! This is always to be seen. I have rolled my hump[1] (*roulé ma bosse*),' he said, using the slang expression with imperturbable seriousness, 'in all parts of the world; I have known brave men—famous ones! *Allez!*[2] . . . He drank carelessly. . . . 'Brave—you conceive—in the Service—one has got to be—the trade demands it (*le métier veut ça*). Is it not so?' he appealed to me reasonably. '*Eh bien!*[3] Each of them—I say each of

1. Traveled around.
2. Enough! (exclamation of impatience).
3. Ah well.

them, if he were an honest man—*bien entendu*[4]—would confess that there is a point—there is a point—for the best of us—there is somewhere a point when you let go everything (*vous lâchez tout*). And you have got to live with that truth—do you see? Given a certain combination of circumstances, fear is sure to come. Abominable funk (*un trac épouvantable*). And even for those who do not believe this truth there is fear all the same—the fear of themselves. Absolutely so. Trust me. Yes. Yes. . . . At my age one knows what one is talking about—*que diable!*[5] . . . He had delivered himself of all this as immovably as though he had been the mouthpiece of abstract wisdom, but at this point he heightened the effect of detachment by beginning to twirl his thumbs slowly. 'It's evident—*parbleu!*' he continued; 'for, make up your mind as much as you like, even a simple headache or a fit of indigestion (*un dérangement d'estomac*) is enough to . . . Take me, for instance—I have made my proofs. *Eh bien!* I, who am speaking to you, once . . .'

"He drained his glass and returned to his twirling. 'No, no; one does not die of it,' he pronounced finally, and when I found he did not mean to proceed with the personal anecdote, I was extremely disappointed; the more so as it was not the sort of story, you know, one could very well press him for. I sat silent, and he too, as if nothing could please him better. Even his thumbs were still now. Suddenly his lips began to move. 'That is so,' he resumed placidly. 'Man is born a coward (*L'homme est né poltron*).[6] It is a difficulty—*parbleu!* It would be too easy otherwise. But habit—habit—necessity—do you see?—the eye of others—*voilà*.[7] One puts up with it. And then the example of others who are no better than yourself, and yet make good countenance. . . .'

"His voice ceased.

" 'That young man—you will observe—had none of these inducements—at least at the moment,' I remarked.

"He raised his eyebrows forgivingly: 'I don't say; I don't say. The young man in question might have had the best dispositions—the best dispositions,' he repeated, wheezing a little.

" 'I am glad to see you taking a lenient view,' I said. 'His own feeling in the matter was—ah!—hopeful, and . . .'

"The shuffle of his feet under the table interrupted me. He drew up his heavy eyelids. Drew up, I say—no other expression can describe the steady deliberation of the act—and at last was disclosed completely to me. I was confronted by two narrow grey circlets, like two tiny steel rings around the profound blackness of the pupils. The sharp glance, coming from that massive body, gave a notion of extreme efficiency, like a razor-edge on a battle-axe. 'Pardon,' he said punctiliously. His

---

4. Of course; understood.
5. What the devil!
6. Perhaps an ironic allusion to the opening words of *Le contrat social* (1762) by the French philosopher Jean-Jacques Rousseau (1712–1778): *"L'homme est né libre"* (Man is born free).
7. That's it.

right hand went up, and he swayed forward. 'Allow me . . . I contended that one may get on knowing very well that one's courage does not come of itself (*ne vient pas tout seul*). There's nothing much in that to get upset about. One truth the more ought not to make life impossible. . . . But the honour—the honour, monsieur! . . . The honour . . . that is real—that is! And what life may be worth when' . . . he got on his feet with a ponderous impetuosity, as a startled ox might scramble up from the grass . . . 'when the honour is gone—*ah ça! par exemple*[8]—I can offer no opinion. I can offer no opinion—because—monsieur—I know nothing of it.'

"I had risen too, and, trying to throw infinite politeness into our attitudes, we faced each other mutely, like two china dogs on a mantelpiece. Hang the fellow! he had pricked the bubble. The blight of futility that lies in wait for men's speeches had fallen upon our conversation, and made it a thing of empty sounds. 'Very well,' I said, with a disconcerted smile; 'but couldn't it reduce itself to not being found out?' He made as if to retort readily, but when he spoke he had changed his mind. 'This, monsieur, is too fine for me—much above me—I don't think about it.' He bowed heavily over his cap, which he held before him by the peak, between the thumb and the forefinger of his wounded hand. I bowed too. We bowed together: we scraped our feet at each other with much ceremony, while a dirty specimen of a waiter looked on critically, as though he had paid for the performance. 'Serviteur,'[9] said the Frenchman. Another scrape. 'Monsieur' . . . 'Monsieur.' . . . The glass door swung behind his burly back. I saw the southerly buster get hold of him and drive him down wind with his hand to his head, his shoulders braced, and the tails of his coat blown hard against his legs.

"I sat down again alone and discouraged—discouraged about Jim's case. If you wonder that after more than three years it had preserved its actuality, you must know that I had seen him only very lately. I had come straight from Samarang, where I had loaded a cargo for Sydney: an utterly uninteresting bit of business,—what Charley here would call one of my rational transactions,—and in Samarang I had seen something of Jim. He was then working for De Jongh, on my recommendation. Water-clerk. 'My representative afloat,' as De Jongh called him. You can't imagine a mode of life more barren of consolation, less capable of being invested with a spark of glamour—unless it be the business of an insurance canvasser. Little Bob Stanton—Charley here knew him well—had gone through that experience. The same who got drowned afterwards trying to save a lady's-maid in the *Sephora* disaster.[1] A case

8. That's it.
9. [Your] servant.
1. Based on Conrad's personal knowledge of the *Douro* disaster of April 1882, which he later recounted in a 1912 article on the *Titanic*.

of collision on a hazy morning off the Spanish coast—you may remember. All the passengers had been packed tidily into the boats and
shoved clear of the ship, when Bob sheered alongside again and scrambled back on deck to fetch that girl. How she had been left behind I
can't make out; anyhow, she had gone completely crazy—wouldn't leave
the ship—held to the rail like grim death. The wrestling-match could
be seen plainly from the boats; but poor Bob was the shortest chief mate
in the merchant service, and the woman stood five feet ten in her shoes
and was as strong as a horse, I've been told. So it went on, pull devil,
pull baker,[2] the wretched girl screaming all the time, and Bob letting
out a yell now and then to warn his boat to keep well clear of the ship.
One of the hands told me, hiding a smile at the recollection, 'It was for
all the world, sir, like a naughty youngster fighting with his mother.'
The same old chap said that 'At the last we could see that Mr Stanton
had given up hauling at the gal, and just stood by looking at her, watchful
like. We thought afterwards he must've been reckoning that, maybe,
the rush of water would tear her away from the rail by-and-by and give
him a show to save her. We daren't come alongside for our life; and
after a bit the old ship went down all on a sudden with a lurch to
starboard—plop. The suck in was something awful. We never saw anything alive or dead come up.' Poor Bob's spell of shore-life had been
one of the complications of a love affair, I believe. He fondly hoped he
had done with the sea for ever, and made sure he had got hold of all
the bliss on earth, but it came to canvassing[3] in the end. Some cousin
of his in Liverpool put him up to it. He used to tell us his experiences
in that line. He made us laugh till we cried, and, not altogether displeased
at the effect, undersized and bearded to the waist like a gnome, he would
tiptoe amongst us and say, 'It's all very well for you beggars to laugh,
but my immortal soul was shrivelled down to the size of a parched pea
after a week of that work.' I don't know how Jim's soul accommodated
itself to the new conditions of his life—I was kept too busy in getting
him something to do that would keep body and soul together—but I
am pretty certain his adventurous fancy was suffering all the pangs of
starvation. It had certainly nothing to feed upon in this new calling. It
was distressing to see him at it, though he tackled it with a stubborn
serenity for which I must give him full credit. I kept my eye on his
shabby plodding with a sort of notion that it was a punishment for the
heroics of his fancy—an expiation for his craving after more glamour
than he could carry. He had loved too well to imagine himself a glorious
racehorse, and now he was condemned to toil without honour like a
costermonger's[4] donkey. He did it very well. He shut himself in, put
his head down, said never a word. Very well; very well indeed—except

2. Proverbial expression implying a contest of varying fortunes.
3. Soliciting orders.
4. Street vendor's.

for certain fantastic and violent outbreaks, on the deplorable occasions when the irrepressible *Patna* case cropped up. Unfortunately that scandal of the Eastern seas would not die out. And this is the reason why I could never feel I had done with Jim for good.

"I sat thinking of him after the French lieutenant had left, not, however, in connection with De Jongh's cool and gloomy backshop, where we had hurriedly shaken hands not very long ago, but as I had seen him years before in the last flickers of the candle, alone with me in the long gallery of the Malabar House, with the chill and the darkness of the night at his back. The respectable sword of his country's law was suspended over his head. To-morrow—or was it to-day? (midnight had slipped by long before we parted)—the marble-faced police magistrate, after distributing fines and terms of imprisonment in the assault-and-battery case, would take up the awful weapon and smite his bowed neck. Our communion in the night was uncommonly like a last vigil with a condemned man. He was guilty too. He was guilty—as I had told myself repeatedly, guilty and done for; nevertheless, I wished to spare him the mere detail of a formal execution. I don't pretend to explain the reasons of my desire—I don't think I could; but if you haven't got a sort of notion by this time, then I must have been very obscure in my narrative, or you too sleepy to seize upon the sense of my words. I don't defend my morality. There was no morality in the impulse which induced me to lay before him Brierly's plan of evasion—I may call it—in all its primitive simplicity. There were the rupees—absolutely ready in my pocket and very much at his service. Oh! a loan; a loan of course—and if an introduction to a man (in Rangoon) who could put some work in his way. . . . Why! with the greatest pleasure. I had pen, ink, and paper in my room on the first floor. And even while I was speaking I was impatient to begin the letter: day, month, year, 2.30 A.M. . . . for the sake of our old friendship I ask you to put some work in the way of Mr James So-and-so, in whom, &c., &c. . . . I was even ready to write in that strain about him. If he had not enlisted my sympathies he had done better for himself—he had gone to the very fount and origin of that sentiment, he had reached the secret sensibility of my egoism. I am concealing nothing from you, because were I to do so my action would appear more unintelligible than any man's action has the right to be, and—in the second place—to-morrow you will forget my sincerity along with the other lessons of the past. In this transaction, to speak grossly and precisely, I was the irreproachable man; but the subtle intentions of my immorality were defeated by the moral simplicity of the criminal. No doubt he was selfish too, but his selfishness had a higher origin, a more lofty aim. I discovered that, say what I would, he was eager to go through the ceremony of execution; and I didn't say much, for I felt that in argument his youth would tell against me heavily: he believed where I had already ceased to doubt. There was something fine in the wildness of his unexpressed, hardly formulated hope. 'Clear out! Couldn't think of it,' he said, with a shake of the head. 'I make you an offer for which I neither demand nor expect any sort of gratitude,' I said; 'you shall repay the money when convenient, and . . .' 'Awfully good of you,' he muttered without looking up. I watched him narrowly: the future must have appeared horribly uncertain to him; but he did not falter, as though indeed there had been nothing wrong with his heart. I felt angry—not for the first time that night. 'The whole wretched business,' I said, 'is bitter enough, I should think, for a man of your kind . . .' 'It is, it is,' he whispered twice, with his eyes fixed on the floor. It was heartrending. He towered above the light, and I could see the down on his cheek, the colour mantling warm under the smooth skin of his face. Believe me or not, I say it was outrageously heartrending. It provoked me to brutality. 'Yes,' I said; 'and allow me to confess that I am totally unable to imagine what advantage you can expect from this licking of the dregs.' 'Advantage!' he murmured out of his stillness. 'I am dashed if I do,' I said, enraged. 'I've been trying to tell you all there is in it,' he went on slowly, as if meditating something unanswerable. 'But after all, it is *my* trouble.' I opened my mouth to retort, and discovered suddenly that I'd lost all confidence in myself; and it was as if he too had given me up, for he mumbled like a man thinking half aloud. 'Went away . . . went into hospitals. . . . Not one of them would face it. . . . They! . . .' He moved his hand slightly to imply disdain. 'But I've got to get over this thing, and I mustn't shirk any of it or . . . I won't shirk any of it.' He was silent. He gazed as though he had been haunted. His unconscious face reflected the passing expressions of scorn, of despair, of resolution,—reflected them in turn, as a magic mirror would reflect the gliding passage of unearthly shapes. He lived surrounded by deceitful ghosts, by austere shades. 'Oh! nonsense, my dear fellow,' I began. He had a movement of impatience. 'You don't seem to understand,' he said incisively; then looking at me without a wink, 'I may have jumped, but I don't run away.' 'I meant no offence,' I said; and added stupidly, 'Better men than you have found it expedient to run, at times.' He coloured all over, while in my confusion I half-choked myself with my own tongue. 'Perhaps so,' he said at last; 'I am not good enough; I can't afford it. I am bound to fight this thing down—I am fighting it *now*.' I got out of my chair and felt stiff all over. The silence was embarrassing, and to put an end to it I imagined nothing better but to remark, 'I had no idea it was so late,' in an airy tone. . . . 'I dare say you have had enough of this,' he said brusquely: 'and to tell you the truth'—he began to look round for his hat—'so have I.'

"Well! he had refused this unique offer. He had struck aside my helping hand; he was ready to go now, and beyond the balustrade the night seemed to wait for him very still, as though he had been marked down for its prey. I heard his voice. 'Ah! here it is.' He had found his

hat. For a few seconds we hung in the wind. 'What will you do after
—after . . .' I asked very low. 'Go to the dogs as likely as not,' he
answered in a gruff mutter. I had recovered my wits in a measure, and
judged best to take it lightly. 'Pray remember,' I said, 'that I should like
very much to see you again before you go.' 'I don't know what's to
prevent you. The damned thing won't make me invisible,' he said with
intense bitterness,—'no such luck.' And then at the moment of taking
leave he treated me to a ghastly muddle of dubious stammers and movements, to an awful display of hesitations. God forgive him—me! He
had taken it into his fanciful head that I was likely to make some difficulty as to shaking hands. It was too awful for words. I believe I shouted
suddenly at him·as you would bellow to a man you saw about to walk
over a cliff; I remember our voices being raised, the appearance of a
miserable grin on his face, a crushing clutch on my hand, a nervous
laugh. The candle spluttered out, and the thing was over at last, with
a groan that floated up to me in the dark. He got himself away somehow.
The night swallowed his form. He was a horrible bungler. Horrible. I
heard the quick crunch-crunch of the gravel under his boots. He was
running. Absolutely running, with nowhere to go to. And he was not
yet four-and-twenty."

Chapter XIV

"I slept little, hurried over my breakfast, and after a slight hesitation
gave up my early morning visit to my ship. It was really very wrong of
me, because, though my chief mate was an excellent man all round,
he was the victim of such black imaginings that if he did not get a letter
from his wife at the expected time he would go quite distracted with
rage and jealousy, lose all grip on the work, quarrel with all hands, and
either weep in his cabin or develop such a ferocity of temper as all but
drove the crew to the verge of mutiny. The thing had always seemed
inexplicable to me: they had been married thirteen years; I had a glimpse
of her once, and, honestly, I couldn't conceive a man abandoned enough
to plunge into sin for the sake of such an unattractive person. I don't
know whether I have not done wrong by refraining from putting that
view before poor Selvin: the man made a little hell on earth for himself,
and I also suffered indirectly, but some sort of, no doubt, false delicacy
prevented me. The marital relations of seamen would make an interesting subject, and I could tell you instances. . . . However, this is not
the place, nor the time, and we are concerned with Jim—who was
unmarried. If his imaginative conscience or his pride; if all the extravagant ghosts and austere shades that were the disastrous familiars[1] of his

1. Intimate associates; also communicating spirits.

youth would not let him run away from the block, I, who of course can't be suspected of such familiars, was irresistibly impelled to go and see his head roll off. I wended my way towards the court. I didn't hope to be very much impressed or edified, or interested or even frightened —though, as long as there is any life before one, a jolly good fright now and then is a salutary discipline. But neither did I expect to be so awfully depressed. The bitterness of his punishment was in its chill and mean atmosphere. The real significance of crime is in its being a breach of faith with the community of mankind, and from that point of view he was no mean traitor, but his execution was a hole-and-corner affair. There was no high scaffolding, no scarlet cloth (did they have scarlet cloth on Tower Hill?[2] They should have had), no awe-stricken multitude to be horrified at his guilt and be moved to tears at his fate—no air of sombre retribution. There was, as I walked along, the clear sunshine, a brilliance too passionate to be consoling, the streets full of jumbled bits of colour like a damaged kaleidoscope: yellow, green, blue, dazzling white, the brown nudity of an undraped shoulder, a bullock-cart with a red canopy, a company of native infantry in a drab body with dark heads marching in dusty laced boots, a native policeman in a sombre uniform of scanty cut and belted in patent leather, who looked up at me with orientally pitiful eyes as though his migrating spirit were suffering exceedingly from that unforeseen—what d'ye call 'em?—avatar —incarnation. Under the shade of a lonely tree in the courtyard, the villagers connected with the assault case sat in a picturesque group, looking like a chromo-lithograph[3] of a camp in a book of Eastern travel. One missed the obligatory thread of smoke in the foreground and the pack-animals grazing. A blank yellow wall rose behind overtopping the tree, reflecting the glare. The court-room was sombre, seemed more vast. High up in the dim space the punkahs were swaying short to and fro, to and fro. Here and there a draped figure, dwarfed by the bare walls, remained without stirring amongst the rows of empty benches, as if absorbed in pious meditation. The plaintiff, who had been beaten, —an obese chocolate-coloured man with shaved head, one fat breast bare and a bright yellow caste-mark above the bridge of his nose,—sat in pompous immobility: only his eyes glittered, rolling in the gloom, and the nostrils dilated and collapsed violently as he breathed. Brierly dropped into his seat looking done up, as though he had spent the night in sprinting on a cinder-track. The pious sailing-ship skipper appeared excited and made uneasy movements, as if restraining with difficulty an impulse to stand up and exhort us earnestly to prayer and repentance. The head of the magistrate, delicately pale under the neatly arranged hair, resembled the head of a hopeless invalid after he had been washed

2. Site of the Tower of London, ancient fortress on the east side of the City of London, famous as a prison and place of execution.
3. Colored print.

and brushed and propped up in bed. He moved aside the vase of flowers—a bunch of purple with a few pink blossoms on long stalks—and seizing in both hands a long sheet of bluish paper, ran his eye over it, propped his forearms on the edge of the desk, and began to read aloud in an even, distinct, and careless voice.

"By Jove! For all my foolishness about scaffolds and heads rolling off—I assure you it was infinitely worse than a beheading. A heavy sense of finality brooded over all this, unrelieved by the hope of rest and safety following the fall of the axe. These proceedings had all the cold vengefulness of a death-sentence, and the cruelty of a sentence of exile. This is how I looked at it that morning—and even now I seem to see an undeniable vestige of truth in that exaggerated view of a common occurrence. You may imagine how strongly I felt this at the time. Perhaps it is for that reason that I could not bring myself to admit the finality. The thing was always with me, I was always eager to take opinion on it, as though it had not been practically settled: individual opinion—international opinion—by Jove! That Frenchman's, for instance. His own country's pronouncement was uttered in the passionless and definite phraseology a machine would use, if machines could speak. The head of the magistrate was half hidden by the paper, his brow was like alabaster.

"There were several questions before the court. The first as to whether the ship was in every respect fit and seaworthy for the voyage. The court found she was not. The next point, I remember, was, whether up to the time of the accident the ship had been navigated with proper and seamanlike care. They said Yes to that, goodness knows why, and then they declared that there was no evidence to show the exact cause of the accident. A floating derelict probably. I myself remember that a Norwegian barque bound out with a cargo of pitch-pine had been given up as missing about that time, and it was just the sort of craft that would capsize in a squall and float bottom up for months—a kind of maritime ghoul on the prowl to kill ships in the dark. Such wandering corpses are common enough in the North Atlantic, which is haunted by all the terrors of the sea,—fogs, icebergs, dead ships bent upon mischief, and long sinister gales that fasten upon one like a vampire till all the strength and the spirit and even hope are gone, and one feels like the empty shell of a man. But there—in those seas—the incident was rare enough to resemble a special arrangement of a malevolent providence, which, unless it had for its object the killing of a donkeyman and the bringing of worse than death upon Jim, appeared an utterly aimless piece of devilry. This view occurring to me took off my attention. For a time I was aware of the magistrate's voice as a sound merely; but in a moment it shaped itself into distinct words . . . 'in utter disregard of their plain duty,' it said. The next sentence escaped me somehow, and then . . . 'abandoning in the moment of danger the lives and property confided to their charge' . . . went on the voice evenly, and stopped. A pair of

eyes under the white forehead shot darkly a glance above the edge of
the paper. I looked for Jim hurriedly, as though I had expected him to
disappear. He was very still—but he was there. He sat pink and fair and
extremely attentive. 'Therefore, . . .' began the voice emphatically. He
stared with parted lips, hanging upon the words of the man behind the
desk. These came out into the stillness wafted on the wind made by
the punkahs, and I, watching for their effect upon him, caught only
the fragments of official language. . . . 'The Court . . . Gustav So-and-
so . . . master . . . native of Germany, . . . James So-and-so . . . mate
. . . certificates cancelled.' A silence fell. The magistrate had dropped
the paper, and, leaning sideways on the arm of his chair, began to talk
with Brierly easily. People started to move out; others were pushing in,
and I also made for the door. Outside I stood still, and when Jim passed
me on his way to the gate, I caught at his arm and detained him. The
look he gave discomposed me as though I had been responsible for his
state: he looked at me as if I had been the embodied evil of life. 'It's all
over,' I stammered. 'Yes,' he said thickly. 'And now let no man . . .'
He jerked his arm out of my grasp. I watched his back as he went away.
It was a long street, and he remained in sight for some time. He walked
rather slow, and straddling his legs a little, as if he had found it difficult
to keep a straight line. Just before I lost him I fancied he staggered a
bit.

   " 'Man overboard,' said a deep voice behind me. Turning round, I
saw a fellow I knew slightly, a West Australian; Chester[4] was his name.
He, too, had been looking after Jim. He was a man with an immense
girth of chest, a rugged, clean-shaved face of mahogany colour, and two
blunt tufts of iron-grey, thick, wiry hairs on his upper lip. He had been
pearler, wrecker, trader, whaler too, I believe; in his own words—
anything and everything a man may be at sea, but a pirate. The Pacific,
north and south, was his proper hunting-ground; but he had wandered
so far afield looking for a cheap steamer to buy. Lately he had
discovered—so he said—a guano[5] island somewhere, but its approaches
were dangerous, and the anchorage, such as it was, could not be considered safe, to say the least of it. 'As good as a gold-mine,' he would
exclaim. 'Right bang in the middle of the Walpole Reefs, and if it's true
enough that you can get no holding-ground anywhere in less than forty
fathom, then what of that? There are the hurricanes, too. But it's a first-
rate thing. As good as a gold-mine—better! Yet there's not a fool of
them that will see it. I can't get a skipper or a shipowner to go near the
place. So I made up my mind to cart the blessed stuff myself.' . . . This
was what he required a steamer for, and I knew he was just then ne-

4. Chester and Robinson were sailors well known in Conrad's day; they sailed in Australian
waters.
5. The manure of seabirds, found especially on certain islands of the Pacific and used as fertilizer.

gotiating enthusiastically with a Parsee firm for an old, brig-rigged, sea-anachronism of ninety horse-power. We had met and spoken together several times. He looked knowingly after Jim. 'Takes it to heart?' he asked scornfully. 'Very much,' I said. 'Then he's no good,' he opined. 'What's all the to-do about? A bit of ass's skin.[6] That never yet made a man. You must see things exactly as they are—if you don't, you may just as well give in at once. You will never do anything in this world. Look at me. I made it a practice never to take anything to heart.' 'Yes,' I said, 'you see things as they are.' 'I wish I could see my partner coming along, that's what I wish to see,' he said. 'Know my partner? Old Robinson. Yes; *the* Robinson. Don't *you* know? The notorious Robinson. The man who smuggled more opium and bagged more seals in his time than any loose Johnny now alive. They say he used to board the sealing-schooners up Alaska way when the fog was so thick that the Lord God, He alone, could tell one man from another. Holy-Terror Robinson. That's the man. He is with me in that guano thing. The best chance he ever came across in his life.' He put his lips to my ear. 'Cannibal? —well, they used to give him the name years and years ago. You remember the story? A shipwreck on the west side of Stewart Island; that's right; seven of them got ashore, and it seems they did not get on very well together. Some men are too cantankerous for anything—don't know how to make the best of a bad job—don't see things as they are —as they *are*, my boy! And then what's the consequence? Obvious! Trouble, trouble; as likely as not a knock on the head; and serve 'em right too. That sort is the most useful when it's dead. The story goes that a boat of Her Majesty's ship *Wolverine* found him kneeling on the kelp, naked as the day he was born, and chanting some psalm-tune or other; light snow was falling at the time. He waited till the boat was an oar's length from the shore, and then up and away. They chased him for an hour up and down the boulders, till a marine flung a stone that took him behind the ear providentially and knocked him senseless. Alone? Of course. But that's like that tale of sealing-schooners; the Lord God knows the right and the wrong of that story. The cutter did not investigate much. They wrapped him in a boat-cloak and took him off as quick as they could, with a dark night coming on, the weather threatening, and the ship firing recall guns every five minutes. Three weeks afterwards he was as well as ever. He didn't allow any fuss that was made on shore to upset him; he just shut his lips tight, and let people screech. It was bad enough to have lost his ship, and all he was worth besides, without paying attention to the hard names they called him. That's the man for me.' He lifted his arm for a signal to some one down the street. 'He's got a little money, so I had to let him into my thing. Had to! It

---

6. Parchment (as for a Merchant Service certificate).

would have been sinful to throw away such a find, and I was cleaned out myself. It cut me to the quick, but I could see the matter just as it was, and if I *must* share—thinks I—with any man, then give me Robinson. I left him at breakfast in the hotel to come to court, because I've an idea. . . . Ah! Good morning, Captain Robinson. . . . Friend of mine, Captain Robinson.'

"An emaciated patriarch in a suit of white drill, a solah topi with a green-lined rim on a head trembling with age, joined us after crossing the street in a trotting shuffle, and stood propped with both hands on the handle of an umbrella. A white beard with amber streaks hung lumpily down to his waist. He blinked his creased eyelids at me in a bewildered way. 'How do you do? how do you do?' he piped amiably, and tottered. 'A little deaf,' said Chester aside. 'Did you drag him over six thousand miles to get a cheap steamer?' I asked. 'I would have taken him twice round the world as soon as look at him,' said Chester with immense energy. 'The steamer will be the making of us, my lad. Is it my fault that every skipper and shipowner in the whole of blessed Australasia turns out a blamed fool? Once I talked for three hours to a man in Auckland. "Send a ship," I said, "send a ship. I'll give you half of the first cargo for yourself, free gratis for nothing—just to make a good start." Says he, "I wouldn't do it if there was no other place on earth to send a ship to." Perfect ass, of course. Rocks, currents, no anchorage, sheer cliff to lay to, no insurance company would take the risk, didn't see how he could get loaded under three years. Ass! I nearly went on my knees to him. "But look at the thing as it is," says I. "Damn rocks and hurricanes. Look at it as it is. There's guano there, Queensland sugar-planters would fight for—fight for on the quay, I tell you." . . . What can you do with a fool? . . . "That's one of your little jokes, Chester," he says. . . . Joke! I could have wept. Ask Captain Robinson here. . . . And there was another shipowning fellow—a fat chap in a white waistcoat in Wellington, who seemed to think I was up to some swindle or other. "I don't know what sort of fool you're looking for," he says, "but I am busy just now. Good morning." I longed to take him in my two hands and smash him through the window of his own office. But I didn't. I was as mild as a curate. "Think of it," says I. "*Do* think it over. I'll call to-morrow." He grunted something about being "out all day." On the stairs I felt ready to beat my head against the wall from vexation. Captain Robinson here can tell you. It was awful to think of all that lovely stuff lying waste under the sun—stuff that would send the sugar-cane shooting sky-high. The making of Queensland! The making of Queensland! And in Brisbane, where I went to have a last try, they gave me the name of a lunatic. Idiots! The only sensible man I came across was the cabman who drove me about. A broken-down swell he was, I fancy. Hey! Captain Robinson? You remember I told you about my cabby in Brisbane—don't you? The chap had a wonderful eye for things. He saw it all in a jiffy. It was a real pleasure to talk with him. One evening after a devil of a day amongst shipowners I felt so bad that, says I, "I must get drunk. Come along; I must get drunk, or I'll go mad." "I am your man," he says; "go ahead." I don't know what I would have done without him. Hey! Captain Robinson.'

"He poked the ribs of his partner. 'He! he! he!' laughed the Ancient, looked aimlessly down the street, then peered at me doubtfully with sad, dim pupils. . . . 'He! he! he!' . . . He leaned heavier on the umbrella, and dropped his gaze on the ground. I needn't tell you I had tried to get away several times, but Chester had foiled every attempt by simply catching hold of my coat. 'One minute. I've a notion.' 'What's your infernal notion?' I exploded at last. 'If you think I am going in with you . . .' 'No, no, my boy. Too late, if you wanted ever so much. We've got a steamer.' 'You've got the ghost of a steamer,' I said. 'Good enough for a start—there's no superior nonsense about us. Is there, Captain Robinson?' 'No! no! no!' croaked the old man without lifting his eyes, and the senile tremble of his head became almost fierce with determination. 'I understand you know that young chap,' said Chester, with a nod at the street from which Jim had disappeared long ago. 'He's been having grub with you in the Malabar last night—so I was told.'

"I said that was true, and after remarking that he too liked to live well and in style, only that, for the present, he had to be saving of every penny—'none too many for the business! Isn't that so, Captain Robinson?'—he squared his shoulders and stroked his dumpy moustache, while the notorious Robinson, coughing at his side, clung more than ever to the handle of the umbrella, and seemed ready to subside passively into a heap of old bones. 'You see, the old chap has all the money,' whispered Chester confidentially. 'I've been cleaned out trying to engineer the dratted thing. But wait a bit, wait a bit. The good time is coming.' . . . He seemed suddenly astonished at the signs of impatience I gave. 'Oh, crakee!'[7] he cried; 'I am telling you of the biggest thing that ever was, and you . . .' 'I have an appointment,' I pleaded mildly. 'What of that?' he asked with genuine surprise; 'let it wait.' 'That's exactly what I am doing now,' I remarked; 'hadn't you better tell me what it is you want?' 'Buy twenty hotels like that,' he growled to himself; 'and every joker boarding in them too—twenty times over.' He lifted his head smartly. 'I want that young chap.' 'I don't understand,' I said. 'He's no good, is he?' said Chester crisply. 'I know nothing about it,' I protested. 'Why, you told me yourself he was taking it to heart,' argued Chester. 'Well, in my opinion a chap who . . . Anyhow, he can't be much good; but then you see I am on the look-out for somebody, and I've just got a thing that will suit him. I'll give him a job on my island.' He nodded significantly. 'I'm going to dump forty coolies there—if I've to steal 'em.

7. Originally an oath (Christ), but by this time merely a jocular slang exclamation of surprise, admiration, etc.

Somebody must work the stuff. Oh! I mean to act square: wooden shed,
corrugated-iron roof—I know a man in Hobart who will take my bill at
six months for the materials. I do. Honour bright. Then there's the
water-supply. I'll have to fly round and get somebody to trust me for
half-a-dozen second-hand iron tanks. Catch rain-water, hey? Let him
take charge. Make him supreme boss over the coolies. Good idea, isn't
it? What do you say?' 'There are whole years when not a drop of rain
falls on Walpole,' I said, too amazed to laugh. He bit his lip and seemed
bothered. 'Oh, well, I will fix up something for them—or land a supply.
Hang it all! That's not the question.'

"I said nothing. I had a rapid vision of Jim perched on a shadowless
rock, up to his knees in guano, with the screams of sea-birds in his ears,
the incandescent ball of the sun above his head; the empty sky and the
empty ocean all a-quiver, simmering together in the heat as far as the
eye could reach. 'I wouldn't advise my worst enemy . . .' I began.
'What's the matter with you?' cried Chester; 'I mean to give him a good
screw[8]—that is, as soon as the thing is set going, of course. It's as easy
as falling off a log. Simply nothing to do; two six-shooters in his belt
. . . Surely he wouldn't be afraid of anything forty coolies could do—
with two six-shooters and he the only armed man too! It's much better
than it looks. I want you to help me to talk him over.' 'No!' I shouted.
Old Robinson lifted his bleared eyes dismally for a moment, Chester
looked at me with infinite contempt. 'So you wouldn't advise him?' he
uttered slowly. 'Certainly not,' I answered, as indignant as though he
had requested me to help murder somebody; 'moreover, I am sure
he wouldn't. He is badly cut up, but he isn't mad as far as I know.'
'He is no earthly good for anything,' Chester mused aloud. 'He would
just have done for me. If you only could see a thing as it is, you would
see it's the very thing for him. And besides . . . Why! it's the most
splendid, sure chance . . .' He got angry suddenly 'I must have a man.
There! . . .' He stamped his foot and smiled unpleasantly. 'Anyhow, I
could guarantee the island wouldn't sink under him—and I believe he
is a bit particular on that point.' 'Good morning,' I said curtly. He looked
at me as though I had been an incomprehensible fool. . . . 'Must be
moving, Captain Robinson,' he yelled suddenly into the old man's ear.
'These Parsee Johnnies are waiting for us to clinch the bargain.' He took
his partner under the arm with a firm grip, swung him round, and,
unexpectedly, leered at me over his shoulder. 'I was trying to do him a
kindness,' he asserted, with an air and tone that made my blood boil.
'Thank you for nothing—in his name,' I rejoined. 'Oh! you are devilish
smart,' he sneered; 'but you are like the rest of them. Too much in the
clouds. See what *you* will do with him.' 'I don't know that I want to do
anything with him.' 'Don't you?' he spluttered; his grey moustache

---

8. Salary, wages. The metaphor implies the employer's attempts to lower the rate, or the em-
   ployee's efforts to force higher payment, of the salary, which has to be screwed out.

bristled with anger, and by his side the notorious Robinson, propped on the umbrella, stood with his back to me, as patient and still as a worn-out cab-horse. 'I haven't found a guano island,' I said. 'It's my belief you wouldn't know one if you were led right up to it by the hand,' he riposted quickly; 'and in this world you've got to see a thing first, before you can make use of it. Got to see it through and through at that, neither more nor less.' 'And get others to see it too,' I insinuated, with a glance at the bowed back by his side. Chester snorted at me. 'His eyes are right enough—don't you worry. He ain't a puppy.' 'Oh dear, no!' I said. 'Come along, Captain Robinson,' he shouted, with a sort of bullying deference under the rim of the old man's hat; the Holy Terror gave a submissive little jump. The ghost of a steamer was waiting for them, Fortune on that fair isle! They made a curious pair of Argonauts.[9] Chester strode on leisurely, well set up, portly, and of conquering mien; the other, long, wasted, drooping, and hooked to his arm, shuffled his withered shanks with desperate haste."

Chapter XV

"I did not start in search of Jim at once, only because I had really an appointment which I could not neglect. Then, as ill-luck would have it, in my agent's office I was fastened upon by a fellow fresh from Madagascar with a little scheme for a wonderful piece of business. It had something to do with cattle and cartridges and a Prince Ravonalo something; but the pivot of the whole affair was the stupidity of some admiral—Admiral Pierre, I think. Everything turned on that, and the chap couldn't find words strong enough to express his confidence. He had globular eyes starting out of his head with a fishy glitter, bumps on his forehead, and wore his long hair brushed back without a parting. He had a favourite phrase which he kept on repeating triumphantly, 'The minimum of risk with the maximum of profit is my motto. What?' He made my head ache, spoiled my tiffin, but got his own out of me all right; and as soon as I had shaken him off, I made straight for the water-side. I caught sight of Jim leaning over the parapet of the quay. Three native boatmen quarrelling over five annas were making an awful row at his elbow. He didn't hear me come up, but spun round as if the slight contact of my finger had released a catch. 'I was looking,' he stammered. I don't remember what I said, not much anyhow, but he made no difficulty in following me to the hotel.

"He followed me as manageable as a little child, with an obedient air, with no sort of manifestation, rather as though he had been waiting for me there to come along and carry him off. I need not have been so

---

9. The mythical Greek heroes who accompanied Jason on board the ship *Argo* to Colchis to recover the Golden Fleece.

surprised as I was at his tractability. On all the round earth, which to some seems so big and that others affect to consider as rather smaller than a mustard-seed, he had no place where he could—what shall I say?—where he could withdraw. That's it! Withdraw—be alone with his loneliness. He walked by my side very calm, glancing here and there, and once turned his head to look after a Sidiboy fireman in a cutaway coat and yellowish trousers, whose black face had silky gleams like a lump of anthracite coal. I doubt, however, whether he saw anything, or even remained all the time aware of my companionship, because if I had not edged him to the left here, or pulled him to the right there, I believe he would have gone straight before him in any direction till stopped by a wall or some other obstacle. I steered him into my bedroom, and sat down at once to write letters. This was the only place in the world (unless, perhaps, the Walpole Reef—but that was not so handy) where he could have it out with himself without being bothered by the rest of the universe. The damned thing—as he had expressed it—had not made him invisible, but I behaved exactly as though he were. No sooner in my chair I bent over my writing-desk like a medieval scribe, and, but for the movement of the hand holding the pen, remained anxiously quiet. I can't say I was frightened; but I certainly kept as still as if there had been something dangerous in the room, that at the first hint of a movement on my part would be provoked to pounce upon me. There was not much in the room—you know how these bedrooms are—a sort of four-poster bedstead under a mosquito-net, two or three chairs, the table I was writing at, a bare floor. A glass door opened on an upstairs verandah, and he stood with his face to it, having a hard time with all possible privacy. Dusk fell; I lit a candle with the greatest economy of movement and as much prudence as though it were an illegal proceeding. There is no doubt that he had a very hard time of it, and so had I, even to the point, I must own, of wishing him to the devil, or on Walpole Reef at least. It occurred to me once or twice that, after all, Chester was, perhaps, the man to deal effectively with such a disaster. That strange idealist had found a practical use for it at once—unerringly, as it were. It was enough to make one suspect that, maybe, he really could see the true aspect of things that appeared mysterious or utterly hopeless to less imaginative persons. I wrote and wrote; I liquidated all the arrears of my correspondence, and then went on writing to people who had no reason whatever to expect from me a gossipy letter about nothing at all. At times I stole a sidelong glance. He was rooted to the spot, but convulsive shudders ran down his back; his shoulders would heave suddenly. He was fighting, he was fighting—mostly for his breath, as it seemed. The massive shadows, cast all one way from the straight flame of the candle, seemed possessed of gloomy consciousness; the immobility of the furniture had to my furtive eye an air of attention. I was becoming fanciful in the midst of my industrious scribbling; and though, when the scratching of my pen stopped for a moment, there was complete silence and stillness in the room, I suffered from that profound disturbance and confusion of thought which is caused by a violent and menacing uproar—of a heavy gale at sea, for instance. Some of you may know what I mean: that mingled anxiety, distress, and irritation with a sort of craven feeling creeping in—not pleasant to acknowledge, but which gives a quite special merit to one's endurance. I don't claim any merit for standing the stress of Jim's emotions; I could take refuge in the letters; I could have written to strangers if necessary. Suddenly, as I was taking up a fresh sheet of notepaper, I heard a low sound, the first sound that, since we had been shut up together, had come to my ears in the dim stillness of the room. I remained with my head down, with my hand arrested. Those who have kept vigil by a sick-bed have heard such faint sounds in the stillness of the night watches, sounds wrung from a racked body, from a weary soul. He pushed the glass door with such force that all the panes rang: he stepped out, and I held my breath, straining my ears without knowing what else I expected to hear. He was really taking too much to heart an empty formality which to Chester's rigorous criticism seemed unworthy the notice of a man who could see things as they were. An empty formality; a piece of parchment. Well, well. As to an inaccessible guano deposit, that was another story altogether. One could intelligibly break one's heart over that. A feeble burst of many voices mingled with the tinkle of silver and glass floated up from the dining-room below; through the open door the outer edge of the light from my candle fell on his back faintly; beyond all was black; he stood on the brink of a vast obscurity, like a lonely figure by the shore of a sombre and hopeless ocean. There was the Walpole Reef in it—to be sure—a speck in the dark void, a straw for the drowning man. My compassion for him took the shape of the thought that I wouldn't have liked his people to see him at that moment. I found it trying myself. His back was no longer shaken by his gasps; he stood straight as an arrow, faintly visible and still; and the meaning of this stillness sank to the bottom of my soul like lead into the water, and made it so heavy that for a second I wished heartily that the only course left open for me were to pay for his funeral. Even the law had done with him. To bury him would have been such an easy kindness! It would have been so much in accordance with the wisdom of life, which consists in putting out of sight all the reminders of our folly, of our weakness, of our mortality; all that makes against our efficiency—the memory of our failures, the hints of our undying fears, the bodies of our dead friends. Perhaps he did take it too much to heart. And if so then— Chester's offer. . . . At this point I took up a fresh sheet and began to write resolutely. There was nothing but myself between him and the dark ocean. I had a sense of responsibility. If I spoke, would that motionless and suffering youth leap into the obscurity—clutch at the straw?

I found out how difficult it may be sometimes to make a sound. There is a weird power in a spoken word. And why the devil not? I was asking myself persistently while I drove on with my writing. All at once, on the blank page, under the very point of the pen, the two figures of Chester and his antique partner, very distinct and complete, would dodge into view with stride and gestures, as if reproduced in the field of some optical toy. I would watch them for a while. No! They were too fantasmal and extravagant to enter into any one's fate. And a word carries far— very far—deals destruction through time as the bullets go flying through space. I said nothing; and he, out there with his back to the light, as if bound and gagged by all the invisible foes of man, made no stir and made no sound."

Chapter XVI

"The time was coming when I should see him loved, trusted, admired, with a legend of strength and prowess forming round his name as though he had been the stuff of a hero. It's true—I assure you; as true as I'm sitting here talking about him in vain. He, on his side, had that faculty of beholding at a hint the face of his desire and the shape of his dream, without which the earth would know no lover and no adventurer. He captured much honour and an Arcadian happiness[1] (I won't say anything about innocence) in the bush, and it was as good to him as the honour and the Arcadian happiness of the streets to another man. Felicity, felicity—how shall I say it?—is quaffed out of a golden cup in every latitude: the flavour is with you—with you alone, and you can make it as intoxicating as you please. He was of the sort that would drink deep, as you may guess from what went before. I found him, if not exactly intoxicated, then at least flushed with the elixir at his lips. He had not obtained it at once. There had been, as you know, a period of probation amongst infernal ship-chandlers, during which he had suffered and I had worried about—about—my trust—you may call it. I don't know that I am completely reassured now, after beholding him in all his brilliance. That was my last view of him—in a strong light, dominating, and yet in complete accord with his surroundings—with the life of the forests and with the life of men. I own that I was impressed, but I must admit to myself that after all this is not the lasting impression. He was protected by his isolation, alone of his own superior kind, in close touch with Nature, that keeps faith on such easy terms with her lovers. But I cannot fix before my eye the image of his safety. I shall always remember him as seen through the open door of my room, taking, perhaps, too much to heart the mere consequences of his failure. I am pleased, of

1. Like the happiness of the inhabitants of Arcadia, a pastoral district of ancient Greece.

course, that some good—and even some splendour—came out of my endeavours; but at times it seems to me it would have been better for my peace of mind if I had not stood between him and Chester's confoundedly generous offer. I wonder what his exuberant imagination would have made of Walpole islet—that most hopelessly forsaken crumb of dry land on the face of the waters. It is not likely I would ever have heard, for, I must tell you, that Chester, after calling at some Australian port to patch up his brig-rigged sea-anachronism, steamed out into the Pacific with a crew of twenty-two hands all told, and the only news having a possible bearing upon the mystery of his fate was the news of a hurricane which is supposed to have swept in its course over the Walpole shoals, a month or so afterwards. Not a vestige of the Argonauts ever turned up; not a sound came out of the waste. Finis! The Pacific is the most discreet of live, hot-tempered oceans: the chilly Antarctic can keep a secret too, but more in the manner of a grave.

"And there is a sense of blessed finality in such discretion, which is what we all more or less sincerely are ready to admit—for what else is it that makes the idea of death supportable? End! Finis! the potent word that exorcises from the house of life the haunting shadow of fate. This is what—notwithstanding the testimony of my eyes and his own earnest assurances—I miss when I look back upon Jim's success. While there's life there is hope, truly; but there is fear too. I don't mean to say that I regret my action, nor will I pretend that I can't sleep o' nights in consequence; still the idea obtrudes itself that he made so much of his disgrace while it is the guilt alone that matters. He was not—if I may say so—clear to me. He was not clear. And there is a suspicion he was not clear to himself either. There were his fine sensibilities, his fine feelings, his fine longings—a sort of sublimated, idealised selfishness. He was—if you allow me to say so—very fine; very fine—and very unfortunate. A little coarser nature would not have borne the strain; it would have had to come to terms with itself—with a sigh, with a grunt, or even with a guffaw; a still coarser one would have remained invulnerably ignorant and completely uninteresting.

"But he was too interesting or too unfortunate to be thrown to the dogs, or even to Chester. I felt this while I sat with my face over the paper and he fought and gasped, struggling for his breath in that terribly stealthy way, in my room; I felt it when he rushed out on the verandah as if to fling himself over—and didn't; I felt it more and more all the time he remained outside, faintly lighted on the background of night, as if standing on the shore of a sombre and hopeless sea.

"An abrupt heavy rumble made me lift my head. The noise seemed to roll away, and suddenly a searching and violent glare fell on the blind face of the night. The sustained and dazzling flickers seemed to last for an unconscionable time. The growl of the thunder increased steadily while I looked at him, distinct and black, planted solidly upon the shores

of a sea of light. At the moment of greatest brilliance the darkness leaped
back with a culminating crash, and he vanished before my dazzled eyes
as utterly as though he had been blown to atoms. A blustering sigh
passed; furious hands seemed to tear at the shrubs, shake the tops of the
trees below, slam doors, break window-panes all along the front of the
building. He stepped in, closing the door behind him, and found me
bending over the table: my sudden anxiety as to what he would say was
very great, and akin to a fright. 'May I have a cigarette?' he asked. I
gave a push to the box without raising my head. 'I want—want—
tobacco,' he muttered. I became extremely buoyant. 'Just a moment,'
I grunted pleasantly. He took a few steps here and there. 'That's over,'
I heard him say. A single distant clap of thunder came from the sea like
a gun of distress. 'The monsoon breaks up early this year,' he remarked
conversationally, somewhere behind me. This encouraged me to turn
round, which I did as soon as I had finished addressing the last envelope.
He was smoking greedily in the middle of the room, and though he
heard the stir I made, he remained with his back to me for a time.

" 'Come—I carried it off pretty well,' he said, wheeling suddenly.
'Something's paid off—not much. I wonder what's to come.' His face
did not show any emotion, only it appeared a little darkened and swollen,
as though he had been holding his breath. He smiled reluctantly as it
were, and went on while I gazed up at him mutely. . . . 'Thank you,
though—your room—jolly convenient—for a chap—badly hipped.'[2]
. . . The rain pattered and swished in the garden; a water-pipe (it must
have had a hole in it) performed just outside the window a parody of
blubbering woe with funny sobs and gurgling lamentations, interrupted
by jerky spasms of silence. . . . 'A bit of shelter,' he mumbled and
ceased.

"A flash of faded lightning darted in through the black framework of
the windows and ebbed out without any noise. I was thinking how I
had best approach him (I did not want to be flung off again) when he
gave a little laugh. 'No better than a vagabond now' . . . the end of the
cigarette smouldered between his fingers . . . 'without a single—single,'
he pronounced slowly; 'and yet . . .' He paused; the rain fell with
redoubled violence. 'Some day one's bound to come upon some sort of
chance to get it all back again. Must!' he whispered distinctly, glaring
at my boots.

"I did not even know what it was he wished so much to regain, what
it was he had so terribly missed. It might have been so much that it was
impossible to say. A piece of ass's skin, according to Chester. . . . He
looked up at me inquisitively. 'Perhaps. If life's long enough,' I muttered
through my teeth with unreasonable animosity. 'Don't reckon too much
on it.'

---

2. Melancholy, bored, depressed; originally, suffering from hypochondria.

" 'Jove! I feel as if nothing could ever touch me,' he said in a tone of sombre conviction. 'If this business couldn't knock me over, then there's no fear of there being not enough time to—climb out, and . . .' He looked upwards.

"It struck me that it is from such as he that the great army of waifs and strays is recruited, the army that marches down, down into all the gutters of the earth. As soon as he left my room, that 'bit of shelter,' he would take his place in the ranks, and begin the journey toward the bottomless pit. I at least had no illusions; but it was I, too, who a moment ago had been so sure of the power of words, and now was afraid to speak, in the same way one dares not move for fear of losing a slippery hold. It is when we try to grapple with another man's intimate need that we perceive how incomprehensible, wavering, and misty are the beings that share with us the sight of the stars and the warmth of the sun. It is as if loneliness were a hard and absolute condition of existence; the envelope of flesh and blood on which our eyes are fixed melts before the out-stretched hand, and there remains only the capricious, unconsolable, and elusive spirit that no eye can follow, no hand can grasp. It was the fear of losing him that kept me silent, for it was borne upon me suddenly and with unaccountable force that should I let him slip away into the darkness I would never forgive myself.

" 'Well. Thanks—once more. You've been—er—uncommonly— really there's no word to . . . Uncommonly! I don't know why, I am sure. I am afraid I don't feel as grateful as I would if the whole thing hadn't been so brutally sprung on me. Because at bottom . . . you, yourself . . .' He stuttered.

" 'Possibly,' I struck in. He frowned.

" 'All the same, one is responsible.' He watched me like a hawk.

" 'And that's true, too,' I said.[3]

" 'Well. I've gone with it to the end, and I don't intend to let any man cast it in my teeth without—without—resenting it.' He clenched his fist.

" 'There's yourself,' I said with a smile—mirthless enough, God knows—but he looked at me menacingly. 'That's my business,' he said. An air of indomitable resolution came and went upon his face like a vain and passing shadow. Next moment he looked a dear good boy in trouble, as before. He flung away the cigarette. 'Good-bye,' he said, with the sudden haste of a man who had lingered too long in view of a pressing bit of work waiting for him; and then for a second or so he made not the slightest movement. The downpour fell with the heavy uninterrupted rush of a sweeping flood, with a sound of unchecked over-whelming fury that called to one's mind the images of collapsing bridges, of uprooted trees, of undermined mountains. No man could breast the

3. So Gloucester responds to Edgar's statement, "Ripeness is all" (*King Lear* 5.2.12).

colossal and headlong stream that seemed to break and swirl against the
dim stillness in which we were precariously sheltered as if on an island.
The perforated pipe gurgled, choked, spat, and splashed in odious rid-
icule of a swimmer fighting for his life. 'It is raining,' I remonstrated,
'and I . . .' 'Rain or shine,' he began brusquely, checked himself, and
walked to the window. 'Perfect deluge,' he muttered after a while: he
leaned his forehead on the glass. 'It's dark, too.'

" 'Yes, it is very dark,' I said.

"He pivoted on his heels, crossed the room, and had actually opened
the door leading into the corridor before I leaped up from my chair.
'Wait,' I cried, 'I want you to . . .' 'I can't dine with you again to-night,'
he flung at me, with one leg out of the room already. 'I haven't the
slightest intention of asking you,' I shouted. At this he drew back his
foot, but remained mistrustfully in the very doorway. I lost no time in
entreating him earnestly not to be absurd; to come in and shut the door."

Chapter XVII

"He came in at last; but I believe it was mostly the rain that did it; it
was falling just then with a devastating violence which quieted down
gradually while we talked. His manner was very sober and set; his bearing
was that of a naturally taciturn man possessed by an idea. My talk was
of the material aspect of his position; it had the sole aim of saving him
from the degradation, ruin, and despair that out there close so swiftly
upon a friendless, homeless man; I pleaded with him to accept my help;
I argued reasonably: and every time I looked up at that absorbed smooth
face, so grave and youthful, I had a disturbing sense of being no help
but rather an obstacle to some mysterious, inexplicable, impalpable
striving of his wounded spirit.

" 'I suppose you intend to eat and drink and to sleep under shelter in
the usual way,' I remember saying with irritation. 'You say you won't
touch the money that is due to you.' . . . He came as near as his sort
can to making a gesture of horror. (There were three weeks and five
days' pay owing him as mate of the *Patna*.) 'Well, that's too little to
matter anyhow; but what will you do to-morrow? Where will you turn?
You must live . . .' 'That isn't the thing,' was the comment that escaped
him under his breath. I ignored it, and went on combating what I
assumed to be the scruples of an exaggerated delicacy. 'On every conceivable ground,' I concluded, 'you must let me help you.' 'You can't,'
he said very simply and gently, and holding fast to some deep idea which
I could detect shimmering like a pool of water in the dark, but which
I despaired of ever approaching near enough to fathom. I surveyed his
well-proportioned bulk. 'At any rate,' I said, 'I am able to help what I

can see of you. I don't pretend to do more.' He shook his head sceptically without looking at me. I got very warm. 'But I can,' I insisted. 'I can do even more. I *am* doing more. I am trusting you . . .' 'The money . . .' he began. 'Upon my word you deserve being told to go to the devil,' I cried, forcing the note of indignation. He was startled, smiled, and I pressed my attack home. 'It isn't a question of money at all. You are too superficial,' I said (and at the same time I was thinking to myself: Well, here goes! And perhaps he is, after all). 'Look at the letter I want you to take. I am writing to a man of whom I've never asked a favour, and I am writing about you in terms that one only ventures to use when speaking of an intimate friend. I make myself unreservedly responsible for you. That's what I am doing. And really if you will only reflect a little what that means . . .'

"He lifted his head. The rain had passed away; only the water-pipe went on shedding tears with an absurd drip, drip outside the window. It was very quiet in the room, whose shadows huddled together in corners, away from the still flame of the candle flaring upright in the shape of a dagger; his face after a while seemed suffused by a reflection of a soft light as if the dawn had broken already.

" 'Jove!' he gasped out. 'It is noble of you!'

"Had he suddenly put out his tongue at me in derision, I could not have felt more humiliated. I thought to myself—Serve me right for a sneaking humbug. . . . His eyes shone straight into my face, but I perceived it was not a mocking brightness. All at once he sprang into jerky agitation, like one of those flat wooden figures that are worked by a string. His arms went up, then came down with a slap. He became another man altogether. 'And I had never seen,' he shouted; then suddenly bit his lip and frowned. 'What a bally[1] ass I've been,' he said very slow in an awed tone. . . . 'You are a brick!'[2] he cried next in a muffled voice. He snatched my hand as though he had just then seen it for the first time, and dropped it at once. 'Why! this is what I—you—I . . .' he stammered, and then with a return of his old stolid, I may say mulish, manner he began heavily, 'I would be a brute now if I . . .' and then his voice seemed to break. 'That's all right,' I said. I was almost alarmed by this display of feeling, through which pierced a strange elation. I had pulled the string accidentally, as it were; I did not fully understand the working of the toy. 'I must go now,' he said. 'Jove! You *have* helped me. Can't sit still. The very thing . . .' He looked at me with puzzled admiration. 'The very thing . . .'

"Of course it was the thing. It was ten to one that I had saved him from starvation—of that peculiar sort that is almost invariably associated with drink. This was all. I had not a single illusion on that score, but looking at him, I allowed myself to wonder at the nature of the one he

1. Schoolboy slang equivalent of "damned"; originally a euphemism for *bloody*.
2. Fine fellow.

had, within the last three minutes, so evidently taken unto his bosom. I had forced into his hand the means to carry on decently the serious business of life, to get food, drink, and shelter of the customary kind, while his wounded spirit, like a bird with a broken wing, might hop and flutter into some hole, to die quietly of inanition there. This is what I had thrust upon him: a definitely small thing; and—behold!—by the manner of its reception it loomed in the dim light of the candle like a big, indistinct, perhaps a dangerous shadow. 'You don't mind me not saying anything appropriate,' he burst out. 'There isn't anything one could say. Last night already you had done me no end of good. Listening to me—you know. I give you my word I've thought more than once the top of my head would fly off . . .' He darted—positively darted— here and there, rammed his hands into his pockets, jerked them out again, flung his cap on his head. I had no idea it was in him to be so airily brisk. I thought of a dry leaf imprisoned in an eddy of wind, while a mysterious apprehension, a load of indefinite doubt, weighed me down in my chair. He stood stock-still, as if struck motionless by a discovery. 'You have given me confidence,' he declared soberly. 'Oh! for God's sake, my dear fellow—don't!' I entreated, as though he had hurt me. 'All right. I'll shut up now and henceforth. Can't prevent me thinking though. . . . Never mind! . . . I'll show yet . . .' He went to the door in a hurry, paused with his head down, and came back, stepping deliberately. 'I always thought that if a fellow could begin with a clean slate. . . . And now you . . . in a measure . . . yes . . . clean slate.' I waved my hand, and he marched out without looking back; the sound of his footfalls died out gradually behind the closed door—the unhesitating tread of a man walking in broad daylight.

"But as to me, left alone with the solitary candle, I remained strangely unenlightened. I was no longer young enough to behold at every turn the magnificence that besets our insignificant footsteps in good and in evil. I smiled to think that, after all, it was yet he, of us two, who had the light. And I felt sad. A clean slate, did he say? As if the initial word of each our destiny were not graven in imperishable characters upon the face of a rock."

Chapter XVIII

"Six months afterwards my friend (he was a cynical, more than middle-aged bachelor, with a reputation for eccentricity, and owned a rice-mill) wrote to me, and judging, from the warmth of my recommendation, that I would like to hear, enlarged a little upon Jim's perfections. These were apparently of a quiet and effective sort. 'Not having been able so far to find more in my heart than a resigned toleration for any individual of my kind, I have lived till now alone in a house that even in this steaming climate could be considered as too big for one man. I have had him to live with me for some time past. It seems I haven't made a mistake.' It seemed to me on reading this letter that my friend had found in his heart more than tolerance for Jim—that there were the beginnings of active liking. Of course he stated his grounds in a characteristic way. For one thing, Jim kept his freshness in the climate. Had he been a girl—my friend wrote—one could have said he was blooming—blooming modestly—like a violet, not like some of these blatant tropical flowers. He had been in the house for six weeks, and had not as yet attempted to slap him on the back, or address him as 'old boy,' or try to make him feel a superannuated fossil. He had nothing of the exasperating young man's chatter. He was good-tempered, had not much to say for himself, was not clever by any means, thank goodness—wrote my friend. It appeared, however, that Jim was clever enough to be quietly appreciative of his wit, while, on the other hand, he amused him by his naïveness. 'The dew is yet on him, and since I had the bright idea of giving him a room in the house and having him at meals I feel less withered myself. The other day he took it into his head to cross the room with no other purpose but to open a door for me; and I felt more in touch with mankind than I had been for years. Ridiculous, isn't it? Of course I guess there is something—some awful little scrape—which you know all about—but if I am sure that it is terribly heinous, I fancy one could manage to forgive it. For my part, I declare I am unable to imagine him guilty of anything much worse than robbing an orchard. *Is it* much worse? Perhaps you ought to have told me; but it is such a long time since we both turned saints that you may have forgotten we too had sinned in our time? It may be that some day I shall have to ask you, and then I shall expect to be told. I don't care to question him myself till I have some idea what it is. Moreover, it's too soon as yet. Let him open the door a few times more for me. . . .' Thus my friend. I was trebly pleased—at Jim's shaping so well, at the tone of the letter, at my own cleverness. Evidently I had known what I was doing. I had read characters aright, and so on. And what if something unexpected and wonderful were to come of it? That evening, reposing in a deck-chair under the shade of my own poop awning (it was in Hong-Kong harbour), I laid on Jim's behalf the first stone of a castle in Spain.[1]

"I made a trip to the northward, and when I returned I found another letter from my friend waiting for me. It was the first envelope I tore open. 'There are no spoons missing, as far as I know,' ran the first line; 'I haven't been interested enough to inquire. He is gone, leaving on the breakfast-table a formal little note of apology, which is either silly or heartless. Probably both—and it's all one to me. Allow me to say, lest

1. Imaginary scheme not likely to be realized.

you should have some more mysterious young men in reserve, that I have shut up shop, definitely and for ever. This is the last eccentricity I shall be guilty of. Do not imagine for a moment that I care a hang; but he is very much regretted at tennis-parties, and for my own sake I've told a plausible lie at the club. . . .' I flung the letter aside and started looking through the batch on my table, till I came upon Jim's handwriting. Would you believe it? One chance in a hundred! But it is always that hundredth chance! That little second engineer of the *Patna* had turned up in a more or less destitute state and got a temporary job of looking after the machinery of the mill. 'I couldn't stand the familiarity of the little beast,' Jim wrote from a seaport seven hundred miles south of the place where he should have been in clover. 'I am now for the time with Egström & Blake,[2] ship-chandlers, as their— well—runner, to call the thing by its right name. For reference I gave them your name, which they know of course, and if you could write a word in my favour it would be a permanent employment.' I was utterly crushed under the ruins of my castle, but of course I wrote as desired. Before the end of the year my new charter took me that way, and I had an opportunity of seeing him.

"He was still with Egström & Blake, and we met in what they called 'our parlour' opening out of the store. He had that moment come in from boarding a ship, and confronted me head down, ready for a tussle. 'What have you got to say for yourself?' I began as soon as we had shaken hands. 'What I wrote you—nothing more,' he said stubbornly. 'Did the fellow blab—or what?' I asked. He looked up at me with a troubled smile. 'Oh no! He didn't. He made it a kind of confidential business between us. He was most damnably mysterious whenever I came over to the mill; he would wink at me in a respectful manner—as much as to say we know what we know. Infernally fawning and familiar—and that sort of thing . . .' He threw himself into a chair and stared down his legs. 'One day we happened to be alone and the fellow had the cheek to say, "Well, Mr James"—I was called Mr James there as if I had been the son—"here we are together once more. This is better than the old ship—ain't it?" . . . Wasn't it appalling, eh? I looked at him, and he put on a knowing air. "Don't you be uneasy, sir," he says. "I know a gentleman when I see one, and I know how a gentleman feels. I hope, though, you will be keeping me on this job. I had a hard time of it too, along of that rotten old *Patna* racket." Jove! It was awful. I don't know what I should have said or done if I had not just then heard Mr Denver calling me in the passage. It was tiffin-time, and we walked together

2. Perhaps the Singapore ship chandlers McAlister & Co., housed in the same building with Emmerson's Tiffin-Rooms, where ships' officers and traders like Captain William Lingard congregated. See Norman Sherry, *Conrad's Eastern World* (Cambridge: Cambridge UP, 1966) 21–23, 80–84.

across the yard and through the garden to the bungalow. He began to chaff[3] me in his kindly way . . . I believe he liked me . . .'

"Jim was silent for a while.

" 'I know he liked me. That's what made it so hard. Such a splendid man! . . . That morning he slipped his hand under my arm. . . . He, too, was familiar with me.' He burst into a short laugh, and dropped his chin on his breast. 'Pah! When I remembered how that mean little beast had been talking to me,' he began suddenly in a vibrating voice, 'I couldn't bear to think of myself . . . I suppose you know . . .' I nodded. . . . 'More like a father,' he cried; his voice sank. 'I would have had to tell him. I couldn't let it go on—could I?' 'Well?' I murmured, after waiting a while. 'I preferred to go,' he said slowly; 'this thing must be buried.'

"We could hear in the shop Blake upbraiding Egström in an abusive, strained voice. They had been associated for many years, and every day from the moment the doors were opened to the last minute before closing, Blake, a little man with sleek, jetty hair and unhappy, beady eyes, could be heard rowing his partner incessantly with a sort of scathing and plaintive fury. The sound of that everlasting scolding was part of the place like the other fixtures; even strangers would very soon come to disregard it completely unless it be perhaps to mutter 'Nuisance,' or to get up suddenly and shut the door of the 'parlour.' Egström himself, a raw-boned, heavy Scandinavian, with a busy manner and immense blonde whiskers, went on directing his people, checking parcels, making out bills or writing letters at a stand-up desk in the shop, and comported himself in that clatter exactly as though he had been stone-deaf. Now and again he would emit a bothered perfunctory 'Sssh,' which neither produced nor was expected to produce the slightest effect. 'They are very decent to me here,' said Jim. 'Blake's a little cad, but Egström's all right.' He stood up quickly, and walking with measured steps to a tripod telescope standing in the window and pointed at the roadstead, he applied his eye to it. 'There's that ship which has been becalmed outside all the morning has got a breeze now and is coming in,' he remarked patiently; 'I must go and board.' We shook hands in silence, and he turned to go. 'Jim!' I cried. He looked round with his hand on the lock. 'You—you have thrown away something like a fortune.' He came back to me all the way from the door. 'Such a splendid old chap,' he said. 'How could I? How could I?' His lips twitched. '*Here* it does not matter.' 'Oh! you —you—' I began, and had to cast about for a suitable word, but before I became aware that there was no name that would just do, he was gone. I heard outside Egström's deep gentle voice saying cheerily, 'That's the *Sarah W. Granger*, Jimmy. You must manage to be first aboard'; and

3. Tease.

directly Blake struck in, screaming after the manner of an outraged
cockatoo, 'Tell the captain we've got some of his mail here. That'll fetch
him. D'ye hear, Mister What's-your-name?' And there was Jim answering Egström with something boyish in his tone. 'All right. I'll make
a race of it.' He seemed to take refuge in the boat-sailing part of that
sorry business.

"I did not see him again that trip, but on my next (I had a six months'
charter) I went up to the store. Ten yards away from the door Blake's
scolding met my ears, and when I came in he gave me a glance of utter
wretchedness; Egström, all smiles, advanced, extending a large bony
hand. 'Glad to see you, Captain. . . . Sssh. . . . Been thinking you
were about due back here. What did you say, sir? . . . Sssh. . . . Oh!
him! He has left us. Come into the parlour.' . . . After the slam of the
door Blake's strained voice became faint, as the voice of one scolding
desperately in a wilderness. . . . 'Put us to a great inconvenience, too.
Used us badly—I must say . . .' 'Where's he gone to? Do you know?'
I asked. 'No. It's no use asking either,' said Egström, standing bewhis-
kered and obliging before me with his arms hanging down his sides
clumsily, and a thin silver watch-chain looped very low on a rucked-
up⁴ blue serge waistcoat. 'A man like that don't go anywhere in particular.' I was too concerned at the news to ask for the explanation of
that pronouncement, and he went on. 'He left—let's see—the very day
a steamer with returning pilgrims from the Red Sea put in here with
two blades of her propeller gone. Three weeks ago now.' 'Wasn't there
something said about the *Patna* case?' I asked, fearing the worst. He
gave a start, and looked at me as if I had been a sorcerer. 'Why, yes!
How do you know? Some of them were talking about it here. There
was a captain or two, the manager of Vanlo's engineering shop at the
harbour, two or three others, and myself. Jim was in here too, having
a sandwich and a glass of beer; when we are busy—you see, captain—
there's no time for a proper tiffin. He was standing by this table eating
sandwiches, and the rest of us were round the telescope watching that
steamer come in; and by-and-by Vanlo's manager began to talk about
the chief of the *Patna*; he had done some repairs for him once, and
from that he went on to tell us what an old ruin she was, and the money
that had been made out of her. He came to mention her last voyage,
and then we all struck in. Some said one thing and some another—not
much—what you or any other man might say; and there was some
laughing. Captain O'Brien of the *Sarah W. Granger*, a large, noisy old
man with a stick—he was sitting listening to us in this arm-chair here
—he let drive suddenly with his stick at the floor, and roars out,
"Skunks!" . . . Made us all jump. Vanlo's manager winks at us and
asks, "What's the matter, Captain O'Brien?" "Matter! matter!" the old

4. Drawn or worked into wrinkles or creases; puckered.

man began to shout; "what are you Injuns laughing at? It's no laughing matter. It's a disgrace to human natur'—that's what it is. I would despise being seen in the same room with one of those men. Yes, sir!" He seemed to catch my eye like, and I had to speak out of civility. "Skunks!" says I, "of course, Captain O'Brien, and I wouldn't care to have them here myself, so you're quite safe in this room, Captain O'Brien. Have a little something cool to drink." "Dam' your drink, Egström," says he, with a twinkle in his eye; "when I want a drink I will shout for it. I am going to quit. It stinks here now." At this all the others burst out laughing, and out they go after the old man. And then, sir, that blasted Jim he puts down the sandwich he had in his hand and walks round the table to me; there was his glass of beer poured out quite full. "I am off," he says—just like this. "It isn't half-past one yet," says I; "you might snatch a smoke first." I thought he meant it was time for him to go down to his work. When I understood what he was up to, my arms fell—so! Can't get a man like that every day, you know, sir; a regular devil for sailing a boat; ready to go out miles to sea to meet ships in any sort of weather. More than once a captain would come in here full of it, and the first thing he would say would be, "That's a reckless sort of a lunatic you've got for water-clerk, Egström. I was feeling my way in at daylight under short canvas when there comes flying out of the mist right under my forefoot a boat half under water, sprays going over the mast-head, two frightened niggers on the bottom boards, a yelling fiend at the tiller. Hey! hey! Ship ahoy! ahoy! Captain! Hey! hey! Egström & Blake's man first to speak to you! Hey! hey! Egström & Blake! Hallo! hey! whoop! Kick the niggers—out reefs—a squall on at the time—shoots ahead whooping and yelling to me to make sail and he would give me a lead in—more like a demon than a man. Never saw a boat handled like that in all my life. Couldn't have been drunk—was he? Such a quiet, soft-spoken chap too—blush like a girl when he came on board. . . ." I tell you, Captain Marlow, nobody had a chance against us with a strange ship when Jim was out. The other ship-chandlers just kept their old customers, and . . .'

"Egström appeared overcome with emotion.

" 'Why, sir—it seemed as though he wouldn't mind going a hundred miles out to sea in an old shoe to nab a ship for the firm. If the business had been his own and all to make yet, he couldn't have done more in that way. And now . . . all at once . . . like this! Thinks I to myself: "Oho! a rise in the screw—that's the trouble—is it? All right," says I, "no need of all that fuss with me, Jimmy. Just mention your figure. Anything in reason." He looks at me as if he wanted to swallow something that stuck in his throat. "I can't stop with you." "What's that blooming joke?" I asks. He shakes his head, and I could see in his eye he was as good as gone already, sir. So I turned to him and slanged him till all was blue. "What is it you're running away from?" I asks. "Who has been getting at you? What scared you? You haven't as much sense as a rat; they don't clear out from a good ship. Where do you expect to get a better berth?—you this and you that." I made him look sick, I can tell you. "This business ain't going to sink," says I. He gave a big jump. "Good-bye," he says, nodding at me like a lord; "you ain't half a bad chap, Egström. I give you my word that if you knew my reasons you wouldn't care to keep me." "That's the biggest lie you ever told in your life," says I; "I know my own mind." He made me so mad that I had to laugh. "Can't you really stop long enough to drink this glass of beer here, you funny beggar, you?" I don't know what came over him; he didn't seem able to find the door; something comical, I can tell you, captain. I drank the beer myself. "Well, if you're in such a hurry, here's luck to you in your own drink," says I; "only, you mark my words, if you keep up this game you'll very soon find that the earth ain't big enough to hold you—that's all." He gave me one black look, and out he rushed with a face fit to scare little children.'

"Egström snorted bitterly, and combed one auburn whisker with knotty fingers. 'Haven't been able to get a man that was any good since. It's nothing but worry, worry, worry in business. And where might you have come across him, captain, if it's fair to ask?'

" 'He was the mate of the *Patna* that voyage,' I said, feeling that I owed some explanation. For a time Egström remained very still, with his fingers plunged in the hair at the side of his face, and then exploded. 'And who the devil cares about that?' 'I dare say no one,' I began . . . 'And what the devil is he—anyhow—for to go on like this?' He stuffed suddenly his left whisker into his mouth and stood amazed. 'Jee!' he exclaimed, 'I told him the earth wouldn't be big enough to hold his caper.' "[5]

Chapter XIX

"I have told you these two episodes at length to show his manner of dealing with himself under the new conditions of his life. There were many others of the sort, more than I could count on the fingers of my two hands. They were all equally tinged by a high-minded absurdity of intention which made their futility profound and touching. To fling away your daily bread[1] so as to get your hands free for a grapple with a ghost may be an act of prosaic heroism. Men had done it before (though we who have lived know full well that it is not the haunted soul but the hungry body that makes an outcast), and men who had eaten and meant to eat every day had applauded the creditable folly. He was indeed

5. Activity (derogatory term).
1. Allusion to Jesus' phrase in the Lord's Prayer (Matthew 6.11).

unfortunate, for all his recklessness could not carry him out from under the shadow. There was always a doubt of his courage. The truth seems to be that it is impossible to lay the ghost of a fact. You can face it or shirk it—and I have come across a man or two who could wink at their familiar shades. Obviously Jim was not of the winking sort; but what I could never make up my mind about was whether his line of conduct amounted to shirking his ghost or to facing him out.

"I strained my mental eyesight only to discover that, as with the complexion of all our actions, the shade of difference was so delicate that it was impossible to say. It might have been flight and it might have been a mode of combat. To the common mind he became known as a rolling stone, because this was the funniest part: he did after a time become perfectly known, and even notorious, within the circle of his wanderings (which had a diameter of, say, three thousand miles), in the same way as an eccentric character is known to a whole countryside. For instance, in Bankok, where he found employment with Yucker Brothers,[2] charterers and teak merchants, it was almost pathetic to see him go about in sunshine hugging his secret, which was known to the very up-country logs on the river. Schomberg,[3] the keeper of the hotel where he boarded, a hirsute Alsatian of manly bearing and an irrepressible retailer of all the scandalous gossip of the place, would, with both elbows on the table, impart an adorned version of the story to any guest who cared to imbibe knowledge along with the more costly liquors. 'And, mind you, the nicest fellow you could meet,' would be his generous conclusion; 'quite superior.' It says a lot for the casual crowd that frequented Schomberg's establishment that Jim managed to hang out in Bankok for a whole six months. I remarked that people, perfect strangers took to him as one takes to a nice child. His manner was reserved, but it was as though his personal appearance, his hair, his eyes, his smile, made friends for him wherever he went. And, of course, he was no fool. I heard Siegmund Yucker (native of Switzerland), a gentle creature ravaged by a cruel dyspepsia, and so frightfully lame that his head swung through a quarter of a circle at every step he took, declare appreciatively that for one so young he was 'of great gabasidy,' as though it had been a mere question of cubic contents. 'Why not send him up country?' I suggested anxiously. (Yucker Brothers had concessions and teak forests in the interior.) 'If he has capacity, as you say, he will soon get hold of the work. And physically he is very fit. His health is always excellent.' 'Ach! It's a great ting in dis goundry to be vree vrom tispep-shia,' sighed poor Yucker enviously, casting a stealthy glance at the pit of his ruined

2. Jucker, Sigg and Co. were teak merchants in Bangkok.
3. Plays an important role in Conrad's "Falk" (1903) and *Victory* (1915). Schomberg's hotel was probably suggested by the smaller of two European hotels in Bangkok, the Universal, owned and managed by Schulmaker and Ulrich. The name Schomberg, however, belongs to a Singapore broker.

stomach. I left him drumming pensively on his desk and muttering, 'Es ist ein Idee. Es ist ein Idee.' Unfortunately, that very evening an unpleasant affair took place in the hotel.

"I don't know that I blame Jim very much, but it was a truly regrettable incident. It belonged to the lamentable species of bar-room scuffles, and the other party to it was a cross-eyed Dane of sorts whose visiting-card recited under his misbegotten name: first lieutenant in the Royal Siamese Navy. The fellow, of course, was utterly hopeless at billiards, but did not like to be beaten, I suppose. He had had enough to drink to turn nasty after the sixth game, and make some scornful remark at Jim's expense. Most of the people there didn't hear what was said, and those who had heard seemed to have had all precise recollection scared out of them by the appalling nature of the consequences that immediately ensued. It was very lucky for the Dane that he could swim, because the room opened on a verandah and the Menam flowed below very wide and black. A boat-load of Chinamen, bound, as likely as not, on some thieving expedition, fished out the officer of the King of Siam, and Jim turned up at about midnight on board my ship without a hat. 'Everybody in the room seemed to know,' he said, gasping yet from the contest, as it were. He was rather sorry, on general principles, for what had happened, though in this case there had been, he said, 'no option.' But what dismayed him was to find the nature of his burden as well known to everybody as though he had gone about all that time carrying it on his shoulders. Naturally after this he couldn't remain in the place. He was universally condemned for the brutal violence, so unbecoming a man in his delicate position; some maintained he had been disgracefully drunk at the time; others criticised his want of tact. Even Schomberg was very much annoyed. 'He is a very nice young man,' he said argumentatively to me, 'but the lieutenant is a first-rate fellow too. He dines every night at my *table d'hôte*,[4] you know. And there's a billiard-cue broken. I can't allow that. First thing this morning I went over with my apologies to the lieutenant, and I think I've made it all right for myself; but only think, captain, if everybody started such games! Why, the man might have been drowned! And here I can't run out into the next street and buy a new cue. I've got to write to Europe for them. No, no! A temper like that won't do!' . . . He was extremely sore on the subject.

"This was the worst incident of all in his—his retreat. Nobody could deplore it more than myself; for if, as somebody said hearing him mentioned, 'Oh yes! I know. He has knocked about a good deal out here,' yet he had somehow avoided being battered and chipped in the process. This last affair, however, made me seriously uneasy, because if his exquisite sensibilities were to go the length of involving him in pot-

---

4. French phrase denoting a common table for guests at a hotel or restaurant. The meal there is customarily paid for at a set rate.

house shindies,[5] he would lose his name of an inoffensive, if aggravating, fool, and acquire that of a common loafer. For all my confidence in him I could not help reflecting that in such cases from the name to the thing itself is but a step. I suppose you will understand that by that time I could not think of washing my hands of him.[6] I took him away from Bankok in my ship, and we had a longish passage. It was pitiful to see how he shrank within himself. A seaman, even if a mere passenger, takes an interest in a ship, and looks at the sea-life around him with the critical enjoyment of a painter, for instance, looking at another man's work. In every sense of the expression he is 'on deck'; but my Jim, for the most part, skulked down below as though he had been a stowaway. He infected me so that I avoided speaking on professional matters, such as would suggest themselves naturally to two sailors during a passage. For whole days we did not exchange a word; I felt extremely unwilling to give orders to my officers in his presence. Often, when alone with him on deck or in the cabin, we didn't know what to do with our eyes.

"I placed him with De Jongh, as you know, glad enough to dispose of him in any way, yet persuaded that his position was now growing intolerable. He had lost some of that elasticity which had enabled him to rebound back into his uncompromising position after every overthrow. One day, coming ashore, I saw him standing on the quay; the water of the roadstead and the sea in the offing made one smooth ascending plane, and the outermost ships at anchor seemed to ride motionless in the sky. He was waiting for his boat, which was being loaded at our feet with packages of small stores for some vessel ready to leave. After exchanging greetings, we remained silent—side by side. 'Jove!' he said suddenly, 'this is killing work.'

"He smiled at me; I must say he generally could manage a smile. I made no reply. I knew very well he was not alluding to his duties; he had an easy time of it with De Jongh. Nevertheless, as soon as he had spoken I became completely convinced that the work was killing. I did not even look at him. 'Would you like,' said I, 'to leave this part of the world altogether; try California or the West Coast? I'll see what I can do . . .' He interrupted me a little scornfully. 'What difference would it make?' . . . I felt at once convinced that he was right. It would make no difference; it was not relief he wanted; I seemed to perceive dimly that what he wanted, what he was, as it were, waiting for, was something not easy to define—something in the nature of an opportunity. I had given him many opportunities, but they had been merely opportunities to earn his bread. Yet what more could any man do? The position struck me as hopeless and poor Brierly's saying recurred to me, 'Let him creep twenty feet underground and stay there.' Better that, I thought, than

5. Rows, fracases in low taverns.
6. Pilate literally washed his hands of responsibility for Jesus' death (Matthew 27.24).

this waiting above ground for the impossible. Yet one could not be sure even of that. There and then, before his boat was three oars' lengths away from the quay, I had made up my mind to go and consult Stein[7] in the evening.

"This Stein was a wealthy and respected merchant. His 'house' (because it was a house, Stein & Co., and there was some sort of partner who, as Stein said, 'looked after the Moluccas') had a large inter-island business, with a lot of trading posts established in the most out-of-the-way places for collecting the produce. His wealth and his respectability were not exactly the reasons why I was anxious to seek his advice. I desired to confide my difficulty to him because he was one of the most trustworthy men I had ever known. The gentle light of a simple, unwearied, as it were, and intelligent good-nature illumined his long hairless face. It had deep downward folds, and was pale as of a man who had always led a sedentary life—which was indeed very far from being the case. His hair was thin, and brushed back from a massive and lofty forehead. One fancied that at twenty he must have looked very much like what he was now at threescore. It was a student's face; only the eyebrows nearly all white, thick and bushy, together with the resolute searching glance that came from under them, were not in accord with his, I may say, learned appearance. He was tall and loose-jointed; his slight stoop, together with an innocent smile, made him appear benevolently ready to lend you his ear; his long arms with pale big hands had rare deliberate gestures of a pointing out, demonstrating kind. I speak of him at length, because under this exterior, and in conjunction with an upright and indulgent nature, this man possessed an intrepidity of spirit and a physical courage that could have been called reckless had it not been like a natural function of the body—say good digestion, for instance—completely unconscious of itself. It is sometimes said of a man that he carries his life in his hand. Such a saying would have been inadequate if applied to him; during the early part of his existence in the East he had been playing ball with it. All this was in the past, but I knew the story of his life and the origin of his fortune. He was also a naturalist of some distinction, or perhaps I should say a learned collector. Entomology was his special study. His collection of *Buprestidœ* and *Longicorns*[8]—beetles all—horrible miniature monsters, looking malevolent in death and immobility, and his cabinet of butterflies, beautiful and hovering under the glass of cases on lifeless wings, had spread his fame far over the earth. The name of this merchant, adventurer, sometime adviser of a Malay sultan (to whom he never alluded otherwise than as 'my poor Mohammed Bonso'),[9] had, on account of a few bushels

7. Probably based on various naturalists and on the trader Captain William Lingard. See below, pp. 365–66.
8. Two groups of beetles: one, brilliantly colored; the other, having long antennae.
9. The name comes from *Memoirs of a Malayan Family*, transcribed by W. Marsden, London, 1830.

of dead insects, become known to learned persons in Europe, who could have had no conception, and certainly would not have cared to know anything, of his life or character. I, who knew, considered him an eminently suitable person to receive my confidences about Jim's difficulties as well as my own."

Chapter XX

"Late in the evening I entered his study, after traversing an imposing but empty dining-room very dimly lit. The house was silent. I was preceded by an elderly grim Javanese servant in a sort of livery of white jacket and yellow sarong, who, after throwing the door open, exclaimed low, 'O master!' and stepping aside, vanished in a mysterious way as though he had been a ghost only momentarily embodied for that particular service. Stein turned round with the chair, and in the same movement his spectacles seemed to get pushed up on his forehead. He welcomed me in his quiet and humorous voice. Only one corner of the vast room, the corner in which stood his writing-desk, was strongly lighted by a shaded reading-lamp, and the rest of the spacious apartment melted into shapeless gloom like a cavern. Narrow shelves filled with dark boxes of uniform shape and colour ran round the walls, not from floor to ceiling, but in a sombre belt about four feet broad—catacombs of beetles. Wooden tablets were hung above at irregular intervals. The light reached one of them, and the word *Coleoptera*[1] written in gold letters glittered mysteriously upon a vast dimness. The glass cases containing the collection of butterflies were ranged in three long rows upon slender-legged little tables. One of these cases had been removed from its place and stood on the desk, which was bestrewn with oblong slips of paper blackened with minute handwriting.

" 'So you see me—so,' he said. His hand hovered over the case where a butterfly in solitary grandeur spread out dark bronze wings, seven inches or more across, with exquisite white veinings and a gorgeous border of yellow spots. 'Only one specimen like this they have in *your* London, and then—no more. To my small native town this my collection I shall bequeath. Something of me. The best.'

"He bent forward in the chair and gazed intently, his chin over the front of the case. I stood at his back. 'Marvellous,' he whispered, and seemed to forget my presence. His history was curious. He had been born in Bavaria, and when a youth of twenty-two had taken an active part in the revolutionary movement of 1848.[2] Heavily compromised, he managed to make his escape, and at first found a refuge with a poor

---

1. A large order of winged beetles and weevils.
2. A series of revolutions throughout Europe, variously motivated. In Germany the dominant motives were constitutional and nationalist.

republican watchmaker in Trieste. From there he made his way to
Tripoli with a stock of cheap watches to hawk about,—not a very great
opening truly, but it turned out lucky enough, because it was there he
came upon a Dutch traveller—a rather famous man, I believe, but I
don't remember his name. It was that naturalist who, engaging him as
a sort of assistant, took him to the East. They travelled in the Archipelago[3] together and separately, collecting insects and birds, for four
years or more. Then the naturalist went home, and Stein, having no
home to go to, remained with an old trader[4] he had come across in his
journeys in the interior of Celebes—if Celebes may be said to have an
interior. This old Scotsman, the only white man allowed to reside in
the country at the time, was a privileged friend of the chief ruler of
Wajo States, who was a woman. I often heard Stein relate how that
chap, who was slightly paralysed on one side, had introduced him to
the native court a short time before another stroke carried him off. He
was a heavy man with a patriarchal white beard, and of imposing stature.
He came into the council-hall where all the rajahs, pangerans, and
headmen were assembled, with the queen, a fat wrinkled woman (very
free in her speech, Stein said), reclining on a high couch under a canopy.
He dragged his leg, thumping with his stick, and grasped Stein's arm,
leading him right up to the couch. 'Look, queen, and you rajahs, this
is my son,' he proclaimed in a stentorian voice. 'I have traded with your
fathers, and when I die he shall trade with you and your sons.'

"By means of this simple formality Stein inherited the Scotsman's
privileged position and all his stock-in-trade, together with a fortified
house on the banks of the only navigable river in the country. Shortly
afterwards the old queen, who was so free in her speech, died, and the
country became disturbed by various pretenders to the throne. Stein
joined the party of a younger son, the one of whom thirty years later
he never spoke otherwise but as 'my poor Mohammed Bonso.' They
both became the heroes of innumerable exploits; they had wonderful
adventures, and once stood a siege in the Scotsman's house for a month,
with only a score of followers against a whole army. I believe the natives
talk of that war to this day. Meantime, it seems, Stein never failed to
annex on his own account every butterfly or beetle he could lay hands
on. After some eight years of war, negotiations, false truces, sudden
outbreaks, reconciliation, treachery, and so on, and just as peace seemed
at last permanently established, his 'poor Mohammed Bonso' was as-
sassinated at the gate of his own royal residence while dismounting in

3. The Malay Archipelago, the largest group of islands in the world, including Sumatra, Borneo,
   Java, Celebes (now Sulawesi), New Guinea, the Moluccas, and the Philippines.
4. Probably Francis James Secretan, a Singapore merchant whose ships traded throughout the
   Dutch East Indies. When Secretan died in 1864, his trading interests devolved upon Captain
   William Lingard, a hero of Conrad's who appears as Captain Tom Lingard in *Almayer's Folly*
   (1895), *An Outcast of the Islands* (1896), and *The Rescue* (1920). See Sherry, *Conrad's Eastern
   World*, 91–96.

the highest spirits on his return from a successful deer-hunt. This event rendered Stein's position extremely insecure, but he would have stayed perhaps had it not been that a short time afterwards he lost Mohammed's sister ('my dear wife the princess,' he used to say solemnly), by whom he had had a daughter—mother and child both dying within three days of each other from some infectious fever. He left the country, which this cruel loss had made unbearable to him. Thus ended the first and adventurous part of his existence. What followed was so different that, but for the reality of sorrow which remained with him, this strange past must have resembled a dream. He had a little money; he started life afresh, and in the course of years acquired a considerable fortune. At first he had travelled a good deal amongst the islands, but age had stolen upon him, and of late he seldom left his spacious house three miles out of town, with an extensive garden, and surrounded by stables, offices, and bamboo cottages for his servants and dependants, of whom he had many. He drove in his buggy every morning to town, where he had an office with white and Chinese clerks. He owned a small fleet of schooners and native craft, and dealt in island produce on a large scale. For the rest he lived solitary, but not misanthropic, with his books and his collection, classing and arranging specimens, corresponding with entomologists in Europe, writing up a descriptive catalogue of his treasures. Such was the history of the man whom I had come to consult upon Jim's case without any definite hope. Simply to hear what he would have to say would have been a relief. I was very anxious, but I respected the intense, almost passionate, absorption with which he looked at a butterfly, as though on the bronze sheen of these frail wings, in the white tracings, in the gorgeous markings, he could see other things, an image of something as perishable and defying destruction as these delicate and lifeless tissues displaying a splendour unmarred by death.

" 'Marvellous!' he repeated, looking up at me. 'Look! The beauty—but that is nothing—look at the accuracy, the harmony. And so fragile! And so strong! And so exact! This is Nature—the balance of colossal forces. Every star is so—and every blade of grass stands so—and the mighty Kosmos in perfect equilibrium produces—this. This wonder; this masterpiece of Nature—the great artist.'

" 'Never heard an entomologist go on like this,' I observed cheerfully. 'Masterpiece! And what of man?'

" 'Man is amazing, but he is not a masterpiece,' he said, keeping his eyes fixed on the glass case. 'Perhaps the artist was a little mad. Eh? What do you think? Sometimes it seems to me that man is come where he is not wanted, where there is no place for him; for if not, why should he want all the place? Why should he run about here and there making a great noise about himself, talking about the stars, disturbing the blades of grass? . . .'

" 'Catching butterflies,' I chimed in.

"He smiled, threw himself back in his chair, and stretched his legs. 'Sit down,' he said. 'I captured this rare specimen myself one very fine morning. And I had a very big emotion. You don't know what it is for a collector to capture such a rare specimen. You can't know.'

"I smiled at my ease in a rocking-chair. His eyes seemed to look far beyond the wall at which they stared; and he narrated how, one night, a messenger arrived from his 'poor Mohammed,' requiring his presence at the 'residenz'—as he called it—which was distant some nine or ten miles by a bridle-path over a cultivated plain, with patches of forest here and there. Early in the morning he started from his fortified house, after embracing his little Emma, and leaving the 'princess,' his wife, in command. He described how she came with him as far as the gate, walking with one hand on the neck of his horse; she had on a white jacket, gold pins in her hair, and a brown leather belt over her left shoulder with a revolver in it. 'She talked as women will talk,' he said, 'telling me to be careful, and to try to get back before dark, and what a great wickedness it was for me to go alone. We were at war, and the country was not safe; my men were putting up bullet-proof shutters to the house and loading their rifles, and she begged me to have no fear for her. She could defend the house against anybody till I returned. And I laughed with pleasure a little. I liked to see her so brave and young and strong. I too was young then. At the gate she caught hold of my hand and gave it one squeeze and fell back. I made my horse stand still outside till I heard the bars of the gate put up behind me. There was a great enemy of mine, a great noble—and a great rascal too—roaming with a band in the neighbourhood. I cantered for four or five miles; there had been rain in the night, but the mists had gone up, up—and the face of the earth was clean; it lay smiling to me, so fresh and innocent—like a little child. Suddenly somebody fires a volley—twenty shots at least it seemed to me. I hear bullets sing in my ear, and my hat jumps to the back of my head. It was a little intrigue, you understand. They got my poor Mohammed to send for me and then laid that ambush. I see it all in a minute, and I think——This wants a little management. My pony snort, jump, and stand, and I fall slowly forward with my head on his mane. He begins to walk, and with one eye I could see over his neck a faint cloud of smoke hanging in front of a clump of bamboos to my left. I think——Aha! my friends, why you not wait long enough before you shoot? This is not yet *gelungen*.[5] Oh no! I get hold of my revolver with my right hand—quiet—quiet. After all, there were only seven of these rascals. They get up from the grass and start running with their sarongs tucked up, waving spears above their heads, and yelling to each other to look out and catch the horse, because I was dead. I let them come as close as the door here, and then bang, bang, bang—take aim each

5. Successful.

time too. One more shot I fire at a man's back, but I miss. Too far already. And then I sit alone on my horse with the clean earth smiling at me, and there are the bodies of three men lying on the ground. One was curled up like a dog, another on his back had an arm over his eyes as if to keep off the sun, and the third man he draws up his leg very slowly and makes it with one kick straight again. I watch him very carefully from my horse, but there is no more—*bleibt ganz ruhig*— keep still, so. And as I looked at his face for some sign of life I observed something like a faint shadow pass over his forehead. It was the shadow of this butterfly. Look at the form of the wing. This species fly high with a strong flight. I raised my eyes and I saw him fluttering away. I think——Can it be possible? And then I lost him. I dismounted and went on very slow, leading my horse and holding my revolver with one hand and my eyes darting up and down and right and left, everywhere! At last I saw him sitting on a small heap of dirt ten feet away. At once my heart began to beat quick. I let go my horse, keep my revolver in one hand, and with the other snatch my soft felt hat off my head. One step. Steady. Another step. Flop! I got him! When I got up I shook like a leaf with excitement, and when I opened these beautiful wings and made sure what a rare and so extraordinary perfect specimen I had, my head went round and my legs became so weak with emotion that I had to sit on the ground. I had greatly desired to possess myself of a specimen of that species when collecting for the professor. I took long journeys and underwent great privations; I had dreamed of him in my sleep, and here suddenly I had him in my fingers—for myself! In the words of the poet' (he pronounced it 'boet')—

> ' "So halt' ich's endlich denn in meinen Händen,
>   Und nenn' es in gewissem Sinne mein." '[6]

He gave to the last word the emphasis of a suddenly lowered voice, and withdrew his eyes slowly from my face. He began to charge a long-stemmed pipe busily and in silence, then, pausing with his thumb on the orifice of the bowl, looked again at me significantly.

" 'Yes, my good friend. On that day I had nothing to desire; I had greatly annoyed my principal enemy; I was young, strong; I had friend-ship; I had the love' (he said 'lof') 'of woman, a child I had, to make my heart very full—and even what I had once dreamed in my sleep had come into my hand too!

"He struck a match, which flared violently. His thoughtful placid face twitched once.

" 'Friend, wife, child,' he said slowly, gazing at the small flame— 'phoo!' The match was blown out. He sighed and turned again to the glass case. The frail and beautiful wings quivered faintly, as if his breath

6. "I hold it, then, at length within my hands, / And in a certain sense can call it mine" (Goethe, *Torquato Tasso* 1.3.393–94, from the translation by Anna Swanwick, 1882).

had for an instant called back to life that gorgeous object of his dreams.

" 'The work,' he began suddenly, pointing to the scattered slips, and in his usual gentle and cheery tone, 'is making great progress. I have been this rare specimen describing. . . . Na! And what is your good news?'

" 'To tell you the truth, Stein,' I said with an effort that surprised me, 'I came here to describe a specimen. . . .'

" 'Butterfly?' he asked, with an unbelieving and humorous eagerness.

" 'Nothing so perfect,' I answered, feeling suddenly dispirited with all sorts of doubts. 'A man!'

" 'Ach so!' he murmured, and his smiling countenance, turned to me, became grave. Then after looking at me for a while he said slowly, 'Well—I am a man too.'

"Here you have him as he was; he knew how to be so generously encouraging as to make a scrupulous man hesitate on the brink of confidence; but if I did hesitate it was not for long.

"He heard me out, sitting with crossed legs. Sometimes his head would disappear completely in a great eruption of smoke, and a sympathetic growl would come out from the cloud. When I finished he uncrossed his legs, laid down his pipe, leaned forward towards me earnestly with his elbows on the arms of his chair, the tips of his fingers together.

" 'I understand very well. He is romantic.'

"He had diagnosed the case for me, and at first I was quite startled to find how simple it was; and indeed our conference resembled so much a medical consultation—Stein, of learned aspect sitting in an arm-chair before his desk; I, anxious, in another, facing him, but a little to one side—that it seemed natural to ask—

" 'What's good for it?'

"He lifted up a long forefinger.

" 'There is only one remedy! One thing alone can us from being ourselves cure!' The finger came down on the desk with a smart rap. The case which he had made to look so simple before became if possible still simpler—and altogether hopeless. There was a pause. 'Yes,' said I, 'strictly speaking, the question is not how to get cured, but how to live.'

"He approved with his head, a little sadly as it seemed. 'Ja! ja! In general, adapting the words of your great poet: That is the question.[7] . . .' He went on nodding sympathetically. . . . 'How to be! Ach! How to be.'

"He stood up with the tips of his fingers resting on the desk.

" 'We want in so many different ways to be,' he began again. 'This magnificent butterfly finds a little heap of dirt and sits still on it; but man he will never on his heap of mud keep still. He want to be so, and

---

7. "To be, or not to be, that is the question" (*Hamlet* 3.1.55).

again he want to be so.' . . . He moved his hand up, then down. . . .
'He wants to be a saint, and he wants to be a devil—and every time he
shuts his eyes he sees himself as a very fine fellow—so fine as he can
never be. . . . In a dream. . . .'

"He lowered the glass lid, the automatic lock clicked sharply, and
taking up the case in both hands he bore it religiously away to its place,
passing out of the bright circle of the lamp into the ring of fainter
light—into shapeless dusk at last. It had an odd effect—as if these few
steps had carried him out of this concrete and perplexed world. His tall
form, as though robbed of its substance, hovered noiselessly over invisible
things with stooping and indefinite movements; his voice, heard in that
remoteness where he could be glimpsed mysteriously busy with immaterial cares, was no longer incisive, seemed to roll voluminous and
grave—mellowed by distance.

" 'And because you not always can keep your eyes shut there comes
the real trouble—the heart pain—the world pain. I tell you, my friend,
it is not good for you to find you cannot make your dream come true,
for the reason that you not strong enough are, or not clever enough.
Ja! . . . And all the time you are such a fine fellow too! *Wie? Was?
Gott im Himmel!*[8] How can that be? Ha! ha! ha!'

"The shadow prowling amongst the graves of butterflies laughed
boisterously.

" 'Yes! Very funny this terrible thing is. A man that is born falls into
a dream like a man who falls into the sea. If he tries to climb out into
the air as inexperienced people endeavour to do, he drowns—*nicht
wahr?*[9] . . . No! I tell you! The way is to the destructive element submit
yourself, and with the exertions of your hands and feet in the water
make the deep, deep sea keep you up. So if you ask me—how to be?'

"His voice leaped up extraordinarily strong, as though away there in
the dusk he had been inspired by some whisper of knowledge. 'I will
tell you! For that too there is only one way.'

"With a hasty swish swish of his slippers he loomed up in the ring of
faint light, and suddenly appeared in the bright circle of the lamp. His
extended hand aimed at my breast like a pistol; his deep-set eyes seemed
to pierce through me, but his twitching lips uttered no word, and the
austere exaltation of a certitude seen in the dusk vanished from his face.
The hand that had been pointing at my breast fell, and by-and-by,
coming a step nearer, he laid it gently on my shoulder. There were
things, he said mournfully, that perhaps could never be told, only he
had lived so much alone that sometimes he forgot—he forgot. The light
had destroyed the assurance which had inspired him in the distant
shadows. He sat down and, with both elbows on the desk, rubbed his
forehead. 'And yet it is true—it is true. In the destructive element

8. Yes! ° ° ° How? What? God in Heaven!
9. Isn't that true?

immerse.' . . . He spoke in a subdued tone, without looking at me, one hand on each side of his face. 'That was the way. To follow the dream, and again to follow the dream—and so—*ewig*[1]—*usque ad finem*.[2] . . .' The whisper of his conviction seemed to open before me a vast and uncertain expanse, as of a crepuscular horizon on a plain at dawn—or was it, perchance, at the coming of the night? One had not the courage to decide; but it was a charming and deceptive light, throwing the impalpable poesy of its dimness over pitfalls—over graves. His life had begun in sacrifice, in enthusiasm for generous ideas; he had travelled very far, on various ways, on strange paths, and whatever he followed it had been without faltering, and therefore without shame and without regret. In so far he was right. That was the way, no doubt. Yet for all that the great plain on which men wander amongst graves and pitfalls remained very desolate under the impalpable poesy of its crepuscular light, overshadowed in the centre, circled with a bright edge as if surrounded by an abyss full of flames. When at last I broke the silence it was to express the opinion that no one could be more romantic than himself.

"He shook his head slowly, and afterwards looked at me with a patient and inquiring glance. It was a shame, he said. There we were sitting and talking like two boys, instead of putting our heads together to find something practical—a practical remedy—for the evil—for the great evil—he repeated, with a humorous and indulgent smile. For all that, our talk did not grow more practical. We avoided pronouncing Jim's name as though we had tried to keep flesh and blood out of our discussion, or he were nothing but an erring spirit, a suffering and nameless shade. 'Na!' said Stein, rising. 'To-night you sleep here, and in the morning we shall do something practical—practical. . . .' He lit a two-branched candlestick and led the way. We passed through empty dark rooms, escorted by gleams from the lights Stein carried. They glided along the waxed floors, sweeping here and there over the polished surface of a table, leaped upon a fragmentary curve of a piece of furniture, or flashed perpendicularly in and out of distant mirrors, while the forms of two men and the flicker of two flames could be seen for a moment stealing silently across the depths of a crystalline void. He walked slowly a pace in advance with stooping courtesy; there was a profound, as it were a listening, quietude on his face; the long flaxen locks mixed with white threads were scattered thinly upon his slightly bowed neck.

1. Forever.
2. "Until the end." A proverbial Latin phrase found several times in the Vulgate Bible, as in the following passage: "For we are made partakers of Christ, if we hold the beginning of our confidence steadfast unto the end" (Hebrews 3.14). See also the November 9, 1891, letter to Conrad from his uncle and guardian, Tadeusz Bobrowski: "I have gone through a lot, I have suffered over my own fate and the fate of my family and my Nation, and perhaps just because of these sufferings and disappointments I have developed in myself this calm outlook on the problem of life, whose motto, I venture to say, was, is, and will be 'usque ad finem' " (*Conrad's Polish Background*, ed. Zdzisław Najder [London: Oxford UP, 1964] 155).

" 'He is romantic—romantic,' he repeated. 'And that is very bad—
very bad. . . . Very good, too,' he added. 'But *is he?*' I queried.

" '*Gewiss,*'[3] he said, and stood still holding up the candelabrum, but
without looking at me. 'Evident! What is it that by inward pain makes
him know himself? What is it that for you and me makes him—exist?'

"At that moment it was difficult to believe in Jim's existence—starting
from a country parsonage, blurred by crowds of men as by clouds of
dust, silenced by the clashing claims of life and death in a material
world—but his imperishable reality came to me with a convincing, with
an irresistible force! I saw it vividly, as though in our progress through
the lofty silent rooms amongst fleeting gleams of light and the sudden
revelations of human figures stealing with flickering flames within unfathomable and pellucid depths, we had approached nearer to absolute
Truth, which, like Beauty itself, floats elusive, obscure, half submerged,
in the silent still waters of mystery. 'Perhaps he is,' I admitted with a
slight laugh, whose unexpectedly loud reverberation made me lower my
voice directly; 'but I am sure you are.' With his head dropping on his
breast and the light held high he began to walk again. 'Well—I exist
too,' he said.

"He preceded me. My eyes followed his movements, but what I did
see was not the head of the firm, the welcome guest at afternoon re-
ceptions, the correspondent of learned societies, the entertainer of stray
naturalists; I saw only the reality of his destiny, which he had known
how to follow with unfaltering footsteps, that life begun in humble
surroundings, rich in generous enthusiasms, in friendship, love, war—
in all the exalted elements of romance. At the door of my room he
faced me. 'Yes,' I said, as though carrying on a discussion, 'and amongst
other things you dreamed foolishly of a certain butterfly; but when one
fine morning your dream came in your way you did not let the splendid
opportunity escape. Did you? Whereas he . . .' Stein lifted his hand.
'And do you know how many opportunities I let escape; how many
dreams I had lost that had come in my way?' He shook his head regretfully. 'It seems to me that some would have been very fine—if I had
made them come true. Do you know how many? Perhaps I myself don't
know.' 'Whether his were fine or not,' I said, 'he knows of one which
he certainly did not catch.' 'Everybody knows of one or two like that,'
said Stein; 'and that is the trouble—the great trouble. . . .'

"He shook hands on the threshold, peered into my room under his
raised arm. 'Sleep well. And to-morrow we must do something
practical—practical. . . .'

"Though his own room was beyond mine I saw him return the way
he came. He was going back to his butterflies."

---

3. Of course.

132

Chapter XXI

"I don't suppose any of you have ever heard of Patusan?"[1] Marlow resumed, after a silence occupied in the careful lighting of a cigar. "It does not matter; there's many a heavenly body in the lot crowding upon us of a night that mankind had never heard of, it being outside the sphere of its activities and of no earthly importance to anybody but to the astronomers who are paid to talk learnedly about its composition, weight, path—the irregularities of its conduct, the aberrations of its light,—a sort of scientific scandal-mongering. Thus with Patusan. It was referred to knowingly in the inner government circles in Batavia, especially as to its irregularities and aberrations, and it was known by name to some few, very few, in the mercantile world. Nobody, however, had been there, and I suspect no one desired to go there in person— just as an astronomer, I should fancy, would strongly object to being transported into a distant heavenly body, where, parted from his earthly emoluments, he would be bewildered by the view of an unfamiliar heavens. However, neither heavenly bodies nor astronomers have anything to do with Patusan. It was Jim who went there. I only meant you to understand that had Stein arranged to send him into a star of the fifth magnitude the change could not have been greater. He left his earthly failings behind him and what sort of reputation he had, and there was a totally new set of conditions for his imaginative faculty to work upon. Entirely new, entirely remarkable. And he got hold of them in a remarkable way.

"Stein was the man who knew more about Patusan than anybody else. More than was known in the government circles I suspect. I have no doubt he had been there, either in his butterfly-hunting days or later on, when he tried in his incorrigible way to season with a pinch of romance the fattening dishes of his commercial kitchen. There were very few places in the Archipelago he had not seen in the original dusk of their being, before light (and even electric light) had been carried into them for the sake of better morality and—and—well—the greater profit too. It was at breakfast of the morning following our talk about Jim that he mentioned the place, after I had quoted poor Brierly's remark: 'Let him creep twenty feet underground and stay there.' He looked up at me with interested attention, as though I had been a rare insect. 'This could be done too,' he remarked, sipping his coffee. 'Bury him in some sort,' I explained. 'One doesn't like to do it of course, but it would be

---

1. Geographically speaking, Conrad had in mind the Teunom River area on the northwest coast of Sumatra. For specific details, however, Conrad was using the Berau delta he personally knew in Dutch East Borneo. The native settlement of Berau is now called Tandjong Redeb and lies some thirty-four miles up the river from the Celebes Sea. He probably took the name Patusan from an account of the destruction of a large pirate stronghold by that name in Sarawak, North Borneo, in Captain the Hon. Henry Keppel's *Expedition to Borneo* (London, 1846) 2.76–92. See below, pp. 358–63 and pp. 378–79.

the best thing, seeing what he is.' 'Yes; he is young,' Stein mused. 'The youngest human being now in existence,' I affirmed. '*Schön.*² There's Patusan,' he went on in the same tone. . . .'And the woman is dead now,' he added incomprehensibly.

"Of course I don't know that story; I can only guess that once before Patusan had been used as a grave for some sin, transgression, or misfortune. It is impossible to suspect Stein. The only woman that had ever existed for him was the Malay girl he called 'My wife the princess,' or, more rarely, in moments of expansion, 'the mother of my Emma.' Who was the woman he had mentioned in connection with Patusan I can't say; but from his allusions I understand she had been an educated and very good-looking Dutch-Malay girl, with a tragic or perhaps only a pitiful history, whose most painful part no doubt was her marriage with a Malacca Portuguese who had been clerk in some commercial house in the Dutch colonies. I gathered from Stein that this man was an unsatisfactory person in more ways than one, all being more or less indefinite and offensive. It was solely for his wife's sake that Stein had appointed him manager of Stein & Co.'s trading post in Patusan; but commercially the arrangement was not a success, at any rate for the firm, and now the woman had died, Stein was disposed to try another agent there. The Portuguese, whose name was Cornelius, considered himself a very deserving but ill-used person, entitled by his abilities to a better position. This man Jim would have to relieve. 'But I don't think he will go away from the place,' remarked Stein. 'That has nothing to do with me. It was only for the sake of the woman that I . . . But as I think there is a daughter left, I shall let him, if he likes to stay, keep the old house.'

"Patusan is a remote district of a native-ruled state, and the chief settlement bears the same name. At a point on the river about forty miles from the sea, where the first houses come into view, there can be seen rising above the level of the forests the summits of two steep hills very close together, and separated by what looks like a deep fissure, the cleavage of some mighty stroke. As a matter of fact, the valley between is nothing but a narrow ravine; the appearance from the settlement is of one irregularly conical hill split in two, and with the two halves leaning slightly apart. On the third day after the full, the moon, as seen from the open space in front of Jim's house (he had a very fine house in the native style when I visited him), rose exactly behind these hills, its diffused light at first throwing the two masses into intensely black relief, and then the nearly perfect disc, glowing ruddily, appeared, gliding upwards between the sides of the chasm, till it floated away above the summits, as if escaping from a yawning grave in gentle triumph. 'Wonderful effect,' said Jim by my side. 'Worth seeing. Is it not?'

2. Fine.

"And this question was put with a note of personal pride that made me smile, as though he had had a hand in regulating that unique spectacle. He had regulated so many things in Patusan—things that would have appeared as much beyond his control as the motions of the moon and the stars.

"It was inconceivable. That was the distinctive quality of the part into which Stein and I had tumbled him unwittingly, with no other notion than to get him out of the way; out of his own way, be it understood. That was our main purpose, though, I own, I might have had another motive which had influenced me a little. I was about to go home for a time; and it may be I desired, more than I was aware of myself, to dispose of him—to dispose of him, you understand—before I left. I was going home, and he had come to me from there, with his miserable trouble and his shadowy claim, like a man panting under a burden in a mist. I cannot say I had ever seen him distinctly—not even to this day, after I had my last view of him; but it seemed to me that the less I understood the more I was bound to him in the name of that doubt which is the inseparable part of our knowledge. I did not know so much more about myself. And then, I repeat, I was going home—to that home distant enough for all its hearthstones to be like one hearthstone, by which the humblest of us has the right to sit. We wander in our thousands over the face of the earth, the illustrious and the obscure, earning beyond the seas our fame, our money, or only a crust of bread; but it seems to me that for each of us going home must be like going to render an account. We return to face our superiors, our kindred, our friends— those whom we obey, and those whom we love; but even they who have neither, the most free, lonely, irresponsible and bereft of ties,—even those for whom home holds no dear face, no familiar voice,—even they have to meet the spirit that dwells within the land, under its sky, in its air, in its valleys, and on its rises, in its fields, in its waters and its trees—a mute friend, judge, and inspirer. Say what you like, to get its joy, to breathe its peace, to face its truth, one must return with a clear conscience. All this may seem to you sheer sentimentalism; and indeed very few of us have the will or the capacity to look consciously under the surface of familiar emotions. There are the girls we love, the men we look up to, the tenderness, the friendships, the opportunities, the pleasures! But the fact remains that you must touch your reward with clean hands, lest it turn to dead leaves, to thorns, in your grasp. I think it is the lonely, without a fireside or an affection they may call their own, those who return not to a dwelling but to the land itself, to meet its disembodied, eternal, and unchangeable spirit—it is those who understand best its severity, its saving power, the grace of its secular[3] right to our fidelity, to our obedience. Yes! few of us understand, but

3. Existing through centuries.

we all feel it though, and I say *all* without exception, because those who do not feel do not count. Each blade of grass has its spot on earth whence it draws its life, its strength; and so is man rooted to the land from which he draws his faith together with his life. I don't know how much Jim understood; but I know he felt, he felt confusedly but powerfully, the demand of some such truth or some such illusion—I don't care how you call it, there is so little difference, and the difference means so little. The thing is that in virtue of his feeling he mattered. He would never go home now. Not he. Never. Had he been capable of picturesque manifestations he would have shuddered at the thought and made you shudder too. But he was not of that sort, though he was expressive enough in his way. Before the idea of going home he would grow desperately stiff and immovable, with lowered chin and pouted lips, and with those candid blue eyes of his glowering darkly under a frown, as if before something unbearable, as if before something revolting. There was imagination in that hard skull of his, over which the thick clustering hair fitted like a cap. As to me, I have no imagination (I would be more certain about him today, if I had), and I do not mean to imply that I figured to myself the spirit of the land uprising above the white cliffs of Dover, to ask me what I—returning with no bones broken, so to speak—had done with my very young brother.[4] I could not make such a mistake. I knew very well he was of those about whom there is no inquiry; I had seen better men go out, disappear, vanish utterly, without provoking a sound of curiosity or sorrow. The spirit of the land, as becomes the ruler of great enterprises, is careless of innumerable lives. Woe to the stragglers! We exist only in so far as we hang together. He had straggled in a way; he had not hung on; but he was aware of it with an intensity that made him touching, just as a man's more intense life makes his death more touching than the death of a tree. I happened to be handy, and I happened to be touched. That's all there is to it. I was concerned as to the way he would go out. It would have hurt me if, for instance, he had taken to drink. The earth is so small that I was afraid of, some day, being waylaid by a blear-eyed, swollen-faced, besmirched loafer, with no soles to his canvas shoes, and with a flutter of rags about the elbows, who, on the strength of old acquaintance, would ask for a loan of five dollars. You know the awful jaunty bearing of these scarecrows coming to you from a decent past, the rasping careless voice, the half-averted impudent glances—those meetings more trying to a man who believes in the solidarity of our lives than the sight of an impenitent death-bed to a priest. That, to tell you the truth, was the only danger I could see for him and for me; but I also mistrusted my want of imagination. It might even come to something worse, in some way it was beyond my powers of fancy to foresee. He wouldn't let me forget how

4. See Genesis 4.9: "And the Lord said unto Cain, where is Abel thy brother?"

imaginative he was, and your imaginative people swing farther in any direction, as if given a longer scope of cable in the uneasy anchorage of life. They do. They take to drink too. It may be I was belittling him by such a fear. How could I tell? Even Stein could say no more than that he was romantic. I only knew he was one of us. And what business had he to be romantic? I am telling you so much about my own instinctive feelings and bemused reflections because there remains so little to be told of him. He existed for me, and after all it is only through me that he exists for you. I've led him out by the hand; I have paraded him before you. Were my commonplace fears unjust? I won't say—not even now. You may be able to tell better, since the proverb has it that the onlookers see most of the game. At any rate, they were superfluous. He did not go out, not at all; on the contrary, he came on wonderfully, came on straight as a die and in excellent form, which showed that he could stay as well as spurt. I ought to be delighted, for it is a victory in which I had taken my part; but I am not so pleased as I would have expected to be. I ask myself whether his rush had really carried him out of that mist in which he loomed interesting if not very big, with floating outlines—a straggler yearning inconsolably for his humble place in the ranks. And besides, the last word is not said—probably shall never be said. Are not our lives too short for that full utterance which through all our stammerings is of course our only and abiding intention? I have given up expecting those last words, whose ring, if they could only be pronounced, would shake both heaven and earth. There is never time to say our last word—the last word of our love, of our desire, faith, remorse, submission, revolt. The heaven and the earth must not be shaken, I suppose—at least, not by us who know so many truths about either. My last words about Jim shall be few. I affirm he had achieved greatness; but the thing would be dwarfed in the telling, or rather in the hearing. Frankly, it is not my words that I mistrust, but your minds. I could be eloquent were I not afraid you fellows had starved your imaginations to feed your bodies. I do not mean to be offensive; it is respectable to have no illusions—and safe—and profitable—and dull. Yet you too in your time must have known the intensity of life, that light of glamour created in the shock of trifles, as amazing as the glow of sparks struck from a cold stone—and as short-lived, alas!"

Chapter XXII

"The conquest of love, honour, men's confidence—the pride of it, the power of it, are fit materials for a heroic tale; only our minds are struck by the externals of such a success, and to Jim's successes there were no externals. Thirty miles of forest shut it off from the sight of an indifferent world, and the noise of the white surf along the coast overpowered the voice of fame. The stream of civilisation, as if divided on a headland a hundred miles north of Patusan, branches east and south-east, leaving its plains and valleys, its old trees and its old mankind, neglected and isolated, such as an insignificant and crumbling islet between the two branches of a mighty, devouring stream. You find the name of the country pretty often in collections of old voyages. The seventeenth-century traders went there for pepper, because the passion for pepper seemed to burn like a flame of love in the breast of Dutch and English adventurers about the time of James the First. Where wouldn't they go for pepper! For a bag of pepper they would cut each other's throats without hesitation, and would forswear their souls, of which they were so careful otherwise: the bizarre obstinacy of that desire made them defy death in a thousand shapes—the unknown seas, the loathsome and strange diseases; wounds, captivity, hunger, pestilence, and despair. It made them great! By heavens! it made them heroic; and it made them pathetic too in their craving for trade with the inflexible death levying its toll on young and old. It seems impossible to believe that mere greed could hold men to such a steadfastness of purpose, to such a blind persistence in endeavour and sacrifice. And indeed those who adventured their persons and lives risked all they had for a slender reward. They left their bones to lie bleaching on distant shores, so that wealth might flow to the living at home. To us, their less tried successors, they appear magnified, not as agents of trade but as instruments of a recorded destiny, pushing out into the unknown in obedience to an inward voice, to an impulse beating in the blood, to a dream of the future. They were wonderful; and it must be owned they were ready for the wonderful. They recorded it complacently in their sufferings, in the aspect of the seas, in the customs of strange nations, in the glory of splendid rulers.

"In Patusan they had found lots of pepper, and had been impressed by the magnificence and the wisdom of the Sultan; but somehow, after a century of chequered intercourse, the country seems to drop gradually out of the trade. Perhaps the pepper had given out. Be it as it may, nobody cares for it now; the glory has departed, the Sultan is an imbecile youth with two thumbs on his left hand and an uncertain and beggarly revenue extorted from a miserable population and stolen from him by his many uncles.

"This of course I have from Stein. He gave me their names and a short sketch of life and character of each. He was as full of information about native states as an official report, but infinitely more amusing. He *had* to know. He traded in so many, and in some districts—as in Patusan, for instance—his firm was the only one to have an agency by special permit from the Dutch authorities. The Government trusted his discretion, and it was understood that he took all the risks. The men he employed understood that too, but he made it worth their while apparently. He was perfectly frank with me over the breakfast-table in the morning. As far as he was aware (the last news was thirteen months old he stated precisely), utter insecurity for life and property was the normal condition. There were in Patusan antagonistic forces,[1] and one of them was Rajah Allang,[2] the worst of the Sultan's uncles, the governor of the river, who did the extorting and the stealing, and ground down to the point of extinction the country-born Malays, who, utterly defenceless, had not even the resource of emigrating—'For indeed,' as Stein remarked, 'where could they go, and how could they get away?' No doubt they did not even desire to get away. The world (which is circumscribed by lofty impassable mountains) has been given into the hand of the highborn, and this Rajah they knew: he was of their own royal house. I had the pleasure of meeting the gentleman later on. He was a dirty, little, used-up old man with evil eyes and a weak mouth, who swallowed an opium pill every two hours, and in defiance of common decency wore his hair uncovered and falling in wild stringy locks about his wizened grimy face. When giving audience he would clamber upon a sort of narrow stage erected in a hall like a ruinous barn with a rotten bamboo floor, through the cracks of which you could see, twelve or fifteen feet below, the heaps of refuse and garbage of all kinds lying under the house. That is where and how he received us when, accompanied by Jim, I paid him a visit of ceremony. There were about forty people in the room, and perhaps three times as many in the great courtyard below. There was constant movement, coming and going, pushing and murmuring, at our backs. A few youths in gay silks glared from the distance; the majority, slaves and humble dependants, were half naked, in ragged sarongs, dirty with ashes and mud-stains. I had never seen Jim look so grave, so self-possessed, in an impenetrable, impressive way. In the midst of these dark-faced men, his stalwart figure in white apparel, the gleaming clusters of his fair hair, seemed to catch all the sunshine that trickled through the cracks in the closed shutters of that dim hall, with its walls of mats and a roof of thatch. He appeared like a creature not only of another kind but of another essence. Had they not seen him come up in a canoe they might have thought he had descended upon them from the clouds. He did, however, come in a crazy dug-out, sitting (very still and with his knees together, for fear of overturning the thing)—sitting

1. According to Jerry Allen in *The Sea Years of Joseph Conrad* (Garden City, N.Y.: Doubleday, 1965), the history of Berau is roughly as follows. By the beginning of the nineteenth century, when records were first kept, Berau had long been under the control of Malay Moslems who had subdued the native, pagan, forest-Dyaks. After a protracted civil war, the district of Sambaliung became an independent sultanate in 1844, the remainder becoming the sultanate of Gunung Tabur. Sporadically, these two sultanates, facing each other across the river, continued to wage war. In 1882, when the sultan of Gunung Tabur died, his son being too young to rule, his father's first cousin, Hadji Adji Kuning, became regent. By 1887, when Conrad stopped several times in Berau, the regent was levying exorbitant duty on all exports, mistreating the native population, and fomenting new trouble with the sultan of Sambaliung.
2. The name comes from Major Fred McNair's *Perak and the Malays* (London, 1878). The names of Doramin and Tamb' Itam ("black messenger") come from the same source.

on a tin box—which I had lent him—nursing on his lap a revolver of the navy pattern—presented by me on parting—which, through an interposition of Providence, or through some wrong-headed notion, that was just like him, or else from sheer instinctive sagacity, he had decided to carry unloaded. That's how he ascended the Patusan river. Nothing could have been more prosaic and more unsafe, more extravagantly casual, more lonely. Strange, this fatality that would cast the complexion of a flight upon all his acts, of impulsive unreflecting desertion—of a jump into the unknown.

"It is precisely the casualness of it that strikes me most. Neither Stein nor I had a clear conception of what might be on the other side when we, metaphorically speaking, took him up and hove him over the wall with scant ceremony. At the moment I merely wished to achieve his disappearance; Stein characteristically enough had a sentimental motive. He had a notion of paying off (in kind, I suppose) the old debt he had never forgotten. Indeed he had been all his life especially friendly to anybody from the British Isles. His late benefactor, it is true, was a Scot—even to the length of being called Alexander M'Neil—and Jim came from a long way south of the Tweed;[3] but at the distance of six or seven thousand miles Great Britain, though never diminished, looks foreshortened enough even to its own children to rob such details of their importance. Stein was excusable, and his hinted intentions were so generous that I begged him most earnestly to keep them secret for a time. I felt that no consideration of personal advantage should be allowed to influence Jim; that not even the risk of such influence should be run. We had to deal with another sort of reality. He wanted a refuge, and a refuge at the cost of danger should be offered him—nothing more.

"Upon every other point I was perfectly frank with him, and I even (as I believed at the time) exaggerated the danger of the undertaking. As a matter of fact I did not do it justice; his first day in Patusan was nearly his last—would have been his last if he had not been so reckless or so hard on himself and had condescended to load that revolver. I remember, as I unfolded our precious scheme for his retreat, how his stubborn but weary resignation was gradually replaced by surprise, interest, wonder, and by boyish eagerness. This was a chance he had been dreaming of. He couldn't think how he merited that I . . . He would be shot if he could see to what he owed . . . And it was Stein, Stein the merchant, who . . . but of course it was me he had to . . . I cut him short. He was not articulate, and his gratitude caused me inexplicable pain. I told him that if he owed this chance to any one especially, it was to an old Scot of whom he had never heard, who had died many years ago, of whom little was remembered besides a roaring voice and a rough sort of honesty. There was really no one to receive his thanks. Stein was

3. A river forming part of the border between Scotland and England.

passing on to a young man the help he had received in his own young days, and I had done no more than to mention his name. Upon this he coloured, and, twisting a bit of paper in his fingers, he remarked bashfully that I had always trusted him.

"I admitted that such was the case, and added after a pause that I wished he had been able to follow my example. 'You think I don't?' he asked uneasily, and remarked in a mutter that one had to get some sort of show first; then brightening up, and in a loud voice he protested he would give me no occasion to regret my confidence, which—which . . .

" 'Do not misapprehend,' I interrupted. 'It is not in your power to make me regret anything.' There would be no regrets; but if there were, it would be altogether my own affair: on the other hand, I wished him to understand clearly that this arrangement, this—this—experiment, was his own doing; he was responsible for it and no one else. 'Why? Why!' he stammered, 'this is the very thing that I' . . . I begged him not to be dense, and he looked more puzzled than ever. He was in a fair way to make life intolerable to himself. . . . 'Do you think so?' he asked disturbed; but in a moment added confidently, 'I was going on though. Was I not?' It was impossible to be angry with him: I could not help a smile, and told him that in the old days people who went on like this were on the way of becoming hermits in a wilderness. 'Hermits be hanged!' he commented with engaging impulsiveness. Of course he didn't mind a wilderness. . . . 'I was glad of it,' I said. That was where he would be going to. He would find it lively enough, I ventured to promise. 'Yes, yes,' he said keenly. He had shown a desire, I continued inflexibly, to go out and shut the door after him. . . . 'Did I?' he interrupted in a strange access of gloom that seemed to envelop him from head to foot like the shadow of a passing cloud. He was wonderfully expressive after all. Wonderfully! 'Did I?' he repeated bitterly. 'You can't say I made much noise about it. And I can keep it up too—only, confound it! you show me a door.' . . . 'Very well. Pass on,' I struck in. I could make him a solemn promise that it would be shut behind him with a vengeance. His fate, whatever it was, would be ignored, because the country, for all its rotten state, was not judged ripe for interference. Once he got in, it would be for the outside world as though he had never existed. He would have nothing but the soles of his two feet to stand upon, and he would have first to find his ground at that. 'Never existed—that's it, by Jove,' he murmured to himself. His eyes, fastened upon my lips, sparkled. If he had thoroughly understood the conditions, I concluded, he had better jump into the first gharry he could see and drive on to Stein's house for his final instructions. He flung out of the room before I had fairly finished speaking."

Chapter XXIII

"He did not return till next morning. He had been kept to dinner and for the night. There never had been such a wonderful man as Mr Stein. He had in his pocket a letter for Cornelius ('the Johnnie who's going to get the sack,' he explained with a momentary drop in his elation), and he exhibited with glee a silver ring, such as natives use, worn down very thin and showing faint traces of chasing.

"This was his introduction to an old chap called Doramin—one of the principal men out there—a big pot—who had been Mr Stein's friend in that country where he had all these adventures. Mr Stein called him 'war-comrade.' War-comrade was good. Wasn't it? And didn't Mr Stein speak English wonderfully well? Said he had learned it in Celebes—of all places! That was awfully funny. Was it not? He did speak with an accent—a twang—did I notice? That chap Doramin had given him the ring. They had exchanged presents when they parted for the last time. Sort of promising eternal friendship. He called it fine—did I not? They had to make a dash for dear life out of the country when that Mohammed—Mohammed—What's-his-name had been killed. I knew the story, of course. Seemed a beastly shame, didn't it? . . .

"He ran on like this, forgetting his plate, with a knife and fork in hand (he had found me at tiffin), slightly flushed, and with his eyes darkened many shades, which was with him a sign of excitement. The ring was a sort of credential. ('It's like something you read of in books,' he threw in appreciatively), and Doramin would do his best for him. Mr Stein had been the means of saving that chap's life on some occasion; purely by accident, Mr Stein had said, but he—Jim—had his own opinion about that. Mr Stein was just the man to look out for such accidents. No matter. Accident or purpose, this would serve his turn immensely. Hoped to goodness the jolly old beggar had not gone off the hooks meantime.[1] Mr Stein could not tell. There had been no news for more than a year; they were kicking up no end of an all-fired row amongst themselves, and the river was closed. Jolly awkward, this; but, no fear; he would manage to find a crack to get in.

"He impressed, almost frightened me with his elated rattle. He was voluble like a youngster on the eve of a long holiday with a prospect of delightful scrapes, and such an attitude of mind in a grown man and in this connection had in it something phenomenal, a little mad, dangerous, unsafe. I was on the point of entreating him to take things seriously when he dropped his knife and fork (he had begun eating, or rather swallowing food, as it were, unconsciously), and began a search all round his plate. The ring! The ring! Where the devil . . . Ah! Here it was . . . He closed his big hand on it, and tried all his pockets one

1. Lost his reason.

after another. Jove! wouldn't do to lose the thing. He meditated gravely over his fist. Had it? Would hang the bally affair round his neck! And he proceeded to do this immediately, producing a string (which looked like a bit of a cotton shoe-lace) for the purpose. There! That would do the trick! It would be the deuce if . . . He seemed to catch sight of my face for the first time, and it steadied him a little. I probably didn't realise, he said with a naïve gravity, how much importance he attached to that token. It meant a friend; and it is a good thing to have a friend. He knew something about that. He nodded at me expressively, but before my disclaiming gesture he leaned his head on his hand and for a while sat silent, playing thoughtfully with the bread-crumbs on the cloth . . . 'Slam the door—that was jolly well put,' he cried, and jumping up, began to pace the room, reminding me by the set of the shoulders, the turn of his head, the headlong and uneven stride, of that night when he had paced thus, confessing, explaining—what you will—but, in the last instance, living—living before me, under his own little cloud, with all his unconscious subtlety which could draw consolation from the very source of sorrow. It was the same mood, the same and different, like a fickle companion that to-day guiding you on the true path, with the same eyes, the same step, the same impulse, to-morrow will lead you hopelessly astray. His tread was assured, his straying, darkened eyes seemed to search the room for something. One of his footfalls somehow sounded louder than the other—the fault of his boots probably—and gave a curious impression of an invisible halt in his gait. One of his hands was rammed deep into his trousers' pocket, the other waved suddenly above his head. 'Slam the door!' he shouted. 'I've been waiting for that. I'll show yet . . . I'll . . . I'm ready for any confounded thing . . . I've been dreaming of it . . . Jove! Get out of this. Jove! This is luck at last . . . You wait. I'll . . .'

"He tossed his head fearlessly, and I confess that for the first and last time in our acquaintance I perceived myself unexpectedly to be thoroughly sick of him. Why these vapourings? He was stumping about the room flourishing his arm absurdly, and now and then feeling on his breast for the ring under his clothes. Where was the sense of such exaltation in a man appointed to be a trading-clerk, and in a place where there was no trade—at that? Why hurl defiance at the universe? This was not a proper frame of mind to approach any undertaking; an improper frame of mind not only for him, I said, but for any man. He stood still over me. Did I think so? he asked, by no means subdued, and with a smile in which I seemed to detect suddenly something insolent. But then I am twenty years his senior. Youth *is* insolent; it is its right—its necessity; it has got to assert itself, and all assertion in this world of doubts is a defiance, is an insolence. He went off into a far corner, and coming back, he, figuratively speaking, turned to rend me. I spoke like that because I—even I, who had been no end kind to him—even I remembered—remembered—against him—what—what had happened. And what about others—the—the—world. Where's the wonder he wanted to get out, meant to get out, meant to stay out—by heavens! And I talked about proper frames of mind!

"'It is not I or the world who remember,' I shouted. 'It is you—you, who remember.'

"He did not flinch, and went on with heat, 'Forget everything, everybody, everybody.' . . . His voice fell . . . 'But you,' he added.

"'Yes—me too—if it would help,' I said, also in a low tone. After this we remained silent and languid for a time as if exhausted. Then he began again, composedly, and told me that Mr Stein had instructed him to wait for a month or so, to see whether it was possible for him to remain, before he began building a new house for himself, so as to avoid 'vain expense.' He did make use of funny expressions—Stein did. 'Vain expense' was good. . . . Remain? Why! of course. He would hang on. Let him only get in—that's all; he would answer for it he would remain. Never get out. It was easy enough to remain.

"'Don't be foolhardy,' I said, rendered uneasy by his threatening tone. 'If you only live long enough you will want to come back.'

"'Come back to what?' he asked absently, with his eyes fixed upon the face of a clock on the wall.

"I was silent for a while. 'Is it to be never, then?' I said. 'Never,' he repeated dreamily without looking at me, and then flew into sudden activity. 'Jove! Two o'clock, and I sail at four!'

"It was true. A brigantine of Stein's was leaving for the westward that afternoon, and he had been instructed to take his passage in her, only no orders to delay the sailing had been given. I suppose Stein forgot. He made a rush to get his things while I went aboard my ship, where he promised to call on his way to the outer roadstead. He turned up accordingly in a great hurry and with a small leather valise in his hand. This wouldn't do, and I offered him an old tin trunk of mine supposed to be water-tight, or at least damp-tight. He effected the transfer by the simple process of shooting out the contents of his valise as you would empty a sack of wheat. I saw three books in the tumble; two small, in dark covers, and a thick green-and-gold volume—a half-crown complete Shakespeare. 'You read this?' I asked. 'Yes. Best thing to cheer up a fellow,' he said hastily. I was struck by this appreciation, but there was no time for Shakespearian talk. A heavy revolver and two small boxes of cartridges were lying on the cuddy-table. 'Pray take this,' I said. 'It may help you to remain.' No sooner were these words out of my mouth than I perceived what grim meaning they could bear. 'May help you to get in,' I corrected myself remorsefully. He however was not troubled by obscure meanings; he thanked me effusively and bolted out, calling Good-bye over his shoulder. I heard his voice through the ship's side urging his boatmen to give way, and looking out of the stern-port I saw the boat rounding under the counter. He sat in her leaning forward, exciting his men with voice and gestures; and as he had kept the revolver in his hand and seemed to be presenting it at their heads, I shall never forget the scared faces of the four Javanese, and the frantic swing of their stroke which snatched that vision from under my eyes. Then turning away, the first thing I saw were the two boxes of cartridges on the cuddy-table. He had forgotten to take them.

"I ordered my gig manned at once; but Jim's rowers, under the impression that their lives hung on a thread while they had that madman in the boat, made such excellent time that before I had traversed half the distance between the two vessels I caught sight of him clambering over the rail, and of his box being passed up. All the brigantine's canvas was loose, her mainsail was set, and the windlass was just beginning to clink as I stepped upon her deck: her master, a dapper little half-caste of forty or so, in a blue flannel suit, with lively eyes, his round face the colour of lemon-peel, and with a thin little black moustache drooping on each side of his thick, dark lips, came forward smirking. He turned out, notwithstanding his self-satisfied and cheery exterior, to be of a careworn temperament. In answer to a remark of mine (while Jim had gone below for a moment) he said, 'Oh yes. Patusan.' He was going to carry the gentleman to the mouth of the river, but would 'never ascend.' His flowing English seemed to be derived from a dictionary compiled by a lunatic. Had Mr Stein desired him to 'ascend,' he would have 'reverentially'—(I think he wanted to say respectfully—but devil only knows)—'reverentially made objects for the safety of properties.' If disregarded, he would have presented 'resignation to quit.' Twelve months ago he had made his last voyage there, and though Mr Cornelius 'propitiated many offertories' to Mr Rajah Allang and the 'principal populations,' on conditions which made the trade 'a snare and ashes in the mouth,' yet his ship had been fired upon from the woods by 'irresponsive parties' all the way down the river; which causing his crew 'from exposure to limb to remain silent in hidings,' the brigantine was nearly stranded on a sandbank at the bar, where she 'would have been perishable beyond the act of man.' The angry disgust at the recollection, the pride of his fluency, to which he turned an attentive ear, struggled for the possession of his broad simple face. He scowled and beamed at me, and watched with satisfaction the undeniable effect of his phraseology. Dark frowns ran swiftly over the placid sea, and the brigantine, with her fore-topsail to the mast and her main-boom amidships, seemed bewildered amongst the cat's-paws. He told me further, gnashing his teeth, that the Rajah was a 'laughable hyæna' (can't imagine how he got hold of hyænas); while somebody else was many times falser than the 'weapons of a crocodile.' Keeping one eye on the movements of his crew forward, he let loose his volubility—comparing the place to a 'cage of beasts made ravenous by long impenitence.' I fancy he meant impunity. He had no

intention, he cried, to 'exhibit himself to be made attached purposefully to robbery.' The long-drawn wails, giving the time for the pull of the men catting the anchor, came to an end, and he lowered his voice. 'Plenty too much enough of Patusan,' he concluded, with energy.

"I heard afterwards he had been so indiscreet as to get himself tied up by the neck with a rattan halter to a post planted in the middle of a mud-hole before the Rajah's house. He spent the best part of a day and a whole night in that unwholesome situation, but there is every reason to believe the thing had been meant as a sort of joke. He brooded for a while over that horrid memory, I suppose, and then addressed in a quarrelsome tone the man coming aft to the helm. When he turned to me again it was to speak judicially, without passion. He would take the gentleman to the mouth of the river at Batu Kring (Patusan town 'being situated internally,' he remarked, 'thirty miles'). But in his eyes, he continued—a tone of bored, weary conviction replacing his previous voluble delivery—the gentleman was already 'in the similitude of a corpse.' 'What? What do you say?' I asked. He assumed a startlingly ferocious demeanour, and imitated to perfection the act of stabbing from behind. 'Already like the body of one deported,' he explained, with the insufferably conceited air of his kind after what they imagine a display of cleverness. Behind him I perceived Jim smiling silently at me, and with a raised hand checking the exclamation on my lips.

"Then, while the half-caste, bursting with importance, shouted his orders, while the yards swung creaking and the heavy boom came surging over, Jim and I, alone as it were, to leeward of the mainsail, clasped each other's hands and exchanged the last hurried words. My heart was freed from that dull resentment which had existed side by side with interest in his fate. The absurd chatter of the half-caste had given more reality to the miserable dangers of his path than Stein's careful statements. On that occasion the sort of formality that had been always present in our intercourse vanished from our speech; I believe I called him 'dear boy,' and he tacked on the words 'old man' to some half-uttered expression of gratitude, as though his risk set off against my years had made us more equal in age and in feeling. There was a moment of real and profound intimacy, unexpected and short-lived like a glimpse of some everlasting, of some saving truth. He exerted himself to soothe me as though he had been the more mature of the two. 'All right, all right,' he said rapidly and with feeling. 'I promise to take care of myself. Yes; I won't take any risks. Not a single blessed risk. Of course not. I mean to hang out. Don't you worry; Jove! I feel as if nothing could touch me. Why! this is luck from the word Go. I wouldn't spoil such a magnificent chance!' . . . A magnificent chance! Well, it *was* magnificent, but chances are what men make them, and how was I to know. As he had said, even I—even I remembered—his—his misfortune against him. It was true. And the best thing for him was to go.

"My gig had dropped in the wake of the brigantine, and I saw him aft detached upon the light of the westering sun, raising his cap high above his head. I heard an indistinct shout, 'You—shall—hear—of—me.' Of me, or from me, I don't know which. I think it must have been *of* me. My eyes were too dazzled by the glitter of the sea below his feet to see him clearly; I am fated never to see him clearly; but I can assure you no man could have appeared less 'in the similitude of a corpse,' as that half-caste croaker had put it. I could see the little wretch's face, the shape and colour of a ripe pumpkin, poked out somewhere under Jim's elbow. He too raised his arm as if for a downward thrust. *Absit omen!*"[2]

Chapter XXIV

"The coast of Patusan (I saw it nearly two years afterwards) is straight and sombre, and faces a misty ocean. Red trails are seen like cataracts of rust streaming under the dark-green foliage of bushes and creepers clothing the low cliffs. Swampy plains open out at the mouth of rivers, with a view of jagged blue peaks beyond the vast forests. In the offing a chain of islands, dark, crumbling shapes, stand out in the everlasting sunlit haze like the remnants of a wall breached by the sea.

"There is a village of fisher-folk at the mouth of the Batu Kring branch of the estuary.[1] The river, which had been closed so long, was open then, and Stein's little schooner, in which I had my passage, worked her way up in three tides without being exposed to a fusilade from 'irresponsive parties.' Such a state of affairs belonged already to ancient history, if I could believe the elderly headman of the fishing village, who came on board to act as a sort of pilot. He talked to me (the second white man he had ever seen) with confidence, and most of his talk was about the first white man he had ever seen. He called him Tuan Jim, and the tone of his references was made remarkable by a strange mixture of familiarity and awe. They, in the village, were under that lord's special protection, which showed that Jim bore no grudge. If he had warned me that I would hear of him it was perfectly true. I was hearing of him. There was already a story that the tide had turned two hours before its time to help him on his journey up the river. The talkative old man himself had steered the canoe and had marvelled at the phenomenon. Moreover, all the glory was in his family. His son and his son-in-law had paddled; but they were only youths without experience, who did not notice the speed of the canoe till he pointed out to them the amazing fact.

"Jim's coming to that fishing village was a blessing; but to them, as

2. Evil omens aside (a proverbial Latin saying).
1. Navigation maps show a Batu Point at the mouth of the Berau River. In Malay *batu* means rock, and *kring* means dry.

to many of us, the blessing came heralded by terrors. So many generations had been released since the last white man had visited the river that the very tradition had been lost. The appearance of the being that descended upon them and demanded inflexibly to be taken up to Patusan was discomposing; his insistence was alarming; his generosity more than suspicious. It was an unheard-of request. There was no precedent. What would the Rajah say to this? What would he do to them? The best part of the night was spent in consultation; but the immediate risk from the anger of that strange man seemed so great that at last a cranky dug-out was got ready. The women shrieked with grief as it put off. A fearless old hag cursed the stranger.

"He sat in it, as I've told you, on his tin box, nursing the unloaded revolver on his lap. He sat with precaution—than which there is nothing more fatiguing—and thus entered the land he was destined to fill with the fame of his virtues, from the blue peaks inland to the white ribbon of surf on the coast. At the first bend he lost sight of the sea with its labouring waves for ever rising, sinking, and vanishing to rise again— the very image of struggling mankind,—and faced the immovable forests rooted deep in the soil, soaring towards the sunshine, everlasting in the shadowy might of their tradition, like life itself. And his opportunity sat veiled by his side like an Eastern bride waiting to be uncovered by the hand of the master. He too was the heir of a shadowy and mighty tradition! He told me, however, that he had never in his life felt so depressed and tired as in that canoe. All the movement he dared to allow himself was to reach, as it were by stealth, after the shell of half a cocoanut floating between his shoes, and bale some of the water out with a carefully restrained action. He discovered how hard the lid of a block-tin case was to sit upon. He had heroic health; but several times during that journey he experienced fits of giddiness, and between whiles he speculated hazily as to the size of the blister the sun was raising on his back. For amusement he tried by looking ahead to decide whether the muddy object he saw lying on the water's edge was a log of wood or an alligator. Only very soon he had to give that up. No fun in it. Always alligator. One of them flopped into the river and all but capsized the canoe. But this excitement was over directly. Then in a long empty reach he was very grateful to a troop of monkeys who came right down on the bank and made an insulting hullabaloo on his passage. Such was the way in which he was approaching greatness as genuine as any man ever achieved. Principally, he longed for sunset; and meantime his three paddlers were preparing to put into execution their plan of delivering him up to the Rajah.

" 'I suppose I must have been stupid with fatigue, or perhaps I did doze off for a time,' he said. The first thing he knew was his canoe coming to the bank. He became instantaneously aware of the forest having been left behind, of the first houses being visible higher up, of a stockade on his left, and of his boatmen leaping out together upon a low point of land and taking to their heels. Instinctively he leaped out after them. At first he thought himself deserted for some inconceivable reason, but he heard excited shouts, a gate swung open, and a lot of people poured out, making towards him. At the same time a boat full of armed men appeared on the river and came alongside his empty canoe, thus shutting off his retreat.

" 'I was too startled to be quite cool—don't you know? and if that revolver had been loaded I would have shot somebody—perhaps two, three bodies, and that would have been the end of me. But it wasn't. . . .' 'Why not?' I asked. 'Well, I couldn't fight the whole population, and I wasn't coming to them as if I were afraid of my life,' he said, with just a faint hint of his stubborn sulkiness in the glance he gave me. I refrained from pointing out to him that they could not have known the chambers were actually empty. He had to satisfy himself in his own way. . . . 'Anyhow it wasn't,' he repeated good-humouredly, 'and so I just stood still and asked them what was the matter. That seemed to strike them dumb. I saw some of these thieves going off with my box. That long-legged old scoundrel Kassim (I'll show him to you to-morrow) ran out fussing to me about the Rajah wanting to see me. I said, "All right." I too wanted to see the Rajah, and I simply walked in through the gate and—and—here I am.' He laughed, and then with unexpected emphasis, 'And do you know what's the best in it?' he asked. 'I'll tell you. It's the knowledge that had I been wiped out it is this place that would have been the loser.'

"He spoke thus to me before his house on that evening I've mentioned—after we had watched the moon float away above the chasm between the hills like an ascending spirit out of a grave; its sheen descended, cold and pale, like the ghost of dead sunlight. There is something haunting in the light of the moon; it has all the dispassionateness of a disembodied soul, and something of its inconceivable mystery. It is to our sunshine which—say what you like—is all we have to live by, what the echo is to the sound: misleading and confusing whether the note be mocking or sad. It robs all forms of matter—which, after all, is our domain—of their substance, and gives a sinister reality to shadows alone. And the shadows were very real around us, but Jim by my side looked very stalwart, as though nothing—not even the occult power of moonlight—could rob him of his reality in my eyes. Perhaps, indeed, nothing could touch him since he had survived the assault of the dark powers. All was silent, all was still; even on the river the moonbeams slept as on a pool. It was the moment of high water, a moment of immobility that accentuated the utter isolation of this lost corner of the earth. The houses crowding along the wide shining sweep without ripple or glitter, stepping into the water in a line of jostling, vague, grey, silvery forms mingled with black masses of shadow, were like a spectral herd of shapeless creatures pressing forward to drink in a spectral and lifeless stream. Here and there a red gleam twinkled within the bamboo walls, warm, like a living spark, significant of human affections, of shelter, of repose.

"He confessed to me that he often watched these tiny warm gleams go out one by one, that he loved to see people go to sleep under his eyes, confident in the security of to-morrow. 'Peaceful here, hey?' he asked. He was not eloquent, but there was a deep meaning in the words that followed. 'Look at these houses; there's not one where I am not trusted. Jove! I told you I would hang on. Ask any man, woman, or child . . .' He paused. 'Well, I am all right anyhow.'

"I observed quickly that he had found that out in the end. I had been sure of it, I added. He shook his head. 'Were you?' He pressed my arm lightly above the elbow. 'Well, then—you were right.'

"There was elation and pride, there was awe almost, in that low exclamation. 'Jove!' he cried, 'only think what it is to me.' Again he pressed my arm. 'And you asked me whether I thought of leaving. Good God! I! want to leave! Especially now after what you told me of Mr Stein's . . . Leave! Why! That's what I was afraid of. It would have been—it would have been harder than dying. No—on my word. Don't laugh. I must feel—every day, every time I open my eyes—that I am trusted—that nobody has a right—don't you know? Leave! For where? What for? To get what?'

"I had told him (indeed it was the main object of my visit) that it was Stein's intention to present him at once with the house and the stock of trading goods, on certain easy conditions which would make the transaction perfectly regular and valid. He began to snort and plunge at first. 'Confound your delicacy!' I shouted. 'It isn't Stein at all. It's giving you what you had made for yourself. And in any case keep your remarks for M'Neil—when you meet him in the other world. I hope it won't happen soon. . . .' He had to give in to my arguments, because all his conquests, the trust, the fame, the friendships, the love,—all these things that made him master had made him a captive too. He looked with an owner's eye at the peace of the evening, at the river, at the houses, at the everlasting life of the forests, at the life of the old mankind, at the secrets of the land, at the pride of his own heart; but it was they that possessed him and made him their own to the innermost thought, to the slightest stir of blood, to his last breath.

"It was something to be proud of. I too was proud—for him, if not so certain of the fabulous value of the bargain. It was wonderful. It was not so much of his fearlessness that I thought. It is strange how little account I took of it: as if it had been something too conventional to be at the root of the matter. No. I was more struck by the other gifts he had displayed. He had proved his grasp of the unfamiliar situation, his intellectual alertness in that field of thought. There was his readiness

too! Amazing. And all this had come to him in a manner like keen
scent to a well-bred hound. He was not eloquent, but there was a dignity
in this constitutional reticence, there was a high seriousness in his stammerings. He had still his old trick of stubborn blushing. Now and then,
though, a word, a sentence, would escape him that showed how deeply,
how solemnly, he felt about that work which had given him the certitude
of rehabilitation. That is why he seemed to love the land and the people
with a sort of fierce egoism, with a contemptuous tenderness."

Chapter XXV

" 'This is where I was prisoner for three days,' he murmured to me (it
was on the occasion of our visit to the Rajah), while we were making
our way slowly through a kind of awestruck riot of dependants across
Tunku Allang's courtyard. 'Filthy place, isn't it? And I couldn't get
anything to eat either, unless I made a row about it, and then it was
only a small plate of rice and a fried fish not much bigger than a
stickleback—confound them! Jove! I've been hungry prowling inside this
stinking enclosure with some of these vagabonds shoving their mugs
right under my nose. I had given up that famous revolver of yours at
the first demand. Glad to get rid of the bally thing. Looked like a fool
walking about with an empty shooting-iron in my hand.' At that moment
we came into the presence, and he became unflinchingly grave and
complimentary with his late captor. Oh! magnificent! I want to laugh
when I think of it. But I was impressed too. The old disreputable Tunku
Allang could not help showing his fear (he was no hero, for all the tales
of his hot youth he was fond of telling); and at the same time there was
a wistful confidence in his manner towards his late prisoner. Note! Even
where he would be most hated he was still trusted. Jim—as far as I could
follow the conversation—was improving the occasion by the delivery of
a lecture. Some poor villagers had been waylaid and robbed while on
their way to Doramin's house with a few pieces of gum or bee's-wax
which they wished to exchange for rice. 'It was Doramin who was a
thief,' burst out the Rajah. A shaking fury seemed to enter that old frail
body. He writhed weirdly on his mat, gesticulating with his hands and
feet, tossing the tangled strings of his mop—an impotent incarnation of
rage. There were staring eyes and dropping jaws all around us. Jim began
to speak. Resolutely, coolly, and for some time he enlarged upon the
text that no man should be prevented from getting his food and his
children's food honestly. The other sat like a tailor at his board, one
palm on each knee, his head low, and fixing Jim through the grey hair
that fell over his very eyes. When Jim had done there was a great stillness.
Nobody seemed to breathe even; no one made a sound till the old Rajah

sighed faintly, and looking up, with a toss of his head, said quickly, 'You hear, my people! No more of these little games.' This decree was received in profound silence. A rather heavy man, evidently in a position of confidence, with intelligent eyes, a bony, broad, very dark face, and a cheerily officious manner (I learned later on he was the executioner), presented to us two cups of coffee on a brass tray, which he took from the hands of an inferior attendant. 'You needn't drink,' muttered Jim very rapidly. I didn't perceive the meaning at first, and only looked at him. He took a good sip and sat composedly, holding the saucer in his left hand. In a moment I felt excessively annoyed. 'Why the devil,' I whispered, smiling at him amiably, 'do you expose me to such a stupid risk?' I drank, of course, there was nothing for it, while he gave no sign, and almost immediately afterwards we took our leave. While we were going down the courtyard to our boat, escorted by the intelligent and cheery executioner, Jim said he was very sorry. It was the barest chance, of course. Personally he thought nothing of poison. The remotest chance. He was—he assured me—considered to be infinitely more useful than dangerous, and so . . . 'But the Rajah is afraid of you abominably. Anybody can see that,' I argued with, I own, a certain peevishness, and all the time watching anxiously for the first twist of some sort of ghastly colic. I was awfully disgusted. 'If I am to do any good here and preserve my position,' he said, taking his seat by my side in the boat, 'I must stand the risk: I take it once every month, at least. Many people trust me to do that—for them. Afraid of me. That's just it. Most likely he is afraid of me because I am not afraid of his coffee.' Then showing me a place on the north front of the stockade where the pointed tops of several stakes were broken, 'This is where I leaped over on my third day in Patusan. They haven't put new stakes there yet. Good leap, eh?' A moment later we passed the mouth of a muddy creek. 'This is my second leap. I had a bit of a run and took this one flying, but fell short. Thought I would leave my skin there. Lost my shoes struggling. And all the time I was thinking to myself how beastly it would be to get a jab with a bally long spear while sticking in the mud like this. I remember how sick I felt wriggling in that slime. I mean really sick—as if I had bitten something rotten.'

"That's how it was—and the opportunity ran by his side, leaped over the gap, floundered in the mud . . . still veiled. The unexpectedness of his coming was the only thing, you understand, that saved him from being at once dispatched with krisses and flung into the river. They had him, but it was like getting hold of an apparition, a wraith, a portent. What did it mean? What to do with it? Was it too late to conciliate him? Hadn't he better be killed without more delay? But what would happen then? Wretched old Allang went nearly mad with apprehension and through the difficulty of making up his mind. Several times the council was broken up, and the advisers made a break helter-skelter for the door and out on to the verandah. One—it is said—even jumped down to the ground—fifteen feet, I should judge—and broke his leg. The royal governor of Patusan had bizarre mannerisms, and one of them was to introduce boastful rhapsodies into every arduous discussion, when, getting gradually excited, he would end by flying off his perch with a kriss in his hand. But, barring such interruptions, the deliberations upon Jim's fate went on night and day.

"Meanwhile he wandered about the courtyard, shunned by some, glared at by others, but watched by all, and practically at the mercy of the first casual ragamuffin with a chopper, in there. He took possession of a small tumble-down shed to sleep in; the effluvia of filth and rotten matter incommoded him greatly: it seems he had not lost his appetite though, because—he told me—he had been hungry all the blessed time. Now and again 'some fussy ass' deputed from the council-room would come out running to him, and in honeyed tones would administer amazing interrogatories. 'Were the Dutch coming to take the country? Would the white man like to go back down the river? What was the object of coming to such a miserable country? The Rajah wanted to know whether the white man could repair a watch?' They did actually bring out to him a nickel clock of New England make, and out of sheer unbearable boredom he busied himself in trying to get the alarum to work. It was apparently when thus occupied in his shed that the true perception of his extreme peril dawned upon him. He dropped the thing—he says—'like a hot potato,' and walked out hastily, without the slightest idea of what he would, or indeed could, do. He only knew that the position was intolerable. He strolled aimlessly beyond a sort of ramshackle little granary on posts, and his eyes fell on the broken stakes of the palisade; and then—he says—at once, without any mental process as it were, without any stir of emotion, he set about his escape as if executing a plan matured for a month. He walked off carelessly to give himself a good run, and when he faced about there was some dignitary with two spearmen in attendance close at his elbow ready with a question. He started off 'from under his very nose,' went over 'like a bird,' and landed on the other side with a fall that jarred all his bones and seemed to split his head. He picked himself up instantly. He never thought of anything at the time; all he could remember—he said—was a great yell; the first houses of Patusan were before him four hundred yards away; he saw the creek, and as it were mechanically put on more pace. The earth seemed fairly to fly backwards under his feet. He took off from the last dry spot, felt himself flying through the air, felt himself, without any shock, planted upright in an extremely soft and sticky mudbank. It was only when he tried to move his legs and found he couldn't that, in his own words, 'he came to himself.' He began to think of the 'bally long spears.' As a matter of fact, considering that the people inside the stockade had to run to the gate, then get down to the landing-place, get into boats, and pull round a point of land, he had more advance than he imagined. Besides, it being low water, the creek was without water—you couldn't call it dry,—and practically he was safe for a time from everything but a very long shot perhaps. The higher firm ground was about six feet in front of him. 'I thought I would have to die there all the same,' he said. He reached and grabbed desperately with his hands, and only succeeded in gathering a horrible cold shiny heap of slime against his breast—up to his very chin. It seemed to him he was burying himself alive, and then he struck out madly, scattering the mud with his fists. It fell on his head, on his face, over his eyes, into his mouth. He told me that he remembered suddenly the courtyard, as you remember a place where you had been very happy years ago. He longed—so he said—to be back there again, mending the clock. Mending the clock—that was the idea. He made efforts, tremendous sobbing gasping efforts, efforts that seemed to burst his eyeballs in their sockets and make him blind, and culminating into one mighty supreme effort in the darkness to crack the earth asunder, to throw it off his limbs— and he felt himself creeping feebly up the bank. He lay full length on the firm ground and saw the light, the sky. Then as a sort of happy thought the notion came to him that he would go to sleep. He will have it that he *did* actually go to sleep; that he slept—perhaps for a minute, perhaps for twenty seconds, or only for one second, but he recollects distinctly the violent convulsive start of awakening. He remained lying still for a while, and then he arose muddy from head to foot and stood there, thinking he was alone of his kind for hundreds of miles, alone, with no help, no sympathy, no pity to expect from any one, like a hunted animal. The first houses were not more than twenty yards from him; and it was the desperate screaming of a frightened woman trying to carry off a child that started him again. He pelted straight on in his socks, be-plastered with filth out of all semblance to a human being. He traversed more than half the length of the settlement. The nimbler women fled right and left, the slower men just dropped whatever they had in their hands, and remained petrified with dropping jaws. He was a flying terror. He says he noticed the little children trying to run for life, falling on their little stomachs and kicking. He swerved between two houses up a slope, clambered in desperation over a barricade of felled trees (there wasn't a week without some fight in Patusan at that time), burst through a fence into a maize-patch, where a scared boy flung a stick at him, blundered upon a path, and ran all at once into the arms of several startled men. He just had breath enough to gasp out, 'Doramin! Doramin!' He remembers being half-carried, half-rushed to the top of the slope, and in a vast enclosure with palms and fruit-trees being run up to a large man sitting massively in a chair in the midst of the greatest possible commotion and excitement. He fumbled in mud and clothes to produce the ring, and, finding himself suddenly on his back, wondered who had knocked him down. They had simply let him go—don't you know?—but he couldn't stand. At the foot of the slope random shots were fired, and above the roofs of the settlement there rose a dull roar of amazement. But he was safe. Doramin's people were barricading the gate and pouring water down his throat; Doramin's old wife, full of business and commiseration, was issuing shrill orders to her girls. 'The old woman,' he said softly, 'made a to-do over me as if I had been her own son. They put me into an immense bed—her state bed—and she ran in and out wiping her eyes to give me pats on the back. I must have been a pitiful object. I just lay there like a log for I don't know how long.'

"He seemed to have a great liking for Doramin's old wife. She on her side had taken a motherly fancy to him. She had a round, nut-brown, soft face, all fine wrinkles, large, bright red lips (she chewed betel assiduously), and screwed up, winking, benevolent eyes. She was constantly in movement, scolding busily and ordering unceasingly a troop of young women with clear brown faces and big grave eyes, her daughters, her servants, her slave-girls. You know how it is in these households: it's generally impossible to tell the difference. She was very spare, and even her ample outer garment, fastened in front with jewelled clasps, had somehow a skimpy effect. Her dark bare feet were thrust into yellow straw slippers of Chinese make. I have seen her myself flitting about with her extremely thick, long, grey hair falling about her shoulders. She uttered homely shrewd sayings, was of noble birth, and was eccentric and arbitrary. In the afternoon she would sit in a very roomy armchair, opposite her husband, gazing steadily through a wide opening in the wall which gave an extensive view of the settlement and the river.

"She invariably tucked up her feet under her, but old Doramin sat squarely, sat imposingly as a mountain sits on a plain. He was only of the *nakhoda* or merchant class, but the respect shown to him and the dignity of his bearing were very striking. He was the chief of the second power in Patusan. The immigrants from Celebes (about sixty families that, with dependants and so on, could muster some two hundred men 'wearing the kriss') had elected him years ago for their head. The men of that race are intelligent, enterprising, revengeful, but with a more frank courage than the other Malays, and restless under oppression. They formed the party opposed to the Rajah. Of course the quarrels were for trade. This was the primary cause of faction fights, of the sudden outbreaks that would fill this or that part of the settlement with smoke, flame, the noise of shots and shrieks. Villages were burnt, men were dragged into the Rajah's stockade to be killed or tortured for the crime of trading with anybody else but himself. Only a day or two before Jim's arrival several heads of households in the very fishing village that was afterwards taken under his especial protection had been driven over the cliffs by a party of the Rajah's spearmen, on suspicion of having been collecting edible birds' nests for a Celebes trader. Rajah Allang pretended to be the only trader in his country, and the penalty for the breach of the monopoly was death; but his idea of trading was indistinguishable from the commonest forms of robbery. His cruelty and rapacity had no other bounds than his cowardice, and he was afraid of the organised power of the Celebes men, only—till Jim came—he was not afraid enough to keep quiet. He struck at them through his subjects, and thought himself pathetically in the right. The situation was complicated by a wandering stranger, an Arab half-breed, who, I believe, on purely religious grounds, had incited the tribes in the interior (the bush-folk, as Jim himself called them) to rise, and had established himself in a fortified camp on the summit of one of the twin hills. He hung over the town of Patusan like a hawk over a poultry-yard, but he devastated the open country. Whole villages, deserted, rotted on their blackened posts over the banks of clear streams, dropping piecemeal into the water the grass of their walls, the leaves of their roofs, with a curious effect of natural decay as if they had been a form of vegetation stricken by a blight at its very root. The two parties in Patusan were not sure which one this partisan most desired to plunder. The Rajah intrigued with him feebly. Some of the Bugis settlers, weary with endless insecurity, were half inclined to call him in. The younger spirits amongst them, chaffing, advised to 'get Sherif Ali with his wild men and drive the Rajah Allang out of the country.' Doramin restrained them with difficulty. He was growing old, and, though his influence had not diminished, the situation was getting beyond him. This was the state of affairs when Jim, bolting from the Rajah's stockade, appeared before the chief of the Bugis, produced the ring, and was received, in a manner of speaking, into the heart of the community."

Chapter XXVI

"Doramin was one of the most remarkable men of his race I had ever seen. His bulk for a Malay was immense, but he did not look merely fat; he looked imposing, monumental. This motionless body clad in rich stuffs, coloured silks, gold embroideries; this huge head, enfolded in a red-and-gold headkerchief; the flat, big, round face, wrinkled, furrowed, with two semicircular heavy folds starting on each side of wide, fierce nostrils, and enclosing a thick-lipped mouth; the throat like a bull; the vast corrugated brow overhanging the staring proud eyes,—made a whole that, once seen, can never be forgotten. His impassive repose (he seldom stirred a limb when once he sat down) was like a display of dignity. He was never known to raise his voice. It was a hoarse and powerful murmur, slightly veiled as if heard from a distance. When he walked, two short, sturdy young fellows, naked to the waist, in white sarongs and with black skull-caps on the backs of their heads, sustained his elbows: they would ease him down and stand behind his chair till he wanted to rise, when he would turn his head slowly, as if with difficulty, to the right and to the left, and then they would catch him under his armpits and help him up. For all that, there was nothing of a cripple about him: on the contrary, all his ponderous movements were like manifestations of a mighty deliberate force. It was generally believed he consulted his wife as to public affairs; but nobody, as far as I know, had ever heard them exchange a single word. When they sat in state by the wide opening it was in silence. They could see below them in the declining light the vast expanse of the forest country, a dark sleeping sea of sombre green undulating as far as the violet and purple range of mountains; the shining sinuosity of the river like an immense letter S of beaten silver; the brown ribbon of houses following the sweep of both banks, overtopped by the twin-hills uprising above the nearer tree-tops. They were wonderfully contrasted: she, light, delicate, spare, quick, a little witch-like, with a touch of motherly fussiness in her repose; he, facing her, immense and heavy, like a figure of a man roughly fashioned of stone, with something magnanimous and ruthless in his immobility. The son of these old people was a most distinguished youth.

"They had him late in life. Perhaps he was not really so young as he looked. Four- or five-and-twenty is not so young when a man is already father of a family at eighteen. When he entered the large room, lined and carpeted with fine mats, and with a high ceiling of white sheeting, where the couple sat in state surrounded by a most deferential retinue, he would make his way straight to Doramin, to kiss his hand—which the other abandoned to him, majestically—and then would step across to stand by his mother's chair. I suppose I may say they idolised him, but I never caught them giving him an overt glance. Those, it is true, were public functions. The room was generally thronged. The solemn formality of greetings and leave-takings, the profound respect expressed in gestures, on the faces, in the low whispers, is simply indescribable. 'It's well worth seeing,' Jim had assured me while we were crossing the river, on our way back. 'They are like people in a book, aren't they?' he said triumphantly. 'And Dain Waris[1]—their son—is the best friend (barring you) I ever had. What Mr Stein would call a good "war-comrade." I was in luck. Jove! I was in luck when I tumbled amongst them at my last gasp.' He meditated with bowed head, then rousing himself he added—

" 'Of course I didn't go to sleep over it, but . . .' He paused again. 'It seemed to come to me,' he murmured. 'All at once I saw what I had to do . . .'

1. Malay word for *heir*.

"There was no doubt that it had come to him; and it had come through war, too, as is natural, since this power that came to him was the power to make peace. It is in this sense alone that might so often *is* right. You must not think he had seen his way at once. When he arrived the Bugis community was in a most critical position. 'They were all afraid,' he said to me—'each man afraid for himself; while I could see as plain as possible that they must do something at once if they did not want to go under one after another, what between the Rajah and that vagabond Sherif.' But to see that was nothing. When he got his idea he had to drive it into reluctant minds, through the bulwarks of fear, of selfishness. He drove it in at last. And that was nothing. He had to devise the means. He devised them—an audacious plan; and his task was only half done. He had to inspire with his own confidence a lot of people who had hidden and absurd reasons to hang back; he had to conciliate imbecile jealousies, and argue away all sorts of senseless mistrusts. Without the weight of Doramin's authority, and his son's fiery enthusiasm, he would have failed. Dain Waris, the distinguished youth, was the first to believe in him; theirs was one of those strange, profound, rare friendships between brown and white, in which the very difference of race seems to draw two human beings closer by some mystic element of sympathy. Of Dain Waris, his own people said with pride that he knew how to fight like a white man. This was true; he had that sort of courage—the courage in the open, I may say,—but he had also a European mind. You meet them sometimes like that, and are surprised to discover unexpectedly a familiar turn of thought, an unobscured vision, a tenacity of purpose, a touch of altruism. Of small stature, but admirably well proportioned, Dain Waris had a proud carriage, a polished, easy bearing, a temperament like a clear flame. His dusky face, with big black eyes, was in action expressive, and in repose thoughtful. He was of a silent disposition; a firm glance, an ironic smile, a courteous deliberation of manner seemed to hint at great reserves of intelligence and power. Such beings open to the Western eye, so often concerned with mere surfaces, the hidden possibilities of races and lands over which hangs the mystery of unrecorded ages. He not only trusted Jim, he understood him, I firmly believe. I speak of him because he had captivated me. His—if I may say so—his caustic placidity, and, at the same time, his intelligent sympathy with Jim's aspirations, appealed to me. I seemed to behold the very origin of friendship. If Jim took the lead, the other had captivated his leader. In fact, Jim the leader was a captive in every sense. The land, the people, the friendship, the love, were like the jealous guardians of his body. Every day added a link to the fetters of that strange freedom. I felt convinced of it, as from day to day I learned more of the story.

"The story! Haven't I heard the story? I've heard it on the march, in camp (he made me scour the country after invisible game); I've listened to a good part of it on one of the twin-summits, after climbing the last hundred feet or so on my hands and knees. Our escort (we had volunteer followers from village to village) had camped meantime on a bit of level ground half-way up the slope, and in the still breathless evening the smell of wood-smoke reached our nostrils from below with the penetrating delicacy of some choice scent. Voices also ascended, wonderful in their distinct and immaterial clearness. Jim sat on the trunk of a felled tree, and pulling out his pipe began to smoke. A new growth of grass and bushes was springing up; there were traces of an earthwork under a mass of thorny twigs. 'It all started from here,' he said, after a long and meditative silence. On the other hill, two hundred yards across a sombre precipice, I saw a line of high blackened stakes, showing here and there ruinously—the remnants of Sherif Ali's impregnable camp.

"But it had been taken, though. That had been his idea. He had mounted Doramin's old ordnance on the top of that hill; two rusty iron 7-pounders, a lot of small brass cannon—currency cannon. But if the brass guns represent wealth, they can also, when crammed recklessly to the muzzle, send a solid shot to some little distance. The thing was to get them up there. He showed me where he had fastened the cables, explained how he had improvised a rude capstan out of a hollowed log turning upon a pointed stake, indicated with the bowl of his pipe the outline of the earthwork. The last hundred feet of the ascent had been the most difficult. He had made himself responsible for success on his own head. He had induced the war party to work hard all night. Big fires lighted at intervals blazed all down the slope, 'but up here,' he explained, 'the hoisting gang had to fly around in the dark.' From the top he saw men moving on the hillside like ants at work. He himself on that night had kept on rushing down and climbing up like a squirrel, directing, encouraging, watching all along the line. Old Doramin had himself carried up the hill in his arm-chair. They put him down on the level place upon the slope, and he sat there in the light of one of the big fires—'amazing old chap—real old chieftain,' said Jim, 'with his little fierce eyes—a pair of immense flintlock pistols on his knees. Magnificent things, ebony, silver-mounted, with beautiful locks and a calibre like an old blunderbuss. A present from Stein, it seems—in exchange for that ring, you know. Used to belong to good old M'Neil. God only knows how *he* came by them. There he sat, moving neither hand nor foot, a flame of dry brushwood behind him, and lots of people rushing about, shouting and pulling round him—the most solemn, imposing old chap you can imagine. *He* wouldn't have had much chance if Sherif Ali had let his infernal crew loose at us and stampeded my lot. Eh? Anyhow, he had come up there to die if anything went wrong. No mistake! Jove! It thrilled me to see him there—like a rock. But the Sherif must have thought us mad, and never troubled to come and see how we got on. Nobody believed it could be done. Why! I think the very chaps who pulled and shoved and sweated over it did not believe it could be done! Upon my word I don't think they did. . . .'

"He stood erect, the smouldering brier-wood in his clutch, with a smile on his lips and a sparkle in his boyish eyes. I sat on the stump of a tree at his feet, and below us stretched the land, the great expanse of the forests, sombre under the sunshine, rolling like a sea, with glints of winding rivers, the grey spots of villages, and here and there a clearing, like an islet of light amongst the dark waves of continuous tree-tops. A brooding gloom lay over this vast and monotonous landscape; the light fell on it as if into an abyss. The land devoured the sunshine; only far off, along the coast, the empty ocean, smooth and polished within the faint haze, seemed to rise up to the sky in a wall of steel.

"And there I was with him, high in the sunshine on the top of that historic hill of his. He dominated the forest, the secular gloom, the old mankind. He was like a figure set up on a pedestal, to represent in his persistent youth the power, and perhaps the virtues, of races that never grow old, that have emerged from the gloom. I don't know why he should always have appeared to me symbolic. Perhaps this is the real cause of my interest in his fate. I don't know whether it was exactly fair to him to remember the incident which had given a new direction to his life, but at that very moment I remembered very distinctly. It was like a shadow in the light."

Chapter XXVII

"Already the legend had gifted him with supernatural powers. Yes, it was said, there had been many ropes cunningly disposed, and a strange contrivance that turned by the efforts of many men, and each gun went up tearing slowly through the bushes, like a wild pig rooting its way in the undergrowth, but, . . . and the wisest shook their heads. There was something occult in all this, no doubt; for what is the strength of ropes and men's arms? There is a rebellious soul in things which must be overcome by powerful charms and incantations. Thus old Sura—a very respectable householder of Patusan—with whom I had a quiet chat one evening. However, Sura was a professional sorcerer also, who attended all the rice sowings and reapings for miles around for the purpose of subduing the stubborn souls of things. This occupation he seemed to think a most arduous one, and perhaps the souls of things are more stubborn than the souls of men. As to the simple folk of outlying villages, they believed and said (as the most natural thing in the world) that Jim had carried the guns up the hill on his back—two at a time.

"This would make Jim stamp his foot in vexation and exclaim with an exasperated little laugh, 'What can you do with such silly beggars?

They will sit up half the night talking bally rot, and the greater the lie the more they seem to like it.' You could trace the subtle influence of his surroundings in this irritation. It was part of his captivity. The earnestness of his denials was amusing, and at last I said, 'My dear fellow, you don't suppose *I* believe this.' He looked at me quite startled. 'Well, no! I suppose not,' he said, and burst into a Homeric peal of laughter. 'Well, anyhow the guns were there, and went off all together at sunrise. Jove! You should have seen the splinters fly,' he cried. By his side Dain Waris, listening with a quiet smile, dropped his eyelids and shuffled his feet a little. It appears that the success in mounting the guns had given Jim's people such a feeling of confidence that he ventured to leave the battery under charge of two elderly Bugis who had seen some fighting in their day, and went to join Dain Waris and the storming-party who were concealed in the ravine. In the small hours they began creeping up, and when two-thirds of the way up, lay in the wet grass waiting for the appearance of the sun, which was the agreed signal. He told me with what impatient anguishing emotion he watched the swift coming of the dawn; how, heated with the work and the climbing, he felt the cold dew chilling his very bones; how afraid he was he would begin to shiver and shake like a leaf before the time came for the advance. 'It was the slowest half-hour in my life,' he declared. Gradually the silent stockade came out on the sky above him. Men scattered all down the slope were crouching amongst the dark stones and dripping bushes. Dain Waris was lying flattened by his side. 'We looked at each other,' Jim said, resting a gentle hand on his friend's shoulder. 'He smiled at me as cheery as you please, and I dared not stir my lips for fear I would break out into a shivering fit. 'Pon my word, it's true! I had been streaming with perspiration when we took cover—so you may imagine . . .' He declared, and I believe him, that he had no fears as to the result. He was only anxious as to his ability to repress these shivers. He didn't bother about the result. He was bound to get to the top of that hill and stay there, whatever might happen. There could be no going back for him. Those people had trusted him implicitly. Him alone! His bare word. . . .

"I remember how, at this point, he paused with his eyes fixed upon me. 'As far as he knew, they never had an occasion to regret it yet,' he said. 'Never. He hoped to God they never would. Meantime—worse luck!—they had got into the habit of taking his word for anything and everything. I could have no idea! Why, only the other day an old fool he had never seen in his life came from some village miles away to find out if he should divorce his wife. Fact. Solemn word. That's the sort of thing . . . He wouldn't have believed it. Would I? Squatted on the verandah chewing betel-nut, sighing and spitting all over the place for more than an hour, and as glum as an undertaker before he came out with that dashed conundrum. That's the kind of thing that isn't so funny

as it looks. What was a fellow to say?—Good wife?—Yes. Good wife
—old though. Started a confounded long story about some brass pots.
Been living together for fifteen years—twenty years—could not tell. A
long, long time. Good wife. Beat her a little—not much—just a little,
when she was young. Had to—for the sake of his honour. Suddenly in
her old age she goes and lends three brass pots to her sister's son's wife,
and begins to abuse him every day in a loud voice. His enemies jeered
at him; his face was utterly blackened. Pots totally lost. Awfully cut up
about it. Impossible to fathom a story like that; told him to go home,
and promised to come along myself and settle it all. It's all very well to
grin, but it was the dashedest nuisance! A day's journey through the
forest, another day lost in coaxing a lot of silly villagers to get at the
rights of the affair. There was the making of a sanguinary shindy in
the thing. Every bally idiot took sides with one family or the other, and
one-half of the village was ready to go for the other half with anything
that came handy. Honour bright! No joke! . . . Instead of attending to
their bally crops. Got him the infernal pots back of course—and pacified
all hands. No trouble to settle it. Of course not. Could settle the deadliest
quarrel in the country by crooking his little finger. The trouble was to
get at the truth of anything. Was not sure to this day whether he had
been fair to all parties. It worried him. And the talk! Jove! There didn't
seem to be any head or tail to it. Rather storm a twenty-foot-high old
stockade any day. Much! Child's play to that other job. Wouldn't take
so long either. Well, yes; a funny set out, upon the whole—the fool
looked old enough to be his grandfather. But from another point of view
it was no joke. His word decided everything—ever since the smashing
of Sherif Ali. An awful responsibility,' he repeated. 'No, really—joking
apart, had it been three lives instead of three rotten brass pots it would
have been the same. . . .'

"Thus he illustrated the moral effect of his victory in war. It was in
truth immense. It had led him from strife to peace, and through death
into the innermost life of the people; but the gloom of the land spread
out under the sunshine preserved its appearance of inscrutable, of secular
repose. The sound of his fresh young voice (it's extraordinary how very
few signs of wear he showed) floated lightly, and passed away over the
unchanged face of the forests like the sound of the big guns on that cold
dewy morning when he had no other concern on earth but the proper
control of the chills in his body. With the first slant of sun-rays along
these immovable tree-tops the summit of one hill wreathed itself, with
heavy reports, in white clouds of smoke, and the other burst into an
amazing noise of yells, war-cries, shouts of anger, of surprise, of dismay.
Jim and Dain Waris were the first to lay their hands on the stakes. The
popular story has it that Jim with a touch of one finger had thrown down
the gate. He was, of course, anxious to disclaim this achievement. The
whole stockade—he would insist on explaining to you—was a poor affair

(Sherif Ali trusted mainly to the inaccessible position); and, anyway, the thing had been already knocked to pieces and only hung together by a miracle. He put his shoulder to it like a little fool and went in head over heels. Jove! If it hadn't been for Dain Waris, a pock-marked tattooed vagabond would have pinned him with his spear to a baulk of timber like one of Stein's beetles. The third man in, it seems, had been Tamb' Itam, Jim's own servant. This was a Malay from the north, a stranger who had wandered into Patusan, and had been forcibly detained by Rajah Allang as paddler of one of the state boats. He had made a bolt of it at the first opportunity, and finding a precarious refuge (but very little to eat) amongst the Bugis settlers, had attached himself to Jim's person. His complexion was very dark, his face flat, his eyes prominent and injected with bile. There was something excessive, almost fanatical, in his devotion to his 'white lord.' He was inseparable from Jim like a morose shadow. On state occasions he would tread on his master's heels, one hand on the haft of his kriss, keeping the common people at a distance by his truculent brooding glances. Jim had made him the headman of his establishment, and all Patusan respected and courted him as a person of much influence. At the taking of the stockade he had distinguished himself greatly by the methodical ferocity of his fighting. The storming party had come on so quick—Jim said—that notwithstanding the panic of the garrison, there was a 'hot five minutes hand-to-hand inside that stockade, till some bally ass set fire to the shelters of boughs and dry grass, and we all had to clear out for dear life.'

"The rout, it seems, had been complete. Doramin, waiting immovably in his chair on the hillside, with the smoke of the guns spreading slowly above his big head, received the news with a deep grunt. When informed that his son was safe and leading the pursuit, he, without another sound, made a mighty effort to rise; his attendants hurried to his help, and, held up reverently, he shuffled with great dignity into a bit of shade, where he laid himself down to sleep, covered entirely with a piece of white sheeting. In Patusan the excitement was intense. Jim told me that from the hill, turning his back on the stockade with its embers, black ashes, and half-consumed corpses, he could see time after time the open spaces between the houses on both sides of the stream fill suddenly with a seething rush of people and get empty in a moment. His ears caught feebly from below the tremendous din of gongs and drums; the wild shouts of the crowd reached him in bursts of faint roaring. A lot of streamers made a flutter as of little white, red, yellow birds amongst the brown ridges of roofs. 'You must have enjoyed it,' I murmured, feeling the stir of sympathetic emotion.

" 'It was . . . it was immense! Immense!' he cried aloud, flinging his arms open. The sudden movement startled me as though I had seen him bare the secrets of his breast to the sunshine, to the brooding forests, to the steely sea. Below us the town reposed in easy curves upon the banks of a stream whose current seemed to sleep. 'Immense!' he repeated for a third time, speaking in a whisper, for himself alone.

"Immense! No doubt it was immense; the seal of success upon his words, the conquered ground for the soles of his feet, the blind trust of men, the belief in himself snatched from the fire, the solitude of his achievement. All this, as I've warned you, gets dwarfed in the telling. I can't with mere words convey to you the impression of his total and utter isolation. I know, of course, he was in every sense alone of his kind there, but the unsuspected qualities of his nature had brought him in such close touch with his surroundings that this isolation seemed only the effect of his power. His loneliness added to his stature. There was nothing within sight to compare him with, as though he had been one of those exceptional men who can be only measured by the greatness of their fame; and his fame, remember, was the greatest thing around for many a day's journey. You would have to paddle, pole, or track a long weary way through the jungle before you passed beyond the reach of its voice. Its voice was not the trumpeting of the disreputable goddess we all know—not blatant—not brazen. It took its tone from the stillness and gloom of the land without a past, where his word was the one truth of every passing day. It shared something of the nature of that silence through which it accompanied you into unexplored depths, heard continuously by your side, penetrating, far-reaching—tinged with wonder and mystery on the lips of whispering men."

Chapter XXVIII

"The defeated Sherif Ali fled the country without making another stand, and when the miserable hunted villagers began to crawl out of the jungle back to their rotting houses, it was Jim who, in consultation with Dain Waris, appointed the headmen. Thus he became the virtual ruler of the land. As to old Tunku Allang, his fears at first had known no bounds. It is said that at the intelligence of the successful storming of the hill he flung himself, face down, on the bamboo floor of his audience-hall, and lay motionless for a whole night and a whole day, uttering stifled sounds of such an appalling nature that no man dared approach his prostrate form nearer than a spear's length. Already he could see himself driven ignominiously out of Patusan, wandering, abandoned, stripped, without opium, without his women, without followers, a fair game for the first comer to kill. After Sherif Ali his turn would come, and who could resist an attack led by such a devil? And indeed he owed his life and such authority as he still possessed at the time of my visit to Jim's idea of what was fair alone. The Bugis had been extremely anxious to pay off old scores, and the impassive old Doramin cherished the hope of yet seeing his son ruler of Patusan. During one of our interviews he deliberately allowed me to get a glimpse of this secret ambition. Nothing could be finer in its way than the dignified wariness of his approaches. He himself—he began by declaring—had used his strength in his young days, but now he had grown old and tired. . . . With his imposing bulk and haughty little eyes darting sagacious, inquisitive glances, he reminded one irresistibly of a cunning old elephant; the slow rise and fall of his vast breast went on powerful and regular, like the heave of a calm sea. He too, as he protested, had an unbounded confidence in Tuan Jim's wisdom. If he could only obtain a promise! One word would be enough! . . . His breathing silences, the low rumblings of his voice, recalled the last efforts of a spent thunderstorm.

"I tried to put the subject aside. It was difficult, for there could be no question that Jim had the power; in his new sphere there did not seem to be anything that was not his to hold or to give. But that, I repeat, was nothing in comparison with the notion, which occurred to me, while I listened with a show of attention, that he seemed to have come very near at last to mastering his fate. Doramin was anxious about the future of the country, and I was struck by the turn he gave to the argument. The land remains where God had put it, but white men—he said—they come to us and in a little while they go. They go away. Those they leave behind do not know when to look for their return. They go to their own land, to their people, and so this white man too would. . . . I don't know what induced me to commit myself at this point by a vigorous 'No, no.' The whole extent of this indiscretion became apparent when Doramin, turning full upon me his face, whose expression, fixed in rugged deep folds, remained unalterable, like a huge brown mask, said that this was good news indeed, reflectively; and then wanted to know why.

"His little, motherly witch of a wife sat on my other hand, with her head covered and her feet tucked up, gazing through the great shutter-hole. I could only see a straying lock of grey hair, a high cheek-bone, the slight masticating motion of the sharp chin. Without removing her eyes from the vast prospect of forests stretching as far as the hills, she asked me in a pitying voice why was it that he so young had wandered from his home, coming so far, through so many dangers? Had he no household there, no kinsmen in his own country? Had he no old mother, who would always remember his face? . . .

"I was completely unprepared for this. I could only mutter and shake my head vaguely. Afterwards I am perfectly aware I cut a very poor figure trying to extricate myself out of this difficulty. From that moment, however, the old *nakhoda* became taciturn. He was not very pleased, I fear, and evidently I had given him food for thought. Strangely enough, on the evening of that very day (which was my last in Patusan) I was once more confronted with the same question, with the unanswerable why of Jim's fate. And this brings me to the story of his love.

"I suppose you think it is a story that you can imagine for yourselves. We have heard so many such stories, and the majority of us don't believe them to be stories of love at all. For the most part we look upon them as stories of opportunities: episodes of passion at best, or perhaps only of youth and temptation, doomed to forgetfulness in the end, even if they pass through the reality of tenderness and regret. This view mostly is right, and perhaps in this case too. . . . Yet I don't know. To tell this story is by no means so easy as it should be—were the ordinary standpoint adequate. Apparently it is a story very much like the others: for me, however, there is visible in its background the melancholy figure of a woman, the shadow of a cruel wisdom buried in a lonely grave, looking on wistfully, helplessly, with sealed lips. The grave itself, as I came upon it during an early morning stroll, was a rather shapeless brown mound, with an inlaid neat border of white lumps of coral at the base, and enclosed within a circular fence made of split saplings, with the bark left on. A garland of leaves and flowers was woven about the heads of the slender posts—and the flowers were fresh.

"Thus, whether the shadow is of my imagination or not, I can at all events point out the significant fact of an unforgotten grave. When I tell you besides that Jim with his own hands had worked at the rustic fence, you will perceive directly the difference, the individual side of the story. There is in his espousal of memory and affection belonging to another human being something characteristic of his seriousness. He had a conscience, and it was a romantic conscience. Through her whole life the wife of the unspeakable Cornelius had no other companion, confidante, and friend but her daughter. How the poor woman had come to marry the awful little Malacca Portuguese—after the separation from the father of her girl—and how that separation had been brought about, whether by death, which can be sometimes merciful, or by the merciless pressure of conventions, is a mystery to me. From the little which Stein (who knew so many stories) had let drop in my hearing, I am convinced that she was no ordinary woman. Her own father had been a white; a high official; one of the brilliantly endowed men who are not dull enough to nurse a success, and whose careers so often end under a cloud. I suppose she too must have lacked the saving dulness —and her career ended in Patusan. Our common fate . . . for where is the man—I mean a real sentient man—who does not remember vaguely having been deserted in the fulness of possession by some one or something more precious than life? . . . our common fate fastens upon the women with a peculiar cruelty. It does not punish like a master, but inflicts lingering torment, as if to gratify a secret, unappeasable spite. One would think that, appointed to rule on earth, it seeks to revenge itself upon the beings that come nearest to rising above the trammels of

earthly caution; for it is only women who manage to put at times into
their love an element just palpable enough to give one a fright—an
extra-terrestrial touch. I ask myself with wonder—how the world can
look to them—whether it has the shape and substance *we* know, the air
we breathe! Sometimes I fancy it must be a region of unreasonable
sublimities seething with the excitement of their adventurous souls,
lighted by the glory of all possible risks and renunciations. However, I
suspect there are very few women in the world, though of course I am
aware of the multitudes of mankind and of the equality of sexes—in
point of numbers, that is. But I am sure that the mother was as much
of a woman as the daughter seemed to be. I cannot help picturing to
myself these two, at first the young woman and the child, then the old
woman and the young girl, the awful sameness and the swift passage of
time, the barrier of forest, the solitude and the turmoil round these two
lonely lives, and every word spoken between them penetrated with sad
meaning. There must have been confidences, not so much of fact, I
suppose, as of innermost feeling,—regrets—fears—warnings, no doubt:
warnings that the younger did not fully understand till the elder was
dead—and Jim came along. Then I am sure she understood much—
not everything—the fear mostly it seems. Jim called her by a word that
means precious, in the sense of a precious gem—jewel. Pretty, isn't it?
But he was capable of anything. He was equal to his fortune, as he—
after all—must have been equal to his misfortune. Jewel he called her;
and he would say this as he might have said 'Jane,' don't you know,
with a marital, homelike, peaceful effect. I heard the name for the first
time ten minutes after I had landed in his courtyard, when, after nearly
shaking my arm off, he darted up the steps and began to make a joyous,
boyish disturbance at the door under the heavy eaves. 'Jewel! O! Jewel.
Quick! Here's a friend come,' . . . and suddenly peering at me in
the dim verandah, he mumbled earnestly, 'You know—this—no confounded nonsense about it—can't tell you how much I owe to her—
and so—you understand—I—exactly as if . . .' His hurried, anxious
whispers were cut short by the flitting of a white form within the house,
a faint exclamation, and a child-like but energetic little face with delicate
features and a profound attentive glance peeped out of the inner gloom,
like a bird out of the recess of a nest. I was struck by the name, of course;
but it was not till later on that I connected it with an astonishing rumour
that had met me on my journey, at a little place on the coast about 230
miles south of Patusan River. Stein's schooner, in which I had my
passage, put in there, to collect some produce, and, going ashore, I
found to my great surprise that the wretched locality could boast of a
third-class deputy-assistant resident, a big, fat, greasy, blinking fellow of
mixed descent, with turned out, shiny lips. I found him lying extended
on his back in a cane chair, odiously unbuttoned, with a large green
leaf of some sort on the top of his steaming head, and another in his

hand which he used lazily as a fan. . . . Going to Patusan? Oh yes.
Stein's Trading Company. He knew. Had a permission? No business of
his. It was not so bad there now, he remarked negligently, and, he went
on drawling, 'there's some sort of white vagabond has got in there, I
hear. . . . Eh? What you say? Friend of yours? So! . . . Then it was
true there was one of these *verdammte*[1]—What was he up to? Found
his way in, the rascal. Eh? I had not been sure. Patusan—they cut
throats there—no business of ours.' He interrupted himself to groan.
'Phoo! Almighty! The heat! The heat! Well, then, there might be something in the story too, after all, and . . .' He shut one of his beastly
glassy eyes (the eyelid went on quivering) while he leered at me atro-
ciously with the other. 'Look here,' says he mysteriously, 'if—do you
understand?—if he has really got hold of something fairly good—none
of your bits of green glass—understand?—I am a Government official
—you tell the rascal . . . Eh? What? Friend of yours?' . . . He continued
wallowing calmly in the chair . . . 'You said so; that's just it; and I am
pleased to give you the hint. I suppose you too would like to get something out of it? Don't interrupt. You just tell him I've heard the tale,
but to my Government I have made no report. Not yet. See? Why make
a report? Eh? Tell him to come to me if they let him get alive out of
the country. He had better look out for himself. Eh? I promise to ask
no questions. On the quiet—you understand? You too—you shall get
something from me. Small commission for the trouble. Don't interrupt.
I am a Government official, and make no report. That's business. Understand? I know some good people that will buy anything worth having,
and can give him more money than the scoundrel ever saw in his life.
I know his sort.' He fixed me steadfastly with both his eyes open, while
I stood over him utterly amazed, and asking myself whether he was mad
or drunk. He perspired, puffed, moaning feebly, and scratching himself with such horrible composure that I could not bear the sight long
enough to find out. Next day, talking casually with the people of the
little native court of the place, I discovered that a story was travelling
slowly down the coast about a mysterious white man in Patusan who
had got hold of an extraordinary gem—namely, an emerald of an enormous size, and altogether priceless. The emerald seems to appeal more
to the Eastern imagination than any other precious stone. The white
man had obtained it, I was told, partly by the exercise of his wonderful
strength and partly by cunning, from the ruler of a distant country,
whence he had fled instantly, arriving in Patusan in utmost distress, but
frightening the people by his extreme ferocity, which nothing seemed
able to subdue. Most of my informants were of the opinion that the
stone was probably unlucky,—like the famous stone of the Sultan of
Succadana,[2] which in the old times had brought wars and untold ca-

1. Damned.
2. One of the largest diamonds in the world.

lamities upon that country. Perhaps it was the same stone—one couldn't say. Indeed the story of a fabulously large emerald is as old as the arrival of the first white men in the Archipelago; and the belief in it is so persistent that less than forty years ago there had been an official Dutch inquiry into the truth of it. Such a jewel—it was explained to me by the old fellow from whom I heard most of this amazing Jim-myth—a sort of scribe to the wretched little Rajah of the place;—such a jewel, he said, cocking his poor purblind eyes up at me (he was sitting on the cabin floor out of respect), is best preserved by being concealed about the person of a woman. Yet it is not every woman that would do. She must be young—he sighed deeply—and insensible to the seductions of love. He shook his head sceptically. But such a woman seemed to be actually in existence. He had been told of a tall girl, whom the white man treated with great respect and care, and who never went forth from the house unattended. People said the white man could be seen with her almost any day; they walked side by side, openly, he holding her arm under his—pressed to his side—thus—in a most extraordinary way. This might be a lie, he conceded, for it was indeed a strange thing for any one to do: on the other hand, there could be no doubt she wore the white man's jewel concealed upon her bosom."

Chapter XXIX

"This was the theory of Jim's marital evening walks. I made a third on more than one occasion, unpleasantly aware every time of Cornelius, who nursed the aggrieved sense of his legal paternity, slinking in the neighbourhood with that peculiar twist of his mouth as if he were perpetually on the point of gnashing his teeth. But do you notice how, three hundred miles beyond the end of telegraph cables and mail-boat lines, the haggard utilitarian lies of our civilisation wither and die, to be replaced by pure exercises of imagination, that have the futility, often the charm, and sometimes the deep hidden truthfulness, of works of art? Romance had singled Jim for its own—and that was the true part of the story, which otherwise was all wrong. He did not hide his jewel. In fact, he was extremely proud of it.

"It comes to me now that I had, on the whole, seen very little of her. What I remember best is the even, olive pallor of her complexion, and the intense blue-black gleams of her hair, flowing abundantly from under a small crimson cap she wore far back on her shapely head. Her movements were free, assured, and she blushed a dusky red. While Jim and I were talking, she would come and go with rapid glances at us, leaving on her passage an impression of grace and charm and a distinct suggestion of watchfulness. Her manner presented a curious combination of shyness and audacity. Every pretty smile was succeeded swiftly by a look of silent, repressed anxiety, as if put to flight by the recollection of some abiding danger. At times she would sit down with us and, with her soft cheek dimpled by the knuckles of her little hand, she would listen to our talk; her big clear eyes would remain fastened on our lips, as though each pronounced word had a visible shape. Her mother had taught her to read and write; she had learned a good bit of English from Jim, and she spoke it most amusingly, with his own clipping, boyish intonation. Her tenderness hovered over him like a flutter of wings. She lived so completely in his contemplation that she had acquired something of his outward aspect, something that recalled him in her movements, in the way she stretched her arm, turned her head, directed her glances. Her vigilant affection had an intensity that made it almost perceptible to the senses; it seemed actually to exist in the ambient matter of space, to envelop him like a peculiar fragrance, to dwell in the sunshine like a tremulous, subdued, and impassioned note. I suppose you think that I too am romantic, but it is a mistake. I am relating to you the sober impressions of a bit of youth, of a strange uneasy romance that had come in my way. I observed with interest the work of his—well—good fortune. He was jealously loved, but why she should be jealous, and of what, I could not tell. The land, the people, the forests were her accomplices, guarding him with vigilant accord, with an air of seclusion, of mystery, of invincible possession. There was no appeal, as it were; he was imprisoned within the very freedom of his power, and she, though ready to make a footstool of her head for his feet, guarded her conquest inflexibly—as though he were hard to keep. The very Tamb' Itam, marching on our journeys upon the heels of his white lord, with his head thrown back, truculent and be-weaponed like a janissary,[1] with kriss, chopper, and lance (besides carrying Jim's gun); even Tamb' Itam allowed himself to put on the airs of uncompromising guardianship, like a surly devoted jailer ready to lay down his life for his captive. On the evenings when we sat up late, his silent, indistinct form would pass and repass under the verandah, with noiseless footsteps, or lifting my head I would unexpectedly make him out standing rigidly erect in the shadow. As a general rule he would vanish after a time, without a sound; but when we rose he would spring up close to us as if from the ground, ready for any orders Jim might wish to give. The girl too, I believe, never went to sleep till we had separated for the night. More than once I saw her and Jim through the window of my room come out together quietly and lean on the rough balustrade—two white forms very close, his arm about her waist, her head on his shoulder. Their soft murmurs reached me, penetrating, tender, with a calm sad note in the stillness of the night, like a self-communion of one being carried on in two tones.

---

1. A soldier (originally a slave) in the Turkish sultan's guard; i.e., a bodyguard.

Later on, tossing on my bed under the mosquito-net, I was sure to hear slight creakings, faint breathing, a throat cleared cautiously—and I would know that Tamb' Itam was still on the prowl. Though he had (by the favour of the white lord) a house in the compound, had 'taken wife,' and had lately been blessed with a child, I believe that, during my stay at all events, he slept on the verandah every night. It was very difficult to make this faithful and grim retainer talk. Even Jim himself was answered in jerky short sentences, under protest as it were. Talking, he seemed to imply, was no business of his. The longest speech I heard him volunteer was one morning when, suddenly extending his hand towards the courtyard, he pointed at Cornelius and said, 'Here comes the Nazarene.' I don't think he was addressing me, though I stood at his side; his object seemed rather to awaken the indignant attention of the universe. Some muttered allusions, which followed, to dogs and the smell of roast-meat, struck me as singularly felicitous. The courtyard, a large square space, was one torrid blaze of sunshine, and, bathed in intense light, Cornelius was creeping across in full view with an inexpressible effect of stealthiness, of dark and secret slinking. He reminded one of everything that is unsavoury. His slow laborious walk resembled the creeping of a repulsive beetle, the legs alone moving with horrid industry while the body glided evenly. I suppose he made straight enough for the place where he wanted to get to, but his progress with one shoulder carried forward seemed oblique. He was often seen circling slowly amongst the sheds, as if following a scent; passing before the verandah with upward stealthy glances; disappearing without haste round the corner of some hut. That he seemed free of the place demonstrated Jim's absurd carelessness or else his infinite disdain, for Cornelius had played a very dubious part (to say the least of it) in a certain episode which might have ended fatally for Jim. As a matter of fact, it had redounded to his glory. But everything redounded to his glory; and it was the irony of his good fortune that he, who had been too careful of it once, seemed to bear a charmed life.

"You must know he had left Doramin's place very soon after his arrival—much too soon, in fact, for his safety, and of course a long time before the war. In this he was actuated by a sense of duty; he had to look after Stein's business, he said. Hadn't he? To that end, with an utter disregard of his personal safety, he crossed the river and took up his quarters with Cornelius. How the latter had managed to exist through the troubled times I can't say. As Stein's agent, after all, he must have had Doramin's protection in a measure; and in one way or another he had managed to wriggle through all the deadly complications, while I have no doubt that his conduct, whatever line he was forced to take, was marked by that abjectness which was like the stamp of the man. That was his characteristic; he was fundamentally and outwardly abject, as other men are markedly of a generous, distinguished, or venerable appearance. It was the element of his nature which permeated all his acts and passions and emotions; he raged abjectly, smiled abjectly, was abjectly sad; his civilities and his indignations were alike abject. I am sure his love would have been the most abject of sentiments—but can one imagine a loathsome insect in love? And his loathsomeness too was abject, so that a simply disgusting person would have appeared noble by his side. He has his place neither in the background nor in the foreground of the story; he is simply seen skulking on its outskirts, enigmatical and unclean, tainting the fragrance of its youth and of its naïveness.

"His position in any case could not have been other than extremely miserable, yet it may very well be that he found some advantages in it. Jim told me he had been received at first with an abject display of the most amicable sentiments. 'The fellow apparently couldn't contain himself for joy,' said Jim with disgust. 'He flew at me every morning to shake both my hands—confound him! but I could never tell whether there would be any breakfast. If I got three meals in two days I considered myself jolly lucky, and he made me sign a chit for ten dollars every week. Said he was sure Mr Stein did not mean him to keep me for nothing. Well—he kept me on nothing as near as possible. Put it down to the unsettled state of the country, and made as if to tear his hair out, begging my pardon twenty times a-day, so that I had at last to entreat him not to worry. It made me sick. Half the roof of his house had fallen in, and the whole place had a mangy look, with wisps of dry grass sticking out and the corners of broken mats flapping on every wall. He did his best to make out that Mr Stein owed him money on the last three years' trading, but his books were all torn, and some were missing. He tried to hint it was his late wife's fault. Disgusting scoundrel! At last I had to forbid him to mention his late wife at all. It made Jewel cry. I couldn't discover what became of all the trade-goods; there was nothing in the store but rats, having a high old time amongst a litter of brown paper and old sacking. I was assured on every hand that he had a lot of money buried somewhere, but of course could get nothing out of him. It was the most miserable existence I led there in that wretched house. I tried to do my duty by Stein, but I had also other matters to think of. When I escaped to Doramin old Tunku Allang got frightened and returned all my things. It was done in a roundabout way, and with no end of mystery, through a Chinaman who keeps a small shop here; but as soon as I left the Bugis quarter and went to live with Cornelius it began to be said openly that the Rajah had made up his mind to have me killed before long. Pleasant, wasn't it? And I couldn't see what there was to prevent him if he really *had* made up his mind. The worst of it was, I couldn't help feeling I wasn't doing any good either for Stein or for myself. Oh! it was beastly—the whole six weeks of it.' "

Chapter XXX

"He told me further that he didn't know what made him hang on—but of course we may guess. He sympathised deeply with the defenceless girl, at the mercy of that 'mean, cowardly scoundrel.' It appears Cornelius led her an awful life, stopping only short of actual ill-usage, for which he had not the pluck, I suppose. He insisted upon her calling him father—'and with respect too—with respect,' he would scream, shaking a little yellow fist in her face. 'I am a respectable man, and what are you? Tell me—what are you? You think I am going to bring up somebody else's child and not be treated with respect? You ought to be glad I let you. Come—say Yes, father. . . . No? . . . You wait a bit.' Thereupon he would begin to abuse the dead woman, till the girl would run off with her hands to her head. He pursued her, dashing in and out and round the house and amongst the sheds, would drive her into some corner, where she would fall on her knees stopping her ears, and then he would stand at a distance and declaim filthy denunciations at her back for half an hour at a stretch. 'Your mother was a devil, a deceitful devil—and you too are a devil,' he would shriek in a final outburst, pick up a bit of dry earth or a handful of mud (there was plenty of mud around the house), and fling it into her hair. Sometimes, though, she would hold out full of scorn, confronting him in silence, her face sombre and contracted, and only now and then uttering a word or two that would make the other jump and writhe with the sting. Jim told me these scenes were terrible. It was indeed a strange thing to come upon in a wilderness. The endlessness of such a subtly cruel situation was appalling—if you think of it. The respectable Cornelius (Inchi 'Nelyus the Malays called him, with a grimace that meant many things) was a much-disappointed man. I don't know what he had expected would be done for him in consideration of his marriage; but evidently the liberty to steal, and embezzle, and appropriate to himself for many years and in any way that suited him best, the goods of Stein's Trading Co. (Stein kept the supply up unfalteringly as long as he could get his skippers to take it there) did not seem to him a fair equivalent for the sacrifice of his honourable name. Jim would have enjoyed exceedingly thrashing Cornelius within an inch of his life; on the other hand, the scenes were of so painful a character, so abominable, that his impulse would be to get out of earshot, in order to spare the girl's feelings. They left her agitated, speechless, clutching her bosom now and then with a stony, desperate face, and then Jim would lounge up and say unhappily, 'Now—come—really—what's the use—you must try to eat a bit,' or give some such mark of sympathy. Cornelius would keep on slinking through the doorways, across the verandah and back again, as mute as a fish, and with malevolent, mistrustful, underhand glances. 'I can stop

his game,' Jim said to her once. 'Just say the word.' And do you know
what she answered? She said—Jim told me impressively—that if she
had not been sure he was intensely wretched himself, she would have
found the courage to kill him with her own hands. 'Just fancy that! The
poor devil of a girl, almost a child, being driven to talk like that,' he
exclaimed in horror. It seemed impossible to save her not only from
that mean rascal but even from herself! It wasn't that he pitied her so
much, he affirmed; it was more than pity; it was as if he had something
on his conscience, while that life went on. To leave the house would
have appeared a base desertion. He had understood at last that there
was nothing to expect from a longer stay, neither accounts nor money,
nor truth of any sort, but he stayed on, exasperating Cornelius to the
verge, I won't say of insanity, but almost of courage. Meantime he felt
all sorts of dangers gathering obscurely about him. Doramin had sent
over twice a trusty servant to tell him seriously that he could do nothing
for his safety unless he would recross the river again and live amongst
the Bugis as at first. People of every condition used to call, often in the
dead of night, in order to disclose to him plots for his assassination. He
was to be poisoned. He was to be stabbed in the bath-house. Arrangements were being made to have him shot from a boat on the river. Each
of these informants professed himself to be his very good friend. It was
enough—he told me—to spoil a fellow's rest for ever. Something of the
kind was extremely possible—nay, probable—but the lying warnings
gave him only the sense of deadly scheming going on all around him,
on all sides, in the dark. Nothing more calculated to shake the best of
nerve. Finally, one night, Cornelius himself, with a great apparatus of
alarm and secrecy, unfolded in solemn wheedling tones a little plan
wherein for one hundred dollars—or even for eighty; let's say eighty—
he, Cornelius, would procure a trustworthy man to smuggle Jim out of
the river, all safe. There was nothing else for it now—if Jim cared a
pin for his life. What's eighty dollars? A trifle. An insignificant sum.
While he, Cornelius, who had to remain behind, was absolutely courting
death by this proof of devotion to Mr Stein's young friend. The sight of
his abject grimacing was—Jim told me—very hard to bear: he clutched
at his hair, beat his breast, rocked himself to and fro with his hands
pressed to his stomach, and actually pretended to shed tears. 'Your blood
be on your own head,' he squeaked at last, and rushed out. It is a curious
question how far Cornelius was sincere in that performance. Jim confessed to me that he did not sleep a wink after the fellow had gone. He
lay on his back on a thin mat spread over the bamboo flooring, trying
idly to make out the bare rafters, and listening to the rustlings in the
torn thatch. A star suddenly twinkled through a hole in the roof. His
brain was in a whirl; but, nevertheless, it was on that very night that he
matured his plan for overcoming Sherif Ali. It had been the thought of
all the moments he could spare from the hopeless investigation into

Stein's affairs, but the notion—he says—came to him then all at once. He could see, as it were, the guns mounted on the top of the hill. He got very hot and excited lying there; sleep was out of the question more than ever. He jumped up, and went out barefooted on the verandah. Walking silently, he came upon the girl, motionless against the wall, as if on the watch. In his then state of mind it did not surprise him to see her up, nor yet to hear her ask in an anxious whisper where Cornelius could be. He simply said he did not know. She moaned a little, and peered into the campong. Everything was very quiet. He was possessed by his new idea, and so full of it that he could not help telling the girl all about it at once. She listened, clapped her hands lightly, whispered softly her admiration, but was evidently on the alert all the time. It seems he had been used to make a confidante of her all along—and that she on her part could and did give him a lot of useful hints as to Patusan affairs there is no doubt. He assured me more than once that he had never found himself the worse for her advice. At any rate, he was proceeding to explain his plan fully to her there and then, when she pressed his arm once, and vanished from his side. Then Cornelius appeared from somewhere, and perceiving Jim, ducked sideways, as though he had been shot at, and afterwards stood very still in the dusk. At last he came forward prudently, like a suspicious cat. 'There were some fishermen there—with fish,' he said in a shaky voice. 'To sell fish—you understand.' . . . It must have been then two o'clock in the morning—a likely time for anybody to hawk fish about!

"Jim, however, let the statement pass, and did not give it a single thought. Other matters occupied his mind, and besides he had neither seen nor heard anything. He contented himself by saying, 'Oh!' absently, got a drink of water out of a pitcher standing there, and leaving Cornelius a prey to some inexplicable emotion—that made him embrace with both arms the worm-eaten rail of the verandah as if his legs had failed—went in again and lay down on his mat to think. By-and-by he heard stealthy footsteps. They stopped. A voice whispered tremulously through the wall, 'Are you asleep?' 'No! What is it?' he answered briskly, and there was an abrupt movement outside, and then all was still, as if the whisperer had been startled. Extremely annoyed at this, Jim came out impetuously, and Cornelius with a faint shriek fled along the verandah as far as the steps, where he hung on to the broken banister. Very puzzled, Jim called out to him from the distance to know what the devil he meant. 'Have you given your consideration to what I spoke to you about?' asked Cornelius, pronouncing the words with difficulty, like a man in the cold fit of a fever. 'No!' shouted Jim in a passion. 'I have not, and I don't intend to. I am going to live here, in Patusan.' 'You shall d-d-die h-h-here,' answered Cornelius, still shaking violently, and in a sort of expiring voice. The whole performance was so absurd and provoking that Jim didn't know whether he ought to be amused or angry. 'Not till I have seen you tucked away, you bet,' he called out, exasperated yet ready to laugh. Half seriously (being excited with his own thoughts, you know) he went on shouting, 'Nothing can touch me! You can do your damnedest.' Somehow the shadowy Cornelius far off there seemed to be the hateful embodiment of all the annoyances and difficulties he had found in his path. He let himself go—his nerves had been over-wrought for days—and called him many pretty names,— swindler, liar, sorry rascal: in fact, carried on in an extraordinary way. He admits he passed all bounds, that he was quite beside himself— defied all Patusan to scare him away—declared he would make them all dance to his own tune yet, and so on, in a menacing, boasting strain. Perfectly bombastic and ridiculous, he said. His ears burned at the bare recollection. Must have been off his chump in some way. . . . The girl, who was sitting with us, nodded her little head at me quickly, frowned faintly, and said, 'I heard him,' with childlike solemnity. He laughed and blushed. What stopped him at last, he said, was the silence, the complete deathlike silence, of the indistinct figure far over there, that seemed to hang collapsed, doubled over the rail in a weird immobility. He came to his senses, and ceasing suddenly, wondered greatly at himself. He watched for a while. Not a stir, not a sound. 'Exactly as if the chap had died while I had been making all that noise,' he said. He was so ashamed of himself that he went indoors in a hurry without another word, and flung himself down again. The row seemed to have done him good though, because he went to sleep for the rest of the night like a baby. Hadn't slept like that for weeks. 'But *I* didn't sleep,' struck in the girl, one elbow on the table and nursing her cheek. 'I watched.' Her big eyes flashed, rolling a little, and then she fixed them on my face intently."

Chapter XXXI

"You may imagine with what interest I listened. All these details were perceived to have some significance twenty-four hours later. In the morning Cornelius made no allusion to the events of the night. 'I suppose you will come back to my poor house,' he muttered surlily, slinking up just as Jim was entering the canoe to go over to Doramin's campong. Jim only nodded, without looking at him. 'You find it good fun, no doubt,' muttered the other in a sour tone. Jim spent the day with the old *nakhoda*, preaching the necessity of vigorous action to the principal men of the Bugis community, who had been summoned for a big talk. He remembered with pleasure how very eloquent and persuasive he had been. 'I managed to put some backbone into them that time, and no mistake,' he said. Sherif Ali's last raid had swept the outskirts of the settlement, and some women belonging to the town had been carried off to the stockade. Sherif Ali's emissaries had been seen in the market-place the day before, strutting about haughtily in white cloaks, and boasting of the Rajah's friendship for their master. One of them stood forward in the shade of a tree, and, leaning on the long barrel of a rifle, exhorted the people to prayer and repentance, advising them to kill all the strangers in their midst, some of whom, he said, were infidels and others even worse—children of Satan in the guise of Moslems. It was reported that several of the Rajah's people amongst the listeners had loudly expressed their approbation. The terror amongst the common people was intense. Jim, immensely pleased with his day's work, crossed the river again before sunset.

"As he had got the Bugis irretrievably committed to action, and had made himself responsible for success on his own head, he was so elated that in the lightness of his heart he absolutely tried to be civil with Cornelius. But Cornelius became wildly jovial in response, and it was almost more than he could stand, he says, to hear his little squeaks of false laughter, to see him wriggle and blink, and suddenly catch hold of his chin and crouch low over the table with a distracted stare. The girl did not show herself, and Jim retired early. When he rose to say good-night, Cornelius jumped up, knocking his chair over, and ducked out of sight as if to pick up something he had dropped. His good-night came huskily from under the table. Jim was amazed to see him emerge with a dropping jaw, and staring, stupidly frightened eyes. He clutched the edge of the table. 'What's the matter? Are you unwell?' asked Jim. 'Yes, yes, yes. A great colic in my stomach,' says the other; and it is Jim's opinion that it was perfectly true. If so, it was, in view of his contemplated action, an abject sign of a still imperfect callousness for which he must be given all due credit.

"Be it as it may, Jim's slumbers were disturbed by a dream of heavens like brass resounding with a great voice, which called upon him to Awake! Awake! so loud that, notwithstanding his desperate determination to sleep on, he did wake up in reality. The glare of a red spluttering conflagration going on in mid-air fell on his eyes. Coils of black thick smoke curved round the head of some apparition, some unearthly being, all in white, with a severe, drawn, anxious face. After a second or so he recognised the girl. She was holding a dammar torch at arm's-length aloft, and in a persistent, urgent monotone she was repeating, 'Get up! Get up! Get up!'

"Suddenly he leaped to his feet; at once she put into his hand a revolver, his own revolver, which had been hanging on a nail, but loaded this time. He gripped it in silence, bewildered, blinking in the light. He wondered what he could do for her.

"She asked rapidly and very low, 'Can you face four men with this?' He laughed while narrating this part at the recollection of his polite alacrity. It seems he made a great display of it. 'Certainly—of course—

certainly—command me.' He was not properly awake, and had a notion of being very civil in these extraordinary circumstances, of showing his unquestioning, devoted readiness. She left the room, and he followed her; in the passage they disturbed an old hag who did the casual cooking of the household, though she was so decrepit as to be hardly able to understand human speech. She got up and hobbled behind them, mumbling toothlessly. On the verandah a hammock of sail-cloth, belonging to Cornelius, swayed lightly to the touch of Jim's elbow. It was empty.

"The Patusan establishment, like all the posts of Stein's Trading Company, had originally consisted of four buildings. Two of them were represented by two heaps of sticks, broken bamboos, rotten thatch, over which the four corner-posts of hardwood leaned sadly at different angles: the principal storeroom, however, stood yet, facing the agent's house. It was an oblong hut, built of mud and clay: it had at one end a wide door of stout planking, which so far had not come off the hinges, and in one of the side walls there was a square aperture, a sort of window, with three wooden bars. Before descending the few steps the girl turned her face over her shoulder and said quickly, 'You were to be set upon while you slept.' Jim tells me he experienced a sense of deception. It was the old story. He was weary of these attempts upon his life. He had had his fill of these alarms. He was sick of them. He assured me he was angry with the girl for deceiving him. He had followed her under the impression that it was she who wanted his help, and now he had half a mind to turn on his heel and go back in disgust. 'Do you know,' he commented profoundly, 'I rather think I was not quite myself for whole weeks on end about that time?' 'Oh yes. You were though,' I couldn't help contradicting.

"But she moved on swiftly, and he followed her into the courtyard. All its fences had fallen in a long time ago; the neighbours' buffaloes would pace in the morning across the open space, snorting profoundly, without haste; the very jungle was invading it already. Jim and the girl stopped in the rank grass. The light in which they stood made a dense blackness all round, and only above their heads there was an opulent glitter of stars. He told me it was a beautiful night—quite cool, with a little stir of breeze from the river. It seems he noticed its friendly beauty. Remember this is a love story I am telling you now. A lovely night seemed to breathe on them a soft caress. The flame of the torch streamed now and then with a fluttering noise like a flag, and for a time this was the only sound. 'They are in the storeroom waiting,' whispered the girl; 'they are waiting for the signal.' 'Who's to give it?' he asked. She shook the torch, which blazed up after a shower of sparks. 'Only you have been sleeping so restlessly,' she continued in a murmur; 'I watched your sleep, too.' 'You!' he exclaimed, craning his neck to look about him. 'You think I watched on this night only!' she said, with a sort of despairing indignation.

"He says it was as if he had received a blow on the chest. He gasped. He thought he had been an awful brute somehow, and he felt remorseful, touched, happy, elated. This, let me remind you again, is a love story; you can see it by the imbecility, not a repulsive imbecility, the exalted imbecility of these proceedings, this station in torchlight, as if they had come there on purpose to have it out for the edification of concealed murderers. If Sherif Ali's emissaries had been possessed—as Jim remarked—of a pennyworth of spunk, this was the time to make a rush. His heart was thumping—not with fear—but he seemed to hear the grass rustle, and he stepped smartly out of the light. Something dark, imperfectly seen, flitted rapidly out of sight. He called out in a strong voice, 'Cornelius! O Cornelius!' A profound silence succeeded: his voice did not seem to have carried twenty feet. Again the girl was by his side. 'Fly!' she said. The old woman was coming up; her broken figure hovered in crippled little jumps on the edge of the light; they heard her mumbling, and a light, moaning sigh. 'Fly!' repeated the girl excitedly. 'They are frightened now—this light—the voices. They know you are awake now—they know you are big, strong, fearless . . .' 'If I am all that,' he began; but she interrupted him: 'Yes—to-night! But what of to-morrow night? Of the next night? Of the night after—of all the many, many nights? Can I be always watching?' A sobbing catch of her breath affected him beyond the power of words.

"He told me that he had never felt so small, so powerless—and as to courage, what was the good of it, he thought. He was so helpless that even flight seemed of no use; and though she kept on whispering, 'Go to Doramin, go to Doramin,' with feverish insistence, he realised that for him there was no refuge from that loneliness which centupled all his dangers except—in her. 'I thought,' he said to me, 'that if I went away from her it would be the end of everything somehow.' Only as they couldn't stop there for ever in the middle of that courtyard, he made up his mind to go and look into the storehouse. He let her follow him without thinking of any protest, as if they had been indissolubly united. 'I am fearless—am I?' he muttered through his teeth. She restrained his arm. 'Wait till you hear my voice,' she said, and, torch in hand, ran lightly round the corner. He remained alone in the darkness, his face to the door: not a sound, not a breath came from the other side. The old hag let out a dreary groan somewhere behind his back. He heard a high-pitched almost screaming call from the girl. 'Now! Push!' He pushed violently; the door swung with a creak and a clatter, disclosing to his intense astonishment the low dungeon-like interior illuminated by a lurid, wavering glare. A turmoil of smoke eddied down upon an empty wooden crate in the middle of the floor, a litter of rags and straw tried to soar, but only stirred feebly in the draught. She had thrust the light through the bars of the window. He saw her bare round arm extended and rigid, holding up the torch with the steadiness of an iron bracket. A conical ragged heap of old mats cumbered a distant corner almost to the ceiling, and that was all.

"He explained to me that he was bitterly disappointed at this. His fortitude had been tried by so many warnings, he had been for weeks surrounded by so many hints of danger, that he wanted the relief of some reality, of something tangible that he could meet. 'It would have cleared the air for a couple of hours at least, if you know what I mean,' he said to me. 'Jove! I had been living for days with a stone on my chest.' Now at last he had thought he would get hold of something, and—nothing! Not a trace, not a sign of anybody. He had raised his weapon as the door flew open, but now his arm fell. 'Fire! Defend yourself,' the girl outside cried in an agonising voice. She, being in the dark and with her arm thrust in to the shoulder through the small hole, couldn't see what was going on, and she dared not withdraw the torch now to run round. 'There's nobody here!' yelled Jim contemptuously, but his impulse to burst into a resentful exasperated laugh died without a sound: he had perceived in the very act of turning away that he was exchanging glances with a pair of eyes in the heap of mats. He saw a shifting gleam of whites. 'Come out!' he cried in a fury, a little doubtful, and a dark-faced head, a head without a body, shaped itself in the rubbish, a strangely detached head, that looked at him with a steady scowl. Next moment the whole mound stirred, and with a low grunt a man emerged swiftly, and bounded towards Jim. Behind him the mats as it were jumped and flew, his right arm was raised with a crooked elbow, and the dull blade of a kriss protruded from his fist held off, a little above his head. A cloth wound tight round his loins seemed dazzlingly white on his bronze skin; his naked body glistened as if wet.

"Jim noted all this. He told me he was experiencing a feeling of unutterable relief, of vengeful elation. He held his shot, he says, deliberately. He held it for the tenth part of a second, for three strides of the man—an unconscionable time. He held it for the pleasure of saying to himself, That's a dead man! He was absolutely positive and certain. He let him come on because it did not matter. A dead man, anyhow. He noticed the dilated nostrils, the wide eyes, the intent, eager stillness of the face, and then he fired.

"The explosion in that confined space was stunning. He stepped back a pace. He saw the man jerk his head up, fling his arms forward, and drop the kriss. He ascertained afterwards that he had shot him through the mouth, a little upwards, the bullet coming out high at the back of the skull. With the impetus of his rush the man drove straight on, his face suddenly gaping disfigured, with his hands open before him gropingly, as though blinded, and landed with terrific violence on his forehead, just short of Jim's bare toes. Jim says he didn't lose the smallest detail of all this. He found himself calm, appeased, without rancour, without uneasiness, as if the death of that man had atoned for everything.

The place was getting very full of sooty smoke from the torch, in which the unswaying flame burned blood-red without a flicker. He walked in resolutely, striding over the dead body, and covered with his revolver another naked figure outlined vaguely at the other end. As he was about to pull the trigger, the man threw away with force a short heavy spear, and squatted submissively on his hams, his back to the wall and his clasped hands between his legs. 'You want your life?' Jim said. The other made no sound. 'How many more of you?' asked Jim again. 'Two more, Tuan,' said the man very softly, looking with big fascinated eyes into the muzzle of the revolver. Accordingly two more crawled from under the mats, holding out ostentatiously their empty hands."

Chapter XXXII

"Jim took up an advantageous position and shepherded them out in a bunch through the doorway: all that time the torch had remained vertical in the grip of a little hand, without so much as a tremble. The three men obeyed him, perfectly mute, moving automatically. He ranged them in a row. 'Link arms!' he ordered. They did so. 'The first who withdraws his arm or turns his head is a dead man,' he said. 'March!' They stepped out together, rigidly; he followed, and at the side the girl, in a trailing white gown, her black hair falling as low as her waist, bore the light. Erect and swaying, she seemed to glide without touching the earth; the only sound was the silky swish and rustle of the long grass. 'Stop!' cried Jim.

"The river-bank was steep; a great freshness ascended, the light fell on the edge of smooth dark water frothing without a ripple; right and left the shapes of the houses ran together below the sharp outlines of the roofs. 'Take my greetings to Sherif Ali—till I come myself,' said Jim. Not one head of the three budged. 'Jump!' he thundered. The three splashes made one splash, a shower flew up, black heads bobbed convulsively, and disappeared; but a great blowing and spluttering went on, growing faint, for they were diving industriously, in great fear of a parting shot. Jim turned to the girl, who had been a silent and attentive observer. His heart seemed suddenly to grow too big for his breast and choke him in the hollow of his throat. This probably made him speechless for so long, and after returning his gaze she flung the burning torch with a wide sweep of the arm into the river. The ruddy fiery glare, taking a long flight through the night, sank with a vicious hiss, and the calm soft starlight descended upon them, unchecked.

"He did not tell me what it was he said when at last he recovered his voice. I don't suppose he could be very eloquent. The world was still, the night breathed on them, one of those nights that seem created for the sheltering of tenderness, and there are moments when our souls, as if freed from their dark envelope, glow with an exquisite sensibility that makes certain silences more lucid than speeches. As to the girl, he told me, 'She broke down a bit. Excitement—don't you know. Reaction. Deucedly tired she must have been—and all that kind of thing. And—and—hang it all—she was fond of me, don't you see. . . . I too . . . didn't know, of course . . . never entered my head . . .'

"Then he got up and began to walk about in some agitation. 'I—I love her dearly. More than I can tell. Of course one cannot tell. You take a different view of your actions when you come to understand, when you are *made* to understand every day that your existence is necessary—you see, absolutely necessary—to another person. I am made to feel that. Wonderful. But only try to think what her life has been. It is too extravagantly awful! Isn't it? And me finding her here like this—as you may go out for a stroll and come suddenly upon somebody drowning in a lonely dark place. Jove! No time to lose. Well, it is a trust too . . . I believe I am equal to it . . .'

"I must tell you the girl had left us to ourselves some time before. He slapped his chest. 'Yes! I feel that, but I believe I am equal to all my luck!' He had the gift of finding a special meaning in everything that happened to him. This was the view he took of his love-affair; it was idyllic, a little solemn, and also true, since his belief had all the unshakable seriousness of youth. Some time after, on another occasion, he said to me, 'I've been only two years here, and now, upon my word, I can't conceive being able to live anywhere else. The very thought of the world outside is enough to give me a fright; because, don't you see,' he continued, with downcast eyes watching the action of his boot busied in squashing thoroughly a tiny bit of dried mud (we were strolling on the river-bank)—'Because I have not forgotten why I came here. Not yet!'

"I refrained from looking at him, but I think I heard a short sigh; we took a turn or two in silence. 'Upon my soul and conscience,' he began again, 'if such a thing can be forgotten, then I think I have a right to dismiss it from my mind. Ask any man here' . . . his voice changed. 'Is it not strange,' he went on in a gentle, almost yearning tone, 'that all these people, all these people who would do anything for me, can never be made to understand? Never! If you disbelieved me I could not call them up. It seems hard, somehow. I am stupid, am I not? What more can I want? If you ask them who is brave—who is true—who is just—who is it they would trust with their lives?—they would say, Tuan Jim. And yet they can never know the real, real truth . . .'

"That's what he said to me on my last day with him. I did not let a murmur escape me: I felt he was going to say more, and come no nearer to the root of the matter. The sun, whose concentrated glare dwarfs the earth into a restless mote of dust, had sunk behind the forest, and the diffused light from an opal sky seemed to cast upon a world without shadows and without brilliance the illusion of a calm and pensive greatness. I don't know why, listening to him, I should have noted so distinctly the gradual darkening of the river, of the air; the irresistible slow work of the night settling silently on all the visible forms, effacing the outlines, burying the shapes deeper and deeper, like a steady fall of impalpable black dust.

" 'Jove!' he began abruptly, 'there are days when a fellow is too absurd for anything; only I know I can tell you what I like. I talk about being done with it—with the bally thing at the back of my head . . . Forgetting . . . Hang me if I know! I can think of it quietly. After all, what has it proved? Nothing. I suppose you don't think so . . .'

"I made a protesting murmur.

" 'No matter,' he said. 'I am satisfied . . . nearly. I've got to look only at the face of the first man that comes along, to regain my confidence. They can't be made to understand what is going on in me. What of that? Come! I haven't done so badly.'

" 'Not so badly,' I said.

" 'But all the same, you wouldn't like to have me aboard your own ship—hey?'

" 'Confound you!' I cried. 'Stop this.'

" 'Aha! You see,' he said, crowing, as it were, over me placidly. 'Only,' he went on, 'you just try to tell this to any of them here. They would think you a fool, a liar, or worse. And so I can stand it. I've done a thing or two for them, but this is what they have done for me.'

" 'My dear chap,' I cried, 'you shall always remain for them an insoluble mystery.' Thereupon we were silent.

" 'Mystery,' he repeated, before looking up. 'Well, then let me always remain here.'

"After the sun had set, the darkness seemed to drive upon us, borne in every faint puff of the breeze. In the middle of a hedged path I saw the arrested, gaunt, watchful, and apparently one-legged silhouette of Tamb' Itam; and across the dusky space my eye detected something white moving to and fro behind the supports of the roof. As soon as Jim, with Tamb' Itam at his heels, had started upon his evening rounds, I went up to the house alone, and unexpectedly, found myself waylaid by the girl, who had been clearly waiting for this opportunity.

"It is hard to tell you what it was precisely she wanted to wrest from me. Obviously it would be something very simple—the simplest impossibility in the world; as, for instance, the exact description of the form of a cloud. She wanted an assurance, a statement, a promise, an explanation—I don't know how to call it: the thing has no name. It was dark under the projecting roof, and all I could see were the flowing lines of her gown, the pale small oval of her face, with the white flash of her teeth, and, turned towards me, the big sombre orbits of her eyes, where there seemed to be a faint stir, such as you may fancy you can detect when you plunge your gaze to the bottom of an immensely deep well. What is it that moves there? you ask yourself. Is it a blind monster or only a lost gleam from the universe? It occurred to me—don't laugh— that all things being dissimilar, she was more inscrutable in her childish ignorance than the Sphinx propounding childish riddles to wayfarers.[1] She had been carried off to Patusan before her eyes were open. She had grown up there; she had seen nothing, she had known nothing, she had no conception of anything. I ask myself whether she were sure that anything else existed. What notions she may have formed of the outside world is to me inconceivable: all that she knew of its inhabitants were a betrayed woman and a sinister pantaloon.[2] Her lover also came to her from there, gifted with irresistible seductions; but what would become of her if he should return to these inconceivable regions that seemed always to claim back their own? Her mother had warned her of this with tears, before she died . . .

"She had caught hold of my arm firmly, and as soon as I had stopped she had withdrawn her hand in haste. She was audacious and shrinking. She feared nothing, but she was checked by the profound incertitude and the extreme strangeness—a brave person groping in the dark. I belonged to this Unknown that might claim Jim for its own at any moment. I was, as it were, in the secret of its nature and of its intentions—the confidant of a threatening mystery—armed with its power perhaps! I believe she supposed I could with a word whisk Jim away out of her very arms: it is my sober conviction she went through agonies of apprehension during my long talks with Jim; through a real and intolerable anguish that might have conceivably driven her into plotting my murder, had the fierceness of her soul been equal to the tremendous situation it had created. This is my impression, and it is all I can give you: the whole thing dawned gradually upon me, and as it got clearer and clearer I was overwhelmed by a slow incredulous amazement. She made me believe her, but there is no word that on my lips could render the effect of the headlong and vehement whisper, of the soft, passionate tones, of the sudden breathless pause and the appealing movement of the white arms extended swiftly. They fell; the ghostly figure swayed like a slender tree in the wind, the pale oval of the face drooped; it was impossible to distinguish her features, the darkness of the eyes was unfathomable; two wide sleeves uprose in the dark like unfolding wings, and she stood silent, holding her head in her hands."

---

1. The sphinx would ask Thebans the following riddle and, whenever they failed, would carry off and devour one of them: "What is that which is four-footed, three-footed, and two-footed?" Oedipus guessed correctly that it was man, crawling in infancy, using a cane in old age, and otherwise walking.
2. A pantomime character, a buffoon, usually a vicious old dotard, the butt and accomplice of the clown.

Chapter XXXIII

"I was immensely touched: her youth, her ignorance, her pretty beauty, which had the simple charm and the delicate vigour of a wild-flower, her pathetic pleading, her helplessness, appealed to me with almost the strength of her own unreasonable and natural fear. She feared the unknown as we all do, and her ignorance made the unknown infinitely vast. I stood for it, for myself, for you fellows, for all the world that neither cared for Jim nor needed him in the least. I would have been ready enough to answer for the indifference of the teeming earth but for the reflection that he too belonged to this mysterious unknown of her fears, and that, however much I stood for, I did not stand for him. This made me hesitate. A murmur of hopeless pain unsealed my lips. I began by protesting that I at least had come with no intention to take Jim away.

"Why did I come, then? After a slight movement she was as still as a marble statue in the night. I tried to explain briefly: friendship, business; if I had any wish in the matter it was rather to see him stay. . . . 'They always leave us,' she murmured. The breath of sad wisdom from the grave which her piety wreathed with flowers seemed to pass in a faint sigh. . . . Nothing, I said, could separate Jim from her.

"It is my firm conviction now; it was my conviction at the time; it was the only possible conclusion from the facts of the case. It was not made more certain by her whispering in a tone in which one speaks to oneself, 'He swore this to me.' 'Did you ask him?' I said.

"She made a step nearer. 'No. Never!' She had asked him only to go away. It was that night on the river-bank, after he had killed the man —after she had flung the torch in the water because he was looking at her so. There was too much light, and the danger was over then—for a little time—for a little time. He said then he would not abandon her to Cornelius. She had insisted. She wanted him to leave her. He said that he could not—that it was impossible. He trembled while he said this. She had felt him tremble. . . . One does not require much imagination to see the scene, almost to hear their whispers. She was afraid for him too. I believe that then she saw in him only a predestined victim of dangers which she understood better than himself. Though by nothing but his mere presence he had mastered her heart, had filled all her thoughts, and had possessed himself of all her affections, she underestimated his chances of success. It is obvious that at about that time everybody was inclined to underestimate his chances. Strictly speaking he didn't seem to have any. I know this was Cornelius's view. He confessed that much to me in extenuation of the shady part he had played in Sherif Ali's plot to do away with the infidel. Even Sherif Ali himself, as it seems certain now, had nothing but contempt for the white man. Jim was to be murdered mainly on religious grounds, I believe. A simple act of piety (and so far infinitely meritorious), but otherwise without much importance. In the last part of this opinion Cornelius concurred. 'Honourable sir,' he argued abjectly on the only occasion he managed to have me to himself—'Honourable sir, how was I to know? Who was he? What could he do to make people believe him? What did Mr Stein mean sending a boy like that to talk big to an old servant? I was ready to save him for eighty dollars. Only eighty dollars. Why didn't the fool go? Was I to get stabbed myself for the sake of a stranger?' He grovelled in spirit before me, with his body doubled up insinuatingly and his hands hovering about my knees, as though he were ready to embrace my legs. 'What's eighty dollars? An insignificant sum to give to a defenceless old man ruined for life by a deceased she-devil.' Here he wept. But I anticipate. I didn't that night chance upon Cornelius till I had had it out with the girl.

"She was unselfish when she urged Jim to leave her, and even to leave the country. It was his danger that was foremost in her thoughts —even if she wanted to save herself too—perhaps unconsciously: but then look at the warning she had, look at the lesson that could be drawn from every moment of the recently ended life in which all her memories were centred. She fell at his feet—she told me so—there by the river, in the discreet light of stars which showed nothing except great masses of silent shadows, indefinite open spaces, and trembling faintly upon the broad stream made it appear as wide as the sea. He had lifted her up. He lifted her up, and then she would struggle no more. Of course not. Strong arms, a tender voice, a stalwart shoulder to rest her poor lonely little head upon. The need—the infinite need—of all this for the aching heart, for the bewildered mind;—the promptings of youth —the necessity of the moment. What would you have? One under-stands—unless one is incapable of understanding anything under the sun. And so she was content to be lifted up—and held. 'You know— Jove! this is serious—no nonsense in it!' as Jim had whispered hurriedly with a troubled concerned face on the threshold of his house. I don't know so much about nonsense, but there was nothing light-hearted in their romance: they came together under the shadow of a life's disaster, like knight and maiden meeting to exchange vows amongst haunted ruins. The starlight was good enough for that story, a light so faint and remote that it cannot resolve shadows into shapes, and show the other shore of a stream. I did look upon the stream that night and from the very place; it rolled silent and as black as Styx[1]: the next day I went away, but I am not likely to forget what it was she wanted to be saved from when she entreated him to leave her while there was time. She told me what it was, calmed—she was now too passionately interested

1. A river of Hades.

for mere excitement—in a voice as quiet in the obscurity as her white half-lost figure. She told me, 'I didn't want to die weeping.' I thought I had not heard aright.

" 'You did not want to die weeping?' I repeated after her. 'Like my mother,' she added readily. The outlines of her white shape did not stir in the least. 'My mother had wept bitterly before she died,' she explained. An inconceivable calmness seemed to have risen from the ground around us, imperceptibly, like the still rise of a flood in the night, obliterating the familiar landmarks of emotions. There came upon me, as though I had felt myself losing my footing in the midst of waters, a sudden dread, the dread of the unknown depths. She went on explaining that, during the last moments, being alone with her mother, she had to leave the side of the couch to go and set her back against the door, in order to keep Cornelius out. He desired to get in, and kept on drumming with both fists, only desisting now and again to shout huskily, 'Let me in! Let me in! Let me in!' In a far corner upon a few mats the moribund woman, already speechless and unable to lift her arm, rolled her head over, and with a feeble movement of her hand seemed to command— No! No! and the obedient daughter, setting her shoulders with all her strength against the door, was looking on. 'The tears fell from her eyes—and then she died,' concluded the girl in an imperturbable monotone, which more than anything else, more than the white statuesque immobility of her person, more than mere words could do, troubled my mind profoundly with the passive, irremediable horror of the scene. It had the power to drive me out of my conception of existence, out of that shelter each of us makes for himself to creep under in moments of danger, as a tortoise withdraws within its shell. For a moment I had a view of a world that seemed to wear a vast and dismal aspect of disorder, while, in truth, thanks to our unwearied efforts, it is as sunny an arrangement of small conveniences as the mind of man can conceive. But still—it was only a moment: I went back into my shell directly. One *must*—don't you know?—though I seemed to have lost all my words in the chaos of dark thoughts I had contemplated for a second or two beyond the pale. These came back too very soon, for words also belong to the sheltering conception of light and order which is our refuge. I had them ready at my disposal before she whispered softly, 'He swore he would never leave me, when we stood there alone! He swore to me!' . . . 'And is it possible that you—you! do not believe him?' I asked, sincerely reproachful, genuinely shocked. Why couldn't she believe? Wherefore this craving for incertitude, this clinging to fear, as if incertitude and fear had been the safeguards of her love. It was monstrous. She should have made for herself a shelter of inexpugnable peace out of that honest affection. She had not the knowledge—not the skill perhaps. The night had come on apace; it had grown pitch-dark where we were, so that without stirring she had faded like the intangible form of a wistful and perverse spirit. And suddenly I heard her quiet whisper again, 'Other men had sworn the same thing.' It was like a meditative comment on some thoughts full of sadness, of awe. And she added, still lower if possible, 'My father did.' She paused the time to draw an inaudible breath. 'Her father too.' . . . These were the things she knew! At once I said, 'Ah! but he is not like that.' This, it seemed, she did not intend to dispute; but after a time the strange still whisper wandering dreamily in the air stole into my ears. 'Why is he different? Is he better? Is he . . .' 'Upon my word of honour,' I broke in, 'I believe he is.' We subdued our tones to a mysterious pitch. Amongst the huts of Jim's workmen (they were mostly liberated slaves from the Sherif's stockade) somebody started a shrill, drawling song. Across the river a big fire (at Doramin's, I think) made a glowing ball, completely isolated in the night. 'Is he more true?' she murmured. 'Yes,' I said.

'More true than any other man,' she repeated in lingering accents. 'Nobody here,' I said, 'would dream of doubting his word—nobody would dare—except you.'

"I think she made a movement at this. 'More brave,' she went on in a changed tone. 'Fear will never drive him away from you,' I said a little nervously. The song stopped short on a shrill note, and was succeeded by several voices talking in the distance. Jim's voice too. I was struck by her silence. 'What has he been telling you? He has been telling you something?' I asked. There was no answer. 'What is it he told you?' I insisted.

" 'Do you think I can tell you? How am I to know? How am I to understand?' she cried at last. There was a stir. I believe she was wringing her hands. 'There is something he can never forget.'

" 'So much the better for you,' I said gloomily.

" 'What is it? What is it?' She put an extraordinary force of appeal into her supplicating tone. 'He says he had been afraid. How can I believe this? Am I a mad woman to believe this? You all remember something! You all go back to it. What is it? You tell me! What is this thing? Is it alive?—is it dead? I hate it. It is cruel. Has it got a face and a voice—this calamity? Will he see it—will he hear it? In his sleep perhaps when he cannot see me—and then arise and go. Ah! I shall never forgive him. My mother had forgiven—but I, never! Will it be a sign—a call . . .'

"It was a wonderful experience. She mistrusted his very slumbers—and she seemed to think I could tell her why! Thus a poor mortal seduced by the charm of an apparition might have tried to wring from another ghost the tremendous secret of the claim the other world holds over a disembodied soul astray amongst the passions of this earth. The very ground on which I stood seemed to melt under my feet. And it was so simple too; but if the spirits evoked by our fears and our unrest have ever to vouch for each other's constancy before the forlorn magicians

that we are, then I—I alone of us dwellers in the flesh—have shuddered
in the hopeless chill of such a task. A sign, a call! How telling in its
expression was her ignorance. A few words! How she came to know
them, how she came to pronounce them, I can't imagine. Women find
their inspiration in the stress of moments that for us are merely awful,
absurd, or futile. To discover that she had a voice at all was enough to
strike awe into the heart. Had a spurned stone cried out in pain it could
not have appeared a greater and more pitiful miracle. These few sounds
wandering in the dark had made their two benighted lives tragic to my
mind. It was impossible to make her understand. I chafed silently at my
impotence. And Jim, too—poor devil! Who would need him? Who
would remember him? He had what he wanted. His very existence
probably had been forgotten by this time. They had mastered their fates.
They were tragic.

"Her immobility before me was clearly expectant, and my part was
to speak for my brother from the realm of forgetful shades. I was deeply
moved at my responsibility and at her distress. I would have given
anything for the power to soothe her frail soul, tormenting itself in its
invincible ignorance like a small bird beating about the cruel wires of
a cage. Nothing easier than to say, Have no fear! Nothing more difficult.
How does one kill fear, I wonder? How do you shoot a spectre through
the heart, slash off its spectral head, take it by its spectral throat? It is
an enterprise you rush into while you dream, and are glad to make your
escape with wet hair and every limb shaking. The bullet is not run, the
blade not forged, the man not born; even the winged words of truth
drop at your feet like lumps of lead. You require for such a desperate
encounter an enchanted and poisoned shaft dipped in a lie too subtle
to be found on earth. An enterprise for a dream, my masters!

"I began my exorcism with a heavy heart, with a sort of sullen anger
in it too. Jim's voice, suddenly raised with a stern intonation, carried
across the courtyard, reproving the carelessness of some dumb sinner by
the river-side. Nothing—I said, speaking in a distinct murmur—there
could be nothing, in that unknown world she fancied so eager to rob
her of her happiness, there was nothing neither living nor dead, there
was no face, no voice, no power, that could tear Jim from her side. I
drew breath and she whispered softly, 'He told me so.' 'He told you the
truth,' I said. 'Nothing,' she sighed out, and abruptly turned upon me
with a barely audible intensity of tone. 'Why did you come to us from
out there? He speaks of you too often. You make me afraid. Do you—
do you want him?' A sort of stealthy fierceness had crept into our hurried
mutters. 'I shall never come again,' I said bitterly. 'And I don't want
him. No one wants him.' 'No one,' she repeated in a tone of doubt.
'No one,' I affirmed, feeling myself swayed by some strange excitement.
'You think him strong, wise, courageous, great—why not believe him

to be true too? I shall go to-morrow—and that is the end. You shall never be troubled by a voice from there again. This world you don't know is too big to miss him. You understand? Too big. You've got his heart in your hand. You must feel that. You must know that.' 'Yes, I know that,' she breathed out, hard and still, as a statue might whisper.

"I felt I had done nothing. And what is it that I had wished to do? I am not sure now. At the time I was animated by an inexplicable ardour, as if before some great and necessary task—the influence of the moment upon my mental and emotional state. There are in all our lives such moments, such influences, coming from the outside, as it were, irresistible, incomprehensible—as if brought about by the mysterious conjunctions of the planets. She owned, as I had put it to her, his heart. She had that and everything else—if she could only believe it. What I had to tell her was that in the whole world there was no one who ever would need his heart, his mind, his hand. It was a common fate, and yet it seemed an awful thing to say of any man. She listened without a word, and her stillness now was like the protest of an invincible unbelief. What need she care for the world beyond the forests? I asked. From all the multitudes that peopled the vastness of that unknown there would come, I assured her, as long as he lived, neither a call nor a sign for him. Never. I was carried away. Never! Never! I remember with wonder the sort of dogged fierceness I displayed. I had the illusion of having got the spectre by the throat at last. Indeed the whole real thing has left behind the detailed and amazing impression of a dream. Why should she fear? She knew him to be strong, true, wise, brave. He was all that. Certainly. He was more. He was great—invincible—and the world did not want him, it had forgotten him, it would not even know him.

"I stopped; the silence over Patusan was profound, and the feeble dry sound of a paddle striking the side of a canoe somewhere in the middle of the river seemed to make it infinite. 'Why?' she murmured. I felt that sort of rage one feels during a hard tussle. The spectre was trying to slip out of my grasp. 'Why?' she repeated louder; 'tell me!' And as I remained confounded, she stamped with her foot like a spoilt child. 'Why? Speak.' 'You want to know,' I asked in a fury. 'Yes!' she cried. 'Because he is not good enough,' I said brutally. During the moment's pause I noticed the fire on the other shore blaze up, dilating the circle of its glow like an amazed stare, and contract suddenly to a red pinpoint. I only knew how close to me she had been when I felt the clutch of her fingers on my forearm. Without raising her voice, she threw into it an infinity of scathing contempt, bitterness, and despair.

" 'This is the very thing he said. . . . You lie!'

"The last two words she cried at me in the native dialect. 'Hear me out!' I entreated; she caught her breath tremulously, flung my arm away. 'Nobody, nobody is good enough,' I began with the greatest earnestness.

I could hear the sobbing labour of her breath frightfully quickened. I hung my head. What was the use? Footsteps were approaching; I slipped away without another word. . . ."

Chapter XXXIV

Marlow swung his legs out, got up quickly, and staggered a little, as though he had been set down after a rush through space. He leaned his back against the balustrade and faced a disordered array of long cane-chairs. The bodies prone in them seemed startled out of their torpor by his movement. One or two sat up as if alarmed; here and there a cigar glowed yet; Marlow looked at them all with the eyes of a man returning from the excessive remoteness of a dream. A throat was cleared; a calm voice encouraged negligently, "Well."

"Nothing," said Marlow with a slight start. "He had told her—that's all. She did not believe him—nothing more. As to myself, I do not know whether it be just, proper, decent for me to rejoice or to be sorry. For my part, I cannot say what I believed—indeed I don't know to this day, and never shall probably. But what did the poor devil believe himself? Truth shall prevail—don't you know, *Magna est veritas et*[1] . . . Yes, when it gets a chance. There is a law, no doubt—and likewise a law regulates your luck in the throwing of dice. It is not Justice the servant of men, but accident, hazard, Fortune—the ally of patient Time—that holds an even and scrupulous balance. Both of us had said the very same thing. Did we both speak the truth—or one of us did— or neither? . . ."

Marlow paused, crossed his arms on his breast, and in a changed tone—

"She said we lied. Poor soul! Well—let's leave it to Chance, whose ally is Time, that cannot be hurried, and whose enemy is Death, that will not wait. I had retreated—a little cowed, I must own. I had tried a fall[2] with fear itself and got thrown—of course. I had only succeeded in adding to her anguish the hint of some mysterious collusion, of an inexplicable and incomprehensible conspiracy to keep her for ever in the dark. And it had come easily, naturally, unavoidably, by his act, by her own act! It was as though I had been shown the working of the implacable destiny of which we are the victims—and the tools. It was appalling to think of the girl whom I had left standing there motionless; Jim's footsteps had a fateful sound as he tramped by, without seeing me, in his heavy laced boots. 'What? No lights!' he said in a loud, surprised voice. 'What are you doing in the dark—you two?' Next moment he

---

1. From the Vulgate Bible: "Magna est veritas et praevalet" (I Esdras 4.41). The King James translation is: "Great is Truth, and mighty above all things."
2. Entered a bout of wrestling.

caught sight of her, I suppose. 'Hallo, girl!' he cried cheerily. 'Hallo, boy!' she answered at once, with amazing pluck.

"This was their usual greeting to each other, and the bit of swagger she would put into her rather high but sweet voice was very droll, pretty, and childlike. It delighted Jim greatly. This was the last occasion on which I heard them exchange this familiar hail, and it struck a chill into my heart. There was the high sweet voice, the pretty effort, the swagger; but it all seemed to die out prematurely, and the playful call sounded like a moan. It was too confoundedly awful. 'What have you done with Marlow?' Jim was asking; and then, 'Gone down—has he? Funny I didn't meet him. . . . You there, Marlow?'

"I didn't answer. I wasn't going in—not yet at any rate. I really couldn't. While he was calling me I was engaged in making my escape through a little gate leading out upon a stretch of newly cleared ground. No; I couldn't face them yet. I walked hastily with lowered head along a trodden path. The ground rose gently, the few big trees had been felled, the undergrowth had been cut down and the grass fired. He had a mind to try a coffee-plantation there. The big hill, rearing its double summit coal-black in the clear yellow glow of the rising moon, seemed to cast its shadow upon the ground prepared for that experiment. He was going to try ever so many experiments; I had admired his energy, his enterprise, and his shrewdness. Nothing on earth seemed less real now than his plans, his energy, and his enthusiasm; and raising my eyes, I saw part of the moon glittering through the bushes at the bottom of the chasm. For a moment it looked as though the smooth disc, falling from its place in the sky upon the earth, had rolled to the bottom of that precipice: its ascending movement was like a leisurely rebound; it disengaged itself from the tangle of twigs; the bare contorted limb of some tree, growing on the slope, made a black crack right across its face. It threw its level rays afar as if from a cavern, and in this mournful eclipse-like light the stumps of felled trees uprose very dark, the heavy shadows fell at my feet on all sides, my own moving shadow, and across my path the shadow of the solitary grave perpetually garlanded with flowers. In the darkened moonlight the interlaced blossoms took on shapes foreign to one's memory and colours indefinable to the eye, as though they had been special flowers gathered by no man, grown not in this world, and destined for the use of the dead alone. Their powerful scent hung in the warm air, making it thick and heavy like the fumes of incense. The lumps of white coral shone round the dark mound like a chaplet of bleached skulls, and everything around was so quiet that when I stood still all sound and all movement in the world seemed to come to an end.

"It was a great peace, as if the earth had been one grave, and for a time I stood there thinking mostly of the living who, buried in remote places out of the knowledge of mankind, still are fated to share in its

tragic or grotesque miseries. In its noble struggles too—who knows? The
human heart is vast enough to contain all the world. It is valiant enough
to bear the burden, but where is the courage that would cast it off?

"I suppose I must have fallen into a sentimental mood; I only know
that I stood there long enough for the sense of utter solitude to get hold
of me so completely that all I had lately seen, all I had heard, and the
very human speech itself, seemed to have passed away out of existence,
living only for a while longer in my memory, as though I had been the
last of mankind. It was a strange and melancholy illusion, evolved half-
consciously like all our illusions, which I suspect only to be visions of
remote unattainable truth, seen dimly. This was, indeed, one of the
lost, forgotten, unknown places of the earth; I had looked under its
obscure surface; and I felt that when to-morrow I had left it for ever, it
would slip out of existence, to live only in my memory till I myself
passed into oblivion. I have that feeling about me now; perhaps it is that
feeling which has incited me to tell you the story, to try to hand over
to you, as it were, its very existence, its reality—the truth disclosed in
a moment of illusion.

"Cornelius broke upon it. He bolted out, vermin-like, from the long
grass growing in a depression of the ground. I believe his house was
rotting somewhere near by, though I've never seen it, not having been
far enough in that direction. He ran towards me upon the path; his feet,
shod in dirty white shoes, twinkled on the dark earth; he pulled himself
up, and began to whine and cringe under a tall stove-pipe hat. His
dried-up little carcass was swallowed up, totally lost, in a suit of black
broadcloth. That was his costume for holidays and ceremonies, and it
reminded me that this was the fourth Sunday I had spent in Patusan.
All the time of my stay I had been vaguely aware of his desire to confide
in me, if he only could get me all to himself. He hung about with an
eager craving look on his sour yellow little face; but his timidity had
kept him back as much as my natural reluctance to have anything to
do with such an unsavoury creature. He would have succeeded, nevertheless, had he not been so ready to slink off as soon as you looked at
him. He would slink off before Jim's severe gaze, before my own, which
I tried to make indifferent, even before Tamb' Itam's surly, superior
glance. He was perpetually slinking away; whenever seen he was seen
moving off deviously, his face over his shoulder, with either a mistrustful
snarl or a woe-begone, piteous, mute aspect; but no assumed expression
could conceal this innate irremediable abjectness of his nature, any
more than an arrangement of clothing can conceal some monstrous
deformity of the body.

"I don't know whether it was the demoralisation of my utter defeat
in my encounter with a spectre of fear less than an hour ago, but I let
him capture me without even a show of resistance. I was doomed to be
the recipient of confidences, and to be confronted with unanswerable

questions. It was trying; but the contempt, the unreasoned contempt, the man's appearance provoked, made it easier to bear. He couldn't possibly matter. Nothing mattered, since I had made up my mind that Jim, for whom alone I cared, had at last mastered his fate. He had told me he was satisfied . . . nearly. This is going further than most of us dare. I—who have the right to think myself good enough—dare not. Neither does any of you here, I suppose? . . ."

Marlow paused, as if expecting an answer. Nobody spoke.

"Quite right," he began again. "Let no soul know, since the truth can be wrung out of us only by some cruel, little, awful catastrophe. But he is one of us, and he could say he was satisfied . . . nearly. Just fancy this! Nearly satisfied. One could almost envy him his catastrophe. Nearly satisfied. After this nothing could matter. It did not matter who suspected him, who trusted him, who loved him, who hated him—especially as it was Cornelius who hated him.

"Yet after all this was a kind of recognition. You shall judge of a man by his foes as well as by his friends, and this enemy of Jim was such as no decent man would be ashamed to own, without, however, making too much of him. This was the view Jim took, and in which I shared; but Jim disregarded him on general grounds. 'My dear Marlow,' he said, 'I feel that if I go straight nothing can touch me. Indeed I do. Now you have been long enough here to have a good look round—and, frankly, don't you think I am pretty safe. It all depends upon me, and, by Jove! I have lots of confidence in myself. The worst thing he could do would be to kill me, I suppose. I don't think for a moment he would. He couldn't, you know—not if I were myself to hand him a loaded rifle for the purpose, and then turn my back on him. That's the sort of thing he is. And suppose he would—suppose he could? Well—what of that? I didn't come here flying for my life—did I? I came here to set my back against the wall, and I am going to stay here . . .'

" 'Till you are *quite* satisfied,' I struck in.

"We were sitting at the time under the roof in the stern of his boat; twenty paddles flashed like one, ten on a side, striking the water with a single splash, while behind our backs Tamb' Itam dipped silently right and left, and stared right down the river, attentive to keep the long canoe in the greatest strength of the current. Jim bowed his head, and our last talk seemed to flicker out for good. He was seeing me off as far as the mouth of the river. The schooner had left the day before, working down and drifting on the ebb, while I had prolonged my stay overnight. And now he was seeing me off.

"Jim had been a little angry with me for mentioning Cornelius at all. I had not, in truth, said much. The man was too insignificant to be dangerous, though he was as full of hate as he could hold. He had called me 'honourable sir' at every second sentence, and had whined at my elbow as he followed me from the grave of his 'late wife' to the gate of

Jim's compound. He declared himself the most unhappy of men, a victim, crushed like a worm; he entreated me to look at him. I wouldn't turn my head to do so; but I could see out of the corner of my eye his obsequious shadow gliding after mine, while the moon, suspended on our right hand, seemed to gloat serenely upon the spectacle. He tried to explain—as I've told you—his share in the events of the memorable night. It was a matter of expediency. How could he know who was going to get the upper hand? 'I would have saved him, honourable sir! I would have saved him for eighty dollars,' he protested in dulcet tones, keeping a pace behind me. 'He has saved himself,' I said, 'and he has forgiven you.' I heard a sort of tittering, and turned upon him; at once he appeared ready to take to his heels. 'What are you laughing at?' I asked, standing still. 'Don't be deceived, honourable sir!' he shrieked, seemingly losing all control over his feelings. '*He* save himself! He knows nothing, honourable sir—nothing whatever. Who is he? What does he want here—the big thief? What does he want here? He throws dust into everybody's eyes; he throws dust into your eyes, honourable sir; but he can't throw dust into my eyes. He is a big fool, honourable sir.' I laughed contemptuously, and, turning on my heel, began to walk on again. He ran up to my elbow and whispered forcibly, 'He's no more than a little child here—like a little child—a little child.' Of course I didn't take the slightest notice, and seeing the time pressed, because we were approaching the bamboo fence that glittered over the blackened ground of the clearing, he came to the point. He commenced by being abjectly lachrymose. His great misfortunes had affected his head. He hoped I would kindly forget what nothing but his troubles made him say. He didn't mean anything by it; only the honourable sir did not know what it was to be ruined, broken down, trampled upon. After this introduction he approached the matter near his heart, but in such a rambling, ejaculatory, craven fashion, that for a long time I couldn't make out what he was driving at. He wanted me to intercede with Jim in his favour. It seemed, too, to be some sort of money affair. I heard time and again the words, 'Moderate provision—suitable present.' He seemed to be claiming value for something, and he even went the length of saying with some warmth that life was not worth having if a man were to be robbed of everything. I did not breathe a word, of course, but neither did I stop my ears. The gist of the affair, which became clear to me gradually, was in this, that he regarded himself as entitled to some money in exchange for the girl. He had brought her up. Somebody else's child. Great trouble and pains—old man now—suitable present. If the honourable sir would say a word. . . . I stood still to look at him with curiosity, and fearful lest I should think him extortionate, I suppose, he hastily brought himself to make a concession. In consideration of a 'suitable present' given at once, he would, he declared, be willing to undertake the charge of the girl, 'without any other provision—when the time came for the gentleman to go home.' His little yellow face, all crumpled as though it had been squeezed together, expressed the most anxious, eager avarice. His voice whined coaxingly, 'No more trouble —natural guardian—a sum of money . . .'

"I stood there and marvelled. That kind of thing, with him, was evidently a vocation. I discovered suddenly in his cringing attitude a sort of assurance, as though he had been all his life dealing in certitudes. He must have thought I was dispassionately considering his proposal, because he became as sweet as honey. 'Every gentleman made a provision when the time came to go home,' he began insinuatingly. I slammed the little gate. 'In this case, Mr Cornelius,' I said, 'the time will never come.' He took a few seconds to gather this in. 'What!' he fairly squealed. 'Why,' I continued from my side of the gate, 'haven't you heard him say so himself? He will never go home.' 'Oh! this is too much,' he shouted. He would not address me as 'honoured sir' any more. He was very still for a time, and then without a trace of humility began very low: 'Never go—ah! He—he—he comes here devil knows from where—comes here—devil knows why—to trample on me till I die—ah—trample' (he stamped softly with both feet), 'trample like this—nobody knows why—till I die. . . .' His voice became quite extinct; he was bothered by a little cough; he came up close to the fence and told me, dropping into a confidential and piteous tone, that he would *not* be trampled upon. 'Patience—patience,' he muttered, striking his breast. I had done laughing at him, but unexpectedly he treated me to a wild cracked burst of it. 'Ha!·ha! ha! We shall see! We shall see! What? Steal from me! Steal from me everything! Everything! Everything!' His head drooped on one shoulder, his hands were hanging before him lightly clasped. One would have thought he had cherished the girl with surpassing love, that his spirit had been crushed and his heart broken by the most cruel of spoliations. Suddenly he lifted his head and shot out an infamous word. 'Like her mother—she is like her deceitful mother. Exactly. In her face too. In her face. The devil!' He leaned his forehead against the fence, and in that position uttered threats and horrible blasphemies in Portuguese in very weak ejaculations, mingled with miserable plaints and groans, coming out with a heave of the shoulders as though he had been overtaken by a deadly fit of sickness. It was an inexpressibly grotesque and vile performance, and I hastened away. He tried to shout something after me. Some disparagement of Jim, I believe—not too loud though, we were too near the house. All I heard distinctly was, 'No more than a little child—a little child.' "

Chapter XXXV

"But next morning, at the first bend of the river shutting off the houses of Patusan, all this dropped out of my sight bodily, with its colour, its design, and its meaning, like a picture created by fancy on a canvas, upon which, after long contemplation, you turn your back for the last time. It remains in the memory motionless, unfaded, with its life arrested, in an unchanging light. There are the ambitions, the fears, the hate, the hopes, and they remain in my mind just as I had seen them —intense and as if for ever suspended in their expression. I had turned away from the picture and was going back to the world where events move, men change, light flickers, life flows in a clear stream, no matter whether over mud or over stones. I wasn't going to dive into it; I would have enough to do to keep my head above the surface. But as to what I was leaving behind, I cannot imagine any alteration. The immense and magnanimous Doramin and his little motherly witch of a wife, gazing together upon the land and nursing secretly their dreams of parental ambition; Tunku Allang, wizened and greatly perplexed; Dain Waris, intelligent and brave, with his faith in Jim, with his firm glance and his ironic friendliness; the girl, absorbed in her frightened, suspicious adoration; Tamb' Itam, surly and faithful; Cornelius, leaning his forehead against the fence under the moonlight—I am certain of them. They exist as if under an enchanter's wand. But the figure round which all these are grouped—that one lives, and I am not certain of him. No magician's wand can immobilise him under my eyes. He is one of us.

"Jim, as I've told you, accompanied me on the first stage of my journey back to the world he had renounced, and the way at times seemed to lead through the very heart of untouched wilderness. The empty reaches sparkled under the high sun; between the high walls of vegetation the heat drowsed upon the water, and the boat, impelled vigorously, cut her way through the air that seemed to have settled dense and warm under the shelter of lofty trees.

"The shadow of the impending separation had already put an immense space between us, and when we spoke it was with an effort, as if to force our low voices across a vast and increasing distance. The boat fairly flew; we sweltered side by side in the stagnant superheated air; the smell of mud, of marsh, the primeval smell of fecund earth, seemed to sting our faces; till suddenly at a bend it was as if a great hand far away had lifted a heavy curtain, had flung open an immense portal. The light itself seemed to stir, the sky above our heads widened, a far off murmur reached our ears, a freshness enveloped us, filled our lungs, quickened our thoughts, our blood, our regrets—and, straight ahead, the forests sank down against the dark-blue ridge of the sea.

"I breathed deeply, I revelled in the vastness of the opened horizon, in the different atmosphere that seemed to vibrate with the toil of life, with the energy of an impeccable world. This sky and this sea were open to me. The girl was right—there was a sign, a call in them—something to which I responded with every fibre of my being. I let my eyes roam through space, like a man released from bonds who stretches his cramped limbs, runs, leaps, responds to the inspiring elation of freedom. 'This is glorious!' I cried, and then I looked at the sinner by my side. He sat with his head sunk on his breast and said 'Yes,' without raising his eyes, as if afraid to see writ large on the clear sky of the offing the reproach of his romantic conscience.

"I remember the smallest details of that afternoon. We landed on a bit of white beach. It was backed by a low cliff wooded on the brow, draped in creepers to the very foot. Below us the plain of the sea, of a serene and intense blue, stretched with a slight upward tilt to the thread-like horizon drawn at the height of our eyes. Great waves of glitter blew lightly along the pitted dark surface, as swift as feathers chased by the breeze. A chain of islands sat broken and massive facing the wide estuary, displayed in a sheet of pale glassy water reflecting faithfully the contour of the shore. High in the colourless sunshine a solitary bird, all black, hovered, dropping and soaring above the same spot with a slight rocking motion of the wings. A ragged, sooty bunch of flimsy mat hovels was perched over its own inverted image upon a crooked multitude of high piles the colour of ebony. A tiny black canoe put off from amongst them with two tiny men, all black, who toiled exceedingly, striking down at the pale water: and the canoe seemed to slide painfully on a mirror. This bunch of miserable hovels was the fishing village that boasted of the white lord's especial protection, and the two men crossing over were the old headman and his son-in-law. They landed and walked up to us on the white sand, lean, dark-brown as if dried in smoke, with ashy patches on the skin of their naked shoulders and breasts. Their heads were bound in dirty but carefully folded headkerchiefs, and the old man began at once to state a complaint, voluble, stretching a lank arm, screwing up at Jim his old bleared eyes confidently. The Rajah's people would not leave them alone; there had been some trouble about a lot of turtles' eggs his people had collected on the islets there—and leaning at arm's-length upon his paddle, he pointed with a brown skinny hand over the sea. Jim listened for a time without looking up, and at last told him gently to wait. He would hear him by-and-by. They withdrew obediently to some little distance, and sat on their heels, with their paddles lying before them on the sand; the silvery gleams in their eyes followed our movements patiently: and the immensity of the outspread sea, the stillness of the coast, passing north and south beyond the limits of my vision, made up one colossal Presence watching us four dwarfs isolated on a strip of glistening sand.

" 'The trouble is,' remarked Jim moodily, 'that for generations these beggars of fishermen in that village there had been considered as the Rajah's personal slaves—and the old rip can't get it into his head that . . .'

"He paused. 'That you have changed all that,' I said.

" 'Yes. I've changed all that,' he muttered in a gloomy voice.

" 'You have had your opportunity,' I pursued.

" 'Have I?' he said. 'Well, yes. I suppose so. Yes. I have got back my confidence in myself—a good name—yet sometimes I wish . . . No! I shall hold what I've got. Can't expect anything more.' He flung his arm out towards the sea. 'Not out there anyhow.' He stamped his foot upon the sand. 'This is my limit, because nothing less will do.'

"We continued pacing the beach. 'Yes, I've changed all that,' he went on, with a sidelong glance at the two patient squatting fishermen; 'but only try to think what it would be if I went away. Jove! can't you see it? Hell loose. No! To-morrow I shall go and take my chance of drinking that silly old Tunku Allang's coffee, and I shall make no end of fuss over these rotten turtles' eggs. No. I can't say—enough. Never. I must go on, go on for ever holding up my end, to feel sure that nothing can touch me. I must stick to their belief in me to feel safe and to—to' . . . He cast about for a word, seemed to look for it on the sea . . . 'to keep in touch with' . . . His voice sank suddenly to a murmur . . . 'with those whom, perhaps, I shall never see any more. With—with—you, for instance.'

"I was profoundly humbled by his words. 'For God's sake,' I said, 'don't set me up, my dear fellow; just look to yourself.' I felt a gratitude, an affection, for that straggler whose eyes had singled me out, keeping my place in the ranks of an insignificant multitude. How little that was to boast of, after all! I turned my burning face away; under the low sun, glowing, darkened and crimson, like an ember snatched from the fire, the sea lay outspread, offering all its immense stillness to the approach of the fiery orb. Twice he was going to speak, but checked himself; at last, as if he had found a formula—

" 'I shall be faithful,' he said quietly. 'I shall be faithful,' he repeated, without looking at me, but for the first time letting his eyes wander upon the waters, whose blueness had changed to a gloomy purple under the fires of sunset. Ah! he was romantic, romantic. I recalled some words of Stein's. . . . 'In the destructive element immerse! . . . To follow the dream, and again to follow the dream—and so—always—*usque ad finem* . . .' He was romantic, but none the less true. Who could tell what forms, what visions, what faces, what forgiveness he could see in the glow of the west! . . . A small boat, leaving the schooner, moved slowly, with a regular beat of two oars, towards the sandbank to take me off. 'And then there's Jewel,' he said, out of the great silence of earth, sky, and sea, which had mastered my very thoughts so that his voice made me start. 'There's Jewel.' 'Yes,' I murmured. 'I need not tell you what she is to me,' he pursued. 'You've seen. In time she will come to understand . . .' 'I hope so,' I interrupted. 'She trusts me, too,' he mused, and then changed his tone. 'When shall we meet next, I wonder?' he said.

" 'Never—unless you come out,' I answered, avoiding his glance. He didn't seem to be surprised; he kept very quiet for a while.

" 'Good-bye, then,' he said, after a pause. 'Perhaps it's just as well.'

"We shook hands, and I walked to the boat, which waited with her nose on the beach. The schooner, her mainsail set and jib-sheet to windward, curveted on the purple sea; there was a rosy tinge on her sails. 'Will you be going home again soon?' asked Jim, just as I swung my leg over the gunwale. 'In a year or so if I live,' I said. The forefoot grated on the sand, the boat floated, the wet oars flashed and dipped once, twice. Jim, at the water's edge, raised his voice, 'Tell them . . .' he began. I signed to the men to cease rowing, and waited in wonder. Tell who? The half-submerged sun faced him; I could see its red gleam in his eyes that looked dumbly at me. . . . 'No—nothing,' he said, and with a slight wave of his hand motioned the boat away. I did not look again at the shore till I had clambered on board the schooner.

"By that time the sun had set. The twilight lay over the east, and the coast, turned black, extended infinitely its sombre wall that seemed the very stronghold of the night; the western horizon was one great blaze of gold and crimson in which a big detached cloud floated dark and still, casting a slaty shadow on the water beneath, and I saw Jim on the beach watching the schooner fall off and gather headway.

"The two half-naked fishermen had arisen as soon as I had gone; they were no doubt pouring the plaint of their trifling, miserable, oppressed lives into the ears of the white lord, and no doubt he was listening to it, making it his own, for was it not a part of his luck—the luck 'from the word Go'—the luck to which he had assured me he was so completely equal. They too, I should think, were in luck, and I was sure their pertinacity would be equal to it. Their dark-skinned bodies vanished on the dark background long before I had lost sight of their protector. He was white from head to foot, and remained persistently visible with the stronghold of the night at his back, the sea at his feet, the opportunity by his side—still veiled. What do you say? Was it still veiled? I don't know. For me that white figure in the stillness of coast and sea seemed to stand at the heart of a vast enigma. The twilight was ebbing fast from the sky above his head, the strip of sand had sunk already under his feet, he himself appeared no bigger than a child—then only a speck, a tiny white speck, that seemed to catch all the light left in a darkened world. . . . And, suddenly, I lost him. . . ."

Chapter XXXVI

With these words Marlow had ended his narrative, and his audience had broken up forthwith, under his abstract, pensive gaze. Men drifted off the verandah in pairs or alone without loss of time, without offering a remark, as if the last image of that incomplete story, its incompleteness itself, and the very tone of the speaker, had made discussion vain and comment impossible. Each of them seemed to carry away his own impression, to carry it away with him like a secret; but there was only one man of all these listeners who was ever to hear the last word of the story. It came to him at home, more than two years later, and it came contained in a thick packet addressed in Marlow's upright and angular handwriting.

The privileged man opened the packet, looked in, then, laying it down, went to the window. His rooms were in the highest flat of a lofty building, and his glance could travel afar beyond the clear panes of glass, as though he were looking out of the lantern of a lighthouse. The slopes of the roofs glistened, the dark broken ridges succeeded each other without end like sombre, uncrested waves, and from the depths of the town under his feet ascended a confused and unceasing mutter. The spires of churches, numerous, scattered haphazard, uprose like beacons on a maze of shoals without a channel; the driving rain mingled with the falling dusk of a winter's evening; and the booming of a big clock on a tower, striking the hour, rolled past in voluminous, austere bursts of sound, with a shrill vibrating cry at the core. He drew the heavy curtains.

The light of his shaded reading-lamp slept like a sheltered pool, his footfalls made no sound on the carpet, his wandering days were over. No more horizons as boundless as hope, no more twilights within the forests as solemn as temples, in the hot quest for the Ever-undiscovered Country over the hill, across the stream, beyond the wave. The hour was striking! No more! No more!—but the opened packet under the lamp brought back the sounds, the visions, the very savour of the past —a multitude of fading faces, a tumult of low voices, dying away upon the shores of distant seas under a passionate and unconsoling sunshine. He sighed and sat down to read.

At first he saw three distinct enclosures. A good many pages closely blackened and pinned together; a loose square sheet of greyish paper with a few words traced in a handwriting he had never seen before, and an explanatory letter from Marlow. From this last fell another letter, yellowed by time and frayed on the folds. He picked it up and, laying it aside, turned to Marlow's message, ran swiftly over the opening lines, and, checking himself, thereafter read on deliberately, like one approaching with slow feet and alert eyes the glimpse of an undiscovered country.

". . . I don't suppose you've forgotten," went on the letter. "You alone have showed an interest in him that survived the telling of his story, though I remember well you would not admit he had mastered his fate. You prophesied for him the disaster of weariness and of disgust with acquired honour, with the self-appointed task, with the love sprung from pity and youth. You had said you knew so well 'that kind of thing,' its illusory satisfaction, its unavoidable deception. You said also—I call to mind—that 'giving your life up to them' (*them* meaning all of mankind with skins brown, yellow, or black in colour) 'was like selling your soul to a brute.' You contended that 'that kind of thing' was only endurable and enduring when based on a firm conviction in the truth of ideas racially our own, in whose name are established the order, the morality of an ethical progress. 'We want its strength at our backs,' you had said. 'We want a belief in its necessity and its justice, to make a worthy and conscious sacrifice of our lives. Without it the sacrifice is only forgetfulness, the way of offering is no better than the way to perdition.' In other words, you maintained that we must fight in the ranks or our lives don't count. Possibly! You ought to know—be it said without malice —you who have rushed into one or two places single-handed and came out cleverly, without singeing your wings. The point, however, is that of all mankind Jim had no dealings but with himself, and the question is whether at the last he had not confessed to a faith mightier than the laws of order and progress.

"I affirm nothing. Perhaps you may pronounce—after you've read. There is much truth—after all—in the common expression 'under a cloud.' It is impossible to see him clearly—especially as it is through the eyes of others that we take our last look at him. I have no hesitation in imparting to you all I know of the last episode that, as he used to say, had 'come to him.' One wonders whether this was perhaps that supreme opportunity, that last and satisfying test for which I had always suspected him to be waiting, before he could frame a message to the impeccable world. You remember that when I was leaving him for the last time he had asked whether I would be going home soon, and suddenly cried after me, 'Tell them . . .' I had waited—curious I'll own, and hopeful too—only to hear him shout, 'No—nothing.' That was all then—and there will be nothing more; there will be no message, unless such as each of us can interpret for himself from the language of facts, that are so often more enigmatic than the craftiest arrangement of words. He made, it is true, one more attempt to deliver himself; but that too failed, as you may perceive if you look at the sheet of greyish foolscap[1]

1. Common term for sheets of legal-size paper, so called from the watermark of a fool's cap and bells originally marking this type of paper.

enclosed here. He had tried to write; do you notice the commonplace hand? It is headed 'The Fort, Patusan.' I suppose he had carried out his intention of making out of his house a place of defence. It was an excellent plan: a deep ditch, an earth wall topped by a palisade, and at the angles guns mounted on platforms to sweep each side of the square. Doramin had agreed to furnish him the guns; and so each man of his party would know there was a place of safety, upon which every faithful partisan could rally in case of some sudden danger. All this showed his judicious foresight, his faith in the future. What he called 'my own people'—the liberated captives of the Sherif—were to make a distinct quarter of Patusan, with their huts and little plots of ground under the walls of the stronghold. Within he would be an invincible host in himself. 'The Fort, Patusan.' No date, as you observe. What is a number and a name to a day of days? It is also impossible to say whom he had in his mind when he seized the pen: Stein—myself—the world at large—or was this only the aimless startled cry of a solitary man confronted by his fate? 'An awful thing has happened,' he wrote before he flung the pen down for the first time; look at the ink blot resembling the head of an arrow under these words. After a while he had tried again, scrawling heavily, as if with a hand of lead, another line. 'I must now at once . . .' The pen had spluttered, and that time he gave it up. There's nothing more; he had seen a broad gulf that neither eye nor voice could span. I can understand this. He was overwhelmed by the inexplicable; he was overwhelmed by his own personality—the gift of that destiny which he had done his best to master.

"I send you also an old letter—a very old letter. It was found carefully preserved in his writing-case. It is from his father, and by the date you can see he must have received it a few days before he joined the *Patna*. Thus it must be the last letter he ever had from home. He had treasured it all these years. The good old parson fancied his sailor son. I've looked in at a sentence here and there. There is nothing in it except just affection. He tells his 'dear James' that the last long letter from him was very 'honest and entertaining.' He would not have him 'judge men harshly or hastily.' There are four pages of it, easy morality and family news. Tom had 'taken orders.' Carrie's husband had 'money losses.' The old chap goes on equably trusting Providence and the established order of the universe, but alive to its small dangers and its small mercies. One can almost see him, grey-haired and serene in the inviolable shelter of his book-lined, faded, and comfortable study, where for forty years he had conscientiously gone over and over again the round of his little thoughts about faith and virtue, about the conduct of life and the only proper manner of dying; where he had written so many sermons, where he sits talking to his boy, over there, on the other side of the earth. But what of the distance. Virtue is one all over the world, and there is only one faith, one conceivable conduct of life, one manner of dying. He hopes his 'dear James' will never forget that 'who once gives way to temptation, in the very instant hazards his total depravity and everlasting ruin. Therefore resolve fixedly never, through any possible motives, to do anything which you believe to be wrong.'[2] There is also some news of a favourite dog; and a pony, 'which all you boys used to ride,' had gone blind from old age and had to be shot. The old chap invokes Heaven's blessing; the mother and all the girls then at home send their love. . . . No, there is nothing much in that yellow frayed letter fluttering out of his cherishing grasp after so many years. It was never answered, but who can say what converse he may have held with all these placid, colourless forms of men and women peopling that quiet corner of the world as free of danger or strife as a tomb, and breathing equably the air of undisturbed rectitude. It seems amazing that he should belong to it, he to whom so many things 'had come.' Nothing ever came to them; they would never be taken unawares, and never be called upon to grapple with fate. Here they all are, evoked by the mild gossip of the father, all these brothers and sisters, bone of his bone and flesh of his flesh,[3] gazing with clear unconscious eyes, while I seem to see him, returned at last, no longer a mere white speck at the heart of an immense mystery, but of full stature, standing disregarded amongst their untroubled shapes, with a stern and romantic aspect, but always mute, dark—under a cloud.

"The story of the last events you will find in the few pages enclosed here. You must admit that it is romantic beyond the wildest dreams of his boyhood, and yet there is to my mind a sort of profound and terrifying logic in it, as if it were our imagination alone that could set loose upon us the might of an overwhelming destiny. The imprudence of our thoughts recoils upon our heads; who toys with the sword shall perish by the sword.[4] This astounding adventure, of which the most astounding part is that it is true, comes on as an unavoidable consequence. Something of the sort had to happen. You repeat this to yourself while you marvel that such a thing could happen in the year of grace[5] before last. But it has happened—and there is no disputing its logic.

"I put it down here for you as though I had been an eyewitness. My information was fragmentary, but I've fitted the pieces together, and there is enough of them to make an intelligible picture. I wonder how he would have related it himself. He has confided so much in me that at times it seems as though he must come in presently and tell the story in his own words, in his careless yet feeling voice, with his offhand manner, a little puzzled, a little bothered, a little hurt, but now and

2. Here Conrad draws upon a March 1790 letter from the Reverend William Hazlitt to his son: "But he who once gives way to any known vice, in the very instant hazards his total depravity and total ruin. You must, therefore, fixedly resolve never, through any possible motives, to do anything which you believe to be wrong."
3. See Adam's words about Eve's creation: "This is now bone of my bones, and flesh of my flesh" (Genesis 2.23).
4. See Jesus' words: "all they that take the sword shall perish with the sword" (Matthew 26.52).
5. Any year of the Christian Era.

then by a word or a phrase giving one of these glimpses of his very own self that were never any good for purposes of orientation. It's difficult to believe he will never come. I shall never hear his voice again, nor shall I see his smooth tan-and-pink face with a white line on the forehead, and the youthful eyes darkened by excitement to a profound, unfathomable blue."

Chapter XXXVII

"It all begins with a remarkable exploit of a man called Brown, who stole with complete success a Spanish schooner out of a small bay near Zamboanga. Till I discovered the fellow my information was incomplete, but most unexpectedly I did come upon him a few hours before he gave up his arrogant ghost. Fortunately he was willing and able to talk between the choking fits of asthma, and his racked body writhed with malicious exultation at the bare thought of Jim. He exulted thus at the idea that he had 'paid out the stuck-up beggar after all.' He gloated over his action. I had to bear the sunken glare of his fierce crow-footed eyes if I wanted to know; and so I bore it, reflecting how much certain forms of evil are akin to madness, derived from intense egoism, inflamed by resistance, tearing the soul to pieces, and giving factitious vigour to the body. The story also reveals unsuspected depths of cunning in the wretched Cornelius, whose abject and intense hate acts like a subtle inspiration, pointing out an unerring way towards revenge.

" 'I could see directly I set my eyes on him what sort of a fool he was,' gasped the dying Brown. 'He a man! Hell! He was a hollow sham. As if he couldn't have said straight out, "Hands off my plunder!" blast him! That would have been like a man! Rot his superior soul! He had me there—but he hadn't devil enough in him to make an end of me. Not he! A thing like that letting me off as if I wasn't worth a kick! . . .' Brown struggled desperately for breath. . . . 'Fraud. . . . Letting me off. . . . And so I did make an end of him after all. . . .' He choked again. . . . 'I expect this thing'll kill me, but I shall die easy now. You . . . you here. . . . I don't know your name—I would give you a five-pound note if—if I had it—for the news—or my name's not Brown. . . .' He grinned horribly. . . . 'Gentleman Brown.'

"He said all these things in profound gasps, staring at me with his yellow eyes out of a long, ravaged, brown face; he jerked his left arm; a pepper-and-salt matted beard hung almost into his lap; a dirty ragged blanket covered his legs. I had found him out in Bankok through that busy-body Schomberg, the hotel-keeper, who had, confidentially, directed me where to look. It appears that a sort of loafing, fuddled vagabond—a white man living amongst the natives with a Siamese woman—had considered it a great privilege to give a shelter to the last days of the famous Gentleman Brown. While he was talking to me in the wretched hovel, and, as it were, fighting for every minute of his life, the Siamese woman, with big bare legs and a stupid coarse face, sat in a dark corner chewing betel stolidly. Now and then she would get up for the purpose of shooing a chicken away from the door. The whole hut shook when she walked. An ugly yellow child, naked and pot-bellied like a little heathen god, stood at the foot of the couch, finger in mouth, lost in a profound and calm contemplation of the dying man.

"He talked feverishly; but in the middle of a word, perhaps, an invisible hand would take him by the throat, and he would look at me dumbly with an expression of doubt and anguish. He seemed to fear that I would get tired of waiting and go away, leaving him with his tale untold, with his exultation unexpressed. He died during the night, I believe, but by that time I had nothing more to learn.

"So much as to Brown, for the present.

"Eight months before this, coming into Samarang, I went as usual to see Stein. On the garden side of the house a Malay on the verandah greeted me shyly, and I remembered that I had seen him in Patusan, in Jim's house, amongst other Bugis men who used to come in the evening to talk interminably over their war reminiscences and to discuss State affairs. Jim had pointed him out to me once as a respectable petty trader owning a small seagoing native craft, who had showed himself 'one of the best at the taking of the stockade.' I was not very surprised to see him, since any Patusan trader venturing as far as Samarang would naturally find his way to Stein's house. I returned his greeting and passed on. At the door of Stein's room I came upon another Malay in whom I recognised Tamb' Itam.

"I asked him at once what he was doing there; it occurred to me that Jim might have come on a visit. I own I was pleased and excited at the thought. Tamb' Itam looked as if he did not know what to say. 'Is Tuan Jim inside?' I asked impatiently. 'No,' he mumbled, hanging his head for a moment, and then with sudden earnestness, 'He would not fight. He would not fight,' he repeated twice. As he seemed unable to say anything else, I pushed him aside and went in.

"Stein, tall and stooping, stood alone in the middle of the room between the rows of butterfly cases. 'Ach! is it you, my friend?' he said sadly, peering through his glasses. A drab sack-coat[1] of alpaca hung, unbuttoned, down to his knees. He had a Panama hat on his head, and there were deep furrows on his pale cheeks. 'What's the matter now?' I asked nervously. 'There's Tamb' Itam there. . . .' 'Come and see the girl. Come and see the girl. She is here,' he said, with a half-hearted show of activity. I tried to detain him, but with gentle obstinacy he

1. Short, loose-fitting wool coat.

would take no notice of my eager questions. 'She is here, she is here,' he repeated, in great perturbation. 'They came here two days ago. An old man like me, a stranger—*sehen sie*[2]—can not do much. . . . Come this way. . . . Young hearts are unforgiving. . . .' I could see he was in utmost distress. . . . 'The strength of life in them, the cruel strength of life. . . .' He mumbled, leading me round the house; I followed him, lost in dismal and angry conjectures. At the door of the drawing-room he barred my way. 'He loved her very much,' he said interrogatively, and I only nodded, feeling so bitterly disappointed that I would not trust myself to speak. 'Very frightful,' he murmured. 'She can't understand me. I am only a strange old man. Perhaps you . . . she knows you. Talk to her. We can't leave it like this. Tell her to forgive him. It was very frightful.' 'No doubt,' I said, exasperated at being in the dark; 'but have *you* forgiven him?' He looked at me queerly. 'You shall hear,' he said, and opening the door, absolutely pushed me in.

"You know Stein's big house and the two immense reception-rooms, uninhabited and uninhabitable, clean, full of solitude and of shining things that look as if never beheld by the eye of man? They are cool on the hottest days, and you enter them as you would a scrubbed cave underground. I passed through one, and in the other I saw the girl sitting at the end of a big mahogany table, on which she rested her head, the face hidden in her arms. The waxed floor reflected her dimly as though it had been a sheet of frozen water. The rattan screens were down, and through the strange greenish gloom made by the foliage of the trees outside a strong wind blew in gusts, swaying the long draperies of windows and doorways. Her white figure seemed shaped in snow; the pendent crystals of a great chandelier clicked above her head like glittering icicles. She looked up and watched my approach. I was chilled as if these vast apartments had been the cold abode of despair.

"She recognised me at once, and as soon as I had stopped looking down at her: 'He has left me,' she said quietly; 'you always leave us— for your own ends.' Her face was set. All the heat of life seemed withdrawn within some inaccessible spot in her breast. 'It would have been easy to die with him,' she went on, and made a slight weary gesture as if giving up the incomprehensible. 'He would not! It was like a blindness—and yet it was I who was speaking to him; it was I who stood before his eyes; it was at me that he looked all the time! Ah! you are hard, treacherous, without truth, without compassion. What makes you so wicked? Or is it that you are all mad?'

"I took her hand; it did not respond, and when I dropped it, it hung down to the floor. That indifference, more awful than tears, cries, and reproaches, seemed to defy time and consolation. You felt that nothing you could say would reach the seat of the still and benumbing pain.

2. You see.

"Stein had said, 'You shall hear.' I did hear. I heard it all, listening with amazement, with awe, to the tones of her inflexible weariness. She could not grasp the real sense of what she was telling me, and her resentment filled me with pity for her—for him too. I stood rooted to the spot after she had finished. Leaning on her arm, she stared with hard eyes, and the wind passed in gusts, the crystals kept on clicking in the greenish gloom. She went on whispering to herself: 'And yet he was looking at me! He could see my face, hear my voice, hear my grief! When I used to sit at his feet, with my cheek against his knee and his hand on my head, the curse of cruelty and madness was already within him, waiting for the day. The day came! . . . and before the sun had set he could not see me any more—he was made blind and deaf and without pity, as you all are. He shall have no tears from me. Never, never. Not one tear. I will not! He went away from me as if I had been worse than death. He fled as if driven by some accursed thing he had heard or seen in his sleep. . . .'

"Her steady eyes seemed to strain after the shape of a man torn out of her arms by the strength of a dream. She made no sign to my silent bow. I was glad to escape.

"I saw her once again, the same afternoon. On leaving her I had gone in search of Stein, whom I could not find indoors; and I wandered out, pursued by distressful thoughts, into the gardens, those famous gardens of Stein, in which you can find every plant and tree of tropical lowlands. I followed the course of the canalised stream, and sat for a long time on a shaded bench near the ornamental pond, where some waterfowl with clipped wings were diving and splashing noisily. The branches of casuarina trees behind me swayed lightly, incessantly, reminding me of the soughing of fir trees at home.

"This mournful and restless sound was a fit accompaniment to my meditations. She had said he had been driven away from her by a dream,—and there was no answer one could make her—there seemed to be no forgiveness for such a transgression. And yet is not mankind itself, pushing on its blind way, driven by a dream of its greatness and its power upon the dark paths of excessive cruelty and of excessive devotion? And what is the pursuit of truth—after all?

"When I rose to get back to the house I caught sight of Stein's drab coat through a gap in the foliage, and very soon at a turn of the path I came upon him walking with the girl. Her little hand rested on his forearm, and under the broad, flat rim of his Panama hat he bent over her, grey-haired, paternal, with compassionate and chivalrous deference. I stood aside, but they stopped, facing me. His gaze was bent on the ground at his feet; the girl, erect and slight on his arm, stared sombrely beyond my shoulder with black, clear, motionless eyes. 'Schrecklich,' he murmured. 'Terrible! Terrible! What can one do?' He seemed to be appealing to me, but her youth, the length of the days suspended over her head, appealed to me more; and suddenly, even as I realised that nothing could be said, I found myself pleading his cause for her sake. 'You must forgive him.' I concluded, and my own voice seemed to me muffled, lost in an irresponsive deaf immensity. 'We all want to be forgiven,' I added after a while.

" 'What have I done?' she asked with her lips only.

" 'You always mistrusted him,' I said.

" 'He was like the others,' she pronounced slowly.

" 'Not like the others,' I protested, but she continued evenly, without any feeling—

" 'He was false.' And suddenly Stein broke in. 'No! no! no! My poor child! . . .' He patted her hand lying passively on his sleeve. 'No! no! Not false! True! true! true!' He tried to look into her stony face. 'You don't understand. Ach! Why you do not understand? . . . Terrible,' he said to me. 'Some day she *shall* understand.'

" 'Will *you* explain?' I asked, looking hard at him. They moved on.

"I watched them. Her gown trailed on the path, her black hair fell loose. She walked upright and light by the side of the tall man, whose long shapeless coat hung in perpendicular folds from the stooping shoulders, whose feet moved slowly. They disappeared beyond that spinney (you may remember) where sixteen different kinds of bamboo grow together, all distinguishable to the learned eye. For my part, I was fascinated by the exquisite grace and beauty of that fluted grove, crowned with pointed leaves and feathery heads, the lightness, the vigour, the charm as distinct as a voice of that unperplexed luxuriating life. I remember staying to look at it for a long time, as one would linger within reach of a consoling whisper. The sky was pearly grey. It was one of those overcast days so rare in the tropics, in which memories crowd upon one—memories of other shores, of other faces.

"I drove back to town the same afternoon, taking with me Tamb' Itam and the other Malay, in whose seagoing craft they had escaped in the bewilderment, fear, and gloom of the disaster. The shock of it seemed to have changed their natures. It had turned her passion into stone, and it made the surly taciturn Tamb' Itam almost loquacious. His surliness, too, was subdued into puzzled humility, as though he had seen the failure of a potent charm in a supreme moment. The Bugis trader, a shy hesitating man, was very clear in the little he had to say. Both were evidently overawed by a sense of deep inexpressible wonder, by the touch of an inscrutable mystery."

There with Marlow's signature the letter proper ended. The privileged reader screwed up his lamp, and solitary above the billowy roofs of the town, like a lighthouse-keeper above the sea, he turned to the pages of the story.

Chapter XXXVIII

"It all begins, as I've told you, with the man called Brown," ran the opening sentence of Marlow's narrative. "You who have knocked about the Western Pacific must have heard of him. He was the show ruffian on the Australian coast—not that he was often to be seen there, but because he was always trotted out in the stories of lawless life a visitor from home is treated to; and the mildest of these stories which were told about him from Cape York to Eden Bay was more than enough to hang a man if told in the right place. They never failed to let you know, too, that he was supposed to be the son of a baronet. Be it as it may, it is certain he had deserted from a home ship in the early gold-digging days, and in a few years became talked about as the terror of this or that group of islands in Polynesia. He would kidnap natives, he would strip some lonely white trader to the very pyjamas he stood in, and after he had robbed the poor devil, he would as likely as not invite him to fight a duel with shot-guns on the beach—which would have been fair enough as these things go, if the other man hadn't been by that time already half-dead with fright. Brown was a latter-day buccaneer, sorry enough, like his more celebrated prototypes; but what distinguished him from his contemporary brother ruffians, like Bully Hayes or the mellifluous Pease,[1] or that perfumed, Dundreary-whiskered,[2] dandified scoundrel known as Dirty Dick, was the arrogant temper of his misdeeds and a vehement scorn for mankind at large and for his victims in particular. The others were merely vulgar and greedy brutes, but he seemed moved by some complex intention. He would rob a man as if only to demonstrate his poor opinion of the creature, and he would bring to the shooting or maiming of some quiet, unoffending stranger a savage and vengeful earnestness fit to terrify the most reckless of desperadoes. In the days of his greatest glory he owned an armed barque, manned by a mixed crew of Kanakas and runaway whalers, and boasted, I don't know with what truth, of being financed on the quiet by a most respectable firm of copra merchants. Later on he ran off—it was reported—with the wife of a missionary, a very young girl from Clapham[3] way, who had married the mild, flat-footed fellow in a moment of enthusiasm, and suddenly transplanted to Melanesia, lost her bearings somehow. It was a dark story. She was ill at the time he carried her off, and died on board his ship. It is said—as the most wonderful part of the tale—that over her body he gave way to an outburst of sombre and violent grief. His luck left him, too, very soon after. He lost his ship on some rocks

---

1. Captain William Henry Hayes of Cleveland, Ohio, and Lieutenant George Pease, briefly of the United States Navy, were notorious South Sea adventurers and pirates. They both died violently in the 1870s.
2. Long flowing side-whiskers separated by shaven chin.
3. Residential district of London, south of the Thames; home in the early nineteenth century of a distinguished group of Evangelical, anti–slave trade philanthropists.

off Malaita, and disappeared for a time as though he had gone down
with her. He is heard of next at Nuka-Hiva, where he bought an old
French schooner out of Government service. What creditable enterprise
he might have had in view when he made that purchase I can't say, but
it is evident that what with High Commissioners, consuls, men-of-war,
and international control, the South Seas were getting too hot to hold
gentlemen of his kidney. Clearly he must have shifted the scene of his
operations farther west, because a year later he plays an incredibly audacious, but not a very profitable part, in a serio-comic business in
Manila Bay, in which a peculating governor and an absconding treasurer
are the principal figures; thereafter he seems to have hung around the
Philippines in his rotten schooner, battling with an adverse fortune, till
at last, running his appointed course, he sails into Jim's history, a blind
accomplice of the Dark Powers.

"His tale goes that when a Spanish patrol cutter captured him he was
simply trying to run a few guns for the insurgents. If so, then I can't
understand what he was doing off the south coast of Mindanao. My
belief, however, is that he was blackmailing the native villages along
the coast. The principal thing is that the cutter, throwing a guard on
board, made him sail in company towards Zamboanga. On the way,
for some reason or other, both vessels had to call at one of these new
Spanish settlements—which never came to anything in the end—where
there was not only a civil official in charge on shore, but a good stout
coasting schooner lying at anchor in the little bay; and this craft, in
every way much better than his own, Brown made up his mind to steal.

"He was down on his luck—as he told me himself. The world he
had bullied for twenty years with fierce, aggressive disdain, had yielded
him nothing in the way of material advantage except a small bag of
silver dollars, which was concealed in his cabin so that 'the devil himself
couldn't smell it out.' And that was all—absolutely all. He was tired of
his life, and not afraid of death. But this man, who would stake his
existence on a whim with a bitter and jeering recklessness, stood in
mortal fear of imprisonment. He had an unreasoning cold-sweat, nerve-
shaking, blood-to-water-turning sort of horror at the bare possibility of
being locked up—the sort of terror a superstitious man would feel at
the thought of being embraced by a spectre. Therefore the civil official
who came on board to make a preliminary investigation into the capture,
investigated arduously all day long, and only went ashore after dark,
muffled up in a cloak, and taking great care not to let Brown's little all
clink in its bag. Afterwards, being a man of his word, he contrived (the
very next evening, I believe) to send off the Government cutter on some
urgent bit of special service. As her commander could not spare a prize
crew, he contented himself by taking away before he left all the sails of
Brown's schooner to the very last rag, and took good care to tow his two
boats on to the beach a couple of miles off.

"But in Brown's crew there was a Solomon Islander, kidnapped in his youth and devoted to Brown, who was the best man of the whole gang. That fellow swam off to the coaster—five hundred yards or so—with the end of a warp made up of all the running gear unrove for the purpose. The water was smooth, and the bay dark, 'like the inside of a cow,' as Brown described it. The Solomon Islander clambered over the bulwarks with the end of the rope in his teeth. The crew of the coaster—all Tagals—were ashore having a jollification in the native village. The two shipkeepers left on board woke up suddenly and saw the devil. It had glittering eyes and leaped quick as lightning about the deck. They fell on their knees, paralysed with fear, crossing themselves and mumbling prayers. With a long knife he found in the caboose the Solomon Islander, without interrupting their orisons, stabbed first one, then the other; with the same knife he set to sawing patiently at the coir cable till suddenly it parted under the blade with a splash. Then in the silence of the bay he let out a cautious shout, and Brown's gang, who meantime had been peering and straining their hopeful ears in the darkness, began to pull gently at their end of the warp. In less than five minutes the two schooners came together with a slight shock and a creak of spars.

"Brown's crowd transferred themselves without losing an instant, taking with them their firearms and a large supply of ammunition. They were sixteen in all: two runaway blue-jackets, a lanky deserter from a Yankee man-of-war, a couple of simple, blond Scandinavians, a mulatto of sorts, one bland Chinaman who cooked—and the rest of the nondescript spawn of the South Seas. None of them cared; Brown bent them to his will, and Brown, indifferent to gallows, was running away from the spectre of a Spanish prison. He didn't give them the time to trans-ship enough provisions; the weather was calm, the air was charged with dew, and when they cast off the ropes and set sail to a faint off-shore draught there was no flutter in the damp canvas; their old schooner seemed to detach itself gently from the stolen craft and slip away silently, together with the black mass of the coast, into the night.

"They got clear away. Brown related to me in detail their passage down the Straits of Macassar. It is a harrowing and desperate story. They were short of food and water; they boarded several native craft and got a little from each. With a stolen ship Brown did not dare to put into any port, of course. He had no money to buy anything, no papers to show, and no lie plausible enough to get him out again. An Arab barque, under the Dutch flag, surprised one night at anchor off Poulo Laut, yielded a little dirty rice, a bunch of bananas, and a cask of water; three days of squally, misty weather from the north-east shot the schooner across the Java Sea. The yellow muddy waves drenched that collection of hungry ruffians. They sighted mail-boats moving on their appointed

routes; passed well-found[4] home ships with rusty iron sides anchored in
the shallow sea waiting for a change of weather or the turn of the tide;
an English gunboat, white and trim, with two slim masts, crossed their
bows one day in the distance; and on another occasion a Dutch corvette,
black and heavily sparred, loomed up on their quarter, steaming dead
slow in the mist. They slipped through unseen or disregarded, a wan,
sallow-faced band of utter outcasts, enraged with hunger and hunted by
fear. Brown's idea was to make for Madagascar, where he expected, on
grounds not altogether illusory, to sell the schooner in Tamatave, and
no questions asked, or perhaps obtain some more or less forged papers
for her. Yet before he could face the long passage across the Indian
Ocean food was wanted—water too.

"Perhaps he had heard of Patusan—or perhaps he just only happened
to see the name written in small letters on the chart—probably that of
a largish village up a river in a native state, perfectly defenceless, far
from the beaten tracks of the sea and from the ends of submarine cables.
He had done that kind of thing before—in the way of business; and this
now was an absolute necessity, a question of life and death—or rather
of liberty. Of liberty! He was sure to get provisions—bullocks—rice—
sweet-potatoes. The sorry gang licked their chops. A cargo of produce
for the schooner perhaps could be extorted—and, who knows—some
real ringing coined money! Some of these chiefs and village headmen
can be made to part freely. He told me he would have roasted their toes
rather than be baulked. I believe him. His men believed him too. They
didn't cheer aloud, being a dumb pack, but made ready wolfishly.

"Luck served him as to weather. A few days of calm would have
brought unmentionable horrors on board that schooner, but with the
help of land and sea breezes, in less than a week after clearing the Sunda
Straits, he anchored off the Batu Kring mouth within a pistol-shot of
the fishing village.

"Fourteen of them packed into the schooner's long-boat (which was
big, having been used for cargo-work) and started up the river, while
two remained in charge of the schooner with food enough to keep
starvation off for ten days. The tide and wind helped, and early one
afternoon the big white boat under a ragged sail shouldered its way
before the sea breeze into Patusan Reach, manned by fourteen assorted
scarecrows glaring hungrily ahead, and fingering the breach-blocks of
cheap rifles. Brown calculated upon the terrifying surprise of his appearance. They sailed in with the last of the flood; the Rajah's stockade
gave no sign; the first houses on both sides of the stream seemed deserted.
A few canoes were seen up the reach in full flight. Brown was astonished
at the size of the place. A profound silence reigned. The wind dropped
between the houses; two oars were got out and the boat held on up-

4. Well-provided.

stream, the idea being to effect a lodgment in the centre of the town before the inhabitants could think of resistance.

"It seems, however, that the headman of the fishing village at Batu Kring had managed to send off a timely warning. When the long-boat came abreast of the mosque (which Doramin had built: a structure with gables and roof finials of carved coral) the open space before it was full of people. A shout went up, and was followed by a clash of gongs all up the river. From a point above two little brass 6-pounders were discharged, and the round-shot came skipping down the empty reach, spirting glittering jets of water in the sunshine. In front of the mosque a shouting lot of men began firing in volleys that whipped athwart the current of the river; an irregular, rolling fusilade was opened on the boat from both banks, and Brown's men replied with a wild, rapid fire. The oars had been got in.

"The turn of the tide at high water comes on very quickly in that river, and the boat in midstream, nearly hidden in smoke, began to drift back stern foremost. Along both shores the smoke thickened also, lying below the roofs in a level streak as you may see a long cloud cutting the slope of a mountain. A tumult of war-cries, the vibrating clang of gongs, the deep snoring of drums, yells of rage, crashes of volley-firing, made an awful din, in which Brown sat confounded but steady at the tiller, working himself into a fury of hate and rage against those people who dared to defend themselves. Two of his men had been wounded, and he saw his retreat cut off below the town by some boats that had put off from Tunku Allang's stockade. There were six of them, full of men. While he was thus beset he perceived the entrance of the narrow creek (the same which Jim had jumped at low water). It was then brim full. Steering the long-boat in, they landed, and, to make a long story short, they established themselves on a little knoll about 900 yards from the stockade, which, in fact, they commanded from that position. The slopes of the knoll were bare, but there were a few trees on the summit. They went to work cutting these down for a breastwork, and were fairly intrenched before dark; meantime the Rajah's boats remained in the river with curious neutrality. When the sun set the glare of many brushwood blazes lighted on the river-front, and between the double line of houses on the land side threw into black relief the roofs, the groups of slender palms, the heavy clumps of fruit trees. Brown ordered the grass round his position to be fired; a low ring of thin flames under the slow ascending smoke wriggled rapidly down the slopes of the knoll; here and there a dry bush caught with a tall, vicious roar. The conflagration made a clear zone of fire for the rifles of the small party, and expired smouldering on the edge of the forests and along the muddy bank of the creek. A strip of jungle luxuriating in a damp hollow between the knoll and the Rajah's stockade stopped it on that side with a great crackling and detonations of bursting bamboo stems. The sky was sombre, velvety, and swarming with stars. The blackened ground smoked quietly with low creeping wisps, till a little breeze came on and blew everything away. Brown expected an attack to be delivered as soon as the tide had flowed enough again to enable the war-boats which had cut off his retreat to enter the creek. At any rate he was sure there would be an attempt to carry off his long-boat, which lay below the hill, a dark high lump on the feeble sheen of a wet mud-flat. But no move of any sort was made by the boats in the river. Over the stockade and the Rajah's buildings Brown saw their lights on the water. They seemed to be anchored across the stream. Other lights afloat were moving in the reach, crossing and recrossing from side to side. There were also lights twinkling motionless upon the long walls of houses up the reach, as far as the bend, and more still beyond, others isolated inland. The loom of the big fires disclosed buildings, roofs, black piles as far as he could see. It was an immense place. The fourteen desperate invaders lying flat behind the felled trees raised their chins to look over at the stir of that town that seemed to extend up-river for miles and swarm with thousands of angry men. They did not speak to each other. Now and then they would hear a loud yell, or a single shot rang out, fired very far somewhere. But round their position everything was still, dark, silent. They seemed to be forgotten, as if the excitement keeping awake all the population had nothing to do with them, as if they had been dead already."

Chapter XXXIX

"All the events of that night have a great importance, since they brought about a situation which remained unchanged till Jim's return. Jim had been away in the interior for more than a week, and it was Dain Waris who had directed the first repulse. That brave and intelligent youth ('who knew how to fight after the manner of white men') wished to settle the business off-hand, but his people were too much for him. He had not Jim's racial prestige and the reputation of invincible, supernatural power. He was not the visible, tangible incarnation of unfailing truth and of unfailing victory. Beloved, trusted, and admired as he was, he was still one of *them*, while Jim was one of *us*. Moreover, the white man, a tower of strength in himself, was invulnerable, while Dain Waris could be killed. Those unexpressed thoughts guided the opinions of the chief men of the town who elected to assemble in Jim's fort for deliberation upon the emergency as if expecting to find wisdom and courage in the dwelling of the absent white man. The shooting of Brown's ruffians was so far good or lucky that there had been half-a-dozen casualties amongst the defenders. The wounded were lying on the verandah tended by their women-folk. The women and children from the lower part of the town had been sent into the fort at the first alarm. There Jewel was in command, very efficient and high-spirited, obeyed by Jim's 'own people,' who, quitting in a body their little settlement under the stockade, had gone in to form the garrison. The refugees crowded round her; and through the whole affair, to the very disastrous last, she showed an extraordinary martial ardour. It was to her that Dain Waris had gone at once at the first intelligence of danger, for you must know that Jim was the only one in Patusan who possessed a store of gunpowder. Stein, with whom he had kept up intimate relations by letters, had obtained from the Dutch Government a special authorisation to export five hundred kegs of it to Patusan. The powder-magazine was a small hut of rough logs covered entirely with earth, and in Jim's absence the girl had the key. In the council, held at eleven o'clock in the evening in Jim's dining-room, she backed up Waris's advice for immediate and vigorous action. I am told that she stood up by the side of Jim's empty chair at the head of the long table and made a warlike impassioned speech, which for the moment extorted murmurs of approbation from the assembled head-men. Old Doramin, who had not showed himself outside his own gate for more than a year, had been brought across with great difficulty. He was, of course, the chief man there. The temper of the council was very unforgiving, and the old man's word would have been decisive; but it is my opinion that, well aware of his son's fiery courage, he dared not pronounce the word. More dilatory counsels prevailed. A certain Haji Saman pointed out at great length that 'these tyrannical and ferocious men had delivered themselves to a certain death in any case. They would stand fast on their hill and starve, or they would try to regain their boat and be shot from ambushes across the creek, or they would break and fly into the forest and perish singly there.' He argued that by the use of proper stratagems these evil-minded strangers could be destroyed without the risk of a battle, and his words had a great weight, especially with the Patusan men proper. What un-settled the minds of the townfolk was the failure of the Rajah's boats to act at the decisive moment. It was the diplomatic Kassim who represented the Rajah at the council. He spoke very little, listened smilingly, very friendly and impenetrable. During the sitting messengers kept arriving every few minutes almost, with reports of the invaders' proceedings. Wild and exaggerated rumours were flying: there was a large ship at the mouth of the river with big guns and many more men—some white, others with black skins and of bloodthirsty appearance. They were com-ing with many more boats to exterminate every living thing. A sense of near, incomprehensible danger affected the common people. At one moment there was a panic in the courtyard amongst the women; shriek-ing; a rush; children crying—Haji Saman went out to quiet them. Then a fort sentry fired at something moving on the river, and nearly killed a villager bringing in his women-folk in a canoe together with the best of his domestic utensils and a dozen fowls. This caused more confusion. Meantime the palaver[1] inside Jim's house went on in the presence of the girl. Doramin sat fierce-faced, heavy, looking at the speakers in turn, and breathing slow like a bull. He didn't speak till the last, after Kassim had declared that the Rajah's boats would be called in because the men were required to defend his master's stockade. Dain Waris in his father's presence would offer no opinion, though the girl entreated him in Jim's name to speak out. She offered him Jim's own men in her anxiety to have these intruders driven out at once. He only shook his head, after a glance or two at Doramin. Finally, when the council broke up it had been decided that the houses nearest the creek should be strongly occupied to obtain the command of the enemy's boat. The boat itself was not to be interfered with openly, so that the robbers on the hill should be tempted to embark, when a well-directed fire would kill most of them, no doubt. To cut off the escape of those who might survive, and to prevent more of them coming up, Dain Waris was ordered by Doramin to take an armed party of Bugis down the river to a certain spot ten miles below Patusan, and there form a camp on the shore and blockade the stream with the canoes. I don't believe for a moment that Doramin feared the arrival of fresh forces. My opinion is that his conduct was guided solely by his wish to keep his son out of harm's way. To prevent a rush being made into the town the construction of a stockade was to be commenced at daylight at the end of the street on the left bank. The old Nakhoda declared his intention to command there himself. A distribution of powder, bullets, and percussion-caps was made immediately under the girl's supervision. Several messengers were to be dispatched in different directions after Jim, whose exact whereabouts were unknown. These men started at dawn, but before that time Kassim had managed to open communications with the besieged Brown.

"That accomplished diplomatist and confidant of the Rajah, on leaving the fort to go back to his master, took into his boat Cornelius, whom he found slinking mutely amongst the people in the courtyard. Kassim had a little plan of his own and wanted him for an interpreter. Thus it came about that towards morning Brown, reflecting upon the desperate nature of his position, heard from the marshy overgrown hollow an amicable, quavering, strained voice crying—in English—for permission to come up, under a promise of personal safety and on a very important errand. He was overjoyed. If he was spoken to he was no longer a hunted wild beast. These friendly sounds took off at once the awful stress of vigilant watchfulness as of so many blind men not knowing whence the deathblow might come. He pretended a great reluctance. The voice declared itself 'a white man—a poor, ruined, old man who had been living here for years.' A mist, wet and chilly, lay on the slopes of the

1. Conference, with much talk.

hill, and after some more shouting from one to the other, Brown called out, 'Come on, then, but alone, mind!' As a matter of fact—he told me, writhing with rage at the recollection of his helplessness—it made no difference. They couldn't see more than a few yards before them, and no treachery could make their position worse. By-and-by Cornelius, in his week-day attire of a ragged dirty shirt and pants, barefooted, with a broken-rimmed pith hat on his head, was made out vaguely, sidling up to the defences, hesitating, stopping to listen in a peering posture. 'Come along! You are safe,' yelled Brown, while his men stared. All their hopes of life became suddenly centred in that dilapidated, mean new-comer, who in profound silence clambered clumsily over a felled tree-trunk, and shivering, with his sour, mistrustful face, looked about at the knot of bearded, anxious, sleepless desperadoes.

"Half an hour's confidential talk with Cornelius opened Brown's eyes as to the home affairs of Patusan. He was on the alert at once. There were possibilities, immense possibilities; but before he would talk over Cornelius's proposals he demanded that some food should be sent up as a guarantee of good faith. Cornelius went off, creeping sluggishly down the hill on the side of the Rajah's palace, and after some delay a few of Tunku Allang's men came up, bringing a scanty supply of rice, chillies, and dried fish. This was immeasurably better than nothing. Later on Cornelius returned accompanying Kassim, who stepped out with an air of perfect good-humoured trustfulness, in sandals, and muffled up from neck to ankles in dark-blue sheeting. He shook hands with Brown discreetly, and the three drew aside for a conference. Brown's men, recovering their confidence, were slapping each other on the back, and cast knowing glances at their captain while they busied themselves with preparations for cooking.

"Kassim disliked Doramin and his Bugis very much, but he hated the new order of things still more. It had occurred to him that these whites, together with the Rajah's followers, could attack and defeat the Bugis before Jim's return. Then, he reasoned, general defection of the townfolk was sure to follow, and the reign of the white man who protected poor people would be over. Afterwards the new allies could be dealt with. They would have no friends. The fellow was perfectly able to perceive the difference of character, and had seen enough of white men to know that these new-comers were outcasts, men without country. Brown preserved a stern and inscrutable demeanour. When he first heard Cornelius's voice demanding admittance, it brought merely the hope of a loophole for escape. In less than an hour other thoughts were seething in his head. Urged by an extreme necessity, he had come there to steal food, a few tons of rubber or gum may be, perhaps a handful of dollars, and had found himself enmeshed by deadly dangers. Now in consequence of these overtures from Kassim he began to think of stealing the whole country. Some confounded fellow had apparently accomplished

something of the kind—single-handed at that. Couldn't have done it
very well though. Perhaps they could work together—squeeze everything
dry and then go out quietly. In the course of his negotiations with Kassim
he became aware that he was supposed to have a big ship with plenty
of men outside. Kassim begged him earnestly to have this big ship with
his many guns and men brought up the river without delay for the
Rajah's service. Brown professed himself willing, and on this basis
the negotiation was carried on with mutual distrust. Three times in the
course of the morning the courteous and active Kassim went down to
consult the Rajah and came up busily with his long stride. Brown, while
bargaining, had a sort of grim enjoyment in thinking of his wretched
schooner, with nothing but a heap of dirt in her hold, that stood for an
armed ship, and a Chinaman and a lame ex-beachcomber of Levuka
on board, who represented all his many men. In the afternoon he
obtained further doles of food, a promise of some money, and a supply
of mats for his men to make shelters for themselves. They lay down and
snored, protected from the burning sunshine; but Brown, sitting fully
exposed on one of the felled trees, feasted his eyes upon the view of the
town and the river. There was much loot there. Cornelius, who had
made himself at home in the camp, talked at his elbow, pointing out
the localities, imparting advice, giving his own version of Jim's character,
and commenting in his own fashion upon the events of the last three
years. Brown, who, apparently indifferent and gazing away, listened
with attention to every word, could not make out clearly what sort of
man this Jim could be. 'What's his name? Jim! Jim! That's not enough
for a man's name.' 'They call him,' said Cornelius scornfully, 'Tuan
Jim here. As you may say Lord Jim.' 'What is he? Where does he come
from?' inquired Brown. 'What sort of man is he? Is he an Englishman?'
'Yes, yes, he's an Englishman. I am an Englishman too. From Malacca.
He is a fool. All you have to do is to kill him and then you are king
here. Everything belongs to him,' explained Cornelius. 'It strikes me he
may be made to share with somebody before very long,' commented
Brown half aloud. 'No, no. The proper way is to kill him the first chance
you get, and then you can do what you like,' Cornelius would insist
earnestly. 'I have lived for many years here, and I am giving you a
friend's advice.'

"In such converse and in gloating over the view of Patusan, which
he had determined in his mind should become his prey, Brown whiled
away most of the afternoon, his men, meantime, resting. On that day
Dain Waris's fleet of canoes stole one by one under the shore farthest
from the creek, and went down to close the river against his retreat. Of
this Brown was not aware, and Kassim, who came up the knoll an hour
before sunset, took good care not to enlighten him. He wanted the white
man's ship to come up the river, and this news, he feared, would be

discouraging. He was very pressing with Brown to send the 'order,' offering at the same time a trusty messenger, who for greater secrecy (as he explained) would make his way by land to the mouth of the river and deliver the 'order' on board. After some reflection Brown judged it expedient to tear a page out of his pocket-book, on which he simply wrote, 'We are getting on. Big job. Detain the man.' The stolid youth selected by Kassim for that service performed it faithfully, and was rewarded by being suddenly tipped, head first, into the schooner's empty hold by the ex-beach-comber and the Chinaman, who thereupon hastened to put on the hatches. What became of him afterwards Brown did not say."

Chapter XL

"Brown's object was to gain time by fooling with Kassim's diplomacy. For doing a real stroke of business he could not help thinking the white man was the person to work with. He could not imagine such a chap (who must be confoundedly clever after all to get hold of the natives like that) refusing a help that would do away with the necessity for slow, cautious, risky cheating, that imposed itself as the only possible line of conduct for a single-handed man. He, Brown, would offer him the power. No man could hesitate. Everything was in coming to a clear understanding. Of course they would share. The idea of there being a fort—all ready to his hand—a real fort, with artillery (he knew this from Cornelius), excited him. Let him only once get in and . . . He would impose modest conditions. Not too low, though. The man was no fool, it seemed. They would work like brothers till, . . . till the time came for a quarrel and a shot that would settle all accounts. With grim impatience of plunder he wished himself to be talking with the man now. The land already seemed to be his to tear to pieces, squeeze, and throw away. Meantime Kassim had to be fooled for the sake of food first—and for a second string. But the principal thing was to get something to eat from day to day. Besides, he was not averse to begin fighting on that Rajah's account, and teach a lesson to those people who had received him with shots. The lust of battle was upon him.

"I am sorry that I can't give you this part of the story, which of course I have mainly from Brown, in Brown's own words. There was in the broken, violent speech of that man, unveiling before me his thoughts with the very hand of Death upon his throat, an undisguised ruthlessness of purpose, a strange vengeful attitude towards his own past, and a blind belief in the righteousness of his will against all mankind, something of that feeling which could induce the leader of a horde of wandering cut-throats to call himself proudly the Scourge of God.[1] No doubt the natural senseless ferocity which is the basis of such a character was exasperated by failure, ill-luck, and the recent privations, as well as by the desperate position in which he found himself; but what was most remarkable of all was this, that while he planned treacherous alliances, had already settled in his own mind the fate of the white man, and intrigued in an overbearing, offhand manner with Kassim, one could perceive that what he had really desired, almost in spite of himself, was to play havoc with that jungle town which had defied him, to see it strewn over with corpses and enveloped in flames. Listening to his pitiless, panting voice, I could imagine how he must have looked at it from the hillock, peopling it with images of murder and rapine. The part nearest to the creek wore an abandoned aspect, though as a matter of fact every house concealed a few armed men on the alert. Suddenly beyond the stretch of waste ground, interspersed with small patches of low dense bush, excavations, heaps of rubbish, with trodden paths between, a man, solitary and looking very small, strolled out into the deserted opening of the street between the shut-up, dark, lifeless buildings at the end. Perhaps one of the inhabitants, who had fled to the other bank of the river, coming back for some object of domestic use. Evidently he supposed himself quite safe at that distance from the hill on the other side of the creek. A light stockade, set up hastily, was just round the turn of the street, full of his friends. He moved leisurely. Brown saw him, and instantly called to his side the Yankee deserter, who acted as a sort of second in command. This lanky, loose-jointed fellow came forward, wooden-faced, trailing his rifle lazily. When he understood what was wanted from him a homicidal and conceited smile uncovered his teeth, making two deep folds down his sallow, leathery cheeks. He prided himself on being a dead shot. He dropped on one knee, and taking aim from a steady rest through the unlopped branches of a felled tree, fired, and at once stood up to look. The man, far away, turned his head to the report, made another step forward, seemed to hesitate, and abruptly got down on his hands and knees. In the silence that fell upon the sharp crack of the rifle, the dead shot, keeping his eyes fixed upon the quarry, guessed that 'this there coon's[2] health would never be a source of anxiety to his friends any more.' The man's limbs were seen to move rapidly under his body in an endeavour to run on all-fours. In that empty space arose a multitudinous shout of dismay and surprise. The man sank flat, face down, and moved no more. 'That showed them what we could do,' said Brown to me. 'Struck the fear of sudden death into them. That was what we wanted. They were two hundred to one, and this gave them

1. Christopher Marlowe applies the phrase to the ruthless hero of his play *Tamburlaine the Great* (1590), the shepherd-robber who, through conquest, rises to be emperor, his ferocity softened only by his love of the captive Zenocrate.
2. Black's (derogatory term, U.S., from *raccoon*).

something to think over for the night. Not one of them had an idea of such a long shot before. That beggar belonging to the Rajah scooted down-hill with his eyes hanging out of his head.'

"As he was telling me this he tried with a shaking hand to wipe the thin foam on his blue lips. 'Two hundred to one. Two hundred to one . . . strike terror, . . . terror, terror, I tell you. . . .' His own eyes were starting out of their sockets. He fell back, clawing the air with skinny fingers, sat up again, bowed and hairy, glared at me sideways like some man-beast of folk-lore, with open mouth in his miserable and awful agony before he got his speech back after that fit. There are sights one never forgets.

"Furthermore, to draw the enemy's fire and locate such parties as might have been hiding in the bushes along the creek, Brown ordered the Solomon Islander to go down to the boat and bring an oar, as you send a spaniel after a stick into the water. This failed, and the fellow came back without a single shot having been fired at him from anywhere. 'There's nobody,' opined some of the men. It is 'onnatural,' remarked the Yankee. Kassim had gone, by that time, very much impressed, pleased too, and also uneasy. Pursuing his tortuous policy, he had dispatched a message to Dain Waris warning him to look out for the white men's ship, which, he had had information, was about to come up the river. He minimised its strength and exhorted him to oppose its passage. This double-dealing answered his purpose, which was to keep the Bugis forces divided and to weaken them by fighting. On the other hand, he had in the course of that day sent word to the assembled Bugis chiefs in town, assuring them that he was trying to induce the invaders to retire; his messages to the fort asked earnestly for powder for the Rajah's men. It was a long time since Tunku Allang had had ammunition for the score or so of old muskets rusting in their arm-racks in the audience-hall. The open intercourse between the hill and the palace unsettled all the minds. It was already time for men to take sides, it began to be said. There would soon be much bloodshed, and thereafter great trouble for many people. The social fabric of orderly, peaceful life, when every man was sure of to-morrow, the edifice raised by Jim's hands, seemed on that evening ready to collapse into a ruin reeking with blood. The poorer folk were already taking to the bush or flying up the river. A good many of the upper class judged it necessary to go and pay their court to the Rajah. The Rajah's youths jostled them rudely. Old Tunku Allang, almost out of his mind with fear and indecision, either kept a sullen silence or abused them violently for daring to come with empty hands: they departed very much frightened; only old Doramin kept his countrymen together and pursued his tactics inflexibly. Enthroned in a big chair behind the improvised stockade he issued his orders in a deep veiled rumble, unmoved, like a deaf man, in the flying rumours.

"Dusk fell, hiding first the body of the dead man, which had been left lying with arms outstretched as if nailed to the ground, and then the revolving sphere of the night rolled smoothly over Patusan and came to a rest, showering the glitter of countless worlds upon the earth. Again, in the exposed part of the town big fires blazed along the only street, revealing from distance to distance upon their glares the falling straight lines of roofs, the fragments of wattled walls jumbled in confusion, here and there a whole hut elevated in the glow upon the vertical black stripes of a group of high piles; and all this line of dwellings, revealed in patches by the swaying flames, seemed to flicker tortuously away up-river into the gloom at the heart of the land. A great silence, in which the looms of successive fires played without noise, extended into the darkness at the foot of the hill; but the other bank of the river, all dark save for a solitary bonfire at the river-front before the fort, sent out into the air an increasing tremor that might have been the stamping of a multitude of feet, the hum of many voices, or the fall of an immensely distant waterfall. It was then, Brown confessed to me, while, turning his back on his men, he sat looking at it all, that notwithstanding his disdain, his ruthless faith in himself, a feeling came over him that at last he had run his head against a stone wall. Had his boat been afloat at the time, he believed he would have tried to steal away, taking his chances of a long chase down the river and of starvation at sea. It is very doubtful whether he would have succeeded in getting away. However he didn't try this. For another moment he had a passing thought of trying to rush the town, but he perceived very well that in the end he would find himself in the lighted street, where they would be shot down like dogs from the houses. They were two hundred to one—he thought, while his men, huddling round two heaps of smouldering embers, munched the last of the bananas and roasted the few yams they owed to Kassim's diplomacy. Cornelius sat amongst them dozing sulkily.

"Then one of the whites remembered that some tobacco had been left in the boat, and, encouraged by the impunity of the Solomon Islander, said he would go to fetch it. At this all the others shook off their despondency. Brown applied to, said, 'Go, and be d—d to you,' scornfully. He didn't think there was any danger in going to the creek in the dark. The man threw a leg over the tree-trunk and disappeared. A moment later he was heard clambering into the boat and then clambering out. 'I've got it,' he cried. A flash and a report at the very foot of the hill followed. 'I am hit,' yelled the man. 'Look out, look out—I am hit,' and instantly all the rifles went off. The hill squirted fire and noise into the night like a little volcano, and when Brown and the Yankee with curses and cuffs stopped the panic-stricken firing, a profound, weary groan floated up from the creek, succeeded by a plaint whose heartrending sadness was like some poison turning the blood cold in the veins. Then a strong voice pronounced several distinct incomprehensible words somewhere beyond the creek. 'Let no one fire,' shouted Brown. 'What does it mean?' . . . 'Do you hear on the hill? Do you hear? Do you hear?' repeated the voice three times. Cornelius translated, and then prompted the answer. 'Speak,' cried Brown, 'we hear.' Then the voice, declaiming in the sonorous inflated tone of a herald, and shifting continually on the edge of the vague waste-land, proclaimed that between the men of the Bugis nation living in Patusan and the white men on the hill and those with them, there would be no faith, no compassion, no speech, no peace. A bush rustled; a haphazard volley rang out. 'Dam' foolishness,' muttered the Yankee, vexedly grounding the butt. Cornelius translated. The wounded man below the hill, after crying out twice, 'Take me up! take me up!' went on complaining in moans. While he had kept on the blackened earth of the slope, and afterwards crouching in the boat, he had been safe enough. It seems that in his joy at finding the tobacco he forgot himself and jumped out on her off-side, as it were. The white boat, lying high and dry, showed him up; the creek was no more than seven yards wide in that place, and there happened to be a man crouching in the bush on the other bank.

"He was a Bugis of Tondano only lately come to Patusan, and a relation of the man shot in the afternoon. That famous long shot had indeed appalled the beholders. The man in utter security had been struck down, in full view of his friends, dropping with a joke on his lips, and they seemed to see in the act an atrocity which had stirred a bitter rage. That relation of his, Si-Lapa by name, was then with Doramin in the stockade only a few feet away. You who know these chaps must admit that the fellow showed an unusual pluck by volunteering to carry the message, alone, in the dark. Creeping across the open ground, he had deviated to the left and found himself opposite the boat. He was startled when Brown's man shouted. He came to a sitting position with his gun to his shoulder, and when the other jumped out, exposing himself, he pulled the trigger and lodged three jagged slugs point-blank into the poor wretch's stomach. Then, lying flat on his face, he gave himself up for dead, while a thin hail of lead chopped and swished the bushes close on his right hand; afterwards he delivered his speech shouting, bent double, dodging all the time in cover. With the last word he leaped sideways, lay close for a while, and afterwards got back to the houses unharmed, having achieved on that night such a renown as his children will not willingly allow to die.

"And on the hill the forlorn band let the two little heaps of embers go out under their bowed heads. They sat dejected on the ground with compressed lips and downcast eyes, listening to their comrade below. He was a strong man and died hard, with moans now loud, now sinking to a strange confidential note of pain. Sometimes he shrieked, and again, after a period of silence, he could be heard muttering deliriously a long and unintelligible complaint. Never for a moment did he cease.

"'What's the good?' Brown had said unmoved once, seeing the Yankee, who had been swearing under his breath, prepare to go down. 'That's so,' assented the deserter, reluctantly desisting. 'There's no encouragement for wounded men here. Only his noise is calculated to make all the others think too much of the hereafter, cap'n.' 'Water!' cried the wounded man in an extraordinary clear vigorous voice, and then went off moaning feebly. 'Ay, water. Water will do it,' muttered the other to himself, resignedly. 'Plenty by-and-by. The tide is flowing.'

"At last the tide flowed, silencing the plaint and the cries of pain, and the dawn was near when Brown, sitting with his chin in the palm of his hand before Patusan, as one might stare at the unscalable side of a mountain, heard the brief ringing bark of a brass 6-pounder far away in town somewhere. 'What's this?' he asked of Cornelius, who hung about him. Cornelius listened. A muffled roaring shout rolled down-river over the town; a big drum began to throb, and others responded, pulsating and droning. Tiny scattered lights began to twinkle in the dark half of the town, while the part lighted by the loom of fires hummed with a deep and prolonged murmur. 'He has come,' said Cornelius. 'What? Already? Are you sure?' Brown asked. 'Yes! yes! Sure. Listen to the noise.' 'What are they making that row about?' pursued Brown. 'For joy,' snorted Cornelius; 'he is a very great man, but all the same, he knows no more than a child, and so they make a great noise to please him, because they know no better.' 'Look here,' said Brown, 'How is one to get at him?' 'He shall come to talk to you,' Cornelius declared. 'What do you mean? Come down here strolling as it were?' Cornelius nodded vigorously in the dark. 'Yes. He will come straight here and talk to you. He is just like a fool. You shall see what a fool he is.' Brown was incredulous. 'You shall see; you shall see,' repeated Cornelius. 'He is not afraid—not afraid of anything. He will come and order you to leave his people alone. Everybody must leave his people alone. He is like a little child. He will come to you straight.' Alas! he knew Jim well—that 'mean little skunk,' as Brown called him to me. 'Yes, certainly,' he pursued with ardour, 'and then, captain, you tell that tall man with a gun to shoot him. Just you kill him, and you will frighten everybody so much that you can do anything you like with them afterwards—get what you like—go away when you like. Ha! ha! ha! Fine . . . ' He almost danced with impatience and eagerness; and Brown, looking over his shoulder at him, could see, shown up by the pitiless dawn, his men drenched with dew, sitting amongst the cold ashes and the litter of the camp, haggard, cowed, and in rags."

Chapter XLI

"To the very last moment, till the full day came upon them with a spring, the fires on the west bank blazed bright and clear; and then Brown saw in a knot of coloured figures motionless between the advanced houses a man in European clothes, in a helmet, all white. 'That's him; look! look!' Cornelius said excitedly. All Brown's men had sprung up and crowded at his back with lustreless eyes. The group of vivid colours and dark faces with the white figure in their midst were observing the knoll. Brown could see naked arms being raised to shade the eyes and other brown arms pointing. What should he do? He looked around, and the forests that faced him on all sides walled the cock-pit of an unequal contest. He looked once more at his men. A contempt, a weariness, the desire of life, the wish to try for one more chance—for some other grave—struggled in his breast. From the outline the figure presented it seemed to him that the white man there, backed up by all the power of the land, was examining his position through binoculars. Brown jumped up on the log, throwing his arms up, the palms outwards. The coloured group closed round the white man, and fell back twice before he got clear of them, walking slowly alone. Brown remained standing on the log till Jim, appearing and disappearing between the patches of thorny scrub, had nearly reached the creek; then Brown jumped off and went down to meet him on his side.

"They met, I should think, not very far from the place, perhaps on the very spot, where Jim took the second desperate leap of his life—the leap that landed him into the life of Patusan, into the trust, the love, the confidence of the people. They faced each other across the creek, and with steady eyes tried to understand each other before they opened their lips. Their antagonism must have been expressed in their glances; I know that Brown hated Jim at first sight. Whatever hopes he might have had vanished at once. This was not the man he had expected to see. He hated him for this—and in a checked flannel shirt with sleeves cut off at the ·elbows, grey bearded, with a sunken, sun-blackened face—he cursed in his heart the other's youth and assurance, his clear eyes and his untroubled bearing. That fellow had got in a long way before him! He did not look like a man who would be willing to give anything for assistance. He had all the advantages on his side—possession, security, power; he was on the side of an overwhelming force! He was not hungry and desperate, and he did not seem in the least afraid. And there was something in the very neatness of Jim's clothes, from the white helmet to the canvas leggings and the pipeclayed shoes,[1] which in Brown's sombre irritated eyes seemed to belong to things he had in the very shaping of his life contemned and flouted.

---

1. Whitened with a certain clay that is also used for making pipes.

" 'Who are you?' asked Jim at last, speaking in his usual voice. 'My name's Brown,' answered the other loudly. 'Captain Brown. What's yours?' and Jim after a little pause went on quietly, as if he had not heard: 'What made you come here?' 'You want to know,' said Brown bitterly. 'It's easy to tell. Hunger. And what made you?'

" 'The fellow started at this,' said Brown, relating to me the opening of this strange conversation between those two men, separated only by the muddy bed of a creek, but standing on the opposite poles of that conception of life which includes all mankind—'The fellow started at this and got very red in the face. Too big to be questioned, I suppose. I told him that if he looked upon me as a dead man with whom you may take liberties, he himself was not a whit better off really. I had a fellow up there who had a bead drawn on him all the time, and only waited for a sign from me. There was nothing to be shocked at in this. He had come down of his own freewill. "Let us agree," said I, "that we are both dead men, and let us talk on that basis, as equals. We are all equal before death," I said. I admitted I was there like a rat in a trap, but we had been driven to it, and even a trapped rat can give a bite. He caught me up in a moment. "Not if you don't go near the trap till the rat is dead." I told him that sort of game was good enough for these native friends of his, but I would have thought him too white to serve even a rat so. Yes, I had wanted to talk with him. Not to beg for my life, though. My fellows were—well—what they were—men like himself, anyhow. All we wanted from him was to come on in the devil's name and have it out. "God d—n it," said I, while he stood there as still as a wooden post, "you don't want to come out here every day with your glasses to count how many of us are left on our feet. Come. Either bring your infernal crowd along or let us go out and starve in the open sea, by God! You have been white once, for all your tall talk of this being your own people and you being one with them. Are you? And what the devil do you get for it; what is it you've found here that is so d—d precious? Hey? You don't want us to come down here perhaps—do you? You are two hundred to one. You don't want us to come down into the open. Ah! I promise you we shall give you some sport before you've done. You talk about me making a cowardly set[2] upon unoffending people. What's that to me that they are unoffending, when I am starving for next to no offence? But I am not a coward. Don't you be one. Bring them along or, by all the fiends, we shall yet manage to send half of your unoffending town to heaven with us in smoke!" '

"He was terrible—relating this to me—this tortured skeleton of a man drawn up together with his face over his knees, upon a miserable bed in that wretched hovel, and lifting his head to look at me with malignant triumph.

2. Attack.

" 'That's what I told him—I knew what to say,' he began again, feebly at first, but working himself up with incredible speed into a fiery utterance of his scorn. 'We aren't going into the forest to wander like a string of living skeletons dropping one after another for ants to go to work upon us before we are fairly dead. Oh no! . . . "You don't deserve a better fate," he said. "And what do you deserve," I shouted at him, "you that I find skulking here with your mouth full of your responsibility, of innocent lives, of your infernal duty? What do you know more of me than I know of you? I came here for food. D'ye hear?—food to fill our bellies. And what did *you* come for? What did you ask for when you came here? We don't ask you for anything but to give us a fight or a clear road to go back whence we came. . . ." "I would fight with you now," says he, pulling at his little moustache. "And I would let you shoot me, and welcome," I said. "This is as good a jumping-off place for me as another. I am sick of my infernal luck. But it would be too easy. There are my men in the same boat—and, by God, I am not the sort to jump out of trouble and leave them in a d—d lurch," I said. He stood thinking for a while and then wanted to know what I had done ("out there" he says, tossing his head down-stream) to be hazed about[3] so. "Have we met to tell each other the story of our lives?" I asked him. "Suppose you begin. No? Well, I am sure I don't want to hear. Keep it to yourself. I know it is no better than mine. I've lived—and so did you, though you talk as if you were one of those people that should have wings so as to go about without touching the dirty earth. Well—it is dirty. I haven't got any wings. I am here because I was afraid once in my life. Want to know what of? Of a prison. That scares me, and you may know it—if it's any good to you. I won't ask you what scared you into this infernal hole, where you seem to have found pretty pickings. That's your luck and this is mine—the privilege to beg for the favour of being shot quickly, or else kicked out to go free and starve in my own way." . . .'

"His debilitated body shook with an exultation so vehement, so assured, and so malicious that it seemed to have driven off the death waiting for him in that hut. The corpse of his mad self-love uprose from rags and destitution as from the dark horrors of a tomb. It is impossible to say how much he lied to Jim then, how much he lied to me now—and to himself always. Vanity plays lurid tricks with our memory, and the truth of every passion wants some pretence to make it live. Standing at the gate of the other world in the guise of a beggar, he had slapped this world's face, he had spat on it, he had thrown upon it an immensity of scorn and revolt at the bottom of his misdeeds. He had overcome them all—men, women, savages, traders, ruffians, missionaries—and Jim—'that beefy-faced beggar.' I did not begrudge him this triumph in

3. Harassed.

articulo mortis,[4] this almost posthumous illusion of having trampled all
the earth under his feet. While he was boasting to me, in his sordid
and repulsive agony, I couldn't help thinking of the chuckling talk relating to the time of his greatest splendour when, during a year or more,
Gentleman Brown's ship was to be seen, for many days on end, hovering
off an islet befringed with green upon azure, with the dark dot of the
mission-house on a white beach; while Gentleman Brown, ashore, was
casting his spells over a romantic girl for whom Melanesia had been too
much, and giving hopes of a remarkable conversion to her husband.
The poor man, some time or other, had been heard to express the
intention of winning 'Captain Brown to a better way of life.' . . . 'Bag
Gentleman Brown for Glory'—as a leery-eyed loafer expressed it once
—'just to let them see up above what a Western Pacific trading skipper
looks like.' And this was the man, too, who had run off with a dying
woman, and had shed tears over her body. 'Carried on like a big baby,'
his then mate was never tired of telling, 'and where the fun came in
may I be kicked to death by diseased Kanakas if *I* know. Why, gents!
She was too far gone when he brought her aboard to know him; she
just lay there on her back in his bunk staring at the beam with awful
shining eyes—and then she died. Dam' bad sort of fever, I guess. . . .'
I remembered all these stories while, wiping his matted lump of a beard
with a livid hand, he was telling me from his noisome couch how he
got round, got in, got home, on that confounded, immaculate, don't-
you-touch-me sort of fellow. He admitted that he couldn't be scared,
but there was a way, 'as broad as a turnpike, to get in and shake his
twopenny soul around and inside out and upside down—by God!' "

Chapter XLII

"I don't think he could do more than perhaps look upon that straight
path. He seemed to have been puzzled by what he saw, for he interrupted
himself in his narrative more than once to exclaim, 'He nearly slipped
from me there. I could not make him out. Who was he?' And after
glaring at me wildly he would go on, jubilating and sneering. To me
the conversation of these two across the creek appears now as the deadliest kind of duel on which Fate looked on with her cold-eyed knowledge
of the end. No, he didn't turn Jim's soul inside out, but I am much
mistaken if the spirit so utterly out of his reach had not been made to
taste to the full the bitterness of that contest. These were the emissaries
with whom the world he had renounced was pursuing him in his
retreat—white men from 'out there' where he did not think himself
good enough to live. This was all that came to him—a menace, a shock,

4. At the point of death (Latin).

a danger to his work. I suppose it is this sad, half-resentful, half-resigned feeling, piercing through the few words Jim said now and then, that puzzled Brown so much in the reading of his character. Some great men owe most of their greatness to the ability of detecting in those they destine for their tools the exact quality of strength that matters for their work; and Brown, as though he had been really great, had a satanic gift of finding out the best and the weakest spot in his victims. He admitted to me that Jim wasn't of the sort that can be got over by truckling, and accordingly he took care to show himself as a man confronting without dismay ill-luck, censure, and disaster. The smuggling of a few guns was no great crime, he pointed out. As to coming to Patusan, who had the right to say he hadn't come to beg? The infernal people here let loose at him from both banks without staying to ask questions. He made the point brazenly, for, in truth, Dain Waris's energetic action had prevented the greatest calamities; because Brown told me distinctly that, perceiving the size of the place, he had resolved instantly in his mind that as soon as he had gained a footing he would set fire right and left, and begin by shooting down everything living in sight, in order to cow and terrify the population. The disproportion of forces was so great that this was the only way giving him the slightest chance of attaining his ends—he argued in a fit of coughing. But he didn't tell Jim this. As to the hardships and starvation they had gone through, these had been very real; it was enough to look at his band. He made, at the sound of a shrill whistle, all his men appear standing in a row on the logs in full view, so that Jim could see them. For the killing of the man, it had been done—well, it had—but was not this war, bloody war—in a corner? and the fellow had been killed cleanly, shot through the chest, not like that poor devil of his lying now in the creek. They had to listen to him dying for six hours, with his entrails torn with slugs. At any rate this was a life for a life. . . . And all this was said with the weariness, with the recklessness of a man spurred on and on by ill-luck till he cares not where he runs. When he asked Jim, with a sort of brusque despairing frankness, whether he himself—straight now—didn't understand that when 'it came to saving one's life in the dark, one didn't care who else went—three, thirty, three hundred people'—it was as if a demon had been whispering advice in his ear. 'I made him wince,' boasted Brown to me. 'He very soon left off coming the righteous over me. He just stood there with nothing to say, and looking as black as thunder—not at me—on the ground.' He asked Jim whether he had nothing fishy in his life to remember that he was so damnedly hard upon a man trying to get out of a deadly hole by the first means that came to hand—and so on, and so on. And there ran through the rough talk a vein of subtle reference to their common blood, an assumption of common experience; a sickening suggestion of common guilt, of secret knowledge that was like a bond of their minds and of their hearts.

"At last Brown threw himself down full length and watched Jim out of the corners of his eyes. Jim on his side of the creek stood thinking and switching his leg. The houses in view were silent as if a pestilence had swept them clean of every breath of life; but many invisible eyes were turned, from within, upon the two men with the creek between them, a stranded white boat, and the body of the third man half sunk in the mud. On the river canoes were moving again, for Patusan was recovering its belief in the stability of earthly institutions since the return of the white lord. The right bank, the platforms of the houses, the rafts moored along the shores, even the roofs of bathing-huts, were covered with people that, far away out of earshot and almost out of sight, were straining their eyes towards the knoll beyond the Rajah's stockade. Within the wide irregular ring of forests, broken in two places by the sheen of the river, there was a silence. 'Will you promise to leave the coast?' Jim asked. Brown lifted and let fall his hand, giving everything up as it were—accepting the inevitable. 'And surrender your arms?' Jim went on. Brown sat up and glared across. 'Surrender our arms! Not till you come to take them out of our stiff hands. You think I am gone crazy with funk? Oh no! That and the rags I stand in is all I have got in the world, besides a few more breech-loaders on board; and I expect to sell the lot in Madagascar, if I ever get so far,—begging my way from ship to ship.'

"Jim said nothing to this. At last, throwing away the switch he held in his hand, he said, as if speaking to himself, 'I don't know whether I have the power. . . .' 'You don't know! And you wanted me just now to give up my arms! That's good, too,' cried Brown. 'Suppose they say one thing to you, and do the other thing to me.' He calmed down markedly 'I daresay you have the power, or what's the meaning of all this talk?' he continued. 'What did you come down here for? To pass the time of day?'

" 'Very well,' said Jim, lifting his head suddenly after a long silence. 'You shall have a clear road or else a clear fight.' He turned on his heel and walked away.

"Brown got up at once, but he did not go up the hill till he had seen Jim disappear between the first houses. He never set his eyes on him again. On his way back he met Cornelius slouching down with his head between his shoulders. He stopped before Brown. 'Why didn't you kill him?' he demanded in a sour, discontented voice. 'Because I could do better than that,' Brown said with an amused smile. 'Never! never!' protested Cornelius with energy. 'Couldn't. I have lived here for many years.' Brown looked up at him curiously. There were many sides to the life of that place in arms against him; things he would never find out. Cornelius slunk past dejectedly in the direction of the river. He was now leaving his new friends; he accepted the disappointing course of events with a sulky obstinacy which seemed to draw more together his little yellow old face; and as he went down he glanced askant here and there, never giving up his fixed idea.

"Henceforth events move fast without a check, flowing from the very hearts of men like a stream from a dark source, and we see Jim amongst them, mostly through Tamb' Itam's eyes. The girl's eyes had watched him too, but her life is too much entwined with his: there is her passion, her·wonder, her anger, and, above all, her fear and her unforgiving love. Of the faithful servant, uncomprehending as the rest of them, it is the fidelity alone that comes into play; a fidelity and a belief in his lord so strong that even amazement is subdued to a sort of saddened acceptance of a mysterious failure. He has eyes only for one figure, and through all the mazes of bewilderment he preserves his air of guardianship, of obedience, of care.

"His master came back from his talk with the white men, walking slowly towards the stockade in the street. Everybody was rejoiced to see him return, for while he was away every man had been afraid not only of him being killed, but also of what would come after. Jim went into one of the houses, where old Doramin had retired, and remained alone for a long time with the head of the Bugis settlers. No doubt he discussed the course to follow with him then, but no man was present at the conversation. Only Tamb' Itam, keeping as close to the door as he could, heard his master say, 'Yes. I shall let all the people know that such is my wish; but I spoke to you, O Doramin, before all the others, and alone; for you know my heart as well as I know yours and its greatest desire. And you know well also that I have no thought but for the people's good.' Then his master, lifting the sheeting in the doorway, went out, and he, Tamb' Itam, had a glimpse of old Doramin within, sitting in the chair with his hands on his knees, and looking between his feet. Afterwards he followed his master to the fort, where all the principal Bugis and Patusan inhabitants had been summoned for a talk. Tamb' Itam himself hoped there would be some fighting. 'What was it but the taking of another hill?' he exclaimed regretfully. However, in the town many hoped that the rapacious strangers would be induced, by the sight of so many brave men making ready to fight, to go away. It would be a good thing if they went away. Since Jim's arrival had been made known before daylight by the gun fired from the fort and the beating of the big drum there, the fear that had hung over Patusan had broken and subsided like a wave on a rock, leaving the seething foam of excitement, curiosity, and endless speculation. Half of the population had been ousted out of their homes for purposes of defence, and were living in the street on the left side of the river, crowding round the fort, and in momentary expectation of seeing their abandoned dwellings on the threatened bank burst into flames. The general anxiety was to see the matter settled quickly. Food, through Jewel's care, had been served out to the refugees. Nobody knew what their white man would do. Some remarked that it was worse than in Sherif Ali's war. Then many people did not care; now everybody had something to lose. The movements of canoes passing to and fro between the two parts of the town were watched with interest. A couple of Bugis war-boats lay anchored in the middle of the stream to protect the river, and a thread of smoke stood at the bow of each; the men in them were cooking their mid-day rice when Jim, after his interviews with Brown and Doramin, crossed the river and entered by the water-gate of his fort. The people inside crowded round him so that he could hardly make his way to the house. They had not seen him before, because on his arrival during the night he had only exchanged a few words with the girl, who had come down to the landing-stage for the purpose, and had then gone on at once to join the chiefs and the fighting men on the other bank. People shouted greetings after him. One old woman raised a laugh by pushing her way to the front madly and enjoining him in a scolding voice to see to it that her two sons who were with Doramin did not come to harm at the hands of the robbers. Several of the bystanders tried to pull her away, but she struggled and cried, 'Let me go. What is this, O Muslims? This laughter is unseemly. Are they not cruel, bloodthirsty robbers bent on killing?' 'Let her be,' said Jim, and as a silence fell suddenly, he said slowly, 'Everybody shall be safe.' He entered the house before the great sigh, and the loud murmurs of satisfaction, had died out.

"There's no doubt his mind was made up that Brown should have his way clear back to the sea. His fate, revolted, was forcing his hand. He had for the first time to affirm his will in the face of outspoken opposition. 'There was much talk, and at first my master was silent,' Tamb' Itam said. 'Darkness came, and then I lit the candles on the long table. The chiefs sat on each side, and the lady remained by my master's right hand.'

"When he began to speak, the unaccustomed difficulty seemed only to fix his resolve more immovably. The white men were now waiting for his answer on the hill. Their chief had spoken to him in the language of his own people, making clear many things difficult to explain in any other speech. They were erring men whom suffering had made blind to right and wrong. It is true that lives had been lost already, but why lose more? He declared to his hearers, the assembled heads of the people, that their welfare was his welfare, their losses his losses, their mourning his mourning.[1] He looked round at the grave listening faces and told them to remember that they had fought and worked side by side. They knew his courage . . . Here a murmur interrupted him . . . And that he had never deceived them. For many years they had dwelt together. He loved the land and the people living in it with a very great love. He was ready to answer with his life for any harm that should come to them

1. Compare Ruth's words to her mother-in-law, Naomi: "thy people shall be my people, and thy God my God: Where thou diest, will I die, and there will I be buried" (Ruth 1.16–17).

if the white men with beards were allowed to retire. They were evil-doers, but their destiny had been evil too. Had he ever advised them ill? Had his words ever brought suffering to the people? he asked. He believed that it would be best to let these whites and their followers go with their lives. It would be a small gift. 'I whom you have tried and found always true ask you to let them go.' He turned to Doramin. The old *nakhoda* made no movement. 'Then,' said Jim, 'call in Dain Waris, your son, my friend, for in this business I shall not lead.' "

Chapter XLIII

"Tamb' Itam behind his chair was thunderstruck. The declaration produced an immense sensation. 'Let them go because this is best in my knowledge, which has never deceived you,' Jim insisted. There was a silence. In the darkness of the courtyard could be heard the subdued whispering, shuffling noise of many people. Doramin raised his heavy head and said that there was no more reading of hearts than touching the sky with the hand, but—he consented. The others gave their opinion in turn. 'It is best,' 'Let them go,' and so on. But most of them simply said that they 'believed Tuan Jim.'

"In this simple form of assent to his will lies the whole gist of the situation; their creed, his truth; and the testimony to that faithfulness which made him in his own eyes the equal of the impeccable men who never fall out of the ranks. Stein's words, 'Romantic!—Romantic!' seem to ring over those distances that will never give him up now to a world indifferent to his failings and his virtues, and to that ardent and clinging affection that refuses him the dole of tears in the bewilderment of a great grief and of eternal separation. From the moment the sheer truthfulness of his last three years of life carries the day against the ignorance, the fear, and the anger of men, he appears no longer to me as I saw him last—a white speck catching all the dim light left upon a sombre coast and the darkened sea—but greater and more pitiful in the loneliness of his soul, that remains even for her who loved him best a cruel and insoluble mystery.

"It is evident that he did not mistrust Brown; there was no reason to doubt the story, whose truth seemed warranted by the rough frankness, by a sort of virile sincerity in accepting the morality and the consequences of his acts. But Jim did not know the almost inconceivable egotism of the man which made him, when resisted and foiled in his will, mad with the indignant and revengeful rage of a thwarted autocrat. But if Jim did not mistrust Brown, he was evidently anxious that some misunderstanding should not occur, ending perhaps in collision and bloodshed. It was for this reason that directly the Malay chiefs had gone he asked Jewel to get him something to eat, as he was going out of the fort to take command in the town. On her remonstrating against this on the score of his fatigue, he said that something might happen for which he would never forgive himself. 'I am responsible for every life in the land,' he said. He was moody at first; she served him with her own hands, taking the plates and dishes (of the dinner-service presented him by Stein) from Tamb' Itam. He brightened up after a while; told her she would be again in command of the fort for another night. 'There's no sleep for us, old girl,' he said, 'while our people are in danger.' Later on he said jokingly that she was the best man of them all. 'If you and Dain Waris had done what you wanted, not one of these poor devils would be alive to-day.' 'Are they very bad?' she asked, leaning over his chair. 'Men act badly sometimes without being much worse than others,' he said after some hesitation.

"Tamb' Itam followed his master to the landing-stage outside the fort. The night was clear but without a moon, and the middle of the river was dark, while the water under each bank reflected the light of many fires 'as on a night of Ramadan,'[1] Tamb' Itam said. War-boats drifted silently in the dark lane or, anchored, floated motionless with a loud ripple. That night there was much paddling in a canoe and walking at his master's heels for Tamb' Itam: up and down the street they tramped, where the fires were burning, inland on the outskirts of the town where small parties of men kept guard in the fields. Tuan Jim gave his orders and was obeyed. Last of all they went to the Rajah's stockade, which a detachment of Jim's people manned on that night. The old Rajah had fled early in the morning with most of his women to a small house he had near a jungle village on a tributary stream. Kassim, left behind, had attended the council with his air of diligent activity to explain away the diplomacy of the day before. He was considerably cold-shouldered, but managed to preserve his smiling, quiet alertness, and professed himself highly delighted when Jim told him sternly that he proposed to occupy the stockade on that night with his own men. After the council broke up he was heard outside accosting this and that departing chief, and speaking in a loud, gratified tone of the Rajah's property being protected in the Rajah's absence.

"About ten or so Jim's men marched in. The stockade commanded the mouth of the creek, and Jim meant to remain there till Brown had passed below. A small fire was lit on the flat, grassy point outside the wall of stakes, and Tamb' Itam placed a little folding-stool for his master. Jim told him to try and sleep. Tamb' Itam got a mat and lay down a little way off; but he could not sleep, though he knew he had to go on an important journey before the night was out. His master walked to and fro before the fire with bowed head and with his hands behind his

1. In the Mohammedan year, the ninth month, on each day of which, from dawn to sunset, strict fasting is practiced, and all activities are reduced; cooking fires are lighted only at night.

back. His face was sad. Whenever his master approached him Tamb' Itam pretended to sleep, not wishing his master to know he had been watched. At last his master stood still, looking down on him as he lay, and said softly, 'It is time.'

"Tamb' Itam arose directly and made his preparations. His mission was to go down the river, preceding Brown's boat by an hour or more, to tell Dain Waris finally and formally that the whites were to be allowed to pass out unmolested. Jim would not trust anybody else with that service. Before starting, Tamb' Itam, more as a matter of form (since his position about Jim made him perfectly known), asked for a token. 'Because, Tuan,' he said, 'the message is important, and these are thy very words I carry.' His master first put his hand into one pocket, then into another, and finally took off his forefinger Stein's silver ring, which he habitually wore, and gave it to Tamb' Itam. When Tamb' Itam left on his mission, Brown's camp on the knoll was dark but for a single small glow shining through the branches of one of the trees the white men had cut down.

"Early in the evening Brown had received from Jim a folded piece of paper on which was written, 'You get the clear road. Start as soon as your boat floats on the morning tide. Let your men be careful. The bushes on both sides of the creek and the stockade at the mouth are full of well-armed men. You would have no chance, but I don't believe you want bloodshed.' Brown read it, tore the paper into small pieces, and, turning to Cornelius, who had brought it, said jeeringly, 'Good-bye, my excellent friend.' Cornelius had been in the fort, and had been sneaking around Jim's house during the afternoon. Jim chose him to carry the note because he could speak English, was known to Brown, and was not likely to be shot by some nervous mistake of one of the men as a Malay, approaching in the dusk, perhaps might have been.

"Cornelius didn't go away after delivering the paper. Brown was sitting up over a tiny fire; all the others were lying down. 'I could tell you something you would like to know,' Cornelius mumbled crossly. Brown paid no attention. 'You did not kill him,' went on the other, 'and what do you get for it? You might have had money from the Rajah, besides the loot of all the Bugis houses, and now you get nothing.' 'You had better clear out from here,' growled Brown, without even looking at him. But Cornelius let himself drop by his side and began to whisper very fast, touching his elbow from time to time. What he had to say made Brown sit up at first, with a curse. He had simply informed him of Dain Waris's armed party down the river. At first Brown saw himself completely sold and betrayed, but a moment's reflection convinced him that there could be no treachery intended. He said nothing, and after a while Cornelius remarked, in a tone of complete indifference, that there was another way out of the river which he knew very well. 'A good thing to know, too,' said Brown, pricking up his ears; and Cornelius began to talk of what went on in town and repeated all that had been said in council, gossiping in an even undertone at Brown's ear as you talk amongst sleeping men you do not wish to wake. 'He thinks he has made me harmless, does he? mumbled Brown very low. . . . 'Yes. He is a fool. A little child. He came here and robbed me,' droned on Cornelius, 'and he made all the people believe him. But if something happened that they did not believe him any more, where would he be? And the Bugis Dain who is waiting for you down the river there, captain, is the very man who chased you up here when you first came.' Brown observed nonchalantly that it would be just as well to avoid him, and with the same detached, musing air Cornelius declared himself acquainted with a backwater broad enough to take Brown's boat past Waris's camp. 'You will have to be quiet,' he said as an afterthought, 'for in one place we pass close behind his camp. Very close. They are camped ashore with their boats hauled up.' 'Oh, we know how to be as quiet as mice. Never fear,' said Brown. Cornelius stipulated that in case he were to pilot Brown out, his canoe should be towed. 'I'll have to get back quick,' he explained.

"It was two hours before the dawn when word was passed to the stockade from outlying watchers that the white robbers were coming down to their boat. In a very short time every armed man from one end of Patusan to the other was on the alert, yet the banks of the river remained so silent that but for the fires burning with sudden blurred flares the town might have been asleep as if in peacetime. A heavy mist lay very low on the water, making a sort of illusive grey light that showed nothing. When Brown's long-boat glided out of the creek into the river, Jim was standing on the low point of land before the Rajah's stockade —on the very spot where for the first time he put his foot on Patusan shore. A shadow loomed up, moving in the greyness, solitary, very bulky, and yet constantly eluding the eye. A murmur of low talking came out of it. Brown at the tiller heard Jim speak calmly: 'A clear road. You had better trust to the current while the fog lasts; but this will lift presently.' 'Yes, presently we shall see clear,' replied Brown.

"The thirty or forty men standing with muskets at ready outside the stockade held their breath. The Bugis owner of the prau, whom I saw on Stein's verandah, and who was amongst them, told me that the boat, shaving the low point close, seemed for a moment to grow big and hang over it like a mountain. 'If you think it worth your while to wait a day outside,' called out Jim, 'I'll try to send you down something—a bullock, some yams—what I can.' The shadow went on moving. 'Yes. Do,' said a voice, blank and muffled out of the fog. Not one of the many attentive listeners understood what the words meant; and then Brown and his men in their boat floated away, fading spectrally without the slightest sound.

"Thus Brown, invisible in the mist, goes out of Patusan elbow to elbow with Cornelius in the stern-sheets of the long-boat. 'Perhaps you shall get a small bullock,' said Cornelius. 'Oh yes. Bullock. Yam. You'll get it if *he* said so. He always speaks the truth. He stole everything I had. I suppose you like a small bullock better than the loot of many houses.' 'I would advise you to hold your tongue, or somebody here may fling you overboard into this damned fog,' said Brown. The boat seemed to be standing still; nothing could be seen, not even the river alongside, only the water-dust flew and trickled, condensed, down their beards and faces. It was weird, Brown told me. Every individual man of them felt as though he were adrift alone in a boat, haunted by an almost imperceptible suspicion of sighing, muttering ghosts. 'Throw me out, would you? But I would know where I was,' mumbled Cornelius surlily. 'I've lived many years here.' 'Not long enough to see through a fog like this,' Brown said, lolling back with his arm swinging to and fro on the useless tiller. 'Yes. Long enough for that,' snarled Cornelius. 'That's very useful,' commented Brown. 'Am I to believe you could find that backway you spoke of blindfold, like this?' Cornelius grunted. 'Are you too tired to row?' he asked after a silence. 'No, by God!' shouted Brown suddenly. 'Out with your oars there.' There was a great knocking in the fog, which after a while settled into a regular grind of invisible sweeps against invisible thole-pins. Otherwise nothing was changed, and but for the slight splash of a dipped blade it was like rowing a balloon car[2] in a cloud, said Brown. Thereafter Cornelius did not open his lips except to ask querulously for somebody to bale out his canoe, which was towing behind the long-boat. Gradually the fog whitened and became luminous ahead. To the left Brown saw a darkness as though he had been looking at the back of the departing night. All at once a big bough covered with leaves appeared above his head, and ends of twigs, dripping and still, curved slenderly close alongside. Cornelius, without a word, took the tiller from his hand."

Chapter XLIV

"I don't think they spoke together again. The boat entered a narrow by-channel, where it was pushed by the oar-blades set into crumbling banks, and there was a gloom as if enormous black wings had been outspread above the mist that filled its depth to the summits of the trees. The branches overhead showered big drops through the gloomy fog. At a mutter from Cornelius, Brown ordered his men to load. 'I'll give you a chance to get even with them before we're done, you dismal cripples,

2. The earliest balloonists carried oars and tried to propel their balloons by rowing.

you,' he said to his gang. 'Mind you don't throw it away—you hounds.'
Low growls answered that speech. Cornelius showed much fussy concern
for the safety of his canoe.

"Meantime Tamb' Itam had reached the end of his journey. The fog
had delayed him a little, but he had paddled steadily, keeping in touch
with the south bank. By-and-by daylight came like a glow in a ground
glass globe. The shores made on each side of the river a dark smudge,
in which one could detect hints of columnar forms and shadows of
twisted branches high up. The mist was still thick on the water, but a
good watch was being kept, for as Tamb' Itam approached the camp
the figures of two men emerged out of the white vapour, and voices
spoke to him boisterously. He answered, and presently a canoe lay
alongside, and he exchanged news with the paddlers. All was well. The
trouble was over. Then the men in the canoe let go their grip on the
side of his dug-out and incontinently fell out of sight. He pursued his
way till he heard voices coming to him quietly over the water, and saw,
under the now lifting, swirling mist, the glow of many little fires burning
on a sandy stretch, backed by lofty thin timber and bushes. There again
a look-out was kept, for he was challenged. He shouted his name as the
two last sweeps of his paddle ran his canoe up on the strand. It was a
big camp. Men crouched in many little knots under a subdued murmur
of early morning talk. Many thin threads of smoke curled slowly on the
white mist. Little shelters, elevated above the ground, had been built
for the chiefs. Muskets were stacked in small pyramids, and long spears
were stuck singly into the sand near the fires.

"Tamb' Itam, assuming an air of importance, demanded to be led to
Dain Waris. He found the friend of his white lord lying on a raised
couch made of bamboo, and sheltered by a sort of shed of sticks covered
with mats. Dain Waris was awake, and a bright fire was burning before
his sleeping place, which resembled a rude shrine. The only son of
Nakhoda Doramin answered his greeting kindly. Tamb' Itam began by
handing him the ring which vouched for the truth of the messenger's
words. Dain Waris, reclining on his elbow, bade him speak and tell all
the news. Beginning with the consecrated formula, 'The news is good,'
Tamb' Itam delivered Jim's own words. The white men, departing with
the consent of all the chiefs, were to be allowed to pass down the river.
In answer to a question or two Tamb' Itam then reported the proceedings
of the last council. Dain Waris listened attentively to the end, toying
with the ring which ultimately he slipped on the forefinger of his right
hand. After hearing all he had to say he dismissed Tamb' Itam to have
food and rest. Orders for the return in the afternoon were given immediately. Afterwards Dain Waris lay down again, open-eyed, while his
personal attendants were preparing his food at the fire, by which Tamb'
Itam also sat talking to the men who lounged up to hear the latest

intelligence from the town. The sun was eating up the mist. A good watch was kept upon the reach of the main stream where the boat of the whites was expected to appear every moment.

"It was then that Brown took his revenge upon the world which, after twenty years of contemptuous and reckless bullying, refused him the tribute of a common robber's success. It was an act of cold-blooded ferocity, and it consoled him on his death-bed like a memory of an indomitable defiance. Stealthily he landed his men on the other side of the island opposite to the Bugis camp, and led them across. After a short but quite silent scuffle Cornelius, who had tried to slink away at the moment of landing, resigned himself to show the way where the undergrowth was most sparse. Brown held both his skinny hands together behind his back in the grip of one vast fist, and now and then impelled him forward with a fierce push. Cornelius remained as mute as a fish, abject but faithful to his purpose, whose accomplishment loomed before him dimly. At the edge of the patch of forest Brown's men spread themselves out in cover and waited. The camp was plain from end to end before their eyes, and no one looked their way. Nobody even dreamed that the white men could have any knowledge of the narrow channel at the back of the island. When he judged the moment come, Brown yelled, 'Let them have it,' and fourteen shots rang out like one.

"Tamb' Itam told me the surprise was so great that, except for those who fell dead or wounded, not a soul of them moved for quite an appreciable time after the first discharge. Then a man screamed, and after that scream a great yell of amazement and fear went up from all the throats. A blind panic drove these men in a surging swaying mob to and fro along the shore like a herd of cattle afraid of the water. Some few jumped into the river then, but most of them did so only after the last discharge. Three times Brown's men fired into the ruck,[1] Brown, the only one in view, cursing and yelling, 'Aim low! aim low!'

"Tamb' Itam says that, as for him, he understood at the first volley what had happened. Though untouched he fell down and lay as if dead, but with his eyes open. At the sound of the first shots Dain Waris, reclining on the couch, jumped up and ran out upon the open shore, just in time to receive a bullet in his forehead at the second discharge. Tamb' Itam saw him fling his arms wide open before he fell. Then, he says, a great fear came upon him—not before. The white men retired as they had come—unseen.

"Thus Brown balanced his account with the evil fortune. Notice that even in this awful outbreak there is a superiority as of a man who carries right—the abstract thing—within the envelope of his common desires. It was not a vulgar and treacherous massacre; it was a lesson, a

1. Crowd.

retribution—a demonstration of some obscure and awful attribute of our nature which, I am afraid, is not so very far under the surface as we like to think.

"Afterwards the whites depart unseen by Tamb' Itam, and seem to vanish from before men's eyes altogether; and the schooner, too, vanishes after the manner of stolen goods. But a story is told of a white long-boat picked up a month later in the Indian Ocean by a cargo steamer. Two parched, yellow, glassy-eyed, whispering skeletons in her recognised the authority of a third, who declared that his name was Brown. His schooner, he reported, bound south with a cargo of Java sugar, had sprung a bad leak and sank under his feet. He and his companions were the survivors of a crew of six. The two died on board the steamer which rescued them. Brown lived to be seen by me, and I can testify that he had played his part to the last.

"It seems, however, that in going away they had neglected to cast off Cornelius's canoe. Cornelius himself Brown had let go at the beginning of the shooting, with a kick for a parting benediction. Tamb' Itam, after arising from amongst the dead, saw the Nazarene running up and down the shore amongst the corpses and the expiring fires. He uttered little cries. Suddenly he rushed to the water, and made frantic efforts to get one of the Bugis boats into the water. 'Afterwards, till he had seen me,' related Tamb' Itam, 'he stood looking at the heavy canoe and scratching his head.' 'What became of him?' I asked. Tamb' Itam, staring hard at me, made an expressive gesture with his right arm. 'Twice I struck, Tuan,' he said. 'When he beheld me approaching he cast himself violently on the ground and made a great outcry, kicking. He screeched like a frightened hen till he felt the point; then he was still, and lay staring at me while his life went out of his eyes.'

"This done, Tamb' Itam did not tarry. He understood the importance of being the first with the awful news at the fort. There were, of course, many survivors of Dain Waris's party; but in the extremity of panic some had swum across the river, others had bolted into the bush. The fact is that they did not know really who struck that blow—whether more white robbers were not coming, whether they had not already got hold of the whole land. They imagined themselves to be the victims of a vast treachery, and utterly doomed to destruction. It is said that some small parties did not come in till three days afterwards. However, a few tried to make their way back to Patusan at once, and one of the canoes that were patrolling the river that morning was in sight of the camp at the very moment of the attack. It is true that at first the men in her leaped overboard and swam to the opposite bank, but afterwards they returned to their boat and started fearfully up-stream. Of these Tamb' Itam had an hour's advance."

Chapter XLV

"When Tamb' Itam, paddling madly, came into the town-reach, the women, thronging the platforms before the houses, were looking out for the return of Dain Waris's little fleet of boats. The town had a festive air; here and there men, still with spears or guns in their hands, could be seen moving or standing on the shore in groups. Chinamen's shops had been opened early; but the market-place was empty, and a sentry, still posted at the corner of the fort, made out Tamb' Itam, and shouted to those within. The gate was wide open. Tamb' Itam jumped ashore and ran in headlong. The first person he met was the girl coming down from the house.

"Tamb' Itam, disordered, panting, with trembling lips and wild eyes, stood for a time before her as if a sudden spell had been laid on him. Then he broke out very quickly: 'They have killed Dain Waris and many more.' She clapped her hands, and her first words were, 'Shut the gates.' Most of the fortmen had gone back to their houses, but Tamb' Itam hurried on the few who remained for their turn of duty within. The girl stood in the middle of the courtyard while the others ran about. 'Doramin,' she cried despairingly as Tamb' Itam passed her. Next time he went by he answered her thought rapidly, 'Yes. But we have all the powder in Patusan.' She caught him by the arm, and, pointing at the house, 'Call him out,' she whispered, trembling.

"Tamb' Itam ran up the steps. His master was sleeping. 'It is I, Tamb' Itam,' he cried at the door, 'with tidings that cannot wait.' He saw Jim turn over on the pillow and open his eyes, and he burst out at once. 'This, Tuan, is a day of evil, an accursed day.' His master raised himself on his elbow to listen—just as Dain Waris had done. And then Tamb' Itam began his tale, trying to relate the story in order, calling Dain Waris Panglima, and saying, 'The Panglima then called out to the chief of his own boatmen, "Give Tamb' Itam something to eat" '—when his master put his feet to the ground and looked at him with such a discomposed face that the words remained in his throat.

" 'Speak out,' said Jim. 'Is he dead?' 'May you live long,' cried Tamb' Itam. 'It was a most cruel treachery. He ran out at the first shots and fell.' . . . His master walked to the window and with his fist struck at the shutter. The room was made light; and then in a steady voice, but speaking fast, he began to give him orders to assemble a fleet of boats for immediate pursuit, go to this man, to the other—send messengers; and as he talked he sat down on the bed, stooping to lace his boots hurriedly, and suddenly looked up. 'Why do you stand here?' he asked very red-faced. 'Waste no time.' Tamb' Itam did not move. 'Forgive me, Tuan, but . . . but,' he began to stammer. 'What?' cried his master aloud, looking terrible, leaning forward with his hands gripping the edge of the bed. 'It is not safe for thy servant to go out amongst the people,' said Tamb' Itam, after hesitating a moment.

"Then Jim understood. He had retreated from one world, for a small matter of an impulsive jump, and now the other, the work of his own hands, had fallen in ruins upon his head. It was not safe for his servant to go out amongst his own people! I believe that in that very moment he had decided to defy the disaster in the only way it occurred to him such a disaster could be defied; but all I know is that without a word he came out of his room and sat before the long table, at the head of which he was accustomed to regulate the affairs of his world, proclaiming daily the truth that surely lived in his heart. The dark powers should not rob him twice of his peace. He sat like a stone figure. Tamb' Itam, deferential, hinted at preparations for defence. The girl he loved came in and spoke to him, but he made a sign with his hand, and she was awed by the dumb appeal for silence in it. She went out on the verandah and sat on the threshold, as if to guard him with her body from dangers outside.

"What thoughts passed through his head—what memories? Who can tell. Everything was gone, and he who had been once unfaithful to his trust had lost again all men's confidence. It was then, I believe, he tried to write—to somebody—and gave it up. Loneliness was closing on him. People had trusted him with their lives—only for that; and yet they could never, as he had said, never be made to understand him. Those without did not hear him make a sound. Later, towards the evening, he came to the door and called for Tamb' Itam. 'Well,' he asked. 'There is much weeping. Much anger too,' said Tamb' Itam. Jim looked up at him. 'You know,' he murmured. 'Yes, Tuan,' said Tamb' Itam. 'Thy servant does know, and the gates are closed. We shall have to fight.' 'Fight! What for?' he asked. 'For our lives.' 'I have no life,' he said. Tamb' Itam heard a cry from the girl at the door. 'Who knows?' said Tamb' Itam. 'By audacity and cunning we may even escape. There is much fear in men's hearts too.' He went out, thinking vaguely of boats and of open sea, leaving Jim and the girl together.

"I haven't the heart to set down here such glimpses as she had given me of the hour or more she passed in there wrestling with him for the possession of her happiness. Whether he had any hope—what he expected, what he imagined—it is impossible to say. He was inflexible, and with the growing loneliness of his obstinacy his spirit seemed to rise above the ruins of his existence. She cried 'Fight!' into his ear. She could not understand. There was nothing to fight for. He was going to prove his power in another way and conquer the fatal destiny itself. He came out into the courtyard, and behind him, with streaming hair, wild of face, breathless, she staggered out and leaned on the side of the doorway. 'Open the gates,' he ordered. Afterwards turning to those of his men who were inside, he gave them leave to depart to their homes.

'For how long, Tuan?' asked one of them timidly. 'For all life,' he said, in a sombre tone.

"A hush had fallen upon the town after the outburst of wailing and lamentation that had swept over the river, like a gust of wind from the opened abode of sorrow. But rumours flew in whispers, filling the hearts with consternation and horrible doubts. The robbers were coming back, bringing many others with them, in a great ship, and there would be no refuge in the land for any one. A sense of utter insecurity as during an earthquake pervaded the minds of men, who whispered their suspicions, looking at each other as if in the presence of some awful portent.

"The sun was sinking towards the forests when Dain Waris's body was brought into Doramin's campong. Four men carried it in, covered decently with a white sheet which the old mother had sent out down to the gate to meet her son on his return. They laid him at Doramin's feet, and the old man sat still for a long time, one hand on each knee, looking down. The fronds of palms swayed gently, and the foliage of fruit-trees stirred above his head. Every single man of his people was there, fully armed, when the old *nakhoda* at last raised his eyes. He moved them slowly over the crowd, as if seeking for a missing face. Again his chin sank on his breast. The whispers of many men mingled with the slight rustling of the leaves.

"The Malay who had brought Tamb' Itam and the girl to Samarang was there too. 'Not so angry as many,' he said to me, but struck with a great awe and wonder at the 'suddenness of men's fate, which hangs over their heads like a cloud charged with thunder.' He told me that when Dain Waris's body was uncovered at a sign of Doramin's, he whom they often called the white lord's friend was disclosed lying unchanged with his eyelids a little open as if about to wake. Doramin leaned forward a little more, like one looking for something fallen on the ground. His eyes searched the body from its feet to its head, for the wound maybe. It was in the forehead and small; and there was no word spoken while one of the bystanders, stooping, took off the silver ring from the cold stiff hand. In silence he held it up before Doramin. A murmur of dismay and horror ran through the crowd at the sight of that familiar token. The old *nakhoda* stared at it, and suddenly let out one great fierce cry, deep from the chest, a roar of pain and fury, as mighty as the bellow of a wounded bull, bringing great fear into men's hearts, by the magnitude of his anger and his sorrow that could be plainly discerned without words. There was a great stillness afterwards for a space, while the body was being borne aside by four men. They laid it down under a tree, and on the instant, with one long shriek, all the women of the household began to wail together; they mourned with shrill cries; the sun was setting, and in the intervals of screamed lamentations the high sing-song voices of two old men intoning the Koran chanted alone.

"About this time Jim, leaning on a gun-carriage, looked at the river, and turned his back on the house; and the girl, in the doorway, panting as if she had run herself to a standstill, was looking at him across the yard. Tamb' Itam stood not far from his master, waiting patiently for what might happen. All at once Jim, who seemed to be lost in quiet thought, turned to him and said, 'Time to finish this.'

" 'Tuan?' said Tamb' Itam, advancing with alacrity. He did not know what his master meant, but as soon as Jim made a movement the girl started too and walked down into the open space. It seems that no one else of the people of the house was in sight. She tottered slightly, and about half-way down called out to Jim, who had apparently resumed his peaceful contemplation of the river. He turned round, setting his back against the gun. 'Will you fight?' she cried. 'There is nothing to fight for,' he said; 'nothing is lost.' Saying this he made a step towards her. 'Will you fly?' she cried again. 'There is no escape,' he said, stopping short, and she stood still also, silent, devouring him with her eyes. 'And you shall go?' she said slowly. He bent his head. 'Ah!' she exclaimed, peering at him as it were, 'you are mad or false. Do you remember the night I prayed you to leave me, and you said that you could not? That it was impossible! Impossible! Do you remember you said you would never leave me? Why? I asked you for no promise. You promised unasked—remember.' 'Enough, poor girl,' he said. 'I should not be worth having.'

"Tamb' Itam said that while they were talking she would laugh loud and senselessly like one under the visitation of God. His master put his hands to his head. He was fully dressed as for every day, but without a hat. She stopped laughing suddenly. 'For the last time,' she cried men-acingly, 'will you defend yourself?' 'Nothing can touch me,' he said in a last flicker of superb egoism. Tamb' Itam saw her lean forward where she stood, open her arms, and run at him swiftly. She flung herself upon his breast and clasped him round the neck.

" 'Ah! but I shall hold thee thus,' she cried. . . . 'Thou art mine!'

"She sobbed on his shoulder. The sky over Patusan was blood-red, immense, streaming like an open vein. An enormous sun nestled crim-son amongst the tree-tops, and the forest below had a black and forbid-ding face.

"Tamb' Itam tells me that on that evening the aspect of the heavens was angry and frightful. I may well believe it, for I know that on that very day a cyclone passed within sixty miles of the coast, though there was hardly more than a languid stir of air in the place.

"Suddenly Tamb' Itam saw Jim catch her arms, trying to unclasp her hands. She hung on them with her head fallen back; her hair touched the ground. 'Come here!' his master called, and Tamb' Itam helped to ease her down. It was difficult to separate her fingers. Jim, bending over her, looked earnestly upon her face, and all at once ran to the landing-stage. Tamb' Itam followed him, but turning his head, he saw that she had struggled up to her feet. She ran after them a few steps, then fell down heavily on her knees. 'Tuan! Tuan!' called Tamb' Itam, 'look back;' but Jim was already in a canoe, standing up paddle in hand. He did not look back. Tamb' Itam had just time to scramble in after him when the canoe floated clear. The girl was then on her knees, with clasped hands, at the water-gate. She remained thus for a time in a supplicating attitude before she sprang up. 'You are false!' she screamed out after Jim. 'Forgive me,' he cried. 'Never! Never!' she called back.

"Tamb' Itam took the paddle from Jim's hands, it being unseemly that he should sit while his lord paddled. When they reached the other shore his master forbade him to come any farther; but Tamb' Itam did follow him at a distance, walking up the slope to Doramin's campong.

"It was beginning to grow dark. Torches twinkled here and there. Those they met seemed awestruck, and stood aside hastily to let Jim pass. The wailing of women came from above. The courtyard was full of armed Bugis with their followers, and of Patusan people.

"I do not know what this gathering really meant. Were these preparations for war, or for vengeance, or to repulse a threatened invasion? Many days elapsed before the people had ceased to look out, quaking, for the return of the white men with long beards and in rags, whose exact relation to their own white man they could never understand. Even for those simple minds poor Jim remains under a cloud.

"Doramin, alone, immense and desolate, sat in his armchair with the pair of flintlock pistols on his knees, faced by an armed throng. When Jim appeared, at somebody's exclamation, all the heads turned round together, and then the mass opened right and left, and he walked up a lane of averted glances. Whispers followed him; murmurs: 'He has worked all the evil.' 'He hath a charm.' . . . He heard them—perhaps!

"When he came up into the light of torches the wailing of the women ceased suddenly. Doramin did not lift his head, and Jim stood silent before him for a time. Then he looked to the left, and moved in that direction with measured steps. Dain Waris's mother crouched at the head of the body, and the grey dishevelled hair concealed her face. Jim came up slowly, looked at his dead friend, lifting the sheet, then dropped it without a word. Slowly he walked back.

" 'He came! He came,' was running from lip to lip, making a murmur to which he moved. 'He hath taken it upon his own head,' a voice said aloud. He heard this and turned to the crowd. 'Yes. Upon my head.' A few people recoiled. Jim waited awhile before Doramin, and then said gently, 'I am come in sorrow.' He waited again. 'I am come ready and unarmed,' he repeated.

"The unwieldy old man, lowering his big forehead like an ox under a yoke, made an effort to rise, clutching at the flintlock pistols on his knees. From his throat came gurgling, choking, inhuman sounds, and his two attendants helped him from behind. People remarked that the ring which he had dropped on his lap fell and rolled against the foot of the white man, and that poor Jim glanced down at the talisman that had opened for him the door of fame, love, and success within the wall of forests fringed with white foam, within the coast that under the western sun looks like the very stronghold of the night. Doramin, struggling to keep his feet, made with his two supporters a swaying, tottering group; his little eyes stared with an expression of mad pain, of rage, with a ferocious glitter, which the bystanders noticed, and then, while Jim stood stiffened and with bared head in the light of torches, looking him straight in the face, he clung heavily with his left arm round the neck of a bowed youth, and lifting deliberately his right, shot his son's friend through the chest.

"The crowd, which had fallen apart behind Jim as soon as Doramin had raised his hand, rushed tumultuously forward after the shot. They say that the white man sent right and left at all those faces a proud and unflinching glance. Then with his hand over his lips he fell forward, dead.

"And that's the end. He passes away under a cloud, inscrutable at heart, forgotten, unforgiven, and excessively romantic. Not in the wildest days of his boyish visions could he have seen the alluring shape of such an extraordinary success! For it may very well be that in the short moment of his last proud and unflinching glance, he had beheld the face of that opportunity which, like an Eastern bride, had come veiled to his side.

"But we can see him, an obscure conqueror of fame, tearing himself out of the arms of a jealous love at the sign, at the call of his exalted egoism. He goes away from a living woman to celebrate his pitiless wedding with a shadowy ideal of conduct. Is he satisfied—quite, now, I wonder? We ought to know. He is one of us—and have I not stood up once, like an evoked ghost, to answer for his eternal constancy? Was I so very wrong after all? Now, he is no more, there are days when the reality of his existence comes to me with an immense, with an overwhelming force; and yet upon my honour there are moments too when he passes from my eyes like a disembodied spirit astray amongst the passions of this earth, ready to surrender himself faithfully to the claim of his own world of shades.

"Who knows? He is gone, inscrutable at heart, and the poor girl is leading a sort of soundless, inert life in Stein's house. Stein has aged greatly of late. He feels it himself, and says often that he is 'preparing to leave all this; preparing to leave, . . .' while he waves his hand sadly at his butterflies."

September 1899–July 1900.

Textual History

Lord Jim exists in two partial manuscript versions. The first, entitled "Tuan Jim: A Sketch," consists of twenty-eight holograph pages and is reprinted below. The second partial manuscript version exists in four very unequal fragments: (1) a single holograph leaf at the British Library in London; (2) 357 holograph leaves at the Rosenbach Library in Philadelphia, 4 of these leaves having manuscript material on their verso; (3) 8 holograph leaves at the Huntington Library in San Marino, California; (4) 7 typescript leaves (between holograph pages 318 and 319), also at the Rosenbach. All the variants in these fragments are in the Cambridge Edition of *Lord Jim*, scheduled for completion in 1999.

The printed text of *Lord Jim* went through a series of revisions: from the periodical version in *Blackwood's Magazine* (October 1899 to November 1900) to the first American edition, to the first Canadian edition, to the first English edition (all three book versions appearing in 1900). Conrad made his first, and by far most numerous, revisions directly on the magazine version. The resulting galley proofs apparently went unrevised to Doubleday and McClure in New York for typesetting the American edition. Conrad went on to make minor revisions of these galleys; these revisions were then "incorporated into the typesetting [in Britain] and duplicate mats were made— one set to be sent to W. J. Gage & Company, Limited," Toronto, and the other to William Blackwood and Sons, Edinburgh. After lead plates had been made, Conrad further revised the last ten chapters. These revisions appear only in the first English edition.[1] Many years later, Conrad wrote in a friend's copy of the first American edition: "Set up probably from English proofs but neither revised nor in any other way corrected by me. It is probably much nearer the text of *B'wood's Magazine* than the first English Ed. of book form."[2] Conrad's remark is true only for the last ten chapters; the first thirty-five are, for the reasons given above, much closer to the first English edition.[3]

In 1917, the first of a series of new editions of *Lord Jim* began to appear, each based upon the previous one: the second English (1917), the second American (1920), and the third English (1921). (Several other editions deriving from the second American subsequently appeared before Conrad's death, August 3, 1924.) A letter from Conrad to Reginald Leon in February 1917 sheds some light: "The only edition in which I take interest is the

---

1. Ernest W. Sullivan, *The Several Endings of Joseph Conrad's* Lord Jim (The Joseph Conrad Society, U.K., n.d.) 10. (This pamphlet, with its precise account of the sequence and significance of Conrad's revisions of the novel's first book editions, is reprinted below.)

2. Quoted by John Dozier Gordon, *Joseph Conrad: The Making of a Novelist* (Cambridge: Harvard UP, 1940) 155.

3. Mr. and Mrs. Kenneth Lincoln apprised me of this fact long ago, but we did not know why.

Collected Edition (limited to 1000 sets in England and in the U.S.) which Doubleday, Page in New York and Wm. Heinemann are going to publish after the war. . . . For the text, it will be exactly the text of the English first editions freed from misprints and with, perhaps, a few (very few) verbal alterations."[4] The two identical limited editions implied in this letter became ultimately the handsome, frequently reprinted, second American Doubleday "Sun Dial" edition of 1920 and the genuinely limited Heinemann, third English edition of 1921. Because of Conrad's letter and because the Heinemann not only came out later than the "Sun Dial" edition but also incorporates virtually all the revisions made in the "Sun Dial" and adds some more, I used the Heinemann edition as my copy-text for the first Norton Critical Edition of *Lord Jim*.

Since then, however, Donald Rude has informed me that the definitive, limited editions Conrad envisioned in 1917 did not turn out as planned. They were neither based on the first English edition nor were they apparently produced under Conrad's direct and continuing supervision. Rude referred me to Ernest W. Sullivan, who convincingly urged using the first English edition as copy-text for *Lord Jim*. This I have done for my second Norton Critical Edition. Such a choice is not without its complications. Although I know of no direct evidence that Conrad himself had a hand in the revisions for the second English edition, some of the changes are obvious improvements in sense, grammar, and idiom. Also, and very interestingly, a set of corrected page proofs for the third English edition exists in the Rosenbach Library. The proofs contain Conrad's initials, in what looks to me to be his handwriting, and some of the handwritten corrections also seem to me to be in his hand.

For this edition, then, I have used the first English edition of *Lord Jim* as the copy-text and have relied upon my old, full collation of the three principal editions: the periodical, the first English, and the third English. All discrepancies among these three have been checked against the second English and the second American editions. Ernest W. Sullivan, who has collated all the editions of *Lord Jim* for his forthcoming Cambridge Edition, has, with great generosity, pointed out to me a large number of mistakes, mostly of omission, that I made a quarter of a century ago. Sullivan has also provided the variants in the first American edition. As in the first Norton Critical Edition, so in this second edition, the textual notes make available to readers all the verbal variants I have found and indicate the ones I have accepted. It is my belief that Conrad intended Marlow to use standard idiomatic English, but sometimes Conrad erred. For example, in Chapter XXII, Marlow, in the first English Edition says, "the last news were thirteen months old." The second English gives "was," and I accept that revision. Similarly, the second English changes "Theirs was one of these strange, profound, rare friendships" to "one of those," and I accept the revision. Or, consider the first sentence of Chapter XXI. The first English, second English, and second American editions read: " 'I don't suppose any of you had ever heard of Patusan?' " On the Rosenbach page proofs of the third English edition, "had" is changed to "have," a revision that I accept. Indeed, "had" is changed several other times on the page proofs to "has" or "have." In the

4. Quoted by Eloise Knapp Hay, *The Political Novels of Joseph Conrad* (Chicago: U of Chicago P, 1963) 181–82n.

same paragraph, Marlow says of Jim: "He left his earthly failings behind him and that sort of reputation he had . . ." The Rosenbach page proofs sensibly (to me) change "that sort" to "what sort." Thus I accept changes from the first to the second English edition if they seem to me unquestionable improvements. Moreover, I tend (like Robert Hampson in the Penguin Classics Edition) to accept virtually all of the handwritten corrections on the Rosenbach page proofs. (The initials "RP" in the Textual Notes designate all the Rosenbach page proof corrections.)

By far the most interesting and most numerous (nearly four hundred) substantive revisions of *Lord Jim* occur between the periodical version and the first English edition. This is hardly surprising, since Conrad's conception of the novel changed radically while he was writing it, probably after it was already appearing in *Blackwood's Magazine*. (From an intended 20,000 words in four installments, the novel swelled to 120,000 words in fourteen installments.) The most sizable revisions occur in the first half of the novel: Conrad made seventeen drastic cuts (passages from five to fifty-seven lines in length) and well over fifty cuts of one to three lines. Of these major cuts and changes, perhaps the most significant have to do with Jim's psychology. Apparently Conrad felt that he had been too explicit in the periodical version, that later in the novel he had sufficiently dramatized his conceptions, and that therefore the explicit statements ought to go. Conrad also lowered Jim's age from twenty-six to twenty-four, made Cornelius into Jewel's stepfather rather than her real father, and, as Sullivan points out, humanized Gentleman Brown. The revisions of the periodical version illuminate every aspect of Conrad's artistry, especially his sensitivity to tone and his ear for rhythm. Some of the alterations simply correct the inevitable minor mistakes of someone writing — amazingly — in his third (or possibly fourth) language. (Conrad, born of Polish parents, early learned French, and perhaps some German; he did not hear English spoken until he was twenty.) The subsequent revisions that I accept are virtually all of the grammatical sort: twenty-four from the first English to the second English; two from the second English to the second American; forty-two from the second American to the third English as made on the Rosenbach proof sheets; and five others from the second American to the third English. No doubt some of my emendations are debatable, and the editors of the forthcoming Cambridge Edition will surely present careful arguments for their choices. Meanwhile, readers of this second Norton Critical Edition can make up their own minds. To the best of my ability and the resources at my command, I have provided readers with the materials that they need to decide.

Punctuation is a different matter. The manuscripts, the periodical version, and the first English edition are very lightly punctuated. The first American and the later editions are more and more heavily punctuated, the third English much the most heavily. Almost surely all these additions are the result of publishing house styling and not Conrad's intention. Therefore, I have tended to keep the punctuation of the first English edition except where it is misleading, as in the occasional case of quotation marks. In those rare cases, I have accepted later punctuation. Some of the punctuation marks entered into the Rosenbach proofs have also been kept. Since some of the mistakes in the spelling of foreign words in the first English edition are corrected in subsequent editions and since the remaining misspellings do not seem to me to be expressive of authorial intention, I have followed the Penguin edition in silently correcting the spelling of French and German words and in regularizing foreign words spelled inconsistently in the first edition. But I have not meddled with inconsistencies that seem to reflect the vagaries of spoken English, e.g. "dam' " for "damn" or "damned."

To repeat, in this Norton text I attempt to follow as closely as possible Conrad's intentions in the first English edition. I do, however, accept certain revisions in later editions that seem obvious improvements and likely to have been in accord with Conrad's wishes. Emendations are indicated by an asterisk. I do not meddle with grammatical errors when they persist in all editions.

Lord Jim exists in the following complete printed states, published during Conrad's lifetime:

P The periodical text published in fourteen installments in *Blackwood's Magazine*, CLXVI–CLXVIII (October 1899 to November 1900).

A^1 The first American edition, published by Doubleday and McClure Co., New York, 1900. *The National Union Catalogue* lists impressions of 1903, 1905, 1909, and some eleven more, up to 1928.

E^1 The first English edition, published by William Blackwood and Sons, Edinburgh and London, October 15, 1900. It went through many subsequent impressions: December 1900, 1904, 1905, 1914, 1915, 1917, and some ten more, up to 1948. The first English edition is the copy-text for this Norton Critical Edition.

E^2 The second English edition, with the "Author's Note" for the first time, published by J. M. Dent and Sons Ltd., London and Toronto, 1917. The Heinemann edition lists a second impression in 1918 and a third in 1920. The second English edition is the copy-text for the "Author's Note" for this Norton Critical Edition.

A^2 The second American edition, volume four of *The Works of Joseph Conrad*, "The Sun Dial Edition," published by Doubleday, Page and Company, Garden City, New York, 1920. Although the Library of Congress lists this edition as "limited to seven hundred and thirty-five copies," many subsequent impressions have been taken, two of which are listed below.

E^3 The third English edition, volume four of *The Works of Joseph Conrad*, "printed from type that has been distributed," and "limited to 780 sets, of which 750 are for sale and 30 for presentation," published by William Heinemann, London, 1921.

[RP Corrected page proofs of the third English edition, housed in the Rosenbach Library in Philadelphia.]

A^{2a} Volume five, *The Works of Joseph Conrad*, "The Uniform Edition," J. M. Dent and Sons Ltd., London and Toronto, 1923. Not a new edition, it derives from the Doubleday "Sun Dial," probably, according to Bruce Harkness,[5] from a duplicate set of plates. It was reprinted in 1926; in 1946, as part of the "Collected Edition," it appeared with five additional pages of biographical and bibliographical material. It is still

---

5. *Conrad's "Heart of Darkness" and the Critics* (San Francisco: Wadsworth, 1960) 161–63.

in print. (In 1925, both Gresham, London, and John Grant, Edinburgh and London, also reprinted *The Works*.)

A²ᵇ The earliest American reprinting of the "Sun Dial" that I have seen, the "Personal," published by Doubleday, Page and Company, Garden City, New York, 1923. (The *National Union Catalogue* lists a 1920 reprinting of *Lord Jim*, by Odyssey Press, and two more in 1921, by Franklin Watts and the "Sun Dial Library," all of New York.) Also in 1923 appeared the "Concord Edition." The "Canterbury Edition" came out in 1924, the year of Conrad's death; the expensive "Memorial Edition" appeared in 1925 but must have been planned earlier (and not, I hope, as a "memorial"), since Conrad signed the leaves of ninety-nine sets; the "Kent Edition" was issued in both 1925 and 1926. Other impressions have since appeared. There is no evidence that Conrad had a hand in any of these. The "Personal" differs from the "Sun Dial" in only about twenty-five instances, all of which could have been printers' sophistications.

Textual Notes

(*Subtitle*) **A Tale** *P* A Sketch A¹, A²ᵇ A Romance (*E²* has A Romance on the spine. Ed.)
*6.9–10 *E³* **Lord Jim** (*Ital.*) RP *E²*, A² Lord Jim
 6.22 **he's** *E³* he is
*6.29 *E³* **1917** RP *E²* June 1917
 8.34 **glass** *E³* grass
 10.10 **laid** A² lad
*11.32 *E³* **has** RP *P*, A¹, *E¹*, *E²*, A² had
*14.31 *E²*, A², *E³* **Strait** *P*, A¹, *E¹* Straits
 17.5 **days. From** *P* days. What could happen that he was not able to master and subdue? . . . and the end of his days was very, very far. Nothing prevented him from believing himself as steadfast as the Atlas bearing up a world, and as invulnerable as the stars. He dared the future as though the Unattainable that dwells beyond the retreating line of the horizon had been lying in the hollow of his palm. From
*17.21 *E³* **an heroic** RP *P*, A¹, *E¹*, *E²*, A² a heroic
 18.36 **drink** *E³* drunk
 20.13 **liquid fire** A¹ fire
*21.2 *E³* **if** RP *P*, A¹, *E¹*, *E²*, A² it
 21.33 **stabbed. The** *P* stabbed, and those questions that stretched his soul on the rack. The
 22.3,4 **anything! [¶]" After** *P* anything—as if facts mattered in the face of terrors! After
 23.4 **things. The** *P* things. There had been a peculiar awfulness in the calm of the sea, in the serenity of the sky, in the words pronounced, in the gestures made, in the silence of a passive world, in the sleep of an unconscious crowd. The
 23.35 **him. He** *P* him. Those men would never know the truth, nobody would ever know the truth; there could be no truth in a simple yes or no. At that moment he was less concerned about himself than at any time since the inquiry began, but he despaired of his power to show the truth, and it was a great despair. He
 23.38 **damp** *P* hot
 24.21 **wayfarer** *P* wanderer
 24.21 **wilderness** *P* desert
 26.17 **tragic as well, began** *P* tragic began
 27.2 **into** A², *E³* in
 27.19 **his head** *P* round
 28.13 **safe. I've** *P* safe! Oh, I've

28.30 **sling, and a** *P* sling; a
28.32 **who looked** *P* and looking
29.26 **face over** *P* face of regret over
30.20 **are** *P* get
30.22 **condemnation** A^2, E^3 condemnations
30.31 **a pose** E^2, A^2, E^3 pose
31.28 **has** *P* had
31.31 **shall** E^3 will
32.11,12 **a case** A^2, E^3 the case
*32.28 E^2, A^2, E^3 **those** *P*, A^1, E^1 these
32.31 **a droll and fearsome effect** *P* an effect of fearsome drollery
32.31 **those** *P* the
32.32 **one** *P* you
32.32 **to** *P* would
32.32,33 **the little box on wheels to** *P* that the little box on wheels would
32.40 **snorted** *P* snorting
*33.40 E^3 **moustaches** *P*, A^1, E^1, E^2, A^2 moustache
35.14 **the ghost** *P* the uprisen ghost
36.9 **get a smoke** *P* smoke it
36.19 **down a** *P* down the tube of a
*36.20 E^2, A^2, E^3 **shoulder** *P*, A^1, E^1 shoulders
36.40 **and** *P* and thereupon
37.8 **enabled me to compose my distracted** *P* was sweeter than balm to my lacerated
37.15 **Four** *P* Seven
38.23 **That's the man.** *P* Didn't you?
38.29 **him. He** *P* him, and had the face of a man sitting out of (*sic*) dull farce in a theatre. He
38.30 **never in his life** *P* never
*38.32 E^2, A^2, E^3 **those** *P*, A^1, E^1 these
38.32 **know nothing** *P* in the whole of their lives know no moment
.38.40 **price. I** *P* price. The serenity of his confidence in himself was intolerable. He had the selfish conceit of a clever boy, bound in the thick hide of a rhinoceros. I
39.21 **case. The verdict must have been** *P* case, probing his own soft spot—accused, tribunal, judge, and executioner in one. The verdict was
39.24 **was no doubt** *P* must have been
39.26,27 **live. I am in a position to know that it** *P* live. It
39.34 **in his relations** *P* in relation
40.11 **would have** *P* ought to have
40.32 **dial to run, and** *P* dial, and
41.18 **him once** *P* him do once
42.18,19 **so far gone as** *P* abandoned enough
42.27 **are** A^2 are are
42.31 **afterwards** A^1 afterward
42.43 **inexpressibly** A^1 inexpressible
43.13 **on** A^1 upon
45.17 **an insect** *P* a beetle
47.17 **about. 'You** *P* about. I was so taken up in wondering what obscure processes were taking place within him, that I did not even attempt to recall any external event which might have been the cause of his only too clear intention to create a scandalous disturbance in this, of all places in the world. 'You
47.24,25 **nature.** *P* nature. Some quality exaggerated into a defect was hurrying him into it. He was carried away; he would be blundering all his life. He was a helpless victim of his mental and physical organisation, about to give himself horribly away, and pathetically ignorant of the curse. All these notions were the outcome of sudden impression rather than of reflection. I
47.34 **his own eyes** *P* his eyes
47.37 **do. But** *P* do or what to say. But
47.38 **was a blackness** A^2, E^3 was blackness
48.11,12 **given himself away utterly** *P* utterly given himself away
48.26 **looking** A^1 looked
48.40 **tears. I** *P* tears. He turned to me, and I thought he would speak, but I
48.43,44 **appeasement? Who** *P* appeasement? The eye of man can't follow nor the mind of man conceive the crooked ways of another man's thoughts; these naïve perversities of reasoning, inspired by the desperation of self-love, kept up by preposterous hopes, arriving at astonishing, at incredible conclusions. Who
49.1 **case. He** *P* case. He had humiliated himself only to be baffled. He
49.24 **meaning? 'You** *P* meaning? Was he a slave to unparalleled stupidity or master of the most consummate dissimulation? 'You

49.28 **view of him** *P* vista, a new horizon
49.32,33 **views he let me have of himself** *P* new vistas he gave me
50.14 **over** *P* across
50.15 **floor; now** *P* floor, ministering obsequiously to those ravenous appetites from over the sea; now
50.17 **wit embroidering** *P* wit, established during the passage, embroidering
50.24 **acquaintance. It** *P* acquaintance, without my being able to imagine where he could have found, within himself, a spot isolated enough for the digging of that convenient grave. It
50.35 **weather. My** *P* weather. I was erecting theories as unstable as castles in Spain,—theories which, I instinctively felt, would be each of them found false, the common fate of all generalisations about men who are only partly in nature. Theirs is always a special case. This was a special case. My
50.37 **him. He** *P* him. We had been conversing as coolly of vital matters as though there had been no sense of morality left on earth, and my remark was made with all the propriety of a dining-room indifference. He
51.6 **ships** A^1 the ships
51.12,13 **chair; I** *P* chair for fear of snapping the fine-spun thread of his confidence. I
51.13,14 **He would be confident and depressed all in the same breath,** *P* His imagination—a rare thing, the last thing I would have suspected him of—was what was wrong with him. Twenty times in the course of his narrative he would give himself away by some word, gesture, or exclamation, and take himself back with a strange unconsciousness that, upon my word, would make my blood run cold. He would be confident and depressed all in the same breath; it was as though the physical wellbeing produced by food and drink, the chance of open talk, the soothing effect of good tobacco, had overlaid the subtle despair in his mind,
52.14 **mistake was** *P* mistake on the part of any man was
53.7,8 **distinction. As** *P* distinction. He astonished me by the suggestiveness of his expressions. He was uncommon; he made you feel this, not by his argumentation—there was not a beggarly two-pennyworth of logic in him—but by the spirit of subtle resentment that pervaded his narrative, changing it into an *ex-parte* presentation of his case against something indefinite, against the world at large, against some universal and disembodied might that had used him ill. As
53.10,11 **imagine. I** [Quotation mark deleted from copy-text. Ed.] *P* imagine. The disembodied might had selected him for the object of a scurvy trick; he had given himself away before the menacing posture of the indefinite and got nothing for it—not even the consolation of knowing he had saved his life. "I
53.13 **Sailors'** *P* Sailor's
53.45 **last! A** *P* last! Oh, he got there without question. A
54.14 **it. Presently** *P* it. He had infinite resources within him to ward off any attack I could deliver. Presently
54.27 **globe-lamp** A^2, E^3 bulk-lamp
*54.34 E^3 **straightway** RP *P*, E^1, E^2, A^2 straight away A^1 straightaway
54.42,43 **ladder.** *P* ladder. "It was very curious to note that he did not understand in the least the deep significance of the incident. It meant that the tension of his brain was already too great to allow it to take proper care of the balance of his body. He mentioned the fact casually enough but for a shade of uneasy irritation, as if there had been some inherent and terrifying quality in sailcloth which had been put forth unfairly against his fortitude. In this serious emergency his liability to be startled by trifles was coming to the surface. His imagination was plunging, and ready to bolt with him. He had a narrow escape there, he said in an injured tone. He might, he pointed out, have fallen down the hatchway and broken his leg—'and where would I have been then, with the ship sinking?' he added, with odious innocence. "He
54.43 **confessed that** *P* confessed
55.10 **fortunate** A^1 unfortunate
55.29 **do. It** *P* do. It was too cruel. It
55.35 **re-forming** E^3 reforming
56.14 **know** A^1 know that
*56.17 A^2, E^3 **arms** *P*, A^1, E^1, E^2 arm
56.24 **peaceful** *P* resigned
56.32 **well** *P* best
56.37 **water take** A^2, E^3 water to take
57.11 **commented** A^1 continued
57.38 **grabbed** *P* snatched at
57.43 **this. The** *P* this; it savoured of the impossible and at the same time carried conviction, extorted a wondering assent. The
58.8 **whispering** *P* screeching
58.36 **below? And the timber—the timber! Would** *P* below? Would
61.17 **black** E^3 back

*61.26 E^2, A^2, E^3 **those** P, A^1, E^1 these
61.26 **deception** P lie
61.26 **where** A^2, E^3 which
61.29 **bridge, as far** P bridge, far
61.33 **beside** P besides
62.12 **Not the** A^2 Not in the
62.24 **shrunk** A^1 shrunken
62.24 **darker** P dark
64.7 **thick** P fat
64.23 **suddenly,** P then
64.33 **extreme aversion** A^1 aversion
65.44 **self-command** E^2, A^2, E^3 self-control
66.4 **stem** P stern
66.25 **events. Twice** P events. They stood before me indubitably true, but a little distorted, as if seen by the sinister glow of his burning contempt. It fell on the sky, on the earth, on the ship, on the men—on himself too—oh yes! on himself too: only he seemed honestly confident of his erect attitude in the general wreck of decent appearances. Twice
67.40 **nor** A^1 or
*68.35 E^3 **me all this** RP P, A^1, E^1 me of all this E^2, A^2 me all of this
69.3 **is** P was
69.20 **living** P live
69.23 **could** P couldn't
69.23 **boat. . . . I** P boat, and—I
70.9 **wished** E^3 wish
70.21 **a deluge** A^1 the deluge
70.30 **that abomination** A^1 the abomination
70.36 **Another** P A man
71.41 **creepers** A^1 the creepers
72.45 **oar** A^2, E^3 oars
73.8 **stooped** E^2, A^2, E^3 stopped
73.10 **uninterrupted, a little** E^3 uninterrupted, little RP
73.16 **abominations** A^1 abomination
*73.32 E^3 **your hand** RP P, A^1, E^1, E^2, A^2 his hand
*73.36 E^3 **make it out** RP P, A^1, E^1, E^2, A^2 make out
*73.37,38 E^3 **It saved** RP P, A^1, E^1, E^2, A^2 It has saved
74.30 **muttered** E^3 muttering
74.32 **back to his oar. I** P back. I
75.2 **capital. On the vivid stars the high corner of the Harbour Office stood** P capital, with vivid stars between, and to the left the high corner of the Harbour Office coming
75.22 **that made** P that had made
*75.22 E^3 **took** RP P, A^1, E^1, E^2, A^2 taken
*75.31 A^2, E^3 **hatred** P, A^1, E^1, E^2 hate
75.38 **triumph, are** P triumph all over the world's surface, are
76.13 **last** P least
78.12 **couldn't! All** P couldn't! There is a time in my life when I had forgotten what sleep was made of, what the word meant; that there was a state in which I could be unconscious of myself. All
78.37 **passing. 'Do** P passing,—something swift and full of purpose, like a cast of the hand-lead taken in shoaling water. 'Do
*79.11,12 E^3 **a second, glowed** RP P the last time, gleamed A^1, E^1, E^2, A^2 a moment, gleamed
79.15 **was a youngster** P was a boy, fair, frank, silly if you will. A youngster
79.20 **was not** P was
79.30–38 **fire * * * imprecation? What** P fire. There is envy of the past, amusement, and infinite pity. Who could resist it? There is such magnificent vagueness in the impulses that had driven each of us to sea, such a glorious indefiniteness of expectations, such a beautiful greed of adventures that are their own and only reward! In other occupations the youngster knows something; he expects—this—that—the other definite thing. In this he only desires, with all his heart, with all his soul—desires—what? He cannot tell. He does not know. What he gets—well, we won't talk of that; but can one of us restrain a smile? In no other kind of life is the illusion more wide of reality—in no other is the beginning *all* illusion—the disenchantment more swift—the subjugation more complete; and no other has the power to extort bitter love for the sake of unfulfilled hopes. Hadn't we all commenced with the same desire, ended with the same knowledge, carried the memory of the same cherished glamour through the sordid days of imprecation? Well may those few of us who can speak, looking from under the black shadows of sails at the bewitching face of the moonlit sea, whisper to themselves 'Odi et amo.' It is the very truth. The intoxication of charm imagined, the desire of the subtle spirit

for ever escaping, the hate of reality sobering and cruel, are like the shadow of the passionate visitation of the gods—the devouring rage of tenderness entwined with the hot rage of anger. 'Odi et amo' they can say as if speaking to life itself, that for all of us begins with the same glamour, and runs through the days of execration to the obscurity of a common end. What

80.21 **the wrong** E^2, A^2, E^3 wrong
81.8 **meditated** P was meditative
*81.13 P, A^1, E^2, A^2, E^3 **of** E^1 o
*81.26 E^3 **those** RP P, A^1, E^1, E^2, A^2 these
*81.43,44 E^3 **alone—for myself** RP P, A^1, E^1, E^2 alone before myself A^2 alone for myself
82.16 **Ascertained** A^1 Ascertain
*83.5 A^1, E^2, A^2, E^3 **Sailors'** P, E^1 Sailor's
84.41 **a memory** E^3 memory
88.4 **had** A^1 have
88.17 **of the** A^1 of
88.30 **dust. 'I** P dust. He turned away. 'I
88.36 **audibly** A^1 inaudibly
89.6 **meat. What** P meat. I don't know what I expected him to reveal. I certainly expected something. What
89.21–22 **His imperturbable and mature calmness was that of** P In his imperturbable and mature calmness he did look like
90.17 **pronounced finally** P said with finality
90.18 **the personal anecdote** P the anecdote
90.18,19 **disappointed; the more so as it** P disappointed. It
90.25 **it. And** P it. One has got to live—you cannot get away from that. And
90.39 **rings around** P rings sparkling and still around
91.2 **get on knowing very well that one's courage** P live with the knowledge that courage
91.4 **truth the more** P illusion the less
91.35 **then working for** P then with
92.15 **by looking at** P near
92.16 **must've** E^3 must 'ave
92.27 **bearded to the waist like** P bearded like
93.1 **the deplorable** P certain
93.5 **left, not** P left me, not
93.14,15 **neck. Our** P neck. This is metaphoric speech; but at the time our
93.18 **of a formal** P of formal
*93.37 E^3 **will** RP P, A^1, E^1, E^2, A^2 shall
94.4 **repay** A^1 repay me
94.10 **kind . . .' 'It** P kind to swallow. . . .' 'It
94.15 **you can expect** P you expect
94.29 **shades. 'Oh,** P shades. It was startling to have the thought occur to one—as it did, for some reason, occur to me just then—that his flesh and blood were like mine; his brain too, and whatever else goes to the making of a human being—only that I had escaped being played with in just that infernal way. This consideration checked the many wise things I wished to say; but I spoke all the same. 'Oh!
94.36,37 **thing down—I** P thing—I
94.41 **refused this unique** P refused. Refused a unique
95.4 **said, 'that I** P said, 'I
95.20 **four-and-twenty** P six-and-twenty
96.9 **and from** P whose safety rests on fidelity to ideas expressed in law, and to despotic and unexpressed ideals. From
96.34 **and a** A^1 and
96.41 **neatly** P carefully
97.10 **and** A^2, E^3 had all
97.10,11 **exile. This** P exile. Everything would be over for him. Everything but the distress of his thoughts, the mental suffering, the danger, the poignant incertitude of fate, the regret. This
97.25,26 **then they declared** P then declared
97.43 **duty,' it said. The** P duty.' The
98.6 **stillness wafted** P stillness as if wafted
101.43 **I've to** A^2, E^3 I've got to
105.7 **quite** A^2 quiet
105.13 A^1, E^2, A^2, E^3 **have kept** P, E^1 had kept
105.21 **an** A^2, E^3 the
105.35 **were** E^3 was
*106.37 E^2, A^2, E^3 **Nature** P, A^1, E^1 nature
107.45 **shores** E^3 shore
109.8 **toward** A^1, A^2, E^3 towards

109.17 **unconsolable** E^3 inconsolable
109.31 **resenting it.' He** A^2, E^3 resenting.' He
*110.13 E^3 **of asking** RP P, A^1, E^1, E^2, A^2 to ask
*111.25 E^2, A^2, E^3 **those** P, E^1, A^1 these
112.1 **unto** E^2, A^2, E^3 into
*112.10 E^2, A^2, E^3 **had** P, A^1, E^1 have
*115.32 E^3 **has** RP P, A^1 E^1, E^2, A^2 had
116.34 **chief of** P chief engineer of
117.11 **round** A^1 around
117.20 **water-clerk** A^1 a water-clerk
117.42 **stuck** A^2 struck
118.22 **the hair** A^1 his hair
122.18 **like what** P, A^1 like
122.30 **carries** E^3 carried
122.37 **his** A^1 this
122.38 **on lifeless** A^2, E^3 of lifeless
123.3 **life or** A^1 life and
123.39 **found a refuge** E^3 found refuge
125.9 **past** E^2, A^2, E^3 part
125.30 **ear** E^3 ears
127.42 **sighed and turned** P sighed, and with an air of resignation turned
128.14,15 **so generously encouraging** P generously encouraging; so generously
128.17 **legs. Sometimes** P legs and industriously puffing at his pipe. Sometimes
*129.20 E^3 **im** RP P, A^1, E^1, E^2, A^2 in
129.28 **So if you** E^3 So you
130.32 **a table** A^2, E^3 the table
131.33 **seems** E^3 seemed
*132.2 E^3 **have** RP P, A^1, E^1, E^2, A^2 had
132.15 **from** E^3 form
*132.21 E^3 **what** RP P, A^1, E^1, E^2, A^2 that
133.18 **Patusan; but** P Patusan. There they were out of the way, but
133.21 **Cornelius, considered** P Cornelius something—I don't remember—considered
133.32 **forests** E^3 forest
134.33 **conscience** E^2, A^2, E^3 consciousness
135.3 **land** P earth
136.18 **floating** P indecisive
136.21 **for that** P for the
136.39 **power of it, are** P power it gives, are
136.39 **a** E^3 an
136.41 **it** E^2 if
137.10 **James the First** P James I
137.24 **as agents** P agents
137.24 **but as instruments** P but instruments
137.39 **of life** A^2 of the life
*138.2 E^2, A^2, E^3 **was** P, A^1, E^1 were
138.6 **and the stealing** P and stealing
139.26,27 **and a refuge** E^3 and refuge
139.37 **owed** A^2 owned
141.35 **a prospect** A^1 the prospect
143.29 **roadstead** E^2, A^2, E^3 roadster
143.37 **this** E^3 his
144.8 **gig manned at** P gig at
144.29 **the trade** P that trade
144.29 **'a snare** P 'nothing but a snare
145.19 **deported** E^3 departed
145.31 **speech; I** P speech and acts. During that hurried leave-taking I
145.44 **misfortune** E^2, A^2, E^3 misfortunes
146.12 **coast of Patusan (I** P coast (I
146.27 **about** P of
149.7 **hey** E^2, A^2, E^3 eh
*150.19 E^3 **Looked** RP P, A^1, E^1, E^2, A^2 Look
150.34 **impotent** A^2, E^3 important
151.13 **immediately afterwards we** P immediately we
151.15 **Jim** P he
151.17 **considered to be** P considered
151.21 **colic. I** P colic or other. I

151.31 **short. Thought** P short. Plop!—to my waist. Thought
151.33 **while** P when
151.34 **slime** P mud
152.2 **fifteen** P twenty odd
153.10 **over his eyes, into** P in his eyes, in
153.23 **the** P a
153.23,24 **of awakening. He remained lying still for a while, and then he arose** P he gave before he uprose
153.27 **animal** P wild beast
154.15 **benevolent eyes** P benevolent old eyes
154.17 **troop** P whole battalion
*154.45 A^1, E^2, A^2, E^3 **of the Rajah's** P, E^1 of Rajah's
*155.9 A^1, E^2, A^2, E^3 **half-breed** P, E^1 half-bred
156.17 **They were wonderfully contrasted** P It was a wonderful contrast
156.35 **on our way** P and coming
157.2 **war** E^2, A^2, E^3 the war
*157.18 E^2, A^2, E^3 **those** P, A^1, E^1 these
*159.31 E^3 **souls** RP P, A^1, E^1, E^2, A^2 soul
160.7 **off all together** A^2, E^2 off together
161.21 **parties** A^1 the parties
162.6 **had been** P was
162.14 **was inseparable from** P hovered silently round
162.16 **the common** A^1 common
162.26 **had been** P was
*163.14 E^2, A^2, E^3 **those** P, A^1, E^1 these
163.26 **fled** P had fled
*163.29 P, E^2, A^2, E^3 **ruler** E^1, A^1 rule
163.30 **had known** P knew
163.32 **flung** P threw
163.32 **on** P flat on
163.35 **Already he could see** P He saw
163.38,39 **After Sherif Ali his turn would come, and who could resist an attack** P Who could resist men
163.39 **owed his life and such** P owed such
164.13 **His breathing silences** P His silences
164.18 **me, while** P me just then, while
164.31 **motherly witch** P motherly, brown witch
164.34–36 **removing * * * voice** P changing the direction of her eyes, in a pitying voice she asked
165.10 **were the ordinary standpoint** P if the ordinary standpoint were
165.17 **of split** P of young split
165.26,27 **conscience. Through her whole life the** P conscience. The
*165.27,28 E^3 **other companion, confidante, and friend but her daughter** P one but her daughter for companion, confidant, and friend A^1, E^1, E^2, A^2 * * * confidant * * *
165.29 **awful little Malacca** E^2, A^2, E^3 awful Malacca
165.29,30 **after the separation from** P who was in reality
165.30 **that** P the
165.33 **drop in my hearing, I** P drop, I
165.34 **convinced that** P convinced
165.44 **seeks** P seems
166.1 **caution; for it** P caution. It
166.1 **put at times** P put
166.11 **be** P be for them
*166.17 E^2, A^2, E^3 **feelings** P, A^1, E^1 feeling
166.17,18 **warnings, no doubt: warnings that** P warnings—that
166.20 **seems** P seems—the torment of every happiness
166.25 **effect. I** P effect. The romance applied to everyday uses. Oh, he was set afloat in a sea of romance, disported himself, darted here and there, rested immersed in it, with the unconscious ease of a first-rate swimmer. I
166.30 **earnestly** P in a hurry
166.32,33 **anxious whispers were** P earnest whispering was
166.39,40 **schooner, in which I had my passage, put** P schooner put
166.40 **and, going ashore, I** P and I
166.41 **the wretched locality** P it
166.42 **big, fat, greasy** P big, greasy
166.42,43 **of mixed** P of a hopelessly mixed

166.43 **with turned out** *P* with a protruding paunch and turned out

167.3 **now, he remarked negligently, and** *P* now—and

°167.4 *E*³ has RP *P*, *A*¹, *E*¹, *E*², *A*² had

167.4,5 **there, I hear. . . . Eh? What you say?** *P* there . . . Eh? What?

167.5 **Friend** *A*², *E*³ Friends

°167.6 **verdammte** RP *A*², *E*³ *verdamte P*, *A*¹, *E*¹, *E*² *vordamte*

167.7 **rascal. Eh?** *P skelm!*

167.9 **Almighty! The** *P* Almighty! Oh, the

167.19 **yet. See? Why** *P* yet. Why

167.21 **had better look out for himself** *P* better look out for that

167.23,24 **trouble. Don't interrupt. I** *P* trouble. I

167.25 **know some good people** *P* know people

167.26 **can** *P* will

167.27 **both his** *P* both

167.30 **composure that** *P* composure under my eyes that

168.2 **fabulously large emerald** *P* fabulous emerald

168.3 **and the belief in it is so persistent that** *P* while

168.4 **had** *P* had even

168.36,37 **flowing * * * head** *P* . She wore cavalierly a small crimson cap, something like a fez

168.38 **assured** *P* quick

168.40 **charm and** *P* charm, youth and gravity, and

169.3 **At times** *P* Or

169.3 **down with us and** *P* down and

169.5 **would remain fastened** *P* remained fixed intently

169.6 **each pronounced word** *P* our words

169.31 **lay down his life** *P* wait hand and foot, to lay down his life if need be

169.32 **silent, indistinct** *P* dumb vague

169.35 **sound; but when** *P* sound. When

169.37 **The girl** *P* She

170.2 **cautiously—and I** *P* cautiously; I

170.16–18 **space, * * * slinking.** *P* space of beaten earth as hard as asphalt, was one torrid blaze of sunshine, and Cornelius was creeping across with an inexpressible effect of stealthiness, of secret slinking, though he was bathed in intense light, and in full view from the house and every other building within the enclosure.

170.27,28 **played a very dubious part (to say the least of it)** *P* played, to say the least of it, a very dubious part

170.35 **war. In this he** *P* war. He

170.36,37 **end, with an utter disregard of his personal safety, he** *P* end he

170.38 **managed to exist** *P* existed

170.42 **line he was forced to take** *P* it might have been

171.8 **is simply seen skulking on its outskirts, enigmatical and unclean** *P* simply hangs on to it

171.11 **have been** *P* be

171.24 **had a mangy look** *P* seemed mangy

171.25 **the corners of broken mats flapping** *P* broken mats flapping about

171.30 **became** *A*¹ had become

171.37 **done in a roundabout way, and with** *P* done with

171.39 **I left the Bugis quarter and went** *P* I went

°171.41,42 *E*², *A*², *E*³ **there was** *P*, *A*¹, *E*¹ was there

172.10 **not be** *E*², *A*², *E*³ not to be

172.17 **'Your mother** *P* 'She

172.19 **outburst** *P* paroxysm of rage

172.37 **earshot, in order to** *P* earshot, to

172.39 **face, and then Jim** *P* face. Jim

173.8 **affirmed; it** *P* affirmed; he was afraid for her. It

173.10 **appeared a base** *P* been like a

173.14 **gathering obscurely** *P* thickening

173.33 **this** *A*², *E*³ his

173.38,39 **confessed to me that** *P* confesses

173.39 **the fellow** *P* he

173.43 **that very night** *P* that night

174.5 **girl, motionless against** *P* girl standing under

174.10 **idea, and so** *P* idea, so

°174.13 *E*³ **confidante** *P*, *A*¹, *E*¹, *E*², *A*² confidant

174.14 **she on her part could** *P* she could

174.32 **footsteps. They** *P* footsteps outside. They

°174.41 *E*³ **have** RP *P*, *A*¹, *E*¹, *E*², *A*² did

°175.1 E^2, A^2, E^3 **have** P, A^1, E^1 had
°176.22,23 E^3 **emerge with** RP P, A^1, E^1, E^2, A^2 emerge out with
177.3,4 **unquestioning, devoted readiness** P unquestioning readiness
177.30 **pace in the morning across** P pace across
°177.36,37 E^3 **night seemed** RP P, A^1, E^1, E^2, A^2 night that seemed
177.39 **girl** P girl in his ear
179.42 **blinded** P blind
180.1 **sooty smoke from the torch,** P smoke from the torch, thickening like a black fog
°181.8 E^3 **Then** RP P, A^1, E^1, E^2, A^2 There
°181.9 E^3 **can** RP P, A^1, E^1, E^2, A^2 could
181.13 **feel** E^2 tell
°181.13 E^3 **has** RP P, A^1, E^1, E^2, A^2 had
181.37 **disbelieved** A^2, E^3 disbelieve
182.22 **said** A^2, E^3 cried
183.3,4 **there? you ask yourself. Is it a blind monster or only** P there? A blind monster or
°182.6 E^2, A^2, E^3 **Sphinx** P, A^1, E^1 sphinx
184.18 **leave us** P go
184.24 **I said** A^1 said I
184.27 **in** A^1 into
184.37 **affections** P emotions
184.38 **that time** P this time
185.4 **argued** P whimpered
185.7 **talk big** A^1 talk
185.8 **was ready** P meant
186.11,12 **that, during the last moments, being** P that, being
186.14 **desired to get in, and** P had
186.23 **mere** P any
186.31 **still—it** P no matter. It
186.34 **These** P But these
186.34 **too very soon, for** P too, for
186.35 **order** A^1 the order
186.39 **shocked. Why** P shocked, as if I had detected her tampering wantonly with the established
    order of emotions. Why
186.45 **stirring she** A^1 stirrings he
187.18 **this. 'More** P this: the slender white form wavered, as you can see sometimes on a calm
    day a thread of smoke sway slightly and then stand upright again above the embers. 'More
°187.19 P, E^3 **will** RP A^1, E^1, E^2, A^2 shall
187.25 **tell you?** P know?
187.35 **shall** P will
188.15 **Her** E^2 Here
188.31 **reproving the carelessness of some** P reproving some
188.32 **distinct murmur** P distinct forcible murmur
189.5 **hard and still, as a statue might whisper.** P preserving her statuesque immobility.
189.12 **planets. She** P planets. But no matter. She
189.30 **infinite. 'Why?'** P infinite. 'Is that the truth?' she said slowly. 'It is the truth,' I answered,
    in the same low tone. 'Why?'
189.30 **murmured** P asked
189.32 **repeated louder; 'tell** P repeated; 'tell
189.33 **confounded, she** P confounded, thinking with despair that nothing had been done, she
189.33 **stamped with** P stamped once with
189.34,35 **Speak.' 'You want to know,' I asked in a fury. 'Yes!' she cried. 'Because** P Speak.'
    'Because
189.35 **brutally** P roughly
189.42,43 **me out** P me
189.44 **began** P said
°190.27 E^3 **Chance** P, A^1, E^1, E^2, A^2 chance
190.38 **his heavy laced** P his laced
191.41 **movement** A^2, E^3 movements
°192.16 A^1, E^3 **has** RP P, E^1, E^2, A^2 had
192.19 **it. He** P it. Well, he is part of the experience, he too lives in the memory. He
192.30,31 **had kept him back** P baulked him
192.32 **succeeded, nevertheless, had** P succeeded had
192.45 **confronted** A^1 confounded
193.32 **sitting at the time** P sitting
193.32 **of his** E^3 of the
194.9 **protested** P whined

*195.12 E^3 **will** RP P, A^1, E^1, E^2, A^2 shall
195.15 **shouted. He would** P cried, within two feet of me. He did
195.15 **honoured** A^1 honourable
195.16,17 **still for a time, and then without a trace of humility began very low** P still. His voice, without a trace of humility in it, was very low at first
195.22 **me, dropping into a confidential and piteous tone, that** P me in a confidential and piteous whine that
195.34 **in** P in a
195.34,35 **ejaculations, mingled with** P voice, interrupted by
195.37,38 **an inexpressibly grotesque and vile performance, and I hastened away** P inexpressibly dismal and vile, and I left him
196.18 **brave, with his faith in Jim, with** P brave, with
196.19 **and his ironic** P and ironic
196.19,20 **frightened, suspicious adoration** P frightened adoration
196.25 **"Jim, as I've told you,** P "We did not part till late. He
196.26 **very heart of untouched** P heart of a primeval
196.31,32 **trees. "The** P trees. "We conversed little. The
196.36 **till** P then
196.39 **far off** P faint
197.1 **the toil** E^3 a toil
197.10 **of** P that rested upon
197.14,15 **thread-like** A^1 thread-line of the
197.18 **displayed** P which spread itself
197.21 **of flimsy mat** P of mat
197.22 **over** P above
197.22 **a crooked multitude** P a multitude
197.25 **and the canoe** P it
197.26 **This** P The
197.27 **men crossing over were** P men were
197.30,31 **heads were** P hair was
197.31 **headkerchiefs** E^2, A^2, E^3 handkerchiefs
197.32 **complaint, voluble, stretching** P complaint, stretching
197.34 **had been** P was
197.35 **his people had collected** P they had been collecting
197.37 **over** P at
197.38,39 **withdrew obediently to** P withdrew to
197.40 **the silvery gleams in their eyes** P there were silvery gleams in their eyes as they
*198.7 E^3 **Have** RP P, A^1, E^1, E^2, A^2 Had
198.8 **sometimes I wish . . . No! I** P sometimes . . . I
198.22 **whom, perhaps, I** P whom I
199.9 **beach. The** P beach. He followed me. The
199.13 **wet oars flashed and dipped** P oars rose and fell
199.18 **wave** P sign
199.21 **its sombre wall that** P from north and south: its sombre wall
199.22 **night; the** P night; only the
199.22 **one** P a
199.23 **dark and still** P sleepily
199.26 **gone** P left
199.34 **foot, and remained persistently** P foot, persistently
199.38 **ebbing fast from** P ebbing from
199.39 **sunk already** P sunk
199.40 **tiny white speck** P tiny speck
200.3 **off the verandah** P away
200.8 **of all** P of
200.28 **for** A^2, E^3 of
200.34 **He sighed** P He seemed to listen to it, then sighed
201.20 **don't** E^3 can't
201.21 **came** A^1 come
201.25 **laws of order and** P law of an ethical
201.33 **frame** P send
*201.38 E^3 **will** RP P, A^1, E^1, E^2, A^2 shall
*201.38 E^3 **will** RP P, A^1, E^1, E^2, A^2 shall
202.18 **the ink blot resembling** P the blot shaped like
202.30 **treasured** P preserved
*203.22 E^3 **will** RP P, A^1, E^1, E^2, A^2 shall
203.29 **consequence** P, A^1 necessity

203.33 **put it down here** P, A^1 relate it
203.34 **I've fitted** P I've put A^1 I put
204.17 **much** E^3 such
204.32 **here** A^2, E^3 hear
205.10–15 **feverishly; * * * learn.** P, A^1 feverishly with a gleeful ferocity and a savage unforgiving
 contempt for poor Jim; but in the middle of a word, perhaps, an invisible hand would take
 him by the throat, and he would look at me dumbly with a heaving breast and an expression
 of doubt and anguish. You could see his coarse lips turn blue behind the drooping, wiry hairs.
 He seemed to fear that I would get tired of waiting for the end of the choking-fit and go away,
 leaving him with his tale untold, with his exultation unexpressed. Nothing was farther from
 my thoughts; I was only afraid that death, hovering over him, would swoop down suddenly
 and baffle my desire to know. He died during the night, I believe, but by that time I had
 nothing more to learn. "I knew the story before, of course; he had only cleared up an obscure
 point, though the profound blackness of the act cannot be dispelled.
206.36 **and yet it** A^1 and it
206.40 **did not respond** P, A^1 was inert
206.42 **felt that nothing** P felt that it would never exhaust itself, and that nothing
207.2 **said** A^1 told me
*207.23 E^2, A^2, E^3 **those** P, A^1, E^1 these
207.28 **lightly** A^1 slightly
207.29 **of** A^1 of the
207.35,36 **and of** A^1 of
207.44 **black** P, A^1 big
207.46 **of the** A^1 of
*208.28 E^2, A^2, E^3 **those** P, A^1, E^1 these
209.3 **the** A^1 in the
209.9 **let you know, too, that** P, A^1 tell you
210.21 **call at** P, A^1 come-to off
210.32,33 **stood in mortal fear of imprisonment** P, A^1 was mortally afraid of a prison
210.35 **terror** P, A^1 fear
210.39,40 **little all clink in its** P, A^1 dollars clink in their
210.40,41 **(the very next evening, I believe) to** P, A^1 the very next evening, to
210.44 **took good care to tow** P, A^1 towed
211.9 **up suddenly and** P, A^1 up and
211.11 **a long knife** P, A^1 a knife
211.27 **to** A^1 to the
212.23 **their toes** P, A^1 them
*213.15 E^3 **quickly** P, A^1, E^1, E^2, A^2 quick
214.31 **truth** E^3 youth
214.37,38 **expecting to find wisdom and courage in the dwelling** P, A^1 to draw strength from
 the spirit
214.38 **man. The** P, A^1 man. Their temper was unforgiving. The Bugis especially were exasperated. The
214.39 **or** P, A^1 and
215.32 **townfolk** E^2 towns-folk
215.39 **others with** P, A^1 others savages with
215.41 **people** A^1 folk
*216.15 E^3 **cut off the** RP P, A^1, E^1, E^2, A^2 cut the
216.17 **ten** P, A^1 fifteen
217.17,18 **up as** P, A^1 up the hill as
*217.19 E^2, A^2, E^3 **palace** P, A^1, E^1 place
217.24 **dark-blue** P, A^1 white
217.32,33 **defection of the townfolk was** P, A^1 defection was E^2, A^2, E^3 defection of the townsfolk
 was
218.19 **there** E^2, A^2, E^3 here
218.39 **afternoon, his men, meantime, resting** P, A^1 afternoon while his men rested
218.40 **stole** P, A^1 stealing
218.41 **creek, and** P, A^1 creek,
219.10 **became** A^2, E^3 become
219.39 **against** A^1 as against
220.7 **own mind** A^1 mind
220.8 **he had really** P, A^1 he really
220.14 **beyond** P, A^1 far over
220.15 **excavations** A^1 excavation
*221.2 E^3 **scooted** RP P, A^1, E^1, E^2, A^2 scouted
221.4 **on** A^1 from

221.5 **blue lips** P, A^1 blue writhing lips
221.7,8 **skinny fingers** P, A^1 skinny earthy fingers
221.18 **Kassim had** P, A^1 Kassim, indeed, had
221.18 **gone, by that time, very** P, A^1 gone, very
221.43 **deep** A^1 deeply
222.21 **is** A^2, E^3 was
223.14 **finding the tobacco** E^2, A^2, E^3 finding tobacco
224.6 **extraordinary** E^2 extraordinarily
*224.34 E^3 **will** RP P, A^1, E^1, E^2, A^2 shall
225.8 **their midst** A^2, E^3 the midst
226.17 **equal** A^1 equals
226.39 **half of** A^2, E^3 half
228.6 **hovering off** P, A^1 hovering down Erromanga way, off
228.6 **dot** E^3 lot
228.8 **his spells** P, A^1 the spell of his fame
228.11 **intention** P, A^1 hope
228.22 **livid hand** P, A^1 livid bony hand
*229.14 A^1, A^2, E^3 **had** RP P, E^1, E^2 has
229.32 **runs. When** P, A^1 runs. Not a gleam of light, not a break in the mischance. When
229.44 **secret** P, A^1 a secret
229.45 **bond of** A^1 bond to
229.45 **and of their** P, A^1 and their
230.5 **were turned,** P, A^1 watched
230.5 **upon the** P, A^1 the
230.15 **hand** P, A^1 arm
230.19 **is** A^1 are
230.31 **or else** P, A^1 or
231.8 **above** P, A^1 before
231.11 **has** A^1 had
231.16 **had been** P, A^1 was
231.25 **And** P, A^1 But
231.32 **regretfully** P, A^1 mournfully
233.13 **Jim insisted** P, A^1 said Jim
233.14 **could** P, A^1 there could
*233.24 E^3 **failings** RP P, A^1, E^1, E^2, A^2 failing
234.8 **command of the fort** P, A^1 command
234.36 **so** A^1 so of
236.15 **boats** E^2, A^2, E^3 boat
236.32 **the fog lasts** P, A^1 it's so thick
236.39 **something—a bullock** A^2, E^3 something—bullock
236.40 **The shadow** P, A^1 The high shadow
238.13 **alongside, and** P, A^1 alongside of his dug-out, and
238.16,17 **saw, under the now lifting** P, A^1 saw now, under the lifting
238.21 **many little knots** A^2, E^3 many knots
238.22 **subdued** P, A^1 steady
239.18 **even** E^3 ever
239.20,21 **When he judged the moment come, Brown** P, A^1 Both its entrances were so narrow and overgrown that the very natives passing in canoes had to look for them carefully. Brown
239.24 **last** P, A^1 third
240.13 **them. Brown** P, A^1 them. No matter. Brown
240.17 **running** P, A^1 running about
240.23 **staring hard at** E^2, A^2, E^3 staring at
240.26 **kicking. He** P, A^1 kicking. Twice I gave a blow. He
*240.32 E^2, A^2, E^3 **swum** P, A^1, E^1 swam
240.42 **fearfully** P, A^1 hesitatingly
241.19 **despairingly** P, A^1 fearfully
242.11 **heart. The** P, A^1 heart. But he was romantic—romantic—and nevertheless true. The
*242.35 E^3 **she passed** RP P, E^1, E^2, A^2 she has passed A^1 she had passed
242.39 **ear** P, A^1 ears
242.40 **could** P, A^1 did
243.32 **stooping, took** P, A^1 stooping over the body, took
243.34 **ran** E^3 rang
244.7 **Tamb' Itam, advancing with** P, A^1 Tamb' Itam with
244.21 **leave me** P, A^1 go away
244.21 **asked you** P, A^1 asked
244.33 **on his shoulder** P, A^1 violently

244.39 **though** *P*, A[1] but
244.40 **of** *P*, A[1] of the
244.45 **earnestly upon** *P*, A[1] long at
245.15 **met seemed awestruck, and stood** *P*, A[1] met stood
246.34 **he passes from my eyes like** *P*, A[1] I believe him to have been only
246.35 **earth, ready to surrender** *P*, A[1] earth—surrendering
246.43 A[2], *E*[3] **THE END**

A *Lord Jim* Gazetteer and Glossary of Eastern and Nautical Terms†

abaft, aft   At or toward the rear or stern of a ship.

anna   A coin of India equal to one-sixteenth of a rupee, or about two U.S. cents. Indian currency was in use in Singapore at that time.

athwart   Across; transversely.

Apia   A seaport on the island of Upolu in western Samoa.

Aukland (Auckland)   A New Zealand port city on northern North Island, formerly the capital of New Zealand.

Bankok (Bangkok)   The capital of Thailand (then Siam).

barque (bark)   A three-masted vessel with the foremast and mainmast square-rigged and the mizzenmast fore-and-aft-rigged.

Batavia   The former Dutch name of Jakarta, a city in Java.

belaying-pin   A removable wooden or metal pin in the rail of a ship, around which ropes can be fastened.

betel   The nutlike seed of the betel palm. Wrapped with a little lime in the leaves of the betel, it is the chief masticatory of the East Indies; it is a pungent, astringent stimulant and stains the teeth black.

binnacle   A case or box that holds the compass; it is fitted with a lamp for use at night.

block   A pulley or system of pulleys in a frame with a hook or loop for attachment.

blue-jacket   An enlisted man in the navy.

boat-chock   One of the cradles in which a ship's boat rests when it is on the deck.

boat-stretcher   A narrow crosspiece in a boat against which a rower braces his feet.

Bombay   The capital of the state of Bombay, in western India, on the Arabian Sea.

breaking-up yard   A place where ships are dismantled when they become old and unserviceable.

---

† Although this glossary draws heavily upon many modern, standard dictionaries, gazetteers, and dictionaries of slang and of nautical words, it also relies upon certain works closer in time to Conrad's nineteenth-century maritime world: J. J. Moore, *The British Mariner's Vocabulary* (1801); A *Naval Encyclopedia* (Philadelphia, 1881); Albert Barrère and Charles Leland, A *Dictionary of Slang, Jargon and Cant* (1897); Captain Paasch, *From Keel to Truck: Dictionnaire de Marine* (1903); and the ninth (1875) and eleventh (1910) editions of the *Encyclopedia Britannica*.

brigantine A two-masted vessel with the foremast square-rigged and the mainmast fore-and-aft-rigged.

brig-rigged Square-rigged.

Brisbane The capital of Queensland, Australia, near the mouth of the Brisbane River.

Bugis A Malayan people of Celebes and adjacent islands.

bulkhead A vertical partition separating compartments on a ship.

buster A southerly, Australian wind of great violence.

by the head Said of a vessel when it is sunk deeper in the water forward than aft.

caboose A deckhouse where cooking is done.

Calcutta A seaport in northeastern India.

campong A native hamlet or village in a Malay-speaking country.

Cape York A peninsula on the northeastern coast of Australia.

capstan A vertical drum revolving on a spindle, used for exerting power required in heaving on a rope or an anchor-cable.

casuarina A genus of chiefly Australian trees, some species of which grow large and yield heavy hard wood.

catspaw A light breath of air that ripples the surface of a calm sea.

catting Hoisting an anchor from the water's edge to the cathead, i.e., to the strong timber projecting from the bow of the ship. Cat tackle is the tackle by which the anchor is lifted from the water level.

coir A stiff elastic fiber extracted from the outer husk of the coconut.

companion A stairway or companionway.

copra Dried coconut meat, the source of coconut oil.

corvette A sailing vessel with a flat deck and one tier of guns.

counter The part of the ship's stern from the waterline to the overhang.

country ship A vessel owned in an Eastern port, as opposed to a home ship.

cranky Likely to heel, tilt.

cuddy A small cabin, formerly the saloon under the poop deck.

cutter A broad square-stemmed boat for carrying stores and passengers; it is either rowed or sailed.

Dain A Bugis title of distinction.

dammar A resin derived from various evergreen trees in Australia, New Zealand, and the East Indies.

davits A pair of small projecting cranes on the sides or stern of the ship used for suspending, lowering, and hoisting a ship's boats.

donkey-man An operator of a donkey engine, a small auxiliary steam engine, especially one used to power a windlass on shipboard.

Dubash An Indian interpreter.

dug-out A canoe made by hollowing out a log.

dunnage Personal baggage.

Eden A port in southeastern New South Wales, Australia.

eight bells The time at the end of a four-hour watch, when the bell is struck eight times (here, 4 A.M.).

ensign The flag hoisted to indicate the nationality of a vessel.

fall The tackle used in lowering a ship's boat from the davits.

fall off Alter course away from the wind.

Flensborg (Flensburg)   A German city near the Danish border on an islet of the Baltic Sea.

flying moor, running moor   Anchoring by dropping the first anchor while the ship has headway and letting go the second anchor after she has gone farther ahead.

fore-and-aft rig   The general term for all rigs in which sails extend lengthwise of the vessel.

forefoot   The lower extremity of the stem, usually curved, where it joins the keel.

forepeak   That part of the hold in the extreme forward part of the ship.

fore-top   The platform at the top of the forwardmost mast.

fore-topsail   The second sail up on the foremast.

fore-'tween-deck   Space between decks in the forward part of the ship.

gaff   Spar on which a steamship raises her flag.

gather headway   Start to move through the water with increasing speed.

gharry   A horse-drawn cab used especially in India but also in Singapore.

gharry-wallah   A gharry driver.

gig   A long, light ship's boat for oars or sail, usually assigned to the captain.

gripes   The canvas bands and fastenings that secure a lifeboat in its cradle.

gunwale   The upper edge of a boat's side.

Hai-phong (Haiphong)   The main port of Tonkin province, French Indo-China (now Vietnam); it developed rapidly after the French treaty of 1874.

Haji   The name designating a Moslem who has made a pilgrimage, especially to Mecca.

hawser   A rope or cable used for mooring, towing, etc.

head   the bow of a ship.

Hector Bank   A ledge located off the southwestern coast of Borneo.

helm   The apparatus that steers a ship, especially the wheel or tiller.

Hobart   A city in Australia, the capital of Tasmania, in the southeastern part of the island on the Derwent River.

home   England, as in home service, home ships.

hooker   A sailor's term for a clumsy, old-fashioned vessel.

Inchi   A Malay term of address equivalent to Mr.

jib-sheet   The rope that controls the lower corner of the jibsail (triangular sail extending from the foremast to the bowsprit).

Kalashee   A native East Indian sailor.

Kalashee watch   A sailing term for general duty performed by all hands, with no regular watches set.

kanakas   Melanesians imported into Australia as laborers.

Koran   The book composed of writings accepted by Moslems as revelations made to Mohammed by Allah.

kriss   A dagger, often with a serpentine blade, used by the Malays.

lanyard   A short piece of rope or line used on a ship for fastening anything.

lascar   An East Indian sailor.

leeward   Situated on the side turned away from the wind, as opposed to windward.

Levuka   A port town that was the site of the first white settlement in Fiji.

Macassar Straits   The wide channel between Borneo and Celebes.

Madagascar   An island in the Indian Ocean off the southeastern coast of Africa.

main-boom   The spar on which the base of a fore-and-aft mainsail is extended.

main gaff   The spar extending diagonally upward from the afterside of the mainmast near its top.

Malacca   A port on the Strait of Malacca, 125 miles north of Singapore.

Malaita   A volcanic island northeast of Guadalcanal.

Melanesia   A group of islands in the Pacific Ocean northeast of Australia.

Menam   Thai for "main river," old name for the Chao Phraya River, the most important in Thailand. It runs 750 miles from northern Thailand through Bangkok to the Gulf of Siam.

middle watch   The watch on a ship from midnight to 4 A.M.

Mindanao   The second largest island of the Philippines (after Luzon), at the southern end of the archipelago.

mizzenmast   The aftermost mast in all three-masted vessels and the second one from aft in ships having four or five masts.

Moluccas   A large group of islands west of Celebes, formerly part of the Dutch East Indies, now part of Indonesia.

mud-pilot   The pilot who takes ships up the River Thames between Gravesend and the London docks.

nakhoda   The master of a native vessel.

Nazarene   The ordinary Eastern term for a Christian.

New South Wales   A state in southeastern Australia.

Nuka-Hiva   The largest of the Marquesas Islands.

out reefs   Let out the reefs; expose the full sail area to the wind.

outward-bound   Headed away from the home port (London).

pangeran   The Malay term for a regent or headman; a prince.

Panglima   A Malay chief.

Parsees   Members of a Zoroastrian religious sect, descendants of Persians who fled to India in the eighth century to escape Moslem persecution; many are engaged in commercial and clerical pursuits throughout the East.

patent log, taffrail log   A mechanical device used for measuring the distance a vessel has sailed. "In this log . . . the registering cog-wheel work, with its dials, is screwed upon a convenient place on the taffrail, and the propeller towed overboard from it by means of a long line, through which it communicates its motion to the register. . . . A small bell was attached to the register, which would ring automatically at every mile passed" (A *Naval Encyclopedia*, Philadelphia, 1881).

Penang   A British settlement on the Malay peninsula at the northern end of the Strait of Malacca.

peon   Attendant or messenger.

Perim   A British island in the strait of Bab el Mandeb, at the entrance to the Red Sea, ninety-six miles from Aden.

pith hat   Helmet-shaped sun hat made of the dried pith of the East Indian sola herb.

poop   A raised deck at the stern; on sailing ships the poop contains accommodations for the master and officers.

port   Left side of a vessel.

Poulo Laut   An island off the southeast coast of Borneo. *Poulo* means island; *laut* means sea.

prau   The Indonesian name for an undecked native boat, dug-out, or plank-built craft that is rowed, paddled, or sailed.

punkah   An Indian device for fanning a room, usually a frame covered with canvas, suspended from the ceiling, and moved manually by cord and pulley.

purser   Ship's officer who keeps the accounts and has charge of provisions.

quarter   The aftermost portion of a vessel's side.

quartermaster   A petty officer who attends to a ship's helm, binnacle, and signals under the master or navigator.

quay   A landing place at which vessels receive or discharge cargo; usually a solid-masonry wall.

Queensland   A state of northeastern Australia.

rajah   In India, originally a prince or king; also applied to Malay chiefs.

Rangoon   The capital of Burma, at the mouth of the Irrawaddy River.

rattan   A portion of the stem of the rattan palm that is used for walking sticks, wickerwork, and cordage.

reach   A straight portion of a stream or river.

Red Rag   Sailors' term for the Red Ensign, the distinctive flag flown by British merchant ships. It has a red field with a Union Jack in the upper left-hand corner.

reef   To reduce the area of a sail by rolling or folding a certain portion of it and making it fast with small ropes.

Réunion   A French island in the Indian Ocean east of Madagascar.

roads, roadstead   An area of water where ships can ride safely at anchor. More or less open anchorage, it affords less protection than a harbor.

running gear, running rigging   The ropes used in handling spars, sails, etc.; they usually run through blocks or pulleys.

rupee   A silver coin of India worth one shilling four pence, or about thirty-two U.S. cents.

Rushcutters Bay   A bay in New South Wales, Australia, on the eastern side of the capital city of Sydney.

Samarang   A port in northern Java.

schooner   A fore-and-aft-rigged vessel with two or more masts.

screw-pile lighthouse   A lighthouse built on piles sunk by screws on their lower ends, usually on shoals, coral reefs, or sand banks.

serang   The boatswain of an East Indian crew; also, the skipper of a small native boat.

Sherif   A title of descendants of Mohammed through his grandson Husain.

ship   To fix anything in its place; for example, to ship the oars means to place them in their rowlocks.

ship-chandler   A dealer in supplies for ships.

ship-keeper   A caretaker placed on board in charge of a vessel when it is in harbor without a crew.

shoulder straps   Epaulets.

sidiboy   A term for a native personal servant of African descent.

solah topi   Pith helmet.

Solomon Islands   A group of islands in the western Pacific Ocean east of New Guinea. At the time *Lord Jim* was written, the northern islands belonged to Germany, the southern to Great Britain.

Somali coast   A portion of the eastern coast of Africa bounded by the Gulf of Aden and the Indian Ocean.

spar   A general term for any mast, yard, boom, gaff, or the like. Spars are usually round and made of wood or metal.

square-rig   A general term for all rigs where sails are extended by yards running across the vessel. A square-rigged vessel can spread a large amount of canvas, often out-sailing a fore-and-after of the same size and type.

stanchion   A small pillar of wood or iron used for various purposes in a ship, for example, to support the decks, rails, awnings, etc.

starboard   Right side of a vessel.

steerage-way   A rate of motion sufficient to make a boat capable of being steered.

stem   A piece of timber or metal, usually curved, to which the sides of a ship are united at the fore end.

stem-head   The top of a ship's stem.

stern-sheets   That part of a boat between the stern and the aftmost seat of rowers. It is generally furnished with seats to accommodate passengers.

Stettin   A seaport, now Polish but formerly German, on the Oder River not far from the Baltic Sea.

Stewart Island   A part of New Zealand south of South Island.

stroke   The oar nearest the stern, setting the time of the stroke. Keep stroke means row together in a regular rhythm.

Succadana   A region of southeast Borneo.

Sunda Strait   The channel between Java and Sumatra.

taffrail   The rail about a vessel's stern.

taffrail-log   Patent log.

Tagal, Tagalog   One of a predominantly Christian Malayan race, chiefly from central Luzon, Philippine Islands.

Talcahuano   One of Chile's major ports.

Tamatave   A seaport in eastern Madagascar.

Tamil   A member of an ancient Dravidian race, which inhabits southern India and northern Ceylon (now Sri Lanka).

thole-pin   A wooden or steel pin that fits in the gunwale of a boat to keep an oar in place when rowing.

thwart   One of the planks that extend crosswise in an open boat for lateral stiffening and which serve as seats for the oarsmen.

tiller   The bar or lever used to turn the rudder in steering.

Tondano   A town in northeastern Celebes.

top-gallant   The third section of the mast (above the topmast, below the royal mast) and its sail, yards, and braces.

trim   The position of a vessel on the water—i.e., on an even keel and neither bow-heavy nor stern-heavy.

Tunku   A Malay term meaning "My Lord."

Union down   The reversed or upside-down position of a ship's ensign, as displayed for a distress signal.

unreeve   Haul a line or rope out of a block.

Wajo   A small kingdom on the southwestern peninsula of Celebes.

Walpole Reefs, Walpole Island   An uninhabited 310-acre coral island in the southwest Pacific 135 miles east of New Caledonia.

Wapping   A section of London close to the docks.

warp   A rope, attached at one end to a fixed object, and used in hauling or moving a vessel.

water-breaker   A small cask or barrel used in a ship's lifeboat for holding drinking water.

way   The motion or speed of a ship through the water.

Wellington   The capital of New Zealand.

windlass   A revolving cylinder used to raise and lower the anchor.

windsail   A wide tube or funnel of canvas used to convey air for ventilation into the lower compartments of a vessel.

yard   A long spar designed to support and extend a sail.

Zambouanga   A city on the southwestern coast of Mindanao, Philippine Islands.

BACKGROUNDS

The Pent Farm. Frontispiece to *Lord Jim* (Edinburgh and London: John Grant, 1925).

Editor's Note on the Composition of *Lord Jim*

Until 1896, two years before he began *Lord Jim*, Joseph Conrad led a life marked by personal loss, loneliness, and physical hardship. The only child of Polish revolutionaries, he was born December 3, 1857, in Berdyczów, in the Ukraine, and christened Józef Teodor Konrad Korzeniowski. In 1795, Poland had been divided among its three neighbors, Russia, Prussia, and Austria. Russia took the largest portion and oppressed the Poles severely. When Conrad was three, his father was arrested in Warsaw for subversive political activities, and six months later the family was sent into exile in Russia. As a result of the hardships of exile, Conrad lost both parents to tuberculosis: his mother, when he was five; his father, when he was eleven. Five years later, Conrad left Poland permanently in order to become a merchant mariner, based first in France, but soon in England. In 1894, after two decades of service in every rank from able seaman to captain, he left the sea to become a writer. In April of the following year, Conrad published his first novel, *Almayer's Folly*; and in March 1896, he published his second, *An Outcast of the Islands*. That same month he married a young Englishwoman, Jessie George. In January 1898, their first child, Borys, was born.

Although Conrad's third novel, *The Nigger of the "Narcissus,"* is a masterpiece of sea fiction, his real literary breakthrough did not occur until 1898. It was then (probably in April) that Conrad wrote the first pages of a "sketch" entitled "Tuan Jim," which grew into *Lord Jim*. It was then (some time in May) that Conrad invented his marvelous personal narrator, Captain Marlow, for the short story "Youth." And it was then (in mid-December) that Conrad began his great short novel, *Heart of Darkness*, perhaps the first modernist masterpiece in English. Nevertheless, Conrad's most reliable biographer, the Polish scholar Zdzisław Najder, considers the first nine months of 1898 "the most difficult period for Conrad since he left the sea."[1] Unsurprisingly, in light of his tragic personal and political past, Conrad always tended to pessimism and melancholia. Najder convincingly argues that Conrad was even subject to attacks of what would now be called clinical depression. Moreover, five months as a river steamboat officer in the Belgian Congo (now Zaire) in 1891 permanently damaged his health, leaving him chronically ill with malaria and jungle gout for the rest of his life. Additionally, thirty-eight years of transient, unmarried existence must have made Conrad's adjustment to domesticity and fatherhood anything but easy. Still, the overwhelming cause of Conrad's despair at this period was writer's block. Since his honeymoon, Conrad had been struggling with a novel called *The Rescue*, using characters from *Almayer* and *Outcast* and consciously intending the work to be a best-selling romance. By 1898, Conrad had written hundreds of pages of the novel; he was committed to its serial publication in both English and American magazines; he had received substantial monetary advances, and he detested the manuscript. Clearly, work on "Tuan

---

1. Zdzisław Najder, *Joseph Conrad: A Chronicle* (New Brunswick: Rutgers UP, 1983) 227.

Jim" and "Youth" were frantic attempts to escape from *The Rescue*. In fact, the novel was not published until 1920.

However, in September 1898, Conrad suddenly cheered up. Edward Garnett (1868–1937), publisher's reader, critic, and Conrad's first English literary friend, introduced him to a precocious young writer named Ford Madox Hueffer (later Ford Madox Ford, 1873–1939). The two men took to each other instantly and even agreed to collaborate. Ford provided two crucial services to Conrad, one practical and the other personal. Conrad, in his depressed state, longed to vacate his current residence in Essex, northeast of London. Ford generously offered to sublet the house he had leased in South Kent, near the English Channel. The Conrads moved into the Pent Farm in November, and in the ensuing decade there Conrad wrote most of his best works. Importantly, the Pent's location brought him within an easy pony trap ride of three writers he already knew and admired: Stephen Crane, Henry James, and H. G. Wells. Ford, let it be said, quickly rented another house in the neighborhood.[2] Besides providing a congenial dwelling place that Conrad would inhabit longer than any other place he would ever know, Ford provided Conrad with an always available, literarily astute, utterly adoring disciple. Ford's presence encouraged Conrad to talk at length about writing, and Ford's knowledge of both the English language and the English artistic world gave Conrad a security about these matters he previously lacked and worried about. Conrad's impact upon Ford was enormous; it is especially evident in Ford's greatest novel, *The Good Soldier* (1915).[3]

Yet Conrad's writing life was never easy, and the *Lord Jim* years, 1898 to 1900, are no exception. Whether husband, wife, or son, some member of the Conrad household was almost always ill. The disasters that struck Conrad's two oldest friends in England disturbed him greatly as well. Adolph P. Krieger, after years of close friendship and business association, quarreled with Conrad and then, in dire financial straits, showered him with hysterical letters demanding immediate repayment of the sizable debt of £180. G. F. W. Hope's eldest son was found stripped and beaten to death in the Essex marshes in December 1899, and the Conrads rushed to console Hope and his wife. Also during the time of writing *Lord Jim*, Conrad strove to raise money to bring Stephen Crane, ill with tuberculosis, back from Havana, helped get his stories published, and bade him a painful farewell in Dover, a month before Crane's death at a German spa.

Conrad's financial affairs were a shambles. He had spent the Krieger loan plus a £250 advance on a novel (*The Rescue*) he could not finish. Consequently, he found himself writing several works simultaneously in order to pay off old debts and meet current expenses. His letters to William Blackwood and David S. Meldrum, his publisher and editor, repetitively request advances of £10, £20, and £50, propose schemes to borrow money on life insurance, contain promises to write still more books, and suggest selling outright to Blackwood's copyrights on books already published.

Fortunately, Conrad at this time appears to have been vibrating with

---

2. For an enjoyable account of the five writers in their south of England milieu at the turn of the century, see Nicholas Delbanco, *Group Portrait* (New York: William Morrow, 1982).

3. Ford later said that *Lord Jim* "entered into me like the blood in my veins." For an account of Conrad's personal and literary relations with Ford, see Thomas C. Moser, *The Life in the Fiction of Ford Madox Ford* (Princeton: Princeton UP, 1980).

creative energy. While working on *Lord Jim*, he wrote all of "Youth" (1898) and *Heart of Darkness* (1899) and some of *The Rescue* (1920); he collaborated with Ford Madox Hueffer on *The Inheritors* (1900) and *Romance* (1903); he projected "Equitable Division" (*Typhoon*, 1902), "A Seaman" (probably "The End of the Tether," 1902), "Dynamite" (probably *Chance*, 1913), and "First Command" (*The Shadow-Line*, 1917). For all their troubles, the Conrads later looked back fondly to those days when Conrad, in "Youth," discovered Marlow, when they moved to Pent Farm, and when he first published in "Maga" (*Blackwood's Magazine*).

Yet magazine publication provided the greatest menace of all to *Lord Jim's* formal excellence. Difficult as it is to believe, Conrad originally intended the novel to be a story of twenty thousand words, only slightly longer than the thirteen thousand of "Youth" and running to three or four installments in the magazine. Even in November 1899 when Conrad had been planning and working sporadically on "Lord Jim: A Sketch" for eighteen months and when the second installment was already on sale, he envisioned only four or five installments. Instead it took fourteen! Perhaps the crucial moment in the writing occurred shortly after a letter of February 12, 1900, in which Conrad states flatly that, with twenty chapters finished, he will need only two more to complete the story. Since Chapter XX concerns Marlow's visit to Stein, Conrad must still, at so late a date, not have decided to develop fully Jim's life in Patusan. It is hard to imagine how there could have been a Gentleman Brown, or even Jim's death. Although Dickens published his novels serially while he was in the process of writing them, he made elaborate plans before he started. More important, and also unlike Conrad, he subscribed to no Flaubertian ideal of highly wrought novelistic form.

The selections below are intended to show how *Lord Jim* came into being.

ALEXANDER JANTA

[Tuan Jim: A Sketch]†

"THE FEW PAGES I HAVE LAID ASIDE. . . ."[1]

[INTRODUCTION]

In July 1925 the Houghton Library at Harvard acquired a little brown leather album, its cover inlaid with metal and mother-of-pearl. It con-

† From "A Conrad Family Heirloom at Harvard," Ludwik Krzyzanowski, ed., *Joseph Conrad: Centennial Essays* (New York: Polish Institute of Arts and Sciences, 1960) 85–109. Reprinted by permission of the Polish Institute of Arts and Sciences of America. I have deleted some material, including footnotes, more relevant to Conrad's Polish heritage than to *Lord Jim*. "Tuan Jim: A Sketch" almost surely represents Conrad's first thoughts about the story. It was probably in April 1898 when Conrad wrote the first words of the novel in his grandmother's keepsake book. Despite the reference in this manuscript to Jim's retreat to a Malay village, Conrad may initially have intended the "Tuan" to be most ironic and Jim to become not a political hero but a nondescript white trader whose career in Patusan would require only the briefest treatment [*Editor*].

1. Joseph Conrad in his "Author's Note" to the 1917 edition of *Lord Jim*.

tained twenty-five pages of Polish poetry which, according to a statement received at the time of purchase was "in the handwriting of Conrad's mother." It definitely was not. The opening page carries the title *Zbiór różnych wierszy* (Collection of Various Poems) in ornate calligraphy. All the poems in the album have been copied by the same hand, that of a Teofila Bobrowska, who wrote her name at the bottom of the title page.

The album belonged to Joseph Conrad, who made ample use of the blank pages left by Teofila and covered twenty-eight pages[2] with the first draft of *Lord Jim*, here called *Tuan Jim: A Sketch*. One additional page contains a few sentences of the *Rescue*, and another lists tentative titles facing the names Lucas, a critic, and Pawling, Conrad's publisher. The following seven pages have been used for a draft of a play, placed in Italy in the time of the Renaissance.

*   *   *

The album * * * was the possession of his grandmother. She has recorded in it poems of friends and contemporaries of the eighteen twenties, closely linked with Krzemieniec and its Lyceum, an educational institution famous in South Eastern Poland at that time.

The names signed to some of the poems which Teofila selected and copied belong to the minor poets of that time.

The verses set down by Teofila were circulated, as was the custom in those romantic times, in many handwritten copies. Their literary value is, at best, insignificant.

*   *   *

On the verso of page 8 of the album a poem signed by Joseph Korzeniowski has been copied by Teofila. * * * The author of this poem was the novelist known in the latter part of the nineteenth century. * * * Like the other poets in this album, his poetic talent flourished before 1830, ceasing altogether after that year in favor of other interests.

The three stanzas of the Korzeniowski poem are titled "When Would I Be Happy." It says:

> If I would see my parents in old age, their white hair not
>   burdened by any miseries, I would be happy.
> If I would see my beloved one as a good mother and a good wife,
>   I would even be happier.
> But if my visionary forebodings which so often deceive me would
>   bring me back my country, I would be the happiest of men.

The subject of this poem is in line with the teachings and recommendations of [Conrad's] uncle Thaddeus Bobrowski and other friends of Conrad's father. Their influence remained a strong factor in the life of Joseph Conrad after he left Poland. It can be judged from at least

---

2. From the back of p. 15 to p. 29; pagination used here in transcript of text is from figures with which each face of a page in the Bobrowska album, starting with her title page, has been numbered.

two of Conrad's rare Polish letters, one written as a sailor, the other as an author in England.[3] The key to Conrad's development into an English writer could certainly have been found in his numerous letters to his uncle Thaddeus, but they were destroyed in the sack of Kazimierówka during the Bolshevik revolution in 1918.

Possibly Conrad's uncle Thaddeus gave him this album, as he was to sail the seven seas "toward Poland," because of the message contained in the poem of another Korzeniowski transcribed by Conrad's own grandmother. Instead of treating it as a family relic, Conrad, having no other pad to write on at a moment of sudden impulse, used the many blank pages as a notebook.

After his first few books were published and favorably received in England, Eliza Orzeszkowa, the *grande dame* of Polish literature of the time, wrote her now embarrassing, but then stinging attack on Conrad, accusing him of betrayal of his own nation's interest by depriving it of his talent in favor "of the Anglosaxonians."[4] The news of this attack reached Conrad and shocked him deeply.

By understandable association, Orzeszkowa used the name of the novelist Korzeniowski, the author of the poem quoted above, to contrast his writing and his position in Polish letters with that of Conrad. An attack so cruel and so unjustified could conceivably color the whole "sentiment of existence" in a character as sensitive and vulnerable to remorse and doubt as Conrad. A feeling of resentment for anything that reminded him of this experience could even have affected his feelings toward his grandmother's album. Another reason why Conrad may not have displayed this album, once it served him as a notebook, was the lack of reverence or respect with which he had used this precious memento of the dear old lady for scribble in a foreign language, not even remotely corresponding to the calligraphic care with which his grandmother had filled page after page with ornate verse. In the hands of an ill-inspired compatriot, ignorant of the English language and literature, such proof of alleged negligence and abuse by the grandson could once again produce accusations of something in the nature of a sacrilege.

3. Written from Teplitz on August 14, 1883, and first published in *Kuryer Warszawski* on June 13, 1937, this letter signed Konrad Korzeniowski contains the following passage: "I am leaving for London in a few days: not knowing where from there, wherever my fate will take me. In the last few years, that means from the time of my first exam, I haven't been too lucky in my travels. I was drowning, I have burned—otherwise I am all right, courage does not fail me nor does willingness to work and attachment to my profession: with that I always remember your recommendation at the time of my departure from Cracow: Remember—you have said—wherever you will sail, you sail toward Poland. This I never have forgotten and never will forget." * * * Czeslaw Milosz in his "Joseph Conrad in Polish Eyes" (*The Atlantic*, 100th anniversary issue, November 1957) quoted another Conrad letter dating from 1903, in which Conrad wrote to a Polish acquaintance (Kazimierz Waliszewski, author of the first Polish study on Conrad, published in 1904): "In the course of my navigations around the globe, I have never separated myself either in my thoughts or in my heart from my native country and . . . I hope to be received there as a compatriot, in spite of my anglicisation."
4. Published in *Kraj* (St. Petersburg), No. 16 in 1899.

Conrad must have been aware of such dangers after Orzeszkowa's outburst hit him and continued to hurt.

*   *   *

Once the usefulness of the Polish album as a pad for scribbling was ended, he could have discarded it or even made an attempt to destroy it. Jessie Conrad speaks eloquently of his habit of tearing and burning.[5] She could have saved the album and given it away, or Conrad himself could have disposed of it to someone who could not understand its Polish content and Polish significance. It is tempting to speculate about Conrad's attitude toward this family album, until, if ever, we learn its exact story.

It is a matter of additional interest that seven pages following the poem of Joseph Korzeniowski, Conrad began to write the story which was to become a tale about "the acute consciousness of lost honour" as he himself chose to express it in his "Author's Note" to the 1917 edition of Lord Jim.

The transcript of Conrad's Tuan Jim: A Sketch and other English notes in his grandmother's album tell their own story. Here we have a most interesting illustration for many pertinent observations by John D. Gordan, who made a study of his exacting corrections and found in the many disconnected jottings, which mark Conrad's struggle with the language and with the subject of his tale, the characteristic gropings of his imagination for expression.[6] The most significant suggestion for a new light on the origin of Lord Jim comes from the page which faces the opening paragraph of Conrad's text.

It can be found in my transcript from the album in question, on the back of page 14, and is indicative of the fact that Conrad's own statement in the preface to the 1917 edition of Lord Jim was not completely accurate. I refer to the passage in which he said:

> . . . the truth of the matter is that my first thought was of a short story concerned *only* with the pilgrim ship episode; *nothing more.* After writing a few pages, however, I became for some reason discontented and I laid them aside *for a time.* I didn't take them out of the drawer till the late Mr. William Blackwood suggested I should give him something again for his magazine.
>
> *It was only then* that I perceived that the Pilgrim ship episode was a good starting point for a free and wandering tale; that it was an event, too, which could conceivably colour the whole "sentiment of existence" in a simple and sensitive character. But all of these preliminary moods and stirrings of spirit were rather obscure

---

5. "Passion for burning MSS was shared by his father who burned all his MSS before his son's eyes while he lay on his death bed." Jessie Conrad in an unpublished letter to W. T. H. Howe, now in the Berg Collection, New York Public Library.

6. *Joseph Conrad, The Making of a Novelist* (Cambridge: Harvard UP, 1940) 150–73.

at the time, and they do not appear clearer to me now after the lapse of so many years.

The few pages I have laid aside were not without their weight in the choice of subject.[7]

There can hardly be any question that with the transcript of the sketch from his grandmother's album we are facing those few pages which Conrad had "laid aside" and which were not "without their weight in the choice of the subject." In this light they assume a very great significance, indeed.

For it can safely be deduced, now that we have this text under scrutiny, that while he first wrote the title of his intended story *Jim: A Sketch* and underlined it with one bold stroke, after jotting down certain thoughts on the verso of the preceding page, he already had an awareness of the entire scope of the two part story, comprising both the Patna episode and its consequence—Patusan. He could have added *Tuan* to the initial version of the title without turning the page.

Thus, the pages found here were indeed "not without weight in the choice of the subject." What is not accurate in his own subsequent estimate of that weight is the assertion that his first thought was of a short story concerned *only* with the pilgrim ship; *nothing more.*[8] As indicated by the addition of the word *Tuan* to the first version of the title *Jim: A Sketch*, that "first thought" was immediately expanded into a much broader concept, the full scope of *Lord Jim.*

It is noteworthy that the content of the page where this expanded view of Jim's story was recorded, though confused and still groping for a way, leads clearly toward the second part of the future novel and found its place in the ultimate and published version of *Lord Jim.* The third paragraph of the first chapter reads as follows:

> *Afterwards, when his* keen *perception of the Intolerable drove him away* for good from seaports and *white man,* even into the virgin forest, *the Malays of the* jungle *village,* where he had elected to conceal his deplorable faculty, added a word to the monosyllable of his incognito. They called *him Tuan Jim: as one might say—* Lord Jim.

7. Paragraphs 3, 4, and 5 of the "Author's Note" of June 1917, preceding a new edition of *Lord Jim.*

8. We are well aware of Conrad's letter of 1898 to Edward Garnett announcing his plans for a collection of short stories for McClure in America and mentioning *Lord Jim* as one of 20,000 words ° ° ° It goes without saying that the first draft of *Lord Jim* precedes the letter to Garnett and also Orzeszkowa's attack on Conrad, which took place after the publication of his first few books—in 1899. "My hypothesis that *Tuan Jim* was written in Spring 1898 can be supported by the fact that a note concerning *The Rescue* on the back of page 28 of the album refers to Chapter 5 of Part 3, the part Conrad was working on at that time. On the back of pp. 29–31 Conrad scribbled a sketch of Part 1 of a drama, with the action in Renaissance Ferrara; his first dramatic projects originated, as far as we know, under the influence of his talks with Crane in early 1898." Najder, 544, n. 40.

(All the words of this passage found already in the grandmother's Polish album are printed in italics).

Taking into account that Conrad had the habit of reworking even already published texts, * * * the words in question seem to have had considerable importance, surviving, as they did, the evolution of the story from the first scribble in the grandmother's album, through the subsequent rewritings in his manuscript, the typescript, the serial, the corrected serial, until they found a permanent place in the first and all subsequent editions of the completed novel, although he made a number of minor changes, eliminating completely the "provoking and brutal stare" for instance.

While the elements contained in this text recur nowhere else in the first twenty-three chapters of *Lord Jim*, the second paragraph of Chapter 24 shows the elderly headsman of the fishing village at the mouth of the Batu Kring branch of the estuary on the coast of Patusan who, speaking of the first white man he had ever seen, in Conrad's words "called him Tuan Jim."

There is another almost verbatim quotation in the text of the second part of *Lord Jim* from Conrad's notes on the verso of page 14 in Bobrowska's album. Toward the end of the last paragraph but one in Chapter 24 of the forty-five-chapter book, we find Cornelius speaking to Brown, who says: "They call him Tuan Jim here. As you may say Lord Jim."

The transcription[9] of Conrad's writing in the Bobrowska album is made as accurately as it could be read from his penciled, careless, and quick handwriting which looks as if it could not have been written at his desk. It has been copied according to Conrad's own instructions to a typist which can be found on the title page of Chapter 14 (page 308) in the manuscript of *Lord Jim* at the Rosenbach Museum in Philadelphia. It reads: "Where MS illegible leave blank space. Mistakes—repetitions and imperfect sentences to be typed *exactly* as written." (The word has been underlined by Conrad.)

On page 23 of this draft for *Lord Jim* the word count which Conrad was making, and which I have transcribed, jumped suddenly from 1300 to 3300 and is indicative of a number of pages, which must have been written on separate sheets, until Conrad resumed his narrative in the notebook. He stopped counting words altogether with the figure 3500 on page 24, although he continued to write for another 8 pages.

Parentheses in the transcript indicate that the word or sentence enclosed was crossed out by the author. Parentheses have been left empty when erased words were unreadable. Words unreadable in the proper text have been replaced by dots. Where a whole page or paragraph was crossed out, rectangular brackets have been used. All numbers on the margins have been copied as Conrad wrote them.

9. By permission of the Harvard College Library.

TUAN JIM: A SKETCH

page 15

(They called him Jim.)
(By the) All the white men by the waterside and and
(board ships) the captains of the ships in the (   ) road-
steads (   ) called him Jim. He was over six feet and stared
downwards at one with an (   ) air of overbearing watch-
fulness. You felt sometimes that (if you happened) were
you to say something (some) the one special thing which
he did not want to hear, he would (   ) knock you down (   )
without more ado. But as a water-clark of a leading ship
chandler in a certain Eastern port, he was popular

back of page 14

Afterwards when his (he disappea—
(The Malay) red from a)
perception of the intolerable
drove him away from the
haunts of white men, the
Malays of the village where he
(has fancied himself free from
the intolerable) without exercising
his perceptive faculty added (called)
him Tuan Jim—as one (would) might
Lord Jim
He had never to my own
knowledge (born his) (had) been (   ) guilty
of an assault. This provoking
and brutal stare (was the) being only the result
of an exquisite sensibility

back of page 15

[A water-clerk (in the Eastern) need not know anything (   )
under the sun but he must have (   ) ability in the ab-ct and
apply it practically. His work consists in going on board
arriving ships greeting (them) the Capt cheerily, forcing
upon him a card—the business card of his employer—
and, (piloting him) on his first visit ashore, piloting him
without ostentation to a (store where) vast cool shop
where he is received like a brother by men he never saw
before There is a parlour, (bottles cigars) easy chairs,
bottles, cigars and a warmth of welcome that melts the
salt of an eighty days' passage out of the heart.]

⌐ *(where) which is full of things that are eaten and drunk on*
  board ships, where ( ) you can get everything to make her
  seaworthy and beautiful from ( ) chain-hooks for her cable
⌐ *to a pot of gold paint for the carving of her stern*[1] ⌐

16

[*Jim then was a water clerk—When a water-clerk (has*
abstract Ability and is also) has been a seaman and pos-
sesses also abstract Ability he is worth good wages and
(some . . .)]

                          II   Jim.

After two years of training he went to sea and entering
into the regions so well known to his imagination found
them singularly barren of adventures. (It was severe
and monotonous.) The task (of earning his bread) before
him was (severe and monotonous) (prosaic) (with foreseen
demands and a limited outlook.) He made m . . . voyages.
He knew the ( ) magic monotony of existence between sky
and water. He knew the criticism of men the exactions
of the sea

                                      back of page 16

and the prosaic severity of the ( ) daily task (where true
men) that gives bread but whose only reward is in the per-
fect love of the work. He did not ( ) have that reward but
there is nothing more enticing disenchanting and enslaving
than the life at sea. His prospects were good. He was
gentlemanly, steady, tractable (and . . .) with a thorough
knowledge of his duty. And in time . . . young he be-
came chief mate of a fine ship without ever having been
tested by those events of the sea that [(. . . .) *the inner*
worth of a man, the quality of his resistance and the
devotion of . . . . not only to others but even to him-
self.]

17

[(*and the secret bustle of his pretences not only to others*
but (even) also to himself)]
that brings into the light of day the inner worth of a man,
the edge of his temper and the fibre of his stuff; that
(bring to the light) reveal the quality of his resistance and
the secret truth of his pretences not only to others but
also to himself.
150 *Only once ( ) in that time he (had) (he) had again the*
glimpse of the earnestness in the anger of the sea. There
are many shades in the danger of adventures and gales,
and only now and then there appears on the face of facts a

---

1. These four lines were written in the margin of the manuscript [*Editor*].

back of page 17

sinister violence of (purpose) intention (a destination . . .)
a hint of (. . . . certain destruction) mercilessness, that
indefinable something that (   ) enforces upon the mind and
the heart of a man that this complication of accidents or
(or this fury means business) this elemental fury (and is
beyond control malice is there for the purpose of destruc-
tion) is coming at him with a purpose of (destruction)
malice with a strength beyond control and with an
unbridled cruelty that (aims at life), meaning to tear out
from him his hope and his fear, the pain of his fatigue and
his longing for rest; (equally . . .) to (obliterate from
his) smash to destroy to annihilate what he has

18

known, loved, enjoyed or hated what is (precious) priceless
and (hateful) necessary (our memories and our future)
the sunshine, the memories the future—(and by
300 *taking away his life) to sweep the (world) whole precious*
world utterly from his sight by the simple act of taking
his life.
At the beginning of a week of which his Scotch Captain
used to say afterwards, "M'an! it's a complete meeracle
she lived through it," Jim disabled by a falling spar laid
in his berth (   ) dazed with the dull pain (   ) (and what
seemed an eternity) as if at the bottom of an abyss of
unrest. (   ) He was (glad) secretly glad he had not to go
on deck. (The limited capacity for emotion . . .). He
did not care what the end would be and he overvalued

back of 18

[his indifference. (The passive) The exhausted courage
is the result of exhausted emotion and (when the body
rest) in the motionless body imagination, this enemy of
man and the father of terror, rests in a slumber that
resembles the peace of conscious resignation.

seven lines erased

The struggle went on somewhere near . . .
gets dull . . .
the certitude of . . .
to a call on deck . . .
motionless body . . .
             (   ) imagina-
tion, that enemy of man and the father of all terrors, sank
into a slumber that resembled the peace of resignation.]

19

[his indifference. The fact he did not see, he had not to
exert himself and passive courage is easy since it is a sign

that imagination the enemy of man, the father of all
terrors is asleep in a motionless body
As he had not to look menace in the face, as he had not
to exert himself the danger became only a matter of faith,
and imagination the enemy of man the father of all terrors]

back of 19

Indifference. The danger when not seen has the vagueness
(of the Impossible) of our imperfect thoughts. Imagination the enemy of man the father of all terrors must have
something to feed upon, otherwise it sinks to rest (from)
(in) in the . . . of exhausted emotions. One admits
(may or may not . . .) the possibility of being struck from
behind, in sleep, or in the dark, but one does not believe in
it till the blow comes. It is otherwise when meeting danger
with brain, eye and hand. Then it is only (   ) a serenity of
temper, (and a) combined with contempt not of death but
for life (. . . . .)

20

than can (face) meet efficiently the aimed blow. Jim
saw nothing but the (   ) (of his) disorder of his tossed
cabin and the certitude of not being liable to a call on deck.
Once or twice he (felt that anguish at the pit of his stomach) felt uncontrolled anguish grip him bodily as he lay
500   (   ) battened down the only man on board. And the brutal
unintelligence of an existence such (an existence) liable
to the agony of such sensations filled him with a despairing
(anger) desire to escape at all costs. The fine weather
returned. He thought no more about it.
His lameness however persisted and when the ship arrived
at an Eastern port, he had to go the hospital. His recovery
was (so slow that he was left behind) slow and when the
ship left

back of 20

he had to remain. The hospital stood on a hill above the
town and in the white men's ward there were only two
patients beside Jim: (anoth) the purser of a gunboat, who
had broken his leg, and kind of railway contractor from
a neighboring (province who held the doctor for an ass)
province afflicted with some mysterious tropical disease
who held the doctor for an ass and surreptitiously committed debaucheries of patent medicine which his Tamil
boy used to smuggle in with unwearied devotion- - They
chatted, played cards a little (   ) lounged in easy chairs
before the open windows. And the gentle breeze entered
(   ) from the wide windows seemed to bring into the bare
cool room the softness of the sky, the languour of earth the
bewitching breath of the Eastern waters. There were per-

fumes in it and suggestions of endless dreams—Jim (   )
looked daily above

21

700 *(the palms) the thickets of gardens above the roofs of the*
town, above the fronds of palms or that roadstead that is
a thoroughfare to the East, the roadstead dotted (with)
by garlanded isles, (   ) lighted by (with) festal sunshine,
(   ) its ships like toys, (   )

three lines erased

its (   ) brilliant activity wearing the air of a holiday pageant,
with the eternal serenity of the Eastern sky overhead, and
and the eternal (   ) peace of the Eastern seas (spread before
750 *his eyes as far as the horizon) possessing the space as*
far as the horizon.

When he could walk without a stick he descended into
the town to look for some chance to get home. Nothing
offered at once and (   ) while waiting he associated naturally
with (   ) the men men of his calling belonging to the

back of 21

port. These were of two kinds. Some [some of these—not
many—(   ) (energetic faces . . .)
(energy undefaced by the breath of the East, the temper
of buccaneers and the eyes of dreamers, and their lives went
on] very few and seldom seen led mysterious lives, had
800 *an unde . . . energy, the tempers of buccaneers and the*
eyes of dreamers. (   ) They lived in a crazy maze of plans,
hopes, enterprises, ahead of civilization in the dark places
of the sea and their death was the only (   ) event of their
900 *fantastic and fiery existence that had a reasonable pro-*
bability of achievement. Others were (   ) men (   ) who like
himself (   ) thrown there by some accident (   ) became
officers of (the) country ships. They had the horror of
the home service (   ) with its hard conditions (   ) heavy
duties (   ) and the hazard of stormy oceans. They were
attuned to the eteranl peace of the sky and sea. They
loved (a lazy life), short passages, good deck-chairs,

22

1000 *large native crews and other distinction of being white—*
They shuddered at the thought of long days at sea (   ). They
led (   ) (precarious) easy and precarious existences always
on the verge of dismissal, (always engaged) serving China-
men, Arabs, (and) half-castes—would have served the
(devil if he made it easy . . . .) devil had he made it only
easy enough. There was (an air) a suspicion of failure

1100　about them. (　) They talked (always) everlastingly of
　　　(getting) turns of luck; how So-and-So (had) got charge
　　　of a boat (in the China) on the coast of China—a soft
　　　thing; how this one had an easy billet in Japan and that
　　　other one in the Siamese [navy—. . . a soft thing in
　　　China or the billet in Japan, in the Navy of Siam (　) had
　　　the air of being (. .) of being disguises for an uncon-
　　　querable loafing] navy; and in all their words in all their
　　　acts in their looks in their persons could be detected
　　　(an invincible fidelity)

back of 22

　　　[an (　) unconditional surrender to the charm of a loafing
　　　existence.]
　　　[The soft spot, the place of decay, the determination to
(1150)　loaf through existence.
　　　Jim listened for days to (their) the endless professional
(1150)　gossip, (to the jealousies) of these men who as seamen
　　　seemed at first to him (as thin as shadows) unsubstantial
　　　as shadows. Then some responsive chord in his nature was
　　　struck and he let himself go. There was a charm in seeing
1200　all these men well clothed well fed and knowing so little
　　　of danger or toil. And after a few days instead of going
　　　home he secured a berth as chief mate of the (　) 'Patna.']

23

　　　[The 'Patna' was a steamer (lean (as) like a greyhound),
　　　as old as the hills, lean like a greyhound and eaten up with
1300　rust like a kettle on a rubbish heap. She was owned by
　　　a Chinaman, chartered by an Arab and commanded by a
　　　sort of renegade (of) New South Wales German who on
　　　the strength of Bismarcks achievements brutalised those
　　　he was not afraid of and wore (a) a 'blood and iron' air
　　　combined with a bottle-nose and a red moustache]
　　　After she had been painted outside and whitewashed inside
3300　six hundred more or less pilgrims were driven on board of
　　　her (as she lay) with steam up alongside of a wooden quay.

back of 23

[(240)　(　) They streamed aboard over three gangways, they
　(14)　streamed in (moved) urged by (　) faith and the hopes of
(. . . .)　paradise, they streamed in (　) with a great thud and shuffle
　(2 . .)　of bare feet without a word, a murmur or a look
　(3 . .)　back (. . . . .) and when (　) clear of the rails spread on all
　(3 . .)]　sides over the deck, flowed forward and aft, (　) overflowed
　　　down the yawning hatchways filled (　) the innermost
3400　recesses of the ship with their bodies like water fills
　　　a cistern flowing into crevices and crannies. Six hundred
　　　men and women with faiths and hopes with affections
　　　and memories. They had been collected there, coming

*from North and South and from the East (coasting in the
water craft in canoes) after treading (the forests) the
forest paths, descending the rivers, coasting in the shallows,
crossing from island to island, passing through suffering*

24

*meeting strange sights, beset by strange fears, upheld by
one desire. They came (for the) from the jungle, and from
cultivated lands, they came from solitary huts (   ) leaving
(   ) the protection of their rulers, their fields, their clearings,
their prosperity, their poverty, the homes they were born
in and the graves of their fathers. They flowed in (with)*
3500   *the strong men at the head of parties, the (   ) lean old men
(who would never return) pressing forward without a hope
of return, the boys looking on fearlessly with serious eyes,
the little girls with . . . long hair hugging a bunch of
bananas or a small bundle of dried fish the muffled women
pressing (   ) to their breast the long headcloths (   ) sleeping
babies, the unconscious pilgrims of the True Faith.—
—"Look at these cattle" said the german skipper to his
new mate.*

back of 24

*An Arab, the chief of this pious voyage came last. He
walked aboard handsome and grave in his white (   ) gown
and large turban, [a string of beads (rosary) in his hand.]
(   ) His servants followed with lots of luggage and the
Patna (left the) backed away from the wharf.
     She (   ) headed between two islands, crossed oblique by
the (   ) anchoring ground of sailing ships, swung through
half a circle in the shadow*

25

*of a hill and ranged close to a ledge of foaming reefs.
The Arab at the stern recited the prayer of travellers by
sea. He invoked the favour of the Most High. His blessing
on the journey and on the secret purposes of the hearts.
(The sun set) The steamer pounded in the dusk the calm
water of the straits; (The steamer was in clear water) and
far astern (a) of the pilgrim ship*

back of 25

*a three-legged lighthouse planted by unbelievers on a
[perched on a shoal winked maliciously its eye of flame at
her errand of faith.] treacherous shoal seemed to wink at
her its eye of (fire) flame as if in derision of (at) her
errand of faith.
[She went on heading west across the Bay of Bengal.
There was not a cloud]*

26

*[on the sky.—And under the cloudless sky the calm sea
stretched its (   ) motionless and smooth surface.*

*There was not a wave, nor an undulation nor a ripple nor
a splash. And the Patna ploughing through the plain of
lifeless waters left no trace but]*

back of 26

*She went on (for days heading West) out of the Strait
across the Bay, through the One-degree passage. She went
(on for days) under a ( ) cloudless sky, under (sky a
scorching sky) through dazzling days (of) through an
unbroken (serenity) hot serenity, (through) in a fulgor
of sunshine, killing all thought, oppressing the heart, ( )
destroying all impulses of strength and energy. And under
that scorching sky the great sea blue, and profound (lay)
remained without a stir, without a ripple, without a
wrinkle*

27

*(a sea of) viscous, stagnant, dead. The 'Patna' (rolling)
with a slight(ly) list passed over that plain luminous and
smooth unrolling a (long) black ribbon of smoke across
the sky, and on the water a white ribbon of foam, that
vanished (together) at once like the phantom of a track
(left by the phantom of a ship.) traced on a sea without life
by the phantom of a ship.
There were only five white men aboard. The*

back of 27

*Capt, two mates and the engineer; they (lived) had their
berths amidships living, eating, sleeping on the long
(bridge) lower bridge without ever coming down amongst
the live cargo. "(Damn) Dirty rascals. Ferfluchte stink
there" said the Captain.
A crew of Malays with an Old Serang and two tindals
attended to the cleanliness of the ship as best they could.
The awnings covered the (ship) decks from stern to stern
with a white roof. Jim kept his watch. He*

28

*felt himself lulled, overcome conquered by (a feeling of)
an insidious langour of safety and rest. It was sailoring
reduced to its simplest expression. (Only the engineer)
There was nothing to do, nothing but a little navigating.
(To look out) Watchfulness even seemed unnecessary in
(this) such an empty universe. Only the engineers swore
at the heat and the Chinamen stokers would come up
from (below) their fires wildeyed (with) and streaming
with wet as though they had been overboard.
All went well and the ship neared the entrance of the
Red Sea.*

Correspondence Related to *Lord Jim*†

To Edward Garnett   [28 May or 4 June? 1898]

I've sold (I think) the sea thing to B[lackwood] for £35 (13000 words). Meldrum thinks there's no doubt—but still B must see it himself. McClure[1] has been the pink of perfection. "We will be glad to get as much as we can for you in America"—and so on. He is anxious to have a book of short tales. I think *Jim* (20.000) Youth (13.000) A seaman (5.000) Dynamite (5.000)[2] and another story of say 15.000 would make a volume for B here and for McC. there. That is after serial pub*on*. I broached the subject and they seem eager. Have made no conditions but said I would like to know what B. would offer: As to McC. I leave it vague for the present.

The Rescue shall not begin till *October* next. That means bookform for winter season of 1899. A long time to wait—and to find it after all a dead frost—perhaps.

I don't feel a bit more hopeful about the writing of Rescue than before. It's like a curse. I can't *imagine* anything.

To David Meldrum   [4 June 1898]

Last night I posted You the last pages of *Youth*. Here I send the first 18 pages of *Jim: A Sketch* just to let you see what it is like. It will give You an idea of the spirit the thing is conceived in. I rather think it ought to be worked out in no less than 20–25 thousand words. Say *two* numbers of "Maga".[3]

---

† These extracts have been chosen to dramatize how, to Conrad's consternation, the novel grew and grew and also to suggest something of his attitude toward his work in progress. (The entire correspondence of 1898 to 1900 merits reading for the insights it gives into Conrad's psyche, his personal milieu, his precarious financial state, and the complex business of authorship.) The extracts by Conrad come from *The Collected Letters of Joseph Conrad: Volume 2, 1898–1902*, ed. Frederick R. Karl and Laurence Davies (Cambridge: Cambridge UP, 1986) 62–303, *passim*. (Reprinted by permission of Cambridge UP.) Bracketed dates are those provided by Karl and Davies; their detailed reasons for the dating are, however, omitted from this Norton Critical Edition. Karl and Davies mark words that might be taken as misprints with an asterisk. The first two Conrad extracts come from Ivy Walls Farm, Stanford-le-Hope, Essex; the remainder come from Pent Farm, Stanford, near Hythe, Kent. The extracts of letters by Blackwood and Meldrum come from *Joseph Conrad: Letters to William Blackwood and David S. Meldrum*, ed. William Blackburn (Durham: Duke UP, 1958) 25, 40, 61, 78–79, 91–94, 104–05. (Reprinted by permission of Duke UP.) The Norton footnotes to Conrad's correspondence draw heavily, but not exclusively, from Karl and Davies.

1. The "sea thing" is "Youth." "Blackwood accepted the story 9 June (Blackburn, 23)." [Karl and Davies] "McClure" refers either to S. S. McClure (1857–1949), publisher and editor of *McClure's Magazine* (New York), or to his brother Robert, its London representative.

2. " 'Jim' grew into *Lord Jim* and 'Dynamite' into *Chance* (written 1911–12); . . . 'A Seaman' . . . may be 'The sketch of old Captain Loutit' (letter to Meldrum, 22 August 1899)." [Karl and Davies] It grew into "The End of the Tether" (written in 1902).

3. "Maga" is the nickname for *Blackwood's Edinburgh Magazine*, edited by William Blackwood (1836–1912); he was also head of the family publishing house. David S. Meldrum (1864–1940) was the literary advisor in the London office of the firm.

David Meldrum to William Blackwood   27 June 1898

Conrad I liked much better at home than abroad. He is, I think, very
sensible and conscientious. He would be delighted if we arranged to
publish a book of short stories—all of the sea—next spring, if the stories
are ready: if not, then in the following autumn.

David Meldrum to William Blackwood   6 January 1899

I find it no difficulty to understand Conrad's position. It surprises me
that he can get along at all. His long story costs two years' work. He
may get £400 out of it, not more. And we see what he does besides his
long story—two or three short ones each year, bringing in at the most
£100. That means that his total income from his work doesn't exceed
£300. Of course he doesn't attempt the impossible by living in London
on that, but even in the country it must be difficult always to put his
hand on money, if he hasn't any private capital. And I think it very
splendid of him to refuse to do any pot-boiling and hope, for him and
for ourselves too, that it will pay him in the long run.

To William Blackwood   14 Febr. 1899

I have a story *Jim* half-written or one-third written (10.000 words) which
is intended for the volume. There are with *Youth* (13.000) and *H of D*
(38.000?) say 50 to 52 thousand words ready. *Jim* being 20 or 30 thou:
would almost make up matter enough for a book. But—are 3 stories
only, enough? And supposing even I finished *Jim* in time could it go
serially into Maga before the date you contemplate? Besides I thought
of two other stories (more in the 'note' of my 'Maga' work) one of them
being called *First Command*[4] and the other (a sketch) entitled *A Seaman*.
These are not written. They creep about in my head but got to be caught
and tortured into some kind of shape. I think—I think they would turn
out good as good as (they say) *Youth* is. But the whole thing is complicated by my horrible inability to finish the *Rescue* for which McClure
has made arrangements. I must peg away at it.

It seems horribly ungrateful of me to talk about the difficulty of doing
what you wish, but I must face the consequences not of my neglect or
laziness but of positive ill-health which has caused the shameful delay
in writing the R. It is small consolation to think I could *not* help it
though I did my best. My best has been so very bad after all.

—Yet: if in your opinion *Youth*. *H of D* and *Jim* would make a
volume I shall *try* to get *Jim* finished in April (my heart sinks when I
think how days pass and how slow my work is). In that case I would
forego the serial pub: of *Jim* not to delay the appearance of the volume.

---

4. Ancestor of *The Shadow-Line* (1917).

I only can say I shall *try*. I dare say no more after my recent experiences as to being punctual. The Vol of the 3 stories would not be positively bad. Whether you would judge such a publication opportune or not I shall do my best to finish *Jim* in April.

Even in the matter of the title I am unable to answer you decisively. I've not thought of it yet—and it is by no means easy to invent something telling and comprehensive. "Youth and Other Tales" would not do? I wish to convey the notion of something lived through and remembered. *Tales from Memory*(.?) you may think a clumsy title. It is so. I don't seem able to think of anything to-night. Why not: "Three Tales" by Joseph Conrad. Flaubert (mutatis mutandis)[5] published Trois contes.[6] The titles of the three tales could be printed on the cover in small capitals thus: Youth; A Narrative. Heart of Dark: Jim: A sketch. That is only if the vol: is to be of the three stories. Pardon the lenght* of this letter, and the unsatisfactory nature of its contents. I *am* an unsatisfactory person, and to no one more than to myself.

To Edward Garnett   [June 1899]

This is the sort of rot I am writing now. Frankly it is not worth troubling about but still I send you this—the first part of a B'wood story in two parts.

To David Meldrum   6th July 99

Herewith 3 chap:[rs] 31 pp. of Lord Jim, or to speak correctly two complete chapters and as much of the third as is ready.

Confiding in Your friendly offices I ask you for a typewritten copy of this batch for myself, together with the return of my own type. The text is pretty correct as it stands now and any small changes I may wish to make shall wait till I get the proof from Maga. This is not enough for one instalment but I will be sending you pages (a few at a time) and work at it steadily till the end. I trust the end of the month will come together with the end of the story. Youre* good letter has cheered me. The story will improve as it goes on. You will arrange the time for publication with McClure; I should not like to lose the American serial of this story if it can be avoided.

The story will be fully 40000 words and I shall ask Mr Blackwood for £120 which is a little more than the agreed rate but expect to do more work for Maga before the year is out—that is if you want me—and make it right in that way. We must talk this matter over when we meet next as I have had proposals made for a series of short stories (or rather short serials) and would like to know M[r] B'wood's intentions. I may say

5. Necessary changes having been made (Latin).
6. *Three Tales* (1877), by Gustave Flaubert (1821–80). It includes "A Simple Heart," much admired by Conrad and Ford.

at once that I would rather work for *Maga* at a less rate than those people offer me; but some revision of terms must take place. However there is plenty of time for that discussion. The important thing now for me is to get rid of my deplorable Jim with honour and satisfaction to all concerned.

To David Meldrum   31ˢᵗ July 99

Here's the end of Chap III. Chap IV whole and the beginning of Chap V. pp of my type *32 to 50* which I should like to be doubly copied— one set for me and the other for E'burgh.

I shall be sending you MS almost daily if only a few pages at a time keeping it up till the end which, I pray, may be soon but is not in sight yet—not by a long way.

                              *   *   *

These three tales will make a thick vol or I am much mistaken. Jim may turn out longer than *H of D* even. Whether as good?—that's a question. Let us hope.

To David Meldrum   [10/11 August 1899]

As to Jim: I think that September *is* safe *quite*. Strictly speaking you have enough for two instalments now in hand. If you divide in that way the story may run into 4 Noˢ. But even if you distribute the whole into three I am confident of coming to time.[7] This work isn't like the *Rescue* where I aim at purely [a]esthetic (if I dare say so) effects. I am now in tolerable health. There's really nothing to stand in the way of a happy termination of Jim's troubles; and its as likely as not the story will be finished a long time before the second instalment comes out.

If America is in the way of the dates I shall not write any slower for it. I *never mean* to be slow. The stuff comes out at its own rate. I am always ready to put it down; nothing would induce me to lay down my pen if I *feel* a sentence—or even a word ready to my hand. The trouble is that too often—alas!—I've to wait for the sentence—for the word.

What wonder then that during the long blank hours the doubt creeps into the mind and I ask myself whether I am fitted for that work. The worst is that while I am thus powerless to produce my imagination is extremely active: whole paragraphs, whole pages, whole chapters pass through my mind. Everything is there: descriptions, dialogue, reflexion—everything—everything but the belief, the conviction, the only thing needed to make me put pen to paper. I've thought out a volume in a day till I felt sick in mind and heart and gone to bed, completely done up, without having written a line. The effort I put out

---

7. "*Lord Jim* ran for fourteen monthly issues of *Blackwood's*, starting in October; Conrad finished the manuscript in July 1900" [Karl and Davies].

should give birth to masterpieces as big as mountains—and it brings forth a ridiculous mouse now and then.

Therefore I must sell my mice as dear as I can since I must live; that's why I beg you very earnestly to arrange matters so as not to give McClure any excuse for losing my Am: Ser: rights of *Jim*.[8] It looks as if I were very mercenary but, God knows, it is not so. I am impatient of material anxieties and they frighten me too because I feel how mysteriously independent of myself is my power of expression. It is there—I believe—and some thought, and a little insight. All this is there; but I am not as the workmen who can take up and lay down their tools. I am, so to speak, only the agent of an unreliable master.

David Meldrum to William Blackwood   18 August 1899

For the story itself—'let's see the end of it' is what I feel myself saying. I think it will come out as well as the 'Heart of Darkness': both, to my mind, want the 'form' of *Youth*.

To David Meldrum   22 Aug^st 99

I've dispatched today 12 pp. more of Jim—addressed to the office. More would have been sent but my wife not being very well could not type yesterday. They shall be coming in very soon: I am going straight ahead with Jim and am rather pleased with him so far.

To William Blackwood   22 Aug^st 99

I am glad you like Jim so far. Your good opinion gives one confidence. From the nature of things treated the story can not be as dramatic (in a certain sense) as the *H of D*. It is certainly more like *Youth*. It is however longer and more varied. The structure of it is a little loose—this however need not detract from its interest—from the "general reader" point of view. The question of *art* is so endless, so involved and so obscure that one is tempted to turn one's face resolutely away from it. I've certainly an idea—apart from the idea and the subject of the story—which guides me in my writing, but I would be hard put to it if requested to give it out in the shape of a fixed formula. After all in this as in every other human endeavour one is answerable only to one's conscience.

I have this day sent off another 3000 words to your London office. 2000 more are actually written or rather scrawled and awaiting the domestic typewriter. I devote myself exclusively to *Jim*. I find I can't live with more than one story at a time. It's a kind of literary monogamism. You know how desperately slow I work. Scores of notions present

8. "In the United States, *Lord Jim* appeared as a book (Doubleday, McClure), but not as a serial" [Karl and Davies].

themselves—expressions. suggest themselves by the dozen, but the inward voice that decides:—this is well—this is right—is not heard sometimes for days together. And meantime one must live!

To John Galsworthy[9]   2nd Sept. 99

Dear of you to drop me a line to think of me and my work. You have no idea how your interest in me *keeps me up*. I am unutterably weary of thinking, of writing, of seeing of feeling of living.

Jim will be finished end this month. I plod on without much faith. Its money. Thats all.

To Edward Garnett   16th Sept 99

I am writing—it is true—but this is only piling crime upon crime: every line is odious like a bad action. I mean odious to me—because I still have some pretences to the possession of a conscience though my morality is gone to the dogs. I am like a man who has lost his gods. My efforts seem unrelated to anything in heaven and everything under heaven is impalpable to the touch like shapes of mist. Do you see how easy writing must be under such conditions? Do you see? Even writing to a friend—to a person one has heard, touched, drank* with, quar[r]elled with—does not give me a sense of reality. All is illusion— the words written, the mind at which they are aimed, the truth they are intended to express, the hands that will hold the paper, the eyes that will glance at the lines. Every image floats vaguely in a sea of doubt— and the doubt itself is lost in an unexpected universe of incertitudes.

To E. L. Sanderson   12 Oct 99

Style or no style—I am *not* the man. And oh! dear Ted—it *is* a fool's business to write fiction for a living. It is indeed.

It is strange. The unreality of it seems to enter one's real life, penetrate into the bones, make the very heart beats pulsate illusions through the arteries. One's will becomes the slave of hallucinations, responds only to shadowy impulses, waits on imagination alone. A strange state, a trying experience, a kind of fiery trial of untruthfulness. And one goes through it with an exaltation as false as all the rest of it. One goes through it—and there's nothing to show at the end. Nothing! Nothing Nothing!

---

9. While Conrad was first mate of the clipper ship *Torrens*, he made, in 1893, lifelong friendships with two young English passengers: John Galsworthy (1867–1933), who became a very successful novelist and playwright; Edward Lancelot ("Ted") Sanderson (1867–1939), who was a teacher at, and ultimately the headmaster of, a boys' preparatory school.

To David Meldrum   [24 October 1899]

Here's some more Jim. The Jany inst is well advanced if not wholly
finished. I've dispatched the proofs and additional type for the Dec^{er}
Number yesterday, proposing that the inst^t should include Chap VIII if
possible. I hope they will see their way. In that case Jan and Febr
instalments without being unduly long will contain the end of the story.

To Edward Garnett   26 Otc^{er}* 99

Thanks for your letter. If I don't send proofs or type it is because there
is, alas, so little to send and what there is, is not worthy. I *feel* it bad;
and, unless I am hopelessly morbid, I can not be altogether wrong. So
much I am conceited; I fancy that I know a good thing when I see it.

   I am weary of the difficulty of it. The game is not worth the candle;
of course there is no question of throwing up the hand. It must be played
out to the end but it is the other men who hold the trumps and the
prospect is not inspiriting.

                              *   *   *

As to Jim. I entreat you: wait till the 2^d inst: comes out (in a few days)
and I shall send you the two together. The first is too bad to stand alone.
The fifth (and last inst) is not written yet—and what it will be God only
knows.

To E. L. Sanderson   26th Oct. 99

My dearest Ted your letter did me good. It is *great* to hear you talk like
this of my work. I wish I could be sure the partiality of your affection
does not mislead you. Ah my dear fellow. If You knew how ambitious
I am, how my ambition checks my pen at every turn. Doubts assail me
from every side. The doubt of form—the doubt of tendency—a mistrust
of my own conceptions—and scruples of the moral order. Ridiculous
—isn't it? As if my soul mattered to the universe! But even as the ant
bringing its grain of sand to the common edifice may justly think itself
important, so I would like to think that I am doing my appointed work.

To William Blackwood   7 Oct 99

The greater part of the Ja^{ny} inst. is written and practically ready; some
of it in London for a fair copy and seventeen pages on the table before
me to be pecked at, slashed, turned over, for two days more, and depart
for Paternoster Row on Monday. I *am* glad you like it—for tho' the
thing were not absolutely bad it might not have been exactly to your
mind. The beginning wobbles a good deal; I did cut up shamefully the
proofs without being able to put it firmly on its feet; however my little
band of faithfuls professes itself (in various letters) to be immensely

pleased. You express yourself hopefully about the book. You may be sure that none of your kind words are wasted. The man here wants them, wants everything he can get of such genuine encouragement.

To David Meldrum [30 October 1899]

My mind is eased by what you say about Jim's lenght.* It would be to my interest to cut it short as possible, but I would just as soon think of cutting off my head. With kind regards from us both

To William Blackwood 8th Nov 99

I shall *without fail* dispatch tomorrow the corr^d proofs of the Dec^{er} instalment—and also some more typed matter. The last[1] number of Jim is practically ready and Febr is on the way to completion. The March issue will see the end of the story—and of the Vol: * * * Just now it is all for Jim! And no amount of sacrifice seems too much for him.

To Edward Garnett [19 November 1899]

I also send you 2d inst of *Jim*—which is too wretched for words. It would have been less shocking if it had included another chapter.

To Edward Garnett [24 November 1899]

You are a dear good old critic—you are! You've a way of saying things that would make an old sign-post take to writing. You put soul and spunk into me—You, so to speak, bamboozle me into going on—and going on and going on. You can detect the shape of a mangled idea and the shadow of an intention in the worst of one's work—and you make the best of it. You would almost persuade me that I exist. Almost!

To David Meldrum 25 Nov 99.

I am still at Jim. I've sent 6 more pages yesterday. I shall send 7 more today to end Chap XIII. The Story will be finished of course this year. I trust they will give me as much space as possible in the Jan. Febr. & Mch numbers. I shall want all I can get.

To David Meldrum 3^d Dec 99

In the matter of space—if Maga gives room in Jany N^o to all *nearly all* of the copy I am sending to-morrow the end of the story may be divided between the Febr^y and March numbers.

1. Latest; i.e., January issue.

To Hugh Clifford[2]   13th Dec 99

And this brings me naturally to *Jim*. Perfectly right! Your criticism is just and wise but the whole story is made up of such side shows just because the main show is not particularly interesting—or engaging I should rather say. I want to put into that sketch a good many people I've met—or at least seen for a moment—and several things overheard about the world. It is going to be a hash of episodes, little thumbnail sketches of fellows one has rubbed shoulders with and so on. I crave your indulgence; and I think that read in the lump it will be less of a patchwork than it seems now.

To David Meldrum   [17 December 1899]

I send here a MS lot of Jim which would be most of the Febr^y instalment. My poor wife is too taken up just now with domestic worries to be able to type for me and I do not want to stop the trickle of copy.

   The lot published and in proof together at present in Edinburgh amounts to 40000 words already. I trust I am not making myself objectionable by unduly lenghtening* my contribution. * * * I still think I shall finish the story this year.

William Blackwood to Conrad   decr 22. 99

Glad to hear you are within sight of the end. The story I think makes good progress and promises to come out well. It will probably be April before I can publish the last instalment as I was obliged to shorten the January part from what was settled upon, owing to pressure upon my space caused by some long articles which could not be longer delayed.

To William Blackwood   26th Dec 99

The tale progresses and in five more days' time it will be still nearer the end which seems well in view now. I say seems, because I do suffer at times from optical delusions (and others) where my work is concerned.

                              *   *   *

the forthcoming volume [will] be a fat book—and not, perhaps, well balanced to the eye. Still we are in for it now I fancy. *Lord Jim* would have hardly the lenght* and certainly has not the sub[s]tance to stand alone; and the three tales, each being inspired by a similar moral idea (or is it only one of my optical delusions?) will make (in that sense) a homogeneous book. Of the matter I am not ashamed and the mere size

2. Sir Hugh Clifford (1866–1941) was a colonial administrator in Malaya when he wrote one of the first general accounts of Conrad's fiction (p. 396). Clifford subsequently held many administrative posts in the Far East and Africa and was also a prolific writer.

won't, I hope, militate against such commercial success as is within my reach.

To David Meldrum   3ᵈ Jan 1900

I am sending by this post a batch of MS. Lord Jim to end Ch XVII. Of course the chapˢ. are short.

The next batch should be the last, unless I were to forward an instalment before the 15ᵗʰ instᵗ.

L. J. is a rather bad business for me on account of its length that is to say. Otherwise I am pleased with it and, I think, with some shadow of a reason.

But the artistic pleasure is neither here nor there. Bread is the thing.

To William Blackwood and Sons   7 Jan 1900

Herewith further instᵗ of Lord Jim p 376–394. *Chap.xviii.*

I trust You've received all eight previous instᵗˢ p. 342–375 sent by registered packet.

To David Meldrum   [9 January 1900]

I've sent off last Friday another inst of *Jim* Ch XVIII, rather longer than either of the three previous ones. I am driving on with the story and you may expect another Chap: shortly. And then the end! I do wish for the end. After the end a visit to you—if convenient. Even if Jess couldn't come I would take a run up to town. But the pressing necessity to write more hangs over me. I don't know when and how I will ever fight my way back to the *Rescue*. I try not to think of it.

To Edward Garnett   20 Jan. 1900.

You make my head whirl when you write like this. What a letter for a poor devil to get! You've knocked my evening's work on the head; I found it impossible to write any copy. You frighten me; because were I to let you take me up on these heights by your appreciation the fall before my own conscience's smile would be so heavy as to break every bone in my body. And yet what, oh! what would become of me if it were not for your brave words that warm like fire and feed like bread and make me drunk like wine!

No. I didn't know anything about *Jim*; and all I know now is that it pleases you; and I declare as true as there are blind, deaf-mute gods sitting above us (who are so clear-eyed; eloquent and sharp of hearing) I declare it is enough for me; for if you think that because I've not been sending you my MS., your opinion has ceased to be a living factor in my individual and artistic existence, you are lamentably mistaken. I was simply afraid. And I am afraid still. You see the work fragmentarily; and the blessed thing is so defective that even that far within it you can not possibly (with all your penetration and sympathy) you cannot possibly know where I tend and how I shall conclude this most inconclusive attempt. You don't; and the truth is that it is not my depth but my shallowness which makes me so inscrutable (?). Thus, (I go cold to think) the surprise reserved for you will be in the nature of a chair withdrawn from under one; something like a bad joke—it will strike you no doubt. Bad and vile. Now had you taken the whole thing the fall would not have been so heavy, I imagine.

To William Blackwood   12 Febr 1900

I've had an exceedingly rough time of it since the 25th of last month when beginning with a severe fit of malaria I continued with bronchities* and an attack of gout, giving my wife a variety entertainment. The poor woman can hardly stand, and as to myself I managed yesterday to totter downstairs for the first time.

This sorry news will explain my delay in returning proofs of Maga: and book,˙and the stoppage of further copy.

To-day (monday) I send off proofs of chap. xvi and xvii and also proofs of book, up to page 208. I have yet ch xviii in proof, which I shall forward very soon together with two more chaprs of copy. After these another two chapters will see the end of Jim.

You have no idea what an anxious time I had. The illness looked much more serious than it has turned out to be and the thought of 'copy' nearly distracted me. All's well that ends well.

To David Meldrum   14 Febr 1900

In an hour we shall leave here to go to H. G. Wells for two days. It'll do me good I think and perhaps when I get back I shall be able to grapple with pen ink and paper. I haven't done anything yet tho' my head is full (too full) of Jim's end but when it comes to putting it down black on white the brain wanders. When I start 10 days will be enough to finish the thing.

David Meldrum to William Blackwood   16 February 1900

On my return from Edinburgh I got a letter from Conrad that he was ill, and knowing the nervous condition of the man I delayed pressure on him to wind up "Jim". I am sorry that the length of "Jim" doesn't suit *Maga* which I can well understand; but, on the other hand, it makes it a more important story—it is a great story now—and in the annals of *Maga* half a century hence it will be one of the honourable things to record of her that she entertained "Jim." I only wish that "Charlotte"[3] whom you are good enough to honour with permit to follow in "Jim's" steps were at all likely to do the old lady such credit.

To William Blackwood   20th Febr 1900

Many thanks for your letter. When it arrived here I was away in Sandgate (only seven miles from here) staying with H.G. Wells for a much needed change.

It has done me some good so that yesterday I got hold of Jim again. When I get into the stride a fortnight will see the end of the story, though I shall not hurry myself since the end of a story is a very important and difficult part; the *most* difficult for me, to execute—that is. It is always *thought out* before the story is begun.

To Edward Garnett   26 Mch 1900

I am still at *Jim*. I've been beastly ill in Febr[y]. Jessie is hunting all over the house for the *Febr[y]* N[o3] to send you. I am old and sick and in debt—but lately I've found I can still write—*it* comes! *it* comes!—and I am young and healthy and rich.

The question is *will* I ever <u>write</u> anything?

I've been cutting and slashing whole pars out of Jim. How bad Oh! how bad! Why is it that a weary heaven has not pulverised me with a wee little teeny weeny thunderbolt?

To David Meldrum   3 Ap. 1900

I am sending a fresh inst. of *Jim* and now I start to write the last chap.

*   *   *

I've been horribly disappointed by the shortness of the inst[t] in the Ap. N[o] the more so that the break just there destroyed an effect. If one only could do without serial publication! Don't think me an ungrateful beast. Jim is very near my heart. I don't apologise now for springing on M[r] Blackwood such a long affair and for the unfortunate dragging manner of its production. Apologies butter no parsnips—to adapt the popular saying. It won't happen again.

To William Blackwood   12 Ap. 1900

Yesterday I sent off to Edinburgh proofs of Maga and book, together with an instalment of type-written matter, and to London a batch of further MS. I feel the need of telling you that I've done something anyway and to assure you that *Lord Jim has* an end, which last I am

---

3. Meldrum's novel *The Conquest of Charlotte* appeared in *Blackwood's Magazine*, July 1901–July 1902.

afraid you may be beginning to doubt. It has though—and I am now trying to write it out. A dog's life! this writing out, this endlessness of effort and this endless discontent; with remorse, thrown in, for the massacre of so many good intentions.

This by the way. The real object of this letter is to tell you that should you find Jim unconscionably long (for Maga—I mean) I am ready to shorten (what remains) by excision. I am however in such a state of mind about the story—so inextricably mixed up with it in my daily life—that I feel unequal to doing the cutting myself; so, addressing you in your character of Editor of *Maga*, I declare my readiness to make conscientious joints, if the parts that can be taken out are marked for me and the MS with such indications is returned. I would not keep it for more than a day or two—and, as (I trust) you will have the story complete in a week or so, there would be time to look through it before the copy is required for setting up.

William Blackwood to Conrad   April 24th 1900

I was glad to receive a further instalment of "Lord Jim". I have now the pleasure of enclosing you proof in duplicate.

I do not think the story loses anything by the method of telling. I would not recommend any cutting down in these three chapters merely for the sake of bringing the serial issue to an earlier close. The end must now justify the length of the story, & to hurry it up for any reason but the right one be assured would be a mistake. I therefore as heretofore leave you a free hand with regard to it. But do not from anything I have said expand it to a greater length than you have already sketched out.

William Blackwood and Sons to Conrad   15 May 1900

We duly received to-day the revised proof of the Magazine portion of Lord Jim and a further instalment of copy, namely, chapters 28, 29, 30 and the beginning of 31. The story has now exceeded the original estimate of its extent and Mr. Blackwood has had under his consideration the exact publication of Lord Jim and the other two stories "Youth" and Heart of Darkness. The printers started the book form of these stories on a comparatively close page on the understanding the Lord Jim would end with at the latest the June number of Maga. But we now find that even in this close page Lord Jim will run to at least 320 pages and we conclude from the portion you sent today that there is still a further instalment to come which may possibly add 10 pages more to the book. In consultation with Mr. Blackwood to-day he indicates that the proof returned this morning and the new copy will run him into the August number of the magazine at least if not also into September and he suggests that it would be advisable to your interest as well as in his own that Lord Jim should be made a separate volume and be published not later than the middle of September by which time the last instalment will have appeared in Maga or at any rate there will be little more of the serial issue to follow that date.

This suggestion of course somewhat alters the arrangement for the volume "Three tales of Sea and Land" but we presume there will be no difficulty on your part in allowing Youth and Heart of Darkness (which are now set up in type and of which plates have been made) to lie in our hands until you are able to add one or two more stories which would make up a reasonable crown 8vo volume to sell at 6/—or may be 3/6.

To David Meldrum   19th May 1900

Now the proposal has come from Mr Blackwood the thing seems unavoidable. Perhaps the story will please. Perhaps! I would like to know what you think. I am too fond of it myself to be very hopeful. It has not been planned to stand alone. *H of D* was meant in my mind as a foil, and *Youth* was supposed to give the note. All this is foolishness—no doubt. The public does not care—can not possibly care—for foils and notes. But it cares for stories and *Jim* is as near a story as I will ever get. The title will have to be altered to *Lord Jim*. A *tale*—instead of A *sketch*. And yet it is a sketch! I would like to put it as A *simple tale* A *plain tale*—something of the sort—if possible. No matter.

*   *   *

Lord Jim should be considered separately of course. It will be (it seems incredible) of, apparently, 100000 words or very little short of that.

To Ford Madox Ford   Monday [9 July 1900]

I really hope to be done on Thursday and we shall arrive[4] on Monday. I am in a state of excitement. You'll be either struck with what I am doing now or else find it beneath contempt. I don't know anything myself except that it is either hit or miss with it. Devil only knows.

To William Blackwood   [14 July 1900][5]

The last word of Lord Jim is written but before I retire to rest I must with the same impulse, the same dip of the pen as it were say a word to you.

Whatever satisfaction I have now or shall have out of the book I owe

---

4. Ford's and Conrad's families were meeting in Bruges for a vacation together.
5. "This is 'the letter penned after sunrise on the fourteenth' (to Blackwood, 18 July). Meldrum wrote to Blackwood on Saturday, 14 July, 'Fortunately, I was in the office this morning when Conrad called with the conclusion of *Jim*, which went off to the type-writer [i.e., typist] *instanter*. He was, of course, in great spirits' (Blackburn, 104)." [Karl and Davies]

very much to you—not only in the way of material help but in the conditions which you have created for me to work in by your friendly and unwearied indulgence.

I feel I owe you also an apology—many apologies for this long work about which the only thing I am sure of is the good faith I brought to its writing. I can't say much more. I would like to express something that would not be mere banality. But I can't. I've been now for 23 hours at work and feel unable to collect my thoughts.

We should like to leave for Bruges on Wednesday next.[6] The type of the last part of MS will be sent to me here. I must live with the end for a bit. There are many places which a bit* judicious cutting would improve and so on. As there is enough copy set up to go on with I suppose I may take a little time. But it will be only a matter of few days at most. In a few hours I start for London with the last pages. I am too tired to feel either glad or sorry just now. But it is a relief of some sort.

William Blackwood to Conrad   18th July 1900

Your very kind letter of thanks for the help I may have afforded you in the writing of this book has gratified me much and I am only carrying out what has been the desire of all those who have gone before me in our connection with our authors.

To William Blackwood   18th July 1900.

It seems to me that *Lord Jim* as title for the book is meagre—perhaps misleading? Could not a sub-title be invented? I am hammering the sorry remnant of my brain without being able to get sound or sense out of it. Perhaps even thus *Lord Jim: A romance* in one line would be better. I feel it's a poor suggestion.[7]

Another matter, if it is not too late already, has occurred to me. Would it not be better seeing the form of the novel (personal narrative from a third party as it were) to dispense with the word *Chapter* throughout the book, leaving only the Roman numerals. After all, these divisions (some of them very short) are not chapters in the usual sense each carrying the action a step further or embodying a complete episode. I meant them only as pauses—rests for the reader's attention while he is following the development of *one* situation, only *one* really from beginning to end. I fear however that it may be now too late to make the alteration.[8]

6. "They left on Friday, 20 July." [Karl and Davies]
7. "The Blackwood edition calls it *A Tale*; the Doubleday, McClure, *A Romance*." [Karl and Davies]
8. "It was." [Karl and Davies]

To William Blackwood   19th July 1900

The end of Lord Jim in accordance with a meditated resolve is presented
in a bare almost bald relation of matters of fact. The situation—the
problem if you will—of that sensitive nature has been already commented upon, illustrated and contrasted. It is my opinion that in the
working out of the catastrophe psychologic disquisition should have no
place. The reader ought to know enough by that time. I enlarge a little
upon the new character which is introduced (that of Brown the desperate
adventurer) so as to preserve the sense of verisimilitude and for the sake
of final contrast; but all the rest is nothing but a relation of events—
strictly, a narrative.

   Pardon this egotism. My head is full of this thing yet.

To John Galsworthy   [20 July 1900]

The end of *L.J.* has been pulled off with a steady drag of 21 hours. I
sent wife and child out of the house (to London) and sat down at 9 am,
with a desperate resolve to be done with it. Now and then I took a walk
round the house out at one door in at the other. Ten-minute meals. A
great hush. Cigarette ends growing into a mound similar to a cairn over
a dead hero. Moon rose over the barn looked in at the window and
climbed out of sight. Dawn broke, brightened. I put the lamp out and
went on, with the morning breeze blowing the sheets of MS all over
the room. Sun rose. I wrote the last word and went into the dining
room. Six o'clock. I shared a piece of cold chicken with Escamillo[9]
(who was very miserable and in want of sympathy having missed the
child dreadfully all day). Felt very well only sleepy; had a bath at seven
and at 8.30 was on my way to London.

To Edward Garnett   12 Nov 1900

You are great and good.
   Yes! you've put your finger on the plague spot. The division of the
book into two parts which is the basis of your criticism demonstrates to
me once more your amazing insight; and your analysis of the *effect* of
the book puts into words precisely and suggestively the dumb thoughts
of every reader—and my own.
   Such is indeed the effect of the book; the effect which *you* can name
and others can only feel. I admit I strove for a great triumph and I have
only succeeded in giving myself utterly away. Nobody'll see it, but you
have detected me falling back with my lump of clay I had been lugging
up from the very bottom of the pit, with the idea of breathing big life
into it. And all I have done was to let it fall with a silly crash.

9. "Borys's dog, named after the toreador in *Carmen*, a present from Stephen Crane." [Karl and
   Davies]

For what is fundamentally wrong with the book—the cause of the effect—is want of power. I do not mean the 'power' of reviewer's jargon. I mean the want of *illuminating* imagination. I wanted to obtain a sort of lurid light out* the very events. You know what I have done—alas! I haven't been strong enough to breathe the right sort of life into my clay—the *revealing* life.

I've been satanically ambitious, but there's nothing of a devil in me, worse luck. The *Outcast* is a heap of sand, the *Nigger* a splash of water, *Jim* a lump of clay. A stone, I suppose will be my next gift to the impatient mankind—before I get drowned in mud to which even my supreme struggles won't give a simulacrum of life. Poor mankind! Drop a tear for it—but look how infinitely more pathetic *I* am! This Pathos *is* a kind of triumph no criticism can touch. Like the philosopher who crowed at the Universe I shall know when I am utterly squashed. This time I am only very bruised, very sore, very humiliated.

This is the effect of the book upon me; the intimate and personal effect. Humiliation. Not extinction. Not yet. All of you stand by me so nobly that I must still exist. There is *You*, always and never dismayed. I had an amazing note from Lucas. Amazing! This morning a letter came from Henry James.[1] Ah! You rub in the balm till every sore smarts—therefore I exist. The time will come when you shall get tired of tending this true and most well-intentioned sham—and then the end'll come too.

But keep up! keep up! Let me exhort you earnestly to keep up! as long as you can.

I send you the H.J. letter. A draught from the Fountain of Eternal Youth. Wouldn't you think a boy had written it? Such enthusiasm! Wonderful old man, with his record of wonderful work! It is, I believe seriously intended (the letter) as confidential. And to you alone I show it—keep *his* secret for us both. No more now.

Late in his life Conrad wrote in a friend's first English edition of *Lord Jim*:

When I began this story which some people think my best—personally I don't—I formed the resolve to cram as much character and episode into it as it could hold. This explains its great length which the tale itself does not justify.[2]

1. "Like nearly all Conrad's incoming correspondence, the letters from E. V. Lucas" (1868–1938), critic, journalist, humorist, and Henry James (1843–1916), great expatriate American novelist, "have vanished." [Karl and Davies]
2. *The Richard Curle Conrad Collection* (New York: American Art Association, 1927), item 35.

The Division, by Chapters, of the Monthly Installments of *Lord Jim: A Sketch* in *Blackwood's Edinburgh Magazine*

ERNEST W. SULLIVAN

The Several Endings of Joseph Conrad's *Lord Jim*†

Bibliographical evidence demonstrates that two rounds of revision (one at the very last minute) by Joseph Conrad created the different treatments of the final ten chapters in the three first editions of *Lord Jim*: the British first edition [B], *Lord Jim: A Tale* (Edinburgh and London: William Blackwood and Sons, 1900); the American first edition [A], *Lord Jim: A Romance* (New York: Doubleday & McClure Co., 1900); and the Canadian first edition [C], *Lord Jim: A Tale of the Sea* (Toronto: W. J. Gage & Company Limited, 1900). Contrary to what one might expect and contrary to their copyright dates, the American first edition contains the earliest state of the text beyond the point represented by sig. 2A in the British first edition, and the British, the latest. As the chronology of the states of the text and their relationships to each other become clear, so, too, does the significance of the revisions. Chapters thirty-six through forty-five chronicle Jim's demise in an episode dominated by "Gentleman Brown," a nefarious "latter-day buccaneer," South Seas

† (London: The Joseph Conrad Society, n.d.). Reprinted with permission of The Joseph Conrad Society, U.K. One footnote has been deleted.

"ruffian," and "blind accomplice of the Dark Powers" ([B], p. 381). The American and Canadian states of the text characterize Gentleman Brown as a grotesque embodiment of universal Dark Forces; the British first edition, as a recognizably human being. Humanizing Brown shifts the responsibility for Jim's fate from elemental, irrational forces outside himself (and therefore possibly outside his control) to his own human and personal failings.

The relevant bibliographical evidence is not usually complex, but a large amount of such evidence is required to explain the significance of the revisions. To simplify the presentation of the bibliographical evidence, I have divided it into two categories: first, that which establishes the existence of three distinct states of the text, and secondly, that which defines the chronological and other relationships among the three states.

I became aware that a bibliographical problem existed while collating the British first edition against the American first edition which had been typeset in America by Doubleday & McClure; the substantives of these editions generally agree up to sig. 2A of the British first edition (p. 369—chapter thirty-six begins on p. 362), but afterwards, the American first edition substantives disagree one hundred and eight times with those of the British first edition. In an effort to discover the source of these variants, I collated the text of the American first edition against that of the British Serial edition, *Lord Jim: A Sketch* which appeared in thirteen monthly installments in *Blackwood's Edinburgh Magazine* between November of 1899 and November of 1900 (vols. 166–68). I discovered that in the one hundred and eight cases in which the American first edition substantives disagreed with those of the British first edition, seventy-seven times the American first edition agreed with the Serial edition. Since sig. 2A begins a new sheet, I guessed that some delay in printing the British first edition had occurred in the second run of signatures and that Doubleday & McClure had simply grown impatient and used the Serial to set up the American first edition from sig. 2A on. This guess ignored the facts that thirty-one substantive readings from sig. 2A forward in the American first edition could not have come from the Serial edition and others had to have come from the theoretically as yet incomplete British first edition.

Comparison of the early chapters of the British and Canadian first editions on a Hinman collator seemed to confirm my conjecture about a delay by showing that these two editions had been printed with the same plates, or, more probably, with plates made from duplicate mats and were thus identical except for minor mat or plate damage.[1] Apparently, the British (and its Canadian twin) first edition represented Conrad's true intentions, and the American was copied from the Serial edition because the superior British first edition text was not available. Then I collated sig. 2A (p. 369) and discovered not only variant readings, but also that the plate for lines 8–16 in the British first edition differed entirely from the plate used for the corresponding lines 8–15 in the Canadian first edition. Collation of pages 369 to 451 in the British and Canadian first editions showed that while the plates of twenty-nine pages were identical,[2] the other fifty-three pages contained differences requiring resetting three hundred and fifty-seven lines of type and moving one hundred and forty-six pieces of plate. The fact that the Canadian and British first editions used twenty-nine identical plates in pages 369–451 proved that lack of access to the complete, original British first edition could not have caused their differences, as I had conjectured for the differences between the British and American first editions.

Time for a new hypothesis. Since the American and Canadian first editions both departed from the British first edition at the same point, Sig. 2A, I collated them against each other to see if they derived from the same text. From sig. 2A forward, the American and Canadian first editions agreed except for thirty-one substantive variants. These variants are clearly authorial (e.g., "told me" [A] *for* "said" [C], "slightly" [A] *for* "lightly" [C], "folk" [A] *for* "people" [C], "third" [A] *for* "last" [C], "fearfully" [A] *for* "despairingly" [C], "stooping over the body" [A] *for* "stooping" [C], and "sobbed violently" [A] *for* "sobbed on his shoulder" [C], and do not result from compositorial interference at Doubleday & McClure; thus, the American and Canadian first editions could not derive from the same copy-text. At this point, with the colophon and copyright stamp dates for the British and Canadian first editions suggesting that the British first edition preceded the Canadian—British, "*September 1899–July 1900*" and 28 February 1901; Canadian, "*October 1899–July 1900*" and 22 April 1901[3]—and with the American and Canadian first edition versions generally agreeing with each other against the British first edition, I hypothesized that after the British text was

---

1. The following examples of mat or plate damage (or of revisions made on the plates themselves) prove incidentally that the first thirty-five chapters of the Canadian first edition were printed independently in Canada and are not merely sheets run off the British first edition plates and shipped to Canada: province, (B, p. 11, l. 1) *and* province; suddenly (B, p. 179, l. 14) *and* suddenly.; Patusan (B, p. 296, l. 21) *and* Patusan.; thought,' (B, p. 321, l. 12) *and* thought,; some-/how.' (B, p. 321, ll. 13–14) *and* some-/how.; " 'My (B, p. 329, l. 1) *and* My. Pages 1–369 of the British and Canadian first editions were probably printed from duplicate mats made from a single type-setting: mats would have been much easier to ship and much less susceptible to damage than plates would have been.

2. After sig. 2A, the British and Canadian first editions used identical mats to make the plates for pages 370–71, 384, 386–88, 391, 394, 397, 399, 401, 403–14, 423, 428, 430, 441, 444, and 449.

3. Copyright stamp dates from British Library copies C. 70. c. 17. and 012622. ee. 29.

printed, Conrad decided to revise chapters thirty-six to forty-five and sent a list of revisions to America and mats incorporating his revisions for pages 369, 372–83, 385, 389–90, 392–93, 395–96, 398, 400, 402, 415–22, 424–27, 429, 431–40, 442–43, 445–48, and 450–51 to Canada. I envisioned essentially two states of the text: the British first edition and a revised state of the British first edition as embodied in the American and Canadian first editions. This new hypothesis had only two weaknesses: (1) when the American and Canadian first editions did agree with each other and against the British first edition, they agreed with the Serial edition, probably the earliest version of the text,[4] and authors rarely revise to an earlier state of the text; and (2) the thirty-one substantive variants between the American and Canadian first editions remained unexplained.

In an effort to resolve the weaknesses in my hypothesis, I conflated my collations of the Serial edition, and British, American, and Canadian first editions from the point represented by sig. 2A in the British first edition. This conflation deflated all of my previous hypotheses by establishing that the three first editions contain three distinct versions of the text from sig. 2A forward: the British first edition contains seventy-seven unique substantive readings; the American, thirty-one; and although the Canadian has none,[5] the absence of the unique British and American readings proved that it is not directly related to either.

The earlier elimination of the Serial edition as a source for the substantive differences among the British, American, and Canadian first editions and the established presence of three distinct versions of the text defined my bibliographical problem in its final form: the chronological relationship of the three versions and the source(s) of the variants had to be established. Unfortunately, except in rare cases (spelling and grammar errors, etc.) one cannot tell from the variants which are the original readings and which the revised; thus, the evidence provided by the variants which defined the bibliographical problem could not solve the problem.

The key evidence for determining the priority of the three versions came from the plates used in the British and Canadian first editions. We recall that these editions were printed with plates made from duplicate mats up until sig. 2A, but that from sig. 2A onward, three hundred and fifty-seven lines were reset and one hundred and forty-six plate sections relocated to form new plates. Examination on a Hinman collator

---

4. Chapters thirty-six to forty appear in the October 1900 *Blackwood's Edinburgh Magazine*, and forty-one to forty-five in the November 1900 issue.
5. The Canadian first edition reading "hat" (p. 401, l. 2) where the American and British first editions correctly read "that" obviously results from plate damage or improper inking and is thus not a unique reading in the same sense that the thirty-one American and seventy-seven British readings are.

dates the revisions after the text was in plate form—moving lines of moveable type would affect letter position, but the positions of letters in the unreset, but relocated, material remain unchanged. The revised plates would have been constructed as follows: (1) lines requiring revision would have been reset; (2) a new mat would have been made from the new typesetting and a partial plate made; (3) the part of the original plate containing the lines to be revised would be cut out; (4) the unrevised remainder of the original plate and the new partial plate would be aligned to keep the page appearance consistent with that of the unrevised pages; (5) the repositioned partial plates would be soldered to make the new plates and (6) the volume would be printed. One would expect that resetting three hundred and fifty-seven lines plus deleting or adding (depending on which state was the original) approximately thirteen lines of material, not to mention moving and soldering one hundred and forty-six pieces of plate, would produce printed pages containing substantial evidence of plate alteration. The Blackwood printers did an absolutely magnificent job of resetting and plate repair, however, and even on a Hinman collator, the evidence (largely due to paper and plate shrinkage and expansion) from plate section alignment is not conclusive, but even the finest printer could not disguise the effects of adding or deleting thirteen lines of material while simultaneously attempting to utilize as many of the original plates as possible. Thus the facts that all "full" pages in the Canadian first edition have thirty-three lines but that pages 372–78 and 436–37 of the British first edition have thirty-two and that the "incomplete" pages 379, 389, and 416 of the British first edition have fewer lines (2, 1, and 1 fewer respectively) than do the corresponding "incomplete" pages in the Canadian first edition prove the priority of the Canadian first edition state of the text from sig. 2A onward relative to that in the British first edition. Furthermore, the close resemblance of the American first edition to the Canadian suggests its priority relative to the British first edition.

With the priority of the states of the text clarified and with the help of some additional evidence, the exact sequence of revision can be inferred. Given the facts that Conrad marked up chapters thirty-two to thirty-five in a copy of the Serial edition now in the Berg collection at the New York Public Library, that many of his marked changes appear in the three versions of the first edition, and that the Blackwood records (provided to me by Professor Leon Higdon of Texas Tech University) show a credit of six pounds and sixteen shillings for "Maga type used" against a total cost of forty-five pounds and sixteen shillings for the first printing of the British first edition of *Lord Jim*, we can induce that Conrad marked Serial edition copy to serve as setting copy for the British first edition and that approximately sixty of the four hundred and fifty-one pages of the British first edition were set with type (rejustified from a double column format) also used for the later issues of the Serial edition.[6] After the type for the planned British first edition was set from the marked Serial edition copy, galley proofs would have been run off for Conrad to check and to make final revisions prior to pressing the mats for plates. The thirty-one readings in the American first edition which do not derive from the Serial edition and which do not show up in the Canadian and British first editions would be accounted for if the American first edition were set from these unrevised galley proofs, a hypothesis pretty much confirmed by a Conrad note in Richard Curle's copy of the American first edition of *Lord Jim*: "This is the first American edition, set up probably from English proofs, but neither revised nor in any other way corrected by me. It is probably much nearer the text of *B'wood's* Maga. than the first British ed. of book form" (*Notes By Joseph Conrad Written In A Set Of His First Editions In The Possession of Richard Curle With An Introduction and Explanatory Comments* [London: privately printed, 1925], p. 20). The American first edition, then, almost certainly derives from unrevised galley proofs pulled from the typesetting made from the marked Serial edition copy and, as its punctuation shows, heavily house-styled by Doubleday & McClure. The American first edition is thus the earliest state of the text and was very likely printed before Conrad made his final revisions.[7]

Conrad then revised the galley proofs, making the thirty-one minor (but clearly authorial) substantive changes that differentiate the American and Canadian first editions, the revisions were incorporated into the typesetting, and duplicate mats were made—one set to be sent to W. J. Gage & Company Limited for printing the Canadian first edition, and one set retained by William Blackwood and Sons for printing the British first edition. The Canadian first edition was also very probably printed before Conrad made his final round of revisions.

Blackwood then took the mats made from the typesetting of Conrad's revised galley proofs, made lead plates, and ran off what Blackwood must have thought was a last round of galley proofs so that Conrad could check the plates. It is at this last moment before publication, with the text already set in plate form and ready to publish, that Conrad decided

6. The type for the October and November 1900 issues, containing the equivalent of eighty-nine pages of the British first edition, could easily have been saved for use in the October 1900 British first edition.

7. Even though the American first edition almost certainly represents the earliest state of the text of the three first editions, it was not certainly published prior to the British first edition which contains Conrad's final revisions: Conrad wanted very much to make the revisions, but his indifference about his texts published outside England means that he might not have made any effort to furnish Doubleday & McClure with his revisions even if the American first edition was not then set in type: "Conrad always regarded his English book-text as the one that mattered. He was not much concerned about perfecting his text for serial publication and not greatly concerned, even, if the American book-text was not his finally revised one" (Curle, footnote, p. 16).

to re-revise from sig. 2A on. Blackwood's records show a charge of fourteen shillings for "Deleted Matter," ten pounds and six shillings for "Alterations," and four pounds and one shilling for "Stereo mendings"; these charges prove the revisions involved not only resetting type, but also work on the plates—exactly the revision process indicated by the Hinman collator evidence. Thus, the bibliographical evidence establishes that the American first edition represents the earliest state of the text following sig. 2A in the British first edition and that the state of the text in the British first edition represents Conrad's final intentions for the ending of *Lord Jim* at the time of the publication of the three first editions.

With the priority of the states of the text and the order of the revisions clearly established, analysis of Conrad's changing intentions for the ending of *Lord Jim* can proceed. The changes were extensive: there are only thirty-one substantive variants totalling forty-six words between the American and Canadian first editions after the point represented by sig. 2A in the British first edition; however, there are seventy-seven substantive variants between the British first edition and its immediate predecessor, the Canadian first edition, after sig. 2A, and these variants include a total two hundred and ninety-eight words, with thirteen of the variants changing more than five words and ten adding or deleting an entire sentence. A variety of motives prompted the revisions—brevity, clarification, changes in the characterization of Jewel, Jim, Kassim, and Tamb' Itam—but the predominant changed intention, encompassing forty-five of the one hundred and eight substantive variants and one hundred and ninety-nine of the three hundred and forty-four total word changes from the American through the British first editions, involves the characterization of Jim's nemesis, Gentleman Brown, whom we first meet on the page following sig. 2A. That Conrad's major concern in the revisions was the characterization of Gentleman Brown is particularly clear on page 372 of the British and Canadian first editions. Conrad deleted eighty-five words from the description of Brown in the Canadian version. When Conrad's narrator, Marlow, changes the topic from Brown, "So much as to Brown, for the present" (C, 1. 20), the variants cease—the next variant of any sort, accidental or substantive, does not occur until the clearly accidental loss of two periods from an ellipsis on page 373 of the Canadian first edition (1.22).

In both the earlier and later states of the text, Brown is "a blind accomplice of the Dark Powers" (B, p. 381) and "moved by some complex intention" (B, p. 380), but, in the earlier states, Brown embodies a grotesque, superhuman evil, whereas in the British first edition state, Brown has been humanized to the point that the struggle between Brown and Jim becomes a psychological drama rather than a battle against allegorical evil.

In the earlier versions, Brown is a physical grotesque: his physical appearance suggests that he is one of the Dark Powers, not merely their unwitting agent. In the British first edition, Conrad deletes the grotesque elements of Brown's appearance. For example, Conrad eliminates "You could see his coarse lips turn blue behind the drooping, wiry hairs" (Serial, p. 552; A, p. 323; and C, p. 372), drops "writhing" from "his blue writhing lips" (Serial, p. 568; A, p. 349; and C, p. 402)—thereby dropping the satanic implications of "writhing"—and drops "bony" from "livid bony hand" (Serial, p. 691; A, p. 361; and C, p. 416), eliminating an image of Brown as the hand of Death. Deleted early descriptions of Brown's imminent departure from this mortal coil had made Brown seem personally attended by the powers of Death and Destruction: "I was only afraid that death, hovering over him, would swoop down suddenly and baffle my desire to know" (Serial, p. 552; A, p. 324; and C, p. 372).

As Brown becomes less a physical grotesque, less immediately in the physical presence of the Dark Powers, so, too, does he become less a moral grotesque. Conrad deletes the following descriptions of Brown's evil nature: "with a gleeful ferocity and a savage, unforgiving contempt for poor Jim" (Serial, p. 552; A, p. 323; C, p. 372) and "I knew the story before, of course; he [Brown] had only cleared up an obscure point, though the profound blackness of the act [the betrayal of Jim] cannot be dispelled" (Serial, p. 552; A, p. 324; C, p. 372). Brown goes from "roasting them [the Patusan natives]" to "roasting their toes" (B, p. 385), and (though not as a natural consequence) the natives grow less restless about Brown's presence—Conrad deletes "Their temper was unforgiving. The Bugis especially were exasperated" (Serial, p. 562; A, p. 339; and C, p. 390). Brown's motives for his violent and evil actions become more sympathetic (he goes from "fear" to "terror" [B, p. 382] at the thought of going to prison, and, instead of bribing his jailors with mere "dollars," he readily gives up his "little all" [B, p. 382]). Even the missionary husband of the woman Brown is about to run off with moves from a "hope" to an "intention" (B, p. 415) of saving Brown's soul. The later Gentleman Brown is still darkened by sin, but he no longer moves in "profound darkness."

And as Brown becomes less satanic, his superhuman evil powers diminish. Conrad deletes Brown's special powers of observation in finding the back channel from which he and his men attack and kill Dain Waris: "Both its entrances were so narrow and overgrown that the very natives passing in canoes had to look for them carefully" (Serial, p. 703;

A, p. 379; and C, pp. 436–7). Brown's loss of superhuman evil powers also diminishes his ability to work evil in Jim's life—as Brown's exiting boat towers over Jim in the fog, Conrad changes its "high shadow" to a "shadow" (B, p. 432).

Abundant bibliographical evidence, then, demonstrates that while *Blackwood's Edinburgh Magazine* was publishing chapters thirty-six to forty-five in its October and November 1900 issues and the American, Canadian, and British first editions of *Lord Jim* were being published in late 1900, Conrad was having second and third thoughts about the mechanism through which he wanted Jim to meet his end. Conrad changed his characterization of Jim's nemesis, Gentleman Brown, from a grotesque, allegorical embodiment of the Dark Powers to a recognizably human form of evil. This changed characterization of Jim's foe inevitably alters Jim's own nature from Saint George battling supernatural evil to "one of us," just another struggler against the darkness in human nature.

SOURCES

Conrad's Eastern seas. From Norman Sherry, *Conrad's Eastern World* (Cambridge and New York: Cambridge UP, 1966). Reproduced by permission of the publisher.

NORMAN SHERRY

The Pilgrim-Ship Episode†

[*Lord Jim* derives largely from Conrad's experiences as a merchant seaman in those Eastern seas from which, as he wrote, He "carried away into [his] writing life the greatest number of suggestions." Between the years 1883 and 1888, Conrad spent in all only a few months in Eastern waters. He made three visits—March 15 to the beginning of May 1883; September 22 to October 19, 1885; and July 1, 1887, to March 1888. During these visits he came to know only three areas at all well—the port of Singapore; the port of Bangkok, capital of Thailand; and a trading post on the River Berau in Dutch East Borneo. And his knowledge of these areas was further limited by the nature of his calling—that of a mariner, with all it implies of brief contacts with lands and peoples and with that contact further limited, for the most part, to members of the seafaring class.

It is not surprising that his most famous novel of the East should be based on a sea disaster involving a pilgrim ship that was abandoned at sea by her captain and officers. The incident caused a great scandal in London and Singapore, and was the subject of two inquiries, one at Aden and one at Singapore; a debate in the Singapore Legislative Assembly; and a question in the British House of Commons. My first section deals, therefore, with the pilgrim-ship episode and Conrad's contact with it.

For the second part of his novel, Conrad drew on his limited knowledge of conditions at the trading post on the River Berau in Borneo, and the second section here sets out what has been discovered of those conditions. But this knowledge was not sufficient, and Conrad consequently turned to a third source—travel books and accounts of men who had lived most of their lives and often made their fortunes in that part of the world.

Although much of the information that follows is given through documents, it should be remembered that Conrad probably obtained a great deal of his knowledge from what he called "marine shore talk," i.e., the gossip of seamen, and also from his own observation.]

The steamship *Jeddah*, owned by the Singapore Steamship Company, was used to carry Muslim pilgrims from Singapore to Jeddah, an Arabian port on the Red Sea. She left Singapore on July 17, 1880, on one of these trips with almost a thousand pilgrims on board, calling at Penang, crossing the strait of Malacca and the Bay of Bengal, and passing Cape Guardafui on her way to Jeddah.

On August 10 she was reported to have foundered off Cape Guardafui with the loss of all those on board except the captain and officers and

† This essay draws upon materials contained in Norman ·Sherry's *Conrad's Eastern World* (Cambridge and New York: Cambridge, 1966), to whom grateful acknowledgment is made.

a few others. The *Globe*, London, reported the loss with these headlines: DREADFUL DISASTER AT SEA. LOSS OF NEARLY 1000 LIVES. But on the following day it was learned that, after a stormy passage during which the *Jeddah*'s boilers had given trouble and she developed a leak, the ship and her passengers had in fact been abandoned on August 8 by her European captain and officers. They had been picked up by the steamship *Scindia* and taken to Aden, where they reported that the *Jeddah* had foundered. The appearance of the *Jeddah* at Aden a day later, towed in by the steamship *Antenor* with her passengers still on board, sparked a scandal and subsequent inquiry.

These cables were received by Syed Muhammad bin Alsagoff, Managing Director of the Singapore Steamship Company, as reported in the *Singapore Daily Times*, August 12, 1880:

> Aden, 10th August 8:20 P.M.
> *Jeddah* foundered. Self, wife, Syed Omar, 18 others saved.
> Clark[1]

> Aden, 11th August 9:15 P.M.
> *Antenor* towed down here *Jeddah* full of water. All life saved, now in charge of Government. Telegraph further particulars tomorrow. Omar gone Jeddah last night.

The next documents are from the *London Times* of August 11 (second edition) and August 12, 1880:

TERRIBLE DISASTER AT SEA

(REUTER'S TELEGRAM.)

ADEN, AUG. 10.

The steamer Jeddah, of Singapore, bound for Jeddah, with 953 pilgrims on board, foundered off Cape Guardafui on the 8th inst. All on board perished, excepting the captain, his wife, the chief officer, the chief engineer, the assistant engineer, and 16 natives. The survivors were picked up by the steamer Scindia and landed here.

ADEN, AUG. 11, 7.50 P.M.

The Jeddah, which was abandoned at sea with 953 pilgrims on board, did not founder, as reported by the master. She has just arrived here, all safe, in tow of the steamer Antenor.

(FROM LLOYD'S.)

Lloyd's agent at Aden, telegraphing under date August 11, 8.40 p.m., announces that the report of the steamer Jeddah having foundered off Guardafui on the 8th of August, and that upwards of 1,000 lives had been lost, is erroneous. The Jeddah has been

---

1. Joseph Lucas Clark, master of the *Jeddah*.

towed into Aden by the steamer Antenor, belonging to the Ocean Steamship Company. Crew and passengers saved.

The Jeddah, a screw steamer of 1,541 tons, was built at Dumbarton in 1872, and owned by the Singapore Steamship Company, and classed 100 Al.

Following are examples of editorial comment in the London newspapers (The *Times*, *Daily Chronicle*, *Globe*, and *Daily News*) concerning the *Jeddah* incident, all from the August 12, 1880, issues:

London was startled yesterday by the announcement of a disaster which, if true, would have been the most dreadful of recent times. The news was that a ship named the Jeddah, of Singapore, bound for Jeddah, had foundered last Sunday off Cape Guardafui, the easternmost point of Africa, near the Straits of Bab-el-Mandeb, with 953 Mahomedan pilgrims on board. All, it was stated, had perished, excepting the captain, his wife, the chief engineer, the assistant engineer, and sixteen natives. The survivors had been picked up by the steamer Scindia and landed at Aden. There was something very unpleasant in the facts thus stated; for, to the honour of sailors, nothing is more rare than that, in a disaster at sea, the captain and the principal officers of the vessel should be the chief or the sole survivors. Nothing can be more admirable than the manner in which, as a rule, the commanders of vessels stay by them to the end, and insist on being the last rather than the first to be saved. Apart from this consideration, the reported loss of life was unprecedented in such an accident, and would have amounted to more than the average total loss on British vessels during the year. But before we have had time to realize the extent of the disaster, the still stranger news arrives that it has never occurred. A telegram from Aden states that the vessel arrived there yesterday in tow of another steamer. She had been abandoned at sea, but did not founder, as the master had reported. This statement is an immense relief; but, as need hardly be urged, it suggests inquiries of a very painful character. Was the vessel, with this vast number of passengers on board, actually abandoned by the master and some of his chief officers? If she was towed into Aden, she could not have been in a condition which would justify her officers in leaving her at all; and the abandonment of duty which would be involved in such conduct is so disgraceful that we must regard the whole matter as a mystery until full particulars are furnished. It would have been terrible that more than nine hundred helpless pilgrims should have perished at sea. But that they should have been abandoned by the officers of the ship to which they had intrusted themselves, and saved by the accidental services rendered them by another vessel, is scarcely credible. The facts at present before us imply as much; but it will be but just to suspend all judgment on the subject until all the facts are accurately known. (*The Times*)

. . . That she should thus have been abandoned and her living freight left to their fate is one of the most dastardly circumstances we have ever heard of in connection with the perils of the deep. . . . It is to be feared that pilgrim ships are officered by unprincipled and cowardly men who disgrace the traditions of seamanship. We sincerely trust that no Englishman was amongst the boatload of cowards who left the *Jeddah* and her thousand passengers to shift for themselves. (*Daily Chronicle*)

. . . even if the *Jeddah* had afterwards foundered there would have remained an indelible stain of discredit upon the men who had thus run away at the moment of peril. But the fact that the ship was not in any extremity of peril is clearly proved by her eventual safety and the charge becomes thus one of over-timidity as well as simple *laches*. . . . (Evening issue of the *Globe*)

. . . The relief which is felt at the safety of the pilgrims will be modified by a feeling of indignation and horror at what seems the cowardly desertion of their post and trust by the master and seamen of the ship. (*Daily News*)

A *London Times* correspondent reported a letter received from Captain Henry Carter, relating his experiences with pilgrim-ship traffic in general:[2]

THE ABANDONMENT OF THE JEDDAH.

A Correspondent says that, pending the arrival of the details of the reported abandonment of the steamship Jeddah, with between 900 and 1,000 Moslem pilgrims on board, the following extract from a letter written to a friend in London by Captain Henry Carter, of Obelisk fame, shortly before his death on the 10th of January last seems to suggest that the strange desertion of their ship by the captain and his chief officers may only too possibly have been prompted by a natural instinct urging them to trust themselves to the sea rather than face perils of a more dreadful kind. Captain Carter's last employment was in this pilgrim traffic, which, under date November 30th, 1879, on board the steamship King Arthur, then lying in the port of Jeddah, he thus graphically describes:—

"No one who has not witnessed the pilgrims actually *en route* can form the slightest conception of the unromantic and unpic-turesque appearance of these wretched fanatics. It is a pity that some philanthropist will not take the trouble to make the tour, and go on board one of the pilgrim vessels about to start on a voyage to Jeddah. There are horrors on board such a ship which no Chris-

2. *London Times*, August 14, 1880.

tian has ever dreamt of, and none but those who grow rich by such wickedness can form any idea of what goes on in these vessels under the British flag—wickedness worse, by far, than was ever found on board a slaver. Only fancy 1,000 or 1,200 fanatics cooped up on the deck of a small vessel for 18 or 20 days, with no room to move, and little or no fresh air to breathe. There is no medical man to attend their wants when sick, and but a limited stock of medicine on board. I lost seven pilgrims in about 10 days, and I firmly believe that prompt medical treatment by a doctor would have saved them all. Of course, if these wretched beings die *en route* to Mecca, their eternal happiness is assured, so that they generally seem glad to give up the ghost and fly to the realms of joy. I wish you could have seen some of our little scenes of excitement. You must understand that my 'batch' consisted of Turcomans, Arabo-Persians, and Bedouins. They all came on board armed to the teeth, but, of course, I had all their weapons taken charge of by my officers and locked up in safety. I mean all the weapons we saw. They take up their quarters in any part of the ship, and from the moment of embarcation set the captain and officers at defiance. One day I had occasion to give orders for the removal of some luggage, which I found placed on the steering-gear, and which, of course, interfered with the navigation of my vessel. I was informed by my officers that the owners of this luggage refused to shift it, and, on my insisting on obedience to my orders, I found about me 150 cut-throat Arabs, all armed and prepared to resist my authority. Discretion was the better part of valour, for my three officers and myself were the only Englishmen on board, so that the odds were too great, and I quietly gave way. I thus found I had not got possession of all the swords, daggers, and firearms, which grieved me much. We were often alarmed by cries of "Fire!" but on only one occasion was it at all serious. In this instance some of these men had lighted a fire on the bare deck, in order to prepare some tea. Of course, a dry pine deck, with its oakum and pitch, was soon a blaze. Luckily it was the upper deck, so the fire was soon mastered. Had it happened below the result would have been terrible, for the 'tween decks would have filled with smoke, the confusion and panic would have rendered the pumps unworkable, the five boats would have been taken possession of and swamped, and a dense cloud of smoke would have been the quickly vanishing sign of a dreadful disaster. The ship and her living freight would have been among 'the missing.' A shocking scene occurred one very dark night, which convinces me of the utterly savage nature of the men I had to deal with. It was reported to me at 10 P.M. that one of the pilgrims was dead. So I gave orders that the friends of the deceased should take the body to the lee side and prepare it for burial. This was being done, but in carrying the corpse across the deck the bearers happened to disturb some Persians who were asleep. Instantly there was a terrible uproar. Swords, daggers, and bludgeons were brandished; the corpse was nearly torn to pieces; and one of my officers, who attempted to quell the disturbance, was thrown down. An implement, something between a tomahawk and a pickaxe, was aimed at his head, but a friendly hand was near, and his life was saved. I have carefully preserved this formidable weapon as a memento of such happy times. A few years ago a pilgrim vessel was stranded on one of the reefs in the Red Sea, and before any attempt could be made to get the ship off the captain and his officers were tied to the mast, and their throats were cut. When the wreck was discovered their bodies were found in this state, and out of the ship's 500 passengers 450 were drowned."

In a letter to the editor of the *London Times*, George Campbell replied to Captain Carter's statement of two days earlier:[3]

THE ABANDONMENT OF THE JEDDAH.

TO THE EDITOR OF THE TIMES

Sir,—I do not know whether the late Captain Carter, of "Obelisk fame," whose letter appears in *The Times* of to-day, is the man who abandoned or the man who saved the Obelisk, nor can I quite make out whether he most intended to condemn the "wretched fanatics" who sail in pilgrim ships or the avaricious Britishers who make money by sailing ships on board which are "such horrors as no Christian ever dreamt of," but I hope the latter, and certainly the letter of one having the practical experience that he had will have effect in drawing attention to these horrors and to the treatment of the pilgrims illustrated by the shocking, though, happily, not fatal, case of the Jeddah.

I dare say Turcomans and Bedouins, when carried in the dreadful way described by Captain Carter, are a rough and dangerous lot; but I wholly deny that there is any ground for applying such a term as "wretched fanatics" to the ordinary pilgrims from the English and Dutch East Indies. Pilgrimages are not unknown in Europe, and to this day many English and very many Americans flock to Jerusalem. The Indian pilgrims to Mecca and Kerbeleh are generally very decent and quiet Mahomedans with no special fanaticism; but they are very little accustomed to sea-voyaging, and somewhat helpless. There is no reason whatever why they should not be protected against barbarous ill-treatment and horrible arrangements on shipboard such as Captain Carter describes.

Though there was probably never before so pronounced a case as that of the Jeddah, unfortunately this is far from being the first case in which wrecks have been brought before the Indian Government where very large numbers of native passengers have been

3. *London Times*, August 16, 1880.

left to drown while the officers and crew escaped; and on account of many abuses the British-Indian law on the subject has carefully, and, I hope, to some degree effectually, provided for the protection of these poor people. But I know that when I was in office there was not equal protection in the case of vessels sailing from Singapore, and, as the Jeddah came from that colony, I am very anxious to know if the present regulations are sufficient, and if there are the means of insuring a thorough inquiry into and adequate treatment of this case. I have given notice of a question in the House of Commons; but meantime there seems difficulty in ascertaining whether the matter will rest with the British, Indian, or colonial authorities, and whether there is anywhere any central power which has sufficient control in cases of vessels sailing between different jurisdictions. I trust you will do what can be done to draw public attention to this dreadful subject. Remember Captain Carter's statements:—"Wickedness worse by far than was ever found on board a slaver;" "one thousand or 1,200 fanatics cooped up on the deck of a small vessel for 18 or 20 days, with no room to move and little or no fresh air to breathe;" no medical man, very little medicine; great mortality due to these hardships, and occasional desertion by those to whom they are intrusted.

Your obedient servant,

GEORGE CAMPBELL.

[Member of Parliament.]

August 14.

Following is a verbatim reprint of the notice to the British House of Commons to bring the question of the *Jeddah* incident before the members:[4]

House of Commons

Notice given Monday 23rd. August 1880.

Question to be put on Tuesday 24th. August 1880.

By Sir George Campbell—To ask the President of the Board of Trade if he would state where, how, and by whom inquiry will be made into the abandonment of the Steamship "Jeddah" by the Captain and Officers and what is the penal law applicable to any grave dereliction of duty found to have occurred in such a case.

If he will communicate with the India Office regarding the occurrence of several successive cases in past years in which large numbers of native Passengers were drowned while the Officers and Crew escaped and in which a strong suspicion arose that native passengers were not always treated as white Passengers would be and will ascertain whether in consequence of the above mentioned

4. Public Record Office copy of Colonial Office 273/111.

losses the Indian law on the subject was made more stringent *and with what result.*

Whether owing to the neglect of the precautions deemed necessary by the Government of India in the vessels engaged in the Singapore Pilgrim traffic an attempt was made to enforce the Indian Laws on such vessels coming to the port of Aden, but was abandoned owing to the remonstrance of the Colonial Authorities.

And if he will lay upon the Table the regulations on this subject now in force at Singapore *and ascertain whether those regulations are bonâ fide carried out or are evaded by taking additional Passengers outside the limits of the port or otherwise.*

Captain Clark's statement was printed in the *Straits Times Overland Journal*, September 8, 1880:

THE S.S. "JEDDAH"

Captain Clark, lately of the S.S. *Jeddah*, has furnished us with the following statement signed by him of the particulars of the abandonment of that vessel.

"I left Penang on 20th July with a crew of 50 men, 5 European officers and 953 adult pilgrims bound to Jeddah. The weather was heavy and threatening, strong head winds and high seas up to the "1½ degree channel," for two days only we had fine weather. After this (29th July) the weather became very heavy the wind increasing almost to hurricane force at times with a very high cross sea, the ship rolling, pitching and straining heavily. The gale continued with unabating fury and the ship labouring and straining heavily caused the boilers to break adrift from their fastenings on the 6th August. Steps were immediately taken to secure the boilers, but the weather was so bad that all the toms put in were broken up and every connection with the boilers broken. The water rose in the ship very rapidly and the steam pumping power was rendered useless. The deck pumps were all at work and the Hadjis and firemen were bailing the water out of the engine room in buckets. Notwithstanding, the water gained about an inch per hour, and on the 7th, the water still increasing, all the boats were ordered to be prepared and provisioned. On the night of the 7th there was a great difference in the demeanour of the pilgrims, they armed themselves with knives and clubs. About 400 men were clustered all around my cabin on deck and I was informed it was their deliberate intention to murder my wife. I satisfied myself assuredly on this point from the various conversations of the Hadjis and their demeanour left no doubt in my mind as to their intention. At midnight they refused to take the pumps, saying that they would sooner die than pump. I passed my wife through the window of my cabin and got one of the officers to put her in one of the boats. Immediately after this, when starting to lower the boat, a general rush was made by

The Rigging Plan of the S.S. *Jeddah*†

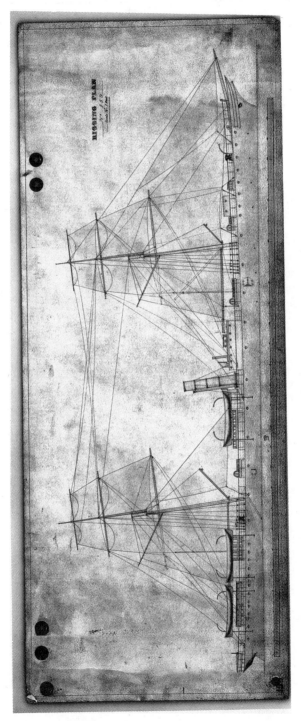

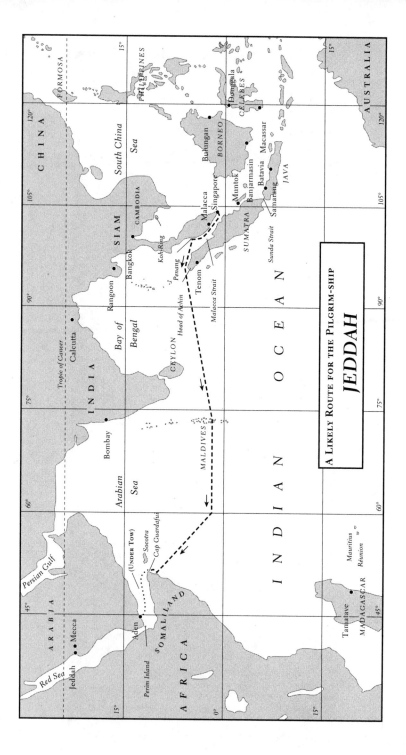

A LIKELY ROUTE FOR THE PILGRIM-SHIP

JEDDAH

A. P. Williams with family at Porthleven [Cornwall] Parsonage, 1868. Williams is at the far right. From Norman Sherry, *Conrad's Eastern World* (Cambridge and New York: Cambridge UP, 1966). Reproduced by permission of Mrs. G. A. Neill.

the pilgrims and I was pushed into the boat during which I received several serious blows. The boat was manned by the Chief Engineer with a boat's crew. The boat went down with a rush, the Chief Mate who was in the ship, was hurled overboard and every effort was made to sink my boat. The Hadjis cut us away from the ship. There was a heavy sea on. The third Engineer jumped or was thrown into the boat during the excitement and attack. I picked up the first officer and took him into my boat. This is all I know personally. It transpired in evidence at the Court of Inquiry that the second mate and 11 others—Hadjis and Crew—who were in another boat, were similarly attacked and the boat cut away, the boat went down and all were drowned. I kept my boat's head hove to sea during the remainder of the night and in the morning I saw no signs of the *Jeddah*. My boat was picked up about 10 A.M. by the *Scindia* and taken to Aden."

(SD.) J. L. CLARK.

A letter to Syed Muhammad bin Alsagoff from his agent in Aden, followed by a report of the reaction in Singapore to the *Jeddah* affair, from the *Straits Times Overland Journal*, September 13, 1880:

From the Daily Times, 8th September

THE S.S. "JEDDAH."

Mr. Syed Mahomed bin Alsagoff, Managing Director of the Singapore, Steam Ship Company, has kindly placed at our disposal the following letter, which we print *verbatim et literatim*, from his Agents in Aden regarding the abandonment of the S.S. *Jeddah*, and which contains the only information he has received on the subject independent of Captain Clark's statement. The telegrams announcing the circumstance, which were received by Mr. Syed Mahomed, have been, it will be remembered, already published:—

Steamer Point,
Aden, August 20th, 1880.

Syed Mahomed Alsagoff, Esq.,
Managing Director
Singapore S.S. Company,
Singapore

Dear Sir,—With deep regret we have to report you the sad circumstances of your good S.S. *Jeddah*.

Captain Clark came with Mr. Omar to our office at about 9 P.M. on the 18th (*sic*) inst., to our surprise, they reported that the S.S. *Jeddah* is foundered this side of the "Socotra" Island, and he himself and his wife, Syed Omar, 1st Mate, 1st Engineer and 21 others arrived per S.S. *Scindia*, and he, Captain Clark gave the Captain of the S.S. *Scindia* Rs. 700 as a remuneration for bringing them with food, &c., supplied to all people.

On the 11th instant at about 6 P.M. it was reported, and came into anchor about 7 P.M., the S.S. *Jeddah*, in tow of Messrs. Alfred Holt's S.S. *Antenor* which was more surprising when it was reported that she had foundered. Immediately on her arrival the authorities ordered the Police Superintendent and Harbour Pilot to go on board, to see what was to be done, and of course our people as well as others went on board for anxiety of the ship and people reported are foundered; the water was only in the Engine room and nowhere else, the bearers of the Boilers broke down and Boilers shifted and whole cause in consequence of the Boilers on one side and the feed pumps gave way, and rapidly the water filled up the Engine room, with pumping of water day and night by passengers they tired after pumping 4 days and nights, and when Captain Clark found that all people on board are tired, they thought the ship must be foundered. The authority, on arrival of the ship, took charge to land passengers and to keep the ship in safe place, and for about 4 or 5 days they put their own men to pump water out of her and to get clean, &c. When your message came to us of course we guaranteed for expenses and to send the passengers to Jeddah and took charge of her and we have had a survey ourselves and Government had another survey on Engine room and Boilers, and the report we forward herein by which you will see what is wanted and we shall be able to do all work here. The second survey we called on the cargo, and glad to say it is not damaged. Copy of survey is herein enclosed. We shall have a Marine Survey on the ship and see what is deficient. At present we can see the sails are all broken in pieces and more lost, 2 life boats are lost, 2 compasses, 2 chronometers are gone, and we have to place whole of these before she is ready for sea. Capt. Clark has left his one chronometer on board.

The Court has finished the trial, and will give verdict this afternoon, and what we have heard is that Captain Clark will lose his certificate, but no one else be injured in any way.

The 2nd Mate is lost by jumping in boat when Captain Clark left the ship, and 3 Khallasees and passengers, in all 18 lives, are lost.

We telegraphed you to send a Captain and we believe you will find a good Captain in Singapore to engage him and send him by a first steamer; it will be much cheaper in long run than to engage here a stray one.

Regarding Officers and Engineers, we shall report you in our next.

Captain Clark has got leave to proceed on, and he is going today to Singapore with his wife per M. M. Co's steamer.

He has Rs. 710 to pay to Captain of the *Scindia* who brought them, which we have debited to the Company.

We shall send you copy of the Court decision on the trial in our next which will give full light on the subject, but it is a bad job done by Captain Clark.

About 300 passengers are already sent away to Rs. 10 each, and we shall send them as the opportunity may offer. The authorities do not like to keep them longer, fearing of sickness breaking out amongst them and may cause an epidemic in the place.

You may rest assured that we shall not fail to do all for the interest of the Company in a most economical way. We have received the credit for $10,000 and will draw as we may require. In meantime we close this in haste as the time of mail is quite near for closing at the Post Office.

> We remain, Dear Sir,
> Yours faithfully,
> Cowasjee Dinshaw & Bros.

From the Daily Times, 10th September
THE S.S. "JEDDAH."

The fame of Captain Clark, who, we believe, is realising his property here with the object of leaving for England, has preceded him. The London newspapers publish the details, eagerly, of his desertion of his ship. For our own part we await the receipt of the evidence given at the Court of Inquiry at Aden, in a spirit of fair play, before we make any comments or draw conclusions. Most persons here have formed their opinions as to Captain Clark's conduct but until the whole of the facts are before us, we prefer to keep silent. The London *Standard* contains the following telegrams and general remarks on the subject. Mr. Syed Mahomed hopes to obtain the copy of the evidence given before the Court of Inquiry by the next mail, he has not received any letter from Aden by this mail:—

Aden, 10th August.—The steamer *Jeddah*, of Singapore, bound for Jeddah, with 953 pilgrims on board, foundered off Cape Guardafui, on the 8th inst. All on board perished excepting the captain, his wife, the chief officer, the chief engineer, the assistant engineer, and 16 natives.

The survivors were picked up by the steamer *Scindia* and landed here.

Aden, 11th August, 7.50 P.M.—*The Jeddah*, which was abandoned at sea with nine hundred and fifty-three pilgrims on board, did not founder as reported by the master. She has just arrived here, all safe, in tow of the steamer *Antenor*.

A court of Inquiry was held at Aden into the cause of the abandonment of the Jeddah.[5]

(No. 896.)

"JEDDAH." (S.S.)

REPORT of a Court of Inquiry held at Aden into the cause of the abandonment of the steamship "JEDDAH."

The steamship "Jeddah," of Singapore, official number 67,990, under British colours of 993$\frac{44}{101}$ tons register, and owned by the Singapore Steamship Company, Limited, Joseph Lucas Clark, master, left Singapore on the 17th July 1880, for Penang.

On arrival at Penang she filled up with pilgrims, making a total complement of 953 as adult passengers, and proceeded on her voyage on the 19th idem for Jeddah direct; she had 600 tons of cargo on board, principally sugar, garron-wood, and general merchandise. Her crew consisted of 50 souls all told, which number included the master, first and second mates, and third engineer, who were Europeans, and with the captain's wife, the only Europeans on board.

The "Jeddah" appears to have experienced heavy weather for the most part of her voyage. On the 3rd August 1880, the wind increased almost to a hurricane, with high breaking sea.

On this date the boilers started from their fastenings and began to work, and steps were subsequently taken to secure them with wedges.

The weather increased in severity until the 6th August; on that day, about 9.30 P.M., the feed valve of the port boiler broke, and the ship had to be stopped for repairs, and the vessel then, it was considered, commenced to leak considerably, having shipped much water previously. As soon as repairs were executed, at 1.30 P.M., the vessel again proceeded under steam, when the feed valve on the starboard boiler also broke; and after again stopping for repair, the ship proceeded at 8.30 P.M. with one boiler only. All hands and passengers were then working at the pumps and baling. As the water appeared to increase, the bilge injection was utilized and the leak reduced; but as that became choked, and the vessel stopped to clear it, the leak increased, it is stated, so rapidly as to put out the fires. In consequence of the quantity of water in the stoke-hole, and from the temporary wedges and supports to the boilers having washed away, and the boilers working backwards and forwards owing to the rolling of the ship, every connection pipe was carried away, and the engine-rooms became untenable and a wreck.

Sail was apparently set as soon as the engines became useless,

5. No. 896, Indian Office Library, London.

but these were blown away, and other sails subsequently set when the wind moderated.

In the meantime pumping and baling was resorted to, and the passengers appear to have given willing assistance after the evening of the 7th August. On that day the master ordered the boats to be got ready, provisioned, armed, and swung out.

Pumping continued on the part of the passengers up to 12 midnight, then apparently some diminution took place. Certain of the crew were then ordered shortly after to man a boat or boats; the bulk of the crew appear to have manned the boats.

At this time the passengers appear to have become partially disorganized, and to have entertained the idea that the boats were going to leave the ship. The master then appears to have decided to hang the starboard lifeboat astern, and to remain in it with his wife and the first engineer and a boat's crew until daylight, being, he states, afraid of his own and his wife's life being attempted if he remained on board. The starboard lifeboat was then about to be lowered, and the captain and his wife and chief engineer got into it. The captain's wife had to pass some 50 feet from the cabin to the boat. When the boat was lowered, the pilgrims commenced to throw boxes, pots and pans, and anything they could lay hands on, into the boat, and pulled the first officer, who was lowering the boat, off the rails; and seeing they could not prevent the lowering of the boat, they attempted to swamp it. The third engineer had in the meantime got into the boat, and the first officer found himself in the water, and was taken into it, and the boat was then cut adrift, and for about a couple of hours the boat's head was kept to the wind and sea, but after that allowed to drive and partially sail before the wind, until at 10 A.M. on the 8th August, it was sighted by the steamship "Scindia," and the persons in it rescued and brought to Aden, where they arrived on the 10th August. On arrival at Aden, the master and others rescued reported the foundering of the "Jeddah" with all on board, and also reported that the second officer and second engineer had been murdered.

After the master left the "Jeddah" it appears that the passengers tried to prevent the second officer leaving the ship, which he appears to have attempted, by leaving the captain's boats and going over to the port side to the boat to which he was appointed, and which was manned and ready for lowering. Two of the passengers, Lojis, and an Arab, appear also to have got into this boat. On the pilgrims ordering the people to come out of the boats, and on their refusal, some of the pilgrims (it cannot be ascertained who) cut the falls, and it fell into the sea bow first from the fore fall being cut first, and all in it appear to have perished.

Shortly after this, the second engineer, who was awoke out of his sleep a little time before by the second officer, and told to go to his boat, proceeded to his boat, also on the port side. This boat was to have been commanded by the first officer, the Lojis, finding this boat also manned with the second engineer in it, got in, and threw all the men back from her into the ship, and would not allow them to leave. They then appear to have resumed pumping and baling, and continued doing so without intermission, gaining on the leak; and on the following morning, 8th August, finding themselves in smooth water, they sighted land and made for it, having had sail set all night. They hoisted signals of distress, and at 3 P.M., when about 7 or 8 miles from land, the wind died away. At about 4.30 P.M., the steamship "Antenor," seeing the signals, bore down on the disabled ship; and the master, after ascertaining the state of affairs, sent his chief mate on board, and took charge, and brought the "Jeddah" in tow to Aden, where both vessels arrived on the afternoon of the 11th August.

The water in the "Jeddah" was considerably reduced by the exertions of the passengers, under the direction of the chief officer of the "Antenor," and that officer on first boarding the ship, and seeing the quantity in her, came to the immediate conclusion that the vessel could be saved. Three sailors, one topman, one syrang, eleven firemen, and one clerk, one fireman working his passage, were all the crew on board the "Jeddah" when brought to Aden, together with the second engineer and supercargo, and 992 passengers—778 men, 147 women, and children 67, not counting infants in arms, were on board.

The above appear to the Court to be, as far as can be ascertained, the circumstances connected with this case; and in reviewing them, and after a patient and careful inquiry into all the details, the Court record the following opinion:—

It appears that the fastenings of the boilers, which are placed athwartships in the "Jeddah," were defective, and in consequence of the rolling of the ship and the heavy sea, these fastenings gave way, and caused a leak by the breaking of the connecting pipes with the ship's bottom. This leak, though serious in itself, was intensified by the vessel shipping large quantities of water, and the boilers having to be blown off or emptied into the ship's bilge on several occasions instead of into the sea, when repairs were being executed. With the rolling of the ship, the quantity of water in the stoke-hole appeared greater than it actually was, and from the engine and donkey-engine being useless, the vessel having water also in the after-hold through the sluice, the actual condition of affairs was thought more serious than was the case; the ship having a leak, and being in a heavy sea. It appears to the Court that sufficient notice was not at once taken of the movement of the boilers, and every available means adopted to secure them as much as possible, immediately it was ascertained that they had shifted and were working.

The chief engineer of the "Jeddah" appears to have treated this matter lightly, and is, in the Court's opinion, primarily responsible for his ignorance in not knowing the extent of the risk and danger run by the boilers moving, and not insisting on all available means being employed at once to stay them.

Had more energetic measures been taken at the outset, it appears just probable to the Court that subsequent events might have been averted. When steam power was no longer available on board the "Jeddah," it appears to the Court that no regular system of reducing the leak was organized by the master. He appears to have come to the conclusion early on the 7th August that the boats would probably be required, and they were prepared and swung out, and the crew engaged in attending to them rather than to the vessel's condition. The firemen, however, appear to have been steadily engaged in working the ash buckets up to midnight of the 7th August.

The master does not appear to have taken his passengers into his confidence or to have endeavoured in the least degree to raise their hopes in any way. On the contrary, it seems he informed them that if they would not pump the vessel would founder, thereby giving no hope. On this point, situated as he was, the Court consider he was wanting in simple judgment, for he had much in his favour to dispel fear and raise the hopes and energies of his passengers, who appeared ready and willing to assist. Land was not far distant, and yet by his act in ordering the boats he led the passengers to believe that the vessel would probably founder, and the boats would be lowered. Although there is conflicting evidence that the master was of this opinion before the Logis had their thoughts averted from the pumping, the master's action after being picked up by the "Scindia," and brought to Aden, and his report of the "Jeddah" having foundered, leads the Court to infer that the master considered the vessel would founder whether pumped and baled out or not. The Court consider he was under the impression from his acts that the "Jeddah" would founder under any circumstances, but, apart from his impressions, his action in ordering the boats to be prepared was an inducement to disturbance, as only about one quarter of the souls on board could have been accommodated in them.

The Court consider that in this the master showed a want of judgment and tact to a most serious extent, and that he caused disorganisation and discontent, not to say despair, at a time when none of these feelings should have been engendered.

The master states that on finding the pilgrims would not work the pumps, shortly after midnight on the 7th and 8th August, and that they appeared altered in demeanour and were some of them armed with knives, he feared that his wife's life and his own would be attempted, as he had been led to infer the same from what he had been told, and consequently very shortly after he found that this was the state of affairs, in place of resorting to measures to restore confidence or to organize any system of defence in case of need, for the protection of the lives of himself and the Europeans on board, which he could easily have done by keeping the bridge with the arms on board, he determined on lowering a boat, in which he intended, he states, first to place his wife and to remain in her himself, to hang astern of the ship until daylight. What the master's intentions were after daylight does not appear. He ordered the boat to be manned, and, after having his wife placed in it, he himself got in and others did also. Up to this time it is evident that no violence or even show of force had been made by the pilgrims to anyone on board; it was only when the boat was being lowered and they became aware of what was taking place, that they appear to have resorted to force, and then not such force as they might have utilized, armed with knives as they were. Failing in preventing the lowering of the boat, the pilgrims proceeded to endeavour to swamp her; two pistol shots were fired in the direction of the pilgrims from the boat by the first officer, and these appear to have prevented any further attempts to swamp the boat, which then was cast off and away from the ship. The passengers, finding other boats were manned, they proceeded to endeavour to prevent their leaving the ship, and, in the case of the second officer's boat, cut it adrift when its inmates would not return on board, and unceremoniously ejected those who had got into the third boat with the second engineer.

The Court consider that the action of the pilgrims tends to prove that they never intended to harm the master and his officers had they remained in the "Jeddah," that their demeanour is accounted for by the evidence that they had made up their minds that they should not be deserted by the only persons capable of protecting and helping them in the circumstances in which they were placed, and consequently they would prevent to the utmost the master or his officers leaving the ship. It is in the Court's opinion more than probable that the master was misled in regard to the real intentions of the pilgrims, but he has himself to blame for not making more certain of these intentions, or waiting for some more clear proof of these intentions than took place. It is to be regretted that the principal witness, Lezed Omar, on this point could not be examined, as he had left Aden for Jeddah the day after his arrival, and before the steamship "Jeddah" was towed in.

There is no evidence before the Court to show that the life of the captain's wife was in danger by reason of any threats made by the pilgrims, and this man, Lezed Omar, alone appears to be the authority of this report, and he is stated to have been in dread himself and much frightened for his own safety.

Doubtless the master on hearing this report, as well as imperfectly understanding the threats actually made by the pilgrims, viz., "that they would not allow any one to leave the ship, and would prevent them to the extent of violence if necessary," the fact of the pilgrims having armed themselves to a certain extent to carry out this threat if need arose, aided by the officious ill-advice of his chief officer, entirely forgot his first duty as a shipmaster, and proceeded to be one of the first instead of the last to leave his disabled vessel to her fate. This last act roused the pilgrims to violence in attempting to swamp his boat, and such the Court consider might naturally have been expected from any body of human beings, even Europeans, situated as the pilgrims were.

With every consideration for the master under the trying circumstances in which he and his crew found themselves placed, the Court is reluctantly compelled to state that they consider that Captain Clark has shown a painful want of nerve as well as the most ordinary judgment, and has allowed his feelings to master the sense of duty it is the pride of every British shipmaster to vaunt, and they consider that in the instances mentioned he has been guilty of gross misconduct in being indirectly the cause of the deaths of the second mate and ten natives, seven crew and three passengers, and in abandoning his disabled ship with nearly 1,000 souls on board to their fate, when by ordinary display of firmness, combined with very little tact in dealing with natives, with whom he is no stranger, he could have ensured their co-operation and gratitude, and saved considerable loss to his owners. The Court must here also remark on the want of anxiety shown by the master for the fate of the "Jeddah," in not doing all in his power to induce the "Scindia" to search for her, as there is little doubt but that a proper statement of facts and little persuasion would have induced the master of the "Scindia" under the circumstances to steam for an hour or so to windward, when the "Jeddah" would certainly have been sighted.

The Court feel compelled to mark their sense of the master, Joseph Lewis Clark's, conduct by ordering, subject to the confirmation of the Bombay Government, that his certificate of competency as master be suspended for a period of three years.

Before concluding, the Court consider it necessary to place on record their disapprobation of the conduct of the first officer of the "Jeddah," Mr. Williams, who may be said to have aided and abetted the master in the abandonment of his vessel. The Court consider it very probable that, but for Mr. William's officious behaviour and unseamanlike conduct, the master would (by the first mate's own showing) have done his duty by remaining on the ship.

Had there been any evidence, except the first mate's own statement, on this point, the Court would have felt constrained to have put him on trial also, they cannot therefore refrain from remarking that they consider that in this instance he has shown himself unfitted for his position as first mate on a crowded pilgrim vessel.

The Court have to regret that, owing to the positive report made of the "Jeddah" having foundered, no steps were taken to detain or record the evidence of the master and officers of the steamship

"Scindia," as to the reasons and causes for their not searching for the steamship "Jeddah" after picking up her master and others. The examination of these witnesses would have completed the evidence which otherwise is not as complete as it might, and very desirable that it should be in this case—the most extraordinary instance known to the Court of the abandonment of a disabled and leaking ship at sea by the master and Europeans, and almost all the crew, with close to 1,000 souls on board when no immediate danger existed of her foundering. The Court consider that it is due to the master of the "Antenor" to place on record their opinion of the contrast of his conduct to that of Captain Clark, and consider him worthy, with his chief officer, Mr. Campbell, of great commendation for their action, not only for rescuing those on board the "Jeddah" from a perilous position and shipwreck, but also for saving a valuable ship and her cargo from loss.

In conclusion the Court consider it is not out of place to remark, that in their estimation nearly 1,000 souls on board a vessel of the tonnage of the "Jeddah" was a greater number than should be allowed by any regulation, especially for a long sea voyage, as taken by the "Jeddah," and at a season when bad weather might naturally have been expected.

(Signed) G. R. GOODFELLOW
Resident and Sessions Judge.

Aden, 20th August 1880
I concur.

(Signed) W. K. THYNNE
Assessor.

Confirmed.

(Signed) JAMES FERGUSSON,
,   Governor of Bombay.

The Merchant Shipping Act, in the case of a Board of Trade certificate, only requires the confirmation of the Local Government with reference to the regularity of the proceedings. Had I been advised that any option rested with it with reference to the details, I should have declined to confirm them, as I think the sentence inadequate to the offence committed by the master of the "Jeddah" as described by the Court.

Assuming that his abandonment of his ship, without necessity, and with the probable loss of an enormous number of helpless people for whose safety he was responsible, was the result rather of cowardice and want of resource than of inhumanity, his subsequent conduct in not doing his utmost to procure them succour showed that latter quality. But in either point of view, he has, in my judgment, shown himself entirely unfit to be entrusted with the charge of life and property at sea.

(Signed)   J.F.

ASSESSOR'S REPORT on the abandonment of the steamship "JEDDAH," of Singapore.

I consider the chief engineer of the "Jeddah" very much to blame for not taking the most active measures to secure the boilers when he first saw them move on the 3rd of August, more especially as the vessel was labouring heavily. When the matter was reported to the master is doubtful, but from the chief engineer's own statement, my opinion is that the engineer did not report to the master the moving of the boilers until the following day; the reason given by the engineer, viz., that the pipes in connection with the boiler were copper and could stand any strain caused by the moving of the boilers, the movement first observed being three-eighths of an inch, but which gradually increased to about two inches, before the boilers became totally useless by all the important pipes breaking, including the donkey engine steam-pipe. Before this happened, the vessel leaked a good deal in the engine-room, and as long as the engines could be worked the leak could be kept down. Had the chief engineer exercised a little judgment, he surely would have known that the movement of the boilers (which was of a jerky nature) was a most dangerous thing, and likely to become more and more dangerous with every heavy roll of the ship, and was a matter which required his most vigilant care from the first. I cannot understand how the engineer could make himself believe that the movement of the boilers (huge masses, each weighing probably not less than 30 tons when filled with water) was a matter of no consequence at first, merely because the movement was only three-eighths of an inch. Common sense might have taught him that the movement was likely to increase with every roll of the ship.

On the 6th August the engines and steam pumps became useless, the ship leaking, but not to any alarming extent. The bilge injection when working being able to keep the leak down; pumps were manned and baling started without any attempt being made to organize the Hadjees into working gangs, with regular reliefs, or replenishing the supply of buckets, by making canvas ones.

At noon of the 7th August, the ship's position was said to be in latitude 11° 55′ north, and longitude 51° 55′ east, "Abdul Kuri" bearing north-east ½ east, true distant about 28 miles. With this position, the bearing of Cape Guardafui would be nearly due west, distant about 35 miles. Shortly after the position of the ship had been ascertained, the order was given to get the boats made ready, which was done before sunset, and crews told off, the engineers and officers were informed what boats they were to go in should the boats leave the ship. Before midnight some of the passengers, it was said, had been heard to say they would kill the captain and his wife. This was reported to the captain. Again it stated that the passengers would use force to prevent the captain from leaving the ship; some of the passengers were observed about midnight to be armed with their knives, stated to be any number from 20 up to 300. The second engineer went to bed at midnight; he did not see any man armed. The captain was warned by the first mate to be careful how he went about the decks, as the passengers might kill him. Up to the time the captain left the ship he was not molested, until he went into the starboard lifeboat at 2:30 A.M. The first and second mates were at the lowering of this boat. The second mate left at once, called the second engineer, and got into his own boat on the port (*i.e.* weather) side, which was all ready for lowering. As the boat was being lowered the falls were cut by the Hadjees, which caused one end of the boat to fall-first, and it is supposed threw the crew out, who were drowned.

Nothing was ever seen of this boat. The Hadjees did what they could to destroy her, they also did what they could to destroy the starboard lifeboat, and I believe knocked the first mate overboard. The distance from the captain's cabin to the starboard lifeboat is stated to be about 40 feet; the captain's wife was passed through one of the windows of the cabin, and either walked along or was carried and put into the boat without being molested, the first mate taking a prominent part in this proceeding.

The first mate of the "Jeddah," according to his own statement, is greatly to blame in doing what he could to demoralize the master, by advising him to leave the ship, telling him his life was in danger, also his wife's life; that he, the master, was sure to be killed if he remained on board; and that he, the first mate, did thrust the master into the boat. The mate worked on the fears of the master for the safety of his wife, and by so doing hurried the master into leaving the ship.

From noon of the 7th until the "Jeddah" was picked up by the "Antenor" she was on the port tack under short canvass, blowing hard from the south, steering west, every hour bringing the vessel nearer to a weather shore, where smooth water might be expected. When the master left the ship at 2:30 A.M. on the 8th August, he must have been distant from Cape Guardafui about 10 miles, judging from the position of the vessel at noon of the 7th of August, viz., latitude 11° 55′ north, and longitude 51° 55′ east; and her approximate position at 4:30 P.M. of the 8th August, viz., latitude 12° north, and longitude 51° 6′ east, when the "Antenor" steered for her and picked her up.

When the "Scindia" picked up the starboard lifeboat the "Jeddah" would be distant about 22 miles, bearing from the "Scindia" about south-south-west.

The "Jeddah" having been towed into Aden harbour on the 11th instant, with the water reduced nearly two feet in the afterhold, proved there was nothing hopeless in the state of the ship when abandoned.

1. I am of the opinion the master was not compelled to leave the "Jeddah."

2. That the master left the "Jeddah" against the will of his passengers.

3. That no disturbance took place until it became known that the master was leaving the ship, and that such disturbance was confined to damaging the boats and occupants when lowering and when lowered by throwing at and into the boats anything which first came to hand, and by cutting the boats' falls.

4. That by leaving the ship the master was the means of causing the loss of 11 [*sic*] lives, and the ship to be abandoned by the major portion of her crew, thereby greatly increasing the danger of the vessel being lost with all on board had she been leaking very badly. The master concluded she had foundered about three hours after he left her, as he was unable to see her at daylight.

5. The master of the "Jeddah," when picked up by the "Scindia," was guilty of great cruelty in not representing matters in such a way to the master of the "Scindia" as would have induced him to steam dead to windward, or in such a direction as might have been considered best to look for the "Jeddah," more especially as the master before leaving had no expectation of her foundering soon.

6. A vessel with upwards of 1,000 souls on board is a charge of great responsibility, and makes it more binding if possible on the master to remain on board to the very last, and by so doing tend to inspire his crew and passengers with courage and determination to save the ship if possible, and by so doing, their lives and property.

I am of opinion had the master's wife not been on board the master would not have deserted his ship.

I am of opinion had the master received proper assistance and advice from his first mate, he, the master, would not have left the ship.

I am of opinion had the master not left the "Jeddah" no lives would have been lost.

I am further of opinion that the first mate should not be permitted to go in the ship again.

The master of the "Antenor" states he passed Cape Guardafui about 3:30 P.M., 3' distant, and steered N. 62° W., true, until he sighted the "Jeddah" at 4.30, Cape Guardafui being distant about 14 miles, bearing S. 60° west. This bearing is wrong, and should be, according to the course steered, about south 46° east.

Given under my hand at Aden, on this the 20th day of August 1880.

(Signed)   W. K. Thynne, Assessor,
Port Officer, Aden.

These findings of the Court of Inquiry of August 20 were published in full in the *Straits Times Overland Journal* the following month, on September 13. In the same issue of the paper was the comment:

> Public excitement has risen to fever heat here in surveying the conduct of Captain Clark, who is well known here, and his officers and engineers in deserting the S.S. *Jeddah*.

There is no doubt that if the Governor or the Secretary of State could have taken criminal action against Captain Clark and Chief Officer Williams they would have done so. In a *Straits Settlement Dispatch* from Governor Weld on September 20, 1880, there is a reference to the indignation felt in Singapore at "the dastardly conduct of the Captain and the greater part at least of his officers," but Weld admits that for want of witnesses they are unable to prosecute. The Board of Trade held the same view, and the sentence—suspension of certificate for three years for Captain Clark and a reprimand for Chief Officer Williams—seemed to them to be totally inadequate, as is evident in the following letter the Board sent to the Under Secretary of State, India Office:[6]

> The misconduct of the Master in deserting his ship with 1,000 lives on board, and not only taking no step to send them assistance, but, on the contrary, reporting falsely that she "had foundered, and that the second officer and the second engineer had been murdered," deserves the severest punishment which could be inflicted by law, and even if the Authorities at Aden had no power to take steps for the criminal prosecution of Mr. Joseph Lucas Clark, there can be no doubt that the Court should by cancelling his Certificate, have done all in their power to prevent him from again having command of a British Ship.

Apart from Captain Clark, only one other member of the *Jeddah*'s crew returned to Singapore: Chief Officer Augustine Podmore Williams, whose conduct had been criticized so severely at the Aden inquiry; he arrived on Wednesday, September 15, 1880, on the S. S. *Naples* from Aden. Only the day before his arrival, the Singapore Legislative Council had debated a motion to have the master of the *Jeddah* arrested and retired, and an account of the debate appeared in the *Singapore Daily Times* on September 16. A. P. Williams was to be the only member of the *Jeddah*'s European crew to remain in Singapore. The attitude of the others is suggested by a letter from Charles Baldwin, the chief engineer of the *Jeddah*, to a resident of Singapore, which was published in the *Straits Times Overland Journal* on October 2, 1880.

6. Register of Letters written for 1881, M. T. 4/300 no. 2777.

THE S.S. "JEDDAH."

The following is a copy of a private letter, dated Jeddah 16th September, received by a resident here from Mr. Baldwin, who was Chief Engineer of the vessel when she was abandoned:—

I little thought when the *Jeddah* left Singapore, that the run would terminate so unfortunately. In fact everything went so well for the three weeks we were under steam that I had begun to congratulate myself on the evident decrease in the consumption, and the continued easy working of the engines. But pride goeth before a fall. And it was a considerable shock my pride got one morning when we were within eighty miles of the African coast, the feed check valve chests gave way one after the other. The cast iron brackets supporting the port boiler broke in pieces allowing the boiler to come down two inches on to the fore and after beams, breaking the pipe communicating from the donkey and main boilers to the donkey engine and breaking the bolts holding the main blow down cock to the ship's bottom, causing a leak which in the course of the next twenty four hours let in water enough to lift the plates and bearers in stoke hole and engine-room, and which water with every roll of the ship surged into the furnaces, and returned in streams from the tube doors of the boiler to leeward. I kept the bilge injection open as long as we could get a turn out of the engines, but when the last valve chest gave way, and no means remained for pumping water into the boilers, and our store room flooded, and all but knocked to pieces, and six feet of water to navigate about in and the three of us half drowned, and knocked up for want of sleep, I was at last compelled to own we could do no more and set the firemen to draw water in ashbuckets up the ventilator. I had had the carpenter down trying to stay the boilers from shifting, but the weight of the boilers and superheater and water, combined with the impetus of the rolling of the ship, crushed the wooden blocks like so much dry tinder, and allowed the boilers a travel of about one and a half inches. For myself and the other engineers, I believe we were perfectly justified in acting as we did. Poor Scott in the hurry had got in the wrong boat, from which he was hauled by the Hadjis and I believe would have been knocked under but for the interposition of Ali the supercargo. Had there been more Europeans left on board when the Captain and Syed Omar left the ship, there would have been more scrimages, and but one Ali. However the whole affair was bad enough to make me decide to have no more to do with the *Jeddah*, and so I told the Agent in Aden, who telegraphed for another Chief, and last Tuesday Mr. J. C. Anderson arrived here with Capt. Craig and the mates. The Agent offered to continue my pay if I would give a hand for a few days which I have done fixing new angle iron brackets under the boilers, and assisting generally. I leave this to-morrow or next day for home. The *Jeddah* is also going to London, and the Agent has offered me a free passage, but I prefer paying my way in another steamer. And so will finish other two years of seagoing, the one dark feature in which is the drowning of our second mate and fourteen others while attempting to lower their boat.

The following are extracts from the report on the action for salvage brought by Alfred Holt, managing partner of the Ocean Steam Ship Company of Liverpool, owners of the British steamship *Antenor*, against the steamship *Jeddah*, her cargo and freight, in the Vice Admiralty Court of the Straits Settlement on October 17, 1881, before Sir Thomas Sidgreaves, Kt., Chief Justice.[7]

On the 8th August, at 5 P.M., the *Antenor*, an iron screw steamship of 1,644 tons, bound on a voyage from Shanghai to London, and with a full complement of 680 passengers, sighted a vessel which subsequently proved to be the *Jeddah*, flying signals of distress. The signals of distress were, on one mast, "We are sinking;" on another, "Send immediate assistance." The flying of the first signal was denied by the defendants' reply, but was clearly proved not only by the witnesses called on behalf of the plaintiffs, but by one of the witnesses, Mahomed Khan, clerk on board the *Jeddah*, called by the defendants. A boat containing the first mate, the boatswain, and four of the crew of the *Antenor*, was sent, and on boarding her they found the *Jeddah* in a very disabled condition. According to the Act on Petition framed upon the affidavits of the Captain and Chief Officer of the *Antenor*, "the Engines were totally disabled, and the Engine fires put out; there were 7 or 8 feet of water in the vessel, and everything on board was in confusion, and all persons on board were panic stricken until the arrival on board of the First Mate and Boatswain of the *Antenor*. The boilers on board were adrift and had broken from their fastenings, and all the pipe connections with the boilers were broken, and no steam-power on board could be used. The steam-pipes on board could not be used, and all fires were out. The position was about 13 miles to the westward of Cape Guardafui and about 9 miles from the African coast. She was under foretopsail jib, and fore and main topsails, and was heading for some bluffs 1,300 feet high on the Coast of Africa. There was an East wind blowing, with a heavy ground swell, and the vessel was being driven through the water in a quasi derelict condition at the rate of 2½ to 3 knots an hour towards the coast. A heavy surf was breaking on the coast, and it was becoming rapidly dark as the sun set at 6 P.M." After the Chief Mate had ascertained by personal observation the state of things on board the *Jeddah*, he returned to the *Antenor* and reported to the Captain. It must be admitted that the Captain found himself confronted with a task of

---

7. Printed in *Cases Heard and Determined in Her Majesty's Supreme Court of the Straits Settlements 1808–1884*, edited and reported by James William Norton Kyshe, Esq., Acting Registrar of the said court in Malacca, 3 vols., Singapore, 1886, II, 37–42.

no ordinary difficulty. In command of a ship with a valuable cargo and a full complement of passengers on board, whose interests and those of his owners he was first bound to consider, and with darkness fast coming on, he had to choose between jeopardizing his own ship, cargo and passengers, or leaving a ship abandoned by the Captain and officers, and with nearly 1,000 souls on board, to the inevitable fate that seemed to await her of foundering at sea or being dashed to pieces on the coast. After a short consultation between the Captain and the Chief Officer, it was decided to make an attempt to save the *Jeddah*. They considered it impossible to take the *Jeddah's* passengers on board the *Antenor*, as the *Antenor* was already full, but they thought that it might be possible to tow her into Aden if they could manage to keep her afloat by inducing the pilgrims to work at the pumps. The Chief Officer returned to the *Jeddah* with the Boatswain and 4 of the crew, after arranging signals with the Captain to be used in case of the *Jeddah* sinking, so as to take them off in time. The boatswain and crew returned to the *Antenor* at 10 P.M., but from that time until the *Jeddah* was successfully towed into Aden, the Chief Officer never left her. Though taking the *Jeddah* in tow was accomplished after considerable difficulty, and with the exercise of much patience, skill, and ingenuity, the Chief Officer steered the *Jeddah* himself until he had taught two of the crew of the *Jeddah* to steer; and he induced the passengers to exert themselves in pumping and baling. The conclusion he had come to at first was, that the ship was sinking when the *Antenor* fell in with her, and that without great exertion in baling and pumping, she must sink.

He says: "I called the headmen amongst the pilgrims together and organised gangs amongst the pilgrims to pump and bale the vessel. This was done, the men constantly relieving one another, and by the evening of the 9th of August, we had gained 6 inches on the water, and during the following night we gained a foot on the water and continued to gain on the water thenceforward until the water was reduced to 3½ feet in the engine room and 5 feet in the after hold."

Upon this point Captain Bragg in his evidence, says:—"On the 9th, as the sun went half way down from the horizon, the Chief Officer telegraphed 'gained 4 inches,' and I called all hands aft to give him a cheer to encourage him—we were corresponding all the time. The question was, whether we could overpower the water, or the water overpower us."

An incident of this sort, slight in itself, yet tends to show the hearty good-will with which the salvors were conducting their operations and how likely it would be that they would reanimate, by their coolness and determination, the failing spirits and flagging energies of the pilgrims.

* * *

Captain Worsley, Master of the Telegraph ship *Sherard Osborne*, says:—"I have been Master Mariner, twenty years;—have commanded sailing ships and steam-ships in all parts of the world. I know the waters about Cape Guardafui. Under the circumstances described in the 5th & 6th paragraphs of J. T. Bragg's affidavit, I should say the *Jeddah* was in great danger. If the *Antenor* had not come up to her, I believe she would have become a total wreck. It would not have been practicable to put her about unless they got the propeller to revolve, *i.e.*, disconnected the propeller; it is not usual to have special disconnecting gear on such ships. She was heading right on to shore, I don't think she could have been steered so as to land on any particular spot on the beach. I should have considered her a hopeless derelict,—worse than a derelict with all those people on board. I don't think she could have been, under the circumstances, brought up under her anchor, if they had let the anchor go. If she had a steam windlass on board I think she would have run an awful risk for fear of the chain carrying away the bows. If it were blowing a gale outside, there would be a heavy ground swell off Cape Guardafui—there would be surf on the shore. I don't think boats would have lived through the surf. I don't know the nature of the bottom—if coral it would be very bad holding. I think that when a ship was left as she was described to be, she was in a helpless state. Second Engineers in ships of this class do not know about the navigation of a ship. The Carpenter is the important man under the Chief Officer as regards anchoring. After hearing the accounts read on the affidavits of Bragg and Campbell of how the *Antenor* got the *Jeddah* off in that night, I think the *Antenor* ran considerable risk; even in smooth water there is a risk of collision in a large steamer going alongside another near enough to take a hawser on board, more particularly when there is a strong current running, as there is there. The darkness would enhance the risk. There was very serious risk to the *Antenor's* screw, so great that unless there was imminent danger I should not attempt it until daylight. If the *Antenor* had snapped her rope and fouled her screw she would have been in danger."

Charles Powell, in his evidence, stated: "Last year I was in command of the *Lusitania*, one of the Orient line, of nearly 4,000 tons. I passed Cape Guardafui on August 7th at noon. We had very stiff weather from Ras Hafun to Guardafui; after we got round Guardafui there was a stiff breeze to the next point to East, I know this coast pretty well. Having heard the position and circumstances of the *Jeddah*, with the native crew and great part of them gone, and with 900 and odd pilgrims on board, I consider she was in great danger. If the *Antenor* had not come up to the *Jeddah*, I certainly think at night-time she would have gone on shore. She was heading for the bluffs. If I had been on board as a passenger I should have considered her case as a very hopeless one. I consider she was in great danger when first sighted, having so much water in her hold; she could not be steered at all. From Mr. Campbell's description, I should say it was blowing a strong breeze; it corresponds with my experience of the day: this was at the height of the monsoon when a strong breeze is generally blowing. If she made any speed at all, it must have been with the help of her canvas; when she was picked up I think she was water-logged. I think she would have gone ashore before daylight. If they had succeeded in getting the anchor down, it was just a chance if they held on: there was danger to the *Antenor* of colliding, and also of getting the hawser foul of her screw—a real danger. If I had been in command of the *Antenor*, I should have considered the position a dangerous one as regards the *Antenor*, and a very risky thing to do."

There can be no doubt, I think, that the *Jeddah* was in imminent danger when she was sighted by the *Antenor*, and that but for the services rendered her by the *Antenor* she would in all probability have foundered or been dashed to pieces, with the loss of every life on board. Taking into consideration the number of the lives thus rescued from the probability of impending death, this is, I believe, a case of life-salvage of a totally unprecedented character.

Conrad's contact with the pilgrim-ship episode stretched over a period of years, and the story probably came to him in varied and vivid forms. No doubt he read most of the details—though not the report of the inquiry at Aden—in the London papers in August 1880. At that time he was staying in London prior to embarking on the *Loch Etive* for Sydney on August 21. His seafaring acquaintances must also have discussed the incident.

His next contact with the tale must have been more vivid. On March 22, 1883, he arrived in Singapore in the S.S. *Sissie*, having been picked up by her after the *Palestine*, on which he was serving as second mate, had been abandoned on a journey from England to Bangkok when her cargo caught fire. The *Palestine* was an extremely old ship, and she sank quickly in calm weather. There was no negligence or cowardice on the part of her captain and crew, as the subsequent Court of Inquiry proved, but it must have seemed significant to Conrad that on his first trip to the East he was involved in an inquiry into the abandonment of a ship, just as the *Jeddah* crew had been involved in Aden. Furthermore, the day before he arrived in Singapore the *Jeddah* had arrived there, and the story of her desertion was no doubt a legend among the seamen. Conrad surely heard of it again, and of the sensation it caused in Singapore, in the very port from which the *Jeddah* had sailed and in which she was then docked.

During his second visit to Singapore, in 1885, he was able to observe something of her later history. The following advertisement appeared in the *Straits Times* of September 8:

> For Sale—The A. I. Steamer "Diamond" of 1,035 nett register carrying about 27,000 piculs dead weight. Engine of 200 horse power, speed 10 knots, with a consumption of 14 tons Cardiff. Built by Wm. Denny & Bros. of Dumbarton. For further particulars apply to M. Alsagoff, Manager, Singapore.

The *Diamond* was the *Jeddah* in disguise. She had not returned to Singapore after the desertion in 1880 until July 25, 1881—a year later. As the *Jeddah* she had then continued on the pilgrim run to Jeddah, but it would seem that her reputation still clung to her, for during 1884 and 1885 she was almost entirely disengaged. Returning from Jeddah on November 7, 1884, she was put up for sale. At this point the owners apparently employed a ruse to get rid of the ship's bad reputation. Her name dropped out of the "Shipping in Harbour" column of the *Straits Times* on February 28, 1885, although she was not listed as having been cleared from the harbor. Significantly, however, the S.S. *Diamond*, with the same tonnage and the same commander—a Captain Geary— was cleared for Palalangan. The Register of Shipping, Harbour Office, Singapore, shows that the *Diamond* was indeed the *Jeddah*, for the date and place of her origin and all other particulars were the same.

Inevitably, Conrad changed the name of the pilgrim ship when he wrote *Lord Jim*, calling it the *Patna*. On January 17, 1888, a 1,149-ton steamer called the *Patna* came into Singapore harbour.[8] At this time Conrad was staying at the Sailors' Home in Singapore (January 4 to January 19, 1888) before leaving on the S. S. *Melita* for Bangkok to take over the command of the bark *Otago*.

There was a particular reason for Conrad's interest in the master of the *Jeddah*, Captain Joseph Lucas Clark. As early as 1872 Clark was carrying pilgrims to Jeddah in the *Sumfoo*. The *Straits Times* of March 7, 1874, reported that Clark took the *Sumfoo* through the Torres Straits. As the first master of a steamer to make this dangerous journey, he was highly praised. Conrad was later to set the same course as commander of the sailing ship *Otago*, and it is extremely likely that he knew of Clark both in this connection and in connection with the *Jeddah*.

The first mate of the *Jeddah* at the time of the desertion was a man called Augustine Podmore Williams. Everything I have been able to discover about him from his descendants and from official and unofficial documents suggests that he was Conrad's inspiration for the whole of the first part of the novel.

---

8. *Straits Times Overland Journal*, January 18, 1888.

Williams' background is, in fact, identical with that of Lord Jim. A. P. Williams came from a parsonage and was one of five sons. His daughter, Mrs. Norah Thornett of Sussex, confirms in a letter (July 13, 1962) that her "father was from a parsonage as mentioned in *Lord Jim* & was one of five sons. He was born at Porthleven, Cornwall on May 22, 1852."

The parsonage at Porthleven was centuries old, and Conrad has given a fairly accurate description of it. The present vicar of Porthleven had this to say about the parsonage in a letter of September 7, 1962:

> I should say that, allowing for a certain amount of "writer's licence," the description of the rectory in *Lord Jim* is of Porthleven Vicarage, as one can see from the garden through the trees Breage Church (very ancient) standing out on a hill about 2 miles away. The Vicarage here is a mixture of brick and stone or granite—mostly granite blocks. The lawn slopes steeply in the front and there is a belt of fir trees, with a small stable and orchard at the back. Of course, the garden is much altered now and there are no green-houses; but the description, on the whole, tallies with Porthleven Vicarage.

According to Miss Nancy Williams of Penzance, the fir trees were planted by her grandfather, A. P. Williams' father. So far as I know he was the first of the Williams family to hold the living. "The old parson" at the time of the *Jeddah* disaster was fifty-seven.

Though A. P. Williams' daughters knew nothing of his early life, it seems likely that he went to a "training ship for officers of the mercantile marine," as did Lord Jim. I have a photograph dated 1868 that was sent to me by his niece, Mrs. Neill. "This antique," she writes, "shows my grandfather and his family." The photograph appears to have been taken at the back of the rectory, probably in the orchard. A. P. Williams, who was then sixteen, is on the extreme left of the family group. He is wearing a uniform of some kind that, with its brass buttons and cap, could be the uniform of a cadet officer of a training ship.

On July 2, 1880, when he was twenty-eight years old, A. P. Williams was taken on at Singapore as first mate of the *Jeddah*. It was not his first appointment as an officer of a ship in the East; prior to this time he had been first mate on the S.S. *Dale* from April 4, 1879, although only for four months. His first chance as chief officer was on the S.S. *Washi* (registered at Hong Kong) for one year, from July 1877 until August 3, 1878. The earliest date I have been able to trace for his arrival in the East is October 3, 1876, when he served on the S.S. *Thales* as second mate.[9]

What must have struck Conrad most forcibly if he met Williams in

9. This information is from Williams' application for a copy of his first mate's certificate, dated 1915. The application is held by the Registry of Shipping and Seamen, Cardiff.

Singapore was that here was no ordinary coward. Williams returned to Singapore, after leaving the *Jeddah,* on the S.S. *Naples,* and the return of one "whose name has been so frequently mentioned in the findings of the Court of Inquiry at Aden" was announced in the *Straits Times Overland Journal* on September 20, 1880. He did not return home as he might have done, for his certificate, unlike that of the master of the *Jeddah,* was not suspended. In spite of the severe censuring he had received both in the report of the inquiry and in the Singapore Legislative Council, William chose to return to a Singapore that was buzzing with news of the desertion—"Public excitement has risen to fever heat" (*Straits Times,* September 13, 1880). In those days the mercantile society in Singapore was so small that there would have been no chance for Williams to lose himself in anonymity, even if he had wished to.

This determination to face it out is also reflected in the letter he wrote to the *Daily Times* in Singapore, printed on September 20, 1880, and reprinted in the *Straits Times* on his return to Singapore:

> To the Editor of the Daily Times.
>
> Sir,—In reading your journal of yesterday's date giving a report of the debate in the Legislative Council regarding the *Jeddah,* I find in Mr. Campbell's speech the following remarks:—"From the evidence adduced at the Court of Inquiry it would seem that his (Captain Clark's) fears were utterly unfounded. However he orders a boat to be lowered, in which he puts his wife, and into which he, with his Chief Officer and the Chief Engineer manage to get."
>
> I am the Chief Officer of the *Jeddah* referred to, and I beg to inform you Mr. Campbell's statement, so far as it refers to me, is untrue. The evidence given before the Court of Inquiry will show that I was thrown overboard by the Hadjis after a severe wound was inflicted on my hand, and that I was afterwards picked up out of the water by Captain Clark and taken into his boat. In official discussions it would be advisable to keep to facts.
>
> I wish to say no more.
>
> > Yours obediently,
> > A. P. Williams,
> > Late S.S. *Jeddah.*

Linked with Williams' attitude is the ideal of the English gentleman. Mrs. Thornett writes in a letter of September 30, 1962, that her "father was conscious of being a gentleman and in some ways a snob. . . . I have the seal of gold with the crest and coat of arms which belonged to my father and I remember he always had this on his watch chain which hung on his waistcoat." What Mrs. Thornett says about the seal is verified by three photographs of Williams I have in my possession. The "seal of gold with the crest and coat of arms" on his watchchain are clearly apparent. The Williams family crest was of a lion passant (walking in profile) bearing a broken chain and the motto *Vinctus Sed-Non Victus* (chained but not conquered).

The conception of what is appropriate to a gentleman probably accounts for the kind of language used by Jim on occasions and particularly in chapters *xvii* and *xxiii*. I have not been able to discover whether this language was typical of A. P. Williams, although an old Singaporean who knew him says he was "very polished in speech—very good mannered." Certainly Jim is given preparatory-school language and enthusiasms that do not at all suit the man we have met earlier narrating the story of his disaster to Captain Marlow. It may have been Conrad's intention to offer a submerged criticism of Lord Jim, indicating his fundamental immaturity, but there is no doubt that Conrad was trying to reproduce the language of a young gentleman. English was not Conrad's native tongue, and preparatory-school slang may have sounded less absurd then than it does now.

Physical likeness between a fictional character and his source is not an easy thing to prove, but Williams had certain outstanding physical features. His height, powerful build, and neat dress are confirmed by Mrs. Thornett. I asked her to compare the description in *Lord Jim* with her memories of her father, and she wrote to me on July 13, 1962 that she had "read *Lord Jim* and it certainly does seem that reference is made to my Father & the description in Chapter 1 seems typical. From my recollection of him as a child, he was powerfully built, very tall and had a deep voice, though gentle at heart." Later, on September 30, 1962, she added: "My father did dress carefully, very neat, all in white, I believe they were called 'tutop' . . . the jackets were buttoned up the front to the neck." A local inhabitant in Singapore has told me that A. P. Williams was a big man, certainly not under six feet—taller, in fact—and broad, while another old Singaporean said he was "bluff, handsome, head up in the air"; my photographs of Williams confirm all this. Mrs. P. Ward of Perth, Australia, stated in a letter August 21, 1962 that her father, A. P. Williams, "had beautiful china-blue eyes."

If Conrad met him in Singapore, Williams must then have been about thirty-one, and twenty-eight at the time of the *Jeddah* incident. The four photographs I have obtained of Williams show him at various stages of his life and certainly in the first two it is possible to trace those less-easy-to-define aspects of manner and stance that were typical of Jim. The first is dated 1868, when Williams was sixteen. He is leaning against a chair, legs crossed and hands in pockets, looking firmly and a little suspiciously into the camera. He is certainly "upstanding, broad-shouldered, with his hands in his pockets" and "clean-limbed, clean-faced, firm on his feet"; given a few years more in age, he might well be the Lord Jim who turned away from the other deserters, looking "unconcerned and unapproachable as only the young can look."

In the second photograph he is probably in his thirties and is photographed in a sitting position, with his wife beside him. The features most noticeable here are his size, powerful build, and direct stare, which could certainly be described as a "kind of dogged self-assertion." He looks out of the photograph with a determined, aggressive pride that is lacking in the younger Williams but that recalls the attitude of Lord Jim when, in his determination not to be called names by any man, he "bullies" Marlow.

Although Williams did not spend years attempting to run away from his past, his later life does have certain similarities with that of Jim. Mrs. Thornett could tell me only that "he was sea-faring to start with and then joined McAlister & Co., as a ship's chandler." On returning to Singapore Williams had obviously tried to continue as a seaman. He was taken on as first officer in the S.S. *Cleator*, a much smaller ship than the *Jeddah*, in January, 1881. He left this ship after two months, and seems to have been unemployed until he joined an even smaller vessel, the S.S. *Vidar*, as first officer in May 1882. This is a most interesting fact, for Conrad himself was first officer on the *Vidar* from August 1887 to January 1888. Williams served on this ship for about the same length of time as Conrad did (May to October 1882) and made the same journeys from Singapore to Berau, the settlement in eastern Borneo on the Berau River that was to become Conrad's source for Patusan. At Berau Williams must have met, as Conrad was to do later, Olmeijer (the original of Almayer), Captain William Lingard (Conrad's Rajah Laut), and Jim Lingard, whose Malay title "Tuan Jim" provided Conrad with the title of his novel. One of Jim Lingard's daughters, who is now living in Singapore, has told me that the Lingard children who were educated in Singapore played with the Williams children, and this suggests a friendship between the two men. The first and second engineers of the *Vidar*, James Allen and John Niven, who appear in *The Shadow-Line*, had been with the *Vidar* at least as early as 1883,[1] and I strongly believe that they joined the *Vidar* earlier than this. Conrad must also have heard of Williams from these two men while he served on the *Vidar*, and then probably have met him as a water-clerk in the port of Singapore.

The first reference to him as a ship chandler's water-clerk is in *Singapore and Straits Directory* of 1884. He was then working for McAlisters, a small but well-known firm in those days and certainly well known today in Singapore. Mrs. Thornett says that her father "was . . . the first man out as the ships came into harbour."

A. P. Williams married in the East, an indication perhaps of his determination to settle here and also of the fact that he had given up the idea of returning home. Mrs. Neill writes that he "shocked and horrified his father—also mine, by marrying a Eurasian! Aunt Jane I

1. *Singapore and Straits Directory*, 1883, p. 96.

A. P. Williams with his wife, Jane Williams, c. 1883. From Norman Sherry, *Conrad's Eastern World* (Cambridge and New York: Cambridge UP, 1966). Reproduced by permission of Miss N. N. Williams.

believe was clever—cultured, of high caste and attractive, and it was apparently a very happy marriage. They had a large family—some black—some white." The record of Williams' marriage is in the registry at St. Andrews Cathedral, Singapore. It records that George Augustine Podmore Williams, aged 30, Master Mariner, married E. Jane Robinson, aged sixteen years, on January 22, 1883.

Williams was still in business in 1915, according to the *Directory*, but in 1916 he died. An obituary appeared in the *Singapore Free Press* on April 20, 1916:

> There passed away yesterday morning, at his residence, Shamrock, Barker Road, Mr. Austin Podmore Williams, who for 27 years was employed at Messrs McAlister & Co., as their chief outside superintendent in the Dubash and Shipchandlery Department. . . . The late Mr. Williams was chief officer of the Singapore Steamship Co.'s *Jeddah*, a pilgrim ship which met with an accident in the Red Sea and was abandoned with about a 1,000 coolies aboard.

In his will are the words: "I desire that my funeral should be quiet, cheap and simple and no fuss made about it." His grave is in the Bidadari Cemetery, Upper Serangoon Road, Singapore. Williams, clearly, regarded himself to the last as a master mariner, in spite of his long years on land, for his headstone was engraved with an anchor.

Although not referred to by name, Singapore is the port that provides the background to the inquiry in *Lord Jim*. It should be remembered that Conrad himself was involved in an inquiry in that port into the loss of the *Palestine* in 1883.

When he reached Singapore for the third time, in the summer of 1887, Conrad spent six weeks in the hospital for treatment of a back injury he had suffered in an accident on board the *Highland Forest*. The European Hospital in Singapore was situated just behind and slightly to the right of the present General Hospital, on a slope some distance from the harbor. Ships at anchor in the harbor can still be seen from the site. Two years before Conrad was in the hospital, convent sisters had been allowed to nurse the sick there. In *The Mirror of the Sea* (1906) Conrad tells how he lay on his back "looking at the fronds of the palm-trees tossing and rustling at the height of the window."

The Harbour Office in Singapore was then a white-fronted building beside the quay, with a pillared portico; the Esplanade, with grass plots facing the sea, is close by; and the bandstand, although no longer in existence, used to be directly opposite Coleman Street, which terminated in the long stretch of the Hotel de l'Europe.

An account of an open-air concert is recorded by Braddell: "The bands used to play . . . twice a week; the chains were taken down opposite

Coleman Street and the carriages were driven in and stood in a circle around the bandstand."[2]

There has never been a Malabar Hotel in Singapore—although there was and is a Malabar Street—but Conrad's description of this hotel in *Lord Jim* corresponds closely to the appearance of the Hotel de l'Europe. Although this hotel is no longer in existence, a photograph in my possession shows that it had a "big dining-room," that its long "front gallery" was used "for coffee and cigars," and that the view from it would be the same as that from the Malabar Hotel: "the riding lights of ships." Indeed the Hotel de l'Europe (described also, although not named, in *The Shadow-Line*), was the only hotel in Singapore that faced the sea; it could be clearly seen from the Harbour Office.

The Sailors' Home, also quite close to the seafront, stood just behind the Hotel de l'Europe. A mercantile marine officer could pay one Malayan dollar per day to stay there, and no doubt this is the sum Conrad himself paid when he stayed at the home (January 4 to January 19, 1877) after he left the S.S. *Vidar*.

The master-attendant who gives a dressing down to the captain of the *Patna* is based on Captain Ellis, the master-attendant in Singapore at that time, a man whom Conrad introduced as a character in "The End of the Tether" and *The Shadow-Line* as well as in *Lord Jim*. Henry Ellis was the man who appointed Conrad to the command of the *Otago*. On July 5, 1963, his grandson, the Reverend Henry Ellis Briscow, wrote to me:

> Captain Henry Ellis was my grandfather. . . . He was a big broad shouldered man with a powerful voice that stuck terror into all his subordinates, whether oriental or occidental; his word was law and he always spoke with the authority of a man who was not accustomed to having his opinions controverted. He ruled with a rod of iron. He had a horror of red tape and did not take kindly to interference from government officials. Henry Ellis had a very violent temper and shouted and roared when things did not go his way. . . . He died of a broken leg because he would not let the doctor put it in splints. He was offered a very good appointment in Venezuela after his retirement in Singapore but was advised not to take it because of his violent temper. This would have eventually led to his being knifed.

Articles about Ellis published in the *Singapore Free Press* (December 5, 1907, and February 20, 1908) confirm some of the aspects of Conrad's fictional portrait:

> He was an Irishman of intensity, a real good man and kindly, but with a quickness of temper that almost set the river on fire. One

2. R. St. J. Braddell, "The Merry Past," *One Hundred Years of Singapore*, 2 vols., London, 1921, II, 495.

minute he would be a stately and dignified official, courteous and gentlemanly; the next he was boiling over with temper and hardly knew what he was doing. Next morning he was all right again and never omitted to make amends for the havoc he had wrought in his haste.

* * *

Captain Ellis was a strong official, blunt and straightforward, standing no nonsense, with a good deal of Irish humor about him and some national touchiness as well. He was by virtue of his office, one of the best known men in Singapore, although in private life he mixed little in Society. . . .

The suicide of the master of the clipper *Cutty Sark* in 1880 was another source for the pilgrim-ship episode of *Lord Jim*.

Conrad may well have heard or read the story of the *Jeddah* and the story of the *Cutty Sark* at the same time. In the *Singapore Straits Times* editorial column on September 20, 1880, there was a report of the motion "touching the abandonment of the S.S. *Jeddah* in open sea by her master and officers when she had over 1,000 souls on board" which was discussed in the Singapore Legislative Assembly. In the same column is the report of the arrival in Singapore of the chief officer of the *Jeddah*, A. P. Williams, just above the following paragraph:

Another painful story from the sea. The British barque *Cutty Sark*, formerly a tea clipper, arrived here on Saturday morning from Anjer, and the second officer, in whose charge she arrived, reports that while at Anjer the chief officer struck a seaman who died from the effects of the blow. The Chief officer, alarmed at the consequences of his act, made his escape. . . .

The only full account of the *Cutty Sark* incident I have been able to obtain is that written by Basil Lubbock, who drew his information from the ship's log and from the narratives of sailors on board at the time. It is likely that he was, in this last instance, drawing upon the kind of hearsay Conrad would have had access to.

The incident on the *Cutty Sark* was as follows. Sydney Smith, the chief mate, gave an order to John Francis, a Negro seaman, which Francis did not obey. Because of the man's insolence and the fact that he threatened Smith with a capstan bar, there was a struggle during which the mate got possession of the capstan bar and brought it down on Francis' head, knocking him unconscious. Francis never regained consciousness and died three days later. According to Lubbock's account of the incident, the mate retired to his cabin for the rest of the passage. When the *Cutty Sark* arrived at Anjer, the mate persuaded his skipper, Captain Wallace, to help him escape, and he was eventually smuggled aboard an American ship, the *Colorado*. The mate was not heard of for two years, but then was found, arrested, tried in London, and sentenced to seven years' imprisonment for manslaughter. Soon after he had helped the mate to escape, Captain Wallace committed suicide.

Lubbock gives an account of Wallace's suicide. Wallace was very upset by the mate's escape:

> Ever since the escape of the mate he had been unable to sleep. . . . Night and day he stood gazing out to sea or walked with bowed head up and down the poop. . . . On the fourth day after leaving Anjer, the watch had just been called at 4 A.M., when the captain, who was standing at the break of the poop with the carpenter, turned to his faithful petty officer and asked if the second mate was on deck.
>
> "Chips" replied that he was just coming up. Whereupon Captain Wallace left the carpenter and walked aft: called the helmsman's attention to the course; then deliberately stepped on to the taffrail and jumped overboard.[3]

A report in the *Singapore Daily Times* of September 18, 1880, on the *Cutty Sark* incident suggests reasons for Wallace's suicide:

> The Captain appears to have assisted the chief officer to escape on board an American ship bound for Saigon and afterwards whether from pangs of conscience or fear of future trouble he threw himself overboard and was drowned.

Wallace was a young and successful skipper. He took his second mate's certificate when he was 21, his first mate's when he was 23, and his master's when he was 24. At twenty-seven he was commander of the famous clipper *Cutty Sark*, and in the same year he committed suicide by walking over the side of the ship. The death of this famous skipper at such an early age, when he was at the height of his career and when there was no strong reason for such an act, must have caused a great deal of speculation.

The Bornean River and Its People†

The second part of *Lord Jim* moves from the *Patna* disaster and the sophisticated Eastern port to the primitive, remote area of the Bornean river, with its two lonely traders and its political intrigue among the native rulers. Conrad himself made such a transition when, on August

---

3. Basil Lubbock, *The Log of the Cutty Sark*, London, 1925, p. 196.
† This essay draws upon materials contained in Norman Sherry's *Conrad's Eastern World* (Cambridge and New York: 1966), to whom grateful acknowledgment is made.

22, 1887, during his last visit to Singapore, he signed on as mate of a trading ship called the *Vidar*. The *Vidar* sailed among the islands of the Southeast Archipelago, calling at ports and making her way up rivers to trading settlements, in particular the post on the River Berau in Dutch East Borneo. This is the settlement called Tandjong Redeb, although it is also referred to in accounts by the names of the two villages on either side of the Berau River, Gunung Tabur and Sambaliung.

Conrad uses the same setting in *Almayer's Folly* (1895) and *An Outcast of the Islands* (1896), but calls the place Sambir; and he also draws upon his knowledge of Berau for "The Lagoon" and "Karain" (1897), "The End of the Tether" (1902), "Freya of the Seven Isles" (1912), and *The Rescue* (1920).

Conrad made only four trips on the *Vidar*, probably spending no more than three days at Tandjong Redeb on each occasion. He could not, therefore, have gained any intimate knowledge of the area and its people, and he must have relied primarily upon observation and hearsay. As might be expected, those aspects of the fictional Patusan which can be shown most conclusively to be based on Berau are ones that would catch the attention of any seaman involved in the navigation of a river and the trading carried on by his vessel. But for specific incidents, personalities, and situations, Conrad appears to have consulted written accounts not only of this area but of other places in the Archipelago, such as the following, from the *Eastern Archipelago Pilot*.[4]

> The KURAN or BERAU RIVER, one of the five principal streams on the east coast of Borneo, is formed by the junction of the rivers Segah and Kalai, which unite opposite the towns of Tabur and Sambaliung, at a distance of 34 miles from the sea. There is an extensive delta at the mouth, the principal channels through which are the Pantai, Garura, Manussur, and Tidung. The first named, which is in fact the mouth of the river of the same name, is one of the most frequented by ships, and its entrance is well defined by several isolated hill tops, which rise from the otherwise low and marshy shore. At Gunong Santul, 26 miles from the sea, the left bank of the river becomes hilly, while on the right bank, and at a distance of about 3 miles, lies a chain of hills from 100 to 160 feet in height, which forms the watershed between the Berau and Pantai rivers. Below Gunong Tabur, the Berau river has a breadth of from 660 to 1,310 yards, its mean depth at ordinary low water being 18 feet, with a minimum depth of 12½ feet at a spot on the west side of Sandang-besar island, known as "Lingard's Cross";[5] in flood the river rises 9 feet.

4. First edition, London, 1893, p. 340.
5. Named after Captain William Lingard, who apparently discovered it. He is the Captain "Tom" Lingard of *Almayer's Folly*, *An Outcast of the Islands*, and *The Rescue*. William Lingard set up a trading post on the river at Tandjong Redeb about 1870 and established Olmeijer (the

Trade.—The principal articles of export are rattan, gutta-percha, and dammar (gum copal), in quantities of about 250 tons, 120 tons, and 300 tons respectively, a year. The principal trade is with Singapore, chiefly in the vessels of Messrs. Lingard & Co., and only a small portion goes to Java or Dutch East India ports. The forests in the Berau lands could furnish an inexhaustable supply of good and fine timber.

Communications.—A tolerably regular steam service between Singapore, Pasir, Berau river, and Bulungan, is maintained by a vessel belonging to an Arab at Singapore, but running under the British flag. There is also irregular steam communication with Makasser, and occasionally with Pontianak.

Another description of the area appeared in the *Straits Times Overland Journal* on March 26, 1883:

Gunong Thabor and Sambaliung, formerly forming together the State of Berouw [Berau] are situated right and left on the Berouw river. The villages therein are insignificant; even the Sultan's house appears miserable. In 1879 only one European resided there, he being a storekeeper from Macassar. There is very little trade, though the soil is very rich and fruitful. Rattans, gutta percha, and coals are the principal products. The inhabitants are lazy and unenterprising. Labour is for women and slaves only. Slaves are met with in almost every house. On the lower river, there is even a large village wholly inhabited by slaves. The authorities allow this, in spite of Art. 115 of the Government reg. whereby slavery in Netherlands India has been abolished. Most of the slaves are fairly well off excepting those who have to work in the mines. The number of these unfortunates yearly sold at Gunong Thabor is estimated at 300. These people are brought or kidnapped from the islands of Sooloo and the other Philippines' and then bartered for gunpowder, muskets, revolvers, lillas cloths, calico, opium, Dutch candles etc.

In 1869, the commandant of H.N.M's steamer *Salak* intercepted a shipment of slaves concealed in four prahus and packed like herrings. This living cargo consisted of young and charming children, a few older beauties (destined for the harem of the Sultan of Gunong Thabor) and several young men, amounting altogether to 34 persons. . . .

Captain Sir Edward Belcher made an excursion up the River Berau in 1845 in search of some British seamen—a Captain Brownrigg and his crew—who had wrecked their ship at the mouth of the Berau and

---

Almayer of *Almayer's Folly*) there, and later, about 1880, his nephew, Jim Lingard. Lingard used only sailing ships and appears eventually to have lost his monopoly of the Berau trade, probably through the intervention of the steamship *Vidar*, owned by Syed Masin Bin Salleh Al Joofree, an Arab in Singapore.

had been taken prisoners by the sultan of Gunung Tabur. Belcher wrote an account of his search for the men in his *Voyage of "H.M.S. Samarang."* The following extracts suggest the kind of topographical and historical detail available to Conrad, and should also be read with the incident of Gentleman Brown in mind.[6]

> About 9, A.M., on the 30th of December, we noticed what at first sight appeared to be a Malay battery, or stockade, constructed upon the summit of a hill which completely commanded the whole reach of the river below this place. * * * we soon discovered that the place was not only without inhabitants, but that the town which had been near it, had been lately burned * * * and the plantain and other fruit trees lately cut down, exhibit[ing] indubitable symptoms of recent war.
>
> *   *   *
>
> In the morning we again moved forward, still without any signs of human beings, although every mile that we advanced the cleared condition of the land, and other objects, satisfied us that we could not be far distant from their dwellings. Shortly before eight, we discovered the first inhabited house, and immediately afterwards the outskirts of the town of Gunung Taboor.
>
> The boats being in a condition for work, with all useless lumber stowed below, we advanced towards the town; it was found to be closely stockaded. * * * On the range of stockade, numbers of small Dutch flags were displayed. On our approach, an ambassador was sent to convey the welcome of the Sultan. * * * as I saw nothing but Dutch colours I was at a loss how to act, until I knew what power held the place; he immediately rejoined, that there were no Dutch here. * * * "the colours you see are Bugis, from Celebes, excepting that large Dutch flag, which was a present from the Governor of Macassar."
>
> *   *   *
>
> He informed me that all the Europeans had been taken away from Sambiliong, the fortified position on the heights, on the opposite side of the river, distant three miles, on the 26th of October last, by a Dutch schooner-of-war, and he produced a Dutch document to that effect.
>
> *   *   *
>
> He further stated, that the English became very troublesome, and although better fed than themselves, were sullen and discontented; that they leagued with the Rajah Muda, his cousin, who had rebelled, and, as he required their aid to work his guns, had seduced them to escape to him, under the promise of sending them safely to Kotai.

6. Sir Edward Belcher, *Narrative of the Voyage of "H.M.S. Samarang,"* 2 vols., London, 1848, I: 212–13, 214–15, 218, 219, 239, 241–42, 279; II: 167–68.

*　*　*

The Rajah Muda, who has established himself, in defiance of the Sultan's authority, at Sambiliong, and assumed the title of *Sultan Muda*, (or young Sultan,) is a cousin of Si Atap, but, as before noticed, having quarrelled about the Europeans, has been closely shut up in his fortress, and will probably be destroyed.

*　*　*

In proof of his anxiety to befriend the English, the Sultan [of Gunung Tabur] offers to give them a separate place within his town to live in, to protect them, to give them a preference in trade, and as a further exhibition of his sincerity to open trading connexions, he gave me a letter under his official seal, containing the list of goods which he would engage as certain cargo, to any vessel which I would send in the May following.

*　*　*

"The next river is a very large one, sometimes called *Barow*, and sometimes *Curan*, from different places near it; the first is an independent state, in alliance with Sooloo, the other is subject to Sooloo. The river has three fathoms at the mouth, but there are several shoals which require a pilot."

This river has been already noticed. It is the Pantai, one of the branches, or properly the main stream, which takes the name of *Brraou*, and gives its name to people of the district, the city being Gunung Taboor. *　*　*

"There is a considerable trade in Cocoa-nuts carried on from *Tuallee*, or *Celebes*, to *Barow*, which they call *Barong*; according to their accounts, the river is very deep within, and the country yields much Bird's nests, and other valuable commodities. But, although the Sooloos agree in the magnitude of the river, they deny that their country is of much consequence with respect to its produce. This river is in the bottom of a deep bay, the land running from thence to the eastward, terminating in a point of red land, called on account of its peculiar colour, *Tanna Mera*, (Red land,) off which are many islands."[7]

*　*　*

I not only used every effort to open trade direct with Gunung Taboor, Tambisan, and Kabatuan; but at my persuasion, two persons have made the attempt; others met me with the observation: "All which you state is very true, and the prices are favourable in the highest degree, *but you cannot warrant half a cargo, even for a small schooner.*" At Gunung Taboor the Sultan bound himself to supply a cargo for one vessel filling up with rattans, Cassia bark, &c., but more he could not promise, as the collection of *one year*. *　*　* until the colony is firmly settled, and piracy annihilated on the range of coast by which trade must pass, this state of affairs will

---

7. Here Belcher is quoting from "Oriental Repertory" by Dalrymple, the explorer.

be slow of arriving; and when it does, still, until the habits of the inland tribes become settled, and they plant for, and send to your market, the same scantiness of tonnage must prevail.

In 1869 the naturalist Alfred Russel Wallace first published an account of his wanderings and discoveries in the Southeast Asian Archipelago during the 1850's and 1860's.[8] Reissued frequently, the work, according to Richard Curle, was Conrad's "intimate friend for many years."[9]

At length, about an hour after noon, we reached our destination—the village of Coupang, situated nearly in the centre of the island—and entered the outer court of a house belonging to one of the chiefs with whom my friend Mr. Ross had a slight acquaintance. Here we were requested to seat ourselves under an open shed with a raised floor of bamboo, a place used to receive visitors and hold audiences. Turning our horses to graze on the luxuriant grass of the courtyard, we waited till the great man's Malay interpreter appeared, who inquired our business and informed us that the Pumbuckle (chief) was at the Rajah's house, but would soon be back. As we had not yet breakfasted, we begged he would get us something to eat, which he promised to do as soon as possible. It was however about two hours before anything appeared, when a small tray was brought containing two saucers of rice, four small fried fish, and a few vegetables. * * *

At length about four o'clock the Pumbuckle made his appearance, and we informed him of our desire to stay with him a few days, to shoot birds and see the country. At this he seemed somewhat disturbed, and asked if we had brought a letter from the Anak Agong (Son of Heaven), which is the title of the Rajah of Lombock. This we had not done, thinking it quite unnecessary; and he then abruptly told us that he must go and speak to his Rajah, to see if we could stay. Hours passed away. The sun set, and it soon became dark, and we got rather hungry as we sat wearily under the shed and no one came. Still hour after hour we waited, till about nine o'clock, the Pumbuckle, the Rajah, some priests, and a number of their followers arrived and took their seats around us. We shook hands, and for some minutes there was a dead silence. Then the Rajah asked what we wanted. * * * questions were asked about my guns, and what powder I had, and whether I used shot or bullets; also what the birds were for, and how I preserved them, and what was done with them in England. Each of my answers and explanations was followed by a low and serious conversation which we could not understand, but the purport of which we could guess. They were evidently quite puzzled, and did not believe a word we had told them. They then inquired if we were really

8. Alfred Russel Wallace, *The Malay Archipelago*, London, 1894, pp. 127–29, 167–68, 173, 236–37, 257–58, 419.
9. Richard Curle, *The Last Twelve Years of Joseph Conrad*, New York, 1928, p. 109.

English, and not Dutch; and although we strongly asserted our
nationality, they did not seem to believe us. * * * At length, about
one in the morning, the whole party rose to depart, and, after
conversing some time at the gate, all went away. We now begged
the interpreter, who with a few boys and men remained about us,
to show us a place to sleep in, at which he seemed very much
surprised, saying he thought we were very well accommodated
where we were. It was quite chilly, and we were very thinly clad
and had brought no blankets, but all we could get after another
hour's talk was a native mat and pillow, and a few old curtains to
hang round three sides of the open shed and protect us a little from
the cold breeze.

* * *

As soon as I was well, I again went to Goa, accompanied by Mr.
Mesman, to beg the Rajah's assistance in getting a small house
built for me near the forest. We found him at a cock-fight in a
shed near his palace, which however he immediately left to receive
us, and walked with us up an inclined plane of boards which serves
for stairs to his house. This was large, well built, and lofty, with
bamboo floor and glass windows. The greater part of it seemed to
be one large hall divided by the supporting posts. Near a window
sat the Queen squatting on a rough wooden arm-chair, chewing
the everlasting sirih and betel-nut, while a brass spittoon by her
side and a sirih-box in front were ready to administer to her wants.
The Rajah seated himself opposite to her in a similar chair, and a
similar spittoon and sirih-box were held by a little boy squatting at
his side. Two other chairs were brought for us. Several young
women, some the Rajah's daughters, others slaves, were standing
about; a few were working at frames making sarongs, but most of
them were idle. * * * Everything had a dingy and faded appearance, very disagreeable and unroyal to a European eye. The only
thing that excited some degree of admiration was the quiet and
dignified manner of the Rajah, and the great respect always paid
to him.

* * *

Close to my house was an inclosed mudhole where three buffaloes
were shut up every night, and the effluvia from which freely entered
through the open bamboo floor.

* * *

About the centre of it is the palace of the Sultan, now a large,
untidy, half-ruinous building of stone. This chief is pensioned by
the Dutch Government, but retains the sovereignty over the native
population of the island, and of the northern part of Gilolo. The
sultans of Ternate and Tidore were once celebrated through the
East for their power and regal magnificence. When Drake visited
Ternate in 1579, the Portuguese had been driven out of the island,

although they still had a settlement at Tidore. He gives a glowing account of the Sultan. * * *

All this glitter of barbaric gold was the produce of the spice trade, of which the Sultans kept the monopoly, and by which they became wealthy. Ternate, with the small islands in a line south of it, as far as Batchian, constitute the ancient Moluccas, the native country of the clove, as well as the only part in which it was cultivated. Nutmegs and mace were procured from the natives of New Guinea and the adjacent islands, where they grew wild; and the profits on spice cargoes were so enormous, that the European traders were glad to give gold and jewels, and the finest manufacturers of Europe or of India, in exchange.

The character of Stein appears to have been built up from a number of sources, including Wallace himself and other people (for example, a German naturalist named Bernstein) mentioned in his book. Following are a description from Wallace of Mr. Mesman, a Macassar-born Dutchman living in Celebes; an account of Wallace's own emotion on finding a rare butterfly; and a reference to Wallace's young assistant, Charles Allen.

[Mr. Mesman] lived in a spacious house near the town, situated in the midst of a grove of fruit trees, and surrounded by a perfect labyrinth of offices, stables, and native cottages occupied by his numerous servants, slaves, or dependants. He usually rose before the sun, and after a cup of coffee looked after his servants, horses, and dogs, till seven, when a substantial breakfast of rice and meat was ready in a cool verandah. Putting on a clean white linen suit, he then drove to town in his buggy, where he had an office, with two or three Chinese clerks who looked after his affairs. His business was that of a coffee and opium merchant. He had a coffee estate at Bontyne, and a small prau which traded to the Eastern islands near New Guinea, for mother-of-pearl and tortoiseshell.

* * *

During my very first walk into the forest at Batchian, I had seen sitting on a leaf out of reach, an immense butterfly of a dark colour marked with white and yellow spots. I could not capture it as it flew away high up into the forest, but I at once saw that it was a female of a new species of Ornithoptera or "bird-winged butterfly," the pride of the Eastern tropics. * * * The next day I went again to the same shrub and succeeded in catching a female, and the day after a fine male. I found it to be as I had expected, a perfectly new and most magnificent species and the most gorgeously coloured butterflies in the world. Fine specimens of the male are more than seven inches across the wings, which are velvety black and fiery orange, the latter colour replacing the green of the allied species. The beauty and brilliancy of this insect are indescribable, and none but a naturalist can understand the intense excitement I experienced when I at length captured it. On taking it out of my net and opening the glorious wings, my heart began to beat violently, the blood rushed to my head, and I felt much more like fainting than I have done when in apprehension of immediate death. I had a headache the rest of the day, so great was the excitement produced by what will appear to most people a very inadequate cause.

* * *

Charles Allen made a voyage to New Guinea * * *. On his return he went to the Sula Islands, and made a very interesting collection, which served to determine the limits of the zoological group of Celebes * * *. His next journey was to Flores and Solor, where he obtained some valuable materials * * *. He afterwards went to Coti on the east coast of Borneo, from which place I was very anxious to obtain collections * * *. On his return thence to Sourabaya in Java, he was to have gone to the entirely unknown Sumba or Sandal-wood Island. Most unfortunately, however, he was seized with a terrible fever on his arrival at Coti, and, after lying there some weeks, was taken to Singapore in a very bad condition, where he arrived after I had left for England. When he recovered he obtained employment in Singapore, and I lost his services as a collector.

Wallace returned home, but Allen remained and prospered in the East. In the *Singapore and Straits Directory* for 1883 he is listed as the manager of the Perseverance Estate, which was owned by a Mr. J. Fisher and extended over a thousand acres. In 1888, Conrad's last year in the East, the *Directory* shows that Allen was by then the owner of the estate. There is a photograph of the estate, said to be about three miles out of Singapore, in *British Malaya: Twentieth Century Impressions.*[1]

Major Fred McNair's book *Perak and the Malays*, from which the following extracts are taken,[2] provided Contrad with accounts of piracy and warfare in the area. In 1873 McNair was one of two British commissioners who, after a pirate attack on a Malay boat, watched the proceedings of the court that tried and punished the pirates, a court "composed of the Viceroy of Salangore, with three Native Commissioners appointed by the Sultan. * * * The sitting of the court took place at a stockade," behind which seven of the eight pirates were executed by the Sultan's kris the next day. Before the trial and execution, a British admiral

had an interview with the Sultan, who was surrounded by his chiefs and people, and in as much state as he was capable of showing. The Admiral, in referring to the barbarity of the Jugra piracy,

1. Ed. Arnold Wright, London, 1908, p. 664.
2. Major Fred McNair, *Perak and the Malays: "Sarong" and "Kris,"* London, 1878, pp. 289, 369–70, 380, 392–93, 400–401, 130–31, 169.

advised and urged upon the Sultan to caution his people against being guilty of such acts in future, pointing out how it was impossible that they could be left unpunished. * * *

The Sultan listened very attentively, and then turning quickly round to his people, he exclaimed: *Dungar lah, jangan kitah main main lagi!*—"Hear now, my people! Don't let us have any more of this little game!"

McNair also describes the murder, on November 2, 1875, of the Resident of Perak, J. W. W. Birch, who had fallen out of favor with the Sultan, and tells of the subsequent fighting.

> * * * the infuriated Malays, armed with spears and krises, made a rush in a body down to the river-bank, where Mr. Birch was ashore at the bathing-house, his orderly being on guard with a revolver. He let his leader, however, be taken completely by surprise. * * * [Mr. Birch] was savagely attacked, some of the Malays driving their keen limbings through the rattan mat that formed a screen, while others went to the end of the bath, and, as the wounded Resident struggled up out of the water, one man cut at him with a sword, when he sank.
>
> * * *
>
> [The Malay Stockade] was a strong place, with deep ditch, earthwork, wattled fence, and pointed bamboos, while it was armed with a large iron gun and a small pivot "lelah."
>
> * * *
>
> Consequent upon the difficulties of the task, and the weight of the guns [two seven-pounders] which had to be dragged [by the British] over and through a variety of serious obstacles, only four miles were advanced in two hours and a half, and at the end of this time the first symptom of the presence of the enemy was found in the shape of several trees felled across the track. * * * Nothing further occurred for a couple of hours, when the advance was again checked by trees felled across the path.
>
> * * *
>
> Captain Channer, with whom was Lieutenant North, R.E., pushed on—his route having been along the bed of a torrent till the way was blocked by felled trees. A rearguard was left to cut through these obstructions; and nothing daunted by the rough nature of the country, Captain Channer threw out men right and left, himself leading the left body of twenty-five men. He had given up his guides, for they evidently knew nothing of the position of the enemy; and trusting to himself, he went on working cautiously through the jungle, till he saw the enemy's smoke and fires, and soon after came upon one of the stockades, and reconnoitered the Malay defences. This jungle fort was composed of logs surrounded

by a palisade, and sharp spiked bamboos were everywhere about the ground.

This was an important moment; for if the Malays had caught sight of the attacking force the alarm would have been given at once; but by using precautions, and watching the enemy, Captain Channer was able to learn the easiest way into the stockade. Then, supported by two Ghoorkhas, he leaped over the palisade, where he could hear the Malays talking inside—no look-out being kept, as the enemy was cooking; and then dashing forward, followed by his two men, he boldly attacked the twenty or thirty who constituted the garrison, shot down one man with his revolver, while the two Ghoorkhas each shot down theirs. Five Malays in all were killed in the first instance, and the remainder of the little flanking party coming up, the enemy, believing themselves to be surrounded, took to flight.

From his limited experience of Borneo, Conrad would hardly have been able to distinguish between Malayan races such as the Malays and the Bugis. The physical characteristics of the two races, from the foreigner's point of view, are very much the same, and other differences relating to character and way of life must have been quite beyond Conrad's knowledge. Yet in his novels he makes distinctions between Malay, Bugis, and Arab. *Perak and the Malays* may well have contributed to this knowledge as well as to the specific characters of Doramin and his wife.

The Bugis are evidently a distinct race from the Malays, and come originally from the southern part of the island of Celebes. They compare most favourably with the Malays proper, being intelligent, courageous, and enterprising; and though very similar to them in appearance, they speak a different language. The Malays fear and respect them above all the other races of the Archipelago; and among them are to be found the principal native traders and merchants. * * * The character given to the Bugis is not always of the best, for he has been termed a beggar, treacherous, given to stealing, braver than a Malay, but not possessing the other's good points, being one who will lay his plans to obtain revenge on the offending party.

The Bugis race has kept itself very distinct from the people amongst whom it dwells, but occasionally inter-marriages take place. One of the most important of late has been that of the well-known Bugis chief of Perak, Nakoda Trong, who led to the hymeneal altar one of the Perak ladies of distinction, Inche Maida, or Princess Maida.

* * *

The house to the left is really the kitchen, while that on the right is, as far as its principal apartment is concerned, fitted up with a

Inche Maida, princess of Perak; her husband, Nakhoda Trong; and attendants. From Norman Sherry, *Conrad's Eastern World* (Cambridge and New York: Cambridge UP, 1966). Reproduced by permission.

bed which occupies about two-thirds of the room. Upon the introduction taking place between [the British] general and princess
[Maida], the lady claimed the former as her guest, and with all the
pride of an English country dame of the last century over her well-
filled ticks, drew his attention to the bed.

Conrad's source for the character of Lord Jim changed once his hero
moved to Patusan. It has been suggested that he derived much material
at this point from reading about Rajah James Brooke of Sarawak, who
was mentioned in all the travelers' tales already cited, as well as others.[3]
Conrad could have found accounts in a number of books of how the
Englishman James Brooke came to Sarawak on the west coast of Borneo,
helped the local governor, Muda Hassim, put down a rebellion, and,
in 1841, became the Rajah of Sarawak. The following extract from *The
Malay Archipelago*[4] is but one suggestion of the kind of inspiration
Brooke might have provided.

A few words in conclusion, about the government of Saráwak.
Sir James Brooke found the Dyaks oppressed and ground down by
the most cruel tyranny. They were cheated by the Malay traders,
and robbed by the Malay chiefs. Their wives and children were
often captured and sold into slavery, and hostile tribes purchased
permission from their cruel rulers to plunder, enslave, and murder
them. Anything like justice or redress for those injuries was utterly
unattainable. From the time Sir James obtained possession of the
country, all this was stopped. Equal justice was awarded to Malay,
Chinaman, and Dyak. The remorseless pirates from the rivers farther east were punished, and finally shut up within their own
territories, and the Dyak, for the first time, could sleep in peace.
His wife and children were now safe from slavery; his house was
no longer burnt over his head; his crops and his fruits were now
his own, to sell or consume as he pleased. And the unknown
stranger who had done all this for them, and asked for nothing in
return, what could he be? How was it possible for them to realize
his motives? Was it not natural that they should refuse to believe
he was a man? for of pure benevolence combined with great power,
they had had no experience among men. They naturally concluded
that he was a superior being, come down upon earth to confer

---

3. Other contemporary writings referring to Brooke are: Captain the Hon. Henry Keppel, *Ex-
pedition to Borneo of H.M.S. Dido for the Suppression of Piracy; with Extracts from the Journal
of James Brooke, Esq. of Sarawak*, London, 1846, and *Visit to the Indian Archipelago, in
H.M. Ship Maeander: with Portions of the Private Journal of Sir James Brooke, K.C.B.,*
London, 1853; Hugh Low, *Sarawak: Inhabitants and Productions*, London, 1848; and Captain
Rodney Mundy, *Narrative of Events in Borneo and Celebes down to the Occupation of
Labuan: from the Journals of James Brooke, Esq. Rajah of Sarawak and Governor of Labuan;
together with a Narrative of the Operations of H.M.S. Iris*, London, 1848. For a full discussion, see John Dozier Gordan, *Joseph Conrad: the Making of a Novelist*, Cambridge, Mass.,
pp. 64–73, and "The Rajah Brooke and Joseph Conrad," *Studies in Philology*, XXXV, 1938,
613–34.
4. Wallace, *op. cit.*, pp. 71–72.

blessings on the afflicted. In many villages where he had not been seen, I was asked strange questions about him. Was he not as old as the mountains? Could he not bring the dead to life? And they firmly believe that he can give them good harvests, and make their fruit-trees bear an abundant crop.

In forming a proper estimate of Sir James Brooke's government, it must ever be remembered that he held Saráwak solely by the goodwill of the native inhabitants. He had to deal with two races, one of whom, the Mahometan Malays, looked upon the other race, the Dyaks, as savages and slaves, only fit to be robbed and plundered. He has effectually protected the Dyaks, and has invariably treated them as, in his sight, equal to the Malays; and yet he has secured the affection and goodwill of both. Notwithstanding the religious prejudices of Mahometans, he has induced them to modify many of their worst laws and customs, and to assimilate their criminal code to that of the civilized world. That his government still continues, after twenty-seven years—notwithstanding his frequent absences from ill-health, notwithstanding conspiracies of Malay chiefs, and insurrections of Chinese gold-diggers, all of which have. been overcome by the support of the native population, and notwithstanding financial, political, and domestic troubles—is due, I believe, solely to the many admirable qualities which Sir James Brooke possessed, and especially to his having convinced the native population, by every action of his life, that he ruled them, not for his own advantage, but for their good.

Since these lines were written, his noble spirit has passed away. But though, by those who knew him not, he may be sneered at as an enthusiastic adventurer, or abused as a hard-hearted despot, the universal testimony of every one who came in contact with him in his adopted country, whether European, Malay, or Dyak, will be, that Rajah Brooke was a great, a wise, and a good ruler—a true and faithful friend—a man to be admired for his talents, respected for his honesty and courage, and loved for his genuine hospitality, his kindness of disposition, and his tenderness of heart.

But surely Conrad observed, at first hand, another James—Captain Lingard's nephew, a young man living in the jungle, isolated, yet with some local standing. At the time Conrad visited Berau, there were certainly two traders there—Charles Olmeijer (a Eurasian), and Jim Lingard. Both appear to have been protégés of Captain William Lingard (who was himself a partial source for Stein in that he was a trader and explorer), who had established the trading post, and both were related to him. It is possible that jealousy existed between them and that Olmeijer saw Jim as a rival.

Traditionally it is believed that Conrad took the name of his hero—Lord Jim—from the Malay title given to young Lingard—Tuan Jim. But there were other characteristics in Jim Lingard that might have

Tuan Jim ("Lord Jim") Lingard in white coat or "tutup."
Photograph taken during the years he lived in Berau as a trader
(John Neilson Conrad Collection).

contributed to Lord Jim. As far as I can gather, Jim Lingard was in love with a native girl, a sea-Dyak. He had as well a remarkable manservant called Lias. His daughter, Mrs. Oehlers of Singapore, has told me that when her father went upriver into the interior Lias always accompanied him, and she recalled that Lias always slept on the verandah of her father's home.

Although Jim Lingard has previously been looked upon as a person of little importance, a letter has survived that shows him as a man of some influence.[5] Mr. Alex Cook, at that time Treasurer General of British North Borneo, describes a visit to the area in 1887:

> I arrived at Balangan (sic) per S.S. Royalist on 31st August: next morning I sent my letter of introduction accompanied by a small present to the Sultan. * * * Wm. James Lingard who is on very friendly terms with the Sultan agreed to go with me.[6]

Finally, it seems to me likely that Conrad was impressed that a man five years younger than himself should be prepared to spend the rest of his life—and he did just that—in such an isolated place. His daughter told me that her father used to say: "I am the only white man on the East Coast."

HANS VAN MARLE AND PIERRE LEFRANC

Ashore and Afloat: New Perspectives on Topography and Geography in Lord Jim†

* * *

In Conrad's novel, the Avondale (82, 133) [52, 82] picks up the master of the Patna, First Mate Jim, and the two engineers (36, 81, 115) [26, 52] in the Gulf of Aden and within less than twenty hours after Jim's jump (133) [82]. In ten days (82) [52] this outward-bound Dale Line steamer (36, 81) [26, 52] takes the foursome to an unnamed Eastern port, where a fortnight later (82) [53] a three-day inquiry (69, 156–57) [45, 96] is held. For more than sixty-five years now, that is since well before Conrad's departure from this world, readers of Lord Jim have been aware of the close resemblance linking the case of his fictional Patna to that of a pilgrim steamer firmly established in maritime history,

---

5. My attention was drawn to this letter by Professor Nicholas Tarling, University of Auckland.
6. Public Record Office, London, F. O. 12/86.
† From Conradiana 20.2 (Summer 1988): 109–35. Reprinted by permission of Texas Tech UP. This article has been edited for publication here. Parenthetical page numbers refer to Lord Jim (New York: Doubleday, 1926); bracketed page numbers refer to this Norton Critical Edition. Other Conrad texts referred to are those of Dent's Collected Edition. Distances have been given in nautical miles.

the *Jeddah*. While still active on scene Conrad never denied the resemblance, contrary to his remonstrances against other similarities pointed out by critics or scholars.

In the last quarter of the nineteenth century no steamer on regular service would ply from the Gulf of Aden to Singapore without coaling at Colombo or an Indian port. Obviously any ship under the Red Ensign would deposit unexpected passengers at her first landfall where the Union Jack was flown. In this case in India, also the only part of the British Empire to boast a Viceroy (39) [28], in those times still residing in Calcutta. Ten days at sea would likewise exclude Singapore (about 3625 miles from Aden) and make Colombo, Madras, and Calcutta successively less likely than Bombay (1650 miles). There are also a couple of geographical clues to be found in the novel as to the identity of the port where the *Avondale* arrives and the inquiry takes place. Marlow asks Chester, a West Australian (161) [98] whether he had dragged old Captain Robinson "over six thousand miles" (163) [100] to this nameless Eastern port, a distance that does not fit Australia-Singapore by any route, but approximates that from Brisbane in Queensland (164–65) [100] to Bombay by way of Torres Strait. Brierly, one of the assessors at the inquiry, "the captain of the crack ship of the Blue Star line . . . the sixteen-knot steel steamer *Ossa*" (57) [38], commits suicide by jumping overboard "less than three days after leaving port" (59) [39] for Shanghai (62, 63) [41]. He does so after having instructed Jones, his first officer, to "alter the course twenty degrees to the southward" within three hours after he had taken over the watch (60, 61) [40]. Such a more southern course is, it is hardly necessary to stress, totally unexplainable anywhere between Singapore and Shanghai.

Sherry's brief for Singapore as the setting of the *Patna* inquiry is largely based on Conrad's familiarity with that port, like Bombay accommodating an Esplanade and a band-stand (39, 40, 42, 120) [28, 30, 75] and Conrad's own appearance before a Court of Inquiry, a one-day proceeding, held in Singapore on 2 April 1883 after the burning of *Palestine*. A quarter century before Sherry, Gordon pleaded the case that the novel's topographical details and terminology point rather to Bombay.[1]

Let us therefore first reassess the latter, somewhat increasing Gordan's scraps of evidence. The local currency of the port is Indian, expressed in annas and rupees (67, 68, 152) [44, 45, 93], whereas the wages of the *Patna*'s second engineer are counted in (Straits) dollars. Sherry is perfectly right in stating that gharries (40, 46–48, 232) [28, 32–33, 140] as a means of local transportation were no less familiar in Singapore than in Bombay, but a gharry-wallah (47) [32]—both nouns borrowed from Hindi—would only be encountered in India as a carriage servant.

1. See Sherry, above, pp. 355–57. John D. Gordan, *Joseph Conrad: The Making of a Novelist* (Cambridge: Harvard UP, 1940) 62–63.

Punkahs (28, 32, 36, 157, 160) [21, 23, 96, 98] and peons (32) [24], too, were known in Singapore as well as in Bombay. Although there was "a small but highly respectable class of Parsee merchants"[2] in Singapore, a Parsee Dubash (35 [26], with Dubash, meaning man of two languages, from Hindi) would act as interpreter on the Indian west coast. And it should be remembered that Bombay was and is the main center of the Parsees, with its Tower of Silence on Malabar Hill where the remains of their dead are exposed to be eaten by vultures. More references to Parsees occur in the novel (161, 168) [99, 102] and the Malabar Hotel or House (42, 76, 151, 165), [30, 49, 93, 101] reminds us of Bombay's hilly southwestern peninsula with Government House at its southern tip.

A Sidiboy (171) [104] Sidi being a Hindi coinage from the Arabic Sayyid (a descendant of the Prophet's daughter)—indicates an African Moslem both on the east coast of his home continent and in western India. This community domiciled in Bombay was sufficiently numerous to figure as a separate category in nineteenth-century city censuses. A solah topi (163) [100], again from Hindi, a sun helmet worn by European civilians, was simply called a topi in Singapore. Tamils (12, 47) [12, 33] were not unknown in Singapore, but are indigenous to India (and Sri Lanka). A plaintiff in court sports a Hindu caste-mark (158) [96]. To invoke also an all-English term: Native infantry (157) [96] did not first appear in Singapore until 1900 (and then not Malay, but Indian), whereas the 1884 Bombay garrison included batallions of both the tenth and the twenty-first regiments of native Infantry of the Indian Army. And to move from English words to silence: Chinese are conspicuously absent in the city where the inquiry is held, although they are part of the local scene in the *Patna*'s home port (13, 14) [13], as are Arabs (13–15) [13; 14]. The pilgrims come, of course, from a Moslem Malay-speaking area, as is witnessed by their campongs and praus (14) [14], "a meticulous precision of statement" (30) [23]. The only Malays actually present at the time of the inquiry are members of the *Patna* crew, "brought over from Aden to give evidence" (97–99) [61–63].

The conclusion seems obvious: Conrad planted a variety of references in *Lord Jim* that could lead knowledgeable readers to assume that the inquiry was meant to be set in India, more precisely Bombay. This also explains how Jim, the water-clerk (5) [8], could move from there "generally farther east" (4) [8], "towards the rising sun" (5) [8]. The novel mentions, in its early pages, Calcutta, Rangoon, Penang, and Batavia by name (5) [8], and later Bankok (198) [119] and Samarang (149) [91], the latter city to the east from Batavia (Jakarta) on the north coast of Java. In fact Calcutta is not mentioned again or even alluded to in the novel's later chapters. Rangoon is clearly Jim's first halting-place after

2. Alfred Russel Wallace, *The Malay Archipelago* (London: Macmillan, 1880) 20–21.

the inquiry (152) [93]. Denver (190) [114], his principal there, owned a rice-mill (187, 189) [112, 114], but may perhaps also have done business as a ship-chandler with a water-clerk in his employ. Penang is not mentioned again either, but fits the requirement of being "a seaport seven hundred miles south" (189) [114] of Rangoon and Jim's second halting-place. Egström & Blake, for whom he worked there, were indeed ship-chandlers and "to call the thing by its right name" had him as their runner (189, see also 194–5) [114, see also 117].

After these "two episodes" among more than a dozen (197) [118] we find Jim in Bankok with "Yucker Brothers, charterers and teak merchants" (198) [119], but without a specific job description. Batavia does crop up a second time (218) [132], but then merely as the seat of the Dutch colonial government. It is, moreover, an unlikely halting-place for Jim, who was taken by Marlow from Bankok to Samarang (also 36, 346, 411) [also 26, 204, 243] and placed with De Jongh as water-clerk (149, 201) [91, 121]. It was from Samarang that Jim set sail for Patusan, his final destination. The circle of his wanderings, described as having "a diameter of, say, three thousand miles" (198) [119], is apparently drawn with Singapore as its center, and in that case Calcutta remains well outside. But the novelist that Conrad had become was, after all, not compiling a haven finding directory for the Indian Ocean and its gulfs and bays.

Why an inquiry set in Bombay, while neither Conrad's newspaper reading on the *Jeddah* case (successively in London, Sydney, and Newcastle, in August 1880, late 1880, and autumn 1881) nor his own experiences in the *Palestine* can have directed his creative imagination so clearly towards India as he was writing *Lord Jim* between 1898 and 1900? Recourse to indisputable biographical details shows that Conrad joined the *Narcissus* in Bombay on 28 April 1884.[3] If we are to rely on Jean-Aubry, his first biographer, Conrad saw her entering the harbor there from the verandah of the local Sailors' Home after previously having toyed with the idea of joining a Persian Gulf steamer.[4] Since the extant records show that Conrad left the *Riversdale* in Madras (with wages paid in rupees) on 17 April 1884 and that the *Narcissus* came into port at Bombay on 23 April, we are on somewhat safe landlubberly ground if we assume that the future novelist travelled by train from Madras via Poona to Bombay, arriving there before the latter date.

* * * Conrad's biographers * * * Jerry Allen and Zdzisław Najder give a departure on 3 June.[5] Bombay newspapers yield more specific

3. See the reproduction of the crew list in Jocelyn Baines, *Joseph Conrad: A Critical Biography* (London: Weidenfield and Nicholson, 1960), following 292.
4. G. Jean-Aubry, *Joseph Conrad: Life and Letters* (London: Heinemann, 1929) 1:76.
5. Jerry Allen, *The Sea Years of Joseph Conrad* (Garden City: Doubleday, 1965) 164, 276, 321. Zdzisław Najder, *Joseph Conrad: A Chronicle* (New Brunswick: Rutgers UP, 1983) 82.

information: port clearance on 4 June, but the actual departure occurred on the fifth.

When we compare the established dates of Conrad's presence in Eastern ports to those of contemporaneous inquiries held there, we find ourselves in * * * Bombay * * * [in] late May 1884: a Court of Inquiry spent three days (Wednesday the 21st, Thursday the 22nd, and Tuesday the 27th of that month) investigating the fate of the *Sir William Armstrong* on her maiden voyage from Newcastle to Bombay. Through plain navigational error she got stranded near Perim at the southern end of the Red Sea, where the *Corrèze*, a French navy transport ship, came to her aid and helped her back to floating. The *Corrèze* was on her way from Toulon to Indo-China, while the French gunboat in *Lord Jim* is bound for home (136) [84], presumably Toulon, the Mediterranean naval base. The *Sir William Armstrong*, under her own power, reached Bombay on 27 April, thus after Conrad's arrival there. It is not at all unlikely that her mishap had earlier been reported by telegram, like that of the *Patna* by "that mysterious cable message" (35) [25]. It so happened that one of the two nautical assessors in the ensuing inquiry was the then master of the *Adowa*, the last ship of Conrad's professional service (1893/94). To quote *Lord Jim*, "all the sailors in the port attended" (56) [38], "everybody connected in any way with the sea was there" (35) [45–46]. The novel also specifies that "The next case was that of assault and battery committed upon a money-lender" (69) [25], which sounds very much like the case heard in Bombay on 21 May 1884 of "assaulting a Native . . . cashier."[6]

* * *

It was also in Bombay that Conrad set eye on the steamer whose name he borrowed for his novel: the *Patna* was there for ten days, from 5 to 15 May 1884. * * * While in Bombay, Conrad may also have been reminded of the *Jeddah* scandal when the *Scindia* had arrived in port on 30 April 1884, for it was she who, almost four years earlier, had rescued the undutiful master of the pilgrim ship and his party of twenty.

Most of these latter details give us cause to notice how Conrad worked experiences from various years into his account of fictional events. There is, so it would seem, a whole web of references and associations that connect the first seventeen chapters of *Lord Jim* with Bombay, but not to the exclusion of Singapore. Elliot, the Master Attendant (38) [27], is clearly modeled on the port official Conrad encountered in Singapore, Captain Henry Ellis. Antonio Mariani with his billiard-room and grog-shop (49) [34] sounds like a wraith of Carlo Mariani, the Maltese hotel keeper in Singapore mentioned in "The End of the Tether." The origin of this bifocal fictional character remains unclear: no Mariani is listed in 1880s directories, either in Bombay or in Singapore. (It may be re-

6. *Times of India*, 22 May 1884.

marked in passing that there is similarly no trace either of the principal shipping master called Archie Ruthvel in *Lord Jim*. 37 [27]).

Two men-of-war, the *Victorieuse*, "the flagship of the French Pacific squadron" (144) [88], and Her Majesty's *Wolverine* (162) [99] are both present in an Australian setting. Hardly a surprise, since Conrad will have recalled them from his first stay in Sydney.[7] Yet another ship, the *Sephora* —the name is also familiar from "The Secret Sharer"—appears in her *Lord Jim* guise (149) [91] as obviously identical with the *Douro* mentioned in Conrad's essay on the loss of the *Titanic* (*Notes on Life and Letters*), a real-world steamer rammed amidships and sunk on the high seas off Cape Finisterre in April 1882. In this case, then, the association is of time rather than place. The *Sarah W. Granger* (192–93) [115, 116] still eludes explanation—but we ought not to forget that Marlow once described his memory as "a mausoleum of proper names" (*Chance*, 69).

The berth Conrad found in Bombay was that of second mate. Marlow, however, is presented as master at the time of the inquiry in *Lord Jim*: he "had a man in the hospital" (48) [33], where a resident surgeon addresses him as Captain (54) [37], and Marlow reports "I . . . gave up my early morning visit to my ship" (156) [95]. Two years later Jones also calls Marlow Captain (59, 61–64) [39, 40–43] and "a long time after . . . in Sydney" (137) [84], "after more than three years" (149) [91], Marlow informs the French lieutenant that he "commanded a merchant vessel at present anchored in Rushcutters' Bay" (144) [88]. If such an encounter belongs to the world of Conrad's biography, it can only be assigned to the six weeks in May-August 1888 he spent in Sydney as master of the *Otago*, four years after his stay in Bombay, yet within the fictional time of *Lord Jim*.

* * *

The conclusion is evident that the inquiry in *Lord Jim* conflates at least three such real-world investigations, not only the one Conrad faced in Singapore after the burning of the *Palestine* (1883) and another he read and heard about—that regarding the abandonment of the *Jeddah* (1880, 1881)—but also the inquiry into the stranding of the *Sir William Armstrong* during which he may well have found himself among the public (1884). The novel appears to contain elements of all three, yet follows none entirely. By way of example: Jim and his fellows are picked up at sea and taken eastward, an event for which there is no parallel in the adventures of the hands of these three real-world ships.

* * *

After his halting-places in seaports (if Bankok can qualify as such) Jim is offered employ up-river as "manager of Stein & Co.'s trading post in Patusan" (220) [133]. He is taken there in a "brigantine of Stein's . . . leaving for the westward" (237) [143]. From Samarang, that is, and so

7. On board the *Duke of Sutherland* from 31 January to 5 July 1879.

on a course towards Sunda Straits, and from there along the west coast
of Sumatra. When Brown later sails "into Jim's history" from Zamboanga
(354) [210] by way of the Straits of Macassar and the Java Sea (356)
[211], he reaches Patusan "with the help of land and sea breezes . . .
after clearing the Sunda Straits" (357) [212]. Indications that show beyond all doubt that Conrad's Patusan is situated somewhere on the west
coast of Sumatra. The location must be very close to the Equator: the
moon rose "gliding upwards between the sides of the chasm . . . of one
irregularly shaped hill split in two, and with the two halves leaning
slightly apart" (220–21) [133]. A vertical rise or almost so, such as can
only be observed on (or very close to) the Equator.[8]

Every reason, therefore, to maintain an earlier identification of the
fictional Patusan with the real-world Teunom (Lat. 4° N). It must be
stressed that Conrad would have become aware of the existence of such
"a remote district" (220) [133] either from newspaper reports read between December 1883 and October 1884, in Port Elizabeth (South
Africa), Bombay, or London or from a book borrowed in the Singapore
Raffles Library in July or August 1887—once more within the same
seminal period in his life reflected in *Lord Jim's* fictional chronology.
It is not altogether clear whether "the distance of six or seven thousand
miles" (230) [139] to Britain is meant to be measured from Patusan or
from Samarang. The actual distance in nautical miles is well over eight
thousand from the latter place and over a thousand less from Teunom,
that is, by way of the Suez Canal.

* * *

The *Patna*'s unnamed port of departure is, very clearly, Singapore.
The allusion to "that roadstead which is a thoroughfare to the East" (12)
[12] can fit no other place, and the seamen stranded there discuss professional opportunities in China, Japan, and Siam (13) [113]. * * *
The ship's route confirms a departure from Singapore. She is carrying
pilgrims bound for Mecca. The "Strait" into whose waters she pounds
"in the dusk" is the Strait of Malacca: the "screw-pile lighthouse . . .
on a treacherous shoal" (15) [14] is the Malacca Strait light-structure
which, in 1879, was described as "a screw-pile lighthouse . . . in 15
feet of water."[9] The anonymous narrator, it will be observed, much
compresses the elements of time and space. This lighthouse stands in
Lat. 2°52′50″ N, Long. 100°58′40″ E, about 200 miles distant from
Singapore. It cannot be "astern" of the ship in the evening that follows
her departure and an interval of at least twenty-four hours has elapsed
of which the narrative gives no hint.

The *Patna* then clears "the Strait" of Malacca and crosses "the bay"
of Bengal. Seamen in the area would feel no need to specify which

8. First pointed out by Hans Lippe, "*Lord Jim*: Some Geographical Observations," *The Conradian*
10 (1985): 135–38.
9. See *China Straits Directory* (1878) 1:93.

Strait and which Bay, but in the case of the latter the reader might expect a capital B. The distance between Singapore and the NW end of the Strait is 620 miles, and that between its end and a point on the ship's route some 170 miles S of Ceylon (which marks the western limit of the Bay) is about 870 miles. An old steamer like the *Patna* would have taken about ten days to log some 1500 miles, but again the narrative is much compressed. The ship is then described as "continuing on her way through the 'One-degree' passage" (15) [14]. This is in error. What is being referred to is the One and Half Degree Channel across the Maldive Islands, in Lat. 1°30' N. The error involves thirty minutes of latitude, i.e. thirty miles, and being that much out in a channel only fifty-two miles wide is potentially dangerous. A ship on course 270 in Lat. 1° N would clear the N shore of Suvadiva Atoll by less than six miles, which might prove insufficient if various factors—a slight error in the latitude at last noon, haze or a moonless night, and unknown currents—combined unfavorably.

*   *   *

The *Patna*'s route, then, makes sense to the crossing of the Maldives, but the situation soon becomes very unclear. The choice of a southern latitude is normal but the actual route followed by the ship remains a mystery. She cannot be simultaneously on course 270 near the Equator and on course 298 or above; nor can she be making straight for points —"Perim," the entrance to "the Red Sea"—which no ship can reach directly from a near-equatorial latitude in the Arabian Sea. Certainly, in any literary account of a ship's passage, completeness is out of the question and technicalities would be disastrous. But if Conrad as a writer is under an obligation to be selective, he is also expected, as a former professional, to be consistent in his choice of facts and in his handling of them: a recently retired seaman writing of a ship's passage would be assumed—and indeed trusted—to get his sea facts always right, with the virtually automatic exactitude inherited from years of practice and responsibility. The notion that Conrad might be silently censuring his narrator for being navigationally confused seems barely worth considering: who could possibly suspect, let alone get hold of, buried criticism of this sort, on technical points, about a narrator who has no existence beyond his function? The alternative possibility arises that this impalpable presence is relaying to us, neutrally and as they come, the impressions and emotions in Jim's mind, whose self-confidence and *hubris* may be such that he is no longer aware of his ship's position and even course. That, certainly, would utterly disqualify him as an officer, but two objections to such a view suggest themselves: implied criticism of this nature would, again, be inaccessible to readers unversed in navigation; and the text does mention that Jim during his watch sometimes glances at "the compass" and at "a chart" (19) [16, 17]. One might alternatively take the view that the pervasive spatial and geographical vagueness, the apparent suspension of a clear perception of time in someone's consciousness in those pages (15–21) [14–18], and above all the extraordinary notion of a ship on two different courses at once, are the type of oddities that one accepts in dreams without noticing them. But an unannounced and unattributed dream which, on examination, cannot be convincingly ascribed either to the narrator or to Jim would be another kind of oddity in these opening chapters. Thus, no satisfactory or acceptable authorial intention can be detected behind the nautical peculiarities under review, and the possibility must be envisaged that, only some five years after his last long voyage on board the *Torrens*, Conrad himself had begun to lose some of his grip on or interest in sea matters, to the extent of becoming careless in his handling of them at his desk.

* * *

One detail * * * disposes the common assumption that the *Patna* is abandoned far out to sea, somewhere in the Arabian Sea: the French lieutenant in charge of her during the towing operations to "Aden" (98, 134) [62, 83] later describes himself as having spent "thirty hours" on board (140, 141, 144) [86, 88]. Those thirty hours must have included the time needed to get "two hawsers on board" (139) [85], and to disembark the passengers, which last operation took twenty-five minutes (142) [87]. The maximum speed at which a ship whose buoyancy has become problematic can be towed in reasonable safety can be estimated at perhaps five knots: an absolute maximum, assuming a very flat sea. The *Jeddah* was towed to Aden over some 330 miles in about 72 hours, average speed 4.58 knots, and the operation was no doubt speeded up by the efficiency of those at the pumps, who by gaining regularly on the water in the hold dispelled any doubts about the ship's buoyancy. Even if one assumes the *Patna* to be towed at five knots for all of thirty hours (which seems excessive: twenty-eight or twenty-nine hours at four knots would seem more likely), that puts her at a maximum distance of 150 miles approximately E of Aden when the tow begins; and she cannot have drifted over many miles during the eight hours or so between her abandonment and her sighting by the French gunboat.

The *Patna*, then, is abandoned by her men well within the Gulf of Aden, which means in turn that someone on board possessed enough navigation and seamanship to make, identify, and round Cape Guardafui —this is a tricky area—within the forty-eight hours before her abandonment. The narrative contains no hint of this. Again, one can understand Conrad's wish not to burden his "pilgrim ship episode" with unnecessary details and complications, but the *Patna* covers the whole distance from the Maldives to a point between 110 and 150 miles E of Aden in an uncomfortable navigational blur.

* * *

Brierly jumps to his death in a highly intriguing navigational void: to the essentially straightforward question, "Where does he jump?" no answer can be offered. The three days, the [Hector] Bank (*any* bank), and the course correction cannot be fitted together and related to a precise area between Bombay or Singapore and Shanghai. Conrad, this time, is recording Marlow's words, which relay Jones's, which echo Brierly's. Since it would seem extraordinary that all the members of this interesting salt water foursome might be passing on to one another and to us strange navigational nonsense, one suspects that it was the retired seaman among them who made the mistakes, getting his times, distances, positions, and courses not only wrong but irreconcilable and intractable. However, a bank which had ceased to exist when Conrad last sailed in or near these waters could be referred to with some freedom in a work of imagination, and it would seem that the nautical coherence that one would expect to find just below the surface of the narrative was disturbed, in Conrad's mind, by a cluster of emotional and imaginative factors in which the light airs, narrow waters, uneasy shallows and tidal streams of Carimata Straits, the scene of the suicide of Wallace of the *Cutty Sark* one month after the abandonment of the *Jeddah*, and the motives and implications of that act as Conrad pondered them over the years, seem mysteriously to converge and to fuse. Some of those factors, with others of like origin in real life, reemerge in "The Secret Sharer": Leggatt's jump and his motives, the very light airs, and the danger from shallows. The Brierly episode may have been caught in, and its telling influenced by, an authorial reverie into which considerations of nautical exactitude did not enter.

A convincing case for locating Patusan in NW Sumatra has been steadily building up since 1940, to which one may perhaps still venture to add something.

Marlow's memorable description of his last glimpse of Jim contains decisive evidence that the coast of Patusan is facing W: the very splendour of the passage seems to have obscured some of the information that it gives. Marlow has returned to his schooner, "the sun [has] set," and "the western horizon [is] one great blaze of gold and crimson." Jim, with "the stronghold of the night at his back," remains visible for some time in the twilight, but darkness gains ground over where he stands and finally engulfs him (335–36) [199]. Two points are clear. Since the sun, with commendable regularity, sets in the west, Jim is standing on a shore E of Marlow. Also, the final vision of Jim as swallowed by Eastern darkness links up with the opening of Marlow's narrative in "Heart of Darkness," and with Conrad's general conception of Western man and civilization as in danger of being submerged by darkness from the East, both out there and in Europe: the sun, which sets in the west, may be setting on the West. The Patusan area, then, cannot extend behind a coast facing E, as the Berau delta does. Moreover, as C. M. Armitage has shown, Brown on board his schooner stolen in Mindanao sails down the Strait of Macassar—and therefore past that delta—*en route* to Poulo Laut and Sunda Straits.

There now is substantial agreement, for textual, contextual, and external reasons, that Patusan corresponds to the river Tenom or Teunom, between Rigaih and Meulabah on the NW coast of Sumatra, about "a hundred miles" SE of the Head of Achin, the "headland" of page 226 [137]. It should also be clear that Conrad, who had never seen that coast, imports the Berau delta as described in his Sambir tales almost *in toto* into this part of Sumatra. Yet there remain slight difficulties in connection with Brown's movements between Poulo Laut (E of the SE point of Borneo), Sunda Straits, and Patusan or Teunom. The distance between the S point of Poulo Laut and the NE entrance to Sunda Straits is about 620 miles, a distance that Brown is reported to have logged in "three days of squally misty weather from the north-east" (356) [211]. That would call for an average speed of some 8.6 knots which in turn would involve fairly long spells at ten knots or more, simply to keep up the rate of speed. It seems most unlikely that a nineteenth-century schooner which is described as "stout" (354) [210] and therefore heavy (as opposed to graceful and fast) could have maintained such speeds over three days, especially in squalls, which bring revolving winds. Similarly, we are told that, "with the help of land and sea breezes," Brown covered "in less than a week" the distance between Sunda Straits and a river mouth below Patusan (357) [212]. The distance between Point Balimbing (just SW of the Straits) and Teunom is about 840 miles. Land and sea breezes abeam can give a sailing vessel a reasonably good push, but they blow with very variable strength for some fourteen hours a day at best, and it would seem quite unlikely that Brown's schooner succeeded in logging ten miles during each of those hours over a six-day period. Conrad, however, may mean that Brown, who was sailing parallel to the coast, took advantage of those breezes whenever there was no wind farther out, it being standard procedure to seek such breezes near the land when there is a flat calm offshore. Conrad, then, must in this instance be given the benefit of the doubt, and full allowance must of course be made for the fact that he has to get Brown and his men all the way from Poulo Laut to far-away Patusan in a minimum number of days, the food and water on board being scarce (356) [211]. Still, one would hardly have expected Brown and his "collection of hungry ruffians" (356) [211] to perform for some ten days on end like a first-class team on board a racing yacht.

Two kinds of imagination appear to have been at work in the writing of *Lord Jim*. On the one hand we recognize what, in a slight adaptation of Coleridge's phrase, can perhaps be called Conrad's shaping power of imagination (cf. "Dejection: An Ode," 1. 86), and can watch with ever-renewed interest identifiable fragments of experience—places, episodes, and people—being combined or fused together in rich and varied patterns. On the other hand, however, at a surprisingly early date after Conrad had left the sea, his handling of sea matters sometimes became uncertain, or vague, or even erratic, and appears to have been perturbed by imaginative factors of another sort. One doubts that he lost interest or ceased to care, but it sometimes would seem that, when the need for quarterdeck exactitude had disappeared, other elements inherited from his sea years or from his make-up made their presence felt: emotions and reveries from a more or less distant past, some of them periodical visitors in the world within.

DWIGHT H. PURDY

The Chronology of *Lord Jim*†

To extrapolate the chronology of a novel can be more than a pedantic exercise. J. E. Tanner has shown how ignorance of the chronology of *Lord Jim* leads to misreadings.[1] Tanner cites two critics who evaluate Marlow's assessment of Jim's end on the basis of his words in Chapter XXI, where Marlow says that Jim " 'achieved greatness.' " But by examining the chronology, Tanner proves that Marlow speaks in that chapter at least a year before he knows anything about Jim's disastrous encounter with Gentleman Brown. Thus Marlow's words in Chapter XXI are no clue to Marlow's final estimate of Jim. Tanner's explication is more than a caveat to critics. It is a good indication of the care with which Conrad must have constructed *Lord Jim*, a testament to Conrad's craftsmanship. As Tanner presents it, the chronology is relatively precise and perfectly consistent. However, the chronology of *Lord Jim* is much more exact than Tanner shows. He neglects the crucial temporal allusion, an allusion that allows us to plot a chronology of astonishing precision and complexity.

The keys to the chronology are Stein and Brierly. To give the reader a grasp of the entire chronology, I will recapitulate what Tanner says of Stein. Marlow tells his auditors that Stein was " 'at threescore' " when he consulted him about Jim. Marlow says, " 'His history was curious. He was born in Bavaria, and when a youth of twenty-two had taken an active part in the revolutionary movement of 1848' " (205) [123]. Stein

† From *Conradiana* 8.1 (1976): 81–82. Reprinted by permission of Texas Tech UP. This article has been edited for publication here. Parenthetical page numbers refer to *Lord Jim* (New York: Doubleday, 1926); bracketed page numbers refer to this Norton Critical Edition.
1. "The Chronology and Enigmatic End of *Lord Jim*," *Nineteenth-Century Fiction* 21.4 (March 1967): 369–80.

was therefore born in 1826, and if " 'threescore' " means exactly sixty, and is not merely a figure of speech for old age, then Marlow confers with Stein in 1886. The penultimate pause in Jim's eastward retreat is Samarang, where Marlow placed Jim with the ship-chandler, De Jongh, three years after the inquiry (149) [91]. It is then that Marlow decides to seek Stein's advice (201–02) [122]. Therefore the inquiry occurs in 1883.

The crucial allusion missed by Tanner concerns Brierly. Tanner says that Brierly commits suicide "early in August of some unspecified year." But the date of the suicide can be fixed exactly—month, day, year, even hour. Given this date, we can plot the events before and after the suicide with remarkable precision. Brierly commits suicide " 'barely' " one week after the inquiry (59) [39], at the age of thirty-two (57) [38]. According to Jones, Brierly's mate on the *Ossa*, Brierly called him into the chart-room at 3:50 a.m. (59) [39]. Brierly fixes the ship's position, writing " 'in his neat figures' " the date and time: " 'seventeen, eight, four a.m.' " (60) [40]. Not long after, Brierly jumps overboard. If he commits suicide six to eight days after the inquiry, the inner and outer limits of " 'barely,' " on August 17, 1883, the last day of the inquiry would be August 9–11, 1883.

We can now establish almost exactly the date of Jim's jump from the *Patna*. After the jump, Jim spends one day in the lifeboat, ten days on the *Avondale*, and two weeks in the Sailors' Home before the inquiry begins (82) [53]. Since the first day of the inquiry would be August 7, 8, or 9 (it lasts three days), Jim leaps from the *Patna* twenty-five days before that date, or on the night of July 13, 14, or 15, 1883. We are also told that Jim was three weeks and five days aboard the *Patna* (182) [110]; therefore the *Patna* set off with its cargo of pilgrims on June 18, 19, or 20, 1883.

Jim goes to Patusan immediately after Marlow's conference with Stein, so he arrives there in 1886. When Gentleman Brown appears, Jim has been in Patusan for three years (367) [218]. Therefore Jim dies in 1889. About Marlow we know that two years elapse between the end of his veranda narrative and the time when the privileged man receives his letters. Marlow tells the privileged man that Jim died " 'in the year of grace before last' " (343) [203], or two years ago. So the story on the veranda and Jim's death occur in the same year.

There is some correspondence between the dates in the novel and those of Conrad's major source for *Lord Jim*, the *Jeddah* incident. The *Jeddah* affair occurred in 1880, three years before the time assigned in the novel. The *Jeddah* set off with its pilgrims on July 17, the *Patna* on June 18, 19, or 20. The captain of the *Jeddah* abandoned her on August 8 and arrived in Aden August 10, the dates of Jim's inquiry. Finally, Brierly's original, Captain Wallace, committed suicide approx-

imately one month after his fictional counterpart and at exactly the same
hour, 4 a.m.[2]

External clues aside, the precision and consistency of the chronology
of *Lord Jim* are far too great to be due to chance alone. Despite the
seemingly haphazard involutions of Conrad's narrative, the chronology
testifies to his consciousness of his craft. * * *

PIERRE LEFRANC

Conradian Backgrounds and Contexts for *Lord Jim*†

The "one short sentence" that contains "the one great secret of the craft"
of the sea provides a starting point. Marlow himself discloses its tenor
a little later when, seeing Jim carried away once more in illusions of
heroism—"Ah! what a chance missed!"—he whisks him back sharply
by saying: "If you had stuck to the ship, you mean!" The mysterious
"short sentence" is the injunction "Stick to the ship!" This, simultaneously, is what "must be driven afresh every day into young heads"
and what lies at the root of Marlow's professional interest in Jim's case.

What might sound like a mere technicality turns out, on inspection,
to be charged with implications. On the surface, the order to stick to
the ship associates a preoccupation with safety and a reminder of basic
duty. So long as a floating ship remains under one's feet, it is generally
safer not to jump, however great the temptation: dozens of ships thought
to be doomed and prematurely abandoned have survived for months.
Moreover, sticking to a ship until she sinks is the only way to make
certain that one will not jump prematurely, thereby abandoning the
ship, passengers, and cargo entrusted to one's care and leaving an un-
manned derelict to float about, a danger to other ships at night. At this
point, however, someone's sensitive mind—no name need be
proposed—begins to raise doubts. What has just been stated implies
that, unless an order is given and can be heard, one's professional honor
may hang on one's precise evaluation of circumstances (which is not
always possible), an ability to make and carry out the right decision
under great stress, and an exceptional sense of timing (in view of the
risk of being sucked into the sea with the sinking ship if one jumps too
late). It also means that duty in its extreme form includes suicide: a
thought worth pondering. Who can say in advance that, whatever the
circumstances and in spite of normal emotions and impulses—fear,
revolt, an "extreme aversion to die," or simply the fear of choking—he

2. Norman Sherry, "Sources" 319–20, 357–58, above.
  † Written especially for this Norton Critical Edition.

will never flinch—never jump? No one, of course, except the blissfully unconscious, the complacent, and all those who live in pretenses or self-illusion. But if this is so, how can judgment be passed on those who have jumped ship by men of whom there can be no certainty that they will never flinch, and in the name of a code that no one can be sure to live up to (if "live" is the word)? Thus it comes about that young men who, in choosing the life of the sea, had not bargained for quite as much, and each of whom has been welcomed into the profession—perhaps a little rapidly—as "one of us," find themselves after a single lapse summarily rejected—"done for," "with nowhere to go"—by older colleagues who cannot be sure that they would do better if and when "the moment comes." (The fact that, for some, it never comes owes everything to luck and nothing to merit.)

It seems no longer necessary to explain whose thoughts we have been following: the issues just surveyed are suggestively examined, in the light of Marlow's experience and observation, in a few dozen brief passages in the first half of *Lord Jim*, some of them just quoted from. Equally worth noting, and surely relevant, is the fact that the injunction "Stick to the ship!" or its flouting underlies an interesting sequence of episodes of sea life found within Conrad's first three years as an officer (1880–1883), which episodes reemerge in his sea tales, in particular the early ones. This sequence of events, including delayed disclosures about some of them, consists of

(1) the premature abandonment of the *Jeddah* by her captain and officers in the Gulf of Aden on 8 August 1880, the news of her successful towing into Aden a few days later, and the report of the official inquiry into the matter on 20 August;

(2) the suicide of Captain Wallace of the *Cutty Sark*, by jumping off his ship in the Straits of Anjer on 9 September 1880;

(3) the sighting in the Atlantic, in the early months of 1881, of an unidentified Danish brig that her men had kept afloat "for weeks" by constant work at the pumps, and who sank in front of them after their rescue by the men of the *Loch Etive*, Conrad among them;

(4) the near sinking of the *Palestine* after she sprang a leak in the chops of the English Channel in December 1881, the constant pumping for days to keep her afloat, and the refusal of her crew to proceed farther in the voyage;

(5) the sinking of the *Douro* off Cape Finisterre minutes after a night collision on 1 April 1882, and the going down with her of her captain and her four officers;

(6) the official confirmation, early in August 1882, that Wallace of the *Cutty Sark* had committed suicide rather than face the dishonor of an inevitable trial: he had helped his first mate to escape after the latter

had had to kill a rebellious crew member in order to save the ship during a "dirty" night; and finally

(7) the abandonment and sinking of the *Palestine*, by now "a mass of fire," in March 1883 and the official inquiry into her loss early in April.

The first three episodes just listed belong to Conrad's time onboard the *Loch Etive*, which had given him his first berth as an officer (the story of the Danish brig is uncorroborated and he may have invented it, but it clearly fits into the pattern and confirms it). The other four incidents took place during his time onboard the *Palestine*, and they mark a palpable crescendo, from episodes discussed or witnessed to episodes in which he was involved, culminating in the slow-motion enacting of the complete script, of the ship in distress, her abandonment, and the subsequent official inquiry, from certificates withdrawn to certificates returned. Now the *Jeddah*, Wallace of the *Cutty Sark*, and the *Douro* reemerge in *Lord Jim*, around the *Patna*, Brierly of the *Ossa*, and Bob Stanton of the *Sephora*. The rescue of the men of the Danish brig is given much prominence in *The Mirror of the Sea*, while the incidents involving the *Palestine* form the basis of "Youth." And there were sequels: in "The End of the Tether," with Captain Whalley tricked by foul play into losing his ship, and going down with her; in "Falk," with Falk sticking to his ship through several nautical Infernos, but at what risk of potential dehumanization? and in "The Secret Sharer," who is none other than an image of Wallace's former first mate climbing onboard the unnamed *Otago* off the river of Bangkok, the night before she sets out on her first voyage under her new master.

To the young untested junior officer that Conrad was in the early 1880s, the sequence of sea incidents summarized above yielded a fairly mixed bag, and the conclusions that could be drawn from it shed more light on what *Lord Jim* and other related stories contain on the underlying issues. There were examples of absolute fidelity to duty, as well as egregious instances of jumping, some almost ludicrous (though always tragic), others of a different nature. The very best men in the profession sometimes jumped: Wallace had just been given, at twenty-seven, the command of one of the finest square-riggers ever launched. Men sometimes went down for wrong reasons, or were tricked into going down. In other cases, considerations of personal honor took precedence over duty: so long as the safety of the ship was ensured, was that wrong? Seamen passed judgment on fellow seamen without being sure that *they* would do better. Landsmen when called upon to judge proved both ignorant and insensitive: Wallace's first mate, who had finally been arrested and tried, had got seven years of penal servitude. There could be no absolutes: circumstances, always, must be inquired into and weighed. And one's personal honor could not be left in the hands of judges blind both to themselves and to others. When he jumps from the unnamed *Otago*, Leggatt, the Secret Sharer, is simultaneously an image of Wallace *and* an image of his first mate, each taking his honor in his own hands, while the new master of the unnamed ship puts his first command at great risk in order to help him, as Wallace had ruined his career to help his first mate make his escape. The code that sometimes demanded suicide left personal honor in another sphere.

The overall pattern just described—the convergence of real-life episodes on a small nexus of issues, and above all the reemergence of both, the episodes and the issues, in several of the sea tales—not only sheds light on the contents and biographical subsoil of *Lord Jim*, but also points very clearly to a good deal of worrying in the Conrad of 1880 to 1883. He—let us call him Korzeniowski—had obtained on 28 May 1880 his first certificate as an officer; he was aware that "a piece of ass's hide" (French *"peau d'âne"*) does not an officer make; and a passage in a Bobrowski letter of June 1880 obviously echoes a Korzeniowski allusion to "many terrible threats [. . .] written [on the certificate] by the gentlemen of the Board Office" in the event of failure in duty. The successive news reports concerning the *Jeddah* reached the British press within the ten days preceding the *Loch Etive*'s departure from London on 21 August 1880. The official report on that incident and the staggering news of the suicide of Wallace became accessible to the men of the *Loch Etive* when they arrived in Sydney in November. All of this, quite inevitably, was discussed in quarterdeck conversations as well as in shore talk, and lofty assertions of unconcern or of unflinching resolve heard during such discussions—some of them quite possibly in juvenile prep school English—are likely to have left Korzeniowski at least puzzled. The crucial question uppermost in *his* mind must have been, Shall I be up to it when the moment comes? Years later, he wrote that during that period he had had "a very vivid comprehension that if I wasn't one of them I was nothing at all." Of course he knew: He would have to "Do or Die"—which was the motto of the *Judea* in "Youth." The sequence of events onboard the *Palestine* may even have brought him some reassurance: he had put this first test behind him.

Any temptation to trespass should of course be resisted, not only out of deference to him but also because any untested young officer is entitled to his worries, which are a sign of health if kept under control (and again, who are we to pass judgment?). But the extraordinary difficulties that confronted Conrad when he began *Lord Jim* can at this point be surveyed. The Korzeniowski subsoil of the story—the heritage of 1880 to 1883—was "confidential information" about himself, to be put quite *beyond* the reader's reach. Some of the doubts concerning the code were virtually subversive: many in the profession lived in illusion or sham; the code, though a necessity, was upheld by fallible men; even death was no certain criterion of duty performed, since in conditions of extreme exhaustion, it sometimes became desirable, as bringing deliverance from it all; the latent protest against moral absolutes could be perceived as reflecting a Roman Catholic fondness for circumstances and excuses; and an intensely Polish sense of personal honor obviously found the idea of others passing judgment utterly distasteful. Also, not far below the surface of the tale floated other substantial doubts, more explicit elsewhere (for instance in *A Personal Record*), about essential notions of conventional morality: What does responsibility mean when so much in individual lives is dictated by accidents and by impulses, both of them aspects of chance, and when some acts are not even willed—they just happen? (This major Conradian theme has not, perhaps, received enough attention.) Is trust possible, and indeed who can be trusted? And, of course, behind the story of Jim, Marlow's interest in it, and Korzeniowski's self-doubt during those years, one senses a deeper interrogation and worry. He had left his native country and chosen the sea, impulsively: Would his punishment and his fate consist in repeating on a ship that first desertion, and had it created, or disclosed, a flaw in him?

The bulk of the evidence suggests that onboard ships he was able to function satisfactorily and even well in conditions of great stress—as on the river Congo—but that disturbing memories and some nightmares returned later to visit him, then to haunt the blank page in front of him: one senses a succession of hard-won victories. It was the very nature— the very *private* nature—of the material that he used for "Youth," *Heart of Darkness*, and *Lord Jim* that rendered not only Marlow, but also the obliqueness, the indirection, the elaborate reticence, the studied incompleteness, and the multiple distancing quite indispensable—leaving us endlessly fascinated, but for long without a clear answer to that simplest of questions, What is *Lord Jim* about? By combining two approaches from outside the "tale," that is, from the biographical and nautical backgrounds and from what other writings contain on the same issues, one can hope to dispel part of the mystery.[1]

1. For Wallace, see *The Times*, 4 August 1882, 4, which gives important details not found in Lubbock. For the *Palestine*, the text of the official report is printed in Sherry, *Conrad's Eastern World*, App. B. About the sinking of the *Douro*, see Charles Hocking, *Dictionary of Disasters at Sea*, London: Lloyd's Register of Shipping, 1969, s.v.; *The Times*, 3 to 12 April 1882 (the lady's maid who would not jump was Lady Becher's maid); and Conrad, *Notes on Life and Letters*, 225–27 (he appears to have discussed the episode in London with a survivor). For the quotation from Bobrowski, see Najder, *Conrad's Polish Background*, 64 (and Najder, *Conrad*, 66). The Conrad quotation about his early years as an officer comes from *NLL*, 183.

CRITICISM

ANONYMOUS

New York Tribune†

If Mr. Conrad's new story excited admiration as it appeared serially in the pages of "Blackwood's Magazine," it exacts a double tribute from the reader now that it is published in book form. Though originally projected on a small scale, its unpremeditated expansion to the form of a full fledged novel has done nothing to spoil the simplicity and balance of the design. It is a long narrative, but it should be read, if possible, at a sitting. Not alone because one idea is dwelt upon with almost painful persistency, but because Mr. Conrad's mode of composition demands it. He makes the whole story fall from the lips of one man, who either states facts as he knew them himself or quotes them from the conversation of others, and despite the amount of material packed into this book one apprehends it best by taking it as an uninterrupted stream of spoken tragedy and eloquence. What the author has to say is absorbing, but even more so is the way in which he says it. Miss Gwendoline Keats, better known as "Zack," has shown in the book called "On Trial" what can be made of an analysis of a coward's nature when the bitter story is expressed in terms of ordinary speech, accented by borrowings from peasant dialect. Mr. Conrad deals with a coward, and he is mercilessly direct in his exposition of the man's most fugitive emotions, but over every page there is flung the indescribable romance of the immemorial East.

Marlow, the suppositious narrator of Jim's half prosaic, half tragic, history, is a student of human nature whose years of traffic on the sea have moulded him to meditative, wistful ways of thinking. The leading points he has to set forth are simple enough. In his boyhood Jim leaves the commonplace English parsonage in which he has been born and brought up. He goes to sea because his imagination has persuaded him that life may thus be made more romantic than he has ever found it at home. After some years fate sends him aboard the steamer Patna, in Oriental waters, as chief mate. The ship leaves port carrying eight hundred native pilgrims. On a night of tropic calm the rotten craft goes to the bottom like a shot, with all hands save a few members of the crew. For Jim there is a choice. He might stay, rouse the sleeping pilgrims and help save some of them. Or he can jump into the single boat that is lowered and escape with the scoundrels who are foully deserting the unconscious people under their charge. Jim jumps, and pays for his

† November 3, 1900: 10.

bodily salvation by years of remorse, in which regret for a specific act of cowardice can never lose the added pang of his infidelity to the ideal of which he has long dreamed. Somewhere in his heart is the germ of strength; somehow, he feels, he can some day atone for his sin. How he atones, how he buries himself in the primeval jungle among natives to whom he becomes a providence and a demi-god, how the life of steadfast truth to which he attains culminates in an episode of almost intolerable bitterness, it were easy to tell in a few words. But Mr. Conrad gives most of his volume to the telling, and justifies himself in making every word magical and precious.

The man Marlow muses like an oracle. He seems to stand immobile before us; there is a gesture now and then; occasionally he shifts his position; often he pauses, relapses into silence, then picks up the narrative again as though it were an effort to detach himself from the myriad memories that come swarming back upon him. He describes Lord Jim—so called by the natives with whom he finds asylum—he gives you Jim's version of this or that moment in the Patna's last hours; he portrays the young native woman who gives her love to the refugee from his own conscience; he lets down at short intervals, like curtains in a theatre, wonderfully painted pictures of luxuriant scenery or of the unmarked sea. It is all a record of little truths; it is a mosaic, formed with zealous solicitude for justice, of the thousand and one facts, emotions, shares of emotion, which in the long run go to make Jim comprehensible, explain his conduct, and make him intensely interesting. It is as accurate as a legal document; Jim's secrets are laid bare as though with the knife of a surgeon. But always it is an oracle that speaks, always the truth comes wrapped about with the awe inspiring atmosphere of a mysterious land and a dark problem of human will and destiny. Sorrow broods over the story. "Lord Jim" is a hard book to read, for it communicates to the reader a grievous sense of man's weakness and of the woe that he can bring down upon his own head. But it is a book of great originality, and it exerts a spell such as is rarely encountered in modern fiction.

ANONYMOUS

Spectator†

It may be that amongst the hundred and twenty-five novels still awaiting notice on our shelves some work of uncommon talent may reveal itself to gladden the heart of the reviewer; in the meantime, we have no

† Spectator 85 (November 24, 1900): 753.

hesitation in pronouncing Mr. Conrad's *Lord Jim* to be the most original, remarkable, and engrossing novel of a season by no means unfruitful of excellent fiction. That it may not strike all readers in this light we readily concede. Mr. Conrad's matter is too detached from "actuality" to please the great and influential section of readers who like their fiction to be spiced with topical allusions, political personalities, or the mundanities of Mayfair,—just now the swing of the pendulum is entirely away from the slums, and almost altogether in the direction of sumptuous interiors. Mr. Conrad, in a word, takes no heed of the vagaries of fashion or of pseudo-culture—he only once mentions an author and only once makes a quotation—he eschews epigrams, avoids politics, and keeps aloof from great cities. His scenes are laid in unfamiliar regions, amid outlandish surroundings. But if you once succumb to the sombre fascination of his narrative—as the present writer did years ago on reading *An Outcast of the Islands*—your thraldom is complete. Several writers have derived literary inspiration from their sojourn in the Malay Archipelago; but Mr. Conrad, beyond all others, has identified himself with the standpoint of the natives, has interpreted their aspirations, illumined their motives, and translated into glowing words the strange glamour of their landscape. Such an achievement, though remarkable in itself, seems to indicate a denationalisation that might inspire a certain amount of distrust. But in the volume before us, though the "noble savage" is once more prominent, the story is half finished before we reach Malaya, and the central figure who rivets our interest throughout, though intensely romantic by temperament, is the son of an English country parson, and throughout all his long exile never loses touch with the sentiment, the ideals, the essential *ethos*, of his race. Jim—"Lord Jim" is merely the translation of the title "Tuan Jim," by which he is known amongst the Malays— is a mate in the merchant service, an engaging, handsome lad, full of confidence in his ability to cope with any emergency, whose career is wrecked at the outset by a sudden act of futile cowardice, unless, indeed, we are to regard it as the result of a temporary mental paralysis. Along with his skipper and the engineers, he deserts what he imagines to be a sinking ship with a freight of eight hundred pilgrims; the derelict is subsequently brought into port, and as a result of the inquiry Jim's certificate is cancelled. A kindly ship's captain at Aden—the narrator of the story—attracted by Jim's frank and engaging personality, bestirs himself in his behalf and procures him a fresh start. But wherever he goes Jim is dogged by the rumour of his past, and he throws up post after post until at last Captain Marlow introduces him to Stein, a trader in the Archipelago, who appoints him his agent at Patusan, an inland village in one of the native States. Here, beyond the ken of civilisation, Jim at last finds the occasion for rehabilitating himself in his own self-esteem. Here, bearing a charmed life, he baffles the plots of the Rajah, overthrows a raiding Arab chieftain, the terror of the neighbourhood, and wins fame by his valour and sagacity. Here also he wins the devoted love of the only white woman in Patusan, the stepdaughter of a Portuguese half-caste, and here, in the words of the narrator, "an obscure conqueror of fame, tearing himself out of the arms of a jealous love at the sign, at the call of his exalted egoism, he passes away under a cloud, inscrutable at heart, forgotten, unforgiven, and excessively romantic." We despair within the limited space at our disposal of conveying any adequate notion of the poignant interest of this strange narrative, the restrained yet fervid eloquence of the style, the vividness of the portraiture, the subtlety of psychological analysis, which are united in Mr. Conrad's latest and greatest work. The wizardry of the Orient is over it all. We can only congratulate him on an achievement at once superlatively artistic in treatment and entirely original in its subject.

HUGH CLIFFORD

The Genius of Mr. Joseph Conrad†

* * * "The Nigger" marks an epoch in Mr. Conrad's literary career, because it proved him to possess, in addition to his other qualities, extraordinary psychological insight of a peculiar kind, and showed that his mind—the mind of the Sclav, more delicate and more subtle than the mind of the Englishman,—was able to analyze human nature in a fashion distinctively its own. Since 1898, three more books have come from Mr. Conrad's pen—"Lord Jim," "Youth," and "Typhoon,"—the first an elaborate psychological study, the others collections of short stories. Space forbids a detailed examination of these volumes, any one of which would suffice to make the reputation of an author. Of the three, "Lord Jim" is the most important, and, indeed, is in some respects the greatest of Mr. Conrad's books. On the other hand, it suffers because we are asked to believe that the story as written was told by the seaman Marlow to his friends after dinner, an illusion which it is impossible to sustain. "Lord Jim" resembles nothing more nearly than some delicate piece of mosaic, of which each of the myriad tiny fragments that compose it is essential to the whole. It is built up, sentence by sentence, paragraph by paragraph, almost word by word, and lacking any phrase it would be marred and incomplete. In a word it is *written*, as in this age of speed and hurry few books are written; but, putting aside all question of its length, the very subtlety of this study of a man's soul makes its delivery by word of mouth in the circumstances described a sheer impossibility. * * *

† *North American Review*, 178 (June 1904): 851.

ALBERT J. GUERARD

Lord Jim†

I

Lord Jim is * * * Conrad's first great impressionist novel. We may recognize various anticipations: the involutions of Our Mutual Friend and The Possessed, the narrator-witnesses and atmospheres of Wuthering Heights and Bleak House, the minute control of the reader's responses to ambiguity in Benito Cereno, even (after all) Madame Bovary's ambivalence. Yet Lord Jim is not really like any of these novels, though it is most like Benito Cereno. It appears at the turn of the century as the first novel in a new form: a form bent on involving and implicating the reader in a psycho-moral drama which has no easy solution, and bent on engaging his sensibilities more strenuously and even more uncomfortably than ever before. An essential novelty, though borrowed perhaps from the mystery or "police" tale, is to force upon the reader an active, exploratory, organizing role; compel him, almost, to collaborate in the writing of the novel. Ford Madox Ford liked to define the impressionist aim as a higher realism: to come closer to actual life by presenting experience as a sensitive witness would receive it—casually, digressively, without logical order. But the game is a more sinister one than that. We certainly do not receive the facts of Lord Jim's life in the order that a citizen and observer of 1880, say Marlow himself, would have received them. The digressive method does indeed convey the "feel" of life. But the impressionist aim is to achieve a fuller truth than realism can, if necessary by "cheating"; and to create in the reader an intricate play of emotion and a rich conflict of sympathy and judgment, a provisional bafflement in the face of experience which turns out to be more complicated than we ever would have dreamed. This aim is present even in the spare and unintellectual The Great Gatsby, certainly in the endless Remembrance of Things Past, even (since everything is present there) in Ulysses. But the culminating triumph of Conradian impressionism is Absalom, Absalom! This austere masterpiece, by complicating each of Conrad's complications, helps us define the earlier experiment. We see the novel developing a musical form. But the main instruments are the reader's mind, feelings, nerves.

"If he keeps on writing the same sort," an early reviewer of Lord Jim remarked, "[Conrad] may arrive at the unique distinction of having few

† From Conrad the Novelist (Cambridge: Harvard UP, 1958). Reprinted by permission of the author. This selection has been edited for publication here. Page numbers refer to this Norton Critical Edition.

readers in his own generation, and a fair chance of several in the next."[1]
The impressionist novel, obscuring story, requires a certain magnitude
and universality if it is to survive its own difficulty; requires these as a
novel say by Trollope does not. *Absalom, Absalom!* is strengthened by
its myths of a doomed family and land under a curse, and by the violence
of Thomas Sutpen's destructive "innocence." Also: who has not been
turned away from a door? And who has not, briefly at least, harbored
an obsessive design? The universality of *Lord Jim* is even more obvious,
since nearly everyone has jumped off some *Patna* and most of us have
been compelled to live on, desperately or quietly engaged in reconciling
what we are with what we would like to be. It may be that Jim should
have required no more than that thickness of paper between the right
and wrong of the affair. Yet he faces "boundary situations" both on
board the *Patna* and in Patusan, and these necessarily involve us. Dorothy Van Ghent argues that the derelict which strikes the *Patna* is an
epiphany and manifestation of " 'dark power' " . . . coincident with and
symbolically identifiable with the impulse that makes Jim jump, an
impulse submerged like the wreck, riding in wait, striking from under."[2]

Even more persuasively, she compares Jim with Oedipus, that other
man of good intentions. The impulse to discriminate between what we
are and what we do, or to dissociate our*selves* from what exists in our
unconscious, is a form ancient enough of making excuses. And the
experience in Patusan, which to some critics seems irrelevant, corresponds to the fairly common dream of a second chance and total break
with the guilty past. "A clean slate, did he say? As if the initial word of
each our destiny were not graven in imperishable characters upon the
face of a rock." Jim can only go to meet that destiny or await it, since
it exists in his temperament; his failure is tragically certain. But he is
one of those great fictional characters whose crime, like Michael Henchard's, makes as well as breaks him. A Henchard who did not sell his
wife would have been a haytrusser to the end of his days; would have
had neither the strength to become mayor of Casterbridge nor the
strength to destroy himself so completely. So too Jim, had the *Patna*
not struck a derelict, would presumably have drifted through life seeking
ever softer and more suspect berths. The first four chapters show him
clearly headed down that path, and content to substitute revery for action.
It is discomforting but true to say that involuntary crime brings him into
the moral universe. At least this: a reader cannot fail to care about a
man of good intentions who deserts a supposedly sinking ship, leaving
eight hundred persons to die.

A further obvious remark on the humanity of great fictions is worth
making, since critics rarely pause to make it: that the Lord Jims and

1. *The Critic* 38 (1901): 138, quoted by John D. Gordan, *Joseph Conrad: The Making of a Novelist* (Cambridge: Harvard UP, 1941) 297.
2. *The English Novel: Form and Function* (New York: Rinehart, 1953) 234.

Thomas Sutpens are more interesting and more attractive to us than they would have been had we met them in "real life." In real life (unaware of Sutpen's childhood or of his grand design) we might have shared all Miss Rosa's distaste for the "demon." Certainly we would have been disgusted by the surface personality of this somber and rude man. And in real life we might have felt toward Jim what Marlow professes to feel only once so strongly: "I perceived myself unexpectedly to be thoroughly sick of him. Why these vapourings?" We might dismiss as intolerable this aggressive yet overly sensitive man in his vanity and his clean white shoes, perpetually thrusting on us his introspections and excuses. We would probably not accept him as "one of us." And would we not, in real life, also turn away from the gross vulgarity of Jay Gatsby and his mass of silk shirts, or from the rugged brutality of Michael Henchard, or from the violent tirades of Ahab, or from the posturings of Emma Bovary, or from the lank ugliness and mad loquacity of Don Quixote? Or from Lear, Macbeth, perhaps even Hamlet? Art induces greater sympathies (but also sterner judgments) than most of us are capable of in the daily conduct of our lives; it compels us to live less indifferently, and frees us from the irrelevant. This does not mean that art, cheating us, is untrue to life, but that it asks for an intensified response to something "like life." In fiction we may, for one thing, be more than once spectators of the same event! The spectator in real life of Jim's death would indeed be inhuman who blamed him for his last "proud and unflinching glance," sent right and left after Doramin's shot. But the novel, especially on a rereading, legitimately asks us to decide whether Jim, still "at the call of his exalted egoism," is really in the clear at this moment; whether he is truly redeemed.

Lord Jim rests, then, on the bedrock of a great story and an important human situation; it has some appeal even for the casual reader who moves through a novel as clumsily as he moves through life. And yet it is, of course, an art novel, a novelist's novel, a critic's novel—perhaps the first important one in England after Tristram Shandy. This means that it becomes a different novel if read very attentively; or, becomes a different novel when read a second or third time. The usual Victorian novel surrenders most of its drama and meaning at a first rapid reading and thereafter becomes inert. If we return to David Copperfield after a year or twenty years and find it a different book from the one we remembered, this is not because the book has changed. It is we who have changed. But certain novels—Benito Cereno as a mild example, Absalom, Absalom! as an extreme one, Lord Jim somewhere between the two—do change. They do become different novels at a second attentive reading. The mere factual mysteries are solved, and no longer preoccupy us. We now know that Don Benito is not a villain, that Thomas Sutpen is the father of Charles Bon, that the Patna did not sink; we cannot twice be made dupes of deceptive appearance to the same degree. But now by the same token we can watch the drama of moral ambiguity as such, and the mechanisms of deception; and we can watch the observers or narrators of the action, their mistakes, their withheld or grudging commitments. The human situation becomes more rather than less complex. Yet we are at the same time somewhat freer to observe art as art: the game of management and grouping and perspective. And matters that merely baffled or exasperated at first, notably the "irrelevant" digressions, assume an ironic or clarifying force. Only at a second reading— only, specifically, when we have come to share most of Marlow's knowledge—can we begin fully to share or imagine his feelings: the horror he would have felt, for instance, during his interview with the dying Gentleman Brown. For we know now, as Marlow knew then, that Brown was responsible for the death of Jim, this "younger brother."

The difference is important and even generic: between the complex art novel and the novel that is, rather, a clear orderly imitation of life; between *Lord Jim* and *Middlemarch* or *Barchester Towers*. A great deal of confusion may be traced to the critic's refusal to recognize this difference as generic, and to his tacit assumption that all novels ought to accomplish whatever they are going to accomplish on a first reading. Normally, I should think, the critic ought to be concerned with the impression *Middlemarch* or *Barchester Towers* might make on an ideally alert first reading; neither novel intends a subtle or deceptive relationship with the reader. But the critic of *Lord Jim* and of most impressionist novels ought to be concerned, and ought to admit this frankly, with both first and subsequent readings, and especially with the latter. For the novel of psycho-moral ambiguity can never, reread, be quite the same book.

No amount of casual rereading, to be sure, will discover *Lord Jim's* full complexity. Isn't this one secret purpose or at least value of Conrad's difficulty, as of Joyce's and Faulkner's: that it makes casual reading less likely? Anyone who truly cares for fiction cares for story, experiences sympathies and repulsions, is interested in places and lives different from his own. We may define a casual reader (and many professional critics are casual readers) as one who cares for little else. And who, above all, identifies very quickly with one of the characters on the basis of the most obvious appeal and thereafter refuses all other appeals. In a word, the reader becomes one of the characters himself; climbs into the book, and, having done so, turns all complex situations into simple ones. It is easy enough to separate the critical from the casual reader of *Lord Jim*, and not merely from that casual reader for the New York Tribune who remarked that "on a night of tropic calm the rotten craft goes to the bottom like a shot, with all hands save a few members of the crew." For the casual reader usually ignores or minimizes the important evidence *against* Lord Jim, is insensitive to ironic overtone and illustrative digression, assumes that Conrad wholly approved of his hero, and is quite certain that Jim "redeemed himself" in Patusan. Thus this casual reader, identifying with Jim so completely, is incapable of responding to the novel's suspended judgments and withheld sympathies; he has committed himself, simply and unequivocally, to a highly equivocal personage. (Very rarely a casual reader is found who goes to the opposite extreme, and develops no sympathy for Jim at all.) So too, since his whole concern is with Jim, the casual reader regards Marlow as no more than an irritating technical device. And he responds not at all to structure and style, to the beauty and meaning inherent in the elaborate ironic play of recurrence and reflexive reference.

But even for a more alert reader, that first reading of *Lord Jim* is very different from a second. Can we remember a genuine first impression, unaffected by our later knowledge of what happened to the *Patna?* The conflict of judgment and sympathy would already exist, but in much simpler terms. Through four chapters, we would listen to an omniscient narrator, who gives us a distinctly ironic portrait of Jim: a man of "exquisite sensibility" who has "elected to conceal" some "deplorable faculty"; who as a boy in training dreamed of rescues but did not act when action was demanded, who could yet return at once to his self-deceptive dreams. And presently we see him on board the *Patna,* the chief mate of a steamer, still dreaming of heroic rescues. We then move to the court of inquiry: see Jim's shame and assume there is some reason for this shame. The officers must have deserted a sinking ship. At what point does our hypothetical first reader realize that the ship didn't sink? On page 35 the crazed chief engineer's remark that he saw her go down is referred to as a "stupid lie"; on page 53 Marlow speaks of an "unforeseen conclusion of the tale" and on the next page interjects, casually: "So that bulkhead held out after all." On page 62: "These sleeping pilgrims were destined to accomplish their whole pilgrimage to the bitterness of some other end." Conceivably our reader might not know what happened until page 83 ("towed successfully to Aden") or even until the French lieutenant refers very specifically to his own role in the salvage. But meanwhile he has come to sympathize with Jim as a conscientious man on a rack, who stayed to face the inquiry. He is hardly prepared to recognize how damaging it is—the evidence of this French lieutenant who stayed on board the *Patna* thirty hours and who recalls that the unloading of the pilgrims at Aden was accomplished in twenty-five minutes. The sympathetic reader is not likely to remember that Jim stayed on board twenty-seven minutes before jumping. These figures (rather deceptive, since the situations were not comparable and lifeboats were lacking) may have a sharply devaluing effect on later readings.

As with large conceptions, so with fine details of texture: a first valid and interesting effect may, on rereading, be replaced by a very different one. Consider, for instance, the elaborate description of the pilgrims streaming onto the *Patna*:

> They streamed aboard over three gangways, they streamed in urged by faith and the hope of paradise, they streamed in with a continuous tramp and shuffle of bare feet, without a word, a murmur, or a look back; and when clear of confining rails spread on all sides over the deck, flowed forward and aft, overflowed down the yawning hatchways, filled the inner recesses of the ship—like water filling a cistern, like water flowing into crevices and crannies, like water rising silently even with the rim.

At a first reading we watch these ghostly pilgrims with some detachment, though they and the rising water are secretly preparing us for disaster at sea; the tenor is "drowned" by the vehicle. In any event this seems to be a matter concerning only the reader and the narrator, who strikes us as rather literary. We are not particularly conscious of Jim as a possible watcher of the scene. But on a second reading we may see these flowing silent pilgrims and this drowning ship only through his eyes. And now the scene reminds us of something we have come to know fairly well: Jim's faculty of "swift and forestalling vision." It prepares us to accept more fully than before the fact that he will be immobilized by his power to imagine these same pilgrims in panic. Thus what had seemed a rather literary comment by a detached narrator is now, intimately, in character with Jim. He, not the author or narrator, is the dangerously "imaginative beggar."

One further example of reflexive reference will indicate how a second reading differs from a first. In Chapter 26, after a brief introduction of the chief Doramin and his son Dain Waris, Marlow summarizes Jim's account of his already legendary exploit: the capture of Sherif Ali's camp. "He has made himself responsible for success on his own head." Not a very disturbing remark, since we know that he was successful. And the portrait of Doramin may seem merely amusing. He is carried up the hill in his armchair, then sits with a pair of flintlock pistols on his knees. "Magnificent things, ebony, silver-mounted, with beautiful locks and a calibre like an old blunderbuss." They were, Jim adds, a present from Stein, in exchange for the talisman ring. All this may seem unimportant and digressive, no more than the small vivid details that confirm a novel's authority and actualize its scenes. But in fact the passage is dropping its associations—"Upon my head" . . . flintlock pistols . . . talisman ring—into the fringes of our consciousness; it is preparing us to respond to the full significance, a hundred and fifty pages later,[3] of Jim's words, "Upon my head." And above all preparing us to recognize and believe the Doramin of the last pages and those pistols on his knees: the deliberateness of the shooting, and the ironic closing of a circle as the ring

3. In this edition, eighty-seven pages later (158 to 245) [*Editor*].

rolls against Jim's foot. Thus the first reading. On a second reading of
Chapter 26 those pistols reflect a light thrown backward; we respond
very strongly to the scene itself and its tragic irony. For it reminds us
—at the very moment that we hear about the greatest active success of
Jim's life, in fact almost his only active success to reach us
dramatically—of how the story will end: with Jim immobilized once
more by a dream, and then immobile in death.

* * *

Lord Jim, then, is an intricate novel about possible emotional and
moral responses to a relatively simple man, even to a "type" of man.
However, it would be a mistake to dwell too much on Jim's simplicity,
or to say that there's "nothing there." For this man repeatedly taken
"unawares," and who is possessed by what he thinks he possesses, offers
a major dramatic image of the will and the personality in conflict, of
the conscious mind betrayed by the unconscious, of the intent rendered
absurd by the deed. The conscious mind discovers, belatedly, what the
betraying dark powers have accomplished: "I had jumped, it seems . . ."
Just so Jim makes his more successful jump over the palisade in Patusan:
"at once, without any mental process as it were, without any stir of
emotion, he set about his escape as if executing a plan matured for a
month." A little more addicted than most men to deliberate revery, Jim
is a little more than most subject to the undeliberate unconscious mind
and its sympathetic or hostile acts. This is best dramatized in the major
scene of crippling identification with Gentleman Brown. But it also
appears very interestingly in his compulsion to make others reënact his
sudden jump from the *Patna*. This may be too elaborate a construction
to put on Jim's act of throwing the crosseyed Dane, now of the Royal
Siamese Navy, into the Menam river. But it does seem to account for
his curious behavior in making the would-be assassins jump into the
river in Patusan. There is a link with the *Patna* incident, in Conrad's
imagination if not in Jim's unconscious, between the torch flung in the
river and the *Patna*'s masthead light, which had seemed to drop "like
a lighted match you throw down."

> "Jump!" he thundered. The three splashes made one splash, a
> shower flew up, black heads bobbed convulsively, and disappeared
> . . . His heart seemed suddenly to grow too big for his breast and
> choke him in the hollow of his throat. This probably made him
> speechless for so long, and after returning his gaze she flung the
> burning torch with a wide sweep of the arm into the river. The
> ruddy fiery glare, taking a long flight through the night, sank with
> a vicious hiss, and the calm soft starlight descended upon them,
> unchecked.

A novelistic portrait may show psychological intuition through its
accurate dramatization of mental processes and significant notation of

behavior. But it may also show it through the efficiency of its often unconscious symbolizing imagination. Significantly enough, if a hat does truly symbolize the personality, Jim turns up on board Marlow's ship without a hat, after throwing the Dane into the river. He has been stripped once again of his disguise, or stripped of his illusion of self. So it is at his most critical hours. He lost his cap, jumping from the *Patna*, and the next day the "sun crept all the way from east to west over my bare head." And when the time comes, at the end, to meet the fatal destiny, he is "fully dressed as for every day, but without a hat." Is it or is it not the *real* Jim who, hatless, takes the disaster "upon his own head" in pride and/or atonement?

Simple Jim may be. But there is nothing simple about Conrad's own understanding of him. We must, as always, except Dostoevsky: the first Freudian novelist and still the greatest dramatist of half-conscious and unconscious processes. And we have seen how The Nigger of the "Narcissus," a symbolist study of identification, prepared the way. Otherwise, *Lord Jim* is perhaps the first major novel solidly built on a true intuitive understanding of sympathetic identification as a psychic process, and as a process which may operate both consciously and less than consciously. The fact that *Lord Jim* takes this process as its center long eluded its readers. But this does not mean that the subject and interest were not unequivocally "there," or that Conrad left matters unreasonably obscure. The fault was ours not his. We may put the case as we must often put it for Dostoevsky: that Conrad dramatized relationships which we could recognize as interesting and perhaps feel to be true, but which we could not accept or explain conceptually.

Dramatically as well as theoretically, *Lord Jim* is a story of sympathies, projections, empathies . . . and loyalties. The central relationship is that of Marlow and Jim. We can see why Jim needs Marlow, as an "ally, a helper, an accomplice." He cannot believe in himself unless he has found another to do so. And he needs a judge, witness, and advocate in the solitude of his battle with himself. All this is evident. But why does Marlow go so far out of his way, very far really, to help Jim? Why does Marlow need Jim? He speaks of the fellowship of the craft, of being his very young brother's keeper, of loyalty to "one of us," of mere curiosity, of a moral need to explore and test a standard of conduct. And we may say with much truth that this is a novel of a moving and enduring friendship between an older and a younger man. But Marlow—in several passages recalling The Nigger of the "Narcissus" 's central comment on identification—acknowledges a more intimate or more selfish alliance. He is loyal to Jim as one must be to another or potential self, to the criminally weak self that may still exist.

> Was it for my own sake that I wished to find some shadow of an
> excuse for that young fellow whom I had never seen before, but

whose appearance alone added a touch of personal concern to the thoughts suggested by the knowledge of his weakness—made it a thing of mystery and terror—like a hint of a destructive fate ready for us all whose youth—in its day—had resembled his youth? I fear that such was the secret motive of my prying.

He appealed to all sides at once—to the side turned perpetually to the light of day, and to that side of us which, like the other hemisphere of the moon, exists stealthily in perpetual darkness, with only a fearful ashy light falling at times on the edge.

If he had not enlisted my sympathies he had done better for himself—he had gone to the very fount and origin of that sentiment, he had reached the secret sensibility of my egoism.

Marlow is not fatally paralyzed or immobilized by this young "double." But Big Brierly is. Brierly is successful, and seems to know nothing of indecision and self-mistrust:

> The sting of life could do no more to his complacent soul than the scratch of a pin to the smooth face of a rock. This was enviable. As I looked at him flanking on one side the unassuming pale-faced magistrate who presided at the inquiry, his self-satisfaction presented to me and to the world a surface as hard as granite. He committed suicide very soon after.
>
> No wonder Jim's case bored him, and while I thought with something akin to fear of the immensity of his contempt for the young man under examination, he was probably holding silent inquiry into his own case. The verdict must have been of unmitigated guilt, and he took the secret of the evidence with him in that leap into the sea.

Insofar as Brierly can explain matters to himself (or to Marlow) he feels humiliated, a white man and seaman, by Jim's evidence given in the presence of natives—"enough to burn a man to ashes with shame." He wants Jim to run away, and offers two hundred rupees to finance the evasion. But professional and racial pride are scarcely sufficient motives for suicide. Marlow sees, in retrospect, that "at bottom poor Brierly must have been thinking of himself" when he wanted Jim to clear out. He had recognized in Jim an unsuspected potential self; he had looked into himself for the first time. "If I understand anything of men, the matter was no doubt of the gravest import, one of those trifles that awaken ideas—start into life some thought with which a man unused to such a companionship finds it impossible to live."

Doubtless Conrad was interested in the case of Brierly (presumably based on the suicide of Captain Wallace of the *Cutty Sark*) in its own right. And for some readers it may exist as one of the many sources of a light thrown obliquely on Jim: possibly (by the very fact of the suicide) to magnify him and give his case importance; possibly (by the integrity of Brierly's last moments as a seaman) to devalue Jim the poor officer. But the episode's chief function is to prepare us to understand (or at least accept) Jim's paralyzed identification with Gentleman Brown and suicidal refusal to fight him; and to prepare us, also, for the deliberateness of Jim's march up to Doramin. The aesthetic principle may be obvious, but the execution of it is seldom easy—to prepare the reader to accept a "strangeness" of major importance and concern by first dramatizing that strangeness in a setting seemingly minor, anecdotal, neutral. And we will need to believe, dramatically if not conceptually, that interview with Gentleman Brown, since it is the direct cause of Jim's death.

The immediate preparation for the interview (Chapters 37–40) shows Conrad's impressionism at its most successful, dramatically speaking. We have an inkling from Brown, on his unclean death-bed, that Jim himself may be dead; we learn from the benumbed Tamb' Itam that Jim "would not fight," and from Jewel that "he had been driven away from her by a dream." Thus in Brown and his cutthroat crew, but also in what we know and recall of Jim's character, we see his destiny approach. It became probable from the moment Brown heard of Jim's power, and started upriver to seek his share of the loot. And thus we are conditioned, during Jim's absence, to see the chief menace of Brown as ruthless and cynical intelligence at the service of pure love of destruction; we expect a combat of wills. And such it turns out to be. "They faced each other across the creek, and with steady eyes tried to understand each other before they opened their lips. Their antagonism must have been expressed in their glances," Marlow suggests. "I know that Brown hated Jim at first sight."

The crafty Brown capitalizes at once on Jim's obvious reluctance to answer questions. He finds a way "as broad as a turnpike, to get in and shake his two penny soul around and inside out and upside down—by God!" He asks Jim what had made him come to Patusan, what had scared him into this infernal hole, and even says something that would inevitably remind Jim of the *Patna*. It is one of the great dramatic scenes in Conrad: the cynical Brown's unerring discovery of his antagonist's weakness. "And there ran through the rough talk a vein of suble reference to their common blood, an assumption of common experience; a sickening suggestion of common guilt, of secret knowledge that was like a bond of their minds and of their hearts." It is a paralyzing, an immobilizing bond; and Jim refuses to fight. According to [Gustav] Morf, Jim immediately identifies himself with Brown, and identification "is characterized always by an extraordinary indulgence for the second self, an indulgence which must of necessity remain incomprehensible to any other person . . . Jim's indulgence for Brown is typical. He simply cannot resist the evil *because the evil is within himself.*" And his "un-

conscious wish is to see Brown (i.e., himself) go off free and powerful . . ."[4]

It could be argued that Morf's phrasing is too blunt; it leaves little
room for exceptions. And identification may lead to hostility rather than
sympathy, as in a condemnation of self by proxy. Still Morf's analysis
(which in 1947 struck me as largely mistaken) now seems more accurate
than my own rationalist explanation: that Jim's hard-won assurance was
destroyed by the fact that the first visitor from the outside world brought
a reminder of the *Patna*, and that Jim was unwilling to shed white men's
blood. These are indeed possible related or additional motives for Jim's
refusal to fight. But the emphasis Morf gives to half-conscious and
unconscious identification is, I am now persuaded, correct. It is at the
center of Conrad's psychology—as it was, almost contemporaneously,
at the center of André Gide's.

II

Not only the characters of a fiction experience such sympathies. The
related central preoccupation of Conrad's technique, the heart of the
impressionist aim, is to invite and control the reader's identifications
and so subject him to an intense rather than passive experience. Marlow's
human task is also the reader's: to achieve a right human relationship
with this questionable younger brother. Marlow must resist an excessive
identification (which would mean abandoning his traditional ethic); he
must maintain a satisfactory balance of sympathy and judgment. No
easy task, since Jim demands total sympathy. "He wanted an ally, a
helper, an accomplice. I felt the risk I ran of being circumvented,
blinded, decoyed, bullied, perhaps, into taking part in a dispute impossible of decision if one had to be fair to all the phantoms in
possession—to the reputable that had its claims and to the disreputable
that had its exigencies." And this is, far more than in most novels, the
reader's moral drama and situation: to be subjected to all the phantoms
in possession, to be exposed to a continuous subtle and flowing interplay
of intellectual appeals to his judgment and poignant appeals to his
sympathy.

The reader must survive this experience and go through this labyrinth
of evidence without the usual guide of an omniscient author or trustworthy author-surrogate. The reader (looking incorrigibly for the author's
convictions and final decisions) is likely to put his trust in Marlow,
including the Marlow who speaks of Jim's "greatness," "truth," and
"constancy." But he does so at his peril. Or he may put his trust, even
more dangerously, in Stein, Jim's fellow-romantic. Stein's wise and
assured tones and his central position in the novel, geographically speaking, have led many readers to assume that he conveys the author's

4. *The Polish Heritage of Joseph Conrad* (London: Sampson, Low, Marston, 1930) 158.

judgment. It would be much more accurate to say that Conrad's moral judgment is isolated, if anywhere, in the austere nameless "privileged man" of Chapter 36, and that his uncorrected sympathy is isolated in Stein. (The "privileged man" would not admit that Jim had mastered his fate, and maintained "that we must fight in the ranks or our lives don't count.") Then to whom and to what should the reader attend, if not to his professed guides? The answer of course is that he should attend, eagerly yet skeptically, to everything: to the moralizing of the guides, yes, but even more to every scrap of evidence they offer by way of anecdote, disgression, example. The reading of this novel is a combat: within the reader, between reader and narrators, between reader and that watching and controlling mind ultimately responsible for the distortions.

Doubtless the common impression left by a first reading is that the formal rational evidence is preponderantly favorable to Jim, and that the novel finally reaches a lenient verdict, even a judgment of "approval." Jim emerges as, simply, a hero and a redeemed man. But the evidence (as we discover on rereading) is by no means preponderantly favorable; and *Lord Jim* is as much a novel about a man who makes excuses as a novel that makes excuses. Our first impression that the novel "approves" Jim turns out to derive not from the area of rational evidence and judgment but from the area of novelistic sympathy; we discover, as we look a little more closely, that Marlow has repeatedly taken us in. He is a considerably more lenient witness than his austere moralizing tone suggests. On various occasions he brings in the damaging evidence (he is, after all, obliged to bring it in) very casually and digressively, as though inviting us to overlook it. So too, when we are inclined to judge harshly, Marlow diverts our attention from the suffering, "burning" Jim to those who merely rot in the background, or who live safely in a world of untested rectitude. "You've been tried." Jim has, at least, been tested and tried. Therefore he exists. Marlow evokes both sympathy and a more lenient judgment whenever he reminds us of those who are safe: Marlow's listeners, or Jim's father sending his four-page letter of "easy morality and family news," or the tourists in the Malabar Hotel where Jim begins his story. Their irrelevance colors our response to Jim's very questionable denial that he was afraid of death: "They were exchanging jocular reminiscences of the donkeys in Cairo. A pale anxious youth stepping softly on long legs was being chaffed by a strutting and rubicund globe-trotter about his purchases in the bazaar. 'No, really—do you think I've been done to that extent?' he inquired very earnest and deliberate." When we return to Jim a moment later, we listen to him more attentively: " 'Some of the crew were sleeping on the number one hatch within reach of my arm,' began Jim again."

Such sudden corrective juxtaposition is at once the novel's characteristic way of redressing a balance of meaning and its chief way of moving us emotionally. It may operate in both directions, of course: correcting an excessive austerity of judgment or correcting an excessive sympathy. The matter is not easy to sum up, and my conclusion is perhaps debatable. But here it is: that on a first reading we are inclined to think Marlow's own judgment of Jim too harsh (since we have missed some of the evidence that led him to that judgment); that on a second reading (because we are discovering that evidence with a force of delayed impact) we may think Marlow's judgment too lenient. In other words, the unfavorable evidence that Marlow had half-concealed through deceptive casualness of manner grows upon us at a second or third reading, and becomes more difficult to discount. But meanwhile our natural sympathy for Jim—the center of attention, the man on the rack, the conscientious sinner, the man who has been "tried"—has correspondingly diminished. We have, in other words, the very reverse of the situation that pertains in *Absalom, Absalom!*, where the favorable evidence has been more than half-concealed. Hence, at a second reading, we think more not less of Thomas Sutpen. But the aesthetic principle, and the implicit assumption that a serious novel like a serious poem is meant to be read more than once, is the same.

The delicate interplay of sympathy and judgment, managed with such ease in the novel itself, is difficult to describe. We may take, as an example of crucial evidence within deceptively unemphasized digression, the testimony of the Malay helmsman in Chapter 8. For some pages we have listened to Jim's own vivid account of his emotions after looking at the bulging bulkhead, and to Marlow's slightly more distant and meditative retelling; together they have taken us as close as we ever come to the original experience of quite understandable fear. We are *there* as Jim, thinking the ship may go at any moment, struggles with the pilgrim importuning him for water to drink; as back on the bridge he finds the officers trying to get one of the boats off the chocks. And at the moment of Jim's most urgent appeal for both sympathy and understanding—"Where was the kindness in making crazy with fright all those people I could not save single-handed—that nothing could save?"—Marlow characteristically withdraws to comment on Jim's longing for ally, helper, accomplice.

In the next paragraphs Marlow holds a very fine balance: reminding us of Jim's self-deceptions and weakness but also of his conscientious shame, magnifying the struggle through allusion and analogy, admitting his own allegiance. The effect at a first reading is to transfer our attention from Jim's dubious acts on board the *Patna* to the magnitude of his present "dispute with an invisible personality." When at last we get back to the *Patna*, Marlow not Jim does the telling, and we can see Jim, a not wholly ignoble figure, standing apart from the other officers and the boat. "The two Malays had meantime remained holding to the wheel"—only thoughtless, immobile figures, not even part of our moral universe. We are quickly diverted from them by the stunning retrospective information that the ship didn't sink. "And still she floated! These sleeping pilgrims were destined to accomplish their whole pilgrimage to the bitterness of some other end." Marlow remarks, casually, that the behavior of the two helmsmen was not "the least wonder of these twenty minutes."

We then move away from the *Patna* to the inquiry, where the two helmsmen were questioned, as for relief from dramatic and moral intensity. It is a moment for attention to flag. The first helmsman, when asked what he thought of matters at the time, says he thought nothing. The second "explained that he had a knowledge of some evil thing befalling the ship, but there had been no order; he could not remember an order; why should he leave the helm?" And the evidence he gives —if we attend to it, as we do on later readings—pricks Jim's balloon. Not the man on the rack and tortured sinner but the old Malayan helmsman devoted to and formed by the honest traditions of the sea is heroic. He defines himself when he pours out the names of skippers and ships. We are reminded of Conrad's pride in "these few bits of paper, headed by the names of a few Scots and English shipmasters."

> To some further questions he jerked back his spare shoulders, and declared it never came into his mind then that the white men were about to leave the ship through fear of death. He did not believe it now. There might have been secret reasons. He wagged his old chin knowingly. Aha! secret reasons. He was a man of great experience, and he wanted *that* white Tuan to know—he turned toward Brierly, who didn't raise his head—that he had acquired a knowledge of many things by serving white men on the sea for a great number of years—and, suddenly, with shaky excitement he poured upon our spell-bound attention a lot of queer-sounding names, names of dead-and-gone skippers, names of forgotten country ships, names of familiar and distorted sound, as if the hand of dumb time had been at work on them for ages. They stopped him at last.

Marlow refers to the helmsman rightly as an "extraordinary and damning witness." But he is silenced, in the novel, very quickly indeed. And we are taken back to the ship. There follow thirty-five pages[5] of a detailed and tormented account of Jim's last minutes on board, of his jump "into an everlasting deep hole," of his harrowing time in the lifeboat with the "three dirty owls" and his day spent apart from them under a burning sun, deliberating whether to die. The reader cannot fail to take Jim's part against theirs, and is more and more tempted to take seriously his assertion that it was not *he* who had jumped. "I told you I jumped; but

5. In this edition, eighteen pages (63 to 81) [*Editor*].

I tell you they were too much for any man. It was their doing as plainly as if they had reached up with a boathook and pulled me over." By the end of Chapter 11, recollecting his debates on suicide, Jim has again threatened to convert the *Patna* episode into an entirely interior affair.

Hence it is high time we return to material matters, to physical things and acts: to what might and might not have been done. And Marlow sweeps us ahead more than three years to his meeting with the French lieutenant of Chapters 12 and 13, who is perhaps the most damning witness and reflector of all. He too appears very casually, within a nominal digression, and I understand he is discounted by some readers as a stuffy and uninteresting figure. Marlow, who in these chapters clearly diverges from Conrad, would have liked so to dismiss him. But his role in the novel may be as crucial as Stein's; the scenes are in a way pendant. For Stein, the intellectual and dreamer who is also a successful man of action, Jim is "romantic"—which is very bad and "also very good." His dream and his anguish are what make him exist. But the French lieutenant, a moving figure of professional competence and integrity, and a man certainly capable of sympathy, at once calls attention to something else: Jim "ran away along with the others." Marlow the observer professes to be irritated by his stolid assurance. But Conrad obviously finds him both likable and admirable, and he has (like a Hemingway figure) the esoteric wound betokening virtue:

> This was absolutely the first gesture I saw him make. It gave me the opportunity to "note" a starred scar on the back of his hand—effect of a gunshot clearly; and, as if my sight had been made more acute by this discovery, I perceived also the seam of an old wound, beginning a little below the temple and going out of sight under the short grey hair at the side of the head—the graze of a spear or the cut of a sabre. He clasped his hands on his stomach again. "I remained on board that—that—my memory is going (*s'en va*). Ah! *Patt-nà. C'est bien ça. Patt-nà. Merci.* It is droll how one forgets. I stayed on board that ship thirty hours."[6]

Time "had left him hopelessly behind with a few poor gifts . . ." But, unlike Jim, he had done what had to be done. And of the thirty hours during which he remained on board the *Patna*, with two quartermasters stationed with axes to cut her clear of the tow if she sank, he chiefly remembers with irritation having had no wine to go with his food. He too was aware of the chief sources of danger, panic among the pilgrims and the "villainous" bulkhead. But he saw them as matters to be taken care of. The way to behave in crisis is to act efficiently. His words are distantly echoed, from one language to another, by Stein's account of an ambush:

6. For instance, the arrow wound of the count in *The Sun Also Rises*.

. . . this manoeuvre eased the strain on the bulkhead, whose state, he expounded with stolid glibness, demanded the greatest care (*éxigeait les plus grands ménagements*).

"It was a little intrigue, you understand. They got my poor Mohammed to send for me and then laid that ambush. I see it all in a minute, and I think—this wants a little management. My pony snort, jump, and stand, and I fall slowly forward with my head on his mane."

At the end of the interview with the French lieutenant, Marlow is "discouraged about Jim's case." Earlier—noting the lieutenant's admission that everyone experiences fear, and his acknowledgment that Jim "might have had the best dispositions"—Marlow was glad to see him take "a lenient view." A suspicious reader might even suppose the lieutenant had begun to confess, on the preceding page, to an act of cowardice similar to Jim's. But the lieutenant means to do no such thing, and he does not take a lenient view. For he has "no opinion" as to what life is like when honor is gone. Hence he has not *acted* in cowardice. "I was confronted," Marlow says,

> by two narrow grey circlets, like two tiny steel rings around the profound blackness of the pupils. The sharp glance, coming from that massive body, gave a notion of extreme efficiency, like a razor-edge on a battle-axe. "Pardon," he said, punctiliously. His right hand went up, and he swayed forward. "Allow me . . . I contended that one may get on knowing very well that one's courage does not come of itself (*ne vient pas tout seul*). There's nothing much in that to get upset about. One truth the more ought not to make life impossible . . . But the honour—the honour, monsieur! . . ."

We do not, even after this second damning witness has spoken, get back to the Malabar House and Jim's narrative at once. Another reflector and witness appears, by way of a digressive development of a modifying clause: Bob Stanton. Marlow has been speaking of Jim's unglamorous mode of life as a water-clerk for De Jongh. Or is the business of an insurance canvasser, which "Little Bob Stanton" had been, even less glamorous? As with the French lieutenant, the introduction is casual and faintly ironic. And then we are told, as though it had no bearing on Jim's case, the story of Stanton's drowning while trying to save a lady's maid in the *Sephora* disaster. He too had done what had to be done. As chief mate he would leave no one on board a sinking ship; Jim had left eight hundred. Stanton reminds us of what the officer is expected to do, irrespective of temptation or mitigating circumstance. And at this point (after seventeen pages[7] of damaging evidence in the guise of digression) we return to Jim and his heroic introspections. "Clear

---

7. In this edition, nine pages (82 to 91) [*Editor*].

out! Couldn't think of it," he replies, when Marlow offers Brierly's plan of escape. But we are less impressed than we would have been before listening to the French lieutenant and before hearing of Stanton's death.

The natural unreflective heroism of the French lieutenant and Stanton thus help to put Jim's reveries of heroism, and his actual failures and excuses, into a clearer perspective. We must remember that in every chapter and on every page the double appeal to sympathy and judgment is made, though one or the other may dominate; we are not being subjected to the blunt regular swings of a pendulum. Still, this is perhaps the point in the first part of the novel where our view of Jim is most severe. The following chapter sets in a strong returning flow of sympathy. We see Jim's formal punishment delivered in a "chill and mean atmosphere. The real significance of crime is in its being a breach of faith with the community of mankind, and from that point of view he was no mean traitor, but his execution was a hole-and-corner affair." In a sense a proper judgment has been passed on Jim's romantic ego and his vulnerable idealism: *certificate canceled.* Then, and almost at once, we see Jim's version of "how to be" in the very different perspective of Chester's gross cynicism: Chester who wants someone "no good" for his guano island, and who regards Jim as "no good" because he takes his downfall to heart. "You must see things exactly as they are"—as Chester's partner Robinson did, who ate his comrades rather than starve, and afterward showed no remorse.[8] Marlow does not accept Chester's proposal. But he vivifies it sufficiently to make us more sympathetic with Jim's plight. And again, though in Marlow's imagination only, we have the "secret sharer" image of the guilty man alone under a burning sun: "I had a rapid vision of Jim perched on a shadowless rock, up to his knees in guano, with the screams of sea-birds in his ears, the incandescent ball of the sun above his head; the empty sky and the empty ocean all a-quiver, shimmering together in the heat as far as the eye could reach." The classic Promethean image of unending punishment magnifies Jim's suffering; it reminds us too of the moral isolation into which he will now enter more deeply than before. And the section ends (Chapters 15,

---

8. *Lord Jim* explores the fine distinctions between guilt and sense of disgrace yet remains ambivalent toward the character who—accepting what he has done as done—lives without remorse. Stein is such a man. But so too is Robinson, who three weeks after his rescue "was as well as ever. He didn't allow any fuss that was made on shore to upset him; he just shut his lips tight, and let people screech. It was bad enough to have lost his ship, and all he was worth besides, without paying attention to the hard names they called him."

In this connection, and though it may reflect only one of several moods, an 1891 letter from Conrad to Marguerite Poradowska is of interest: "Each act of life is final and inevitably produces its consequences in spite of all the weeping and gnashing of teeth and the sorrow of weak souls who suffer as fright grips them when confronted with the results of their own actions. As for myself, I shall never need to be consoled for any act of my life, and this because I am strong enough to judge my conscience rather than be its slave, as the orthodox would like to persuade us to be" (*Letters of Joseph Conrad to Marguerite Poradowska, 1890–1920*, translated and edited by John A. Gee and Paul J. Sturm, [New Haven, Yale UP, 1940] 36). See *The Collected Letters of Joseph Conrad*, Vol. 1, 1861–1897, ed. Frederick R. Karl and Laurence Davies (Cambridge: Cambridge UP, 1983) 95 [*Editor*].

16, 17) with the not unsympathetic picture of Jim's long silent struggle with himself, while Marlow writes letter after letter. "He was rooted to the spot, but convulsive shudders ran down his back; his shoulders would heave suddenly. He was fighting, he was fighting—mostly for his breath, as it seemed." The "idea obtrudes itself that he made so much of his disgrace while it is the guilt alone that matters." Nevertheless the impression left, at the end of this part, is of a kind of stubborn courage.

This then is *Lord Jim's* chief way of provoking in its readers a strong human response and meaningful conflict: to interweave or suddenly juxtapose (rather than group logically and chronologically) the appeals to judgment and sympathy, to criticism and compassion. A man is what he does, which in Jim's case is very little that is not equivocal. But also he "exists" for us by the quality of his feeling and the poignant intensity of his dream. He is not "good enough" (as Marlow tells Jewel, as the Malay helmsman and other witnesses verify) yet his childish romanticism may be preferable to a cynical realism. In any event, as Marlow goes on to say, "nobody is good enough." This is not a relativistic conclusion. It reminds us rather how strong Marlow's moral and community engagement was, against which his brotherly and outlaw sympathy contended.

These peculiar groupings—of incident and witness and evidence, of intellectual and emotional appeal—distinguish *Lord Jim* from most earlier fiction. But imagery also leaves us in provisional and perhaps lasting uncertainty. Is Jim "in the clear"? The novel's chief recurrent image is of substance and reality obscured, often attractively so, by mist or by deceptive light. *Fog, mist, cloud,* and *veil* form a cluster with *moonlight,* and with *dream,* to dramatize certain essential distinctions: between the conscious mind and the unconscious, illusion and reality, the "ego-ideal" and the self's destiny as revealed by its acts. Imagery is supposed to reveal an author's ultimate and perhaps unconscious bias. But much of the imagery here is grouped fairly consciously as part of a multiple appeal to the reader. These images—if they do form a cluster, if we do properly take them together—should help determine the delicate relationship of idealism and self-deception. And hence they should help us to evaluate Stein's advice ("follow the dream") and Jim's ultimate conduct in Patusan, when opportunity comes to his side, veiled like an Eastern bride.

At a first reading all this imagery of nebulosity may magnify and glamorize Jim (as fog magnifies Wordsworth's sheep), and also may be partly responsible for our first impression that Jim is an exceedingly mysterious person. But its later effect may be to persuade us that Stein is not, unequivocally, a spokesman for the author, and to throw still further doubt on Jim's "redemption" in Patusan. "I ask myself whether his rush had really carried him out of that mist in which he loomed interesting if not very big, with floating outlines—a straggler yearning inconsolably for his humble place in the ranks."

The meaning of *mist*, as we look at its various appearances, is clearer than we might have expected. It can refer generally to ambiguity but more centrally refers to the aura of deception and self-deception that surrounds Jim's reality. Now and then Marlow has a "glimpse through a rent in the mist in which he moved and had his being," as Jim says something truly revealing: as he tells of his impulse to go back to the spot of the *Patna*'s abandonment, or as he recognizes the good Marlow does him by listening. But the mists close again at once when Jim refers to his plight as "unfair." Thus we may call the mist his illusion of self or ego-ideal, which is in turn responsible for the deceptions; it may impose the "mask" of a "usual expression." Reality can then appear in an "unconscious grimace," or through rifts caused by the inward struggles. He stumblingly reveals the truth; or, we stumble upon it. "The muscles round his lips contracted into an unconscious grimace that tore through the mask of his usual expression—something violent, short-lived, and illuminating like a twist of lightning that admits the eye for an instant into the secret convolutions of a cloud." The provocative reality in this instance was a fact normally evaded: that he was in the lifeboat with the others. Or, "The mist of his feelings shifted between us, as if disturbed by his struggles, and in the rifts of the immaterial veil he would appear to my staring eyes distinct of form and pregnant with vague appeal like a symbolic figure in a picture." This questionable sentence would suggest that the "real" Jim behind the apparent one has the vague symbolic appeal. Very possibly this dubious phrasing simply came to Conrad, who refused to examine it closely.

Still, we can say that mist, fog, and veil conceal or blur reality. So too does moonlight, whose "occult power" can rob things of their reality: "It is to our sunshine, which—say what you like—is all we have to live by, what the echo is to the sound: misleading and confusing whether the note be mocking or sad. It robs all forms of matter—which, after all, is our domain—of their substance, and gives a sinister reality to shadows alone." Dorothy Van Ghent advances an interesting argument: that the split conical hill on Patusan suggests Jim's spiritual cleavage, and the moon rising between the two halves suggests a "figure of the ego-ideal" with its "illusionariness, and the solitude implied by illusion."[9] The moonlight of Patusan is certainly associated with immobility and isolation, and with times when Jim is seriously entranced by his pride and illusions of success. This moonlight comments on the unreality of his aspirations. So too (when Jim still confuses guilt with disgrace, and thus comes "no nearer to the root of the matter") Marlow notes the "irresistible slow work of the night settling on all the visible forms,

9. *The English Novel* 237. This may be true, though the split hill exists in the "source" of Brooke's memoirs. The imagination makes its significant selections from reality.

effacing the outlines . . ." But if the light of the moon is associated with illusion and a blurring of reality, the dark of the moon can be a very important reality, and one largely responsible for our acts: the unconscious itself. "He appealed to all sides at once—to the side turned perpetually to the light of day, and to that side of us which, like the other hemisphere of the moon, exists stealthily in perpetual darkness, with only a fearful ashy light falling at times on the edge." Whatever their sympathies in the matter, Marlow and Conrad clearly believe that we shall be saved by the sunlight of action and that deceptive half-lights are menacing.

All this (if we are to trust Marlow at all) has an important bearing on Stein's ambiguous advice: to submit yourself to the "destructive element" of the ego-ideal; to attempt through action to realize (or live with?) that illusion of self; to "follow the dream." Jewel remarks, very accurately, that Jim "had been driven away from her by a dream." Marlow's introduction ("one of the most trustworthy men I had ever known") together with Stein's grave tones and the memorably cryptic quality of his utterance create an initial confidence. At a first reading we naturally identify Stein's judgment and Conrad's. But the imagery which occurs to Marlow, immediately after Stein gives his advice, seems to say something very different. It associates Stein and his "conviction" with the half-lights of deception and menacing illusion; it brings Stein down to Jim's level rather than raises Jim to his. We cannot be sure what Conrad thought about Stein. Neither, possibly, could Conrad himself. This is Marlow's comment:

> The whisper of his conviction seemed to open before me a vast and uncertain expanse, as of a crepuscular horizon on a plain at dawn—or was it, perchance, at the coming of the night? One had not the courage to decide; but it was a charming and deceptive light, throwing the impalpable poesy of its dimness over pitfalls—over graves. His life had begun in sacrifice, in enthusiasm for generous ideas; he had travelled very far, on various ways, on strange paths, and whatever he followed it had been without faltering, and therefore without shame and without regret. In so far he was right. That was the way, no doubt. Yet for all that the great plain on which men wander amongst graves and pitfalls remained very desolate under the impalpable poesy of its crepuscular light, overshadowed in the center, circled with a bright edge as if surrounded by an abyss full of flames. When at last I broke the silence it was to express the opinion that no one could be more romantic than himself.

"One had not the courage to decide . . ." The passage, which sounds perilously close to deliberate double talk, probably owes some of its ambiguity to Conrad's inner conflicts discussed in the first chapter. For here the idealist, the skeptic, and the outlaw ("strange paths . . . without regret") all have their say. The ambiguity of Stein's remarks on the "destructive element" (which have regrettably come to mean anything any casual reader wants them to mean) may derive from the same conflicts. Conrad wants both the dreamer and the man who acts to survive: ". . . with the exertions of your hands and feet in the water make the deep, deep sea keep you up." But there is also a rhetorical ambiguity in the famous passage, which derives from our habit of thinking of the ideal or the illusory as "higher," and of air as higher than water. This is no doubt one reason why readers are tempted to equate the "destructive element" with life, action, and so on, and the air with ideal illusion. But the passage, which is prefaced by a reference to the "dream" as the dream of what we would like to be, doesn't say that. The dream is equated with the ideal of self or ego-ideal *and* with the sea *and* with the destructive element:

> "A man that is born falls into a dream like a man who falls into the sea. If he tries to climb out into the air as inexperienced people endeavour to do, he drowns—*nicht wahr?* . . . No! I tell you! The way is to the destructive element submit yourself, and with the exertions of your hands and feet in the water make the deep, deep sea keep you up."

Or: *A man is born ready to create an idealized conception of self, an ego-ideal. If he tries to escape or transcend this conception of self, he collapses. He should accept this ideal and try through action to make it "viable."* (Which is very far from the frequent reading: *man must learn to live with his unideal limitations.*)

But this has become a very dark saying—not only because we think of the ideal as something that transcends, of the ideal as higher, of air as more illusory than water, but also because we think of those who submit to the ego-ideal as "inexperienced" and of those who try to correct it as "experienced." The passage turns out to say something very different from what it appeared to say. There are several possibilities here, including one seldom considered in discussions of famous passages: that Conrad produced without much effort a logically imperfect multiple metaphor, liked the sound of it, and let matters go at that. There is also the possibility that Conrad wanted to show Stein giving confused advice. And there is the very real possibility that Conrad made less distinction between "ego" and "ego-ideal" than we are now accustomed to make. (If the "dream" is equated with "ego" we have less trouble with the climbing into air.) But whether we begin with the ego or with the ideal which, having originated in the ego, carries its own destruction within it, we can probably ascribe to Conrad the pessimism he ascribes to Anatole France:

He knows that our best hopes are irrealisable; that it is the almost incredible misfortune of mankind, but also its highest privilege, to aspire towards the impossible; that men have never failed to defeat their highest aims by the very strength of their humanity which can conceive the most gigantic tasks but leaves them disarmed before their irremediable littleness.[1]

Lord Jim has its great structural innovations and successes. What shall we say of its alleged formal weakness: its apparent break into two separate novels, with the second one inferior to the first? A division into two parts certainly exists: the first concerned with Jim's introspective response to the *Patna* incident, the second with his adventurous "second chance" in Patusan. "You've put your finger on the plague spot," Conrad wrote to Garnett concerning this division.[2] A story of continuing distress or slow deterioration might have been more symmetrical. But the very echoing of the crucial names—*Patna, Patusan*—suggests why we must have that second part. The most remote place and unrelated circumstance discovers, in us, the character with which we set out. "A clean slate, did he say? As if the initial word of each our destiny were not graven in imperishable characters upon the face of a rock." There is an aesthetic reason for the Patusan chapters fully as compelling: that by Chapter 17 a story of passive suffering (though the subject was by no means exhausted) threatened to exhaust the reader. Some outlet in action, or at least the illusion of such an outlet, had become necessary. And it is in fact astonishing to see, as we look back, how little has happened in those seventeen chapters in a fictional present time. We have had Jim's gestures as he talks; Marlow and Jim have had their misunderstanding over "cur"; Marlow has had his conversations with Chester and Brierly and Jim has refused Brierly's offer; Marlow has pressed upon him a letter of recommendation. And that is about all.

At the end of Chapter 17 Jim sets out with renewed confidence; his last words are "clean slate." Chapters 18–20 may be regarded as transitional: the first two on Jim's retreat "in good order towards the rising sun," as he throws up various jobs; the third on the famous interview with Stein, who sends Jim to Patusan. The second part of the novel would then begin with Chapter 21, or at the latest with Chapter 22 and Marlow's forestatement of Jim's initial success in Patusan. And its surface material is that of military and political adventure in a remote exotic setting. We may further divide this "second part" in two. Chapters 22–35 deal with the period of Jim's success and carry us to the end of Marlow's original narrative. Chapters 36–45 deal with the Gentleman Brown incident and Jim's ruin.

It would be pedantic to attach much importance to the fact that *Lord*

1. *Notes on Life and Letters* (New York: Doubleday, Page, 1921) 33.
2. See above, p. 304.

Jim divides into parts (most novels of its length do) or to be seriously concerned about the shocks of transition. For these shocks are slight, and are not to be blamed on Patusan. The major break comes not with the introduction of the Patusan material (Chapters 21, 22) but with the end of Marlow's oral narrative (Chapter 35). The important question is whether the novel and its reader are violated in a serious way: either because the material of the second half contradicts the material of the first and devalues it, or because Conrad imagined this material less well, or because it is intrinsically less interesting, or because it demands from us an entirely different kind of attention. Is there, that is, any damaging change in the delicate relationship of author-material-reader?

These questions must be asked, more specifically, of Chapters 22–35. For this section of the novel, exciting enough at a first reading, does not bear much rereading. The later chapters (36–45), though "adventurous" and "romantic," are very moving; they recover the *authenticity in depth* of the first part. There, once again we are watching character in action; not luck but destiny. And I think this points to the serious weakness of Chapters 22–35: that the adventures—the wearisome matter of getting the guns up the hill, for instance—have nothing to do with the essential Jim. Hence Conrad (who is less interested in or less convinced by this other Jim) gives a disproportionate attention to the Patusan background. Or can we say—following upon Gordan's demonstration that this successful Jim was based to some degree on James Brooke of Sarawak—that Conrad was here too bemused by his sources? For a while the appalling success of the historic Brooke must have made Jim's introspections seem unimportant; the physical perils are emphasized, not the perils of soul. Marlow now and then steps in to remind us that all this fed Jim's romantic egoism, these successes and physical dangers overcome. But for pages on end the reader is allowed to forget this moral problem and theme. We may add that a characteristic mediocrity sets in with the introduction of Jewel in Chapter 28: with women and their frightening "extra-terrestrial touch," the second standard ingredient of exotic romance. But Chapters 25–27 (on the defeat of Sherif Ali) seem the weakest of all on later readings.

The technical problem for Conrad, at this point in the novel, was a grave one. Only a continuation of the impressionistic method, he must have reasoned, could bridge the gap between the two parts: cover not only the separation of Marlow from Jim and the passage of time, but also the sharp change from passive suffering to adventurous action. Perhaps the reader, caught in the old familiar web and involuted structure, would not try to escape? The reasoning was sound enough, so far as it went. Yet the impressionistic method is one real source of our irritation with Chapters 25–27, since it has no intrinsic justification. For the method is designed to evoke complex, wavering, suspended responses to infinitely debatable psycho-moral questions; the intricacies and evasions are justified by the fullness of human involvement. But there is little in the three chapters to warrant such reader involvement. They deal with nothing more ambiguous than practical maneuvers: a military action that did or did not succeed.

But this must not be exaggerated. In a novel of great and subtle artistry this structural flaw is one of the few aesthetic facts easy to detect and isolate, hence easy to overemphasize. There is, for instance, no collapse in style as we move into the Patusan material, only a very slight change to suggest that Conrad's creative relationship to the story has changed. With Chapter 37 Marlow begins to *write*, though nominally for only one reader: the "privileged man." But a slight significant change to a more written style had already occurred in Chapters 21 and 22. It suggests that (as Marlow loses his intimate touch with *listeners*) Conrad's own attitude becomes more detached. The style in Chapter 21 now and then approaches that of *The Mirror of the Sea*: "We wander in our thousands over the face of the earth, the illustrious and the obscure, earning beyond the seas our fame, our money, or only a crust of bread; but it seems to me that for each of us going home must be like going to render an account." The distinction between one style and another is a rather delicate one, especially since the speaking Marlow possesses the richness and variety of a written style and the writing Marlow preserves the best qualities of voice. The first of the following passages, though elaborate, keeps the illusion of a man speaking aloud to men; the second, though it has a quality of voice, is essentially "written." The difference comes, among other things, from a higher degree of abstraction in the second passage. There is more of a "novelistic" impulse in the first, no doubt, but both are well done:

> But she turned her back on them as if in disdain of their fate: she had swung round, burdened, to glare stubbornly at the new danger of the open sea which she so strangely survived to end her days in a breaking-up yard, as if it had been her recorded fate to die obscurely under the blows of many hammers. What were the various ends their destiny provided for the pilgrims I am unable to say; but the immediate future brought, at about nine o'clock next morning, a French gunboat homeward bound from Réunion.

> It seems impossible to believe that mere greed could hold men to such a steadfastness of purpose, to such a blind persistence in endeavour and sacrifice. And indeed those who adventured their persons and lives risked all they had for a slender reward. They left their bones to lie bleaching on distant shores, so that wealth might flow to the living at home. To us, their less tried successors, they appear magnified, not as agents of trade but as instruments of a recorded destiny, pushing out into the unknown in obedience to an inward voice, to an impulse beating in the blood, to a dream of the future.

The second passage, frankly expository and transitional, is not of course typical of the later chapters. But it does suggest the greater distance or at least altered angle from which Conrad now looked at his story. The solitary white man adventuring into the interior, there to traffic with the natives and become their virtual ruler, and who is presently possessed by what he possesses—such a figure had fascinated Conrad from the first. At the two extremes of fortune might be the Georges Antoine Klein, or Kurtz, who died on board the *Roi des Belges* and the James Brooke who became Rajah of Sarawak, founding a dynasty which lasted until very recently, and one of the world's great fortunes. Both—together with an officer of the *Jeddah* who was not fast enough to get away with the others and so stumbled into undeserved heroism, and together with the braggart Jim Lingard whom Conrad had met—may have gone into the dreaming of *Lord Jim*.[3] But Conrad could dream failure more easily than he could dream success. He could imagine magnificently the failure of Kurtz (when he broke away from *Lord Jim* to write "Heart of Darkness"). And he could imagine magnificently Jim's failure and death. What he could not imagine, at the same level of intensity and belief, was Jim's period of success.

Discussions of *Lord Jim*, concerned as they are with interpretative and structural problems, regularly neglect the purely novelistic side of vivid particular creation. Mine has been no exception. Yet without the particulars of place and person, without the finely evoked atmospheres and brilliant minor vignettes, the novel's amount of brooding debate might have become intolerable. Its pleasures in any event would have been different ones. Page by page, *Lord Jim's* consistent great appeal largely depends on its changing of the lens, on its sudden shifts from a distant and often nebulous moral perspective to a grossly and superbly material foreground. Marlow's tendency to make such shifts is his most personal and most useful mannerism. It lends reality to the unsubstantial reveries, as gross substance is bound to do, yet invites us to look at them more critically. But most of all it offers the pleasure of a creative surprise. Thus (to take a fine example of sudden rescue from the vague and vast) Cornelius interrupts Marlow's revery, which once again has indulged its fondness for the old problem of "illusion":

> . . . I have that feeling about me now; perhaps it is that feeling which has incited me to tell you the story, to try to hand over to you, as it were, its very existence, its reality—the truth disclosed in a moment of illusion.
> Cornelius broke upon it. He bolted out, vermin-like, from the long grass growing in a depression of the ground. I believe his house was rotting somewhere near by, though I've never seen it, not having

3. Gordan 57–73.

been far enough in that direction. He ran towards me upon the
path; his feet, shod in dirty white shoes, twinkled on the dark earth:
he pulled himself up, and began to whine and cringe under a tall
stovepipe hat. His dried-up little carcass was swallowed up, totally
lost, in a suit of black broadcloth.

Conrad's success with such minor figures is (as we look back on the
earlier work and forward to *Nostromo*) one of the substantial advances
registered by *Lord Jim*. Cornelius, Marlow remarks, merely skulks on
the "outskirts" of the story. But the account of his trembling attempt to
get rid of Jim is fine dramatic writing. Through a slight narrative distance
(we are never told in so many words what Cornelius intends) we watch
him try to sell Jim protection for eighty dollars, then hover outside the
house in the darkness, apparently waiting to see him killed. We know
his intentions by his behavior when Jim appears unexpectedly: the way
he ducks sideways as though shot at, his panic as he clings to the rail
of the verandah, his "faint shriek" when Jim appears again.

Criticism, it may be, pays too little attention to the vivid minor figure,
and to the pleasure and actualizing effect of the surprise. *Lord Jim*
obviously depends very heavily on intellectual surprise, as the reader is
compelled to make large and sudden adjustments and resolve conflicting
demands. But the lesser surprises are important too. The German captain
of the *Patna*, for instance, reaches us through a series of surprises. He
is created by them. He is dramatically introduced, after a long elevated
passage on the pilgrims coming aboard the *Patna*, by his brief remark:
"Look at dese cattle . . ." And a surprise may be most effective when
it proves to be true in an unexpected way. The fanciful metaphor to
convey his voice has its exactness: "From the thick throat of the commander of the *Patna* came a low rumble, on which the sound of the
word *schwein* fluttered high and low like a capricious feather in a faint
stir of air." Presently we see him (who also is being taken "unawares")
slide into the harbor office and Archie Ruthvel's presence: "something
round and enormous, resembling a sixteen-hundred-weight sugar-
hogshead wrapped in striped flannelette, up-ended in the middle of the
large floor space." And finally we see him drive off in the gharry to the
astonishment of his subordinates, the monstrous fatness somehow
squeezed into that "little box on wheels":

> . . . but it only sank with a click of flattened springs, and suddenly
> one venetian blind rattled down. His shoulders reappeared, jammed
> in the small opening; his head hung out, distended and tossing like
> a captive balloon, perspiring, furious, spluttering. He reached for
> the gharry-wallah with vicious flourishes of a fist as dumpy and red
> as a lump of raw meat. He roared at him to be off, to go on. Where?
> Into the Pacific, perhaps. The driver lashed; the pony snorted,
> reared once, and darted off at a gallop. Where? To Apia? to Hon-

olulu? He had 6,000 miles of tropical belt to disport himself in, and I did not hear the precise address. A snorting pony snatched him into "ewigkeit" in the twinkling of an eye, and I never saw him again . . .

A connected account of *Lord Jim* (unless it is to rival the novel in length) is bound to neglect such fine particulars. Thus a discussion of Chapter 14 must mention Jim's loss of his certificate and the cynicism of Chester's offer. But our living experience of the chapter is no little affected by the plaintiff in the assault case: "an obese chocolate-coloured man with shaved head, one fat breast bare and a bright yellow caste-mark above the bridge of his nose, sat in pompous immobility: only his eyes glittered, rolling in the gloom, and the nostrils dilated and collapsed violently as he breathed." It is affected infinitely more, of course, by the brief portrait of Captain Robinson, who had once been reduced to cannibalism. Chester's story is made vivid in classical fictional ways:

> ". . . a boat of Her Majesty's ship *Wolverine* found [Robinson] kneeling on the kelp, naked as the day he was born, and chanting some psalm-tune or other; light snow was falling at the time. He waited till the boat was an oar's length from the shore, and then up and away. They chased him for an hour up and down the boulders, till a marine flung a stone that took him behind the ear providentially and knocked him senseless. Alone? Of course . . ."

This is fine enough, and credible enough. But the great fictional stroke was to interrupt Chester's talk with the appearance of Captain Robinson himself, a doddering and "amiable" old man:

> An emaciated patriarch in a suit of white drill, a solah topi with a green-lined rim on a head trembling with age, joined us after crossing the street in a trotting shuffle, and stood propped with both hands on the handle of an umbrella. A white beard with amber streaks hung lumpily down to his waist. He blinked his creased eyelids at me in a bewildered way. "How do you do? how do you do?" he piped, amiably, and tottered. "A little deaf," said Chester aside.

The naked chanting Robinson and the Robinson with amber-streaked white beard, the plaintiff with his one fat breast bare and eyes rolling in the gloom, the monstrously fat captain of the *Patna* and the monstrously fat Doramin, the slinking Cornelius and his twinkling white shoes, Gentleman Brown and the "sunken glare of his fierce crow-footed eyes"—all alike remind us of the old paradox: that the successfully achieved grotesque has a kind of fictional reality that the flat and commonplace seldom attains. Conrad will show even more of this novelistic creativity, this intense visual and dramatic surprise, in *Nostromo.*

IAN WATT

Composition and Sources†

*　*　*

The composition of *Lord Jim* is important not only as an example of
the extraordinary difficulties under which Conrad worked, but also because it provides some initial clues both to the narrative form and the
thematic development of the novel.

The Houghton Library at Harvard owns an elegant album in which
Conrad's maternal grandmother copied out twenty-five pages of Polish
poems belonging to the early eighteen-twenties; there remained many
blank pages, and Conrad used twenty-eight of them to write down a
heavily corrected and unfinished draft entitled "Tuan Jim: A Sketch."
This draft is the basis, though not the immediate basis, for the first three
chapters of the printed version of *Lord Jim*. It ends with the *Patna*
steaming towards the entrance of the Red Sea; but there is just enough
to enable us to reconstruct with some plausibility what Conrad had in
mind when he originally thought the narrative would be worked out in
the fifteen or so thousand words needed for two numbers of "Maga."

Like the final version, "Tuan Jim: A Sketch" begins with a visual
impression: and this visual impression seems, as with *Almayer's Folly*,
to represent Conrad's initial creative impetus.[1] In his Author's Note
Conrad recounted: "One sunny morning in the commonplace surroundings of an Eastern roadstead, I saw his form pass by—appealing—
significant—under a cloud—perfectly silent." The short story envisaged
in the sketch would presumably have passed from the impression of Lord
Jim as a water-clerk to an extended flashback of the pilgrim-ship episode;
and Jim would probably have ended up, like Almayer and Willems, as
a contemptible outcast in a Malay village—the second page of the
Harvard manuscript reads: "Afterwards when his perception of the intolerable drove him away from the haunts of white men, the Malays of
the village . . . (called) him Tuan Jim—as one would Lord Jim" (281).

The main difference between the first four chapters of the final version
and the rest of *Lord Jim* is suggested by this last sentence. Conrad's
original attitude to his hero was distant and ironical; Jim is called "Lord"
as a mockingly hyperbolic translation of the honorific "Tuan," a Malay
form of address which is actually used in the sense merely of "Sir" or

---

† From *Conrad in the Nineteenth Century* (Berkeley and Los Angeles: U of California P, 1979).
   Reprinted by permission of Chatto & Windus and the U of California P. This selection has
   been edited for publication here. Parenthetical page numbers refer to this Norton Critical
   Edition.
1. In a 1923 interview Conrad remarked: "I get my hints from a passing face. I saw Lord Jim
   that way" (Dale B. J. Randall, "Conrad Interviews, No. 6: Louis Weitzenkorn," (*Conradiana*
   4 [1972]: 30).

"Master," and is applied to everyone with any claim to authority or status, including that of merely being white.[2] Behind the sketch one can faintly discern a neat structure reminiscent of Daudet or Maupassant, in which a momentary but suggestive glimpse of a local character arouses a narrator's casual interest in how this figure came to be what he now is—a failure; and since the manuscript version contains no suggestion of the "course of light holiday literature" (8) which made Jim want to go to sea, we can assume that in Conrad's original plan Jim was not a romantic.

The mere fact, however, that Conrad could still use much of the early draft suggests that the novel retained one essential quality of the short story; as Conrad wrote to Blackwood after he had finished *Lord Jim*, the novel is "the development of *one* situation, only *one* really from beginning to end" (303). One can see this central unity operating throughout the process of what Conrad called "Jim's expansion"; and it probably accounts for Conrad's fear, which he expressed as late as 26 December 1899, that "*Lord Jim* would have hardly the lenght [sic] and certainly has not the substance to stand alone" (297).

The central section—from chapter five to chapter twenty—is essentially an expansion in narrative form of the opening of "Tuan Jim"; instead of merely reporting a rapid generalised impression of how Jim seemed to "all the white men by the waterside and the captains of the ships," the novel in effect multiplies the single observer who narrates the sketch, and gives a long and penetrating series of reports of interviews with people who are either acquainted with Jim or who illuminate his case. This change from a third-person summary, filtered from the gossip of a seaport, to a full and direct presentation is mainly done through Marlow. He does not occur in the sketch (which may date from before Marlow's first appearance in "Youth"), but must have been decided on fairly soon after Conrad began steady work on *Lord Jim*, and certainly before 31 July 1899, when chapter four and the beginning of chapter five were sent to Meldrum (292). It is Marlow's presence which makes *Lord Jim* almost as different from what we would expect from its first four chapters, as *Heart of Darkness* is from "An Outpost of Progress"; Marlow transforms Jim the outcast into "one of us."[3]

*   *   *

A vivid visual impression of someone, possibly [A. P.] Williams, presumably led Conrad to link the scandal of the *Jeddah* with an individual moral problem; then memories of Jim Lingard and readings about Rajah Brooke added further suggestions for Jim's Borneo career, but

2. Sir Hugh Clifford, a distinguished Malayan civil servant, and a close friend of Conrad, objected to "Lord" as mistranslation of "Tuan" (in his Introduction to the Memorial edition of *Lord Jim* [New York, 1925] viii). But either "Sir" or "Mr." Jim would sound much too flippant, while "Master Jim" would suggest a boy.

3. Conrad said nothing about the mode of narration until after finishing *Lord Jim*, and then he merely described it as "personal narrative from a third party."

what gives Jim his peculiar power to engage our imagination and our affections surely derives from Conrad's own involvement in Jim's fate; in a somewhat more direct sense than with Almayer, another major source of Jim is Conrad himself.

The only specific parallel[4] between the lives of the two men is the course of events which led both of them to yield to the solicitations of "short passages, good deck-chairs, large native crews, and the distinction of being white". Early in 1887 Conrad had signed on as first mate of the *Highland Forest*, a barque; in *The Mirror of the Sea* he relates that in the captain's absence he took charge of loading the cargo at Amsterdam, and that when the captain learned how the cargo had been stowed, he commented: "Well, we shall have a lively time of it this passage, I bet".[5] In fact the *Highland Forest* rolled so badly that some spars did go, and, as Conrad comments, "it was only poetic justice that the chief mate who had made a mistake—perhaps a half-excusable one . . . should pay the penalty." A spar hit Conrad's back; like Jim, he probably "spent many days stretched on his back, dazed, battered, hopeless, and tormented as if at the bottom of an abyss of unrest" (11); and he may even, like Jim, have "felt secretly glad he had not to go on deck." In any case the passage as a whole has the ring of personal experience.

This parallel between Jim and Conrad, however, would only apply to the first part of *Lord Jim*; and in most respects the characters and experiences of Jim and Conrad are very different indeed. Still, the existence of an element of identification—including youthful romantic dreams of heroic adventure—would help to explain why Conrad consistently linked *Lord Jim* to his two autobiographical stories of the period, "Youth" and *Heart of Darkness*. Thus, even at the end of 1899, when the novel was very far advanced, Conrad wrote that "the three tales, each being inspired by a similar moral idea (or is it only one of my optical delusions?) will make (in that sense) a homogeneous book" (297). Here one notices that Conrad admits that he may be wrong in finding a similar moral idea in the three stories; and yet he continued to assert that the three tales belonged together. Even when *Lord Jim* was almost finished he wrote to Blackwood: "It has not been planned to stand alone. *H of D* was meant in my mind as a foil, and *Youth* was supposed to give the note" (302). One can surmise that "Youth" was Conrad's Song of Innocence, and that perhaps *Lord Jim*, which Conrad thought "more like *Youth*" than *Heart of Darkness* (293), was originally intended to strike the same youthful note, though in a more critical spirit. Then there had intervened the writing of *Heart of Darkness*, Conrad's middle-aged Song of Experience. When he came back to *Lord Jim*, he brought

---

4. Though Conrad also confesses that in his days of "youth" and "innocence" his "pensive habits . . . made me sometimes dilatory in my work about the rigging," *The Mirror of the Sea and A Personal Record*, ed. Zdzisław Najder (Oxford: Oxford UP, 1988) 122.

5. *Mirror of the Sea*, ed. Najder, 53.

with him a Marlow who had gone through a second and much deeper experience of disillusionment. This may have transformed Conrad's previous conception, and in effect turned *Lord Jim* into a dialogue between the two Marlows, with Jim as the voice of his earlier innocence, and Marlow confronting him with the disenchanted voice of later experience.

* * *

The Friendship†

In their early meetings Jim was naturally very unsure of where he stood with Marlow, and remained shy in his presence throughout; still, by the time of their last farewell there had been a number of occasions when Jim had managed to express his gratitude and affection in his own inarticulate way. Marlow, on the other hand, never really expressed his affection to Jim. This is partly because of the role Marlow has to play in their relationship; he must be the dull voice of the reality-principle and conventional morality; but there are other reasons. For one thing, as Thoreau said, "It is impossible to say all that we think, even to our truest Friend";[1] for another, there is Marlow's character to be taken account of. He usually gives the impression of being difficult, impatient, impersonal, and emotionally very reticent, even when he has no cause to be reserved. To the auditors of his narrative, for instance, all the explanations Marlow gives underplay the real feelings in his association with Jim: it is the result of mere chance, of curiosity, of a momentary emotional impulse, of his sense of responsibility, or of pity. "There was nothing but myself between him and the dark ocean. I had a sense of responsibility" (105) he says on one occasion; and on another: "I happened to be handy, and I happened to be touched. That's all there is to it" (135).

It is curious that our strongest sense of the depth of Marlow's feelings for Jim comes from the tone of many of his more general reflective passages, passages where Marlow seems so oblivious of his hearers that the writing produces an effect of soliloquy. There is, for instance, the peroration about going home, where Marlow imagines "the spirit of the land uprising above the white cliffs of Dover, to ask me what I—returning with no bones broken, so to speak—had done with my very young brother." The same tendency to be most direct about his feelings when he is thinking aloud is found in Marlow's final letter to the privileged friend about Jim's death: "At times it seems as though he must come in presently and tell the story in his own words. . . . It's difficult

† From *Conrad in the Nineteenth Century*, pp. 334–38.
1. Henry David Thoreau, *A Week on the Concord and Merrimack Rivers* (New York: Scribner's, 1921) 209.

to believe he will never come. I shall never hear his voice again, nor shall I see his smooth tan-and-pink face with a white line on the forehead, and the youthful eyes darkened by excitement to a profound, unfathomable blue" (204).

The friendship of Jim and Marlow is not based on any particular mutuality of understanding or belief. Marlow never tells Jim that his interest in him began largely as a rather abstract moral puzzle; and he never persuades Jim to view his failure as a betrayal, not of himself but of human solidarity. The relationship in general very largely lacks the intellectual closeness or the other elements which are usually thought to constitute the basis of friendship. Marlow and Jim are neither soulmates like David and Jonathan, nor heroic comrades in arms like Roland and Oliver; and there is no question of one offering to sacrifice his life for the other, like Damon and Pythias or Orestes and Pylades. Many of the other standard features of friendship are also absent: there is no equality of age or status; and Marlow and Jim, far from being lifelong friends, do not spend a total of much more than a few weeks in each other's company.

Conrad's novel could hardly have been called "Charlie and Jim," but it is nevertheless the tale of a friendship. That friendship, however, is dominated by elements of separateness, incompleteness, and misunderstanding which are reflections not only of the personal idiosyncrasies of Jim and Marlow but of some of the characteristic social and intellectual divisions of the modern world.

The world of *Lord Jim* is a far cry from that of the much smaller, closer, and more leisurely societies which produced the classical patterns of heroic friendship in Greek epic and the Old Testament. In such warrior societies friendship is essentially a companionship between men who are the preeminent exponents of such virtues as courage, loyalty, and military prowess, which are the common ideals of the community as a whole. Jim and Marlow belong to a society whose scale and diversity are of a vastly greater magnitude, and where personal relations therefore tend to a much greater individual autonomy, and have very little continuity with the activities and values of the social order in general. It is true that the friendship of Marlow and Jim grows out of what are perhaps the two strongest and most universal forms of solidarity which remain in modern society: that of the occupational group, and that of the hierarchy of generations within it. But the depth of their friendship, as we have seen, largely depends on how each feels an internal conflict between his role as a member of a group and his inner self. In this their friendship is really a special case of a very general tendency in modern society for personal relations to begin on the basis of educational and occupational likeness, but to be transformed into a private intimacy which functions as an escape, an alternative, or even as a counterforce, to the public attitudes of their own group, and of society in general.

For Conrad, the question of how to live, in the simplest and most immediate occupational sense, was overwhelmingly important; at the same time, however, his consciousness of its demands sharpened his sense of individual separateness. Conrad's successive exposure to two national and two occupational allegiances had given a very special prominence to this contradiction between the public and the private; if he felt a deeper and more conscious commitment to solidarity, he also felt a deeper and more conscious resentment of its obligations. This contradiction is no doubt reflected in Marlow's continual and uneasy oscillations about his attitude to Jim, and in his somewhat surprising remark that "there is never time to say . . . the last word of our love, of our desire, faith, remorse, submission, revolt" (136). The same contradiction is found in what is most distinctive about Conrad's treatment of his characters and their personal relationships. The characters are intensely individual, but their consciousness is very largely determined by what they do in the world of work, and both their internal conflicts and their relationships with others are deeply and continually subject to the external and internal conditions imposed by collective human activities.

The friendship of Jim and Marlow is representative in this kind of way; it is not an intensification of the usual social or occupational relationships and values, but a private and even collusive alternative to them: to use Durkheim's terms, it is based not on individual likeness but on complementary needs; isolation, separateness, and conflict are the essential bases of its development, its intensity, and its meaning.

The closest literary analogy to the Marlow-Jim relationship is perhaps that portrayed in the oldest of surviving epics, the story of how a more than half divine Sumerian king, Gilgamesh, and a more than half animal man, Enkidu, become close friends. The initial differences between Marlow and Jim are much less, of course, but the development of their friendship is almost as surprising. Some of Marlow's narrative recalls Gilgamesh's threnody when Enkidu dies;[2] and if Jim does not, like Enkidu, come back from the underworld, he lives again and endures as an active presence in Marlow's imagination.

It is probably the sense of mutual need between two such disparate people which gives *Lord Jim* its special appeal. Among Conrad's novels, it is unique in having at its center so rewarding and touching a personal relationship; and this undertone of emotional warmth goes far to qualify the sadness of Jim's life and the gloom of Marlow's meditations. In many of his other works, Conrad's psychological and intellectual distance from the characters prevents us from feeling very deeply for them; our hearts do not go out very fully to Almayer, James Wait, or Kurtz, and if they do to Singleton or some of Conrad's later characters, it is with admiration

---

2. See Alexander Heidel, *The Gilgamesh Epic and Old Testament Parallels* (Chicago: U of Chicago P, 1949) especially 78–79.

rather than intimate emotional identification. In *Lord Jim* there is a more direct pattern of sympathy, both between Marlow and Jim, and between them and the reader. We see how a friendship can subsist despite great differences of age, temperament, and outlook; how there may be no deeper bond than the silent reciprocities of loneliness; how it doesn't matter that Jim has a "commonplace hand" (202) or a schoolboy banality of diction; and how the closest human communion may exist most intensely in no more than "the sound of a faint sigh that passed between us like the flight of a bird in the night" (80).

Yet another of the universal themes in *Lord Jim*, then, is that of the unequal and difficult friendship: and it is made very real because the vividness of Conrad's impressionist presentation of Jim and Marlow has made us participate so deeply in its existential realities, realities which are so distinctively representative of the difficulties and doubts of the modern world; under some conditions, apparently even the mysterious barriers to human understanding can strengthen personal ties; as Marlow puts it: "The less I understood the more I was bound to him in the name of that doubt which is the inseparable part of our knowledge" (134).

It is perhaps the scepticism of Montaigne which gets nearest to expressing the nature of the relationship between Marlow and Jim. Montaigne confesses that, if pressed to explain his friendship with Etienne de la Boétie, he can only reply: "Par ce que c'estoit luy; par ce que c'estoit moy."[3] Because it was him; because it was me. In enacting how Jim is Jim and Marlow Marlow, Conrad portrays a friendship much closer to ordinary experience in the modern world than is to be found in earlier fictional treatments of friendship; and this goes far to explain why *Lord Jim* has become the cherished and enduring work it is.

FREDRIC JAMESON

[Romance and Reification in *Lord Jim*]†

Nothing is more alien to the windless closure of high naturalism than the works of Joseph Conrad. Perhaps for that very reason, even after eighty years, his place is still unstable, undecidable, and his work unclassifiable, spilling out of high literature into light reading and romance,

---

3. "De L'Amitié," *Oeuvres complètes* (Paris: Gallimard, 1962) 187.
† From Fredric Jameson, *The Political Unconscious: Narrative as a Socially Symbolic Act* (Ithaca: Cornell UP, 1981). Reprinted by permission of Cornell UP and Methuen & Co. This selection has been edited for publication here. Parenthetical page numbers refer to this Norton Critical Edition.

reclaiming great areas of diversion and distraction by the most demanding practice of style and *écriture* alike, floating uncertainly somewhere in between Proust and Robert Louis Stevenson. Conrad marks, indeed, a strategic fault line in the emergence of contemporary narrative, a place from which the structure of twentieth-century literary and cultural *institutions* becomes visible as it could not be in the heterogeneity of Balzacian registers, nor even in the discontinuities of the paradigms which furnish materials for what is an increasingly unified narrative apparatus in Gissing. In Conrad we can sense the emergence not merely of what will be contemporary modernism (itself now become a literary institution), but also, still tangibly juxtaposed with it, of what will variously be called popular culture or mass culture, the commercialized cultural discourse of what, in late capitalism, is often described as a media society. This emergence is most dramatically registered by what most readers have felt as a tangible "break" in the narrative of *Lord Jim*, a qualitative shift and diminution of narrative intensity as we pass from the story of the *Patna* and the intricate and prototextual search for the "truth" of the scandal of the abandoned ship, to that more linear account of Jim's later career in Patusan, which, a virtual paradigm of romance as such, comes before us as the prototype of the various "degraded" subgenres into which mass culture will be articulated (adventure story, gothic, science fiction, bestseller, detective story, and the like). But this institutional heterogeneity—not merely a shift between two narrative paradigms, nor even a disparity between two types of narration or narrative organization, but a shift between two distinct cultural spaces, that of "high" culture and that of mass culture—is not the only gap or discontinuity that *Lord Jim* symptomatically betrays. Indeed, we will have occasion to isolate the stylistic practice of this work as a virtually autonomous "instance" in its own right, standing in tension or contradiction with the book's various narrative instances or levels—just as we will insist on the repressed space of a world of work and history and of protopolitical conflict which may in this respect be seen as the trace and the remnant of the content of an older realism, now displaced and effectively marginalized by the emergent modernist discourse. The paradigm of formal history which must now be presupposed is thus evidently more complex than the framework of a movement from Balzacian realism to high realism with which we have previously worked. Schematically, it may be described as a structural breakdown of the older realisms, from which emerges not modernism alone, but rather two literary and cultural structures, dialectically interrelated and necessarily presupposing each other for any adequate analysis: these now find themselves positioned in the distinct and generally incompatible spaces of the institutions of high literature and what the Frankfurt School conveniently termed the "culture industry," that is, the apparatuses for the production of

"popular" or mass culture.[1] That this last is a new term may be dramatically demonstrated by the situation of Balzac, a writer, if one likes,
of "best sellers," but for whom this designation is anachronistic insofar
as no contradiction is yet felt in his time between the production of best
sellers and the production of what will later come to be thought of as
"high" literature.

*   *   *

The privileged place of the strategy of containment in Conrad is the
sea; yet the fact of the sea also allows us to weigh and appreciate the
relative structural difference between the "nascent modernism" that we
will observe in these texts and the more fully achieved and institution-
alized modernisms of the canon. For the sea is both a strategy of containment and a place of real business: it is a border and a decorative
limit, but it is also a highway, out of the world and in it at once, the
repression of work—on the order of the classic English novel of the
country-house weekend, in which human relations can be presented in
all their ideal formal purity precisely because concrete content is rele-
gated to the rest of the week—as well as the absent work-place itself.

So the sea is the place from which Jim can contemplate that dreary
prose of the world which is daily life in the universal factory called
capitalism:

> His station was in the fore-top, and often from there he looked
> down, with the contempt of a man destined to shine in the midst
> of dangers, at the peaceful multitude of roofs cut in two by the
> brown tide of the stream, while scattered on the outskirts of the
> surrounding plain the factory chimneys rose perpendicular against
> a grimy sky, each slender like a pencil, and belching out smoke
> like a volcano. (9)

Jim's externality to this world, his absolute structural distance from it,
can be measured by a process to which we will shortly return, namely
the impulse of Conrad's sentences to transform such realities into impressions. These distant factory spires may be considered the equivalent for
Jim and, in this novelistic project, for Conrad, of the great Proustian
glimpses of the steeples of Martinville (with the one obvious qualification
that the latter are already sheer impression and need neither aesthetic
transformation, nor the Archimedean point of a structural externality,
all the energy of Proustian style now being invested in the meditation
on the object itself).

*   *   *

Yet strategies of containment are not only modes of exclusion; they can
also take the form of repression in some stricter Hegelian sense of the

1. T. W. Adorno and Max Horkheimer, "The Culture Industry," in *Dialectic of Enlightenment*,
trans. J. Cumming (New York: Herder & Herder, 1972) 120–67, and see my "Reification and
Utopia in Mass Culture," *Social Text*, no. 1 (Winter 1979): 130–48.

persistence of the older repressed content beneath the later formalized surface. Indeed, I have argued elsewhere that such vertical repression and layering or sedimentation is the dominant structure of the classical modernistic text.[2] In this respect, too, Conrad, as a merely emergent moment in such a strategy, has suggestive and emblematic things to show us, as witness the following supremely self-conscious art-sentence, whose Flaubertian triplication is a virtual allegory of manifest and latent levels in the text:

> Above the mass of sleepers, a faint and patient sigh at times floated, the exhalation of a troubled dream; and short metallic clangs bursting out suddenly in the depths of the ship, the harsh scrape of a shovel, the violent slam of a furnace-door, exploded brutally, as if the men handling the mysterious things below had their breasts full of fierce anger: while the slim high hull of the steamer went on evenly ahead, without a sway of her bare masts, cleaving continuously the great calm of the waters under the inaccessible serenity of the sky. (16)

Ideology, production, style: on the one hand the manifest level of the content of *Lord Jim*—the moral problem of the "sleepers"—which gives us to believe that the "subject" of this book is courage and cowardice, and which we are meant to interpret in ethical and existentializing terms; on the other, the final consumable verbal commodity—the vision of the ship—the transformation of all these realities into style and the work of what we will call the impressionistic strategy of modernism whose function is to derealize the content and make it available for consumption on some purely aesthetic level; while in between these two, the brief clang from the boiler room that drives the ship marking the presence beneath ideology and appearance of that labor which produces and reproduces the world itself, and which, like the attention of God in Berkeleyan idealism, sustains the whole fabric of reality continuously in being.

*   *   *

So this ground bass of material production continues underneath the new formal structures of the modernist text, as indeed it could not but continue to do, yet conveniently muffled and intermittent, easy to ignore (or to rewrite in terms of the aesthetic, of sense perception, as here of the sounds and sonorous inscription of a reality you prefer not to conceptualize), its permanencies ultimately detectable only to the elaborate hermeneutic geiger counters of the political unconscious and the ideology of form.

This reality of production is, of course, at one with the intermittent vision of the sea's economic function, and with Conrad's unquestionable

---

2. "Modernism and Its Repressed: Robbe-Grillet as Anti-Colonialist," *Diacritics* 6.2 (Summer 1976): 7–14.

and acute sense of the nature and dynamics of imperialist penetration. We will shortly see how even awareness of this latter historical and economic type is "managed" in the text itself. As for the productive relationship of human beings to nature, I will argue that Conrad's consciousness of this ultimate building block of social reality (as well as of its class content under capitalism—the "fierce anger" of the muffled sounds) is systematically displaced in two different ways. The first is by a recoding of the human pole of the labor process in terms of the whole ideological myth of *ressentiment* outlined in our previous chapter. Indeed the narrative of *The Nigger of the "Narcissus,"* with its driving power and ideological passion, may in this respect be characterized as one long tirade against *ressentiment*; the work concludes with the transformation of its villain, Donkin, the epitome of the *homme de ressentiment*, into a labor organizer (who "no doubt earns his living by discoursing with filthy eloquence upon the right of labour to live[3]). The other pole of the labor process, that nature which is its material object and substratum, is then strategically reorganized around one of great conceptual containment strategies of the day, one which we have come to call existentialism, and becomes the pretext for the production of a new metaphysic—a new myth about the "meaning" of life and the absurdity of human existence in the face of a malevolent Nature. These two strategies—*ressentiment* and existentializing metaphysics—allow Conrad to recontain his narrative and to rework it in melodramatic terms, in a subsystem of good and evil which now once again has villains and heroes. So it is no accident that Jim's first experience of the violence of the sea is at once coded for us in existential terms, the sea, the source of this mindless violence, becoming the great adversary of Man, in much the same way that Camus' vision of absurdity rewrites an essentially nonhuman nature into an anthropomorphic character, a vengeful God ("the first assassin, because he made us mortal"):

> Only once in all that time he had again the glimpse of the earnestness in the anger of the sea. That truth is not so often made apparent as people might think. There are many shades in the danger of adventures and gales, and it is only now and then that there appears on the face of facts a sinister violence of intention— that indefinable something which forces it upon the mind and the heart of a man, that this complication of accidents or these elemental furies are coming at him with a purpose of malice, with a strength beyond control, with an unbridled cruelty that means to tear out of him his hope and his fear, the pain of his fatigue and his longing for rest: which means to smash, to destroy, to annihilate all he has seen, known, loved, enjoyed, or hated; all that is priceless and necessary—the sunshine, the memories, the future,—which

3. Joseph Conrad, *The Nigger of the "Narcissus,"* ed. Robert Kimbrough (New York: W. W. Norton, 1979) 107.

means to sweep the whole precious world utterly away from his sight by the simple and appalling act of taking his life. (11)

But if you believe this version of the text, this particular rewriting strategy by which Conrad means to seal off the textual process, then all the rest follows, and *Lord Jim* really becomes what it keeps telling us it is, namely a tale of courage and cowardice, a moral story, and an object-lesson in the difficulties of constructing an existential hero. I will argue that this ostensible or manifest "theme" of the novel is no more to be taken at face value than is the dreamer's immediate waking sense of what the dream was about. Yet as this is a complex argument, which will ultimately be validated only by the rest of the present chapter, I will simply suggest, at this point, that our business as readers and critics of culture is to "estrange" this overt theme in a Brechtian way, and to ask ourselves why we should be expected to assume, in the midst of capitalism, that the aesthetic rehearsal of the problematics of a social value from a quite different mode of production—the feudal ideology of honor—should need no justification and should be expected to be of interest to us. Such a theme must mean *something else*: and this even if we choose to interpret its survival as an "uneven development," a nonsynchronous overlap in Conrad's own values and experience (feudal Poland, capitalist England).

* * *

Yet Conrad is also a late nineteenth-century novelist, and that in a rather different way than has yet been touched on. The affiliations of this particular Conrad are less with Henry James than they are with Proust, and from this perspective his debt to Flaubert becomes equally modified, the relevant texts now being those that practice that hallucinatory imagery in which the positivist theory of perception was anticipated and legitimized *avant la lettre*. What must be stressed here is the intimate dialectical relationship between this properly positivist ideology of the sense datum and the accompanying notion of "consciousness"— a scientific or pseudoscientific theory which is ideological to the degree to which it projects a whole conception of subject-object relations, a whole vision of "human nature" which cannot but be a whole politics and philosophy of history, as well—as well as a whole aesthetic movement ordinarily thought to be in opposition to it (and in fact profoundly antipositivist in spirit), namely impressionism. I will argue, on the one hand, that both positivism as ideological production and impressionism as aesthetic production are first to be understood in terms of the concrete situation to which they are both responses: that of rationalization and reification in late nineteenth-century capitalism. On the other, I want to show that Conrad may best be situated historically if we understand his practice of style as a literary and textual equivalent of the impressionist strategy in painting (hence his kinship with the greatest of all literary impressionists, Proust). But these assertions will be useful only to the degree to which we understand that the impressionistic strategy, although the dominant one for classical modernism, is only one of those structurally available to the modernists (the much rarer expressionism is another): to understand stylistic production this way is to free ourselves from the monotony of the formal history projected by the ideology of modernism itself (each new style is a break with the past, the history of styles is simply the sum total of all of these radical changes and innovations), and to substitute for it the possibility of reading a given style as a projected solution, on the aesthetic or imaginary level, to a genuinely contradictory situation in the concrete world of everyday social life.

To read Conrad's "will to style" as a socially symbolic act involves the practice of *mediation*, an operation that we have already characterized (in Chapter 1) as the invention of an analytic terminology or code which can be applied equally to two or more structurally distinct objects or sectors of being. As we there argued, it is not necessary that these analyses be homologous, that is, that each of the objects in question be seen as doing the same thing, having the same structure or emitting the same message. What is crucial is that, by being able to use the same language about each of these quite distinct objects or levels of an object, we can restore, at least methodologically, the lost unity of social life, and demonstrate that widely distant elements of the social totality are ultimately part of the same global historical process.

In the present case, this means the invention of a description of Conrad's stylistic practice (and of that of impressionist painting) which is adequate in its own terms and does justice to the autonomy or semi-autonomy of aesthetic language, but which at the same time, by articulating the description of a quite different type of reality—in the event, the organization and experience of daily life during the imperialist heyday of industrial capitalism—allows us to think these two distinct realities together in a meaningful way (causality, long the scarecrow used to frighten people away from social mediations of this kind, being only one of the possible meanings, only one of the possible relations that can obtain between such distinct terms).

It has no doubt already become clear to the reader that the mediatory code I have found most useful here is that variously termed rationalization by Weber and reification by Lukács. Yet the reader should also be reminded that Marxism knows a number of other such mediatory codes, the most obvious ones being social class, mode of production, the alienation of labor, commodification, the various ideologies of Otherness (sex or race), and political domination. The strategic selection of reification as a code for the reading and interpretation of Conrad's style does not constitute the choice of one kind of Marxism (let us say, a Lukácsean one) over others, but is instead an option open to all intelligent Marxisms and part of the richness of the Marxian system itself.

* * *

This, then, is my justification in characterizing Conrad's stylistic production as an *aestheticizing strategy*: the term is not meant as moral or political castigation, but is rather to be taken literally, as the designation of a strategy which for whatever reason seeks to recode or rewrite the world and its own data in terms of perception as a semi-autonomous activity. We have already witnessed this process at work in a key place, namely in the sentence that articulated the infrastructure of ship and text—the boiler room—in the language of the sense of hearing, thereby secretly unraveling the very designation of an infrastructure by absorbing it into the final term of the tripartite passage, into the realm of the image, thereby transforming it into an art-commodity which one consumes by way of its own dynamic, that is, by "perceiving" it as image and as sense datum.

* * *

That modernism is itself an ideological expression of capitalism, and in particular, of the latter's reification of daily life, may be granted a local validity. It has at least been possible to show that the objective preconditions of Conrad's modernism are to be found in the increasing fragmentation both of the rationalized external world and of the colonized psyche alike. And surely, there is a sense in which such faithful "expression" of the underlying logic of the daily life of capitalism programs us to it and helps to make us increasingly at home in what would otherwise—for a time traveler from another social formation—be a distressingly alienating reality. Viewed in this way, then, modernism can be seen as a late stage in the bourgeois cultural revolution, as a final and extremely specialized phase of that immense process of superstructural transformation whereby the inhabitants of older social formations are culturally and psychologically retrained for life in the market system.

Yet modernism can at one and the same time be read as a Utopian compensation for everything reification brings with it. We stressed the semi-autonomy of the fragmented senses, the new autonomy and intrinsic logic of their henceforth abstract objects such as color or pure sound; but it is precisely this new semi-autonomy and the presence of these waste products of capitalist rationalization that open up a life space in which the opposite and the negation of such rationalization can be, at least imaginatively, experienced. The increasing abstraction of visual art thus proves not only to express the abstraction of daily life and to presuppose fragmentation and reification; it also constitutes a Utopian compensation for everything lost in the process of the development of capitalism—the place of quality in an increasingly quantified world, the place of the archaic and of feeling amid the desacralization of the market system, the place of sheer color and intensity within the grayness of measurable extension and geometrical abstraction. The perceptual is in this sense a historically new experience, which has no equivalent in older kinds of social life. Meanwhile this vocation of the perceptual, its Utopian mission as the libidinal transformation of an increasingly dessicated and repressive reality, undergoes a final political mutation in the countercultural movements of the 1960s (at which point the ambiguity of the impulse also becomes more pronounced, and the reminder of the accompanying "ideological" value of the perceptual as the expression of psychic fragmentation is once more politically timely). Our present concern is to respect the ambivalent value of Conrad's impressionism, that ambiguity at the very heart of his will to style which alone makes it a complex and interesting historical act, and ensures it a vitality outside the cultural museum. Seen as ideology and Utopia all at once, Conrad's stylistic practice can be grasped as a symbolic act which, seizing on the Real in all of its reified resistance, at one and the same time projects a unique sensorium of its own, a libidinal resonance no doubt historically determinate, yet whose ultimate ambiguity lies in its attempt to stand beyond history.

In arguing for this particular historical and historicizing "reading" of Conrad's style, we have perhaps implied that he is himself unaware of the symbolic social value of his verbal practice. If so, this is an error which we must now correct, for it is certain that—whatever the thoughts and awarenesses of the biographical Conrad—a reflexivity, a self-consciousness of the nature of this symbolic process, is inscribed in the text itself, and most strikingly in *Lord Jim*. This is, indeed, the meaning of the character of Stein, inserted strategically, as one of Jim's series of father figures, between the great bravura unfolding of the *Patna* story and the later romantic adventure in Patusan, where Stein has influence and interests, and where he is able to install the stigmatized Jim, thereby giving him a final chance with destiny.

Stein is thus a pivotal figure from the narrative point of view; but I would argue that this particular plot function is itself merely a figure of a quite different value, and a way of framing the character of Stein in such a way as to make that second or emblematic value momentarily visible to us. The story of Stein, indeed, is the story of the passing of the heroic age of capitalist expansion; it marks the end of the era when individual entrepreneurs were giants, and the setting in place of the worldwide institutions of capitalism in its monopoly stage. Conrad will tell this particular story again; indeed, I will shortly try to show that it is the informing center of *Nostromo* as well. For the moment, however, it is enough to invoke characteristic late nineteenth-century terms like individualism and heroism to understand why such a situation should have fascinated Conrad (who brought his own particular historical "uneven development" and his background as a Pole and a Russian subject to this exploration of the British business empire).

What is of interest to us is, however, not only the symptomatic break in Stein's career—the high adventure of heroic colonialism succeeded by the sedate vocation of the ever more prosperous merchant—but also and in particular the compensatory formation that accompanies such a change of life. For Stein becomes a butterfly collector, that is to say, essentially a collector of images; and the serene melancholy of the collector's passion is surely here to be taken as the same gesture of renunciation, the same withdrawal from life and repudiation of the world that, in *The Hidden God*, Lucien Goldmann has shown to be the symbolic meaning of the invention of Jansenism by that whole class-fraction which was the seventeenth-century *noblesse de robe*:

> I respected the intense, almost passionate absorption with which he looked at a butterfly, as though on the bronze sheen of these frail wings, in the white tracings, in the gorgeous markings, he could see other things, an image of something as perishable and defying destruction as these delicate and lifeless tissues displaying a splendor unmarred by death. (125)

For us, however, the thematics of "death" and the rhetoric of mortality is here but a disguise for the sharper pain of exclusion by history, just as the passion for butterfly collecting must be read as the fable and the allegory of the ideology of the image, and of Conrad's own passionate choice of impressionism—the vocation to arrest the living raw material of life, and by wrenching it from the historical situation in which alone its change is meaningful, to preserve it, beyond time, in the imaginary.

J. HILLIS MILLER

Lord Jim: Repetition as Subversion of Organic Form†

As a first larger-scale example of the intertwining of the two modes of repetition in narrative, I choose Conrad's *Lord Jim*. This falls roughly midway in the historical span from which my seven novels come: from the early Victorian period to the eve of the Second World War. *Lord Jim* provides a particularly overt case of the issues I am investigating; it invites the reader to believe that it may be comprehensible according to some mode of the first, centered form of repetition, while the actual uses of repetition in the text forbid that comprehension. And to begin after the middle of the ninety-year period from which my novels are drawn may help to forestall the assumption that I am tracing a historical development, turn, or evolution from Victorian to modern, or from simple to complex, or from realist to symbolic, or from naive acceptance

† Reprinted by permission of the publishers from *Fiction and Repetition: Seven English Novels* by J. Hillis Miller, Cambridge, MA: Harvard UP, Copyright © 1982 by J. Hillis Miller. This selection has been edited for publication here.

of narrative conventions to sophisticated and self-conscious artistry. The telling of such a literary historical story is itself a narrative open to the same kind of challenges all seven of my novels pose to the notion of a plot with beginning, middle, and end. Each of my novels belongs to a particular moment in English literary history, and in English social and political history too, but my claim is that these contexts do not fully determine the way repetition functions in works written in this moment or that. In each case, rather, as I shall try to show, particular materials—the historical facts of British imperialism in *Lord Jim*, for example, or social conditions in Yorkshire in the early nineteenth century in *Wuthering Heights*—become subject, when they are made into a novel, to the impossibility of telling a story which is a pure example of either of the kinds of repetitive form I have identified in my first chapter. The seven novels interpreted here are variants of this situation. They do not make a historical "progression," or a "degradation" either. My chapters are attempts at readings, not attempts at the construction of a history, unless the demonstration of a movement in place or a series of nonprogressive variations is considered to be a form of history. It may be that the activity of reading, if it is carried out with rigor, tends to inhibit or even make impossible that sort of story we tell ourselves which is given the name "literary history."

Lord Jim, like most works of literature, contains self-interpretative elements. Much of it is an explication of words and signs by means of other words, as narrator follows narrator, or as narration is inserted within narration. The critic who attempts to understand *Lord Jim* becomes another in a series of interpreters. He enters into a process of interpretation in which words bring out the meaning of other words and those words refer to others in their turn. No literary text has a manifest pattern, like the design of a rug, which the eye of the critic can survey from the outside and describe as a spatial form, but the intricacies of multiple narrators and time shifts in *Lord Jim* make this particularly evident. The textuality of a text, a "yarn" spun by Conrad, is the meshing of its filaments as they are interwoven in ways hidden from an objectifying eye. The critic must enter into the text, follow its threads as they weave in and out, appearing and disappearing, crisscrossing with other threads. In doing this he adds his own thread of interpretation to the fabric, or he cuts it in one way or another, so becoming part of its texture or changing it. Only in this way can he hope to identify the evasive center or ground which is not visible as a fixed emblem around which the story is spun, but is paradoxically, as Wallace Stevens says in "A Primitive Like an Orb," a "center on the horizon,"[1] a center which is outside and around rather than within and punctual.

Samuel Taylor Coleridge, that brilliant manipulator of the metaphors

1. *The Collected Poems* (New York: Knopf, 1951) 443.

of Occidental metaphysics, presents an image of the work of art in its rounded unity corresponding to the assumption that there is such an interior center. Aesthetic wholeness in a narrative, he says, must be copied from the wholeness of a universe which circles in time around the motionless center of a God to whose eternal insight all times are co-present:

> The common end of all *narrative*, nay, of *all*, Poems is to convert a *series* into a *Whole*: to make those events, which in real or imagined History move on in a *strait* line, assume to our Understandings a *circular* motion—the snake with it's Tail in its mouth. Hence indeed the almost flattering and yet appropriate Term, Poesy—i.e. poiesis-*making*. Doubtless, to his eye, which alone comprehends all Past and all Future in one eternal Present, what to our short sight appears strait is but part of the great Cycle—just as the calm Sea to us *appears* level, tho' it indeed [be] only a part of a *globe*. Now what the Globe is in Geography, *miniaturing* in order to *manifest* the Truth, such is a Poem to that Image of God, which we were created with, and which still seeks Unity or Revelation of the *One* in and by the *Many*.[2]

The concept of the organic unity of the work of art, as this passage shows, cannot be detached from its theological basis. Nor can it separate itself from mimetic theories of art. Far from asserting the autonomy of the artwork, its way of being self-sufficiently rounded in on itself, Coleridge here describes the poem as an image or a representation, even the representation of a representation. Its globular roundness miniatures not God in his relation to the creation, but the image of God created in our souls which drives us to seek the one in the many. The poem is the image of an image. Moreover, the oneness revealed in and by the many is not intrinsic but extrinsic. It is the center of a circle made up of a series of events which move in sequence but are curved back on themselves, like the fabled snake with its tail in its mouth, by the attraction of that center, just as the soul "in order to be an individual Being . . . must go forth *from* God, yet as the *receding* from *him* is to *proceed* towards Nothingness and Privation, it must still at every step turn back toward him in order to *be* at all—Now, a straight Line, continuously retracted forms of necessity a circular orbit."[3] The creation, the soul, the work of art—all three have the same shape, the same movement, and the same relation to a generative center. They are related in a descending series of analogical equivalences, each a copy of the one above and all able to be defined by the same geometrical or zoological metaphors.

2. Letter to Joseph Cottle, 1815, in *Unpublished Letters of Samuel Taylor Coleridge, Including Certain Letters Republished from Original Sources*, ed. Earl Leslie Griggs II (New Haven: Yale UP, 1933) 128.
3. Ibid. 129.

In place of this kind of doubling, twice removed, of God's universe by the little world of the work of art, Conrad presents for both cosmos and work of literature a structure which has no beginning, no foundation outside itself, and exists only as a self-generated web:

> There is a—let us say—a machine. It evolved itself (I am severely scientific) out of a chaos of scraps of iron and behold!—it knits. I am horrified at the horrible work and stand appalled. I feel it ought to embroider—but it goes on knitting . . . And the most withering thought is that the infamous thing has made itself; made itself without thought, without conscience, without foresight, without eyes, without heart. It is a tragic accident—and it has happened . . . It knits us in and it knits us out. It has knitted time, space, pain, death, corruption, despair and all the illusions—and nothing matters. I'll admit however that to look at the remorseless process is sometimes amusing.[4]

One way of looking at the remorseless process is by way of a novel, but a novel is not for Conrad an *image* of the horrible knitting machine and its work. It is part of the knitting, woven into its web. The infamous machine has made human beings and all their works too, including language and its power of generating or of expressing all the illusions. Works of art, like man's other works, are what they are "in virtue of that truth one and immortal which lurks in the force that made [the machine] spring into existence."[5] Product of the same force which has knit the rest of the universe, a work of art has the same kind of structure. A novel by Conrad, though it invites the reader to hope that he can find a center of the sort Coleridge ascribes to the good work of art, has nothing certainly identifiable outside itself by which it might be measured or from which it might be seen. It has no visible thematic or structuring principle which will allow the reader to find out its secret, explicate it once and for all, untie all its knots and straighten all its threads. The knitting machine cannot be said to be the origin of the cloth it knits, since what the machine knits is itself, knitter and knitted forming one indistinguishable whole without start or finish, continuously self-creating. The cloth exists as the process of its knitting, the twisting of its yarns as they are looped and knotted by a pervasive "force." This force is the truth one and immortal everywhere present but nowhere visible in itself, an energy both of differentiation and of destruction. "It knits us in and it knits us out."

A familiar passage in Conrad's *Heart of Darkness* describes the indirection characteristic of works of literature like *Lord Jim*. The passage uses a variant of the image of the knitted fabric in the letter to Cunninghame Graham. "The yarns of seamen," says the narrator, "have a

4. Letter of Dec. 20, 1897, in *The Collected Letters of Joseph Conrad: Volume 1, 1861–1897*, ed. Frederick R. Karl and Laurence Davies (Cambridge: Cambridge UP, 1983) 425.
5. Ibid.

direct simplicity, the whole meaning of which lies within the shell of a cracked nut. But Marlow was not typical (if his propensity to spin yarns be excepted) and to him the meaning of an episode was not inside like a kernel but outside, enveloping the tale which brought it out only as a glow brings out a haze, in the likeness of one of these misty halos that, sometimes, are made visible by the spectral illumination of moonshine."[6] Though the meaning is outside, it may only be seen by way of the tale which brings it out. This bringing out takes place in the interaction of its different elements in their reference to one another. These the critic must track, circling from one word or image to another within the text. Only in this movement of interpretation does the meaning exist. It is not a central and originating node, like the kernel of a nut, a solid and pre-existing nub. It is a darkness, an absence, a haze invisible in itself and only made visible by the ghostlike indirection of a light which is already derived. It is not the direct light of the sun but the reflected light of the moon which brings out the haze. This visible but secondary light and the invisible haze create a halo of "moonshine" which depends for its existence on the reader's involvement in the play of light and dark which generates it. Does this invitation to believe that there is an explanatory center, without positive identification of that center or even certainty about whether or not it exists, in fact characterize *Lord Jim*? I shall investigate briefly here a series of ways the novel might be interpreted.

The theme of *Lord Jim* is stated most explicitly toward the end of chapter 5, in Marlow's attempt to explain why he concerns himself with Jim:

> Why I longed to go grubbing into the deplorable details of an occurrence which, after all, concerned me no more than as a member of an obscure body of men held together by a community of inglorious toil and by fidelity to a certain standard of conduct, I can't explain. You may call it an unhealthy curiosity if you like; but I have a distinct notion I wished to find something. Perhaps, unconsciously, I hoped I would find that something, some profound and redeeming cause, some merciful explanation, some convincing shadow of an excuse. I see well enough now that I hoped for the impossible—for the laying of what is the most obstinate ghost of man's creation, of the uneasy doubt uprising like a mist, secret and gnawing like a worm, and more chilling than the certitude of death—the doubt of the sovereign power enthroned in a fixed standard of conduct.

Jim is "one of us," an Englishman, son of a country clergyman, a "gentleman," brought up in the British traditions of duty, obedience, quiet faithfulness, and unostentatious courage. Nevertheless, he has

6. *Heart of Darkness*, 3d ed., ed. Robert Kimbrough (New York: W. W. Norton, 1988) 9.

committed the shockingly dishonorable act of deserting his ship and the helpless pilgrims it carried. Jim's desertion seems especially deplorable to Marlow because Jim looks so trustworthy, so perfect an example of the unassuming nobility of the tradition from which he has sprung. "He had no business to look so sound," says Marlow. "I thought to myself —well, if this sort can go wrong like that . . . and I felt as though I could fling down my hat and dance on it from sheer mortification"; "He looked as genuine as a new sovereign, but there was some infernal alloy in his metal" (ch. 5). The descrepancy between what Jim looks like and what he is puts in question for Marlow "the sovereign power enthroned in a fixed standard of conduct." He does not doubt the existence of the standard, the seaman's code of fidelity, obedience, and obscure courage on which the British empire was built. He comes to question the power installed behind this standard and within it. This power, as its defining adjective affirms, justifies the standard as its king—its principle, its source, its law.

If there is no sovereign power enthroned in the fixed standard of conduct then the standard is without validity. It is an all-too-human fiction, an arbitrary code of behavor—"this precious notion of a convention," as Marlow says, "only one of the rules of the game, nothing more" (ch. 7). Nothing matters, and anything is possible, as in that condition of spiritual anarchy which takes over on the ship's boat after Jim and the other officers have deserted the *Patna* and left her to sink with eight hundred men, women, and children. "After the ship's lights had gone," says Jim, "anything might have happened in that boat— anything in the world—and the world no wiser. I felt this, and I was pleased. It was just dark enough, too. We were like men walled up quick in a roomy grave. No concern with anything on earth. Nobody to pass an opinion. Nothing mattered . . . No fear, no law, no sounds, no eyes—not even our own, till—till sunrise at least" (ch. 10). Marlow interprets Jim's words in a way which gives them the widest application to the derelict condition of a man who has lost faith, conviction, his customary material surroundings—whatever has given his world stability and order by seeming to support it from outside. "When your ship fails you," says Marlow, "your whole world seems to fail you; the world that made you, restrained you, taken [sic] care of you. It is as if the souls of men floating on an abyss and in touch with immensity had been set free for any excess of heroism, absurdity, or abomination. Of course, as with belief, thought, love, hate, conviction, or even the visual aspect of material things, there are as many shipwrecks as there are men . . . Trust a boat on the high seas to bring out the Irrational that lurks at the bottom of every thought, sentiment, sensation, emotion" (ch. 10).

Marlow's aim (or Conrad's) seems clear: to find some explanation for Jim's action which will make it still possible to believe in the sovereign power. Many critics think that in the end Marlow (or Conrad) is satisfied, that even Jim is satisfied. The circumstances of Jim's death and his willingness to take responsibility for the death of Dain Waris ("He hath taken it upon his own head"; ch. 45) make up for all Jim has done before. Jim's end re-enthrones the regal power justifying the fixed standard of conduct by which he condemns himself to death.

Matters are not so simple in this novel. For one thing, there is something suspect in Marlow's enterprise of interpretation. "Was it for my own sake," he asks, "that I wished to find some shadow of an excuse for that young fellow whom I had never seen before?" (ch. 5). If so much is at stake for himself, he is likely to find what he wants to find.

Marlow attempts to maintain his faith in the sovereign power in several contradictory ways. One is to discover that there are extenuating circumstances. Perhaps Jim is not all bad. Perhaps he can be excused. Perhaps he can ultimately redeem himself. At other times Marlow suggests that in spite of appearances Jim has a fatal soft spot. He cannot be safely trusted for an instant. If this is so, then he must be condemned in the name of the kingly law determining good and evil, praise and blame. At still other times Marlow's language implies that Jim is the victim of dark powers within himself, powers which also secretly govern the universe outside. If there is no benign sovereign power there may be a malign one, a principle not of light but of blackness, "a destructive fate ready for us all" (ch. 5). If this is the case, there are indeed extenuating circumstances, precisely the "shadow of an excuse." To act according to a fixed standard of conduct which is justified by no sovereign power, as perhaps Jim does in his death, is the truest heroism. It is defiance of the shadowy powers which would undermine everything man finds good. If this is so, Jim's death is nevertheless in one sense still a sham. It is a sham in the sense that it is valued by no extrahuman judge. It is only one way of acting among others.

Perhaps, to pursue this line a little further, the source of all Jim's trouble is his romanticism, that childish image of himself as a hero which has its source in fraudulent literature and sticks with him all his life: "He confronted savages on tropical shores, quelled mutinies on the high seas, and in a small boat upon the ocean kept up the hearts of despairing men—always an example of devotion to duty, and as unflinching as a hero in a book" (ch. 1). Perhaps it is Jim's confidence in this illusory image of himself which is the source of his inability to confront the truth about himself and about the universe. Perhaps this confidence even paradoxically explains his repeated acts of cowardice. It may be that Jim's death is no more than the last of such acts, his last failure to face the dark side of himself which is so rudely brought back before him in the person of Gentleman Brown. His death may be no more than his last attempt to act according to a fictional idea of heroic conduct. Certainly the final paragraphs of the novel show Marlow by no means "satisfied." The ending is a tissue of unanswered questions in which Marlow affirms once more not that Jim is a hero or that Jim is a coward, but that he remains an indecipherable mystery:

> And that's the end. He passes away under a cloud, inscrutable at heart, forgotten, unforgiven, and excessively romantic . . . He goes away from a living woman to celebrate his pitiless wedding with a shadowy ideal of conduct. Is he satisfied—quite, now, I wonder? We ought to know. He is one of us—and have I not stood up once, like an evoked ghost, to answer for his eternal constancy? Was I so very wrong after all? Now he is no more, there are days when the reality of his existence comes to me with an immense, with an overwhelming force; and yet upon my honour there are moments, too, when he passes from my eyes like a disembodied spirit astray amongst the passions of this earth, ready to surrender himself faithfully to the claim of his own world of shades.
>
> Who knows? (Ch. 45)

The ending seems to confirm Marlow's earlier statement that the heart of each man is a dark forest to all his fellows and "loneliness" a "hard and absolute condition of existence": "The envelope of flesh and blood on which our eyes are fixed melts before the out-stretched hand, and there remains only the capricious, unconsolable, and elusive spirit that no eye can follow, no hand can grasp" (ch. 16).

On the other hand, all that seems problematic and inconclusive about *Lord Jim* when it is approached from the point of view of explicit thematic statements and by way of Marlow's interpretation of Jim may be resolved if the reader stands back from Marlow's perspective and looks at the novel as a whole. The detached view may see the truth, according to that proverb Marlow recalls which affirms that "the onlookers see most of the game" (ch. 21). Seen from a distance, *Lord Jim* may turn out to be a pattern of recurrent motifs which reveals more about Jim than Marlow comes to understand. Jim's feeling at his trial that "only a meticulous precision of statement would bring out the true horror behind the face of things" (ch. 4) may be the clue to the aesthetic method of the book. The episodes Marlow and others relate, the language they use, may reveal to the readers of the novel a secret hidden from Marlow, from Jim, and from all the characters, a secret known only to Conrad. He may have chosen this way to show forth the truth because only as a participant in its revelation can the reader understand it.

When *Lord Jim* is approached from the perspective of its narrative structure and its design of recurrent images it reveals itself to be not less but more problematic, more inscrutable, like Jim himself. I have elsewhere argued that temporal form, interpersonal relations, and relations of fiction and reality are three structuring principles fundamental to fiction.[7] *Lord Jim* is an admirable example of the tendency of these in

7. In *The Form of Victorian Fiction* (Notre Dame: U of Notre Dame P, 1968).

their interaction to weave a fabric of words which is incapable of being interpreted unambiguously, as a fixed pattern of meaning, even though the various possibilities of meaning are rigorously delimited by the text.

To begin with the structure of interpersonal relations: Victorian novels were often apparently stabilized by the presence of an omniscient narrator, spokesman for the collective wisdom of the community, though, as my Victorian examples here demonstrate, such a narrator never turns out to be unequivocally the basis of the storytelling when a given Victorian novel is interpreted in detail. Such a narrator, if he were ever to exist, would represent a trustworthy point of view and also a safe vantage point from which to watch the hearts and minds of the characters in their relations to one another. Conrad, as many critics have noted, does not employ a "reliable" narrator. In *Lord Jim* no point of view is entirely trustworthy. The novel is a complex design of interrelated minds, no one of which can be taken as a secure point of reference from which the others may be judged.

The first part of the story is told by an "omniscient" narrator who seems like the narrator of a novel by Trollope or by George Eliot. This first narrator of *Lord Jim* has the same superhuman powers of insight, including direct access to the hero's mind, that is possessed by those earlier Victorian narrators. He relinquishes that access early in the story, as though it could not provide a satisfactory avenue to the truth behind Jim's life. He then returns in chapter 36, after Marlow's narrative to his almost silent auditors is over. He returns to introduce the man who receives the letter which is Marlow's "last word" about Jim. The bulk of the novel is made up of Marlow's telling of Jim's story to the group of listeners in the darkness who are the reader's surrogates. Those listeners stand between the reader and Marlow's telling. "He existed for me," says Marlow, "and after all it is only through me that he exists for you. I've led him out by the hand; I have paraded him before you" (ch. 21).

Many sections of the story are told to Marlow by Jim. In these the reader can see Jim attempting to interpret his experience by putting it into words. This self-interpretation is interpreted once more by Marlow, then by implication interpreted again by Marlow's listeners. The latter appear occasionally as intervening minds, as when one of them says: "You are so subtle, Marlow" (ch. 8). This overlapping of interpretative minds within minds is put in question in its turn, at least implicitly, by the "omniscient" narrator. He surrounds all and perhaps understands all, though he does not give the reader the sort of interpretative help provided by the narrator of *Middlemarch* or of *The Last Chronicle of Barset*. Even so, this narrator may have been brought back briefly near the end of the novel to suggest that the reader might be wise to put in question Marlow's interpretation of Jim, even though the narrator cannot or will not provide the reader with any solid alternative ground on which to stand.

Within Marlow's narrative there are many minor characters—Captain Brierly, the French lieutenant, Chester, Stein—who have their say in the story. They are irreplaceable points of view on Jim within Marlow's point of view. They are sources of parts of his story and offer alternative ways of judging it. Their own stories, moreover, are analogous to Jim's story, though whether in a positive or in a negative way is often hard to tell. Just as the crucial episodes in Jim's life echo one another, the jump from the *Patna* repeating his failure to jump in the small boat when he was in training and being repeated again by his jump over the stockade in Patusan ("Patusan" recalling *Patna*), so Captain Brierly's suicide is a jump ambiguously duplicating Jim's jumps (was it cowardly or an act of heroism following logically from a shattering insight into the truth of things?), while the French lieutenant's courage shows what Jim might have done on the *Patna*, and Stein's strange history echoes Jim's either positively or negatively. Stein appears to be either an unreliable narrator or a trustworthy commentator, depending on one's judgment of his life and personality. Is he a man who has bravely immersed himself in the destructive element to win an ultimate wisdom, or has he withdrawn passively from life to collect his butterflies and to give Marlow and the readers of the novel only misleading clues to the meaning of Jim's life?

Lord Jim is made up of episodes similar in design. In each a man confronts a crisis testing his courage, the strength of his faith in the sovereign power enthroned in a fixed standard of conduct. In each case someone, the man himself or someone else, interprets that test, or rather he interprets the words which the man's reaction to the test has already generated. There is even a parody of this pattern early in the novel, as if to call attention to it as a structuring principle or as a universal way in which men are related to one another. Just as Marlow seeks out the chief engineer of the *Patna* in the hospital "in the eccentric hope of hearing something explanatory of the famous affair from his point of view," so the doctor who is tending the engineer after his brandy debauch says he "never remember[s] being so interested in a case of the jim-jams before." "The head, ah! the head, of course, gone, but the curious part is that there is some sort of method in his raving. I am trying to find out. Most unusual—that thread of logic in such a delirium" (ch. 5). The reader of *Lord Jim*, like the doctor, must seek the thread of logic within a bewildering complexity of words. With these words Conrad attempts to express a truth beyond direct expression in words, "for words also belong to the sheltering conception of light and order which is our refuge" (ch. 33), our refuge from the truth hidden in the darkness. In the sequence of discrete episodes which makes up the novel, no episode serves as the point of origin, the arch-example of the *mythos* of the novel, but each is, by reason of its analogy to other episodes, a repetition of them, each example being as enigmatic as all the others.

A similar complexity characterizes the temporal structure of the novel. Jim says of his memory of watching the other officers struggle to get the *Patna*'s boat in the water: "I ought to have a merry life of it, by God! for I shall see that funny sight a good many times yet before I die" (ch. 9). Of an earlier moment before the officers desert the ship he says: "It was as though I had heard it all, seen it all, gone through it all twenty times already" (ch. 8). Each enactment of a given episode echoes backward and forward indefinitely, creating a pattern of eddying repetition. If there are narrators within narrators there are also times within times —time-shifts, breaks in time, anticipations, retrogressions, retellings, and reminders that a given part of the story has often been told before. Marlow, for example, like the Ancient Mariner, has related Jim's story "many times, in distant parts of the world" (ch. 4). The novel is made up of recurrences in which each part of the story has already happened repeatedly when the reader first encounters it, either in someone's mind, or in someone's telling, or in the way it repeats other similar events in the same person's life or in the lives of others. The temporal structure of the novel is open. *Lord Jim* is a chain of repetitions, each event referring back to others which it both explains and is explained by, while at the same time it prefigures those which will occur in the future. Each exists as part of an infinite regression and progression within which the narrative moves back and forth discontinuously across time seeking unsuccessfully some motionless point in its flow.

It might be argued that the sequence of events as the reader is given them by Conrad, in a deliberately chosen order, is a linear series with a beginning, middle, and end which determines a straightforward development of gradually revealed meaning moving through time as the reader follows word after word and page after page, becoming more and more absorbed in the story and more and more emotionally involved in it. This sequence, it might be argued, generates a determinate meaning. It is true that this linear sequence is shared by any reader and that it establishes a large background of agreement about what happens and even about the meaning of what happens. That Jim jumps from the *Patna* and that this is a morally deplorable act no reader is likely to doubt. But it is also true that the linear sequence of episodes as it is presented to the reader by the various narrators is radically rearranged from the chronological order in which the events actually occurred. This could imply that Conrad, the "omniscient narrator," or Marlow has ordered the episodes in such a way that the best understanding by the reader of a total meaning possessed by one or another of these narrators will be revealed. Or it may imply, as I think it does, that the deeper explanatory meaning behind those facts open to the sunlight, about which anyone would agree, remains hidden, so that any conceivable narrator of these facts or interpreter of them is forced to move back and forth across the facts, putting them in one or another achronological order in the hope that this deeper meaning will reveal itself. The narration in many ways, not least by calling attention to the way one episode repeats another rather than being clearly a temporal advance on it, breaks down the chronological sequence and invites the reader to think of it as a simultaneous set of echoing episodes spread out spatially like villages or mountain peaks on a map. *Lord Jim* too, to borrow the splendid phrase Henry James uses in his review of Conrad's *Chance*, is "a prolonged hovering flight of the subjective over the outstretched ground of the case exposed."[8] Insofar as the novel is this and not the straightforward historical movement suggested by Aristotle's comments on beginning, middle, and end in the *Poetics*, then the sort of metaphysical certainty implicit in Aristotle, the confidence that some *logos* or underlying cause and ground supports the events, is suspended. It is replaced by the image of a consciousness attempting to grope its way to the hidden cause behind a set of enigmatic facts by moving back and forth over them. If the "facts" are determinate (more or less) the novel encourages the reader to seek the "why" behind the events, some "shadow of an excuse." It is here, I am arguing, that the text does not permit the reader to decide among alternative possibilities, even though those possibilities themselves are identified with precise determinate certainty.

The similarities between one episode and another or one character and another in *Lord Jim* no doubt appear to be deliberately designed (whether by Conrad or by Marlow), like most of the cases of repetition discussed in this book. Such repetitions differ from those which are accidental or merely contingent, perhaps even insignificant, although the reader would do well not to be too sure about the existence of insignificant similarities. Moreover, the fact that Conrad probably consciously intended most of the repetitions I discuss here (though certainty about that is of course impossible) may be trivial compared to the way the novel represents human life as happening to fall into repetitive patterns, whether in the life of a single person, as Jim repeats variants of the same actions over and over, or from person to person, as Brierly's jump repeats Jim's jump. The question the novel asks and cannot unequivocally answer is "Why is this?" To say it is because Conrad designed his novel in recurring patterns is to trivialize the question and to give a misplaced answer to it.

Nor can the meaning of the novel be identified by returning to its historical sources, however helpful or even essential these are in establishing a context for our reading. The "source" of *Lord Jim*, as Conrad tells the reader in the Author's Note, was a glimpse of the "real" Jim: "One sunny morning in the commonplace surroundings of an Eastern roadstead, I saw his form pass by—appealing—significant—under a cloud—perfectly silent . . . It was for me, with all the sympathy of

8. "The New Novel" (1914), in *Notes on Novelists* (London: Dent, 1914) 276.

which I was capable, to seek fit words for his meaning." Norman Sherry, in *Conrad's Eastern World*, and Ian Watt, in *Conrad in the Nineteenth Century*, have discussed in detail the historical events which lie behind the novel.[9] *Lord Jim* can be defined as an attempt on Conrad's part to understand the real by way of a long detour through the fictive. To think of *Lord Jim* as the interpretation of history is to recognize that the historical events "behind" the novel exist now as documents, and that these documents too are enigmatic. They are as interesting for the ways in which Conrad changed them as for the ways in which he repeated them exactly. The novel is related to its sources in a pattern of similarity and difference like that of the episodes inside the novel proper. The facts brought to light by Sherry and Watt, for example the "Report of a Court of Inquiry held at Aden into the cause of the abandonment of the steamship 'Jeddah,' "[1] do not serve as a solid and unequivocal point of origin by means of which the novel may be viewed, measured, and understood. The documents are themselves mysterious, as mysterious as the Old Yellow Book on which Browning based *The Ring and the Book* or as the dry, factual account of historical events included at the end of Melville's *Benito Cereno*. In all these cases knowledge of the historical sources makes the story based on them not less but more inscrutable, more difficult to understand. If there are "fit words" for Jim's "meaning" they are to be found only within the novel, not in any texts outside it.

Perhaps, to turn to a last place where an unambiguous meaning may be found, the pattern of images in its recurrences somehow transcends the complexities I have discussed. It may constitute a design lying in the sunlight, ready to be seen and understood. It will be remembered that Conrad attempts above all, as he says in the preface to *The Nigger of the "Narcissus,"* to make us *see*. Matching this is the recurrent image in *Lord Jim* according to which Marlow gets glimpses of Jim through a rift in the clouds. "The views he let me have of himself," says Marlow, "were like those glimpses through the shifting rents in a thick fog—bits of vivid and vanishing detail, giving no connected idea of the general aspect of a country" (ch. 6). The metaphorical structure of the novel may reveal in such disconnected glimpses a secret which cannot be found out by exploring its narrative, temporal, or interpersonal patterns, or by extracting explicit thematic statements.

A network of light and dark imagery manifestly organizes the novel throughout. It is first established insistently near the beginning in the description of the *Patna* steaming across the calm sea: "The *Patna*, with a slight hiss, passed over that plain luminous and smooth, unrolled a black ribbon of smoke across the sky, left behind her on the water a

---

9. (Cambridge: Cambridge UP, 1966) 41–170; (Berkeley and Los Angeles: U of California P, 1979) 259–69.
1. Sherry; see "Sources," pp. 333–43.

white ribbon of foam that vanished at once, like the phantom of a track drawn upon a lifeless sea by the phantom of a steamer" (ch. 2). Black against white, light against dark—perhaps the meaning of *Lord Jim* is to be found in Conrad's manipulation of this binary pattern.

This metaphorical or "symbolic" pattern too is systematically ambiguous, as may be seen by looking at two examples, the description of Jim's visit to Marlow's room after his trial and the description of Marlow's last glimpse of Jim on the shore. The juxtaposition of light and dark offers no better standing ground from which what is equivocal about the rest of the novel may be surveyed and comprehended than any other aspect of the text. The "visual aspect of material things" and the clues it may offer to the meaning of man's life sink in the general shipwreck which puts in doubt the sovereign power enthroned in a fixed standard of conduct:

> He remained outside, faintly lighted on the background of night, as if standing on the shore of a sombre and hopeless sea.
>
> An abrupt heavy rumble made me lift my head. The noise seemed to roll away, and suddenly a searching and violent glare fell on the blind face of the night. The sustained and dazzling flickers seemed to last for an unconscionable time. The growl of the thunder increased steadily while I looked at him, distinct and black, planted solidly upon the shores of a sea of light. At the moment of greatest brilliance the darkness leaped back with a culminating crash, and he vanished before my dazzled eyes as utterly as though he had been blown to atoms. (Ch. 16)

> He was white from head to foot, and remained persistently visible with the stronghold of the night at his back, the sea at his feet, the opportunity by his side—still veiled. What do you say? Was it still veiled? I don't know. For me that white figure in the stillness of coast and sea seemed to stand at the heart of a vast enigma. The twilight was ebbing fast from the sky above his head, the strip of sand had sunk already under his feet, he himself appeared no bigger than a child—then only a speck, a tiny white speck, that seemed to catch all the light left in a darkened world . . . And, suddenly, I lost him. (Ch. 35)

In one of these passages Jim is the light that illuminates the darkness. In the other he is the blackness that stands out against a blinding light which suddenly reveals itself from its hiding place and then disappears. Light changes place with dark; the value placed on dark and light changes place, as light is sometimes the origin of dark, dark sometimes the origin of light. Each such passage, moreover, refers to the others by way of anticipation or recollection, as the first of the texts quoted prefigures the second, but when the reader turns to the other passage it is no easier to understand and itself refers to other such passages. No one of them is the original ground, the basis on which the others may be interpreted. *Lord Jim* is like a dictionary in which the entry under one word refers the reader to another word which refers him to another and then back to the first word again, in an endless circling. Marlow sitting in his hotel room ceaselessly writing letters by the light of a single candle while Jim struggles with his conscience and the thunderstorm prepares in the darkness outside may be taken as an emblem of literature as Conrad sees it. A work of literature is for him in a paradoxical relation to a nonverbal reality it seeks both to uncover and to evade in the creation of its own exclusively verbal realm.

I claim, then, that from whatever angle it is approached *Lord Jim* reveals itself to be a work which raises questions rather than answering them. The fact that it contains its own interpretations does not make it easier to understand. The overabundance of possible explanations only inveigles the reader to share in the self-sustaining motion of a process of interpretation which cannot reach an unequivocal conclusion. This weaving movement of advance and retreat constitutes and sustains the meaning of the text, that evasive center which is everywhere and nowhere in the play of its language.

Marlow several times calls explicit attention to the unendingness of the process by which he and the readers of the novel go over and over the details of Jim's life in an ever-renewed, never-successful attempt to understand it completely and so write "Finis" to his story. "And besides," affirms Marlow apropos of his "last" words about Jim, "the last word is not said,—probably shall never be said. Are not our lives too short for that full utterance which through all our stammerings is of course our only and abiding intention? . . . There is never time to say our last word—the last word of our love, or our desire, faith, remorse, submission, revolt" (ch. 21). The reader will remember here those "last words" of Kurtz ("The horror! The horror!") which Marlow in another story hears and ironically praises for their finality, their power to sum up. If this theme is repeated within *Lord Jim*, these repetitions echo in their turn passages in other novels by Conrad. If *Heart of Darkness* leads to Marlow's recognition that he cannot understand Kurtz as long as he has not followed Kurtz all the way into the abyss of death, the "ending" of *Lord Jim* is Marlow's realization that it is impossible to write "The End" to any story: "End! Finis! the potent word that exorcises from the house of life the haunting shadow of fate. This is what—notwithstanding the testimony of my eyes and his own earnest assurances—I miss when I look back upon Jim's success. While there's life there is hope, truly; but there is fear, too . . . he made so much of his disgrace while it is the guilt alone that matters. He was not—if I may say so—clear to me. He was not clear. And there is a suspicion he was not clear to himself either" (ch. 16). Nor can he, I am arguing, ever be clear to us, except with the paradoxical clarity generated by our recognition that the process of interpreting his story is a ceaseless movement toward a light which always remains hidden in the dark.

Let there be no misunderstanding here. The situation I have just described does not mean that the set of possible explanations for Jim's action is limitless, indeterminate in the sense of being indefinitely multiple and nebulous. The various meanings are not the free imposition of subjective interpretations by the reader, but are controlled by the text. In that sense they are determinate. The novel provides the textual material for identifying exactly what the possible explanations are. The reader is not permitted to go outside the text to make up other possible explanations of his own. The indeterminacy lies in the multiplicity of possible incompatible explanations given by the novel and in the lack of evidence justifying a choice of one over the others. The reader cannot logically have them all, and yet nothing he is given determines a choice among them. The possibilities, moreover, are not just given side by side as entirely separate hypotheses. They are related to one another in a system of mutual implication and mutual contradiction. Each calls up the others, but it does not make sense to have more than one of them.

*   *   *

EDWARD SAID

[The Presentation of Narrative in *Lord Jim*]†

Both in his fiction and in his autobiographical writing Conrad was trying to do something that his experience as a writer everywhere revealed to be impossible. This makes him interesting as the case of a writer whose working reality, his practical and even theoretical competence as a writer, was far in advance of what he was saying. Occurring at the time when he lived and wrote, this irony of Conrad's writing has a critical place in the history of the duplicity of language, which since Nietzsche, Marx, and Freud has made the study of the orders of language so central to the contemporary understanding. Conrad's fate was to write fiction great for its presentation, not only for what it was representing. He was misled by language even as he led language into a dramatization no other author really approached. For what Conrad discovered was that the chasm between words saying and words meaning was widened, not lessened, by a talent for words written. To have chosen to write, then, is to have chosen in a particular way neither to say directly nor to mean exactly

† From *The World, The Text and The Critic* (Cambridge: Harvard UP, 1983). Reprinted by permission of the author. The text has been edited for publication here. Parenthetical page numbers refer to edition used by the author; bracketed page numbers refer to this Noiton Critical Edition.

in the way he had hoped to say or to mean. No wonder that Conrad returned to this problematic concern repeatedly, a concern that his writing dramatized continuously and imaginatively.

*   *   *

Lord Jim is one of the first of Conrad's extended narratives to make knowledge, intelligibility, and vision into functions of utterance. The novel takes off in "the act of intelligent volition" that directs Marlow's eyes to Jim's during the inquiry. After a period of "endless converse with himself" and at a time when "speech was no use to him any longer," Jim at last meets a man whose presence loosens the tongues "of men with soft spots, with hard spots, with hidden plague spots." Marlow not only listened but is "willing to remember Jim at length, in detail and audibly." True, Jim has "influential confidences" to confess, and yet Marlow's propensity to tell and remember is just as important to the book. "With the very first word [of his narrative] Marlow's body, extended at rest in the seat, would become very still, as though his spirit had winged its way back into the lapse of time and were speaking through his lips from the past" (XXI, 33) [24]. Marlow's generosity toward Jim is rooted in precisely that same tendency to romantic projection because of which Jim so embarrassingly prefers courageous voyages in projective inspiration to voyages in actuality. Neither man, whether hearer or storyteller, truly inhabits the world of facts. First Jim and then Marlow wander off "to comprehend the Inconceivable," an activity so urgent and rarefied at the same time that it involves "a subtle and momentous quarrel as to the true essence of life." Ultimately Conrad points out that Jim does not speak to Marlow, but rather in front of him, just as Marlow cannot by definition speak to the reader but only in front of him.

What first seems like a meeting of minds turns into a set of parallel lines. Moreover Marlow explicitly says later that Jim exists for him, as if to say that Jim's confession before Marlow mattered more than *what* Jim confessed (both Marlow and Jim seem equally confused anyway). Only because of that performance—not just because of Jim's exploits in and of themselves—does Jim exist for his listener. I have already commented on Conrad's practice, which is evident in what Marlow says of Jim's enigmatic appearance and his need to talk, of alternating the visual and the oral modes: the way the narrative shows how "Romance had singled out Jim for its own" follows directly from this practice. Jim's appetite for disastrous adventure, like Marlow's narrative, like our attention to the tale, corresponds not to any communicable pattern of linear progress from, say, ambition to accomplishment, but conforms rather to a more abstract impulse. The impulse can find no expression in action, and no image, other than the vague rubric of Romance, conveys the aim of Jim's troubled quest. Forced into the duration of reported speech or utterance, the impulse's exigencies are such relatively ethereal things as pattern, rhythm, phrase, sequence.

But, we are entitled to ask, what is the pressure on Jim that makes him favor death over life, and which urges Marlow and Conrad toward "inconclusive experiences" that reveal less to the reader than any reader is prepared to expect? In all cases the dominating factor is not narrative energy but a fatalistic desire to behold the self passively as an object told about, mused on, puzzled over, marveled at fully, in utterance. That is, having everywhere conceded that one can neither completely realize one's own nor fully grasp someone else's life experience, Jim, Marlow, and Conrad are left with a desire to fashion verbally and approximately their individual experience in the terms unique to each one. Since invariably this experience is either long past or by definition almost impossible, no image can capture this, just as finally no sentence can.

Nevertheless the utterance is spoken, if not only to, then in the presence of, another. Words convey the presence to each other of speaker and hearer but not a mutual comprehension. Each sentence drives a sharper wedge between intention (wanting-to-speak) and communication. Finally wanting-to-speak, a specifically verbal intention, is forced to confront the insufficiency, and indeed the absence, of words for that intention. It is not too extreme to say that in a complex way Conrad is dramatizing the disparity between verbal intention grammatically and formally apprehendable and possible on the one hand and, on the other, verbality itself, as a way of being in the world of language with other human beings. In "Amy Foster," that most poignant of all his stories, the disparity is spelled out in particular human detail. Washed ashore in England, Yanko Goorall lives among people who cannot make him out and to whose language he is always a foreigner:

> These were the people to whom he owed allegiance, and an over-whelming loneliness seemed to fall from the leaden sky of that winter without sunshine. All the faces were sad. He could talk to no one, and had no hope of ever understanding anybody. It was as if these had been the faces of people from the other world— dead people he used to tell me years afterwards. Upon my word, I wonder he did not go mad. He didn't know where he was. Some-where very far from his mountains—somewhere over the water. Was this America, he wondered? . . . The very grass was different, and the trees. All the trees but the three old Norway pines on the bit of lawn before Swaffer's house, and these reminded him of his country. He had been detected once, after dusk, with his forehead against the trunk of one of them, sobbing, and talking to himself. They had been like brothers to him at that time, he affirmed. Everything else was strange . . . Many times have I heard his high-pitched voice from behind the ridge of some sloping sheepwalk, a voice light and soaring, like a lark's but with a melancholy human note, over our fields that hear only the song of birds. And I would be startled myself. Ah! He was different; innocent of heart, and full

of good will, which nobody wanted, this castaway, that, like a man transplanted into another planet, was separated by an immense space from his past and by an immense ignorance of the future. His quick, fervent utterance positively shocked everybody.

Conrad's excruciatingly detailed understanding of this predicament makes this choice of utterance as his way of presenting narratives something far more urgent than a comfortable aesthetic choice. It is clear he believed that only a fully imagined scene between a speaker and a watching hearer could present—continuously, directly, and, since it occurs in story after story, repeatedly—the fundamental divorce he stood for as a writer: the rift between a fully developed but, with regard to other people, only an intentional or latent capacity for complete expression and an inescapable human community. "There are no words for the sort of things I wanted to say" (*Lord Jim*). Hence Conrad's penchant for repeating phrases like "he was one of us" together with reminders of how unique each individual and his experiences were. And the text Conrad worked at ceased simply to be a written document and became instead a distribution of utterances around both sides of the rift. They are held together by the reader's attention to both sides. In its duration for the length of *Lord Jim*, such overarching attention binds together Jim's verbal intention and Marlow's forbearance as a witness. Only in the domain of intention and fantasy to which Conrad's heroes have a fatal attraction can there be completion for schemes of the kind Jim devises for himself; but such a place is apprehendable only during the constantly progressing narrative of his doom and failure. When Marlow sees Jim for the last time, there is this passage:

> "Jim, at the water's edge, raised his voice. "Tell them . . ." he began. I signed to the men to cease rowing, and waited in wonder. Tell who? The half-submerged sun faced him. I could see its red gleam in his eyes that looked dumbly at me . . . "No—nothing," he said, and with a slight wave of his hand motioned the boat away. I did not look again at the shore till I had clambered on board the schooner . . . He was white from head to foot, and remained persistently visible with the stronghold of the night at his back, the sea at his feet, the opportunity by his side—still veiled? I don't know. For me that white figure in the stillness of coast and sea seemed to stand at the heart of a vast enigma. The twilight was ebbing fast from the sky above his head, the strip of sand had sunk already under his feet, he himself appeared no bigger than a child—then only a speck, a tiny white speck that seemed to catch all the light left in a darkened world . . . And suddenly, I lost him." (XXI, 336) [199]

Much is brought together here. Jim's terminal silence indicates that once again "a silent opportunity" takes over his life. He seems for a moment to have become the point of visual, as well as intellectual, reference for which words are both inadequate and never relinquished. Then he disappears. His life is covered over with the few suggestive traces—a letter, an incomplete narrative, a patchy oral report—that Marlow can garner much later. But at least Jim holds the privacy of his being intact.

*   *   *

PHILIP M. WEINSTEIN

"Nothing Can Touch Me": *Lord Jim*†

*   *   *

Despite Conrad's vexation at being considered a writer of sea tales, the relations between the exigent subject and the world he inhabits—the deeper lines of stress in his fiction—indicate the traces of a "maritime" orientation. A basic *donnée* of his imagination is the assertion of human will against a shapeless and unaccommodating natural backdrop. His typical story is of a willed invasion, a precarious attempt to make a foreign medium support a private desire. The humanly willed vs. the naturally given is of course a tension in, as well as a constitutive condition of, all fiction. No art naively engages its object, simply giving voice to nature, free of all convention. What distinguishes Conrad's work from that of his Victorian predecessors in this regard, however, is his uneasiness, his problematic and even debilitating awareness of the artifice in his art. Fictions lie, and he must continually find ways of "tilting" his fictive world, to make it reveal its artifice and thus suggest its unconventional truth. Hence the complexity, not to say perversity, of his approach to his materials, for though the materials are what he must deliver, the conventional forms into which they most readily fall are embarrassingly inappropriate: a betrayal as much as a clarification. The abrupt transitions and extended deviations of his narrative stance serve to keep the materials "undomesticated" by rendering his events and characters opaque in themselves, enigmatic in the view of others (including the reader), and unplaced within any larger unifying setting. Harmony, order, interrelationship—these emerge in Conrad's world (its structure as well as its plots) as willed achievements crafted against an incessant pressure toward entropy and discontinuity. Whether its subject

† From *The Semantics of Desire: Changing Models of Identity from Dickens to Joyce* (Princeton: Princeton UP, 1984). Copyright © 1984 by Princeton UP. Reprinted by permission of Princeton UP. This selection has been edited for publication here. Page references to *Lord Jim* are to this Norton Critical Edition.

be the mastery of the sea (as in all the sea narratives) or the pacification of the land (as in "Heart of Darkness," *Nostromo,* and to a lesser extent *The Secret Agent* and *Under Western Eyes*), the Conrad narrative emphasizes the strain and unlikelihood, the unnaturalness of such a willed enterprise, as set within the overwhelming inertia of an inhuman medium.

* * *

Conrad's best work awakens within his reader a state of disorientation akin to that which he portrays in his characters. The world one enters in his pages is murky, evasive, and incongruent. Perspective shifts unexpectedly from character to character, from scene to scene, from time frame to time frame. On a given two pages in Chapter 5 (26–28) of *Lord Jim* Marlow's narrative moves impressionistically from Jim to the German captain to De Jongh to Archie Ruthvel to a Portuguese half-caste to Captain Elliott and his three daughters' matrimonial problems.[1] These figures loom into and then vanish out of the reader's uncomprehending view. They are present before they have been explained and absent before the explaining is over. Conrad's fiction contains scores of such peripheral floating figures, and they contribute unobtrusively to its effect upon us. They make us take this fictional world as a scene of fleeting, opaque objects, glimpsed in passing rather than prepared for, made transparent, fixed. Thus the impressionistic Conrad narrative may be said to be most "maritime" in its proliferation of peripatetic figures against a background as uncaring and unfocused as the Pacific Ocean.

* * *

A gallery of willful figures, brought by Marlow's narrative suddenly into and then out of focus, enigmatic to the reader, unclear to other characters and often to themselves as well, moving with their private projects within a medium that bonds them intensely without impairing their solitude—such is a rough summary of the phenomenal world of *Lord Jim.* The keynote of its composition, though, is seen less in its shape than heard in its utterance. Rather than condense its speech into the unified and recollected voice of an authoritative narrator, Conrad quotes it. His genius is to make us hear the disjointed multiplicity of its polyglot speakers.

Everyone talks in *Lord Jim;* few achieve verbal coherence. Conrad is extraordinarily alert to the strangeness of speech, the ways in which it wells out of one human subject, reaches stammeringly toward an attendant second subject, then subsides in failure. "The blight of futility

1. Albert J. Guerard's magisterial study of Conrad includes a useful "slow-motion" synopsis of these pages, paragraph by paragraph. Only by slowing down one's critical pace does one register the subversiveness of Conrad's narrative structure in the first half of *Lord Jim.* See Guerard, *Conrad the Novelist* (134–40). Ian Watt in his *Conrad in the Nineteenth Century* also devotes some twenty-five pages to Conrad's extremely flexible deployment of time in *Lord Jim* (286–310).

that lies in wait for men's speeches had fallen upon our conversation, and made it a thing of empty sound" (91). This writer for whom only Polish was native, all other languages being learned—achievements of the will, against the grain—renders sensitively the gap between a feeling and an utterance, a speaker and a listener. Each speaker characteristically deforms the medium of language as he exploits it. The words uttered reflect the speaker but rarely the object he is attempting to describe. "Look at dese cattle" (14) says the German captain, " 'She was full of reptiles' " (35) says the Chief Engineer. " 'Impossible de comprendre—vous concevez' " (85) says the French lieutenant. " 'One thing alone can us from being ourselves cure!' " (128) says Stein. " 'Jove! Get out of this. Jove! This is luck at last. . . . You wait. I'll . . .' " (142) says Jim about to try his chance at Patusan. " 'An awful thing has happened . . . I must now at once . . .' " (202) writes Jim at the end, brokenly, obscurely, making his last futile attempt to explain the impact of Brown upon his destiny.

In each instance the utterance is shaped, if not skewed, by the subjective inflections of the speaker. Even where the language is common, ten men in sufficient distress will speak ten different dialects. At moments of deep need the Conradian psyche verges on inarticulateness, issuing cryptic words about reptiles, stammering broken phrases. Conrad is a master of fragmented utterance. He had doubtless suffered—at any rate he makes us hear—the incapacity of the soul to deliver itself in language. What he portrays is not the transparency of communication but the opacity of frustrated men talking, each in his own idiom and syntax, circling vainly for "that full utterance which through all our stammerings is of course our only and abiding intention" (136).

Utterance in *Lord Jim* is embodied, inflected, opaque. Again and again we wait expectantly with Marlow as a privileged commentator—Brierly, Chester, the French lieutenant, Stein, Cornelius, Brown—draws close and begins to speak. Always the speech reaches toward Jim, fleetingly silhouettes him, then retires extinguished to its subjective point of origin. Speech in Conrad is either teasingly inadequate or radically inadequate. The Pilgrims on the *Patna* understanding nothing of their coming betrayal, the Malay helmsmen hearing the white crew's words but convinced of "secret reasons" for their behavior, Jewel pressing Marlow to explain the enigma of Jim—each of these instances expresses the parochialism of words, their status as simultaneously conveyer and concealer of meaning. There are only words available, and the words are often no better than noises. Discourse is strictly conventional, by way of translation and interpretation. The deep reality remains inaccessible, mute, and would doubtless be unbearable if confronted directly. As Marlow says in "Heart of Darkness," "The inner truth is hidden—luckily, luckily." Against such a world of flickering and isolated figures, each burdened with obscure dreams of self-ratification, speaking each in his own inflected tongue—against, precisely, the murk and slipper-iness of this phenomenal world we need to assess the rigid and simplistic perfection of Conrad's moral code. His people speak many tongues, but his code is a universal grammar.

"One of us"—the group, not the individual, is the source of value, and it is urgent to know quickly if one belongs to it or not. Membership is indicated by a symbolism of shared uniforms, shared skills, shared vocabulary. These surface signs attest to belief in "a few very simple ideas . . . notably . . . the idea of Fidelity".[2] For Fidelity, read rigorous self-restraint in the pursuit of a common goal. The crisis-model implicit in Conrad's moral formulation is a fragile ship in a destructive element. It will *naturally* founder should its crew relax their hold upon them-selves. A successful voyage is a kind of miracle, a continuous repression of the anarchic possibilities of self-release. Neither spoken (and thus subjectively inflected, stammering, ambiguous) nor written, the require-ments of the seaman's code are universally symbolized in the form of a certificate. It is a document as briskly impersonal as the uniforms its followers wear.

Uniforms in Conrad are no picturesque decoration. Their aim is to make uniform, to maintain the conviction of uniformity, to hold in the narcissistic urges of ego-release. "I have a horror of losing even for one moving moment that full possession of myself which is the first condition of good service," Conrad writes in his Preface to A *Personal Record* (xvii). There can be no doubt that the stress is on possession, not self. The hidden impulses of the self represent not a resource to be exploited but a menace to be controlled, kept in uniform ("The inner truth is hidden —luckily, luckily"). Clothing—Jim's, Nostromo's—is almost as eloquent a phenomenon in Conrad's world as the body beneath it is in Lawrence's.

Indeed, when approached close up, Conrad's characters often reveal grotesque bodies. Brown, Robinson, and Cornelius are drawn in broad, aggressively offensive strokes that radiate their author's disgust. But the crowning portrait of physical repulsion is the German captain:

> "The skipper gazed in an inanimate way between his feet: he seemed to be swollen to an unnatural size by some awful disease. . . . His thick, purplish lips came together without a sound, he went off in a resolute waddle to the gharry and began to jerk at the door-handle with such a blind brutality of impatience that I expected to see the whole concern overturned on its side, pony and all. The driver . . . displayed at once all the signs of intense terror . . . looking around from his box at this vast carcass forcing its way into his conveyance. The little machine shook and rocked tumultuously, and the crimson nape of that lowered neck, the size of those strain-ing thighs, the immense heaving of that dingy, striped green-and-

2. *The Mirror of the Sea and A Personal Record*, ed. Zdzisław Najder (Oxford: Oxford UP, 1988) xiv. Subsequent page references appear parenthetically above [*Editor*].

orange back, the whole burrowing effort of that gaudy and sordid
mass troubled one's sense of probability with a droll and fearsome
effect, like one of those grotesque and distinct visions that scare
and fascinate one in a fever. He disappeared." (32)

It is, in several senses, the scene of a misfit. The clothes are not fitting
in themselves, and the body neither fits into them nor into the gharry.
More deeply, spirit cannot conceivably fit into such a body. Conrad
suggests the disease of pure uncontrolled matter. Free to roam about
the vast Pacific, uncoerced by "your verfluchte certificate" (29), the
German captain has "swollen" cancerously along the lines of his worst
susceptibilities. Like all of Conrad's grotesques—and some of Conrad's
protagonists—he has abandoned his native culture, been exposed to a
foreign setting, lost his sustaining bond with a shaping code, and simply
collapsed into himself. His monstrous figure suggests the potential of
unbridled self-release. His body has no internal order. Unharnessed by
any sanction outside itself, it swells into the sordid overripeness of a
"vast carcass." *Mutatis mutandis*, his physical enormity is a figure for
Kurtz's spiritual monstrosity. In the German captain—as in Verloc,
Nikita, and others—Conrad fuses physical obesity with moral deformity
with vocational vagrancy: men faithful only to their internal propensity
lapse into vile bodies.

Such figures suggest the liabilities to which, in Conrad's imagination,
undisciplined flesh is heir. There already exist several studies of the
perverse implications that insinuate themselves into the prose whenever
Conrad dilates on a woman's physical charms. Suffice it to say here that
the erotic body beneath the clothes is explosive material for Conrad.
The complex of feelings—desire and dread, awe and disgust—to which
its depiction gives rise are never artistically mastered.[3]

But with uniforms, with chosen, crafted signs that promise to control
the impulses and vicissitudes of flesh even if they do not guarantee it
—with these he excels. An expression of the conscious will, they bear
the hallmark of Conradian value: they have been painstakingly created.
They represent less a virtue that is indigenous to the human animal
than one he has willed upon himself.[4] And of course it is the encounter

3. Guerard is brief but acute on this cause (among others) for the recurrent failures in Conrad's
art. Thomas Moser's *Joseph Conrad: Achievement and Decline* (Cambridge: Harvard UP, 1957)
is the classic book-length study of Conrad's fiction from a Freudian perspective. Bernard
Meyer's *Joseph Conrad: A Psychoanalytic Biography* (Princeton: Princeton UP, 1967) frankly
exploits the work as a quarry harboring the psyche of its author, but even so it contains some
arresting perceptions for the literary critic. See especially chapters 3–4, 6, 13–15, and the very
suggestive Conrad drawings reproduced and interpreted on 326–32.

4. The conscious will is of course also "indigenous," but my point is that it is a will opposed to
the spontaneous inclinations of the subject, and of secondary rather than primary importance
as a key, so to speak, for interpreting Conrad's imagination. For a cogent opposed view of
these two strains in Conrad's work, see Ian Watt, "Joseph Conrad: Alienation and Commitment." Watt argues that the nihilistic strain is to be seen as part of Conrad's late-Victorian
intellectual inheritance, "the findings of the alienated intellect," whereas the positive strain
of commitment is a product of his immediate experiences as a seaman. In *The English Mind*,
ed. Hugh Sykes Davies and George Watson (Cambridge: Cambridge UP, 1964) 269.

between these Procrustean values and the ambiguous phenomena they fail to control that generates Conrad's tragic novels. I turn now to the crises of identity that beset the protagonist once his uniform has slipped.

* * *

Freud writes in *The Interpretation of Dreams*: "Very rarely does the complexity of human character, driven hither and thither by dynamic forces, submit to a choice between simple alternatives, as our antiquated morality would have us believe" (5:621). The ambivalence of Conrad comes into focus when one sees that he illogically endorses both sides of Freud's polar statement. He knows that character is polymorphous and unpredictable, often disobedient to the trained will. Yet the only schema of assessment that he can accept is the seaman's code based on "our antiquated morality."

As much as Dickens or George Eliot, Conrad relies on the habitual self; as much as Lawrence or Gide, he disbelieves in its efficacy. " 'But habit—habit—necessity—do you see?—the eye of others—*voilà*' " affirms the French lieutenant. Like work itself, habit narcotizes the anxious imagination; it is king in the realm dominated by learned gesture and conscious will. However, Conrad so arranges his fictions that the habits generated by conscious training are insufficient. A surface garment, like protective coloration, habit loses its mediating efficacy the moment the landscape essentially alters; and Conrad's plots insist on such an alteration. Kurtz in the Congo, Jim on a ship about to founder, Decoud on the Great Isabel, Razumov confronted by Haldin—these shattering encounters break through the willed defenses of habit. A propensity deep within the menaced self—deeper than anything learned—is awakened, and against the crisis caused by this intrusive impulse Conrad knows no governing remedy.

In an interesting recent study, Bruce Johnson approaches these crises of identity in the spirit of Sartrean existentialism, claiming as "Conradian assumptions . . . first, that identity, sense of self, must be created continuously by will; second, that the realm of will is also that of morality. Identity does not exist as a given natural fact. . . . If identity were part of established natural certainties, man would indeed be godlike".[5] As the French lieutenant says, " 'it would be too easy otherwise' " (90). Johnson goes on to set up a brilliant contrast between Jim and Stein. Jim believes in

> a predetermined self which, though experience may temporarily frustrate its appearance, will ultimately shine forth. Stein—who, we are told, is instinctively heroic—ironically believes in the contingent self; Jim, who is contingently cowardly or heroic believes in the ordained self. . . . What Stein's advice suggests . . . is that the man who recognizes his contingency, his moment-to-moment

5. Bruce Johnson, *Conrad's Models of Mind* (Minneapolis: U of Minnesota P, 1971) 17. Subsequent page references appear parenthetically [*Editor*].

> formlessness, pursues the ideal as an expression of his humanity.
> To be human is . . . to be unlike the butterfly, not the precise and
> peaceful balance of cosmic forces, but the magnificent imbalance
> of a lust for perfection in a creature aware of his imperfection. To
> pursue the ideal as one's already innate essence is not to *pursue* it
> at all. (60)

This commentary is so illuminating that one quarrels with it in a
spirit of indebtedness. Still, Johnson's Sartrean model is misleading. It
proposes more flexibility, more choice in this matter of identity (and
more smugness in Jim's quest), than Conrad dramatizes. A Schopenhauerian lens is the appropriate one here, for while Conrad does show
identity to be inscribed in the will, this will is not Sartre's instrument,
obedient to the dictates of consciousness. Schopenhauer writes:

> According to my fundamental point of view . . . will is first and
> original; knowledge is merely added to it as an instrument belonging
> to the phenomenon of will. Therefore every man is what he is
> through his will. . . . Through the knowledge which is added to
> it he comes to know in the course of experience *what he is*, i.e.,
> he learns his character. Thus he *knows* himself in consequence of
> and in accordance with the nature of his will, instead of *willing* in
> consequence of and in accordance with his knowing. According to
> the latter view, he would only require to consider how he would
> like best to be, and he would be it. . . . I, on the contrary, say
> that . . . he cannot resolve to be this or that, nor can he become
> other than he is; but he *is* once for all, and he knows in the course
> of experience *what* he is.[6]

This somber notion of identity is a shade—but only a shade—more
deterministic than Conrad's in his major fiction. Essentially, if not
entirely, we harbor what we are within us, and catastrophe releases it:
"A clean slate, did he say? As if the initial word of each our destiny
were not graven in imperishable characters upon the face of a rock!"
(112)[7] *Lord Jim* is a haunting as much as it is a soaring, and if one sees
in it, according to Johnson, "the power of human ego . . . to confer
value upon abstractions and to idealize its own desires" (65), one sees
as well Jim's sustained and hopeless attempt to erase that "initial word"
inscribed in his unconscious will and revealed in his jump. As Dorothy
Van Ghent lucidly puts it, ". . . at no time does he consciously acknowledge that it *was* himself who jumped from the *Patna*—it was

6. Arthur Schopenhauer, *The World as Will and Idea*, in *Schopenhauer: Selections*, ed. Dewitt
H. Parker (New York: Scribner's, 1928) 212. Johnson himself speculates as to whether Conrad's
model of mind is better described in Schopenhauerian or Sartrean terms (126–30).
7. Watt maintains a similar view of the inalterable givens within Conradian identity: "In general
Conrad's novels suggest that he thought character was impervious to full comprehension; it
was also nearly as intractable as circumstance, and equally unlikely to be transformed in
accordance with our wishes" (*Conrad in the Nineteenth Century*, 340).

only his body that had jumped; and his career thenceforth is an attempt to prove before men that the gross fact of the jump belied his identity".[8] * * *

Given his isolation, his exposure, and his idealized self-image, the Conradian protagonist rarely learns from his crises and almost never absorbs what he learns. Nietzsche's advice, "Become who you are," is intolerable to him, for what he has glimpsed in himself is usually his worst possibilities. The willful invader has been involuntarily invaded. Something inside has slipped through the uniform of chosen identity, and he moves not to accommodate the despised intruder but to stiffen trebly his resolve. His nature a door he wants to keep closed, his native culture a past he has abandoned, his isolation now intensifies and he either collapses (like Kurtz and Decoud), sinks deeper into his ego-dream (like Gould and Jim), or engages in a species of conscious role-playing that soon becomes desperate and untenable (like Nostromo and Razumov). In every instance the setting he inhabits freezes into the shape of the crisis scene: Jim and his jump are as inseparable as Nostromo and his hidden silver, Razumov and his betrayed Haldin.

Men so brittle as Conrad's protagonists cannot accommodate stress; they can only resist it or be shattered by it. This I take to be the implication of Conrad's proliferating doubles, invasive figures who express in caricature propensities that the immaculate protagonist cannot afford to acknowledge in himself. Jim's effect on Brierly is duplicated by Brown's effect on Jim. An unbearably besmirching resemblance *in posse*[9] is glimpsed, and *posse*, of course, is the enemy. In Jim's case, Brown intensified a sullying that began with the jump from the *Patna*, for Brown reactivates George:

> "Eight hundred living people, and they were yelling after the one dead man to come down and be saved! 'Jump, George! Jump! Oh, jump!' . . . With the first hiss of rain, and the first gust of wind, they screamed, 'Jump, George! We'll catch you! Jump!' . . . I heard as if I had been on the top of a tower another wild screech, 'Geo-o-o-orge! Oh, jump!' She was going down, down, head first under me . . . I had jumped . . . it seems. . . ." (69)

Jim's account unintentionally but insistently associates himself with George. He jumps into the place reserved for George; more darkly, he jumps into George, at a stroke taking on George's moral obliquity. He carries George within him—a secret sharer—and George is dead. The implication, borne out in a number of ways, is that Jim is dead too. He has ceased to live after the *Patna* disgrace; or, to put it another way, he has fallen outside the aegis of his transcendental identity. His life has lost its unfolding promise, has become (essentially) a suspension. Rooted

8. *The English Novel: Form and Function* (New York: Rinehart, 1953) 233–34.
9. Possible but not actual. Literally, in possibility [*Editor*].

mentally to the time and place of one traumatic scene, he lives to prove
that he will know how to die next time.[1]

The reiterated refrain of "Nothing can touch me" (this phrase or a
slight variant of it occurs at least eight times)[2] points to this death-like
immunity in Jim. His heroism on Patusan is founded on a continual
risking of his life. He once a month drinks the Rajah's possibly poisoned
coffee, and his willingness to die suggests that, in a psychic sense, he
has already conceded his life. " 'Nothing is lost,' " he tells Jewel minutes
before Doramin fires. Everything he could lose has already been lost.
Invaded by the impulse released in the *Patna* disaster, his identity underwent an unsurvivable humiliation: he became not-himself. Having
psychically suffered death already, he is on easy terms with his coming
physical dissolution, and he swells with pleasure at the first death he
can exact in obscure recompense for his own:

> He told me he was experiencing a feeling of unutterable relief, of
> vengeful elation. He held his shot, he says, deliberately. . . . He
> held it for the pleasure of saying to himself, That's a dead man!
> . . . The explosion in that confined space was stunning. . . . He
> saw the man jerk his head up, fling his arms forward, and drop his
> kriss. . . . With the impetus of his rush the man drove straight on,
> his face suddenly gaping disfigured, with his hands open before
> him gropingly, as though blinded. . . . Jim says he didn't lose the
> smallest detail of all this. He found himself calm, appeased, without
> rancour, without uneasiness, as if the death of that man had atoned
> for everything. (179)

Jim relishes this death scene too intensely for it not to relate massively
to his own. His prolonged savoring of this moment in which a dangerous
man is about to be annihilated by his own greater power reverses sat-
isfyingly his earlier nightmare of impotence. "Relief . . . vengeful elation
. . . appeased . . . atoned"—this is the language of a man with a death
inside him, and he is ready to inflict it on others, as he is "heroically"
ready to inflict it on himself. Other people, other places hold no promise
for intimacy but serve only as the setting for this unchanging offer of
his death. Marlow says that on Patusan "all these things that made him
master had made him a captive, too . . . it was they that possessed him
and made him their own to the innermost thought, to the slightest stir
of blood, to his last breath" (149). Jim pledges them his death; he cannot
bring them into his life. In his psychic drama only one figure holds the
stage. Even with Jewel the bond is as limited as it is intense:

1. As though completing a single action that began with his jump from the *Patna*, Jim says
at the moment of crisis to Tamb' Itam (and even more to himself): " 'Time to finish this' "
(244).
2. See 20, 109, 145, 148, 175, 193, 198, 244.

"I—I love her dearly. More than I can tell. Of course one cannot tell. You take a different view of your actions when you come to understand, when you are *made* to understand every day that your existence is necessary—you see, absolutely necessary—to another person." (181)

He loves her for loving him, trusting him, requiring his daily existence. He speaks not of his need of her existence, for he is past needing anyone's existence; all he requires is their immaculate belief.[3] Marlow closes the narrative of Jim's life with a scene that silhouettes vividly his spotless immunity against the tribe's vulnerable humanity. We are shown Doramin, unwieldy, barely able to move, leaning upon "the neck of a bowed youth," a figure of total penetrability: bereft father, betrayed chief, decrepit man, ravaged by his emotions. And we see Jim, finally fixing on them all the "proud and unflinching glance" (246) he has been unable to summon until now. It is the face of a hero—"as unflinching as a hero in a book" the face Jim dreamed of when a boy—[4] and he can summon it now because he has finally paid its price: he carries a bullet through the heart. For an exquisite instant he is perfect, knowing himself to be, securely, and without possibility of change, at one with his own ideal. His death, outrageously withheld by the leap from the *Patna*, heroically offered thereafter, is finally accepted. He dies "with his hand over his lips" (246), as though to still any sound of pain or protest that might sully this immaculate payment.

"Nothing can touch me." Encased in his dream of himself, Jim could be shattered but not touched. His perfection is as inflexible as that of the code he had betrayed. Against both these perfections—Jim's and the code's—we may finally set the frailer values that remain: the communities that are not Community, the truths that are not Truth. These values are implicit in the voice and structure of the novel.

The narrative voice of *Lord Jim* is as tentative and polyvalent as the moral code it refers to is crisp and absolute. Further, the contextual presence of others—their look, talk, and behavior—is as insistently borne in on the reader as it is kept at bay from the hero's idealizing and isolating consciousness. "The infernal joke was being crammed devilishly down his throat," says Marlow, "but—look you—he was not going to admit of any sort of swallowing motion in his gullet" (68). While

3. The Novalis epigraph to *Lord Jim* ("It is certain my conviction gains infinitely, the moment another soul will believe in it") contains *in nuce* this entire point, for it expresses the need of a beleaguered ego, not the hope for a common bond. The belief of "another soul" is indispensable because it corroborates "my conviction." The language of "souls" and "convictions" suggests the often disembodied thinness of Conradian community: a dependence of the fragile subjective self upon a comprehending objective other, not a mutual intimacy between two incarnate subjects.
4. I owe this connection to David Thorburn, *Conrad's Romanticism* (New Haven: Yale UP, 1974) 55.

Jim proudly says No, however, his body does Yes, does Yes continuously and involuntarily. Whatever he may *say*, he swallows.

Community—not the ideal one of his private dream but the actual ones of his embodied life—is always in force, its transactions are continuous. It is not a matter of choice; there is nothing but community. It can be honored or betrayed but not banished. Conrad's figures are helplessly social; they exist together in (to use Melville's words) "a mutual joint-stock company." Whatever contracts the hero acknowledges or ignores, he is contracted up to his neck, and he calls upon these contracts incessantly, unwittingly, to keep himself afloat. The support of others —to be believed by them—is as stringently required as intimacy with them is denied. Surrounding the Conradian roamer—ostensibly alone with his dream—is the unemphasized, often unsought, but ever-present medium (supportive or destructive) of other people. And it is his relation to this medium that determines, at the moment of maximum stress, whether he survives or is shattered.

"We exist only in so far as we hang together" (135), Marlow tells his listeners. " 'Nobody is good enough' " (189), he hurls at Jewel. " 'The example of others who are no better than yourself, and yet make good countenance . . .' " (90), the French lieutenant affirms. Each has his private point of collapse; each borrows from the collective strength of others, even as he lends from his own strength. All human projects require collaboration; and this commerce of continuous, involuntary, even unconscious acts of dependency and support makes up the actual Conradian community. Such a community may be obscured by the hero's grandiose visions, but it is implicit wherever men foregather. Jim therefore starts with alarm when, on board the *Patna*, his gorgeous dreams of achievement are interrupted by the appearance of the German captain:

> Red of face, only half awake, the left eye partly closed, the right staring stupid and glassy. . . . There was something obscene in the sight of his naked flesh . . . the odious and fleshly figure, as though seen for the first time in a revealing moment, fixed itself in his memory for ever as the incarnation of everything vile and base that lurks in the world we love: in our own hearts we trust for our salvation in the men that surround us, in the sights that fill our eyes, in the sounds that fill our ears, and in the air that fills our lungs. (17–18)

So much of the novel is here: the allure of immaculate dreams that satisfy the idealizing will, the vileness of mere motley flesh, the reality of community as something ineluctable—the sound in our ears and the air in our lungs. Jim has unknowingly entrusted himself where he knowingly despises; inundated by bad air and bad sounds, he goes under. Thus betrayed, he turns (unaware) betrayer, for one way of assessing his career is to see it as a recurrent betrayal of real though (for him) sub-ordinate communities—the Pilgrims on the *Patna*, Denver, Egstrom and Blake, Dain Waris, Doramin, Jewel—while in pursuit of an ideal one, glimpsed in a dream, lost in a nightmare. Dedicated to this pursuit, all subsequent situations perceived as ghostly simulacra of his collapse-that-must-be-redeemed, Jim is absolute and untouchable. The figure of flexibility and survival and presence is not Jim but Marlow.

Marlow's moving voice generates the image of community in *Lord Jim*. Digressive, quizzical, judgmental, compassionate, Marlow's talk bodies forth the shape of Conrad's phenomenal world. On the periphery of that talk we find the unchosen presence of others—Chester, Denver, the French lieutenant, Stein, Brown—there for support or damage, but in any case there. And at the center of that talk is Jim—probed, judged, sympathized with, abetted, and yet never fully fathomed. "It is as if loneliness were a hard and absolute condition of existence; the envelope of flesh and blood on which our eyes are fixed melts before the out-stretched hand, and there remains only the capricious, inconsolable, and elusive spirit that no eye can follow, no hand can grasp" (109). In *Lord Jim*'s world of flickering objects and impenetrable motives of stresses that no solitary can withstand and communities that implicate the self without fathoming its secrets or consulting its will, the connective ele-ment is Marlow's voice. Scrupulously unsimplistic, sympathetic and judgmental, his voice insists on supplying both darkness and light, both confusion and clarity; and it thus acknowledges "that doubt which is the inseparable part of our knowledge" (134).

Shortly after finishing *Lord Jim*, Conrad wrote: ". . . in the sphere of an art dealing with a subject matter whose origin and end are alike unknown there is no possible conclusion. The only indisputable truth of life is our ignorance. Besides this there is nothing evident, nothing absolute, nothing uncontradicted. . . ."[5] These words resonate with the grave and unconsoling spirit of *Lord Jim*. Notwithstanding the poignance of Jim's heroic quest, they make explicit the illusion of a transcendental code, and they at least imply the genius of a novel that, unable to reach the authority of a transparent center, expends its energies in opaque approaches, seeking tentatively to touch what it cannot state.

5. Letter of Aug. 2, 1901, to the *New York Times* "Saturday Review," in *The Collected Letters of Joseph Conrad: Volume 2, 1898–1902*, ed. Frederick R. Karl and Laurence Davies (Cam-bridge: Cambridge UP, 1986) 348.

PAUL B. ARMSTRONG

[Monism and Pluralism in *Lord Jim*]†

Conrad similarly oscillates between monism and pluralism, but he is more skeptical than James about the powers of belief as a hermeneutic instrument. In *Lord Jim*, for example, the opening chapters of third-person narration suggest that Jim has an existence independent of what Marlow and others may later think about him. And at the inquiry about the *Patna*, "there was no incertitude as to facts" in Jim's case (56) [37]. But Conrad's novel affirms the autonomy of the real only to throw it into question. Marlow sums up his efforts to understand Jim with this typical complaint: "I wanted to know—and to this day I don't know, I can only guess" (79) [51]. The blockage in Marlow's quest for comprehension shows him and us the prevalence of belief in any act of interpretation. Marlow complains about Jim: "The views he let me have of himself were like those glimpses through the shifting rents in a thick fog—bits of vivid and vanishing detail, giving no connected idea of the general aspect of a country. They fed one's curiosity without satisfying it; they were no good for purposes of orientation. Upon the whole he was misleading" (76) [49]. Marlow's glimpses of Jim remain fragmentary and disconnected. The gaps and contradictions between them hinder the Jamesian composition of parts into a whole, and their refusal to synthesize leaves Marlow without a sense of the consistency among elements in a pattern which is necessary for lucid comprehension.

His inability to make fragments fit together rebounds in turn and questions the trustworthiness of the glimpses themselves precisely because they will not cohere: Is Jim romantic or criminal? Is he courageous in facing the consequences of his acts, or cowardly in resisting the full burden of guilt? Marlow can achieve enough coherence to make Jim roughly comprehensible, but a lingering awareness of gaps in his knowledge and disjunctions in his pattern constantly causes him doubts. Where [James's] Isabel and Strether are deceived because the parts fit together all too well in the constructs they naïvely project, Marlow is blocked because his fragments refuse to compose completely.[1]

† From *The Centennial Review* 27.4 (Fall 1983). Reprinted by permission of *The Centennial Review* and the author. This selection has been edited for publication here. Parenthetical page numbers refer to *Lord Jim* (Garden City: Doubleday, Page, 1924); bracketed page numbers refer to this Norton Critical Edition.

1. I agree with Elsa Nettels that James portrays understanding as an evolving process where, by contrast, Marlow experiences "a succession of moments of insight, isolated, without causal or logical connection." What I have tried to do is to trace this difference to its hermeneutic foundations—namely, their opposite treatments of the relation between wholes and parts. But Nettels oversimplifies their paradoxical attitudes toward reality when she depicts James as a pure believer in and Conrad as a pure skeptic about the discoverability of truth. See the nevertheless very interesting chapter, "The Drama of Perception," in her book *James and Conrad* (Athens: U of Georgia P, 1977) 44–79.

Marlow turns to others to help him decide what to believe about Jim. As he explains, "the thing was always with me, I was always eager to take opinion on it, as though it had not been practically settled: individual opinion—international opinion—by Jove!" (159) [97]. What Marlow finds when he consults others, however, is a veritable conflict of interpretations—from Stein's romantic reading of Jim to Chester's demonic materialistic view, from Brierly's thinly veiled despair about the young man's implications to the cool professionalism of the French lieutenant's assessment, from the resentful animosity of Brown and Cornelius to the disappointed loyalty of Jewel and Tamb' Itam. Each of these attitudes reveals as much about its own rules for interpreting as it does about Jim. One of Conrad's best critics has plausibly argued that "the truth about Jim must be the sum of many perceptions."[2] A further question troubles Marlow, however: What if they do not add up? What if they are incompatible rather than harmonious and complementary?

Instead of advancing Marlow's clarity or certainty about Jim, the rival readings he discovers make the young man increasingly enigmatic. In almost every case, Marlow is as much impressed—if not more—by what an interpretation disguises as by what it discloses. And with such accumulations of blindness, he paradoxically feels at times that he knows less about Jim the more he acquires opinions about him. Each interpretation seems "true," at least to some extent—even the dark views of Brown and Cornelius, who find pretense and vanity in Jim's aloof moral purity. But considered as a group, the readings do not fit together. And because they are finally irreconcilable, they frustrate Marlow's attempt to develop a coherent, comprehensive view of Jim as much as they aid it. Irreducible hermeneutic pluralism thus displaces the monistic assumptions about reality with which the novel began.

Conrad regards belief not only as an epistemological challenge, however, but also as a metaphysical dilemma. Conrad's dual concern with belief as an instrument of knowledge and as evidence of the fragility of human constructs becomes apparent in Marlow's very first encounter with Jim: "There he stood, clean-limbed, clean-faced, firm on his feet, as promising a boy as the sun ever shone on; and, looking at him, knowing all he knew and a little more too, I was as angry as though I had detected him trying to get something out of me by false pretenses. He had no business to look so sound. . . . And note, I did not care a rap about the behaviour of the other two [members of the *Patna*'s crew]. Their persons somehow fitted the tale" (40–41) [28–29]. Marlow is disconcerted by Jim because he is an anomaly—a part inconsistent with Marlow's expectations, given his faith in his community's standard of conduct. Jim defies the set of types by which Marlow customarily composes the world. More is at stake here, however, than Marlow's epis-

2. Thomas C. Moser, *Joseph Conrad: Achievement and Decline* (Cambridge: Harvard UP, 1957) 39.

temological habits. By frustrating his interpretive hypotheses, Jim undermines Marlow's confidence in the fundamental convictions on which his typology rests.

The young man is most disturbing because he introduces Marlow to the possibility of deception in matters he had thought immune to it. The possibility of lying suggests the presence of signs—conventions no stronger or more necessary than our belief in them, a confidence the liar manipulates and betrays.[3] Jim's deception reveals to Marlow that systems of meaning and value he had never doubted are basically conventional, no more substantial or secure than the agreement of their adherents to observe them. They may seem absolute, but they are also arbitrary, since others could always have been adopted in their place. Jim causes Marlow to doubt "the sovereign power enthroned in a fixed standard of conduct" (50) [35]. Because this sovereignty can be counterfeit, it is a convention, not given by divine right. Marlow's hermeneutic crisis in making sense of Jim quickly takes on metaphysical overtones because the failure of his rules for reading his world exposes the contingency of the convictions and conventions on which they are based.

Conrad's combination of monism and pluralism is a reflection of his ceaseless (and potentially unstoppable) oscillation between an intense desire to overcome contingency and an equally compelling recognition that this can never be accomplished. Conrad wishes to discover a single truth that would transcend the variability of the realm of meanings and provide them with a stabilizing, unifying origin. But his pursuit of monism ever turns up new evidence of the world's irreducible pluralism. His often-quoted preface to *The Nigger of the "Narcissus"* describes art's goal as the conquest of the accidental and the inessential in life through the discovery of the necessary and the absolute: "Art itself may be defined as a single-minded attempt to render the highest kind of justice to the visible universe, by bringing to light *the truth, manifold and one*, underlying its every aspect. It is an attempt to find in its forms, in its colours, in its light, in its shadows, in the aspects of matter, and in the facts of life what of each is fundamental, what is enduring and essential—their one illuminating and convincing quality—the very truth of their existence."[4] This quest for essences suggests the temperament of a monist for whom truth is ultimately single, the transcendental signified beneath the multiplicity of signifiers that both disguise and reveal it. But this crucial passage also betrays the sensibility of a pluralist.

Conrad not only calls truth "manifold" as well as "one." He also refrains from claiming that the series of essences disclosed by art will

<hr/>

3. Umberto Eco argues: "Every time there is a lie there is signification. Every time there is signification there is the possibility of using it in order to lie." See Eco, *A Theory of Semiotics* (Bloomington: Indiana UP, 1976) 59.

4. Joseph Conrad, "Preface" to *The Nigger of the "Narcissus"* (1897), in *Joseph Conrad on Fiction*, ed. Walter F. Wright (Lincoln: U of Nebraska P, 1964) 160; emphasis mine.

eventually synthesize into a single "Truth." More subtly but even more tellingly, his lengthy list of plurals at the beginning of the second sentence ("forms," "colours," "shadows," and so on) insistently asserts the world's inherent multiplicity and thereby implicitly undercuts the plea for oneness with which the sentence ends (itself a listing of several elements). If Conrad does discover a final truth, this is the ubiquity of nothingness.[5] But once again monism leads to pluralism because a multiplicity of meanings ensues from the absence of a ground that might limit or unite them.

MARIANNE DE KOVEN

The Destructive Element: *Lord Jim*†

*   *   *

The ambivalence that, as I will argue, generated the most salient features of modernist form was an ambivalence toward the radical remaking of culture and represented these writers' response precisely to [Perry] Anderson's "profoundly ambiguous possible revolutionary outcomes of the downfall of the old order." The downfall of the old order, linked to the radical remaking of culture, was to be the downfall of class, gender, and racial (ethnic, religious) privilege; revolution was to be in the direction of egalitarian leveling on all those fronts. This utter change was embodied in the social-political sphere in the various left-wing revolutionary movements—anarchism, communism, socialism—and in feminism. For the sake of convenience, I will designate these two forces socialism and feminism.[1] The period from 1880 to World War I, during which modernism evolved, encompassed the heyday of these movements on the Anglo-American political scene, allowing of course for important national differences and for specific historical sequences of success and defeat, revolutionary activity and state suppression, and for the diversity of organizations and leaders within these general movements. What I am postulating is a profound connection between this radical history

---

5. For example, see J. Hillis Miller, *Poets of Reality* (1965; rpt. New York: Atheneum, 1969) 13–39; Royal Roussel, *The Metaphysics of Darkness. A Study in the Unity and Development of Conrad's Fiction* (Baltimore: Johns Hopkins UP, 1971); and William W. Bonney, *Thorns and Arabesques: Contexts for Conrad's Fiction* (Baltimore: Johns Hopkins UP, 1980).

† From *Rich and Strange: Gender, History, Modernism.* Copyright © 1991 by Princeton UP. Reprinted by permission of Princeton UP. This selection has been edited for publication here. Parenthetical page numbers refer to this Norton Critical Edition.

1. Perry Anderson, "Modernity and Revolution," *New Left Review* 144 (March–April 1984): 96–113 (reprinted in *Marxism and the Interpretation of Culture,* ed. Cary Nelson and Lawrence Grossberg [Urbana: U of Illinois P, 1988] 317–33). I am using the term "feminism" here anachronistically. For a history of the emergence of twentieth-century feminism from the nineteenth-century woman movement in the United States, see Nancy F. Cott, *The Grounding of Modern Feminism* (New Haven: Yale UP, 1987).

and the development of modernist form. The irresolvable ambivalence (fear and desire in equal portion) of modernist writers concerning their own proposals for the wholesale revision of culture, proposals paralleled in the political sphere by the programs for wholesale social revision promulgated by socialism and feminism, generated the irreducible self-contradiction, what I will call the *sous-rature*,[2] of modernist form. I will argue that male modernists generally feared the loss of their own hegemony implicit in such wholesale revision of culture, while female modernists generally feared punishment for their dangerous desire for that revision.

* * *

Jim dies a sacrifice to his "exalted egoism," going "away from a living woman to celebrate his pitiless wedding with a shadowy ideal of conduct" (246). He chooses at the end the sterility of the bankrupt Western code of masculine honor that makes him "one of us." He is defeated by outmoded patriarchal conventions for masculinity * * *. In *Lord Jim*, * * * the empowered feminine ("a living woman") is the locus of potential for both liberation from those conventions and also for the protagonist's annihilation. * * * the empowered feminine is connected to otherness of race and class, and figurally to water: Stein's famous injunction "in the destructive element immerse" is the best formulation I have seen of modernist *sous-rature*. Accordingly, * * * narrative stance toward the protagonist is perfectly ambivalent: as Albert Guerard says in *Conrad the Novelist*, concerning reader response to Jim, "We must remember that in every chapter and on every page the double appeal to sympathy and judgment is made."

From the beginning, Conrad calls attention to an overdone insistence on Jim's masculinity. * * * "He was an inch, perhaps two," hits us with the force of its strangeness as an introduction to a male protagonist, and the normalizing phrase that follows, "under six feet," does not entirely dispel that strangeness, with its suggestion of extreme tininess, one reading of which is the primal tininess of the infant in relation to the mother. * * * That tininess will reappear in Marlow's description of his last sight of Jim, which I would argue is a womb image: "He was white from head to foot, and remained persistently visible with the stronghold of the night at his back, the sea at his feet . . . that white figure in the stillness of coast and sea seemed to stand at the heart of a vast enigma. . . . he himself appeared no bigger than a child—then only a speck, a tiny white speck, that seemed to catch all the light left in a darkened world" (199).

Marlow focuses on the whiteness "from head to foot" of that fetal "tiny white speck." That whiteness is also emphasized in the novel's opening paragraph: "He was spotlessly neat, apparelled in immaculate

2. Literally, under erasure [*Editor*].

white from shoes to hat" (7). As in *Heart of Darkness*, the maternal feminine is allied with the dark of night and of skin color, while Jim is the dazzling white of an exaggerated version of his racial identity. As Jim's whiteness is overdone, and therefore questionable, so is his masculinity: "His voice was deep, loud, and his manner displayed a kind of dogged self-assertion which had nothing aggressive in it. It seemed a necessity, and it was directed apparently as much at himself as at anybody else" (7). Conrad's description of a water-clerk's job also deliberately calls into question Jim's masculinity: "To the captain he is faithful like a friend and attentive like a son, with the patience of Job, the unselfish devotion of a woman, and the jollity of a boon companion" (7). * * * Conrad is presenting for critique the hegemonic alliance of whiteness and maleness embodied (exaggerated and therefore undermined) in Jim. (Critique, of course, is in equipoise with sympathy, as Guerard says— Jim is, after all, "one of us.")

In the first pages of the book, we also learn that Jim is "Jim—nothing more. He had, of course, another name, but he was anxious that it should not be pronounced" (8). He has literally forfeited the name-of-the-Father, renouncing (or being stripped of) his patriarchal birthright. This forfeiture is emphasized later in the novel, again in a sequence depicting Jim's life as a water-clerk in an Eastern port. First Marlow berates him for having left the surrogate father who would have made his fortune: " 'Oh! you—you—' I began, and had to cast about for a suitable word, but before I became aware that there was no name that would just do, he was gone" (115). Jim's boss then duplicates Marlow's inability to name Jim properly: "D'ye hear, Mister What's-your-name?" (116).

Accordingly, or appropriately, Jim as water-clerk is drifting steadily East, away from his Western (white, imperialist, patriarchal) patrimony, toward (I would argue) the feminine. Thomas Moser has shown that the East was associated with death for Conrad;[3] I see it as also associated with the feminine. The evidence of that association in *Lord Jim* will emerge in the course of this reading. At this point I would like to cite what I see as the clearest evidence in Conrad's oeuvre of the femininity of the East—the passage in "Youth" where Marlow arrives at his first Eastern port * * *

> "And this is how I see the East. . . . I see a bay, a wide bay, smooth as glass and polished like ice, shimmering in the dark. A red light burns far off upon the gloom of the land, and the night is soft and warm. We drag at the oars with aching arms, and suddenly a puff of wind, a puff faint and tepid and laden with strange odours of blossoms, of aromatic wood, comes out of the

3. *Joseph Conrad: Achievement and Decline* (Cambridge: Harvard UP, 1957) 46–47. In *Orientalism* (New York: Pantheon, 1978), Edward Said discusses the West's symbolic association of the East with the feminine.

still night—the first sigh of the East on my face. That I can never forget. It was impalpable and enslaving, like a charm, like a whispered promise of mysterious delight. . . . The scented obscurity of the shore was grouped into vast masses, a density of colossal clumps of vegetation probably—mute and fantastic shapes. And at their foot the semicircle of a beach gleamed faintly, like an illusion. There was not a light, not a stir, not a sound. The mysterious East faced me, perfumed like a flower, silent like death, dark like a grave.

"And I saw weary beyond expression, exulting like a conqueror, sleepless and entranced as if before a profound, a fateful enigma."[4]

The East is a locus of death indeed * * * the fearful maternal origin of life and therefore death, the womb-tomb ("perfumed like a flower, silent like death, dark like a grave"). * * *

Jim is driven farther and farther East by his "keen perception of the Intolerable"—Conrad is, in keeping with his impressionist method, tantalizing us with the intolerable "fact" (the *Patna* story) that Jim's "incognito" is designed to "hide," a fact we are not to learn for quite a while. What we do learn at the outset is that Jim's father, possessor and bequeather of that unspeakable surname, is the seemingly timeless type of the English parson, who "possessed such certain knowledge of the Unknowable as made for the righteousness of people in cottages without disturbing the ease of mind of those whom an unerring Providence enables to live in mansions" (8). In fact the parson-father is the opposite of timeless—he is eminently historical. What he represents seems about to be overthrown, for better and worse, by the twentieth century.

Conrad goes to significant lengths to establish the politics of Jim's situation: the patrimony that he has renounced/from which he is exiled (both are true) is not only almost ludicrously bankrupt ("such certain knowledge of the Unknowable") but, even more important, it is designed to maintain the status quo of class in a manner reminiscent of Marx's analysis of the function of religion in class society. Orthography and parallel structure link Jim's "Intolerable" with his father's "Unknowable." It is more than a truism to say that the most important intention in Conrad's fiction is to show that the Unknowable is not susceptible to any "certain knowledge." Perhaps it is precisely the Father's false and oppressive certainty that makes Western masculinity, with its concomitant race and class dominance, the Intolerable for Jim.

We move quickly from the parsonage of Jim's childhood to the training ship of his early manhood, where he is sent (with portentous irony) when "after a course of light holiday literature his vocation for the sea had declared itself" (8). There we see him in his characteristic posture:

4. Joseph Conrad, "Youth: A Narrative," in "*Youth*" and "*Gaspar Ruiz*" (1902; rpt. London: J. M. Dent, 1963) 37–38.

His station was in the fore-top, and often from there he looked down, with the contempt of a man destined to shine in the midst of dangers, at the peaceful multitude of roofs cut in two by the brown tide of the stream, while scattered on the outskirts of the surrounding plain the factory chimneys rose perpendicular against a grimy sky, each slender like a pencil, and belching out smoke like a volcano. He could see the big ships departing, the broad-beamed ferries constantly on the move, the little boats floating far below his feet, with the hazy splendour of the sea in the distance, and the hope of a stirring life in the world of adventure. (9)

This passage is irresistible to critics with political interests. Jameson uses it to attack modernism's conversion of the grimy "realities" of history to shining impressions, a conversion the impulse toward which he finds in the very rhythm of Conrad's sentences. I have used this passage to begin to define precisely how modernist *sous-rature* works, emphasizing narrative distance from, and irony concerning, Jim's "station . . . in the foretop," which Conrad associates with the "stirring life in the world of adventure" offered by Jim's "course of light holiday literature" * * * It is only from that lofty, self-deluded perch that grimy realities are converted to impressions, and the novel launches at this point precisely a critique of the world of masculine adventure fantasy.

Moreover, the imagery of the description of the factories undercuts this passage's distancing from industrial reality, invoking the explosive, leveling potential of industrial capitalism in the figure of the chimney "belching out smoke like a volcano." At the same time, "slender like a pencil" evokes self-reflexively—the impressionist's admonition to himself—the instability of a superficial, butterfly sort of impressionism that would attempt to fly above all darker, beetle knowledge (one thinks of a preternaturally sundrenched Monet or Renoir).[5] The writing pencil that would convert a smokestack into a pencil is slender indeed. Out of it a volcanic truth will inevitably erupt.

What holds me now in this passage is the "peaceful multitude of roofs cut in two by the brown tide of the stream," a stream that flows toward "the hazy splendour of the sea in the distance." Of course this brown stream severing peaceful roofs prefigures the geography of Jim's Patusanian village, and specifically foreshadows his confrontation with Gentleman Brown straddling that *brown* Eastern stream. "Cut in two" is a figure of some violence, particularly in conjunction with "peaceful multitude." Conrad could have used "divided" or could even have formulated the scene with the river simply running through the town. The

---

5. In the predominant symbolic configuration of this novel, the butterfly is the ideal, or logos-transcendence, while the beetle, ugly and evil but necessary, is earthbound immanence. See Tony Tanner, "Butterflies and Beetles—Conrad's Two Truths," *Chicago Review*, 16 (Winter–Spring 1963): 123–40.

violence of "cut in two" prefigures the violence of Gentleman Brown and of the novel's ending.

I would also argue that the overall tableau, including this violence, has an emblematic quality. It is an emblem of modernist *sous-rature*. The brown stream, the vaginal passage running to the hazy splendour of the oceanic maternal womb, cuts violently through the social-literary status quo, which has all along used this stream to construct itself as homogeneous on the basis of a concealed dualism or bipolarity. The town was built as one town "in two" parts on either side of this stream. But Conrad makes the stream the aggressor, cutting the town in two, and therefore revealing or making visible—putting under erasure—this bipolar structure's construction of its fallacious peace and sense of unity on the suppression of the vaginal passage. * * * The violence of this reinscribed passage ("cut in two") parallels, and is linked to, the violence of the erupting industrial volcanoes—again, the historical forces associated with the construction of modernism are the forces engendering feminism and socialism.

Jim is linked for us subliminally in this passage both to the unstable status quo, associated with the fake world of masculine adventure fantasy, and at the same time to its undoing by means of the modernist making-visible of the violent brown stream. Jim simultaneously embodies the masculine code of honor—what Marlow calls "the sovereign power enthroned in a fixed standard of conduct" (35), his adherence to which makes Jim "one of us"—and also the bankruptcy and spuriousness of that code: he raises for Marlow "*the doubt of* the sovereign power enthroned in a fixed standard of conduct" (italics added). He carries an exaggerated defense of this masculine standard with him as he drifts farther and farther toward the feminine East.

He takes the questionable berth on the *Patna* in the first place as a result of a sequence of events highly significant for this reading. Having failed the training ship test of valor as a direct result of his fantasizing on his perch in the fore-top, he finds the sea devoid of the adventure he seeks. In a horrendous gale, he experiences the "earnestness of the anger of the sea" and is "disabled by a falling spar" (11), a figure suggestive of a simultaneously toppling and punitive masculinity, a double castration (a *falling* spar *disables* Jim). As a result of his importantly unnamed injury, he "spent many days stretched on his back, dazed, battered, hopeless, and tormented as if at the bottom of an abyss of unrest" (11). Helplessness, passivity, and despair are found "at the bottom of an abyss": deprived of (a questionable) conventional masculinity, Jim falls into the abyss of the alienated maternal.

Recovering from this injury in "the white men's ward" (12) of a hospital in an Eastern port, Jim is snared by the lure of the Eastern sexual feminine: "The hospital stood on a hill, and a gentle breeze entering through the windows, always flung wide open, brought into the bare room the softness of the sky, the languor of the earth, the bewitching breath of the Eastern waters. There were perfumes in it, suggestions of infinite repose, the gift of endless dreams" (12). The sexual feminine of the East is just as alienated for this wounded but untested white male as is the abyss of the maternal.

The stage is set for the pivotal drama of the *Patna* episode. The language Conrad uses in introducing the *Patna* is loaded with implications for my concerns here. The eight hundred nonwhite, non-Western pilgrims are clearly linked with feminine water imagery: the pilgrims and the feminine are the colonized, disenfranchised volcanic force that will destroy that spurious white male Western code of honor. They are the destructive element in which Jim at first fails to immerse. * * * The repetitions of "streamed," of "flowed" and "overflowed," and of "like water" make the liquidity of the pilgrims ominous. This pilgrim-water has the same silence of potent otherness as the maternal feminine heart of darkness, like that of the maternal origin a silence filled with compelling nonsymbolic (to these Western ears) language.

The Eastern sea in which the *Patna* floats enacts figurally the drama of gender in patriarchy. During the day, "under a sky scorching and unclouded, enveloped in a fulgor of sunshine that killed all thought, oppressed the heart, withered all impulses of strength and energy"—an exaggeration of overbearing paternal logos comparable to Jim's overdone masculinity—the sea is very clearly an alienated maternal feminine: "under the sinister splendour of that sky the sea, blue and profound, remained still, without a stir, without a ripple, without a wrinkle— viscous, stagnant, dead . . . a lifeless sea . . . an abyss forever open in the wake of the ship" (14–15). But at night, the benign maternal emerges and gains ascendancy * * *:

> The nights descended on her like a benediction. . . . The propeller turned without a check, as though its beat had been part of the scheme of a safe universe; and on each side of the *Patna two deep folds of water* . . . enclosed within their straight and diverging ridges a few white swirls of foam . . . Jim on the bridge was penetrated by the great certitude of unbounded safety and peace that could be read on the silent aspect of nature *like the certitude of fostering love upon the placid tenderness of a mother's face.* (15, italics added)

Conrad could not invoke the benign and sexuate ("two deep folds of water") maternal more explicitly here.

This de-repressed, resplendent and nurturing nighttime sea (and night-time is also, of course, the "time" of the ascendant unconscious as well as of the empowered maternal feminine), not the "viscous, stagnant, dead" sea of patriarchal repression * * * is the enabling "destructive element" of modernism (by metonymy, the empowered rising water of the nighttime sea also includes the nonwhite, non-Western pilgrims, who survive unharmed the nighttime sea's devastating attack on Jim and his fellow officers). In the simultaneity of its enabling and its destroying, Conrad's "in the destructive element immerse" is a succinct formulation of modernist *sous-rature*.

In the *Patna* episode, the maternal "element" proves its "destructive"ness by throwing in the path of the ship the mysterious and deadly obstruction that changes the course of Jim's life, an obstruction that Marlow will call "the suspended menace discovered in the midst of the most perfect security" (61).

*   *   *

Jim's first jump, his jump off the *Patna*, is an initial, failed attempt to come down off his perch "aloft" in the bankrupt, juvenile literary/social text of masculine adventure fantasy. * * * He jumps down toward the destructive element of the repressed maternal, toward the lower (class) and the darker (race) of the cave of the maternal origin. However, he lands not in the destructive element itself but in a lifeboat designed to save him from it, manned by his co-conspirators in maintaining the social status quo. As Stein will instruct him (via Marlow), he can only "follow the dream" authentically if he renounces protection from the destructive element, if he in fact "immerses" in it.

*   *   *

The gendered language Marlow uses to describe the jump confirms Jim's. Marlow quotes Jim and then echoes him:

> "She seemed higher than a wall; she loomed like a cliff over the boat. . . . I wish I could die," he cried. "There was no going back. It was as if I had jumped into a well—into an everlasting deep hole." . . . Nothing could be more true: he had indeed jumped into an everlasting deep hole. . . . He told me it was like being swept by a flood through a cavern. . . . for two or three minutes the end of the world had come through a deluge in a pitchy black-ness.(70) [6]

Jim has jumped into the deep well-hole of the maternal, a hole deathly, inescapable, and overwhelming for him at this stage of the novel. Jim's first encounter with the maternal "abyss" had been entirely involuntary—it came as a result of his being "disabled by a falling spar," his first experience of deprivation of patriarchal masculine power. Its outcome was a passive alienation. In this second encounter counter he jumps voluntarily, though the motivation for the jump

---

6. Note here, for future reference, the glowing red side-light that Jim focuses on after he jumps—"he rolled over, and saw vaguely the ship he had deserted uprising above him, with the red side-light glowing large in the rain like a fire on the brow of a hill seen through a mist" (70)—and its similarity to the red light in the passage in "Youth" associating the East with the feminine: "A red light burns far off upon the gloom of the land, and the night is soft and warm" (37).

is entirely unconscious—he literally does not know what he is doing—and the destructive element he is jumping into is still fully alienated for him, both in his description of it and in the fact that he jumps into the lifeboat that simultaneously saves him from it and binds him to the worst version of the gender-race-class system that re-presses it.

The hideousness of the beetle-skipper with whom Jim has willy-nilly allied himself by jumping into the lifeboat forces the reader to acknowledge the real implications of Jim's betrayal of the pilgrims—his complicity in the attitude toward them ("Look at dese cattle" (14) that allows the officers *including Jim* to abandon ship (Marlow deliberately uses the word "deserted" (70). When Marlow watches Jim as he is on the point of finding out that the *Patna* did not in fact sink, he expects to see him "overwhelmed, confounded, pierced through and through, squirming like an impaled beetle" (30). At the same time, in the lifeboat sequence the beetle-skipper is associated with the tyranny of the phallus and of its oppressive ownership of language (he *becomes* a relentlessly talking erect phallus):

> The skipper started swearing, as hoarse as a crow. He wasn't going to talk at the top of his voice for *my* accommodation. "Are you afraid they will hear you on shore?" I asked. He glared as if he would have liked to claw me to pieces. The chief engineer advised him to humour me. He said I wasn't right in my head yet. The other rose *astern*, like a thick pillar of flesh—and talked—talked. (77, italics added)

* * *

Stein's story of the capture of the rare butterfly specimen he is examining when Marlow finds him is a parable of the impossible dialectic of death and life, immanence and transcendence, feminine and masculine, that is summarized by "in the destructive element immerse." * * *

Stein rides "four or five miles . . . there had been rain in the night, but the mists had gone up, up—and the face of the earth was clean; it lay smiling to me, so fresh and innocent—like a little child" (126). Stein and his princess have a daughter, Emma, a brown girl with a European name. The clean, "innocent" "face of the earth," suggestive of Stein's child (who, with the princess her mother, is shortly to die), immediately becomes the site of treachery and slaughter: an ambush by Stein's enemies. The innocence and freshness are not, however, a delusion or a snare—they *coexist with* treachery and death. Immediately following the phrase "like a little child" comes, "Suddenly somebody fires a volley—twenty shots at least it seemed to me." Stein feigns death, falling forward on his horse's neck, using death to preserve his life. Stein shoots his attackers as they approach him—they believe his ruse—and "then I sit alone on my horse with the clean earth smiling at me, and there are the bodies of three men lying on the ground" (127).

Conrad could not make clearer the coexistence, the cohabitation of the "clean earth smiling" and the death that he carefully makes hideous: "one was curled up like a dog, another on his back had an arm over his eyes as if to keep off the sun, and the third man he draws up his leg very slowly and makes it with one kick straight again" (127).

Now comes the miraculous moment (I feel compelled to report here that it gives me chills every time):

> And as I looked at his face for some sign of life [the man who had horribly kicked his leg] I observed something like a faint shadow pass over his forehead. It was the shadow of this butterfly. Look at the form of the wing. This species fly high with a strong flight. I raised my eyes and I saw him fluttering away. I think—Can it be possible? And then I lost him. . . . At last I saw him sitting on a small heap of dirt ten feet away. . . . I got him! . . . On that day I had nothing to desire . . . even what I had once dreamed in my sleep had come into my hand, too! (127)

Just as he advises Marlow, Stein follows his dream (*the* dream—the unconscious) by immersing in the destructive element. The shadow of the butterfly appears on the forehead of the man Stein has killed. But Stein doesn't actually catch the butterfly—the thing itself rather than its shadow—until it lands "on a small heap of dirt," so suggestive of the maternal feminine as well as of death (the grave). Jim will not be able to follow his dream until he acknowledges his connectedness to the earth, dirt, the feminine: "This magnificent butterfly finds a little heap of dirt and sits still on it; but man he will never on his heap of mud keep still" (128).

Stein, inscribing the modernist moment of social-textual transformation, then rewrites the parable of Plato's cave. I will follow this crucial modernist parable sentence by sentence. "A man that is born falls into a dream like a man who falls into the sea" (129). This dream is the opposite of Jim's fore-top life of adventure fantasy, of escapist wish-fulfillment; this is precisely the falling-down that Jim initiated but avoided when he jumped from the *Patna* not into the destructive element but into the lifeboat. This dream has to do with being born and with the sea: it is the dream again as representation of the realm of the repressed maternal-unconscious, a representation in the image of which modernist form evolved.

"If he tries to climb out into the air as inexperienced people endeavour to do, he drowns—*nicht war?*" (129). Climbing out into the air from a sea-dream into which one falls at birth would seem to figure a positive, appropriate emergence from infancy, the presymbolic, the attachment to the mother's body, into the air, the only element that supports human life. "Climb out" suggests worthy endeavor, and the movement upward from sea to air recapitulates the Platonic trajectory from cave to sunlight. But this attempt to climb out into the air is one that only "inexperienced people" make, and when they do, they drown. As I read this, the time is past, historically, when the sea-dream, the destructive element, the lower-down and darker otherness of gender, race, and class can simply be left behind, remaining suppressed, invisible, and silent. The attempt to maintain that suppression will result in that deadly rising of the water that (figurally) drowned Conrad's unreconstructed representative of upper-class Western white male hegemony, Alvan Hervey, in "The Return." This suppression must be undone, and an alliance must be forged with the ineluctably powerful destructive element.

"No! I tell you! The way is to the destructive element submit yourself, and with the exertions of your hands and feet in the water make the deep, deep sea keep you up" (129). The verbs in this sentence constitute a fabulous conjuncture of passivity and activity, opposition and alliance, submission and manipulation, hostility and awe. The conceit of the entire parable is swimming as opposed to drowning—the "inexperienced" person in the water flails about, desperately attempting to get out, and therefore drowns; the good swimmer attempts to become one with the water, making the movements of "hands and feet" that will keep him afloat. This, however, is only the surface story. The crucial pair of verbs in this sentence is "submit" and "make": only by genuinely jumping into the destructive element, a jump that Stein reformulates on the next page as an immersion—a renunciation of will, mastery, control, dominance—can "you" then harness the power of the destructive element by appropriate "exertions of your hands and feet" and "*make*" it "keep you up." Will can only be exerted effectively in the destructive element *after* submission to it; submission and will conjoined form a productive alliance.

*   *   *

In Patusan, Jim immerses in the destructive element and for a time follows his dream. Again, the destructive element is constituted by dark-skinned race as well as the sexuate maternal feminine.

*   *   *

Marlow distrusts Jim's Patusan triumph. He assumes in this section of the novel a softened, open-minded version of the famous Conradian conservatism, a conservatism enunciated at its extreme point in the beliefs Marlow attributes to the recipient of his letter narrating Jim's end:

> I remember well you would not admit he had mastered his fate. You prophesied for him the disaster of weariness and of disgust with acquired honour, with the self-appointed task, with the love sprung from pity and youth. You had said you knew so well "that kind of thing," its illusory satisfaction, its unavoidable deception. You said also—I call to mind—that "giving your life up to them"

(*them* meaning all of mankind with skins brown, yellow, or black in colour) "was like selling your soul to a brute." You contended that "that kind of thing" was only endurable and enduring when based on a firm conviction in the truth of ideas racially our own, in whose name are established the order, the morality of an ethical progress.(201)

Marlow's tone in reporting this familiar ideology is just ironic enough to distance, but not to detach him from it: "I affirm nothing" (201).

Marlow's own racism (and sexism) are decidedly more tempered than the letter recipient's, but they frame his view of Jim's experience in Patusan. Marlow dislikes Patusan. He describes his first view of it in highly sexual and markedly negative imagery:

The coast of Patusan (I saw it nearly two years afterwards) is straight and sombre, and faces a misty ocean. Red trails are seen like cataracts of rust streaming under the dark green foliage of brushes and creepers clothing the low cliffs. Swampy plains open out at the mouth of rivers, with a view of jagged blue peaks beyond the vast forests. In the offing a chain of islands, dark, crumbling shapes, stand out in the everlasting sunlit haze like the remnants of a wall breached by the sea.(146)

The "red trails . . . like cataracts of rust streaming under the dark green foliage" is as explicit a menstrual image as one is likely to find in Conrad.

Marlow attributes to Jim the gloomy view of Patusanian geography evident in this passage as "pathetic" projection of a cosmic depression:

At the first bend he [Jim] lost sight of the sea with its labouring waves for ever rising, sinking, and vanishing to rise again—the very image of struggling mankind—and faced the immovable forests rooted deep in the soil, soaring towards the sunshine, everlasting in the shadowy might of their tradition, like life itself. And his opportunity sat veiled by his side like an Eastern bride waiting to be uncovered by the hand of the master.(147)

But Jim's "opportunity" proves to be nothing like a veiled Eastern bride, and Jewel herself takes Jim's fate in her hands. The image of the veiled Eastern bride, like the tedious abstraction in the above passage ("the very image of struggling mankind"), bespeaks an uneasiness with the radical implications of Jim's actual experience in Patusan.

* * *

The imagery in which Jim's Patusanian rebirth is embedded reveals the text's positive valuation of the maternal origin that Marlow's anti-female ideology functions to counteract and obscure. This time, when Jim jumps, he actually lands in the destructive element rather than in a "life boat," and he takes refuge with nonwhite, non-Western people of both genders rather than with the degraded, corrupt representatives of his own ruling class, race, and gender. After flying over Tunku Allang's stockade like a butterfly, Jim leaps again. "He took off from the last dry spot, felt himself flying through the air, felt himself, without any shock, planted upright in an extremely soft and sticky mudbank" (152). Jim finally lands on (in) the mud, the mound of earth, as Stein's butterfly does.

In this maternal mudbank he flounders for what seems like an eternity. The description of this floundering is very like a description of a difficult birth: "He made efforts, tremendous sobbing, gasping efforts, efforts that seemed to burst his eyeballs in their sockets and make him blind, and culminating into one mighty supreme effort in the darkness to crack the earth asunder, to throw it off his limbs—and he felt himself creeping feebly up the bank" (153). He has immersed in the destructive element and emerged to follow his shining dream, heroically liberating the village from its oppression by Sherif Ali, with the help of the worthy Bugis of Doramin, *using* the vaginal geography of Patusan's two hills for his daring defeat of that brigand and then becoming Patusan's just and beloved Tuan Jim, with Jewel always at his side. It is significant that the character Conrad emphasizes in Doramin's compound, when Jim first reaches it after his rebirth, is Doramin's "old wife," who is kind to Jim. We have heard nothing of Jim's actual mother, only his parson-father of the unmentionable surname. In his Patusanian rebirth, Jim has acquired a good mother.[7]

The stunning, redeeming, heroic defeat of Sherif Ali could not have occurred without Jewel. Her agency is a crucial goad to the passivity Jim lapses into when he leaves Doramin to take over Stein's company compound after his escape from Rajah Allang's stockade. With the help of her initiative, Jim overcomes Cornelius's corruption of Stein's enter-prise. It is she who takes the lead in the first defeat of Sherif Ali's men, keeping vigil, waking Jim in the night and virtually forcing him to defend himself, thrusting the red torch—the glowing red light of the benign sexuate maternal—through the window of the storehouse in which Sherif Ali's men lie in wait to kill Jim. As the men surrender, one of them calls Jim "Tuan."

In narrating the storehouse episode (reminiscent, of course, of Stein's ambush parable) and in his treatment of Jewel in general, Marlow emphasizes her union with Jim and its redeeming quality: "Their soft murmurs reached me, penetrating, tender . . . like a self-communion of one being carried on in two tones" (169). Further: "he realised that for him there was no refuge from that lone-

---

7. Though Jim describes Doramin's wife as a "little, motherly witch of a wife" with a "sharp chin," Conrad has her speak movingly and with the authority of the "vast prospect": "Without removing her eyes from the vast prospect of forests stretching as far as the hills, she asked me in a pitying voice why was it that he so young had wandered from his home, coming so far, through so many dangers? Had he no household there, no kinsmen in his own country? Had he no old mother, who would always remember his face?" (164).

liness which centupled all his dangers except—in her. 'I thought,' he said to me, 'that if I went away from her it would be the end of everything somehow.' . . . He let her follow him without thinking of any protest, as if they had been indissolubly united" (178). Jim's union with Jewel, a brown woman, is, quite simply, his salvation. When he abandons her to "celebrate his pitiless wedding with a shadowy ideal of conduct," a shadowy ideal that makes him "one of us" and that is elsewhere described as a "firm conviction in the truth of ideas racially our own, in whose name are established the order, the morality of an ethical progress," it *is* "the end of everything."

The narration of Jim's Patusanian triumph unfolds toward Jewel. We get the story of Jim's war against Sherif Ali before "the story of his love" that precedes that war chronologically. This narrative positioning heightens the effect of the storehouse episode, making it, rather than the rout of Sherif Ali, the dramatic culmination of Jim's success. Further, Marlow has much more trouble telling "the story of his love," because it is a different kind of story altogether from the familiar masculine saga of the successful military venture.[8] If it were the kind of love story it seems to the letter recipient to be, Marlow would not have such trouble telling it; it would be just as familiar as the tale of military exploit. Even Conrad's embarrassment and inadequacy in the narration of sexual material would not produce precisely this disclaimer, which I cite in full because of its importance to my argument:

> I suppose you think it [the story of his love] is a story that you can imagine for yourselves. We have heard so many such stories, and the majority of us don't believe them to be stories of love at all. For the most part we look upon them as stories of opportunities: episodes of passion at best, or perhaps only of youth and temptation, doomed to forgetfulness in the end, even if they pass through the reality of tenderness and regret. This view mostly is right, and perhaps in this case, too. . . . [sic] Yet I don't know. To tell this story is by no means so easy as it should be—*were the ordinary standpoint adequate.* Apparently it is a story very much like the others: for me, however, there is visible in its background the melancholy figure of a woman, the shadow of a cruel wisdom buried in a lonely grave, looking on wistfully, helplessly, with sealed lips. The grave itself, as I came upon it during an early morning stroll, was a rather shapeless brown mound, with an inlaid neat border of white lumps of coral at the base, and enclosed within a circular fence made of split saplings, with the bark left on. A garland of leaves and flowers was woven about the heads of the slender posts—and the flowers were fresh. (165, italics added)

8. Also, of course, because of what Moser calls the "uncongenial subject."

"The ordinary standpoint" is not "adequate" to this modernist treatment of the feminine. The conventional love story, which, because it involves a white European man and a brown non-Western woman, does not even qualify to "the majority of us" as a *love* story at all, cannot accommodate this material, *because* there is visible in its background the melancholy figure of a buried, silenced, horribly oppressed woman, whose position in this text is that of the mother.

As always with Conrad, the details of this passage invite explication. The stories that are not love stories at all appear to "the majority of us" as "stories of opportunities"—remember that Jim's "opportunity" was supposed to have been always at his side "like a veiled Eastern bride." However, the story of Jim and Jewel is *not* a story of the kind of "opportunity" Marlow imagines his audience to construct—it is a story of immersion in the destructive element. "The veiled Eastern bride" is just as spurious as the "ordinary standpoint" of "the majority of us." Marlow clearly dissociates himself here from the point of view of "the majority of us" that he is carefully deferring to; that is the entire point of the necessity for Conrad of inventing a new narrative form that problematizes "the ordinary standpoint." The "us" Jim is "one of," the "we" to whom women appear a separate species, "the majority of us" who are so cynical about Jim and Jewel, are precisely the dominant race, gender, and class whose "shadowy ideal of conduct," the "idea racially our own," constitutes the "ordinary standpoint" that this modernist narrative puts under erasure.

The origin of that erasure is figured as the mother's grave, *not* the mother-as-grave. The first emphasis is on the mother herself, "melancholy," "buried in a lonely grave, looking on wistfully, helplessly, with sealed lips." Jewel's mother, the woman's mother rather than the man's, is a figure of pathos rather than terror, whose maternal silence, here at least, is no longer ominous or imposing but rather signals, as in truth it does, suppression.

The description of the mother's grave, the familiar maternal feminine figure of the "shapeless brown mound," reminds us of the crucial mound of earth on which the butterfly alights ("small" or "little heap of dirt," "heap of mud" [127–28]. This brown mound, however, is distinguished by "an inlaid neat border of white lumps of coral at the base." The dread vaginal teeth, seemingly an inevitable component of sexuate maternal figuration for Conrad, have become here harmless, orderly, small, totally nonthreatening, even poignantly decorative. Moreover, they are made of coral: "of his bones are coral made."[9] Without insisting on this point or pushing it too far, I would suggest that this harmless, pathetic grave, garlanded about with fresh leaves and flowers suggesting rebirth, incor-

9. Shakespeare, *The Tempest* 1.2.398. "Sea-change," just below, and De Koven's book title, *Rich and Strange*, are also allusions to Ariel's song in *The Tempest* [*Editor*].

porates the sea-change of the paternal as an element of the modernist impossible dialectic.

We need not rely for this reading of the significance of Jewel's mother on the above passage alone. Jewel tells Marlow that she does not want to die weeping, as her mother did: " 'My mother had wept bitterly before she died,' she explained" (186). This simple statement produces in Marlow a remarkable reaction: "An inconceivable calmness seemed to have risen from the ground around us, imperceptibly, like the still rise of a flood in the night, obliterating the familiar landmarks of emotions. There came upon me, as though I had felt myself losing my footing in the midst of waters, a sudden dread, the dread of the unknown depths" (186). In the clearest possible figuration in light of my argument here, Conrad shows us Marlow feeling the force of the destructive element as a direct result of understanding the oppression of women.

Jewel explains that Cornelius tried to enter her mother's death chamber, but Jewel, at her mother's order, succeeded in keeping him out. As Jewel keeps her shoulder on the door, with Cornelius shoving on the other side and yelling "Let me in! Let me in! Let me in!"

> "The tears fell from her eyes, and then she died," concluded the girl in an imperturbable monotone, which more than anything else, more than the white statuesque immobility of her person, more than mere words could do, troubled my mind profoundly with the passive, irremediable horror of the scene. It had the power to drive me out of my conception of existence, out of that shelter each of us makes for himself to creep under in moments of danger, as a tortoise withdraws within its shell. For a moment I had a view of a world that seemed to wear a vast and dismal aspect of disorder, while, in truth, thanks to our unwearied efforts, it is as sunny an arrangement of small conveniences as the mind of man can conceive. But still—it was only a moment: I went back into my shell directly. One *must*—don't you know?—though I seemed to have lost all my words in the chaos of dark thoughts I had contemplated for a second or two beyond the pale. These came back, too, very soon, for words also belong to the sheltering conception of light and order which is our refuge. (186)

Again, Marlow is intermediary in this novel between convention and the radical rewriting of the social and literary text proposed by modernity, positioned precisely in the space this novel's modernist *sous-rature* defines. He is sufficiently a conventional soul, "one of us," with whom the white male Western reader can identify, by whom he would not feel threatened. Yet he has wider imagination and a larger moral sensibility than "one of us" generally has. He knows at some level that the "truth" of the "sunny arrangement of small conveniences" (a phrase suggesting both logos and technology) is in fact a tortoise shell under which "one *must*" take refuge to protect oneself from that other truth of a vast and dismal disorder, a silent chaos of dark thoughts, associated here, again, not with the mother herself, as in patriarchal ideology, but with the oppression/suppression of the mother (in the person of Cornelius, and, significantly, of the antifemale social convention that forced Jewel's mother to marry him).

Jewel herself is figured as the destructive element. Her eyes are just the same sort of deep well that Jim lands in when he jumps off the *Patna*, and her teeth are not harmless:

> It was dark under the projecting roof, and all I could see were the flowing lines of her gown, the pale, small oval of her face, with the white flash of her teeth, and, turned towards me, the big, sombre orbits of her eyes, where there seemed to be a faint stir, such as you may fancy you can detect when you plunge your gaze to the bottom of an immensely deep well. What is it that moves there? you ask yourself. Is it a blind monster or only a lost gleam from the universe? (182–83)

The destructiveness of the feminine element is a crucial part of the modernist *sous-rature* of this novel. Again, the other truth of which Marlow gets fitful glimpses is horrific to him, terrifying as well as redeeming, as it was to Conrad and to the male modernist writers who followed him. Even the harmless, pathetic grave of the mother can, in a certain cracked moonlight, reacquire its sinister, fearful, death-dealing patriarchal lineaments. Note in the following not only the remarkable chaplet of bleached skulls but also the *coal-black* [vaginal] double summit, the *black* crack across the face of the moon (again, the chained feminine monster is linked to blackness), the cavern, the heavily reiterated shadows, the deathliness, the warm, heavy incense, and the stumps of felled trees—a litany of Conradian alienation from the maternal feminine:

> The big hill rearing its double summit coal-black in the clear, yellow glow of the rising moon, seemed to cast its shadow upon the ground . . . raising my eyes, I saw part of the moon glittering through the bushes at the bottom of the chasm. . . . it disengaged itself from the tangle of twigs; the bare, contorted limb of some tree, growing on the slope, made a black crack right across its face. It threw its level rays afar as if from a cavern, and in this mournful eclipse-like light the stumps of felled trees uprose very dark, the heavy shadows fell at my feet on all sides, my own moving shadow, and across my path the shadow of the solitary grave perpetually garlanded with flowers. In the darkened moonlight the interlaced blossoms took on shapes foreign to one's memory and colours indefinable to the eye, as though they had been special flowers gathered by no

> man, grown not in this world, and destined for the use of the dead
> alone. Their powerful scent hung in the warm air, making it thick
> and heavy like the fumes of incense. The lumps of white coral
> shone round the dark mound like a chaplet of bleached skulls. (191)

The feeling inspired in Marlow by this scene is precisely the "feeling
which has incited me to tell you the story, to try to hand over to you,
as it were, its very existence, its reality—the truth disclosed in a moment
of illusion" (192). "The truth disclosed in a moment of illusion": Conradian impressionism, modernist *sous-rature*.

In the end, Conrad decides that Jim is, after all, too white, too much
one of us, to sustain the remarkable fusion with the brown and the
female that he temporarily achieves in Patusan. In the final sequence
—the written narrative Marlow mails to the novel's ultimate representative of one-of-us-ness—Jim's whiteness, de-emphasized in the previous
section (except for the tiny white speck at the end), suddenly becomes
the most important thing about him, defining his foil relationship to
"Brown": "Brown saw in a knot of coloured figures motionless between
the advanced houses a man in European clothes, in a helmet, all
white"(225). * * *

Jim is ineluctably white, European, a ruler: "Patusan was recovering
its belief in the stability of earthly institutions since the return of the
white lord" (230). He is also, for all his immersion in the river mud,
still (or again) a butterfly susceptible to defeat by the return of his own
repressed beetlehood as embodied in Gentleman Brown, in cahoots with
the ultimate beetle Cornelius. In fact, Brown and Jim meet "not very
far from the place, perhaps on the very spot, where Jim took the second
desperate leap of his life—the leap that landed him into the life of
Patusan, into the trust, the love, the confidence of the people" (225).
Presumably, Conrad's locating Jim's defeat by Brown on that spot
is designed to negate the rebirth, the immersion in the destructive element, that occurred there. I would argue that the negation is not ret-
roactive; that, to put it colloquially, the rebirth was real while it lasted.
It is (not surprisingly) put under erasure rather than proven false. (The
doubles relationship between Jim and Gentleman Brown, down to the
complementarity of their half-names, is too well documented to require
rehearsal here.)

The hegemonic status quo is inadequately reimposed at the end of
this novel. * * * Marlow describes Gentleman Brown as "a blind accomplice of the Dark Powers" (210): Dark Powers have again become
capitalized, returned to their consummate evil and inaccessible otherness. The difference, I would argue, is that the status quo is clearly
reimposed here in the character of a dire and discredited inevitability,
even to the point of Conrad's inviting us to judge Jim negatively for his

adherence to it, his "pitiless wedding with a shadowy ideal of conduct."
I see the relentless emphasis on Jim's whiteness as a measure of Conrad's
disengagement from all that whiteness signifies, a disengagement revealed by his finding it ridiculous even as he invites us to admire it.

I would like to consider in some detail Conrad's treatment of the letter
recipient.[1] He is "the privileged man" (200), privileged because he is
the only one "of all these listeners ever to hear the last word of the story"
(200), but the phrase itself ("privileged man") has other (rather obvious
in relation to my preoccupations here) suggestions. He is important, of
course, because the reader assumes his position at this point in the text.
Until now, the reader was positioned as part of an undefined, anonymous
group of listeners, a situation that more or less reproduces the condition
of actual readership. Now that position changes markedly, and the reader
must deal with the text's pressure simultaneously to identify and resist
identification with a carefully located and specified single character, a
character who, as we have seen, is credited with an extreme version of
hegemonic racism and sexism.

Conrad's description of this man distances us radically from, and
fundamentally discredits, the position we must assume as his co-
recipients of the letter: in other words, our complicity in his "standpoint."
Before he reads the contents of his packet, this man looks out of his
window:

> His rooms were in the highest flat of a lofty building, and his glance
> could travel afar beyond the clear panes of glass, as though he were
> looking out of the lantern of a lighthouse. The slopes of the roofs
> glistened, the dark, broken ridges succeeded each other without
> end like sombre, uncrested waves, and from the depths of the town
> under his feet ascended a confused and unceasing mutter. The
> spires of churches, numerous, scattered haphazard, uprose like
> beacons on a maze of shoals without a channel; the driving rain
> mingled with the falling dusk of a winter's evening; and the booming
> of a big clock on a tower, striking the hour, rolled past in volu-
> minous, austere bursts of sound, with a shrill, vibrating cry at the
> core. He drew the heavy curtains. (200)

This passage recalls Jim's fore-top view of the town and sea at the
beginning of the novel. We have returned to a state of alienation, a
vantage point too high up and too detached: too "privileged." Evidently,
the tone of this passage is entirely different from that early, light, hopeful
(if quietly ominous) fore-top vision. It is bleak and almost despairing,
deathly, the end of the story, overwhelmed by the Dark Powers as figured,
tellingly, in ocean imagery. This man stays high and dry only by drawing
his curtains and *with*drawing from the world into his privilege, a privilege

1. See also Linda M. Shires, "The 'Privileged' Reader and Narrative Methodology in *Lord Jim*,"
Conradiana 17.1 (Winter 1985): 19–30.

synonymous with isolation and moribundity. His windows may be clear, but he can't see through them. "The light of his shaded reading lamp slept like a sheltered pool . . . his wandering days were over" (200). Stein's wandering days were over too, but his reading lamp lit up a corner of his otherwise dark museum of immersion in the destructive element. No heavy curtains shut out the darkness for him.

In the packet this man receives, in addition to the cover letter and long narrative written by Marlow and the fragment written by Jim, is a yellowed old letter from his father that Jim has evidently treasured, "found carefully preserved in his writing-case" (202). Jim has remained faithful, in the end, to the law of the Father. But what to Jim was a profoundly important document, we see, with Marlow's help, as "easy morality and family news . . . The old chap goes on equably trusting Providence and the established order of the universe. . . . One can almost see him, grey-haired and serene in the inviolable shelter of his book-lined, faded, and comfortable study, where for forty years he had conscientiously gone over and over again the round of his little thoughts about faith and virtue" (202). For this shadowy ideal of conduct, these little thoughts about faith and virtue, ideas racially our own, Jim, in his "exalted egoism," "goes away from a living woman." Appropriately, Jim's choice is aligned with the "standpoint" of the "privileged reader," stand-in for the father, and the Father, who "screwed up his lamp, and solitary above the billowy roofs of the town, like a lighthouse-keeper above the sea," ultimate figure of hegemonic, hierarchical masculinity, "turned to the pages of the story" (208).

Jim dies *following* a bankrupt Western masculine code of honor, enforced by the brown ("Brown") man who saved him after his Patu-sanian rebirth; a brown man who kills Jim as a father avenging the death of his own son. * * * The [novel's] central question concerns the efficacy or success of the protagonist's response to the modern challenge to rewrite the social text. Does Jim follow the dream *"usque ad finem"* by immersing successfully in the destructive element, or was his Patu-sanian triumph of fusion with the other always a delusion, Gentleman Brown always waiting in the wings of his own psyche? * * * the question is unanswered, or the answer is "both": the irresolvable ambivalence of modernist *sous-rature* * * * [in which] the twentieth-century challenge to rewrite the social text produced the modernist literary text.

DAPHNA ERDINAST-VULCAN

The Failure of Myth: *Lord Jim*†

The following discussion of *Lord Jim* will focus on the problematic structural rift in the novel, the transition from the story of the *Patna* and its consequences (chapters 1–21) to the story of Patusan (chapters 22–45). Conrad himself had referred to this transition as a "plague spot" in the novel, an epithet which was later followed by an almost unanimous, if qualified to various degrees, critical dismissal of the second part as a regrettable artistic lapse. Thus, when Ian Watt discusses the "intractable contradiction between the basic terms of [Conrad's] previous [i.e. *Patna*] and his present [i.e. Patusan] narrative assumptions," he registers "a sense of reduced complexity and rapid confluence of the narrative elements," and John Batchelor argues that the Patusan part of the novel has "a curiously simple moral polarity, a brightly coloured flatness . . . It is as though the end of *Lord Jim* were drawn from a part of Conrad's mind different from, and shallower than, the consciousness that has created the bulk of the novel."[1]

A somewhat crude but useful distinction can be made between "first generation" and "second generation" critics of the novel.[2] The former group, including eminent scholars like Thomas Moser and A. J. Guerard, largely avoids the ethical problematics of the novel, the unresolved questions posed by the first part, and posits a stable ethical code by which Jim's story is to be judged. Moser's pioneering study is symptomatic of this approach in its definition of Conrad's ethic as founded on the "simple principles" of fidelity, stoic humanism, and solidarity with the community in a godless universe, a moral hierarchy which, according to Moser, is "implicit on every page".[3]

The critics of the latter group, including T. Tanner, C. B. Cox, J. Hillis Miller, and others, regard the novel as a distinctly modernist expression. Having registered the effect of extreme ethical relativism where moral judgement is well-nigh impossible, these "second generation" critics present the open-endedness of the moral dilemmas in the

---

† ©Daphna Erdinast-Vulcan 1991. Reprinted from *Joseph Conrad and the Modern Temper* by Daphna Erdinast-Vulcan (1991) by permission of Oxford UP. This selection has been edited for publication here; asterisks indicate deletions. Parenthetical page numbers refer to The Uniform Edition (London: J. M. Dent, 1923); bracketed page numbers refer to this Norton Critical Edition.

1. Ian Watt, *Conrad in the Nineteenth Century* (Berkeley: U of California P, 1979) 307–8; John Batchelor, *The Edwardian Novelists* (London: Buckworth, 1982) 46.
2. This classification of critical approaches does not pretend to do justice to the complexity and particular insights of the interpretations under discussion, but as the purpose of this discussion is to suggest an alternative approach, I have chosen to resort to this schematic mode of presentation.
3. Thomas C. Moser, *Joseph Conrad: Achievement and Decline* (Cambridge: Harvard UP, 1957) 10–49.

first part of the novel as its ultimate stance. The "meaning" of the novel is thus construed as the Absence of Meaning, the invalidation of all metaphysical, epistemological, and ethical certainties.[4]

My own view is that, while the novel is undoubtedly foregrounded against the spiritual and ethical malaise of modernity, it is not merely a reflection of the modern temper but an active, if desperate, attempt to defeat it by a regression to a mythical mode of discourse. This regression, effected by the transition to Patusan, is at the core of the structural rift in the novel.

The second issue which emerges from the first part of the novel as an axis of critical interpretation is the character of Jim himself. Guerard describes Jim as "a rather adolescent dreamer and 'romantic' with a strong ego-ideal, who prefers solitary reveries of heroism to the shock and bustle of active life. . . . He has a strong visual imagination and vividly foresees the worst. . . . He differs from other introverted dreamers chiefly in the degree of his Bovarysme; he can literally confuse reality and dream at times. . . . He tries to live his dream." Thomas Moser relates Jim to a long line of Conradian heroes: romantic egoists, dreamers who idealize their self-deceptions and distort reality in their obsession with the fixed idea of their own greatness. Berthoud also defines Jim as "unfit for reality" because he has "exchanged his real self with an ideal self" and attributes his jump from the *Patna* to a "prolonged habit of self-deception".[5]

These analyses of Jim's character and his sense of identity are founded on a neat distinction between facts and ideas, truth and fiction, reality and illusion, "real" self and self-ideal, where the first term in each pair of opposites is a reflection of a desired standard, and the second is a form of deviation. I believe that such a distinction, however essential as a working hypothesis in everyday life, is seriously questioned in the novel: through Marlow's distinction between the "facts" and the "truth" in Jim's case (56) [37]; by his realization of "the convention that lurks in all truth and . . . the essential sincerity of falsehood" (93) [59]; by his participation in "the spirit of his [Jim's] illusion" (109) [69] and his reluctant admission of his own part in "the fellowship of . . . illusions" (128) [79].

Marlow, ostensibly the spokesman for solid British common sense and decency, is forced to recognize the optical illusions that turn the most ostensibly tangible sights and sounds into deceptive phantoms (113–15, 135) [70–72, 83]; the grey area between what is "a lie" and what

---

4. Tony Tanner, "Butterflies and Beetles—Conrad's Two Truths," *Chicago Review* 16 (Winter–Spring 1963): 123–40; C. B. Cox, *Joseph Conrad: The Modern Imagination* (London: J. M. Dent & Sons, 1974) 19–44; J. Hillis Miller, *Fiction and Repetition* (Cambridge: Harvard UP, 1982) 22–41.
5. A. J. Guerard, *Conrad the Novelist* (Cambridge: Harvard UP, 1958) 140–41; Moser, *Achievement and Decline* 30–33; Jacques Berthoud, *Joseph Conrad: The Major Phase* (Cambridge: Cambridge UP, 1978) 72–73.

is "not true" (130) [80]; and the inadequacy of the judgement of that "expert in possession of the facts" (146) [89], the admirable French Lieutenant. His final acknowledgement of the universal need for "some such truth or some such illusion—I don't care how you call it, there is so little difference, and the difference means so little" (111) [135], is a painful diagnosis of a state of epistemological uncertainty which is so closely linked to the problem of ethical indeterminacy.

The relationship of these two aspects of the novel is significant: [Alasdair] MacIntyre argues that "man is in his actions and practice, as well as in his fictions, essentially a story-telling animal. He is not essentially, but becomes through his history, a teller of stories that aspire to truth. . . . We enter human society . . . with one or more imputed character-roles into which we have been drafted—and we have to learn what they are in order to be able to understand how others respond to us and how our responses to them are apt to be construed. . . . Mythology, in its original sense, is at the heart of things."[6] According to the narrative view of the self, "the story of my life is always embedded in the story of those communities from which I derive my identity." The predicament of modern ethics results, according to MacIntyre, from "the lack of any such unifying [narrative] conception of a human life" and from its conception of ethics as distinct from and prior to the social context (the narrative) of the individual.[7]

MacIntyre's theory clearly suggests that one's sense of identity and the ethical code by which one chooses to live are both the products of a fictional self-perception (i.e. as assumption of a certain role in a hypothetical narrative). This theory, which defies the traditional distinction between the spheres of ethics and psychology, is illuminating for a reading of *Lord Jim*. The structural rift in the novel, the fault-line between the *Patna* and the Patusan sections, marks the willed effort of the character to enter another story, as it were, to construct his identity and find a new ethical orientation in a different textual sphere.

Jim is leading a fictional life. Like other Conrad characters * * * he constructs his identity in a literary context, viewing himself as a protagonist in an imaginary story. The ethical code he must obey is embedded in the generic conventions of the narrative (the courage of the hero in impossible circumstances), and Jim's self-assigned role in the fiction provides him with a psychological and a moral point of reference. His decision to become a seaman was occasioned by "a course of light holiday literature" (5) [8], and his image of himself as a seaman is nurtured on

6. Alasdair MacIntyre, *After Virtue: A Study in Moral Theory*, 2d ed. (1st ed. 1981; London: Duckworth, 1985) 216. Further page references appear parenthetically below [*Editor*].

7. MacIntyre, *After Virtue* 221–25. A narrative view of the self has been presented by postmodern theorists, such as Lyotard and Butor, but MacIntyre's theory is more relevant to the present discussion because narrative, for him, is not a fictional-and-therefore-fictitious construct. It is a form of ethical, as well as epistemological, mediation between consciousness and world which can be validated by the protagonists' acts.

adventure stories: "He saw himself saving people from sinking ships.
. . . He confronted savages on tropical shores, quelled mutinies on the
high seas, and in a small boat upon the ocean kept up the hearts of
despairing men—always an example of devotion to duty, and as unflinching as a hero in a book" (6) [9]. The use of the adjective "unflinching" in this introductory passage and at the very end of Jim's story
when, with an "unflinching glance," he faces his death, is, as noted by
one of the critics, a framing device designed to illuminate Jim's entire
life as conceived by a single vision.[8]

But as MacIntyre so convincingly argues in his definition of man as
"a story-telling animal," this process (whereby identity is derived from
a role in a narrative view of human life) is not necessarily a pathological
peculiarity. We all construe our sense of identity in terms of our role
in the narrative we are part of, and this fictional identity is not necessarily
fictitious as long as one can maintain some measure of congruence
between the fictional ego-ideal and one's actual conduct. Marlow himself
is forced into an admission of the universal need for some sort of "moral
posture" (41 [29], my emphasis), for some sort of sustaining faith which
may be either truth or illusion (222) [135]. When an individual realizes,
as Jim does after his jump from the *Patna*, that the fictional role has
become manifestly fictitious, that it is no longer tenable, he or she is
bound to experience an identity crisis.

In the situation on board the *Patna* as perceived by the officers, the
sinking of the ship within a few moments from the apparently fatal
collision seemed to be inevitable. Marlow himself is impelled to admit:
"Frankly, had I been there I would not have given as much as a counterfeit farthing for the ship's chances to keep above water to the end of
each successive second. . . . Their escape would trouble me as a prodigiously inexplicable event . . ." (97–8) [62]. The only force that could
have made Jim stay on board would have been an indomitable adherence
to his heroic ego-ideal. His illusion (or ego-ideal) has failed to sustain
him when all other potential supports of his identity—the eye of others,
the possibility of action, the light of day—have been snatched away
from under his feet. His problem is not, as suggested by some, that his
illusion is overwhelmingly strong, but simply that it is *not strong enough*.

I would like, at this point, to introduce the concept of "identifiction"
to denote a literary text or genre on which a fictional character construes
his or her identity. The use of the term might, I hope, indicate the
distinction between a generic model which reflects the intentions of the
author, and a text or a genre which serves as a point of reference for
the characters themselves in the definition of their identity and the
management of their lives. Emma Bovary, whose identi-fiction is the
sentimental novel, is an obvious case in point, but, as already suggested,

8. J. E. Tanner, "The Chronology and the Enigmatic End of *Lord Jim*," *Nineteenth-Century
Fiction* 21.4 (1967): 379.

I believe that a certain degree of *bovarysme* is universal. Emma and Jim are merely extreme cases.

Jim's initial identi-fiction was the Stevensonian adventure story. It had failed him on the *Patna*. His subsequent choice of the heroic epic as a prototext of the Patusan episode in his life can best be understood in terms of MacIntyre's theory again. MacIntyre examines the features of heroic societies in an attempt to understand the Aristotelian formulation of the virtues which is based on the moral order of the (fictional?) heroic age. The virtues in heroic societies—courage, fidelity, friendship—are important not merely as qualities of individuals, but as qualities necessary "to sustain a household and a community":

> Morality and social structure are in fact one and the same in heroic societies. There is only one set of social bonds. Morality as something distinct does not yet exist. Evaluative questions *are* questions of social fact. It is for this reason that Homer speaks of *Knowledge* of what to do and how to judge. Nor are such questions difficult to answer, except in exceptional cases. For the given rules which assign men their place in the social order and with it their identity also prescribe what they owe and what is owed to them and how they are to be treated and regarded if they fail and how they are to treat and regard others if those others fail. Without such a place in the social order, a man would not only be incapable of receiving recognition and response from others; not only would others not know, but he himself would not know who he was.[9]

MacIntyre's comment on the difference between modern society and the heroic society is particularly relevant to Jim's case:

> There is thus the sharpest of contrasts between the emotivist self of modernity and the self of the heroic age. The self of the heroic age lacks precisely that characteristic which we have already seen that some modern philosophers take to be an essential characteristic of human selfhood: the capacity to detach oneself from any particular standpoint or point of view, to step backwards, as it were, and view and judge that standpoint or point of view from the outside. In the heroic society there is no "outside" except that of the stranger. [The freedom of choice of values on which modernity prides itself would appear] from the standpoint of a tradition ultimately rooted in heroic societies . . . more like the freedom of ghosts—of those whose human substance approached vanishing point—than of men.[1]

By moving to Patusan, Jim becomes part of another story, as it were. This new identi-fiction, which is closely modelled on the heroic epic, offers him a new context of psychological and ethical orientation. He

9. MacIntyre, *After Virtue* 123–24.
1. Ibid. 126–27.

turns away from the individualized ethos of modernity, the "ghostly freedom of choice," offered by the multiplicity of voices in the first part of the story, towards the heroic mythical narrative, a fictional genre which is predicated on the ethos of communality.

The heroic-epic model of the Patusan section of *Lord Jim* has been noted by Tony Tanner, who argues that the collision of the two sections is ironical in that even as it presents the passing of the heroic ideals in an "elegiac light," it refuses to take them at their face value. In support of his view of the novel as a modernist reflection of an epistemological and ethical uncertainty, Tanner aptly quotes Ulrich, the unheroic hero of *The Man without Qualities*, who speaks of the unrequited yearning for a "narrative order" in life.[2] I would suggest that Jim's transition to Patusan is, indeed, the last stop in his quest for a "narrative order," but the terms of this narrative order, the heroic-epic or mythical prototext ought to be accepted as valid so long as the fiction is upheld by Jim himself. Only by a willing suspension of our modern disbelief, by a re-enactment of Jim's transition into the mythical mode, can we accommodate the different ethical and aesthetic assumptions of the Patusan section.

Patusan is described by Marlow as "a distant heavenly body," "a star of the fifth magnitude" where Jim can find "a totally new set of conditions for his imaginative faculty to work upon," leaving his "earthly failings behind him" (218) [132]. The local people regard Jim as a "creature of another essence" (229) [138], and the folk stories that evolve around his feats of courage and cunning are patterned on the mythical model, ascribing supernatural powers to the hero in his dealings with his enemies and with nature itself: "There was already a story that the tide had turned two hours before its time to help him on his journey up the river" (242–3) [146]; "As to the simple people of the outlying villages, they believed and said (as the most natural thing in the world) that Jim had carried the guns up the hill on his back—two at a time" (266) [159].

Jim himself seems to accept this mythical version of himself without the slightest touch of self-consciousness. His description of his flight from the Rajah's stockade employs the same epic hyperbole: "He . . . went over 'like a bird' . . . The earth seemed fairly to fly backwards under his feet" (253) [152]. He seems to act upon that mythical concept of himself when he visits the Rajah's camp and drinks the coffee which might be poisoned, as if he were, indeed, immune to poison (251–2) [151]. When Marlow tells him of the legends that have evolved around his victory over Sherif Ali, he denies them earnestly, as if they were not incredible in themselves (266–7) [159–60].

Marlow, amused but slightly irritated by Jim's unconscious propagation of the myth, views that "subtle influence of his surroundings" as

2. Tony Tanner, *Conrad: Lord Jim* (Great Neck: Barron's Educational Series, 1963) 8–12.

"part of his captivity" (266) [160]. But Marlow himself seems to be drawn into the spirit of this illusion just as he was by Jim's experience on board the *Patna*. His own description of Jim is couched in the idiom of the very myth he ridicules: "He had heroic health" (244) [147]; "he . . . burst into a Homeric peal of laughter" (267) [160]. Marlow's scepticism seems to waver before the magic of Jim's conviction: when Jim shows him the moon rising behind the two hills Marlow smiles at the note of "personal pride" with which he relates to the sight, "as though he had had a hand in regulating that unique spectacle." But immediately afterwards he qualifies his irony: "He had regulated so many things in Patusan! Things that would have appeared as much beyond his control as the motions of the moon and the stars" (221) [134]. Marlow himself describes Jim as "the heir of a shadowy and mighty tradition" (244) [147], "a figure set up on a pedestal, to represent in his persistent youth the power, and perhaps the virtues, of races that never grow old" (265) [159]. Jim embraces the heroic virtues: physical courage, fidelity, cunning, and friendship (261, 305) [157, 181]—the virtues which are essential for the maintenance of the community. He creates the community of Patusan as a mythical heroic society, and is, in turn, created by his role in this society, given a new identity and a new name.

A significant illustration of the difference between the modern and the mythical modes of discourse which constitute the *Patna* and the Patusan parts of Jim's story respectively is the relationship between Jim and the natural world. In the first part, nature is perceived as indifferent or viciously hostile to Jim. The *Patna* sails "under a sky scorching and unclouded, enveloped in a fulgor of sunshine that killed all thought, withered all impulses of strength and energy" (15) [14]; the menace of the storm seems to have "a sinister violence of intention . . . a purpose of malice . . . an unbridled cruelty . . ." (10–11) [11]. When Jim tells his story to Marlow, racked with remorse and shame, "the rain pattered and swished in the garden; a water-pipe (it must have had a hole in it) performed just outside the window a parody of blubbering woe with funny sobs and gurgling lamentation, interrupted by jerky spasms of silence . . ." (178) [108], in cruel mockery of Jim's anguish.

This relationship with nature is reversed in Patusan. As I have already noted, it is not only the local myth, spun by the natives, which invests Jim with supernatural powers (242, 266–7, 270) [149, 159–60, 161]. Marlow, too, observes that Jim is "in complete accord with his surroundings—with the life of the forest and with the life of men" (175) [106]. Jim's downfall is sympathetically responded to by nature, to a degree that would induce one to invoke the "pathetic fallacy," were it not so appropriately keyed up to Jim's archetypal stature: "There was a gloom as if enormous black wings had been spread above the mist that filled its depth to the summits of the trees. The branches overhead showered big drops through the gloomy fog" (401) [237]; "The sky over

Patusan was blood-red, immense, streaming like an open vein. An enormous sun nestled crimson amongst the tree-tops, and the forest below had a black and forbidding face" (413) [244]. It is only through a mythical arrangement of our universe—a meaningful narrative order—that we can overcome its essential randomness and indifference.[3]

Another aspect of the mythical mode of discourse, as established in the introductory section, is the feeling that subject and object are linked by a common power or energy, that words have the power to generate reality (hence the importance of spells, vows, and curses), and that objects can be the vehicles of abstract qualities. The distinction between the mythical or metaphoric idiom, which accommodates the concept of *mana* (a magic power which fuses the subject and the object), and the modern mode of discourse which is predicated on a clear-cut distinction between meaning and reality, is illuminating when applied to the history of the ring which had brought Jim into the heart of the community of Patusan, and which is, perhaps, the most significant evidence of what happens to him.

In the world of Patusan, where the poetic or metaphoric is the culturally ascendant language, *the ring is friendship*. It is, in this sense, a charm through which, as in a myth or a fairy-tale, Jim is gifted with the quality of friendship. But as I hope to have established, Jim cannot fully surrender himself to the terms of his own fiction, and the incompleteness of his vision results in a transition to the metonymic phase. In the metonymic phase, *the ring is "put for" friendship*. It is no longer a totem, animated by magic and endowed with a potent power, but a token, a mere symbol. In the latter phase Jim's heroic virtues are not immanent and immutable qualities: They are predicated on his willed application of the metonymic relationship, on his "putting" the ring for friendship. The ring may lose its precarious magic power when he fails, if only for a moment, in his indomitable belief in its power. Indeed, the massacre of Dain Waris and his people, who have trusted to the magic of the ring, is perceived as "a failure of a potent charm" (351) [208], and Jim will have to fulfil his vow and pay with his life in order to reinstate the power of his word.

Another prototext of the Patusan chapters is the Old Testament story of the Garden of Eden. Jim's rebirth from the mud in Patusan enacts a phylogenetic rebirth. Marlow tells Stein that Jim is "the youngest human being now in existence" (219) [133]. Jim has symbolically drowned his identity when he jumped from the *Patna*, and after a few years in the limbo of the coast, he is now sent to Patusan to be reborn as Adam, the man without a history. He wakes up, covered with mud and "alone of his kind" (254) [153] as Adam was when he was created.

3. Lezsek Kolakowski, *The Presence of Myth*, trans. Adam Czerniawski (Chicago: U of Chicago P, 1989) chaps. 7–8.

He meets the woman who is the "refuge from his loneliness" (300) [178] and names her Jewel, as Adam had named Eve (277–8) [166].

The establishment of the Old Testament story as a prototext of the Patusan episode alerts the reader to the possible existence of a serpent in Jim's Garden of Eden. The obvious suspect is Cornelius, who is constantly described in reptilian terms: "*creeping* across in full view with an inexpressible effect of *stealthiness*, of dark and secret *slinking*" (285) [170]; "perpetually slinking away" (324) [192]; "*crushed like a worm . . . his obsequious shadow gliding after mine . . .*" (326 [194], my emphases). The most poignant evidence of Cornelius's position in this Garden of Eden is Marlow's comment about the man's hatred for Jim: "After all this was a kind of recognition. You shall judge of a man by his foes . . ." (325) [193]. The recognition is not merely the immediate antipathy of the crooked man towards the hero—it seems to be a recognition of the ancient rivalry between Adam and the serpent. But this profusion of signals which mark Cornelius as the serpent is not vindicated by the plot. Cornelius's hatred of Jim and his devious manipulations do play a minor part in Jim's downfall, but he has no hand in Jim's fatal decision to let Brown go. He only takes advantage of the disintegration of the Patusan fiction, for which Jim alone is responsible.

The description of Gentleman Brown, the direct catalyst of the process, is also loaded with metaphysical-demonic connotations: "Brown was a latter day buccaneer . . . but what distinguished him from his contemporary brother ruffians . . . was the arrogant temper of his misdeeds and a vehement scorn for mankind at large . . ." (352) [209], "Brown, as though he had been really great, had a satanic gift of finding out the best and the weakest spot in his victims" (385) [229]. But the demonic attributes of Brown are brought into play only by the encounter with Jim and his power of posing as Jim's secret sharer. Shortly before the encounter he is described as a shabby adventurer, a man who, in spite of his glorious notoriety in the past, is clearly headed for failure, and the peculiar story about his love for the missionary's wife who had died in his arms (353) [209] adds a touch of humanizing pathos to his hatred for mankind. Brown is not innately endowed with demonic powers. He attains his demonic stature by his power over Jim.

The real serpent in Jim's Garden of Eden is his own weakness, the wavering of his faith in his own fiction. Earlier in the novel Marlow speculates on that weakness: "The commonest sort of fortitude prevents us from being criminals in a legal sense; it is from weakness unknown, but perhaps suspected, as in some parts of the world you would suspect a *deadly snake in every bush*,—from weakness that may lie hidden, watched or unwatched . . . not one of us is safe" (42–3 [30], my emphasis). Jim's weakness is not, as has been argued by critics, his tendency to live in a fictional realm, but his inability to bring himself to a total surrender to the fiction.

In terms of the biblical prototext, Jim is made to relinquish his identity as Adam and forced back in the role of Cain. Jim was cast into the role of Cain after his desertion of the *Patna*: "He was running. Absolutely running, with nowhere to go to" (155) [95]; '. . . The earth wouldn't be big enough to hold his caper' " (196) [118]. In Patusan he tried to cast off the role of Cain, after having enacted the archetypal punishment, and to regain the wholeness of Adam. Paradoxically, his sympathetic identification with Brown and his inability to kill him or let him die will bring about the death of Dain Waris, his adopted brother, and the collapse of the heroic code.

The allusion to Cain has been noted by critics, but has led them to look for an Abel to match the ostensible biblical story.[4] I believe that the significance of the story lies elsewhere: one must remember that it is Cain who is the forefather of civilization. Abel had no progeny, and his literal murder is, therefore, a literary and cultural ending as well. Cain is the man who had lived on and later founded a city. Civilization is, therefore, Cain's estate by extension. Jim tries to regain the wholeness of Adam in the garden of Eden, but—being human and therefore of Cain's offspring, as Gentleman Brown's apearance brings home to him—he is doomed to fail. He cannot erase the mark of Cain.

With the intrusion of time and memory, in the person of Gentleman Brown, into the mythical (i.e., ahistorical and atemporal) world of Patusan, the fiction created by Jim in an attempt to redeem himself from the role of Cain, is shattered. There are indications, however, even before Brown's arrival, that Jim's escape into the mythical mode is destined to fail, that his own history and the history of his race must eventually disrupt the fictional fabric of Patusan.

Marlow's scepticism about Jim's proposal to "begin with a clean slate" overshadows the entire Patusan episode with its prophetic echo: " 'A clean slate,' did he say? As if the initial word of each our destiny were not graven in imperishable characters upon the face of a rock" (186) [112]. Marlow's foreboding, his awareness of the inevitability of Jim's failure, colours his description of Patusan with an overtone of heavy sadness: "A brooding gloom lay over this vast and monotonous landscape; the light fell on it as if into an abyss. The land devoured the sunshine . . ." (264) [159]; "In the darkened moonlight the interlaced blossoms took on shapes . . . as though they [were] . . . destined for the use of the dead alone. . . . The lumps of white coral shone round the dark mound like a chaplet of bleached skulls . . ." (322) [191]. Jim himself is impelled to admit, even at the height of his success, that he cannot seal himself off in the Patusan fiction: " 'I have not forgotten why I came here. Not yet! . . . they [the people of Patusan] can never know

4. Daniel R. Schwarz, *Conrad: "Almayer's Folly" to "Under Western Eyes"* (Ithaca: Cornell UP, 1980) 90.

the real, real truth . . .' " (305) [181]. This, then, is the source of Jim's weakness, his "snake in the grass."

Patusan is, as noted by critics, a work of art. It is recalled by Marlow as a motionless painting, "fixed and revealed forever," partaking of "that stillness and permanence which is the prerogative of a work of art."[5] It is, in a sense, Jim's own creation, a story of which he is both the author and the protagonist. Marlow's initial description of Jim's inarticulateness is reversed at the end of his story, when he acknowledges the artistic powers of his former protégé: ". . . you must remember he was a finished artist in that peculiar way, he was a gifted poor devil with the faculty of swift and forestalling vision. The sights it showed him had turned him into cold stone" (96) [61], "He . . . had that faculty of beholding at a hint the face of his desire and the shape of his dream, without which the earth would know no lover and no adventurer" (175) [106]. It is this faculty of vision which paralyses Jim on board the *Patna*, but later impels him to attain greatness. Marlow's homage to Jim as an artist is rendered in the very same terms which Conrad himself has used in his artistic manifesto, the famous Preface to *The Nigger of the Narcissus*. Jim is an artist because he can make Marlow see: "His few mumbled words were *enough to make me see* the lower limb of the sun . . . the tremble of a vast ripple . . ." (122–3 [76], my emphasis); "It's extraordinary how he could cast upon you the spirit of his illusion. I listened as if to a tale of black magic. . . . he said 'They shouted'—and involuntarily I pricked up my ears for the ghost of that shout that would be heard directly through the false effect of silence" (109–10) [68–69]. The "real," "objective" silence around the narrator and his listener turns into a false effect by the power of Jim's shared vision.

The regression to the heroic-epic narrative model and to the mythical mode of discourse in the Patusan part of *Lord Jim* is, then, a projection of the protagonist's perception of himself, his own ideological and aesthetic construction of his world. Jim's enactment of the evolutionary process and his rebirth in Patusan take him back to the earliest form of narrative in human history, the heroic epic. Patusan is, for him, not merely a physical haven, but an aesthetic and ethical space, a different narrative mould for his shattered self.

The power of the word which is predominant in the mythical phase, turns into a double-edged weapon in Jim's hands. Jim has, in a mythical sense, created the community of Patusan with his word alone. "Those people had trusted him implicitly. Him alone! His bare word. . . . His word decided everything" (268–9) [160–61]. "His word was the one truth of every passing day" (272) [163]. But, as Marlow cryptically observes,

5. Tanner, *Lord Jim* 49; Schwarz 80–82. However, even those critics who have credited Jim with the creation of Patusan have accounted for his artistry in purely aesthetic terms. The relegation of Patusan to a closed aesthetic sphere establishes a disparity between ethics and aesthetics, a disparity which goes against the grain of Conrad's convictions and obscures the significance of the second part of the novel.

"the imprudence of our thoughts recoils upon our heads; who toys with the sword shall perish by the sword" (342) [203]. In Jim's case one might well be tempted to rephrase this oracular comment as "who toys with the *word* shall perish by the *word*." Jim uses his *mana*, the power of his word, to persuade the people of Patusan to let Brown go. "He . . . told them . . . that he had never deceived them. . . . Had his words ever brought suffering to the people?" (392) [232–33]. His rash vow does eventually recoil on him. He perishes, like a true biblical or mythical hero, by his own word.

Selected Bibliography

An enormous amount has been written about Joseph Conrad and *Lord Jim*. The most useful guides to this material are Bruce E. Teets and Helmut E. Gerber, *Joseph Conrad: An Annotated Bibliography of Writings about Him* (Northern Illinois UP, 1971); Bruce E. Teets, *Joseph Conrad: An Annotated Secondary Bibliography* (Garland, 1990); and Owen Knowles, *An Annotated Critical Bibliography of Joseph Conrad* (Harvester Wheatsheaf, 1992). Additionally, there is the indispensable annual *PMLA Bibliography*, now also available through the computer. Two scholarly journals feature bibliographies and book reviews (as well as articles of high quality): *Conradiana* (Texas Tech UP) and *The Conradian* (Joseph Conrad Society, UK).

There is a great deal of interesting biographical writing about Joseph Conrad. He himself wrote two memoirs: *The Mirror of the Sea* (1906) and, especially valuable, *A Personal Record* (1912). Well on its way to completion is the eight-volume *Collected Letters of Joseph Conrad*, ed. Frederick R. Karl and Laurence Davies (Cambridge UP, 1983 –). Conrad's wife and two sons all wrote reminiscences: Jessie Conrad, *Joseph Conrad As I Knew Him* (1926) and *Joseph Conrad and His Circle* (1935); Borys Conrad, *My Father: Joseph Conrad* (1970); John Conrad, *Joseph Conrad: Times Remembered* (1981). Edward Garnett, Conrad's discoverer, wrote about him in the introduction to his edition: *Letters from Conrad, 1895 to 1924* (1928). Ford Madox Ford, Conrad's literary collaborator and intimate friend of ten years, wrote of him at length in *Joseph Conrad: A Personal Remembrance* (1924) and *Mightier Than the Sword* (1938; published in the United States as *Portraits from Life*, 1937). Richard Curle, a friend during Conrad's later years, published *The Last Twelve Years of Joseph Conrad* (1928). The earliest biography is G. Jean-Aubry's two-volume *Joseph Conrad: Life and Letters* (1927). Subsequent notable biographies include the following: Jocelyn Baines, *Joseph Conrad: A Critical Biography* (1960); Bernard C. Meyer, *Joseph Conrad: A Psychoanalytic Biography* (1967); Norman Sherry, *Conrad and His World* (1972, with 142 illustrations); Frederick R. Karl, *Joseph Conrad: The Three Lives* (1979); Roger Tennant, *Joseph Conrad* (1981); Cedric Watts, *Joseph Conrad: A Literary Life* (1989); John Batchelor, *The Life of Joseph Conrad* (1994). Much excellent biographical commentary appears throughout Ian Watt's *Conrad in the Nineteenth Century* (1979). For Polish family documents, see Zdzisław Najder, ed., *Conrad under Familial Eyes* (1983). The best, fullest biography is also by Najder: *Joseph Conrad: A Chronicle* (1983). The best, most readable biography of medium length is Jeffrey Meyers's *Joseph Conrad* (1991). See, also, an attractive travel book about Conrad in the East: Gavin Young, *In Search of Conrad* (1991).

Many of the major scholarly and critical books and articles on Conrad and *Lord Jim* are excerpted from or referred to in the preceding sections of this book and are not listed below. The First Norton Critical Edition of *Lord Jim* (1968) is a further source of titles. Finally, the works listed below are a personal sampling of other interesting commentaries. General books on Conrad are included only if they contain significant discussions of *Lord Jim*.

Batchelor, John. *Lord Jim*. London: Unwin Hyman, 1988.

Berman, Jeffrey. *Joseph Conrad: Writing as Rescue*. New York: Astra, 1977.

Berthoud, Jacques. *Joseph Conrad: The Major Phase*. Cambridge: Cambridge UP, 1978.

Bloom, Harold, ed. *Joseph Conrad's "Lord Jim"* (Modern Critical Interpretations Series). Edgemont: Chelsea House, 1987.

Conroy, Mark. *Modernism and Authority: Strategies of Legitimation in Flaubert and Conrad*. Baltimore: Johns Hopkins UP, 1985.

Cottom, Daniel. "*Lord Jim*: Destruction Through Time." *Centennial Review* 27 (1983): 10–29.

Cox, C. B. *Joseph Conrad: The Modern Imagination*. London: Dent, 1974.

Dale, Patricia. "A Borrowing from Hazlitt's Father." *Notes and Queries* 10 (1963): 146.

Daleski, H. M. *Joseph Conrad: The Way of Dispossession*. New York: Holmes and Meier, 1977.

Darras, Jacques. *Conrad and the West: Signs of Empire*. London: Macmillan, 1982.

Davidson, Arnold E. *Conrad's Endings: A Study of the Five Major Novels*. Ann Arbor: U of Michigan Research P, 1984.

Dobrinsky, Joseph. *The Artist in Conrad's Fiction: A Psychocritical Study*. Ann Arbor: U of Michigan Research P, 1989.

Ducharme, Robert. "The Power of Culture in *Lord Jim*." *Conradiana* 22 (1990): 3–24.

Fincham, Gail. "The Dialogism of *Lord Jim*." *The Guardian* 22.1–2 (Spring–Winter 1997): 58–74.

Fraser, Gail. *Interweaving Patterns in the Works of Joseph Conrad*. Ann Arbor: U of Michigan Research P, 1988.

Galen, Nina. "Stephen Crane as a Source for Conrad's Jim." *Nineteenth-Century Fiction* 38 (1983): 78–96.

Glassman, Peter J. *Language and Being: Joseph Conrad and the Literature of Personality*. New York: Columbia UP, 1976.

GoGwilt, Christopher. *The Invention of the West: Joseph Conrad and the Double-Mapping of Europe and Empire*. Stanford: Stanford UP, 1995.

Hawthorn, Jeremy. *Joseph Conrad: Language and Fictional Self-Consciousness*. Lincoln: U of Nebraska P, 1979.

Hay, Eloise Knapp. "*Lord Jim* and le Hamlétisme." *L'Époque conradienne* 1990: 9–27.

Hervouet, Yves. *The French Face of Joseph Conrad*. Cambridge: Cambridge UP, 1990.

Hunter, Allan. *Joseph Conrad and the Ethics of Darwinism*. London: Crown Helm, 1983.

Johnson, Bruce. *Conrad's Models of Mind*. Minneapolis: U of Minnesota P, 1971.

Jones, Michael P. *Conrad's Heroism: A Paradise Lost*. Ann Arbor: U of Michigan Research P, 1985.

Kirschner, Paul. *Conrad: The Psychologist as Artist*. Edinburgh: Oliver and Boyd, 1968.

Kuehn, Robert E., ed. *Twentieth Century Interpretations of "Lord Jim."* Englewood Cliffs, NJ: Prentice Hall, 1969.

Lothe, Jakob. *Conrad's Narrative Method*. Oxford: Clarendon P, 1989.

McClure, John A. *Kipling and Conrad: The Colonial Fiction*. Cambridge: Harvard UP, 1981.

Mongia, Padmini. " 'Ghosts of the Gothic': Spectral Women and Colonized Spaces in Conrad's *Lord Jim*." *The Conradian* 17.2 (Spring 1993): 1–16.

Murfin, Ross C. "*Lord Jim*": *After the Truth*. New York: Twayne, 1992.

Nadelhaft, Ruth. *Joseph Conrad* (Feminist Readings Series). Atlantic Highlands, NJ: Humanities, 1991.

Najder, Zdzisław. "*Lord Jim*: A Romantic Tragedy of Honor." *Conradiana* 1 (1968): 1–8.

Nettels, Elsa. *James and Conrad*. Athens: U of Georgia P, 1977.

O'Hanlon, Redmond. *Joseph Conrad and Charles Darwin: The Influence of Scientific Thought on Conrad's Fiction*. Edinburgh: Salamander, 1984.

Parins, James W., Robert J. Dilligan, and Todd K. Bender. *A Concordance to Conrad's "Lord Jim."* New York: Garland, 1976.

Parry, Benita. *Conrad and Imperialism*. London: Macmillan, 1983.

Price, Martin. *Forms of Life: Character and Moral Imagination in the Novel*. New Haven: Yale UP, 1983.

Raval, Suresh. *The Art of Failure: Conrad's Fiction*. Boston: Allen and Unwin, 1986.

Rising, Catharine. *Darkness at Heart: Fathers and Sons in Conrad*. New York: Greenwood, 1990.

Roussel, Royal. *The Metaphysics of Darkness: A Study of the Unity and Development of Conrad's Fiction*. Baltimore: Johns Hopkins UP, 1971.

Schwarz, Daniel R. *Conrad: "Almayer's Folly" to "Under Western Eyes."* Ithaca: Cornell UP, 1980.

Seidel, Michael. *Exile and the Narrative Imagination*. New Haven: Yale UP, 1986.

Sherry, Norman, ed. *Conrad: The Critical Heritage*. London: Routledge, 1973.

Simmons, Alan H., and J. H. Stape, eds. *Lord Jim: Centennial Essays*. Rodopi: Amsterdam, and Atlanta, GA, 2000.

Simons, Kenneth. *The Ludic Imagination: A Reading of Joseph Conrad*. Ann Arbor: U of Michigan Research P, 1985.

Stape, J. H. " 'Gaining Conviction': Conradian Borrowing and the *Patna* Episode in *Lord Jim*." *Conradiana* 25 (1993): 22–34.

Stewart, J. I. M. *Joseph Conrad*. London: Longmans, Green, 1968.

Tarnawski, Wit. *Conrad the Man, the Writer, the Pole: An Essay in Psychological Biography*. London: Polish Cultural Foundation, 1984.

Tenenbaum, Elizabeth Brody. " 'And the woman is dead now': A Reconsideration of Conrad's Stein." *Studies in the Novel* 10 (1978): 335–45.

Thorburn, David. *Conrad's Romanticism*. New Haven: Yale UP, 1974.

Verleun, Jan. *Patna and Patusan Perspectives*. Groningen: Bouma's Boekhuis, 1979.

Watts, Cedric. *A Preface to Conrad*. London: Longman, 1982.

Winner, Anthony. *Culture and Irony: Studies in Joseph Conrad's Major Novels*. Charlottesville: UP of Virginia, 1988.

Wollaeger, Mark A. *Joseph Conrad and the Fictions of Skepticism*. Stanford: Stanford UP, 1990.